RESEARCH
IN EDUCATION

EIGHTH EDITION

RESEARCH
IN EDUCATION

John W. Best
Butler University, Emeritus

James V. Kahn
University of Illinois at Chicago

Allyn and Bacon
Boston • London • Toronto • Sydney • Tokyo • Singapore

Vice President, Education: Nancy Forsyth
Editorial Assistant: Cheryl Ouellette
Marketing Manager: Kris Farnsworth
Sr. Editorial Production Administrator: Susan McIntyre
Editorial Production Service: Ruttle, Shaw & Wetherill, Inc.
Composition Buyer: Linda Cox
Manufacturing Buyer: Suzanne Lareau
Cover Administrator: Suzanne Harbison

Library of Congress Cataloging-in-Publication Data

Best, John W.
    Research in education / John W. Best, James V. Kahn.—8th ed.
      p. cm.
    Includes bibliographical references and index.
    ISBN 0-205-18697-1
    1. Education—Research. I. Kahn, James V., 1948–   . II. Title.
LB1028.B4 1998
370´.7´2—dc21   96-53399
                                                       CIP

Printed in the United States of America

10 9 8 7 6 5 4   RRD   04 03 02 01 00 99

CONTENTS

PART II   *Research Methods   73*

PREFACE

The eighth edition of *Research in Education* has the same goals as the previous editions. The book is meant to be used as a research reference or as a text in an introductory course in research methods. It is appropriate for graduate students enrolled in a research seminar, for those writing a thesis or dissertation, or for those who carry on research as a professional activity. All professional workers should be familiar with the methods of research and the analysis of data. If only as consumers, professionals should understand some of the techniques used in identifying problems, forming hypotheses, constructing and using data-gathering instruments, designing research studies, and employing statistical procedures to analyze data. They should also be able to use this information to interpret and critically analyze research reports that appear in professional journals and other publications.

No introductory course can be expected to confer research competence, nor can any book present all relevant information. Research skill and understanding are achieved only through the combination of coursework and experience. Graduate students may find it profitable to carry on a small-scale study as a way of learning about research.

This edition expands and clarifies a number of ideas presented in previous editions. Additional concepts, procedures, and especially examples have been added. Each of the five methodology chapters has the text of an entire published article following it, which illustrates that type of research. Nothing has been deleted from the seventh edition other than a few examples of research that have been replaced with more recent and appropriate examples. An appendix (B) has been added that contains a data set for use by students in Chapters 10, 11, and 12. This edition has been written to conform to the guidelines of the American Psychological Association's (APA) *Publications Manual* (4th ed.). The writing style suggested in Chapter 3 is also in keeping with the APA manual.

Many of the topics covered in this book may be peripheral to the course objectives of some instructors. We do not suggest that all of the topics in this book be included in a single course. We recommend that instructors use the topics selectively and in the sequence that they find most appropriate. Students can then use the portions remaining in subsequent courses, to assist in carrying out a thesis, and/or as a reference.

This revision benefited from the comments of Professor Kahn's students, who had used the earlier editions of this text. To them and to reviewers Barbara Boe, Carthage College; John A. Jensen, Boston College; Jerry McGee, Sam Houston State; and Gene Gloekner, Colorado State University, we express our appreciation. We also wish to thank Michelle Chapman and Tara O'Brien who assisted in the preparation of this edition. We wish to acknowledge the cooperation of the University of Illinois at Chicago Library and Computer Center; SPSS, Inc.; and SAS Institute, Inc. Finally, we are grateful to our wives, Solveig Ager Best and Kathleen Cuerdon-Kahn, for their encouragement and support.

J.W.B.
J.V.K.

RESEARCH
IN EDUCATION

P A R T I

INTRODUCTION TO EDUCATIONAL RESEARCH: DEFINITIONS, RESEARCH PROBLEMS, PROPOSALS, AND REPORT WRITING

The first three chapters of this book are intended to explore the historical underpinnings of educational research, define some basic concepts, describe the processes of selecting a research problem to be investigated and writing a research proposal, and demonstrate a style of writing that can be used to write research reports, research proposals, and term papers.

Chapter 1 introduces the research endeavor. Such matters as methods of science, the importance of theory, the formulation of hypotheses, sampling techniques, and an overview of the methodologies used in educational research are described. Different types of educational research—historical, quantitative descriptive, qualitative, and experimental—are briefly described.

Chapter 2 describes the process by which a research problem is identified. This is one of the most difficult steps in the research process for beginners and sometimes for experienced researchers as well. This chapter also discusses the ethics of conducting research with humans, including ethic statements by both the American Psychological Association and American Educational Research Association. Finally, some suggestions for library research and how to write a research proposal are presented.

Chapter 3 describes one style for writing a research report, the style of the American Psychological Association. This style was selected because it is the most commonly accepted by journals in the field of education and psychology. The description includes writing style, preparing the manuscript, referencing, tables, and figures. This chapter also briefly describes an approach to evaluating research reports written by others.

1

THE MEANING OF RESEARCH

THE SEARCH FOR KNOWLEDGE

Human beings are the unique product of their creation and evolution. In contrast to other forms of animal life, their more highly developed nervous system has enabled them to develop sounds and symbols (letters and numbers) that make possible the communication and recording of their questions, observations, experiences, and ideas.

It is understandable that their greater curiosity, implemented by their control of symbols, would lead people to speculate about the operation of the universe, the great forces beyond their own control. Over many centuries people began to develop what seemed to be plausible explanations. Attributing the forces of nature to the working of supernatural powers, they believed that the gods manipulated the sun, stars, wind, rain, and lightning at their whim.

The appearance of the medicine man or priest, who claimed special channels of communication with the gods, led to the establishment of a system of religious authority passed on from one generation to another. A rigid tradition developed, and a dogma of nature's processes, explained in terms of mysticism and the authority of the priesthood, became firmly rooted, retarding further search for truth for centuries.

But gradually people began to see that the operations of the forces of nature were not as capricious as they had been led to believe. They began to observe an orderliness in the universe and certain cause-and-effect relationships; they discovered that under certain conditions events could be predicted with reasonable accuracy. However, these explanations were often rejected if they seemed to conflict with the dogma of religious authority. Curious persons who raised questions were often punished and even put to death when they persisted in expressing doubts suggested by such unorthodox explanations of natural phenomena.

This reliance on empirical evidence or personal experience challenged the sanction of vested authority and represented an important step in the direction of scientific inquiry. Such pragmatic observation, however, was largely unsystematic and further limited by the lack of an objective method. Observers were likely to overgeneralize on the basis of incomplete experience or evidence, to ignore complex factors operating simultaneously, or to let their feelings and prejudices influence both their observations and their conclusions.

It was only when people began to think systematically about thinking itself that the era of logic began. The first systematic approach to reasoning, attributed to Aristotle and the Greeks, was the deductive method. The categorical syllogism was one model of thinking that prevailed among early philosophers. Syllogistic reasoning established a logical relationship between a *major premise,* a *minor premise,* and a *conclusion.* A major premise is a self-evident assumption, previously established by metaphysical truth or dogma, that concerns a relationship; a minor premise is a particular case related to the major premise. Given the logical relationship of these premises, the conclusion is inescapable.

A typical Aristotelian categorical syllogism follows:

Major Premise: All men are mortal.
Minor Premise: Socrates is a man.
Conclusion: Socrates is mortal.

This deductive method, moving from the general assumption to the specific application, made an important contribution to the development of modern problem solving. But it was not fruitful in arriving at new truths. The acceptance of incomplete or false major premises that were based on old dogmas or unreliable authority could only lead to error. Semantic difficulties often resulted from shifting definitions of the terms involved.

Centuries later Francis Bacon advocated direct observation of phenomena, arriving at conclusions or generalizations through the evidence of many individual observations. This inductive process of moving from specific observations to the generalization freed logic from some of the hazards and limitations of deductive thinking. Bacon recognized the obstacle that the deductive process placed in the way of discovering new truth: It started with old dogmas that religious or intellectual authorities had already accepted and thus could be expected to arrive at few new truths. These impediments to the discovery of truth, which he termed "idols," were exposed in his *Novum Organum,* written in 1620.

The following story, attributed to Bacon, expresses his revolt against the authority of the written word, an authority that dominated the search for truth during the Middle Ages:

In the year of our Lord, 1432, there arose a grievous quarrel among the brethren over the number of teeth in the mouth of a horse. For thirteen days the disputation raged without ceasing. All the ancient books and chronicles were fetched out, and wonderful and ponderous erudition was made manifest. At the beginning of the fourteenth day a youthful friar of goodly bearing asked his learned superiors for permission to add a word, and straightway, to the wonder of the disputants, whose deep wisdom he sorely vexed, he beseeched them in a manner coarse and unheard of, to look in the mouth of a horse and find answers to their questionings. At this, their dignity being grievously hurt, they waxed exceedingly wroth; and joining in a mighty uproar they flew upon him and smote him hip and thigh and cast him out forthwith. For, said they, "Surely Satan hath tempted this bold neophyte to declare unholy and unheard-of ways of finding truth, contrary to all the teachings of the fathers." After many days of grievous strife the dove of peace sat on the assembly, and they, as one man, declaring the problem to be an everlasting mystery because of a dearth of historical and theological evidence thereof, so ordered the same writ down. (Mees, 1934, pp. 13–14)

The method of inductive reasoning proposed by Bacon, a method new to the field of logic but widely used by the scientists of his time, was not hampered by false premises, by the inadequacies and ambiguities of verbal symbolism, or by the absence of supporting evidence.

But the inductive method alone did not provide a completely satisfactory system for the solution of problems. Random collection of individual observations without a unifying concept or focus often obscured investigations and therefore rarely led to a generalization or theory. Also, the same set of observations can lead to different conclusions and support different, even opposing, theories.

The deductive method of Aristotle and the inductive method of Bacon were fully integrated in the work of Charles Darwin in the nineteenth century. During his early career his observations of animal life failed to lead to a satisfactory theory of man's development. The concept of the struggle for existence in Thomas Malthus's *Essay on Population* intrigued Darwin and suggested the assumption that natural selection explains the origin of different species of animals. This hypothesis provided a needed focus for his investigations. He proceeded to deduce specific consequences suggested by the hypothesis. The evidence he gathered confirmed the hypothesis that biological change in the process of natural selection, in which favorable variations were preserved and unfavorable ones destroyed, resulted in the formation of new species.

The major premise of the older deductive method was gradually replaced by an assumption, or *hypothesis,* that was subsequently tested by the collection and logical analysis of data. This deductive-inductive method is now recognized as an example of a scientific approach.

John Dewey (1938) suggested a pattern that is helpful in identifying the elements of a deductive-inductive process:

A Method of Science

1. Identification and definition of the problem
2. Formulation of a hypothesis—an idea as to a probable solution to the problem, an intelligent guess or hunch
3. Collection, organization, and analysis of data

4. Formulation of conclusions
5. Verification, rejection, or modification of the hypothesis by the test of its consequences in a specific situation

Although this pattern is a useful reconstruction of some methods of scientific inquiry, it is not to be considered the *only* scientific method. There are many ways of applying logic and observation to problem solving. An overly rigid definition of the research process would omit many ways in which researchers go about their tasks. The planning of a study may include a great deal of exploratory activity, which is frequently intuitive or speculative and at times a bit disorderly. Although researchers must eventually identify a precise and significant problem, their object may initially be vague and poorly defined. They may observe situations that seem to suggest certain possible cause-and-effect relationships and even gather some preliminary data to examine for possible relevancy to their vaguely conceived problem. Thus, much research begins with the inductive method. At this stage imagination and much speculation are essential to the formulation of a clearly defined problem that is susceptible to the research process. Many students of research rightly feel that problem identification is one of the most difficult and most crucial steps of the research process.

Frequently researchers are interested in complex problems, the full investigation of which requires a series of studies. This approach is known as *programmatic research* and usually combines the inductive and deductive methods in a continuously alternating pattern. The researcher may begin with a number of observations from which a hypothesis is derived (inductive reasoning). Then the researcher proceeds deductively to determine the consequences that are to be expected if the hypothesis is true. Data are then collected through the inductive method to verify, reject, or modify the hypothesis. Based on the findings of this study, the researcher goes on to formulate more hypotheses to further investigate the complex problem under study. Thus, the researcher is continually moving back and forth between the inductive method of observation and data collection and the deductive method of hypothesizing the anticipated consequences to events.

SCIENCE

The term *science* may be thought of as an approach to the gathering of knowledge rather than as a field or subject matter. Science, put simply, consists of two primary functions: (1) the development of theory and (2) the testing of substantive hypotheses that are deduced from theory. The scientist, therefore, is engaged in the use, modification, and/or creation of theory. The scientist may emphasize an empirical approach in which data collection is the primary method, a rational approach in which logical and deductive reasoning is primary, or a combination of these approaches, which is most common. Regardless of the emphasis the scientist begins with a set of ideas that direct the effort and with a goal that entails the development or testing of theory.

By attempting to apply the rigorous, systematic observation analysis used in the physical and biological sciences to areas of social behavior, the social sciences have grown and have advanced humanity's knowledge of itself. The fields of anthropology, economics, education, political science, psychology, and social psychology have become recognized as sciences by many authorities. To the extent that these fields are founded on scientific methodology, they are sciences. Some reject this concept, still defining science in terms of subject matter rather than methodology. Historically their position can be readily explained. Because scientific methods were first used in the investigation of physical phenomena, tradition has identified science with the physical world. Only within the last century has the methodology of science been applied to the study of various areas of human behavior. Because these are newer areas of investigation, their results have not achieved the acceptance and status that come with the greater maturity and longer tradition of the physical sciences.

The uniformity of nature is a reasonable assumption in the world of physical objects and their characteristics, but in the area of social behavior such assumptions are not warranted. Human nature is much more complex than the sum of its many discrete elements, even if they could be isolated and identified. Because human nature is so complex, it is much more difficult to develop sound theories of human behavior than to predict occurrences in the physical world. Research on human subjects has numerous problems:

1. No two persons are alike in feelings, drives, or emotions. What may be a reasonable prediction for one may be useless for another.
2. No one person is completely consistent from one moment to another. Human behavior is influenced by the interaction of the individual with every changing element in his or her environment, often in a way that is difficult to predict.
3. Human beings are influenced by the research process itself. They are influenced by the attention that is focused on them when under investigation and by the knowledge that their behavior is being observed.
4. The behavioral sciences have been limited by a lack of adequate definition. Accurate operational definitions are essential to the development of a sophisticated science. Such traits as intelligence, learning, hostility, anxiety, or motivation are not directly observable and are generally referred to as "constructs," implying that they are constructions of the scientist's imagination. Constructs cannot be seen, heard, or felt. They can only be inferred by phenomena such as test scores or by observed hostile or aggressive acts, skin responses, pulse rates, or persistence at a task.

But even constructs for which useful descriptive instruments are available account for only limited sources of variation; they yield only partial definitions. For example, intelligence, as defined by a score on an intelligence test, is not a satisfactory measure of the type of intelligence that individuals are called on to demonstrate in a variety of situations outside a formal academic environment.

In the physical sciences many complex constructs have been more effectively defined in operational terms. Time is one such construct: Time is a function of the motion of the earth in relation to the sun, measured by the rotation of a hand on the face of a circular scale in precise units. Weight is a construct involving the laws of gravitation, measured by springs, torsion devices, levers, or electronic adaptations of these instruments.

The instruments that measure such constructs are devised so that they are consistent, to a maximum degree, with known physical laws and forces and yield valid descriptions in a variety of situations. An international bureau prescribes standards for these devices so that they may provide precise operational definitions of the constructs.

Although the problems of discovering theories of human behavior are difficult, it is possible to do so. Behavioral scientists need to carry on their investigations as carefully and rigorously as have physical scientists. However, one must not overestimate the exactness of the physical sciences, for theoretical speculations and probability estimates are also inherent characteristics.

Today we live in a world that has benefited greatly from progress made by the biological and physical sciences. Infant mortality is decreasing, and life expectancy continues to increase. Surgery is now performed on fetuses *in utero* to correct such conditions as hydrocephalus. Children born prematurely weighing less than 1,000 grams (approximately 2 pounds) survive and generally thrive. The Salk and Sabin vaccines have rid the world of poliomyelitis. Many forms of cancer are being conquered by early detection and chemotherapy. Improved nutrition, antibiotics, innovative surgical techniques, and countless other accomplishments allow us to lead longer, healthier lives. Automation and computerization touch every aspect of our lives, changing our work and leisure environments and impacting the type of jobs available. The splitting of the atom, space travel, and developments in the field of electronics such as the laser, superconductivity, and the silicon chip promise still greater changes and adventures that are beyond the scope of most people's imaginations. All these improvements have resulted from the investigation of biological and physical sciences.

However, there is less confidence about the improvement of the nonphysical aspects of our world. Despite all our marvelous gadgets, there is some doubt whether we are happier or more satisfied or whether our basic needs are being fulfilled more effectively today than they were a century ago. The fear of nuclear plant failures and uncertainty about the safe disposal of nuclear waste are uppermost in the minds of people throughout the world. Our apparent inability to solve various social problems raises the specter of malnutrition, terrorism, and illiteracy. There is great concern that our children are not learning sufficiently to compete in our more technologically complex society. Standard scores indicate that high school children are less prepared for college today than were their parents and older siblings.

Scientific methods must be applied with greater vigor and imagination to the behavioral aspects of our culture. The development of the behavioral sciences and their application to education and other human affairs present some of our greatest challenges.

THE RÔLE OF THEORY

At this stage in the discussion, a statement about theory is appropriate. To many people the term *theory* suggests an ivory tower, something unreal and of little practical value. On the contrary, a theory establishes a cause-and-effect relationship between variables with the purpose of explaining and predicting phenomena. Those who engage in pure research devote their energies to the formulation and reformulation of theories and may not be concerned with their practical applications. However, when a theory has been established, it may suggest many applications of practical value. John Dewey once said that there was nothing more practical than a good theory.

Theories about the relationship between the position of the earth and other moving celestial bodies were essential to the successful launching and return of manned space vehicles. Theories of the behavior of gases were essential to the development of refrigeration and air conditioning. Controlled atomic energy could not have been achieved without the establishment of theories about the nature of mass and energy and the structure of the atom. The real purpose of scientific methods is prediction, the discovery of certain theories or generalizations that anticipate future occurrences with maximum probability.

Piaget's theory of cognitive development is a good example of a theory that has been developed with little or no concern for application. Only one of Piaget's many books discussed education in any great detail (Piaget, 1970), and even this book does not deal with the specifics that most teachers desire and need. However, innumerable books, chapters, and articles written by followers of Piaget have explicated the usefulness of his theory for teaching practices from preschool (e.g., Read, 1995; Sophian, 1995) to high school (e.g., Karplus et al., 1977; Staver & Gabel, 1979) and even to higher education (Harcharick, 1993). The theory also has been shown to have implications for teaching children with mental retardation (e.g., Kahn, 1992, 1996; McCormick et al., 1990) and with other disabilities (e.g., Wolinsky, 1970). So although Piaget's aim was to understand the cognitive structures and functioning of children and adults, his theory has been embraced by educators and psychologists who have investigated ways in which it could be used to improve educational practice.

But what do we mean by the term *theory?* A theory is an attempt to develop a general explanation for some phenomenon. A theory defines nonobservable constructs that are inferred from observable facts and events and that are thought to have an effect on the phenomenon under study. A theory describes the relationship among key variables for purposes of explaining a current state or predicting future occurrences. A theory is primarily concerned with explanation and therefore focuses on determining cause-effect relationships.

OPERATIONAL DEFINITIONS OF VARIABLES - things that you manipulate

Such variables as giftedness, academic achievement, and creativity are conceptualizations that are defined in dictionary terms. But because these aspects cannot be observed directly, they are vague and ambiguous and provide a poor basis for identifying variables. Much more precise and unambiguous definitions of variables can be stated in operational form, which stipulates the operation by which they can be observed and measured. Giftedness could be operationally defined as a score that is 2 or more standard deviations above the mean on the *Wechsler Adult Intelligence Scale,* academic achievement as a score on the *Stanford Achievement Test,* or creativity as a score on the *Torrance Tests of Creative Thinking.* When an operational definition is used, there is no doubt about what the researcher means.

To be useful, however, operational definitions must be based on a theory that is generally recognized as valid. Operational terms do not always prove useful in describing variables, for they could conceivably be based on irrelevant behavior. Defining degree of self-esteem in terms of the number of times an individual smiles per minute would not be a useful or realistic definition, even though such behavior could easily be observed and recorded.

THE HYPOTHESIS - statement of what is going to happen

Two important functions that hypotheses serve in scientific inquiry are the development of theory and the statement of parts of an existing theory in testable form. In his now classic chapter, Snow (1973) describes six levels of theory, with the first level being hypothesis formation. At this initial level the theory developer has a hunch based on theory, past experience, observations, and/or information gained from others. A hypothesis is formulated in such a way that this hunch can be tested. Based on the findings of the subsequent research, the hypothesis is supported or rejected and more hypotheses are formulated to continue the process of building a cohesive theory.

The most common use of hypotheses is to test whether an existing theory can be used to solve a problem. In everyday situations those who confront problems often propose informal hypotheses that can be tested directly. For example, when a lamp fails to light when the switch is turned on, several hypotheses come to mind, based on our understanding of electricity and on our past experiences with lamps:

1. The plug is not properly connected to the wall outlet.
2. The bulb is burned out.
3. The fuse is burned out or the circuit breaker has been tripped.
4. There has been a power failure in the neighborhood.

Each of these speculations can be tested directly by checking the plug connection, substituting a bulb known to be in working condition, inspecting the fuse or circuit breaker, or noting whether other lights in the house, or in neighbors' houses, are on.

The Research Hypothesis

The *research* or *scientific hypothesis* is a formal affirmative statement predicting a single research outcome, a tentative explanation of the relationship between two or more variables. For the hypothesis to be testable, the variables must be operationally defined. That is, the researcher specifies what operations were conducted, or tests used, to measure each variable. Thus, the hypothesis focuses the investigation on a definite target and determines what observations, or measures, are to be used.

A number of years ago the hypothesis was formulated that there is a positive causal relationship between cigarette smoking and the incidence of coronary heart disease. This hypothesis proposed a tentative explanation that led to many studies comparing the incidence of heart disease among cigarette smokers and non-smokers. As a result of these extensive studies, the medical profession now generally accepts that this relationship has been established.

In the behavioral sciences the variables may be abstractions that cannot be observed. These variables must be defined operationally by describing some samples of actual behavior that are concrete enough to be observed directly. The relationship between these observable incidents may be deduced as consistent or inconsistent with the consequences of the hypothesis. Thus, the hypothesis may be judged to be probably true or probably false.

For example, one might propose the hypothesis that third-grade children taught the Chisanbop hand-calculating process would learn to perform the basic arithmetic processes more effectively (that is, score higher on a specified measure or test of arithmetic processing) than those using the conventional method. Children would be randomly assigned to two groups, one taught the Chisanbop system (experimental group) and the other using the conventional method (control group). The experiment would be carried on for a period of 9 months. If the hypothesis were true, the experimental group's mean scores on a standardized arithmetic achievement test would be significantly higher than those of the control group.

The Null Hypothesis (H_0)

At the beginning of their study, researchers state an affirmative scientific or research hypothesis as a prediction of the outcome that they propose to test. Most often this research hypothesis suggests that a difference of some kind (e.g., one group will do better than another) will occur. Later, at the stage of the statistical analysis of the observed data, they restate this hypothesis in negative, or null, form. For instance, the previously stated hypothesis, that third-grade children taught the Chisanbop method would score higher on a specified test of arithmetic than those using the conventional method, would be restated: There is no significant difference between the arithmetic achievement of the two groups. Some authors have argued that the null hypothesis cannot possibly be correct (e.g., Cohen, 1990; Murphy, 1990). Frick (1995), on the other hand, argues that if a good faith effort is made to reject the null hypothesis and fails, the null hypothesis can be accepted. Thus, in rare cases the research hypothesis could be the same as the null hypothesis. For instance, Kahn (1985) hypothesized that children with mild mental retardation and children of average intelligence, equated for mental age, would perform similarly on Piagetian tests.

The null hypothesis relates to a statistical method of interpreting conclusions about population characteristics that are inferred from the variable relationships observed in samples. The null hypothesis asserts that observed differences or relationships result merely from chance errors inherent in the sampling process. Most hypotheses are the opposite of the null hypothesis. In such a case if the researcher rejects the null hypothesis, he or she accepts the research hypothesis, concluding that the magnitude of the observed variable relationship is probably too great to attribute to sampling error. The logic of the use of the null hypothesis, which may be confusing to students, is explained in greater detail in the discussions of sampling error and the central limit theorem in Chapter 11.

In a null hypothesis you suggest that no are no differences.

SAMPLING

* State it negatively so that you can prove or disprove it.

The primary purpose of research is to discover principles that have universal application, but to study a whole population to arrive at generalizations would be impracticable, if not impossible. Some populations are so large that their characteristics cannot be measured; before the measurement could be completed, the populations would have changed.

Imagine the difficulty of conducting a reading experiment with all American fifth-grade children as subjects. The study of a population of this size would require the services of thousands of researchers, the expenditure of millions of dollars, and hundreds of thousands of class hours.

Fortunately, the process of sampling makes it possible to draw valid inferences or generalizations on the basis of careful observation of variables within a relatively small proportion of the population. A measured value based on sample data is a *statistic*. A population value inferred from a statistic is a *parameter*.

A *population* is any group of individuals who has one or more characteristics in common that are of interest to the researcher. The population may be all the individuals of a particular type or a more restricted part of that group. All public schoolteachers, all male secondary schoolteachers, all elementary schoolteachers, or all Chicago kindergarten teachers may be populations.

A *sample* is a small proportion of a population selected for observation and analysis. By observing the characteristics of the sample, one can make certain inferences about the characteristics of the population from which it is drawn. Contrary to some popular opinion, samples are not selected haphazardly; they are chosen in a systematically random way so that chance or the operation of probability can be utilized.

This concept of sampling is discussed in more detail in Chapter 6 where we discuss threats to external validity and generalization. For now, we will focus on methods of sampling.

Randomness

The concept of *randomness* has been basic to scientific observation and research. It is based on the assumption that while individual events cannot be predicted with accuracy, aggregate events can. For instance, although it may not predict with great accuracy an individual's academic achievement, it will predict accurately the average academic performance of a group.

Randomization has two important applications in research:

1. Selecting a group of individuals for observation who are representative of the population about which the researcher wishes to generalize, or
2. Equating experimental and control groups in an experiment. Assigning individuals by random assignment is the best method of providing for their equivalence.

It is important to note that a random sample is not necessarily an identical representation of the population. Characteristics of successive random samples drawn from the same population may differ to some degree, but it is possible to estimate their variation from the population characteristics and from each other. The variation, known as *sampling error*, does not suggest that a mistake has been made in the sampling process. Rather, sampling error refers to the chance variations that occur in sampling; with randomization these variations are predictable and taken into account in data-analysis techniques. The topic of sampling error is considered in greater detail in Chapter 11 in the discussion of the central limit theorem, the standard error of the mean, and the level of significance.

The Simple Random Sample

The individual observations or individuals are chosen in such a way that each has an equal chance of being selected, and each choice is independent of any other choice. If researchers wished to draw a sample of 50 individuals from a population of 600 students enrolled in a school, they could place the 600 names in a container and, blindfolded, draw one name at a time until the sample of 50 was selected. This procedure is cumbersome and is rarely used. Rather, a random numbers table or computer-generated list is more common.

Random Numbers

A more convenient way of selecting a random sample or assigning individuals to experimental and control groups so that they are equated is by the use of a table of random numbers. Many such tables have been generated by computers producing a random sequence of digits. *The million random digits with 100,000 normal deviates* of the Rand Corporation (1965) and Fisher and Yates's (1963) *Statistical tables for biological, agricultural and medical research* are frequently used.

When a table is used, it is necessary to assign consecutive numbers to each member of the population from which the sample is to be selected. Then, entering the table at any page, row, or column, the researcher can select the sample from 001 to 999, three digits, and from 0001 to 9999, four digits. When a duplicated number or a number larger than the population size is encountered, it is skipped, and the process continues until the desired sample size is selected.

As an illustration assume that a sample of 30 is to be selected from a serially numbered population of 835. Using a portion of the table of random numbers reproduced here (see Table 1.1), 30 three-digit numbers are selected by reading from left to right. When using the table of random numbers to select a sample, the population members must be numbered serially. Then, entering the table at any page, row, or column at random, the researcher can select the sample by reading to the left, right, up, down, or diagonally. For populations up to 99 in number, two digits are selected; from 001 to 999, three digits; and from 0001 to 9999, four digits.

The sample comprises these 30 numbered members of the population. If this group were to be divided into two equated groups of 15 each, the first 15 could compose one group, and the second 15, the other. There are many varieties of random assignment, such as assigning the odd numbers to one group (1, 3, 5, 7, . . .) and the even numbers (2, 4, 6, 8, . . .) to the other.

For those with access to a computer, many packaged computer programs include the capability to produce a random numbers table. A simple program can generate a table of random numbers designed for a particular study.

It is apparent that to select a random sample, one must not consciously select any particular individual or observation. The size of the sample may or may not be significantly related to its adequacy. A large sample, carelessly selected, may be biased and inaccurate, whereas a smaller one, carefully selected, may be relatively unbiased and accurate enough to make satisfactory inference possible. However, a well-selected large sample is more representative of the population than a well-selected smaller sample. This is explained in greater detail in the discussions of sampling error and the central limit theorem in Chapter 11.

TABLE 1.1   An Abbreviated Table of Random Numbers

50393	13330	92982	07442	63378	02050
09038	31974	22381	24289	72341	61530
82066	06997	44590	23445	72731	61407
91340	84979	39117	89344	46694	95596

The Sample

503	426	197	161	590	~~913~~	444
~~931~~	337	422	530	~~234~~	408	669
333	802	381	820	457	497	
092	050	242	660	273	~~939~~	
~~982~~	090	~~897~~	699	~~161~~	117	
074	383	234	744	407	~~893~~	

In selecting this sample, eight numbers were deleted. Numbers 931, 982, 897, 913, 939, and 893 were deleted because they were larger than the population of 835 described. Numbers 234 and 161 were deleted because they duplicate previous selections.

In addition to caution in the sampling process, definition of the population about which inferences are to be made is extremely important. When the now defunct *Literary Digest* drew its sample for the purpose of predicting the results of the 1936 presidential election, subjects were chosen from the pages of telephone directories and from automobile registration lists. The prediction of Alfred Landon's victory over Franklin D. Roosevelt proved to be wrong, and a postelection analysis revealed that the population for which the prediction was made was not the same population sampled. Large numbers of eligible voters did not own automobiles and were not telephone subscribers and consequently were not included in the sample. In fact, the resulting sample was systematically biased to overrepresent the wealthy and underrepresent the poor and unemployed.

The Systematic Sample

If a population can be accurately listed or is finite, a type of systematic selection will provide what approximates a random sample. A *systematic sample* consists of the selection of each *nth* term from a list. For example, if a sample of 200 were to be selected from a telephone directory with 200,000 listings, one would select the first name by randomly selecting a name from a randomly selected page. Then every thousandth name would be selected until the sample of 200 names was complete. If the last page were reached before the desired number had been selected, the count would continue from the first page of the directory. Systematic samples of automobile owners could be selected in similar fashion from a state licensing bureau list or file or a sample of eighth-grade students from a school attendance roll.

The Stratified Random Sample

At times it is advisable to subdivide the population into smaller homogeneous groups to get more accurate representation. This method results in the *stratified random sample.* For example, in an income study of wage earners in a community, a true sample would approximate the same relative number from each socioeconomic level of the whole community. If, in the community, the proportion were 15% professional workers, 10% managers, 20% skilled workers, and 55% unskilled workers, the sample should include approximately the same proportions to be considered representative. Within each subgroup a random selection should be used. Thus, for a sample of 100, the researcher would randomly select 15 professional workers from the subpopulation of all professional workers in the community, 10 managers from that subpopulation, and so on. This process gives the researcher a more representative sample than one selected from the entire community, which might be unduly weighted by a preponderance of unskilled workers.

In addition to, or instead of socioeconomic status, such characteristics as age, gender, extent of formal education, ethnic origin, religious or political affiliation, or rural-urban residence might provide a basis for choosing a stratified sample. The characteristics of the entire population together with the purposes of the study must be carefully considered before a stratified sample is decided on.

The Area or Cluster Sample

The *area* or *cluster sample* is a variation of the simple random sample that is particularly appropriate when the population of interest is infinite, when a list of the members of the population does not exist, or when the geographic distribution of the individuals is widely scattered. For example, if researchers wanted to survey students in 100 homerooms in secondary schools in a large school district, they could first randomly select 10 schools from all of the secondary schools in the district. Then from a list of homerooms in the 10 schools they could randomly select 100.

A more likely scenario in which cluster sampling would be needed is if, for the purpose of a survey, researchers wanted to select a sample from all public school elementary teachers in the United States. A simple random sample would be impracticable. From the 50 states a random sample of 20 could be selected. From these 20 states all counties could be listed and a random sample of 80 counties selected. From the 80 counties all the school districts could be listed and a random sample of 30 school districts selected. It would not be difficult to compile a list of all elementary teachers from the 30 school districts and to select a random sample of 500 teachers. This successive random sampling of states, counties, school districts, and, finally, of individuals would involve a relatively efficient and inexpensive method of selecting a sample of individuals.

This method of sampling is likely to introduce an element of sample bias because of the unequal size of some of the subsets selected. Only when a simple random sample would be impracticable is this method recommended.

Nonprobability Samples

Nonprobability samples are those that use whatever subjects are available rather than following a specific subject selection process. Some nonprobability sampling procedures may produce samples that do not accurately reflect the characteristics of a population of interest. Such samples may lead to unwarranted generalizations and should not be used if random selection is practicable.

Educational researchers, because of administrative limitations in randomly selecting and assigning individuals to experimental and control groups, often use available classes as samples. The status of groups may be equated by such statistical means as the analysis of covariance (discussed in Chapter 11). In certain types of descriptive studies, the use of available samples may restrict generalizations to similar populations. For example, when a psychology professor uses students from Introduction to Psychology classes as subjects, the professor may safely generalize only to other similar groups of psychology students.

A sample consisting of those who volunteer to participate in a study may represent a biased sample. Volunteers are not representative of a total population because volunteering results in a selection of individuals who are different and who really represent a population of volunteers. In a sense, those who respond to a mailed questionnaire are volunteers and may not reflect the characteristics of all who were on the mailing list. It may be desirable to send another copy of the instrument to nonrespondents with an appeal for their participation.

Sample Size

The bigger the sample, the better the statistics and results.

There is usually a trade-off between the desirability of a large sample and the feasibility of a small one. The ideal sample is large enough to serve as an adequate representation of the population about which the researcher wishes to generalize and small enough to be selected economically—in terms of subject availability and expense in both time and money. There is no fixed number or percentage of subjects that determines the size of an adequate sample. It may depend on the nature of the population of interest or the data to be gathered and analyzed. A national opinion poll randomly selects a sample of about 1,500 subjects as a reflection of the opinions of a population of more than 150 million United States citizens of voting age, with an error factor of 2 to 3%.

Before the second decade of the 20th century, statisticians believed that samples should be relatively large so that the normal probability table could be used to estimate sampling error, explained by the central limit theorem. (See Chapter 11 for a discussion of sampling error and students' distribution.) The work of William Sealy Gosset in 1915, in which he developed data on the probability distribution of small sample means (student's t distribution), led to the effective use of small samples. Gosset's contribution made feasible research studies that necessarily had to be limited to a small number of subjects. Small-sample research has made a significant contribution to statistical analysis of research data, particularly in experimental studies.

Samples of 30 or more are usually considered large samples and those with fewer than 30, small samples. At approximately this sample size of 30, the magnitude of student's t critical values for small samples approaches the z critical values of the normal probability table for large samples. (See Chapter 11 for a discussion of z and t critical values.)

More important than size is the care with which the sample is selected. The ideal method is random selection, letting chance or the laws of probability determine which members of the population are to be selected. When random sampling is employed, whether the sample is large or small, the errors of sampling may be estimated, giving researchers an idea of the confidence that they may place in their findings.

In summary, here are several practical observations about sample size:

1. The larger the sample, the smaller the magnitude of sampling error and the greater likelihood that the sample is representative of the population.
2. Survey studies typically should have larger samples than are needed in experimental studies because the returns from surveys are from those who, in a sense, are volunteers.
3. When samples are to be subdivided into smaller groups to be compared, researchers should initially select large enough samples so that the subgroups are of adequate size for their purpose.

4. In mailed questionnaire studies, because the percentage of responses may be as low as 20 to 30%, a large initial sample should be selected to receive the mailing so that the final number of questionnaires returned is large enough to enable researchers to have a small sampling error.
5. Subject availability and cost factors are legitimate considerations in determining appropriate sample size.

WHAT IS RESEARCH?

How is research related to scientific method? The terms *research* and *scientific method* are sometimes used synonymously in educational discussions. Although it is true that the terms have some common elements of meaning, a distinction is helpful.

For the purposes of this discussion, *research* is considered to be the more formal, systematic, and intensive process of carrying on a scientific method of analysis. Scientific method in problem solving may be an informal application of problem identification, hypothesis formulation, observation, analysis, and conclusion. You could reach a conclusion as to why your car wouldn't start or why a fire occurred in an unoccupied house by employing a scientific method, but the processes involved probably would not be as structured as those of research. Research is a more systematic activity that is directed toward discovery and the development of an organized body of knowledge. *Research may be defined as the systematic and objective analysis and recording of controlled observations that may lead to the development of generalizations, principles, or theories, resulting in prediction and possibly ultimate control of events.*

Because definitions of this sort are rather abstract, a summary of some of the characteristics of research may help to clarify its spirit and meaning.

1. Research is directed toward the solution of a problem. The ultimate goal is to discover cause-and-effect relationships between variables, though researchers often have to settle for the useful discovery of a systematic relationship because the evidence for a cause-and-effect relationship is insufficient.
2. Research emphasizes the development of generalizations, principles, or theories that will be helpful in predicting future occurrences. Research usually goes beyond the specific objects, groups, or situations investigated and infers characteristics of a target population from the sample observed. Research is more than information retrieval, the simple gathering of information. Although many school research departments gather and tabulate statistical information that may be useful in decision making, these activities are not properly termed *research.*
3. Research is based on observable experience or empirical evidence. Certain interesting questions do not lend themselves to research procedures because they cannot be observed. Research rejects revelation and dogma as methods of establishing knowledge and accepts only what can be verified by observation.
4. Research demands accurate observation and description. Researchers may choose to use quantitative measuring devices when appropriate to answer the

question under study. When this is not possible or appropriate to answer the researchers' question using quantitative methods, they may choose from a variety of qualitative or nonquantitative methods to describe their observations. Good research utilizes valid and reliable data-gathering procedures.

5. Research involves gathering new data from primary, or firsthand, sources or using existing data for a new purpose. Teachers frequently assign a so-called research project that involves writing a paper dealing with the life of a prominent person. Students are expected to read a number of encyclopedias, books, or periodical references and to synthesize the information in a written report. This is not research, for the data are not new. Merely reorganizing or restating what is already known and has already been written, valuable as it may be as a learning experience, is not research. It adds nothing to what is known.

6. Although research activity may at times appear somewhat random and unsystematic, it is more often characterized by carefully designed procedures that apply rigorous analysis. Although trial and error are often involved, research is rarely a blind, shotgun investigation or an experiment just to see what happens.

7. Research requires expertise. The researcher knows what is already known about the problem and how others have investigated it. He or she has searched the related literature carefully and is also thoroughly grounded in the terminology, concepts, and technical skills necessary to understand and analyze the data gathered.

8. Research strives to be objective and logical, applying every possible test to validate the procedures employed, the data collected, and the conclusions reached. The researcher attempts to eliminate personal bias. There is no attempt to persuade or to prove an emotionally held conviction. The emphasis is on testing rather than on proving the hypothesis. Although absolute objectivity is as elusive as pure righteousness, the researcher tries to suppress bias and emotion in his or her analysis.

9. Research involves the quest for answers to unsolved problems. Pushing back the frontiers of ignorance is its goal, and originality is frequently the quality of a good research project. However, previous important studies are deliberately repeated, using identical or similar procedures, with different subjects and different settings and at a different time. This process is *replication.* Replication is always desirable to confirm or to raise questions about the conclusions of a previous study.

10. Research is characterized by patient and unhurried activity. It is rarely spectacular, and researchers must expect periodic disappointment and discouragement as they pursue the answers to difficult questions.

11. Research is carefully recorded and reported. Each important term is defined, limiting factors are recognized, procedures are described in detail, references are carefully documented, results are objectively recorded, and conclusions are presented with scholarly caution and restraint. The written report and accompanying data are made available to the scrutiny of associates or other scholars. Any competent scholar will have the information necessary to analyze, evaluate, and even replicate the study.

12. Research sometimes requires courage. The history of science reveals that many important discoveries were made in spite of the opposition of political and religious authorities. The Polish scientist Copernicus (1473–1543) was condemned by church authorities when he announced his conclusion concerning the nature of the solar system. His theory, in direct conflict with the older Ptolemaic theory, held that the sun, not the earth, was the center of the solar system. Copernicus angered supporters of prevailing religious dogma, who viewed his theory as a denial of the story of creation as described in the book of Genesis. Modern researchers in such fields as genetics, sexual behavior, and even business practices have aroused violent criticism from those whose personal convictions, experiences, or observations were in conflict with some of the research conclusions.

The rigorous standards of scientific research are apparent from an examination of these characteristics. The research worker should be a scholarly, imaginative person of the highest integrity, who is willing to spend long hours painstakingly seeking knowledge. However, it must be recognized that researchers are human beings. The ideals that have been listed are probably never completely realized. They are goals to strive for and are not all achieved by every researcher.

Many people have a superficial concept of research, picturing research workers as strange, introverted individuals who, shunning the company of their fellows, find refuge in their laboratories. There, surrounded by test tubes, retorts, beakers, and other gadgets, they carry on their mysterious activities. In reality the picture is quite different. Research is not all mysterious, and it is carried on by thousands of quite normal individuals, more often in teams than alone and very often in the factory, the school, or the community, as well as in the laboratory. Its importance is attested to by the tremendous amounts of time, manpower, and money spent on research by industry, universities, government agencies, and the professions. The key to the cultural development of the Western world has been research, the reduction of areas of ignorance by discovering new truths, which in turn lead to better predictions, better ways of doing things, and new and better products. We recognize the fruits of research: better consumer products, better ways of preventing and treating disease, better ways of understanding the behavior of individuals and groups, and a better understanding of the world in which we live. In the field of education, we identify research with a better understanding of the individual and a better understanding of the teaching–learning process and the conditions and environments under which it is most successfully carried on.

PURPOSES OF RESEARCH

Fundamental or Basic Research

To this point we have described research in its more formal aspects. Research has drawn its pattern and spirit from the physical sciences and has represented a rigorous, structured type of analysis. We have presented the goal of research as the development of theories by the discovery of broad generalizations or principles. We have employed careful sampling procedures to extend the findings beyond the group or situation studied. So far our discussion has shown little concern for the application of the findings to actual problems in areas considered to be the concern of people other than the investigator. Such an approach, which often leads to knowledge for knowledge's sake, is the approach of *basic* or *fundamental research.*

Fundamental research is usually carried on in a laboratory or some other sterile environment, sometimes with animals. This type of research, which generally has no immediate or planned application, may later result in further research of an applied nature.

Applied Research — *try it out !*

Applied research has most of the characteristics of fundamental research, including the use of sampling techniques and the subsequent inferences about the target population. However, its purpose is improving a product or a process—testing theoretical concepts in actual problem situations. Most educational research is applied research, for it attempts to develop generalizations about teaching–learning processes, instructional materials, the behavior of children and ways to modify it, and so on.

Fundamental research in the behavioral sciences may be concerned with the development and testing of theories of behavior. Educational research is concerned with the development and testing of theories of how students and teachers behave in educational settings.

Action Research — *use w/o testing then evaluate results*

Since the late 1930s the fields of social psychology and education have shown great interest in what has been called *action research.* In education this movement has had as its goal the involvement of both research specialist and classroom teacher in the study and application of research to educational problems in a particular classroom setting.

Action research is focused on immediate application, not on the development of theory or on generalization of applications. It has placed its emphasis on a problem here and now in a local setting. Its findings are to be evaluated in terms of local applicability, not universal validity. Its purpose is to improve school practices and at the same time to improve those who try to improve the practices: to combine the research processes, habits of thinking, ability to work harmoniously with others, and professional spirit.

If most classroom teachers are to be involved in research activity, it will probably be in the area of action research. Modest studies may be conducted for the purpose of trying to improve local classroom practices. It is not likely that many teachers will have the time, resources, or technical background to engage in the more formal aspects of research activity. Fundamental research must continue to make its essential contribution to behavioral theory, and applied research to the improvement of educational practices. These activities, however, will be primarily the function of professional researchers, many of them subsidized by universities, private and government agencies, professional associations, and philanthropic foundations.

Many observers have disparaged action research as nothing more than the application of common sense or good management. But whether or not it is worthy of the term *research,* it does apply scientific thinking and methods to real-life problems and represents a great improvement over teachers' subjective judgments and decisions based on folklore and limited personal experiences.

In concluding this discussion it is important to realize that research may be carried on at various levels of complexity. Respectable research studies may be the simple descriptive fact-finding variety that lead to useful generalizations. Actually, many of the early studies in the behavioral sciences were useful in providing needed generalizations about the behavior or characteristics of individuals and groups. Subsequent experimental studies of a more complex nature needed this groundwork information to suggest hypotheses for more precise analysis. For example, descriptive studies of the intellectually gifted, carried on since the early 1920s by the late Lewis M. Terman and his associates, have provided useful generalizations about the characteristics of this segment of the school population. Although these studies did not explain the factors underlying giftedness, they did provide many hypotheses investigated later by more sophisticated experimental methods.

ASSESSMENT, EVALUATION, AND DESCRIPTIVE RESEARCH

The term *descriptive research* has often been used incorrectly to describe three types of investigation that are basically different. Perhaps their superficial similarities have obscured their differences. Each of them employs the process of disciplined inquiry through the gathering and analysis of empirical data, and each attempts to develop knowledge. To be done competently, each requires the expertise of the careful and systematic investigator. A brief explanation may serve to put each one in proper perspective. A more complete discussion can be found in Chapter 5.

Assessment is a fact-finding activity that describes conditions that exist at a particular time. No hypotheses are proposed or tested, no variable relationships are examined, and no recommendations for action are suggested.

The national census is a massive assessment type of investigation conducted by the Bureau of the Census, a division of the United States Department of Commerce. Every 10 years an enumeration of the population is conducted, with data classified by nationality, citizenship, age, gender, race, marital status, educational level, regional and community residence, employment, economic status, births, deaths, and other characteristics. These data provide a valuable basis for social analysis and government action.

In education, assessment may be concerned with the determination of progress that students have made toward educational goals. The *National Assessment of Educational Progress* (NAEP), originally known as the Committee on Assessment of the Progress of Education, has been financed by the National Center for Educational Statistics. Since 1969 a nationwide testing program has been conducted in such fields as science, mathematics, literature, reading, and social studies, in four age groupings, in various geographical areas of the country, in communities of various sizes, and in particular states and has reported interesting evidence of the degree to which learning goals have or have not been realized.

Evaluation is concerned with the application of its findings and implies some judgment of the effectiveness, social utility, or desirability of a product, process, or program in terms of carefully defined and agreed on objectives or values. It may involve recommendations for action. It is not concerned with generalizations that may be extended to other settings. In education it may seek answers to such questions as: How well is the science program developing the competencies that have been agreed on by the faculty curriculum committee? Should the program in vocational or agriculture education be dropped? Are the library facilities adequate? Should the reading textbook series currently in use be retained?

Descriptive research, unlike assessment and evaluation, is concerned with all of the following: hypothesis formulation and testing, the analysis of the relationships between nonmanipulated variables, and the development of generalization. It is this last characteristic that most distinguishes descriptive research from assessment and evaluation. Although assessment and evaluation studies may include other characteristics of descriptive research, only descriptive research has generalization as its goal. Unlike the experimental method, in which variables are deliberately arranged and manipulated through the intervention of the researcher, in descriptive research variables that exist or have already occurred are selected and observed. This process is described as *ex post facto, explanatory observational,* or *causal-comparative research* in Chapter 5. Both descriptive and experimental methods employ careful sampling procedures so that generalizations may be extended to other individuals, groups, times, or settings.

TYPES OF EDUCATIONAL RESEARCH

Any attempt to classify types of educational research poses a difficult problem. The fact that practically every textbook suggests a different system of classification provides convincing evidence that there is no generally accepted scheme. In addition, there is the potential confusion with what we termed the purposes of research (basic, applied, or action) earlier in this chapter. Some would consider this structure as three types of research. However, because little educational research is fundamental, most being applied or action, we present four categories of research methods that are most common in educational research. Any one of these categories could include research studies that are of a basic, applied, or action nature.

To systematize a method of presentation, however, some pattern is desirable. At the risk of seeming arbitrary and with a recognition of the danger of oversimplification, we suggest a framework that might clarify understanding of basic principles of research methodology. It should be noted that the system of classification is not important in itself but has value only in making the analysis of research processes more comprehensible.

Actually, *all* research involves the elements of observation, description, and the analysis of what happens under certain circumstances. A rather simple four-point analysis may be used to classify educational research. Practically all studies fall under one, or a *combination*, of these types:

1. *Historical research* describes *what was.* The process involves investigating, recording, analyzing, and interpreting the events of the past for the purpose of discovering generalizations that are helpful in understanding the past and the present and, to a limited extent, in anticipating the future.
2. *Descriptive research (quantitative)* uses quantitative methods to describe *what is,* describing, recording, analyzing, and interpreting conditions that exist. It involves some type of comparison or contrast and attempts to discover relationships between existing nonmanipulated variables. Some form of statistical analysis is used to describe the results of the study.
3. *Qualitative descriptive research* uses nonquantitative methods to describe *what is.* Qualitative descriptive research uses systematic procedures to discover nonquantifiable relationships between existing variables.
4. *Experimental research* describes *what will be* when certain variables are carefully controlled or manipulated. The focus is on variable relationships. As defined here, deliberate manipulation is always a part of the experimental method.

These four categories are not meant to imply that a study cannot include more than one category. For example, a study might include both quantitative and qualitative methods. At least one entire chapter of this text is devoted to each of these types of research, to techniques of data gathering, and to methods of analysis.

SUMMARY

Human beings' desire to know more about their world has led them from primitive superstition to modern scientific knowledge. From mysticism, dogma, and the limitations of unsystematic observation based on personal experience, they have examined the process of thinking itself to develop the method of deductive–inductive thinking, which has become the foundation of scientific method. Although first applied as a method of the physical sciences, the process of scientific inquiry has also become the prevailing method of the behavioral sciences.

There is no single scientific method because scientists carry on their investigations in a number of ways. However, accuracy of observation and the qualities of imagination, creativity, objectivity, and patience are some of the common ingredients of all scientific methods.

The hypothesis is an essential research device that gives a focus to the investigation and permits researchers to reach probability conclusions. After researchers formulate an affirmative research hypothesis at the outset of their project, they restate the hypothesis in negative, or null, form for the purposes of statistical analysis of their observations. This procedure facilitates inferring population characteristics from observed variable relationships as they relate to the error inherent in the sampling process.

Sampling, a deliberate rather than haphazard method of selecting subjects for observation, enables the scientist to infer conclusions about a population of interest from the observed characteristics of a relatively small number of cases. Simple random, systematic, stratified random, area or cluster, and available (nonprobability) samples have been described. Methods of determining the size of an appropriate sample are suggested, and the sources of sample bias are considered.

Research has been defined as *the systematic and objective analysis and recording of controlled observations that may lead to the development of generalizations, principles, or theories, resulting in prediction and possibly ultimate control of events.* The characteristics of research that may help to clarify its spirit and meaning have been presented.

Fundamental or *basic* research is the formal and systematic process of deductive–inductive analysis, leading to the development of theories. *Applied* research adapts the theories developed through fundamental research to the solution of problems. *Action* research, which may fail to attain the rigorous qualities of fundamental and applied research, attempts to apply the spirit of scientific method to the solution of problems in a particular setting, without any assumptions about the general application of findings beyond the situation studied.

In this chapter we have classified research as historical, descriptive, or experimental, and we have established assessment, evaluation, and descriptive research as three distinct types of investigation. Descriptive research may be either quantitative or qualitative, and experimental research may include groups of subjects or single subjects.

Remember that research is essentially an intellectual and creative activity. The mastery of techniques and processes does not confer research competence, though these skills may help the creative problem solver to reach his or her objectives more efficiently.

EXERCISES

1. Construct two syllogisms:
   a. One that is sound.
   b. One that is faulty. Indicate the nature of the fallacy.

2. Illustrate the application of Dewey's steps in problem solving. Choose one of the problems listed, or one of your own:
   a. brown patches on your lawn
   b. your car won't start when you leave for home
   c. getting an economical buy on canned peaches
   d. most of the members of your class failed an examination

3. Give an example of:
   a. a pure research problem
   b. an applied research problem
   c. an action research problem

4. To what extent have religious institutions resisted the claims of science?

5. Is there necessarily a conflict between the disciplines of the sciences and the humanities?

6. Explain why you agree or disagree with the following statements:
   a. Excessive effort is spent on the development of theories because they don't usually work in real situations.
   b. Science is more properly thought of as a method of problem solving than as a field of knowledge.
   c. Applied research is more important than pure research in contributing to human welfare.

7. How would you select a sample of 40 college students for a morale study from a freshman class of 320?

8. From a metropolitan school district staff directory you wish to select a sample of 300 teachers from a listing of 3,800. Discuss several ways in which the sample could be selected, considering the issues that may be involved.

9. What are the distinctive characteristics of descriptive research as contrasted with:
   a. assessment
   b. evaluation
   c. experimental research

10. How is the term *research* sometimes misused in classroom assignments and television interviews?

REFERENCES

Cohen, J. (1990). Things I have learned (so far). *American Psychologist, 45,* 1304–1312.

Dewey, J. (1938). *Logic: The theory of inquiry.* New York: Holt, Rinehart & Winston.

Fisher, R. A., & Yates, F. (1963). *Statistical tables for biological, agricultural, and medical research.* Edinburgh: Oliver & Boyd.

Frick, R. W. (1995). Accepting the null hypothesis. *Memory and Cognition, 23,* 132–138.

Harcharick, K. (1993). Piaget and the university internship experience. *Journal of Cooperative Education, 29,* 24–32.

Kahn, J. V. (1985). Evidence of the similar-structure hypothesis controlling for organicity. *American Journal of Mental Deficiency, 89,* 372–378.

Kahn, J. V. (1996). Cognitive skills and sign language knowledge of children with severe and profound mental retardation. *Education and Training in Mental Retardation, 31,* 162–168.

Kahn, J. V. (1992). Predicting adaptive behavior of severely and profoundly mentally retarded children with early cognitive measures. *Journal of Intellectual Deficiency Research, 36,* 101–114.

Karplus, R., Lawson, A. E., Wolman, W., Appel, M., Bernoff, R., Howe, A., Rusch, J. J., & Sullivan, F. (1977). *Science teaching and the development of reasoning.* Berkeley: Lawrence Hall of Science, University of California.

Mees, C. E. K. (1934). Scientific thought and social reconstruction. *American Scientist, 22,* 13–14.

McCormick, P. K., Campbell, J. K., Pasnak, R., & Perry, P. (1990). Instruction on Piagetian concepts for children with mental retardation. *Mental Retardation, 28,* 359–366.

Murphy, K. R. (1990). If the null hypothesis is impossible, why test it? *American Psychologist, 45,* 403–404.

Piaget, J. (1970). *Science of education and the psychology of the child.* New York: Viking Press.

Rand Corporation (1965). *A million random digits with 100,000 normal deviates.* New York: Free Press.

Read, L. (1995). Amos bear gets hurt. *Young Children, 50,* 19–23.

Snow, R. E. (1973). Theory construction for research on teaching. In R. M. W. Travers (Ed.), *Second handbook of research on teaching.* Chicago: Rand McNally.

Sophian, C. (1995). Representation and reasoning in early numerical development: Counting, conservation, and comparisons between sets. *Child Development, 66,* 559–577.

Staver, J. R., & Gabel, D. L. (1979). The development and construct validation of a group-administered test of formal thought. *Journal of Research in Science Teaching, 16,* 535–544.

Wolinsky, C. F. (1970). Piaget's theory of perception: Insights for educational practices with children who have perceptual difficulties. In I. J. Athey & D. O. Rubadeau (Eds.), *Educational implications of Piaget's theory.* Waltham, MA: Ginn-Blaisdell.

2

SELECTING A PROBLEM
AND PREPARING
A RESEARCH PROPOSAL

One of the most difficult phases of the graduate research project is the choice of a suitable problem. Beginners are likely to select a problem that is much too broad in scope. This may be due to their lack of understanding of the nature of research and systematic problem-solving activity. It may also be due to their enthusiastic but naive desire to solve an important problem quickly and immediately.

Those who are more experienced know that research is often tedious, painfully slow, and rarely spectacular. They realize that the search for truth and the solution of important problems take a great deal of time and energy and the intensive application of logical thinking. Research makes its contribution to human welfare by countless small additions to knowledge. The researcher has some of the characteristics of the ant, which brings its single grain of sand to the anthill.

Before considering the ways in which problems may be identified, we will discuss a few of the characteristics of research and the activities of the researcher. Research is more often a team endeavor than an individual activity. Researchers working in groups attack problems in different ways, pooling their knowledge and ideas and sharing the results of their efforts. Highly publicized discoveries usually result from the cumulative efforts of many, working as teams over long periods of time. They are rarely the product of a single individual working in isolation.

Great discoveries rarely happen by accident. When they do, the researcher is usually well grounded and possesses the ability, known as *serendipity*, to recognize the significance of these fortunate occurrences. He or she is imaginative enough to seize the opportunity presented and to carry it through to a fruitful conclusion. Pasteur observed that chance favors the prepared mind.

Researchers are specialists rather than generalists. They employ the principle of the rifle rather than the shotgun, analyzing limited aspects of broad problems.

Critics have complained that much social research consists of learning more and more about less and less until the researcher knows everything about nothing. This is a clever statement but an exaggeration. The opposite statement, equally clever and exaggerated, characterizes much ineffective problem solving: learning less and less about more and more until one knows nothing about everything.

There is a danger, however, that research activity may focus on such fragmentary aspects of a problem that it has little relevance to the formulation of a general theory. An analysis of the relationship among a few isolated factors in a complex situation may seem attractive as a research project, but it will make little or no contribution to a body of knowledge. Research is more than compiling, counting, and tabulating data. It involves deducing the consequences of hypotheses through careful observation and the application of rigorous logic.

It is sometimes important to discover that a generalization is probably *not* true. Beginning researchers frequently associate this type of conclusion with a sense of personal failure, for they become emotionally committed to their hypotheses. Research, however, is a process of *testing* rather than *proving*, and it implies an objectivity that lets the data lead where they will.

THE ACADEMIC RESEARCH PROBLEM

Academic research projects have been subjected to much criticism, both by the academic community and by the general public. The academic research project is usually necessary in partial fulfillment of the requirements of a graduate course or for an advanced degree. The initial motivation may not be the desire to engage in research but the practical need of meeting a requirement. The lack of time, financial resources, and inexperience of the student researcher are hindrances to significant contributions. But these projects are often justified on the grounds that once students develop some research competency, they will use their "know-how" to seek solutions to basic problems and will make a contribution to the body of knowledge on which sound practices are based. In addition, to be a competent consumer of others' research, one must be capable of producing research of one's own. Finally, although few such studies make a significant contribution to the development or refinement of knowledge or to the improvement of practice, those that do make an impact, even if only one in twenty, make this endeavor worthwhile. One way to increase the likelihood of the student's research project being theoretically valuable is for the student to work with a faculty member who is conducting research.

When master's degree or doctoral studies are carried on under the close supervision of an advisor or major professor who is devoting his or her energies to research on a significant problem, the student's thesis may make an important contribution. The efforts of the degree candidate can then be directed toward certain restricted phases of the major problem, making possible long-term longitudinal studies. Such studies as those by the late Lewis M. Terman at Stanford University of gifted children, followed over 50 years, represent the cumulative attack that is likely to yield more significant results than the uncoordinated investigations of candidates whose efforts lack this unifying direction and continuity.

However, few graduate students in education are full-time students; consequently, they often have competing demands of teaching, supervising student activities, attending meetings, and participating in administrative activity. This may result in less contact with their advisors and a more independent research project. Thus, most graduate students tend to select practical problems that are closely related to their school experience but are not primarily theoretically based. These studies are often based on the students' school experiences, which may be of greater significance to schoolchildren than the theoretically based research of their faculty.

Levels of Research Projects

In the light of the varied types and purposes of students' projects, choice of a problem will depend on the level at which the research is to be done. Typically, a problem appropriate for a beginner in a first course in research is different from that selected for the more rigorous requirements of the master's thesis or the doctoral dissertation. One way for beginners to make a contribution to the research literature is to have them engage in research with faculty members who have long-term projects under way. The emphasis for these students will be placed on the learning process of the beginning researcher, rather than on his or her unique contribution to education. Through working with a faculty member on extant research, the student will be able to make a contribution and learn at the same time.

Some students choose a first problem that can be expanded later into a more comprehensive treatment at the level of the master's thesis or the doctoral dissertation. The first study thus serves as an exploratory process.

Sources of Problems

The choice of a suitable problem is always difficult. Few beginners possess real problem awareness, and even the more experienced researcher hesitates at this step. It is a serious responsibility to commit oneself to a problem that will inevitably require much time and energy and that is so academically significant. What are the most likely sources to which one may go for a suitable research problem or from which one may develop a sense of problem awareness?

Many of the problems confronted in the classroom, the school, or the community lend themselves to investigation, and they are perhaps more appropriate for the beginning researcher than are problems more remote from his or her own teaching experience. What organizational or management procedures are employed? How is learning material presented? To what extent does one method yield more effective results than another? How do teachers feel about these procedures? How do pupils and parents feel about them? What out-of-school activities and influences seem to affect students and the teaching–learning process? Teachers will discover "acres of diamonds" in their own backyards, and an inquisitive and imaginative mind may discover in one of these problem areas an interesting and worthwhile research project.

Technological changes and curricular developments are constantly bringing forth new problems and new opportunities for research. Perhaps more than ever before, educational innovations are being advocated in classroom organization, in teaching materials and procedures, and in the application of technical devices and equipment. Such innovations as computer-assisted instruction, teaching by television, programmed instruction, modified alphabets, new subject matter concepts and approaches, flexible scheduling, and team teaching need to be carefully evaluated through the research process.

The graduate academic experience should stimulate the questioning attitude toward prevailing practices and effectively promote problem awareness. Classroom lectures, class discussions, seminar reports, and out-of-class exchanges of ideas with fellow students and professors will suggest many stimulating problems to be solved. Students who are fortunate enough to have graduate assistantships have a special opportunity to profit from the stimulation of close professional relationships with faculty members and fellow assistants.

Reading assignments in textbooks, special assignments, research reports, and term papers will suggest additional areas of needed research. Research articles often suggest techniques and procedures for the attack on other problems. A critical evaluation may reveal faults or defects that made published findings inconclusive or misleading. Many research articles suggest problems for further investigation that may prove fruitful.

Consultation with the course instructor, advisor, or major professor is helpful. Although the student should not expect research problems to be assigned, consultation with a faculty member is desirable. Most students feel insecure as they approach the choice of a research problem. They wonder if the problem they may have in mind is significant enough, feasible, and reasonably free of unknown hazards. To expect the beginner to arrive at the advisor's office with a completely acceptable problem is unrealistic. One of the most important functions of the research advisor is to help students clarify their thinking, achieve a sense of focus, and develop a manageable problem from one that may be too vague and complex.

The following list may suggest areas from which research problems may be further defined:

1. Multiculturalism in the classroom
2. Distance instruction
3. Modified alphabets (e.g., Initial Teaching Alphabet)
4. Flexible scheduling
5. Team teaching
6. Evaluation of learning, reporting to parents
7. Student regulation/control
8. Learning styles
9. Peer tutoring

10. Homework policies and practices
11. Field trips
12. School buildings and facilities, lighting, space, safety
13. Extracurricular programs
14. Student out-of-school activities: employment, recreation, cultural activity, reading, television viewing
15. Teacher out-of-school activities: employment, political activity, recreation
16. Uses of the Internet in instruction
17. English as a second language programs
18. New approaches to biology, chemistry, physics
19. Language laboratories: foreign languages, reading
20. Comparison of multiple textbooks
21. Independent study programs
22. Advanced placement program
23. Audiovisual programs
24. Sociometry
25. Health services
26. Guidance-counseling programs
27. Teacher morale: annoyances and satisfactions
28. Teacher welfare: salaries, merit rating, retirement, tenure
29. Educational organizations: local, state, and national; NEA, AFT
30. Inner-city schools, effects of poverty, Head Start, Upward Bound, tutoring
31. Pre-service education of teachers: student teaching
32. Teacher attitudes on a variety of issues, e.g., inclusion of special-needs students
33. In-service programs
34. Effects of racial integration: student, teacher
35. Parochial/private school problems, tax credits
36. Follow-up of graduates, dropouts
37. Religion and education: released time programs, dismissed time, shared time
38. Non-school-sponsored social organizations or clubs
39. School district reorganization
40. Community pressures on the school: academic freedom, controversial issues
41. Legal liability of teachers
42. School vouchers
43. Small schools within large schools
44. Sex education
45. Ability grouping: acceleration, retardation/promotion
46. Special education: speech therapy, clinical services, social services
47. Problems in higher education: selection, prediction of success, graduate programs
48. Work-study programs
49. Attribution of success and failure
50. Comparison of the effectiveness of two teaching methods/procedures

51. Self-image analysis
52. Vocational objectives of students
53. History of an institution, program, or organization
54. Factors associated with the selection of teaching, nursing, or social work as a career
55. Case studies of an interesting student or teacher
56. Socioeconomic status and academic achievement
57. Perceptions of administrative leadership
58. The effect of stress on academic achievement
59. Minimal competency tests for promotion and/or graduation
60. Merit pay for teachers

For those students who are not teachers, some of the problem areas listed may be appropriate in social agency, hospital, or industrial situations. Keep in mind that this list includes general topics that need a great deal of refinement to become a researchable problem. The student usually needs the help of a faculty member in gradually refining the general topic into a useful statement of a research problem.

To take a general topic or problem, such as those listed, and refine it into a researchable problem, the individual needs to define certain components of the problem: the population of interest, the situation, what part of the issue is to be addressed in the first (or next) study, and so forth.

For example, item 49 deals with the issue of attribution of success and failure. To make this a researchable problem requires a good deal of narrowing and refinement. One researchable problem that can be derived from this broad topic (using the approach referred to in the previous paragraph) asks the question, Will college freshmen who are internally focused (attributing their successes and failures to themselves) do better in their first year of college than those who are externally focused (attributing their successes and failures to external factors)? Another equally plausible research question from this same topic is, Do learning-disabled adolescents differ from nondisabled adolescents on a measure of attribution? As can be seen, many researchable problems can be derived from this topic. Only by narrowing the focus (e.g., population, situation, measurements) can a researchable problem be derived. Once the scope of the topic or problem has been narrowed to make it a potentially researchable problem, we can then determine its importance and feasibility.

Evaluating the Problem

Before the proposed research problem can be considered appropriate, several searching questions should be raised. Only when these questions are answered in the affirmative can the problem be considered a good one:

1. Is this the type of problem that can be effectively solved through the process of research? Can relevant data be gathered to test the theory or find the answer to the question under consideration?

2. Is the problem significant? Is an important principle involved? Would the solution make any difference as far as educational theory or practice is concerned? If not, there are undoubtedly more significant problems waiting to be investigated.

3. Is the problem a new one? Is the answer already available? Ignorance of prior studies may lead a student to spend time needlessly on a problem already investigated by some other worker. However, although novelty or originality is an important consideration, simply because a problem has been investigated in the past does not mean that it is no longer worthy of study. At times it is appropriate to replicate (repeat) a study to verify its conclusions or to extend the validity of its findings to a different situation or population. For instance, research with children might be of great importance to replicate with mentally retarded children. Similarly, much cross-cultural research consists of replicating research conducted in one country with samples in another country. For instance, Kohlberg's (1984; Power, Higgins, & Kohlberg, 1989) theory of moral reasoning has been shown to be valid in a number of countries, thereby supporting the universality of the theory.

4. Is research on the problem feasible? After a research project has been evaluated, there remains the problem of suitability for a particular researcher. The student should ask: Although the problem may be a good one, is it a good problem for me? Will I be able to carry it through to a successful conclusion? Some of the questions the students should consider are the following:

    a. Am I competent to plan and carry out a study of this type? Do I know enough about this field to understand its significant aspects and to interpret my findings? Am I skillful enough to develop, administer, and interpret the necessary data-gathering devices and procedures? Am I well grounded in the necessary knowledge of research design and statistical procedures?

    b. Are pertinent data accessible? Are valid and reliable data-gathering devices and procedures available? Will school authorities permit me to contact the students, conduct necessary experiments or administer necessary tests, interview teachers, or have access to important cumulative records? Will I be able to get the sponsorship necessary to open doors that otherwise would be closed to me?

    c. Will I have the necessary financial resources to carry on this study? What will be the expense involved in data-gathering equipment, printing, test materials, travel, and clerical help? If the project is an expensive one, what is the possibility of getting a grant from a philanthropic foundation or from such governmental agencies as the National Institute of Education?

    d. Will I have enough time to complete the project? Will there be time to devise the procedures, select the data-gathering devices, gather and analyze the data, and complete the research report? Because most academic programs impose time limitations, certain worthwhile projects of a longitudinal type are precluded.

e. Will I have the determination to pursue the study despite the difficulties and social hazards that may be involved? Will I be willing to work aggressively when data are difficult to gather and when others are reluctant to cooperate? Controversial problem areas such as sex education and multiculturalism are probably not appropriate for a beginning research project.

THE RESEARCH PROPOSAL

The preparation of a research proposal is an important step in the research process. Many institutions require that a proposal be submitted before any project is approved. This provides a basis for the evaluation of the project and gives the advisor a basis for assistance during the period of his or her direction. It also provides a systematic plan of procedure for the researcher to follow.

The proposal is comparable to the blueprint that an architect prepares before the bids are let and building commences. The initial draft proposal is subject to modification after review by the student and his or her project advisor or committee. Because good research must be carefully planned and systematically carried out, procedures that are improvised from step to step will not suffice. A worthwhile research project is likely to result only from a well-designed proposal.

The seven-part proposal format presented here should not be considered the only satisfactory sequence. In fact, the first five parts are often contained in two major components: the statement of the problem and its significance, and the review of the literature and hypotheses, which might also include definitions, assumptions, limitations, and delimitations. Many institutions and funding agencies suggest or require other formats for the research proposal. Still, most proposal formats include the need for all of the information requested in the seven-part format presented here. When one is submitting a proposal for funding or organizational (e.g., graduate school) approval, it is wise to follow the format suggested by the funding or approval source.

Part 1: The Statement of the Problem
This is often a declarative statement but may be in question form. This attempt to focus on a stated goal gives direction to the research process. It must be limited enough in scope to make a definite conclusion possible. The major statement may be followed by minor statements. The problem areas that were listed earlier in this chapter are not statements of problems. They are merely broad areas of concern from which problems may be derived.

A problem often implies that a controversy or difference of opinion exists. Problems can be derived from theory, prior research results, or personal observation and experience. Most frequently problems are based on a significant concern (e.g., a rate of illiteracy among adults that is unacceptable in modern society) and an insufficient knowledge base regarding what to do about the concern. Examples of problem statements are:

Are children who have attended kindergarten better prepared for first grade?

Participation in high school competitive athletics may conflict with optimal academic performance.

Racial segregation may have a damaging effect on the self-image of minority group children.

Knowledge of participation in an experiment may have a stimulating effect on the reading achievement of participants.

These problem statements involve more than information gathering. They suggest hypotheses and provide a focus for research activity.

Part 2: The Significance of the Problem

It is important that the researcher point out how the solution to the problem or the answer to the question can influence educational theory or practice. That is, the researcher must demonstrate why it is worth the time, effort, and expense required to carry out the proposed research. Careful formulation and presentation of the implications or possible applications of knowledge help to give the project an urgency, justifying its worth.

Failure to include this step in the proposal may well leave the researcher with a problem without significance—a search for data of little ultimate value. Many of the tabulating or "social bookkeeping" research problems should be abandoned if they do not pass the critical test of significance. Perhaps university library shelves would not groan with the weight of so many unread and forgotten dissertations if this criterion of significance had been rigorously applied. With so many gaps in educational theory and so many areas of education practice in need of analysis, there is little justification for the expenditure of research effort on trivial or superficial investigations.

Part 3: Definitions, Assumptions, Limitations, and Delimitations

It is important to define all unusual terms that could be misinterpreted. These definitions help to establish the frame of reference with which the researcher approaches the problem. The variables to be considered should be defined in operational terms. Such expressions as *academic achievement* and *intelligence* are useful concepts, but they cannot be used as criteria unless they are defined as observable samples of behavior. Academic grades assigned by teachers or scores on standardized achievement tests are operational definitions of achievement. A score on a standardized intelligence test is an operational definition of intelligence.

Assumptions are statements of what the researcher believes to be facts but cannot verify. A researcher may state the assumption that the participant observers in the classroom, after a period of three days, will establish rapport with the students and will not have a reactive effect on the behavior to be observed.

Limitations are those conditions beyond the control of the researcher that may place restrictions on the conclusions of the study and their application to other situations. Administrative policies that preclude using more than one class in an experiment, a data-gathering instrument that has not been validated, or the inability to randomly select and assign subjects to experimental and control groups are examples of limitations.

Delimitations are the boundaries of the study. A study of attitudes toward racial minorities may be concerned only with middle-class, fifth-grade pupils, and conclusions are not to be extended beyond this population sampled.

Part 4: Review of Related Literature

A summary of the writings of recognized authorities and of previous research provides evidence that the researcher is familiar with what is already known and what is still unknown and untested. Because effective research is based on past knowledge, this step helps to eliminate the duplication of what has been done and provides useful hypotheses and helpful suggestions for significant investigation. Citing studies that show substantial agreement and those that seem to present conflicting conclusions helps to sharpen and define understanding of existing knowledge in the problem area, provides a background for the research project, and makes the reader aware of the status of the issue. Parading a long list of annotated studies relating to the problem is ineffective and inappropriate. Only those studies that are plainly relevant, competently executed, and clearly reported should be included.

In searching related literature the researcher should note certain important elements:

1. Reports of studies of closely related problems that have been investigated
2. Design of the study, including procedures employed and data-gathering instruments used
3. Populations that were sampled and sampling methods employed
4. Variables that were defined
5. Extraneous variables that could have affected the findings
6. Faults that could have been avoided
7. Recommendations for further research

Capitalizing on the reviews of expert researchers can be fruitful in providing helpful ideas and suggestions. Although review articles that summarize related studies are useful, they do not provide a satisfactory substitute for an independent search. Even though the review of related literature is presented as step 4 in the finished research proposal, the search for related literature is one of the first steps in the research process. It is a valuable guide to defining the problem, recognizing its significance, suggesting promising data-gathering devices, appropriate study design, and sources of data.

Part 5: The Hypothesis

It is appropriate here to formulate a major hypothesis and possibly several minor hypotheses. This approach further clarifies the nature of the problem and the logic underlying the investigation and gives direction to the data-gathering process. A good hypothesis has several basic characteristics:

1. It should be reasonable.
2. It should be consistent with known facts or theories.
3. It should be stated in such a way that it can be tested and found to be probably true or probably false.
4. It should be stated in the simplest possible terms.

The research hypothesis is a tentative answer to a question. It is an educated guess or hunch, generally based on prior research and/or theory, to be subjected to the process of verification or disconfirmation. The gathering of data and the logical analysis of data relationships provide a method of confirming or disconfirming the hypothesis by deducing its consequences.

It is important that the hypothesis be formulated before data are gathered. Suppose that the researcher gathers some data and, on the basis of these, notes something that looks like the basis for an alternative hypothesis. Because any particular set of observations may display an extreme distribution, using such observations to test the hypothesis would possibly lead to an unwarranted conclusion.

The formulation of the hypothesis in advance of the data-gathering process is necessary for an unbiased investigation. It is not inappropriate to formulate additional hypotheses after data are collected, but they should be tested on the basis of new data, not on the old data that suggested them.

Part 6: Methods

This part of the research proposal usually consists of three parts: *subjects, procedures,* and *data analysis.* The *subjects* section details the population from which the researcher plans to select the sample. Variables that are frequently included, depending on the type of project proposed, include chronological age, grade level, socioeconomic status, sex, race, IQ (if other than average), mental age (if significantly different from chronological age), academic achievement level, and other pertinent attributes of the targeted population. The number of subjects desired from the population and how they will be selected are also indicated in this section. The reader should be able to understand exactly from where and how the subjects are to be selected so as to make replication possible.

The *procedures* section outlines the research plan. It describes in detail what will be done, how it will be done, what data will be needed, and what data-gathering devices will be used (see Chapter 9). Again, the detail should be sufficient for the reader to be able to replicate the procedures.

The method of *data analysis* is described in detail in the third part of the methods section. The information given in the data-analysis section should be specific and detailed enough to demonstrate to the reader exactly what is planned. No details should be left open to question.

Part 7: Time Schedule

Although this step may not be required by the study advisor, a time schedule should be prepared so that the researcher can budget his or her time and energy effectively. Dividing the project into manageable parts and assigning dates for their completion help to systematize the study and minimize the natural tendency to procrastinate.

Some phases of the project cannot be started until other phases have been completed. Such parts of the final research report as the review of related literature can be completed and typed while waiting for the data-gathering process to be completed. If the project is complicated, a flow chart or time-task chart may be useful in describing the sequence of events. Because academic research projects usually involve critical time limitations and definite deadlines for filing the completed report, the planning of procedures with definite date goals is important. From time to time the major professor or advisor (or funding agency) may request a progress report. This device also serves as a stimulus, helping the researcher to move systematically toward the goal of a completed project.

ETHICS IN HUMAN EXPERIMENTATION

In planning a research project involving human subjects, it is important for the researcher to consider the ethical guidelines designed to protect his or her subjects. In particular, medical and psychological experimentation using human subjects involves some element of risk, however minor, and raises questions about the ethics of the process. Any set of rules or guidelines that attempts to define ethical limits for human experimentation raises controversy among members of the scientific community and other segments of society. Too-rigid controls may limit the effectiveness of research, possibly denying society the answers to many important questions. On the other hand, without some restraints, experimental practices could cause serious injury and infringe on human rights.

These issues go beyond courtesy or etiquette and concern the appropriate treatment of persons in a free society. Some of these questions have been dealt with by scientists and philosophers, by enactment of legislative bodies, by codes of ethics and professional organizations, or by guidelines established by educational institutions.

In 1974 the U.S. Congress established the National Commission for the Protection of Human Subjects of Biomedical and Behavioral Research to formulate guidelines for the research activities of the National Institutes of Health and the National Institute of Mental Health.

The Commission's 4-year, monthly deliberations, supplemented by discussions held at the Smithsonian Institution's Belmont Conference Center, resulted in the publication of the *Belmont report: Ethical principles and guidelines for the protection of human subjects of research* (1979). A videotape based on the Belmont report (*The Belmont report: Basic ethical principles and their application*) was produced in 1986. This videotape describes the basic ethical principles of conducting research with human subjects, including respect for the persons involved. It illustrates these principles using case studies of actual biomedical and behavioral research.

Universities have established human experiment review committees to advise academic investigators about appropriate procedures and to approve those studies that conform to their ethical guidelines. Most private and governmental funding agencies require such a review prior to awarding of grants. The university may have *ad hoc* committees concerned with a particular study or standing committees that deal with all experimental activities involving the institution or division. In cases where serious risks must be weighed against the potential benefits to society, reviews by both *ad hoc* and institution-wide committees may be deemed necessary. Some faculty researchers have complained that review committees have unduly restricted their experimental activities. It is possible in some cases that particular members of the committee did not have the technical background to make sound judgments outside their own fields of competence. Others have felt that, because the committee assignment demanded so much of their time, they could not contribute their best effort. However, because the human experiment review committee maintains the ethical standards of the institution and supervises the ethical guidelines established by the U.S. government, it serves a critical purpose.

In 1953 the American Psychological Association issued its first code of ethics for psychologists. In 1963 the code was revised, and its preamble contained the following statement:

> *The psychologist believes in the dignity and worth of the individual human being. He is committed to increasing man's knowledge of himself and others. While pursuing this endeavor he protects the welfare of any persons who may seek his services, or any subject, human or animal, that may be the object of his study. He does not use his professional position or relationship, nor does he knowingly permit his own services to be used by others, for purposes inconsistent with these values. While demanding for himself freedom of inquiry and communication, he accepts the responsibility this freedom confers; for competence where he claims it, for objectivity in the report of his findings, and for the consideration of the best interests of his colleagues and of society. (American Psychological Association, 1963, p. 2)*

In 1970 the Board of Directors appointed an *Ad Hoc* Committee on Ethical Standards in Psychological Research to bring the 1963 code up to date in light of changes in the science, in the profession, and in the broader social context in which psychologists practice. The first draft of the committee report was circulated among 18,000 members of the association. About 5,000 responded with suggestions. In addition, journal editors, staff members of research review committees, directors of research organizations, writers on research ethics, and leaders in such special fields as hypnosis were interviewed. These contributions were supplemented by discussions at regional and national meetings of the association. Psychology departments of universities, hospitals, clinics, and government agencies as well as anthropologists, economists, sociologists, lawyers, philosophers, and psychiatrists were consulted.

As a result of these conversations and correspondence with professionals from all scholarly disciplines, a final draft was adopted and published in 1973. In 1978 a Committee for the Protection of Human Subjects in Psychological Research was established and charged with making annual reviews and recommendations regarding the official APA position. These annual reviews led to a revision, which went through a similar process of consultation as the 1973 edition. A final draft that incorporated various suggestions was adopted and published in 1982. Subsequently in August 1992 the American Psychological Association's Council of Representatives adopted the most recent ethical standards. These were published in December 1992. Although these ethical standards include all psychological practices, we describe only those related to research practices. The standards on research ethics published in 1992 were consistent with those published in 1982.

Ten principles were formulated that deal specifically with the experimenter's responsibilities toward participants. In the published reports, *Ethical Principles of Psychologists and Code of Conduct* (American Psychological Association, 1992) and *Ethical Principles in the Conduct of Research with Human Participants* (American Psychological Association, 1982), each principle is stated with discussion of issues, problems, and recommendations for appropriate action. The meticulous care with which this code was developed attests to the concern of this professional organization for ethical practices in psychological research. Readers who are interested in a more complete discussion on ethics in human experimentation are urged to read these reports.

The following discussion, while not a summary of the American Psychological Association (APA) code of ethics, is consistent with the APA code. The guidelines discussed here are not ethical absolutes. Rather, they characterize writing in the field of ethics and a number of professional codes that the authors have examined. The guidelines deal with the following areas of concern: informed consent; invasion of privacy; confidentiality; deception; protection from stress, harm, or danger; and knowledge of outcome.

Informed Consent

Recruitment of volunteers for an experiment should always involve the subjects' complete understanding of the procedures employed, the risks involved, and the demands that may be made on participants. Whenever possible, subjects should also be informed of the purpose of the research. When subjects are not competent to give informed consent due to age, illness, or disability, the informed consent of parents, guardians, or responsible agents must be secured. This freedom to participate or to decline to participate is basic, and it includes the freedom to withdraw from an experiment at any time without penalty. Coercion to participate or to remain as a participant must not be applied, and any exploitation of participants is an unethical practice.

The following are examples of experiment-recruitment practices that might raise ethical questions:

1. Subjects who are inmates of penal institutions volunteer to participate in anticipation of more favorable treatment or recommendation of earlier parole.

2. Medical students who need money are recruited for experiments by offers of financial reward.
3. Participants who do not have the mental capacity to give rational consent—persons who are mentally ill or mentally retarded, or those with reduced capacity—are recruited in institutions or nursing homes.
4. Members of a college class are required to participate in an experiment to meet a course requirement.

In some cases it may be possible to dispense with informed consent, depending on the institutional guidelines and discussion with colleagues. Such instances might include the use of anonymous questionnaires, observations in a natural setting, or archival research.

Invasion of Privacy

Ordinarily it is justifiable to observe and record behavior that is essentially public, behavior that others normally would be in a position to observe. It is an invasion of privacy to observe and record intimate behavior that the subject has reason to believe is private. Concealed observers, cameras, microphones, or the use of private correspondence without the subject's knowledge and permission are invasions of privacy. If these practices are to be employed, the researcher should explain the reasons and secure permission.

This statement is not to suggest that intimate behavior cannot be observed ethically. The sexual behavior studies of Doctors Masters and Johnson are based on observation and recording of the most intimate acts, but subjects volunteered to participate with full knowledge of the purposes and procedures employed. The motivation is based on confidence in the integrity of the researchers and the importance of their scientific contributions to human welfare.

Confidentiality

The ethical researcher holds all information that he or she may gather about the subject in strict confidence, disguising the participant's identity in all records and reports. No one should be in a position to threaten the subject's anonymity nor should any information be released without his or her permission.

Deception

Participants should not be deceived about the purpose or nature of the research unless "justified by the study's prospective scientific, educational, or applied value and that equally effective alternative procedures that do not use deception are not feasible" (American Psychological Association, 1992, p. 1609). Even then the participants should never be deceived about any aspect of the study that might "affect their willingness to participate, such as physical risks, discomfort, or unpleasant emotional experiences" (p. 1609). Finally, any deception must be explained to the subjects at the earliest opportunity, generally immediately after their participation is complete. Studies using deception are given particularly rigorous reviews by institutional review committees.

Protection from Physical and Mental Stress, Harm, or Danger

In using treatments that may have a temporary or permanent effect on the subjects, the researcher must take all precautions to protect their well-being. Treatments are administered under the direction of competent professional practitioners in clinical or research facilities where effective and thorough precautions and safeguards may be assured. Where some risk is unavoidable, the potential benefits may be sufficient to justify the research. A balance needs to be achieved, with benefit outweighing risk, in such a case.

Knowledge of Outcome

The participant has a right to receive an explanation for the reasons for the experimental procedures and the results of the investigation. The researcher may explain the results and their significance orally, in writing, or by informing participants of the issue of the journal in which the report is published.

The American Educational Research Association (AERA) (1992) also has published ethical standards that include sections on research, intellectual ownership, and students and student researchers. The ten ethical standards regarding research include informed consent; honesty between researchers and participants and institutional representatives; sensitivity to local institutional policies; participants' right to withdraw; researchers' not exploiting research populations, subordinates, or students; sensitivity to cultural, religious, gender, and other differences among participants; careful consideration and minimization of techniques that might have negative social consequences (e.g., negative sociometrics); researchers' need to be sensitive to the integrity of ongoing local institutional activities; communication of research findings clearly to appropriate research populations and other stakeholders; and participants' right to anonymity. As the reader will note, there is a great deal of overlap and no conflict between the AERA and APA policies.

Ethical researchers not only observe these ethical guidelines but also take complete responsibility for the actions of their co-experimenters, colleagues, assistants, technical personnel, secretaries, and clerks involved in the project, constantly monitoring their research activities. Researchers have obligations to their subjects, their professional colleagues, and the public. They do not discard unfavorable data that would modify the interpretation of their investigation. They make their data available to their professional peers so that they may verify the accuracy of the results. They honor promises made to subjects as a consideration for their participation in a study. They give appropriate credit to those who have aided them in their investigations, participated in the data analysis, or contributed to the preparation of the research report. They place scientific objectivity above personal advantage and recognize their obligation to society for the advancement of knowledge.

Recently there have been reports in the news media of fraudulent behavior. These news reports have related instances of fraud connected with research funded by the National Institutes of Health, which has its own investigators. These instances of fraudulent behavior have resulted in a great deal of embarrassment for those involved, including a Nobel laureate who co-authored a paper that included fraudulent data (unbeknownst to him) and a prison sentence in at least one case for misappropriation of funds. Some researchers have been known to justify deception, coercion, invasion of privacy, breach of confidentiality, or risks to subjects in the name of science, but one might suspect that the prestige, ambition, or ego of the experimenter was the primary motivation.

USING THE LIBRARY

The student should become thoroughly acquainted with the university library, the location of its varied facilities, and the services it provides. In addition to the traditional card catalog, university libraries have computerized their holdings and have placed terminals in various locations for ease of finding books and periodicals. Many large research-oriented university libraries also permit access to their list of holdings through various terminals and computers throughout campus and through dial-up phone lines from computers with modems.

Sometimes a student learns of a reference that is not available in the local library. Most libraries belong to one of the major shared cataloging systems. The most common of these is the Online Computer Library Center (OCLC) with the holdings of over 3,000 libraries. The list of books and periodicals available and the libraries holding these materials can be quickly accessed on a time-sharing computer system available in most libraries. The student's library requests the books or a photocopy of the article, which is then loaned to the student by the library. Some libraries provide access to WorldCat, which permits users with a university computer account to search OCLC from any computer with a modem.

Finding Related Literature

Students often waste time searching for references in an unsystematic way. The search for references is an ever-expanding process, for each reference may lead to a new list of sources. Researchers may consider these sources as basic:

1. *The Education Index*
2. *Resources in Education*
3. *Current Index to Journals in Education*
4. *Index to Doctoral Dissertations* and *Dissertation Abstracts International*
5. Other specialized indexes or abstracts indicated by the area of investigation (e.g., *Psychological Abstracts, Social Science Citation Index*)

Appendix J lists indexes and abstracts that the student or researcher may use to find articles and books on his or her topic. Many of these databases, including *Resources in Education,* which is a monthly abstract journal of the publications of the Educational Research Information Centers (ERIC), *Exceptional Child Education Resources, Psychological Abstracts,* and dozens of others, can be accessed directly through one of the computer services available to libraries. Virtually all college and university libraries and many public libraries offer this service. The investigator, often independently but sometimes with the help of a librarian, uses key words to let the computer system know which materials are desired. For instance, if a researcher is reviewing the literature that has used Piagetian theory with persons with mental retardation, she or he might use the key words *Piaget* with *mental retardation, mentally retarded,* and *retardation.* The computer then searches all the titles and abstracts for those containing both *Piaget* and one of the other key words. The investigator can then have the titles or titles and abstracts printed, usually at a printer nearby. Sometimes it is possible to download the information to a disk that the researcher keeps.

The specific services that are available at an individual library may include on-line services such as the Illinois Bibliographic Information Service (IBIS), which is available to all subscribing Illinois libraries. Other states and regions offer their own services similar to IBIS. These services offer a wide range of subject-based indexes and abstracts, which can be searched interactively. Also available at many libraries are computers set up with CD-ROM databases for searching one or more abstracts or indexes.

Microfiche

The development of microfiche has been an important contribution to library services by providing economy and convenience of storing and distribution of scholarly materials. A microfiche is a sheet of film that contains images of printed materials. Filmed at a reduction of 1 to 24 or higher, nearly one hundred 8½" × 11" pages of copy can be reproduced on one 4" × 6" film card. Microfiche readers that magnify the images to original or larger copy size are available at libraries. Some microfiche readers provide up to 40× magnification on screens as large as 15" × 21".

Many document-reproduction services supply microfiche to libraries on subscription or by special order. Many documents are produced by ERIC of studies that otherwise may not be published because of their length or other issues. Many of these ERIC documents are written reports of conference presentations or final reports to funding agencies. *Resources in Education* and *The Education Index* as well as the computer search services include ERIC documents along with publications in journals. It is easy to tell if the researcher has located a journal article or ERIC document of interest by the letters preceding the number of the item: *ED* stands for an ERIC document and *EJ* indicates a journal article.

NOTE TAKING

One of the most important research activities of the graduate student is note taking—putting materials in a form that can easily be recalled and used in the future. Notes will result from speeches and lectures, class discussions, conversation, solitary meditation, and reading reference materials. When the graduate student prepares term papers and research reports, the notes that result from reading will be most significant. Without a careful, systematic method of note taking, much of what is read is quickly forgotten.

Reading-reference notes have been classified under four principal categories:

1. *Quotation.* The exact words of an author are reproduced and enclosed in quotation marks. It is essential to copy each statement accurately and to indicate the exact page reference so that the quotations can be properly referenced in the written report.
2. *Paraphrase.* The reader restates the author's thoughts in his or her own words.
3. *Summary.* The reader states in condensed form the contents of the article.
4. *Evaluation.* The reader records his or her own reaction, indicating agreement or disagreement or interpreting the point of view of the writer.

A single note card may include several of these types when it seems appropriate.

A Suggested Method for Taking Notes

1. Skim the reference source before taking any notes. A bird's-eye view is essential before you can decide what material to record and use. Selecting the most significant material is a skill to be cultivated.
2. Use 4" × 6" index cards. They are easily sorted by subject headings and are large enough to include a reasonable amount of material. Some students prefer 5" × 8" cards, which are less convenient to carry but provide more space for notes.
3. File each note card under a definite topic or heading. Place the subject heading at the top of the card for convenient filing. A complete bibliographic citation should be placed at the bottom of the note card. If a book has been used, the call number should be indicated to facilitate library location in the future.
4. Include only one topic on a card. This makes organization of notes flexible. If the notes are lengthy, use consecutively numbered cards and slip a rubber band around them before filing.
5. Be sure that notes are complete and clearly understandable, for they are not likely to be used for some time after they have been taken.
6. Distinguish clearly between a summary, a direct quotation of the author, a reference to the author's source, and an evaluative statement.
7. Do not plan to recopy or type your notes. It wastes time and increases the possibility of error and confusion. Copy your notes carefully the first time.
8. Keep a supply of note cards with you at all times so that you can jot down ideas that come to you while waiting, riding the bus, or listening to a lecture or discussion.
9. Keep a permanent file of your notes. You may find the same notes useful in a number of courses or in writing a number of reports.

When taking notes consider the advisability of making photocopies of book and journal pages so that they can be examined more efficiently at home. The trend toward microfilming and microfiching professional literature will continue as the constantly increasing volume of published materials burdens limited shelf space. In the future journals will likely be offered on computer disk as well. Coin-operated microfilm and microfiche printers are found in most university libraries.

REFERENCES AND BIBLIOGRAPHY

In preparing a journal report, paper, or research proposal the author is expected to include a list of the references that have been cited in the text. Sometimes it is preferable to include additional materials that were used by the author but not actually cited in the paper. In this case the author provides a bibliography that includes all the relevant references, cited or not. This is not in keeping with the American Psychological Association style described and used in this text, which includes only references actually cited. However, other styles of writing and referencing permit or even encourage the listing of all relevant publications.

The most convenient way to assemble and organize references or a bibliography is by the use of bibliography cards. The card includes the names of the author(s), the facts of publication, and the annotation (see Chapter 3 for examples using the American Psychological Association system). Placing the information on cards makes it easy to assemble the authors' names in alphabetical order in the reference section of the report. There are computer programs that store bibliographic information from which the researcher can select those references needed in any given report. Some researchers just keep adding to this list and then select those needed.

Fair Use of Copyrighted Materials

The doctrine of *fair use* has been codified in the *Copyright Law of the United States* (United States Copyright Office, 1994) in section 107. Section 107 contains a list of purposes for which copyrighted material may be reproduced. It also states the circumstances, including the amount of the work and the effect on the value of the material, under which the material can be reproduced. Short quotations of a copyrighted publication may be reproduced without permission in books, articles, and other publications. This is often interpreted as fewer than 250 words (in total) from a book-length work or less than 5% of a journal article. The reproduction of artwork such as a graph or chart needs permission. Permission is not needed for a paraphrase of the original work. However, a paraphrase means a substantial re-writing of the original, not just changing a few words. Whether a quotation or a paraphrase, the researcher needs to provide appropriate reference to the work as discussed in Chapter 3.

THE FIRST RESEARCH PROJECT

Experience has indicated that one way to understand the methodology and processes of research is to engage in research. Such a project may be very modest in nature and necessarily limited by time, the experience of the student, and many other factors associated with the graduate student's other obligations. However, the methodology may be learned by actively engaging in the research process under the careful supervision of the instructor in the beginning course in research. Respectable research projects have been undertaken and reported on within a semester's time, even within an 8-week summer session. Although most of these studies have been of the descriptive-survey type, some simple historical and experimental studies have also been completed. The emphasis must necessarily be placed on the process rather than on the product or its contribution to the improvement of educational practice.

The full-scale project may be either an individual or a group enterprise. Groups of three to five graduate students can profitably work together on the planning of the study. Data-gathering devices may be chosen or constructed through joint enterprise. Data may be gathered within the university graduate class or in the classrooms, schools, or communities in which the group's members teach. However, it is recommended that the next steps—organization and analysis of data and the writing of the final report—be an individual project. There is always the danger in a group project of "letting George do it," and, incidentally, letting George get all the benefit from the experience.

This recommended combination of group effort in the initial stages and individual effort in the later stages represents a compromise that seems effective and enables students to carry through a study in a limited amount of time with reasonable opportunity for personal growth. For some of those who will write a thesis in partial fulfillment of degree requirements, this first project may serve as preparation. For others it may initiate a study capable of subsequent expansion into a thesis or dissertation.

Many research course instructors believe that a more practical requirement would be the preparation of a carefully designed research proposal rather than a limited-scope study. Much can be said for this point of view because the beginning research student is inexperienced, the time is short, and there is a real danger of conveying a superficial concept of sound research.

The following topics were selected by student researchers who were carrying out a project or writing a proposal in partial fulfillment of the requirements of a beginning course in educational research. Most of the topics were short, action-type descriptive studies, not based upon random selection and random assignment of subjects or observations. Notice that the wording of many of the titles did not imply generalization of the conclusions to a wider population. The *primary* purpose was a learning exercise, with a contribution to a field of knowledge being secondary.

Topics Used by Students in a Beginning Graduate Course in Educational Research

1. Student Attitudes about the Use of Theater in an English Class
2. The Reading Skill Development of a Deaf First-Grade Child
3. The Status of Latin in Indiana High Schools
4. Discipline Problems at Washington High School as Viewed by a Group of Seniors

5. Case Study of a Child with Bipolar Disorder
6. The Status of Music in the Western Yearly Meeting of the Society of Friends
7. The Rehabilitation of a Group of Cocaine Addicts in a Federally Funded Drug Treatment Center
8. The Social Development of a 6-Year-Old Autistic Child
9. The Effect of Trial Promotion on the Academic Achievement of a Group of Underachievers
10. The Effects of Parent Visitation on the Reading Performance of a Group of Fourth-Grade Students
11. The Predictive Value of Entrance Examinations at the Methodist School of Nursing
12. The Interests of a 3-Year-Old Boy: A Case Study
13. Survey of Teacher Attitudes Regarding Inclusion of Special Needs Students
14. A Comparison of Regular Classroom and Learning Disabled Children's Expressive Language Skills
15. The Effect of Verbal Mediation on the Mathematical Achievement of Learning Disabled Students
16. The Effect of Teacher Education on Attitudes toward Mainstreaming
17. Effect of Verbalization on Performance and On-Task Behavior of Reading Disabled Children
18. Prevalence of Behavior Problems of Hearing Siblings of Deaf Children
19. The Influence of Kindergarten Experience on the Subsequent Reading Achievement of a Group of Third-Grade Pupils
20. A Sociometric Analysis of Behavior Disordered Adolescents Integrated into Regular High School Classes
21. The Attitudes and Behavior of Freshmen and Seniors Regarding Classroom Dishonesty at Sheridan High School
22. The Attitudes of a Group of Florida School Superintendents toward Mandated Minimum Competency Testing
23. Authority Images of a Selected Group of Inner-City Children
24. The Achievement of Twins, Both Identical and Fraternal, in the Lebanon, Indiana, Metropolitan School District
25. A Follow-up Study of Non-Promoted Students at School #86
26. A History of the Indiana Boys' School, Plainfield, Indiana
27. A Comparative Analysis of the Self-Concepts of a Group of Gifted and Slow-Learning Children
28. The Attitudes of a Group of High School Seniors toward Nuclear Protest Movements
29. The Use of the *Distar* Reading Program with an Autistic Child
30. The Attitudes of a Group of Graduate Students toward Mandated Smoking Restrictions in Public Facilities
31. The Influence of Entering Age on the Subsequent Achievement at First-, Second-, and Third-Grade Levels in Washington Township
32. The Attitudes of a Selected Group of Black and White Parents toward Busing to Achieve Racial Integration

33. A Study of Socioeconomic Status in the Butler–Tarkington Area, a Racially Integrated Community
34. A Follow-Up Study of the 1970 Graduates of Grace Lutheran School
35. The Effect of Title IX, Prohibiting Sex Discrimination in Public Schools, on the Athletic Budgets of Illinois Public Colleges and Universities

For experienced researchers, projects would be more theory-oriented, with conclusions generalized beyond the specific group observed. At this more advanced level a careful process of randomization would be desirable, if not necessary, and the research design would be much more rigorous. The details of some of the more sophisticated procedures are explained in subsequent chapters of this text and in other relevant sources, particularly in discussion of experimental and descriptive research processes, the selection or construction of data-gathering devices, and the statistical analysis of data.

SUBMITTING A RESEARCH PROPOSAL TO A FUNDING AGENCY

Experienced researchers submit research proposals to foundations or government agencies to support their research. These proposals, especially to government agencies, are usually written in response to the agency's Request for Proposals (RFP) on a specific topic (e.g., a national center on literacy) or in a general area (e.g., field-initiated research on populations with disabilities). The RFP (or if there is no RFP, the funding guidelines provided by the agency or foundation) is usually quite specific in the goals and priorities for funding. The RFP also provides guidelines for writing the proposal, including a suggested format and sometimes a copy of the guidelines to be used in rating the proposal. These review guidelines may include the number of points assigned to each component of the grant proposal and what the reviewers should be looking for in the proposal. Usually the significance of the proposed research and the methodology are the two most important components for being successful and receiving a grant.

Because of the highly competitive nature of funded research, it is critical that the proposal author respond carefully to the priorities of the funding agency. In fact, it may be useful to discuss the proposal with a representative of the agency or foundation before completing and submitting it. Agency personnel are surprisingly open and willing to provide suggestions. In addition, a number of foundations will initially review only brief descriptions (one or two pages) of proposed research and then request full proposals only from those descriptions that seem most promising. Government agencies in particular also will provide the author of an unsuccessful grant proposal with the reviewers' comments, which may lead to a greatly improved proposal for future submission. The beginning researcher may find it useful to understand the type of detailed information that a government agency or foundation would expect to receive before committing funds.

Here is a list of suggestions for those who seek financial support:

1. Write the proposal very carefully. A carelessly written proposal suggests to the evaluators that the research project would be carelessly done. It is also useful to follow the format recommended by the agency in writing the proposal.
2. Pay attention to stated goals and priorities of the foundation or agency. It is important to point out how your study would be relevant to these goals.
3. State your problem in such a way that the proposal evaluators, who are capable and experienced in judging research proposals but know nothing about your project, will be able to judge its worth and the likelihood of its contributing to a significant area of knowledge.
4. Indicate how your study will add to or refine present knowledge.
5. State your hypothesis or hypotheses in both conceptual and operational terms and in both substantive and null form.
6. Indicate that you are completely familiar with the field of investigation and are aware of all recent studies in the problem area.
7. Indicate how you propose to test your hypotheses, describing your research design and the data-gathering instruments or procedures that you will use, indicating their known validity and reliability.
8. Describe your sampling procedures, indicating how you will randomly select and randomly assign your subjects or observations or why random selection and assignment is not possible and/or unnecessary.
9. Indicate the confounding variables that must be recognized, and explain how you propose to minimize their influence.
10. Explain the statistical procedures that you will employ, indicating any computer application that you will use.
11. Prepare a budget proposal of the funds required for

    a. wages, including any fringe benefits
    b. purchase or rental of special equipment or supplies
    c. travel expenses
    d. clerical expenses
    e. additional overhead expenses that may be involved
    f. publication costs

12. Provide some tangible evidence of your competence by listing

    a. research projects that you have carried on or in which you have actively participated
    b. your scholarly journal articles, including abstracts of your studies
    c. your academic training and other qualifications

SUMMARY

Academic research projects are usually required in partial fulfillment of the requirements of a course or a degree program. The motivation is not always a genuine desire to engage in research. In addition, limitations of time, money, and experience usually preclude the consideration of problems that could make significant contributions to educational theory and practice.

The choice of a suitable problem is one of the most difficult tasks facing the beginning researcher. Students tend to define problems that are too broad in scope or that deal with too fragmentary aspects of the problem. Consultation with the course instructor or advisor is particularly helpful in identifying a problem that is manageable and significant enough to justify the time and effort that will be required.

Problems are found in the teachers' daily classroom, school, and community experiences. Technological and social changes call for research evidence to chart new courses in educational practice. Graduate academic experience helps to promote problem awareness through classroom activities, the reading of research studies, and interaction with instructors, advisors, and fellow students.

A good research problem has the qualities of significance, originality, and feasibility. The researcher should evaluate a proposed problem in the light of his or her competence, the availability of data, the financial demands of the project, the limitations of time, and the possible difficulties and social hazards involved.

A research proposal is required by many institutions and organizations as a useful basis for determining how a project will be evaluated as well as a guide for the researcher. The proposal contains a clear and concise statement of the problem; the hypothesis or hypotheses involved; a recognition of the significance of the problem; definitions of important terms; assumptions, delimitations, and limitations; a review of related literature; an analysis of proposed research procedures; a reference list; and a time schedule. Some advisors request a report from time to time to evaluate the progress of the investigation.

One way to learn about research is to conduct a study in connection with the beginning research course. Another way is to write a research proposal that may involve all the steps in the research process except the gathering and analysis of data and the formulation of conclusions. Either of these exercises gives a focus to the discussion about research and may help in developing some competence and the research point of view. It may even encourage some teachers to conduct modest studies in their own schools during or after the completion of their graduate programs.

Other issues addressed in this chapter that are of critical importance in conducting research are the ethical nature of research and the fair use of copyrighted material.

EXERCISES

1. The following research topics are faulty or are completely inappropriate. Revise each one, if possible, so that it describes a feasible project or proposal for this course.

   a. The Attitudes of Teachers toward Merit Rating
   b. How to Teach Poetry Most Effectively

    c. The Best Way to Teach Spelling
    d. The Evils of Alcohol
    e. Does Ability Grouping Meet the Needs of Students?
    f. The Adequacy of Law Enforcement
    g. The Hazards of Smoking
    h. Why the Discussion Method Is Better Than the Lecture Method
    i. The Fallacy of Evolution

2. State a hypothesis, first in scientific or research form and then in null or statistical form. Also state the research question that these hypotheses would answer or the problem statement that the hypotheses would address.

3. Define the following terms in operational form:

    a. intelligence
    b. creativity
    c. coordination
    d. authorization
    e. memory

4. In a research study is a hypothesis to be tested always preferable to a question to be remembered? Why or why not?

5. What are some of the more effective ways to find a suitable research problem?

REFERENCES

American Educational Research Association (1992). Ethical standards of the American Educational Research Association. *Educational Researcher, 21,* 23–26.

American Psychological Association (1963). *Ethical standards of psychologists.* Washington, DC: APA.

American Psychological Association (1973). *Ethical principles in the conduct of research with human participants.* Washington, DC: APA.

American Psychological Association (1982). *Ethical principles in the conduct of research with human participants.* Washington, DC: APA.

American Psychological Association (1992). Ethical Principles of Psychologists and Code of Conduct. *American Psychologist, 47,* 1597–1611.

Belmont report: Basic ethical principles and their applications. (1986). Washington, DC: National Library of Medicine.

Belmont report: Ethical principles and guidelines for the protection of human subjects of research. (1979). Washington, DC: Smithsonian Institution, Superintendent of Documents, U.S. Government Printing Office.

Kohlberg, L. (1984). *The psychology of moral development: The nature and validity of moral stages.* San Francisco: Harper & Row.

Power, F. C., Higgins, A., & Kohlberg, L. (1989). *Lawrence Kohlberg's approach to moral education.* New York: Columbia University.

United States Copyright Office. (1994). *Copyright Law of the United States.* Circular 92 Reprinted from Public Law 103–465, December 8, 1994.

3

THE RESEARCH REPORT

Although research reports may differ considerably in scope of treatment, they are expected to follow a conventional pattern of style and form in academic circles. These styles and forms may seem unduly arbitrary to the student. However, they are based on principles of clear organization and presentation, and graduate students in education must be familiar with them if they are to communicate their ideas effectively. In addition, although the format and style suggested in this chapter are particularly appropriate for a research report, the student also may find them useful in writing a review of the literature or a research proposal.

STYLE MANUALS

Some graduate schools or departments have designated an official manual or have established their own style manual to which their theses or dissertations must conform. Students should find out which manual has been officially adopted by their institution or department. Beginning graduate students are disturbed when they discover that these manuals do not always completely agree on matters of typography or format. Careful examination, however, reveals that differences concern minor details. In general, all style manuals basically agree on the principles of correct presentation.

Regardless of which manual is used as a guide, it should be followed consistently in matters of form and style. The information in this chapter is consistent with one of the widely used style manuals, the *Publication Manual*, 4th ed. (1994) of the American Psychological Association. Other manuals commonly used in the social sciences and humanities include *The Chicago Manual of Style*, 14th ed. (1993); the *MLA Handbook for Writers of Research Papers*, 4th ed. (Gibaldi, 1995); *Form and Style: Research Papers, Reports, Theses*, 9th ed. (Slade, Campbell, & Ballou, 1994); and *A Manual for Writers of Term Papers, Theses, and Dissertations*, 6th ed. (Turabian, 1996). For specialized materials two available publications are *The Complete Guide to Citing Government Information Resources: A Manual for Writers and Librarians,* rev. ed. (Garner, 1993) and *Electronic Style: A Guide to Citing Electronic Information* (Li & Crane, 1993).

FORMAT OF THE RESEARCH REPORT

The research report, because of its relative brevity, differs somewhat from a thesis or dissertation. The following outline presents the sequence of topics covered in the typical research report prepared according to the American Psychological Association's (APA) *Publication Manual,* 4th ed. (1994):

I. Title Page
   A. Title
   B. Author's name and affiliation
   C. Running head
   D. Acknowledgments (if any)

II. Abstract

III. Introduction (no heading)
   A. Statement of the problem
   B. Background/review of literature
   C. Purpose and rationale/hypothesis

IV. Method
   A. Subjects
   B. Apparatus or instrumentation (if necessary)
   C. Procedure

V. Results
   A. Tables and figures (as appropriate)
   B. Statistical presentation

VI. Discussion
   A. Support or nonsupport of hypotheses
   B. Practical and theoretical implications
   C. Conclusions

VII. References

VIII. Appendix (if appropriate)

The APA style for typing a manuscript requires double spacing throughout the paper. Additional spaces may set off certain elements such as the running head on the title page, but single spacing should never be used. Leave margins of 1½ inches at the top, bottom, right, and left of every page. Number all pages except the figures. The APA style for typing a manuscript requires double spacing throughout the paper. Begin additional spaces with the title page. The title page and the abstract are on separate pages (pages 1 and 2, respectively). Begin a new page for the introduction, for the references, for each table and figure, and for each appendix.

The first page of the report is the title page and includes the title, author's name, and author's affiliation near the top of the page, separated by double spaces. Toward the bottom of the page are the running head and acknowledgments, separated by a double space.

The title should be concise and should indicate clearly the purposes of the study. One should keep in mind its possible usefulness to the reader, who may scan a bibliography in which it may be listed. The title should not claim more for the study than it actually delivers. It should not be stated so broadly that it seems to provide an answer that cannot be generalized, either from the data gathered or from the methodology employed. For example, in a simple, descriptive, self-concept study of a group of children enrolled in a particular inner-city elementary school, the title should not read, "The Self-Concepts of Inner-City Children." A more appropriate title would be "The Self-Concepts of a Group of Philadelphia Inner-City Children." The first title implies broader generalization than is warranted by the actual study.

The title should be typed in uppercase and lowercase letters, centered, and, when two or more lines are needed, double spaced. The running head, a shortened version of the title, should be a maximum of 50 characters including letters, punctuation, and spaces between words. The running head is typed near the bottom of the page in uppercase letters.

Acknowledgments appear as unnumbered footnotes near the bottom of the title page to indicate the basis of a study (e.g., doctoral dissertation), grant support, review of prior draft of the manuscript, and assistance in conducting the research and/or preparing the manuscript. They should be clearly and directly stated. Figure 3.1 on page 58 illustrates a sample title page of a manuscript that was subsequently published (Kahn, 1982).

The abstract on page 2 of the research report describes the study in 100 to 150 words and includes the problem under study, characteristics of the subjects, the procedures used (e.g., data-gathering techniques, intervention procedures), the findings of the study, and the conclusions reached by the researcher. A good abstract increases the readership of the article because many persons read the abstracts in a journal to decide which articles to read completely.

Main Body of the Report

The main body of the research report has four major sections: *introduction, method, results,* and *discussion.* The first of these sections, the *introduction,* begins a new page (page 3) and, because of its position, does not need a label. A well-written introduction has three components. The researcher must give a clear and definitive statement of the problem. As described in Chapter 2, the problem must indicate the need for the research and why it is important in terms of theory and/or practice.

Moral Reasoning in Irish Children and Adolescents

as Measured by the Defining Issues Test

James V. Kahn

University of Illinois at Chicago

This research was conducted while the author was a
Senior Fulbright-Hays Scholar at University College,
Cork, Ireland and on sabbatical leave from the
University of Illinois at Chicago. I wish to
acknowledge the assistance of the computer facilities
at both universities. I also wish to thank the many
children, teachers, and administrators at the various
schools at which the data reported were collected. I
also wish to thank Rose Naputano for her secretarial
assistance and Larry Nucci for his critical comments.

RUNNING HEAD: IRISH MORAL REASONING

FIGURE 3.1 Example of Title Page

A review of previous literature on the topic is also an essential component of the introduction. The researcher must demonstrate an understanding of the existing literature pertinent to his or her study. However, although an exhaustive review is an appropriate part of a thesis or dissertation, it is not included in a research report. The author should assume that the reader has some knowledge of the field being investigated. Only research pertinent to the issue under investigation should be included. The author also needs to logically connect the previous body of literature with the current work.

The final component of the introduction includes a clear rationale for the proposed hypoyhesis, definitions of the variables investigated and controlled, and a formal statement of each hypothesis. Each hypothesis must be clearly stated as to how it will be tested. Terms must be clear, and predicted outcomes must be measurable. For example, an investigation of an early intervention program with children at high risk for mental retardation should not hypothesize that "The high-risk children in the experimental group will have greater gains in intelligence." We need to know *whom* the high-risk children will be surpassing, and we need to know how *intelligence* is conceptualized. A better hypothesis for this study is, "High-risk children receiving the intervention program will have greater gains in IQ than will their control group peers."

The main body of the report continues with the *method* section, which follows the introduction. It includes two or more subsections and describes in great detail just what the investigator did. This allows the reader to determine how appropriate the procedures were and how much credence to give the results. A well-written method section is sufficiently detailed to enable a reader to replicate the components of the study. The method section is separated from the introduction by the centered heading "Method." Generally, subsections are then labeled at the left margin and underlined. The method section should always include at least two subsections: subjects and procedures.

The subsection on *subjects* needs to identify the participants of the study, the number of persons included in the study, and the means by which the participants were selected. Major demographic characteristics such as age, sex, socioeconomic status, and race are included as they relate to the study. Sufficient information must be provided to permit the reader to replicate the sample.

The *procedures* subsection describes the actual steps carried out in conducting the study. This includes the measurement devices, if no separate section is provided; the experimental treatments; the assignment of subjects to conditions; the order of assessments, if more than one; the time period, if pertinent; and any design features used to control potentially confounding variables. Again, enough information must be provided to permit replication. However, procedures published in detail elsewhere should only be summarized with the citation given for the other publication.

Additional subsections may be included as necessary. For instance, if a battery of complex tests is to be used and described, a separate subsection on instrumentation is appropriate. Complex designs might also be better described in a separate section.

The third section of the main body is *results*. The results section presents the data and the statistical analyses without discussing the implications of the findings. Individual scores or raw data are only presented in single-subject—or very small sample size—studies. All relevant findings are presented including those that do not support the hypothesis. Tables and figures are useful to supplement textual material. They should be used when the data cannot readily be presented in a few sentences in the text. Data in the text and in tables or figures should not be redundant; rather, they should be complementary. The text must indicate what the reader should expect to see in the tables and figures so as to clarify their meaning. The level of significance for statistical analyses should be presented.

Finally, the report's main body concludes with the *discussion* section. After presenting the results the researcher can determine the implications of the study including whether the hypotheses were supported or should be rejected. It is appropriate to discuss both theoretical implications and practical applications of the study. A brief discussion of the limitations of the present investigation and of proposals for future research is appropriate. New hypotheses may be proposed if the data do not support the original hypotheses. The researcher should also include conclusions that reflect whether the original problem is better understood, or even resolved, as a result of this study.

References and Appendices

The reference section of the manuscript begins a new page with the label "References," centered. *References* consists of all documents, including journal articles, books, chapters, technical reports, computer programs, and unpublished works mentioned in the text. A reference section should not be confused with a bibliography: a bibliography contains everything in the reference section *plus* other useful publications not cited in the manuscript. Bibliographies are not generally provided for research reports; only references are usually included.

References are arranged in alphabetical order by the last names of the first-named authors. When no author is listed, the first word of the title or sponsoring organization is used to begin the entry. Each reference starts at the left margin of the page, with subsequent lines double spaced and indented. No extra spaces separate the entries.

An *appendix* is useful in providing detailed information that seems inappropriate or too long for the main body of the paper. Each appendix begins on a new page with the label "Appendix" and its identifying letter, centered. Following this label is the centered title of the appendix and then the material. Materials that generally should be in an appendix include a new computer program, unpublished tests, lengthy treatments unavailable elsewhere, and so on.

THE THESIS OR DISSERTATION

Research theses and dissertations follow the same outline as described for the research report. The major difference between the thesis and dissertation is length and comprehensiveness. Many institutions have their own style manuals for these major research papers; they may require or suggest a certain order of topics, the designating of major (and some minor) sections as a chapter, bibliographies in place of reference sections, and more complete appendices. Because a goal of the thesis or dissertation is to demonstrate the student's knowledge in a particular field, it is more appropriate to be complete and comprehensive rather than concise and brief. Length is not an issue here as it is when submitting an article to a journal. It may even be appropriate to include raw data and computer printouts of the analyses. Students should read their institution's required style manual carefully and speak with their advisor before beginning their theses or dissertations.

STYLE OF WRITING

The research report should have a creative, clear, and concise style. Although the phraseology should be dignified and straightforward, it need not be dull or pedantic. Even the most profound ideas can best be explained in simple language and short, coherent sentences. Slang, hackneyed, or flippant phrases and folksy style should be avoided. Objectivity is the primary goal, not exhortation or persuasion. The research report should describe and explain, rather than convince or move to action. In this respect the research report differs from an essay or feature article.

For years it was considered inappropriate for a researcher to use personal pronouns such as *I, me, we,* and so forth; people thought their use indicated a lack of objectivity. This changed, however, when the second edition of the APA's *Publication Manual* was published in 1974. Personal pronouns should be used when they are appropriate. "I believe" is preferable to "The present author believes. . . ." The writer should, however, refrain from using plural personal pronouns (e.g., *we*) unless there are multiple authors.

Sexist language needs to be avoided. The writer needs to be explicit in identifying the gender referred to. "Sexist bias can occur when pronouns are used carelessly, when the masculine pronoun *he* is used to refer to both sexes, or when the masculine or feminine pronoun is used exclusively to define roles by sex (e.g., 'the nurse . . . she')" (American Psychological Association, 1994, p. 50). The writer needs to be clear whether one or both genders are intended. There are numerous alternatives to the generic "he," the APA *Manual* demonstrates, including rephrasing, use of plurals, and dropping the pronoun.

Only the last names of cited authorities are used. Titles such as *professor, Dr., Mr.,* and *Dean* are omitted. The past tense should be used in describing completed research procedures. Abbreviations may be used only after their referent has been spelled out, with the abbreviation following in parentheses. There are a few exceptions to this rule for well-known abbreviations such as *IQ.*

Discussion of Quantitative Terms

"*Few* in number" and "*less* in quantity" are the preferred forms of expression. Numbers beginning a sentence should always be spelled out. Fractions and numbers less than 10 should be spelled out. Use "one-half," but for all figures with fractions use "4½" or "4.5." *Percent* (meaning "per hundred") is spelled out except in tables and figures and when preceded by arabic numerals ("18%"), unless they begin a sentence. *Percentage* means "proportion." In numbers with more than three digits, commas should mark off thousands or millions (1,324; 12,304,000).

Ordinarily standard statistical formulas are not presented in the research report, nor are computations. If a rather unusual formula is used in the analysis, it is appropriate to include it.

Of course, the ordinary rules of correct usage should prevail. A good dictionary, a spelling guide, a handbook of style, and a thesaurus are helpful references. Too frequently students' work contains errors of spelling, nonagreement between subject and predicate, nonparallel construction, and inconsistent tense sequence. Students who have difficulty in written expression should have a competent friend or relative proofread their copy for correct usage before they type the final manuscript. Inability to write correctly is a serious limitation. Carelessness is an equally great fault.

Writing research reports effectively is not an easy task. Good reports are not written hurriedly. Even skillful and experienced writers revise many times before they submit a manuscript for publication.

REFERENCE FORM

References are cited in the text by giving the last name(s) of the author(s) and the year of the publication or, in the case of unpublished citations, the year the reference was written. If the author's name does not appear in the text, the name and year appear in parentheses, separated by a comma. If the author's name is used in the text, the year follows the name in parentheses. When more than one work is cited in parentheses, the references are separated by semicolons. Page numbers are given, in parentheses, only for direct quotations. See examples of this style of citation throughout this book.

All materials referred to in the text, and only those, are listed alphabetically in the reference section of the manuscript. The *Publication Manual,* 4th ed., of the American Psychological Association (1994) has specific guidelines for the format of various types of work. The following illustrates the form that different types of references should take. Titles underlined may be italicized instead.

1. Book:

   Gardner, H. (1983). <u>Frames of mind: The theory of multiple intelligences</u>. New York: Basic Books.

2. Book with multiple authors:

   Li, X., & Crane, N. B. (1993). <u>Electronic style: A guide to citing electronic information</u>. Westport, CT: Meckler.

3. Book in subsequent edition:

   Marshall, C., & Rossman, G. B. (1995). <u>Designing qualitative research</u> (2nd ed.). Thousand Oaks, CA: Sage.

4. Editor as author:

   Walberg, H. J. & Haertel, G. D. (Eds.). (1990). <u>The international encyclopedia of educational evaluation</u>. New York: Pergamon.

5. No author given:

   <u>Prentice-Hall author's guide</u>. (1978). Englewood Cliffs, NJ: Prentice-Hall.

6. Corporate or association author:

   American Psychological Association. (1994). <u>Publication manual</u> (4th ed.). Washington, DC: Author.

7. Part of a series of books:

   Terman, L. M., & Oden, M. H. (1947). <u>Genetic studies of genius series: Vol. 4. The gifted child grows up</u>. Stanford, CA: Stanford University Press.

8. Chapter in an edited book:

   Wiley, D. E. (1991). Test validity and invalidity reconsidered. In R. E. Snow, & D. E. Wiley (Eds.), <u>Improving inquiry in social science: A volume in honor of Lee J. Cronbach</u>. Hillsdale, N.J.: Lawrence Erlbaum.

9. Journal article:

   Frick, R. W. (1995). Accepting the null hypothesis. <u>Memory and Cognition, 23</u>, 132–138.

10. Magazine article:

    Meer, J. (1984, August). Pet theories. <u>Psychology Today</u>, 60–67.

11. Unpublished paper presented at a meeting:

    O'Shea, R. K., Papoutsis-Kritikos, E., Kahn, J. V., & Baxter, A. (1996, April). <u>Demographic correlates of attendance</u>. Paper presented at the Annual Meeting of the Council for Exceptional Children, Orlando, FL.

12. Thesis or dissertation (unpublished):

    Best, J. W.(1948). <u>An analysis of certain selected factors underlying the choice of teaching as a profession</u>. Unpublished doctoral dissertation, University of Wisconsin, Madison.

13. Unpublished manuscripts:

    Kahn, J. V., Jones, C., & Schmidt, M. (1984). <u>Effect of object preference on sign learnability by severely and profoundly retarded children: A pilot study</u>. Unpublished manuscript, University of Illinois at Chicago.

    Baxter, A. & Kahn, J. V. (1996). <u>Effective early intervention for inner-city infants and toddlers</u>. Manuscript submitted for publication.

14. Article accepted for publication:

> Kahn, J. V. (in press). Cognitive skills and sign language knowledge of children with severe and profound mental retardation. <u>Education and Training in Mental Retardation, 31</u>.

15. Technical report:

> Kahn, J. V. (1981). <u>Training sensorimotor period and language skills with severely retarded children</u>. Chicago, IL: University of Illinois at Chicago. (ERIC Document Reproduction Service No. ED 204 941).

PAGINATION

Page numbers are assigned to each page of the paper or report. The title page does not have a page number typed on it, but a number is allowed for it in the series.

Page numbers are placed in the upper right-hand corner, one inch below the top of the page and aligned with the right margin. Pages are numbered consecutively from the title page, through the abstract, main body of the paper, and references. After the references come the footnotes (if any), tables, figures, and appendices (if any), the numbering of pages continuing in this order.

In addition, each page except the title page has a short title (the running head) typed above the page number (often the first two or three words of the whole title). This is done so that if the pages are separated, they can be identified with the appropriate manuscript.

TABLES

A table is a systematic method of presenting statistical data in vertical columns and horizontal rows according to some classification of subject matter. Tables enable the reader to comprehend and interpret masses of data rapidly and to grasp significant details and relationships at a glance. Tables and figures should be used sparingly; too many overwhelm the reader.

Good tables are relatively simple, concentrating on a limited number of ideas. Including too much data in a table minimizes the value of tabular presentation. It is often advisable to use several tables rather than to include too many details in a single one. It has been said that the mark of a good table is its effectiveness in conveying ideas and relationships independently of the text of the report.

Because each table is on a separate page following the references, the desired placement of the table is indicated by the following method. Text references should identify tables by number rather than by such expressions as "the table above" or "the following table." The author tells the publisher where the table goes by stating "Insert Table [give number] about here." Tables should rarely be carried over to the second or third page. If the table must be continued, the headings should be repeated at the top of each column of data on each page.

Tables should not exceed the page size of the manuscript. Large tables that must be folded into the copy are always cumbersome and cannot be easily refolded and replaced. Large tables should be reduced to manuscript-page size by photocopy or some other process of reproduction. Tables too wide for the page may be turned sideways, with the top facing the left margin of the manuscript.

See Figure 3.2 for a sample of a properly presented table. The word *table* is centered between the page margins and typed in capital letters, followed by the table number in Arabic numerals. Tables are numbered consecutively throughout the entire report or thesis, including those tables that may be placed in the appendix.

TABLE 2

Occupations of Fathers of University
of Wisconsin Seniors Preparing to Teach[a]

Occupations	Men		Women	
	N	%	N	%[b]
Business proprietor	24	23	32	29
Skilled labor	19	18	10	9
Farming	17	17	19	17
Clerical-sales	16	16	18	16
Professional	15	15	20	18
Unskilled labor	6	6	6	5
No data	5	5	7	6
Total	102	100	112	100

[a]Adapted from Best, J. W. (1948). <u>An analysis of certain
selected factors underlying the choice of teaching as a
profession</u>. Unpublished doctoral dissertation,
University of Wisconsin, Madison.

[b]Percentages rounded to equal 100%.

FIGURE 3.2   A Sample Table

The caption or title is placed one double space below the word *table* and centered. No terminal punctuation is used. The main title should be brief, clearly indicating the nature of the data presented. Occasionally a subtitle is used to supplement a briefer main title, denoting such additional information as sources of data and measuring units employed.

Column headings, or box heads, should be clearly labeled, describing the nature and units of measure of the data listed. If percentages are presented, the percentage symbol (%) should be placed at the top of the column, not with the number in the table.

If numbers are shortened by the omission of zeros, that fact should be mentioned in the subtitle ("in millions of dollars," "in thousands of tons"). The "stub," or label, for the rows should be clear and concise, parallel in grammatical structure, and, if possible, no longer than two lines.

Decimal points should always be carried out to the same place (e.g., tenths or hundredths) and aligned in the column. When no data are available for a particular cell, indicate the lack by a dash rather than a zero. When footnotes are needed to explain items in the table, use small letters. Numerical superscripts may be confused with the data contained in the table. Use asterisks to indicate probability levels and place them below the table.

FIGURES

A figure is a device that presents statistical data in graphic form. The term *figure* is applied to a wide variety of graphs, charts, maps, sketches, diagrams, and drawings. When skillfully used, figures present aspects of data in a visualized form that may be clearly and easily understood. Figures are not intended as substitutes for textual description but included to emphasize certain significant relationships.

Many of the qualities listed as characteristics of good tables are equally appropriate when applied to figures:

1. The title should clearly describe the nature of the data presented.
2. Figures should be simple enough to convey a clear idea and should be understandable without the aid of much textual description.
3. Numerical data on which the figure is based should be presented in the text or an accompanying table, if they are not included in the figure itself.
4. Data should be presented carefully and accurately so that oversimplification, misrepresentation, or distortion do not result.
5. Figures should be used sparingly. Too many figures detract from, rather than illuminate, the presentation.
6. Figures follow tables in the order of items in a manuscript. The placement desired in the text is indicated in the same manner used to indicate the placement of tables.

7. Figures should follow, not precede, the related textual discussion.
8. Figures are referred to by number, never as "the figure above" or "the figure below."
9. The title and number of the figure are placed on a separate page preceding the figure in the manuscript.

The Line Graph

The line graph is useful in showing change in data relationships over a period of time. The horizontal axis usually measures the independent variable, the vertical axis, the measured characteristic. Graphic arrangement should proceed from left to right on the horizontal axis and from bottom to top on the vertical. The zero point should always be represented, and scale intervals should be equal. If a part of the scale is omitted, a set of parallel jagged lines should be used, indicating that part of the scale is omitted (see Figure 3.3).

We have devised two figures, a line graph and a bar graph, that depict data relationships presented textually in two journal articles (see Figures 3.4 on page 68 and 3.5 on page 69).

When several lines are drawn, they may be distinguished by using various types of lines—solid, dotted, or alternate dots and dashes. Black ink is used.

A smooth curve cannot be obtained by plotting any data directly. Only when infinite data are obtained will the lines connecting the points approach a curved line. The figure formed by the lines connecting the points is known as a *frequency polygon*.

The Bar Graph or Chart

The bar graph, which can be arranged either horizontally or vertically, represents data by bars of equal width drawn to scale length. The numerical data may be lettered within the bar or outside it. A grid may be used to help quantify the graphic representation. A divided bar graph represents the components of a whole unit in one bar (see Figure 3.6 on page 69).

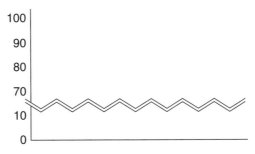

FIGURE 3.3   A Line Graph

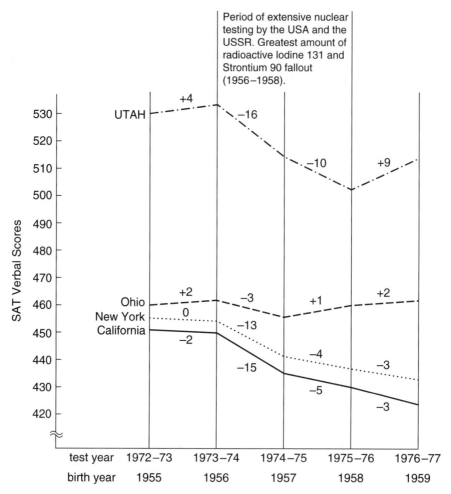

FIGURE 3.4   Mean Verbal SAT Scores, 1972–1977, in Four Selected States

(Graphic representation by the author, adapted from *Kappan*, Interview with Ernest Sternglass, "The Nuclear Radiation/SAT Score Decline Connection," *Phi Delta Kappan, 61* [Nov. 1979], 184.)

    In bar graphs the bars are usually separated by space. If the graph contains a large number of items, the bars may be joined to save space.
    Horizontal bar graphs are usually used to compare components at a particular time. Vertical bars are used to make comparisons at different times.

The Circle, Pie, or Sector Chart

Circle, pie, or sector charts show the division of a unit into its component parts. They are frequently used to explain how a unit of government distributes its share

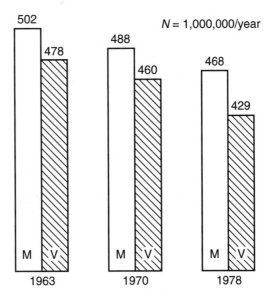

FIGURE 3.5 **Decline of Mean Scholastic Aptitude Test Scores from 1963 to 1978**

(Throughout the 1970s, verbal scores declined .04 standard deviation each year and mathematical scores declined .025 standard deviation.)

of the tax dollar, how an individual spends his or her salary, or any other type of simple percentage distribution.

The radius is drawn vertically, and components are arranged in a clockwise direction in descending order of magnitude. The proportion of data is indicated by the number of degrees in each section of the 360-degree circle (see Figure 3.7 on page 70).

This kind of data should be typed or printed within the segment, if possible. If there is insufficient room for this identification, a small arrow should point from the identification term to the segment.

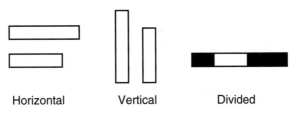

Horizontal   Vertical   Divided

FIGURE 3.6 **Divided Bars for Graphs**

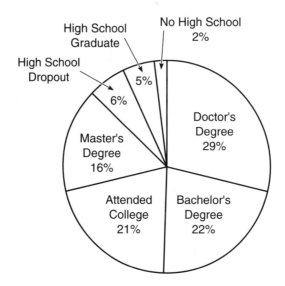

FIGURE 3.7   Educational Backgrounds of 129 American Celebrities Listed in the *Current Biography 1966 Yearbook*

(Adapted from Adela Deming, "The Educational Attainments of Americans Listed in the *Current Biography 1966 Yearbook*." Unpublished report, Butler University, Indianapolis, Indiana, 1967, p. 7.)

Maps

When geographic location or identification is important, maps may be used. Identification may be made by dots, circles, or other symbols, and density or characteristics of areas can be represented by shading or crosshatching. A key or legend should always be supplied if shadings are used.

Organization Charts

To show staff functions, lines of authority, or flow of work within an organization, an organization chart is a helpful graphic device.

Units may be represented by circles, squares, or oblongs, with names lettered within the units. Distinctions between direct and indirect relationships may be indicated by solid and dotted lines. Ordinarily authority, supervision, or movement of materials flow from the top to the bottom of the chart, but variations can be indicated by the use of arrows.

EVALUATING A RESEARCH REPORT

Writing a critical analysis of a research report is a valuable experience for the educational research student. Reports for this purpose may be taken from published collections and periodicals such as the *Educational Researcher,* the *Journal of Educational Research,* or one of the many other publications that publish research reports in education or in the closely related fields of psychology or sociology. Unpublished research reports written by previous educational research students are another source as are the theses or dissertations in the university library. Appendix H provides a checklist for evaluating a manuscript or publication.

Through a critical analysis the student may gain some insight into the nature of a research problem, the methods by which it may be attacked, the difficulties inherent in research, the ways in which data are analyzed and conclusions drawn, and the style of the report.

The following questions suggest a possible structure for the analysis:

1. The Title and Abstract

   a. Are they clear and concise?
   b. Do they promise no more than the study can provide?

2. The Problem and Hypotheses (Introductory Section)

   a. Is the problem clearly stated?
   b. Is the problem properly delimited?
   c. Is the significance of the problem recognized?
   d. Are hypotheses clearly stated and testable?
   e. Are assumptions, limitations, and delimitations stated?
   f. Are important terms defined?

3. Review of Related Literature (Introductory Section)

   a. Is it adequately covered?
   b. Are important findings noted?
   c. Is it well organized?
   d. Is an effective summary provided?
   e. Is the cited literature directly relevant to the problem and hypotheses?

4. Method Section

   a. Is the research design described in detail?
   b. Is it adequate?
   c. Are the samples described in detail?
   d. Are relevant variables recognized?
   e. Are appropriate controls provided to establish experimental validity?
   f. Are data-gathering instruments appropriate?
   g. Are validity and reliability of the instruments established?
   h. Can the sample and procedure be replicated based on the information and references given?

5. Results Section

   a. Is the statistical treatment appropriate?
   b. Is appropriate use made of tables and figures?
   c. Is the analysis of data relationships logical, perceptive, and objective?

6. Discussion Section

    a. Is the discussion clear and concise?
    b. Is the problem/hypothesis restated appropriately?
    c. Is the analysis objective?
    d. Are the findings and conclusions justified by the data presented and analyzed?
    e. Did the author(s) generalize appropriately or too much?

7. Overall Writing

    a. Is it clear, concise, and objective?
    b. Are the parts of the paper properly related to each other?

SUMMARY

The research report follows the conventional pattern of style and form used in academic circles. Although style manuals differ in some of the smaller details, students should be consistent in following the style in the manual required by their institution or in the one that they are permitted to select.

The writing should be clear, concise, and completely objective. Of course, the highest standards of correct usage are expected, and careful proofreading is necessary before the final report is submitted.

Tables and figures may help to make the meaning of the data clear. They should be presented in proper mechanical form and should be carefully designed to present an accurate and undistorted picture.

The evaluation of a research project is a valuable exercise for students of educational research. Using the analytical questions suggested, the critiquing of another researcher's report helps students develop competency in their own research and reporting skills.

REFERENCES

American Psychological Association. (1994). *Publication manual* (4th ed.). Washington, DC: Author.

Garner, D. L., & Smith, D. H. (1993). *The complete guide to citing government information resources: A manual for writers and librarians*, (rev. ed.). Bethesda, MD: Congressional Information Service.

Gibaldi, J. (1995). *MLA handbook for writers of research papers*, (4th ed.). New York: Modern Language Association.

Kahn, J. V. (1982). Moral reasoning in Irish children and adolescents as measured by the Defining Issues Test. *Irish Journal of Psychology, 5,* 96–108.

Kahn, J. V. (1992). Predicting adaptive behavior of severely and profoundly mentally retarded children with early cognitive measures. *Journal of Intellectual Deficiency Research, 36,* 101–114.

Li, X., & Crane, N. B. (1993). *Electronic style: A guide to citing electronic information.* Westport, CT: Meckler.

Slade, C., Campbell, W. G., & Ballou, S. V. (1994). *Form and style: Research papers, reports, and theses,* (9th ed.). Boston: Houghton Mifflin.

The Chicago Manual of Style, (14th ed.). (1993). Chicago: University of Chicago.

Turabian, K. L. (1996). *A manual for writers of term papers, theses, and dissertations,* (6th ed.). Chicago: University of Chicago.

PART II

RESEARCH METHODS

The methodologies of educational research are based, in most instances, on research methods in the behavioral and social sciences, relying most heavily on psychology, sociology, and anthropology. Because research in these fields emphasizes logical-positivism, which uses experimental and quantitative research methods, most educational research also utilizes these methodologies. Still some research concerns may be addressed more appropriately with a phenomenological, or qualitative, research approach derived from the humanities, particularly history and philosophy, or with qualitative methods from the social sciences (e.g., ethnography from anthropology).

Research can be divided into two broad categories: *quantitative research* and *qualitative research.* Quantitative research consists of research in which the data can be analyzed in terms of numbers. An example of quantitative research might be a study comparing two methods of teaching reading to first-grade children because the data used to determine which method is more successful will be a test score. The average score of the children receiving one method is compared to the average score of children receiving the other method. This example is an experimental study (discussed in Chapter 6) if the experimenter randomly assigns the children to the methods, or a descriptive study (Chapter 5) if the children have already received the instruction and the experimenter merely examines the results after the fact. In either case the study is considered quantitative.

Research can also be qualitative; that is, it can describe events and persons scientifically without the use of numerical data. A study consisting of interviews of mothers of handicapped infants to determine how their lives and beliefs were affected by the birth of their handicapped children is an example of qualitative research. Such a study carefully and logically analyzes the responses of the mothers and reports those responses that are consistent as well as those that disagree.

Each of these types of research has advantages and disadvantages. In quantitative research the experimenter has carefully planned the study including the tests, or other data collection instruments. Each subject is identically studied, and there is little room for human bias to create problems with the data. Qualitative research is also planned carefully. Yet qualitative studies leave open the possibility of change, of asking different questions, and of going in the direction that the observation may lead the experimenter. Quantitative research is based more directly on its original plans, and its results are more readily analyzed and interpreted. Qualitative research is more open and responsive to its subject.

Part II of this book is intended to provide the student with a detailed description of a variety of methodologies and data collection procedures used in educational research. New to this edition are reprints of research articles at the end of each of the five research methods chapters (Chapters 4 through 8). One article depicting that type of research appears at the end of each chapter with some comments written in the margins. Each article is also mentioned in the text of that chapter.

Chapter 4 describes the procedures used in historical research. Some historians (including educational historians) use strictly qualitative procedures based on the humanistic research view, whereas others include quantitative procedures from the social science perspective. Both of these approaches are described.

Chapter 5 strives to delineate the variety of descriptive studies (assessment, evaluation, and research) using quantitative methods in educational settings. All descriptive studies are attempts to describe the current state of affairs. Two broad categories of descriptive studies discussed in this chapter, assessment and evaluation studies, are not truly research. They differ from descriptive research in that their goals are not the creation of new, generalizable knowledge. Rather, these important types of studies are interested in the assessment of a given population's status on one or more measures or in the evaluation of the success of a given program or project, respectively.

Chapter 6 describes the variety of research designs utilized in experimental research. Included are true experimental designs using randomization, quasi-experimental designs with no randomization, and pre-experimental designs offering little or no control of confounding variables. This chapter also describes and defines the type of variables used in experimental research (independent, dependent, and confounding), experimental validity and the various threats to it, and the ways in which the diverse research designs control for the various threats to experimental validity.

Chapter 7 provides the reader with information regarding a specific type of experimental research, single-subject research and describes the most commonly used designs and procedures.

Chapter 8 was new to the last edition. Although the topic of qualitative methodologies was included in the previous editions, only a few approaches were covered briefly. This chapter provides a more comprehensive and detailed overview of qualitative research methods, excluding historical methods, which are covered in Chapter 4.

Chapter 9 depicts the tools and methods by which researchers collect data. The procedures described are those used in all types of research discussed in the previous chapters as well as descriptions of reliability and validity for most types of data collection tools including tests, questionnaires, observation, and others.

Although Chapters 5 through 8 separate and describe different approaches to the research endeavor to make it easier for the beginning researcher to understand these procedures, the separation of descriptive research from experimental and quantitative from qualitative is somewhat arbitrary and artificial. For instance, some descriptive research (Chapter 5) can utilize the quasi-experimental designs described in Chapter 6.

More important, quantitative and qualitative research should be thought of as a continuum rather than a mutually exclusive dichotomy. For instance, survey research is described in both Chapters 5 and 8 because it can be used in both quantitative and qualitative research. More to the point, the same survey instrument in the same study can include both quantitative and qualitative items that require different analyses. In addition, as indicated in Chapter 8, some qualitative research methods culminate in some numerical result (e.g., the summing up of the number of instances of interview responses in each response category). Thus, although the reader is being introduced to each of these concepts separately, the good researcher utilizes a variety of these methods in combination during her or his career.

4

HISTORICAL RESEARCH

History is a meaningful record of human achievement. It is not merely a list of chronological events but a truthful integrated account of the relationships between persons, events, times, and places. History is used to understand the past and to try to understand the present in light of past events and developments. History is also used to prevent "reinventing the wheel" every few years. Historical analysis may be directed toward an individual, an idea, a movement, or an institution. However, none of these objects of historical observation can be considered in isolation. People cannot be subjected to historical investigation without some consideration of their interaction with the ideas, movements, and/or institutions of their times. The focus merely determines the points of emphasis toward which historians direct their attention.

Table 4.1 on page 78 illustrates several historical interrelationships taken from the history of education. For example, no matter whether the historian chooses to study the Jesuit Society, religious teaching orders, the Counter-Reformation, or Ignatius of Loyola, each of the other elements appears as a prominent influence or result and as an indispensable part of the account. The interrelationship of this institution, movement, and man makes the study of one in isolation from the others meaningless, if not impossible.

Historical research can be qualitative or quantitative (or a combination). The type of approach should be determined by the issue addressed and the data available. For example, research on the relative school performance during the depression as compared to the years just before it should probably include a quantitative analysis of the school performance data from the two time frames. On the other hand, Whitehead's (1996) description of the life and work of the Reverend Bartholomew Booth from 1760 to 1785 is appropriately qualitative. Those who wish to engage in historical research should read the works of historians about the methods and approaches regarding historical studies in education (e.g., Berkhofer, 1995; Cohen, 1994; Seldon, 1988; Tuchman, 1994).

TABLE 4.1   Some Examples of the Historical Interrelationship Among Men,
           Movements, and Institutions

Men	Movements	Institutions	
		General Type	Name
Ignatius of Loyola	Counter-Reformation	Religious Teaching Order	Society of Jesus, 1534 (Jesuit Society)
Benjamin Franklin Education for Life	Scientific Movement	Academy	Philadelphia Academy, 1751
Daniel Coit Gilman G. Stanley Hall Wm. Rainey Harper	Graduate Study and Research	University Graduate School	Johns Hopkins University, 1876 Clark University, 1887 University of Chicago, 1892
John Dewey	Experimentalism Progressive Education	Experimental School	University of Chicago Elementary School, 1896
W. E. B. Dubois Walter White	Racial Integration in the Public Schools	Persuasion Organization	National Assn. for the Advancement of Colored People, 1909
B. R. Buckingham	Scientific Research Education	Research Periodical, Research Organization	Journal of Ed. Research, 1920 American Educational Research Assn., 1931

THE HISTORY OF AMERICAN EDUCATION

Historical studies deal with almost every aspect of American education. Such investigations have pointed out the important contributions of both educators and statesmen. They have examined the growth and development of colleges and universities, elementary and secondary schools, educational organizations and associations, the rise and decline of educational movements, the introduction of new teaching methods, and the issues persistently confronting American education.

An understanding of the history of education is important to professional workers in this field. It helps them to understand the *how* and *why* of educational movements that have appeared and, in some cases, continue to prevail in the schools. It helps them to evaluate not only lasting contributions but also the fads and "bandwagon" schemes that have appeared on the educational scene only to be discarded.

An examination of many developments of the past confirms the observation that little in education is really new. Practices hailed as innovative are often old ideas that have previously been tried and replaced by something else. Innovators should examine the reasons such practices were discarded and consider whether their own proposals are likely to prove more successful. Several studies, briefly described, illustrate the historical background of some contemporary educational movements and issues.

Organized programs of individualized instruction introduced in a number of school systems in the 1960s are similar in many respects to those introduced in a number of schools in the 1890s and in the first quarter of the 20th century. First introduced at Pueblo, Colorado, and known as the Pueblo Plan, later modified and known as the Winnetka and Dalton Plans, these programs do have common elements. Dispensing with group class activity in academic courses, students were given units of work to complete at their own rate before proceeding to more advanced units. Individual progress based on mastery of subject matter units was the criterion for promotion in or completion of a course. Search (1901) advocated this plan, and his influence on Carleton Washburn in the elementary schools of Winnetka, Illinois, and on Helen Parkhurst in the secondary schools at Dalton, Massachusetts, is generally recognized. Whether the Pueblo, Winnetka, or Dalton plans were fads or sound programs, the fact remains that they disappeared from the schools before reappearing in the 1960s. Although these programs have generally faded away again, they are still highly valued by some involved in the education of gifted students as well as of those with disabilities.

The place of religion in public education is an issue concerning many people. In the period following World War II, in a series of Supreme Court decisions, religious instruction and religious exercises in public schools were declared unconstitutional and in violation of the First Amendment of the United States Constitution. In 1963 in the case of *Abington School District v. Schempp,* the Court held that a Pennsylvania law requiring daily bible reading was in violation of the First Amendment. Much resentment and criticism of the Supreme Court followed this decision, and several efforts have been made to introduce amendments to the Constitution to permit religious exercises in the public schools. This controversy persists to this day with a majority of Americans polled (71%) (Gallop, 1995) believing that prayer in schools would be positive although the majority (70%) would prefer a silent prayer to a spoken one and only 41% would still support prayer in the schools if it offended a large percentage of parents. In addition, this poll indicates that 81% prefer that all major religions be included, with 13% wanting only Christian prayer.

The bible reading issue was also a bitter one more than 100 years ago. The Philadelphia Bible Riots of 1840 (Lannie & Diethorn, 1968) resulted in the deaths of about 45 soldiers and civilians, serious injury to about 140, and property damage to homes and churches valued at nearly $500,000. Nativist/foreign-born, and Catholic–Protestant conflicts produced the tense atmosphere, but the bible reading issue precipitated the riots. It is apparent that prayer is not an issue of recent origin, and an understanding of previous conflicts places the issue in clearer perspective.

Various other historical researchers have studied the impact on American education of Thomas Jefferson, Benjamin Franklin, Calvin Stowe, Catherine Beecher, Horace Mann, Maria Montessori, Henry Barnard, Ella Flagg Young, William Holmes McCuffey, Daniel Coit Gilman, John Dewey, and many other eminent educators. These contributions have been carefully examined in many studies and their importance noted. One study by Thursfield (1945) included many famous individuals from the 19th century. He studied Henry Barnard's *American Journal of Education,* published in 31 massive volumes between 1855 and 1881. He pointed out the *Journal*'s vital contribution to the development of American education. Through its comprehensive treatment of all aspects of education, it provided a readily available medium for the presentation and exchange of ideas of many great educators of the period. It has been stated that almost every educational reform adopted in the last half of the 19th century was largely because of the influence of the *Journal.* Among its contributors were Henry Barnard, Horace Mann, Bronson Alcott, Daniel Coit Gilman, William T. Harris, and Calvin Stowe in addition to many prominent foreign contributors such as Herbert Spencer.

Cremin (1961) examined the reason for the rise and decline of the progressive education movement, including the major changes in philosophy and practices that transformed American education and the forces that brought the movement to a halt in the 1950s. Although some historians differ with his conclusions, Cremin's analysis is the definitive history of progressive education in America.

More recent historical analyses include Weiler's (1994) examination of the role of women in rural school reform in California during the first 40 years of the 20th century. She notes that because the majority of teachers in rural California were women they played a central role in the reforms.

In another recent publication John Hardin Best (1996) reviewed the role of education in the formation of the American South. His review points out the difficulties in conducting historical research and provides insightful conclusions.

In a recent book Moreo (1996) provides a wide-ranging perspective on how schools coped with the depression of the 1930s. Among the material covered this text includes discussions of the attempted reorganization of the New York City public school system, the parental and student complaints of the schools (including the Amish of Pennsylvania), and the impact of the depression on Seattle schools.

Finally Robenstine (1992) studied the effect of French colonial policy on the education of women and minorities in early 18th century Louisiana. As Robenstine states:

> *Within a scant decade of the establishment of New Orleans as a permanent settlement of the Louisiana Territory in 1718, provisions were made for the education of the females of the area—white and minority. While meager efforts had been made to provide education for male youth, those efforts were not well received by the small local population and ultimately were short lived. Consequently, the first lasting element of institutionalized education in French colonial Louisiana, the Ursuline school and convent, put a unique emphasis on female and minority education. How this unusual development merged with, and reflected, colonial political goals is the central concern of this essay. (p. 193)*

One of the major conclusions was that French women were needed to establish and maintain French culture in the colony. Many of the early male settlers had married Native Americans, which the French government wanted to prevent and instead wanted them to marry French women in the future. In addition, they found the Ursuline nuns had a civilizing influence through their education. Thus, political concerns affected educational policy. The complete article by Robenstine appears at the end of this chapter.

These historical studies are examples of but a few of the thousands of books, monographs, and periodical articles depicting the story of American education. In addition to examining these works, students are urged to consult the *History of Education Quarterly,* which presents scholarly book reviews and critical analyses of contemporary historical research.

HISTORY AND SCIENCE

Opinions differ as to whether the activities of the historian can be considered scientific or whether there is such a thing as historical research.

Those who take the negative position point out the following limitations:

1. Although the purpose of science is prediction, the historian cannot usually generalize on the basis of past events. Because past events were often unplanned or did not develop as planned, because there were so many uncontrolled factors, and because the influence of one or a few individuals was so crucial, the same pattern of factors is not repeated.
2. The historian must depend on the reported observations of others, often witnesses of doubtful competence and sometimes of doubtful objectivity.
3. The historian is much like a person trying to complete a complicated jigsaw puzzle with many of the parts missing. On the basis of what is often incomplete evidence, the historian must fill in the gaps by inferring what has happened and why.
4. History does not operate in a closed system such as may be created in the physical science laboratory. The historian cannot control the conditions of observation nor manipulate the significant variables.

The result of these problems is often conflicting "histories" of the same events.

Those who contend that historical investigation has the characteristics of scientific research activity present these arguments:

1. The historian delimits a problem, formulates hypotheses or raises questions to be answered, gathers and analyzes primary data, tests the hypotheses as consistent or inconsistent with the evidence, and formulates generalizations or conclusions.
2. Although the historian may not have witnessed an event or gathered data directly, he or she may have the testimony of a number of witnesses who have observed the event from different vantage points. It is possible that subsequent events have provided additional information not available to contemporary

observers. The historian rigorously subjects the evidence to critical analysis in order to establish its authenticity, truthfulness, and accuracy.

3. Although it is true that the historian cannot control the variables directly, this limitation, and number 2 above, also characterizes most behavioral research, particularly nonlaboratory investigations in sociology, psychology, and economics.

4. In reaching conclusions the historian employs principles of probability similar to those used by physical scientists.

5. The observations of historians may be described in *qualitative* or *quantitative* terms, depending on the subject matter and the approach of the historian. In general, the traditional approach is qualitative, whereas the revisionists use quantitative analyses. The traditional, qualitative approach in many historical studies does not preclude the application of scientific methodology. As Brickman (1982) points out, it simply requires "the synthesis and presentation of the facts in a logically organized form." (p. 91)

Historical Generalization

There is some difference of opinion even among historians as to whether historical investigations can establish generalizations. Most historians would agree that some generalizations are possible, but they disagree on the validity of applying them to different times and places. In 1963 some of the foremost historians of the time came together to provide their opinions on the possible generalization of historical research for a book edited by Gottschalk. Although this book is more than 30 years old, the points made are valid today. In this book Gottschalk (1963) states the case of the comparative historian in this way:

> Sooner or later one or more investigators of a period or area begin to suspect some kind of nexus within the matter of their historical investigation. Though such "hunches," "insights," "guesses," "hypotheses," whatever you may call them, may be rejected out of hand by some of them, the bolder or rasher among them venture to examine the possibility of objective reality of such a nexus, and then it is likely to become a subject of debate and perhaps of eventual refinement to the point of wide recognition in the learned world. The process is not very different from the way analytical scholars in other fields proceed—Darwin, for example, or Freud. If this process serves no other purpose, it at least may furnish propositions upon which to focus future investigations and debates. . . .
>
> But do not these historical syntheses, no matter what their author's intention, invariably have a wider applicability than to any single set of data from which they rose? If Weber was right, isn't it implicit in this concept of the Protestant ethic that where a certain kind of religious attitude prevails there the spirit of capitalism will, or at least may, flourish? . . . If Mahan was right, couldn't victory in war (at least before the invention of the airplane) be regarded as dependent on maritime control? If Turner was right, won't his frontier thesis apply to some

extent to all societies that have frontiers to conquer in the future, as well as it has applied to American society in the past? (pp.121–122)

Finley (1963) adds his comments on generalization:

Ultimately the question at issue is the nature of the historian's function. Is it only to recapture the individual concrete events of a past age, as in a mirror, so that the progress of history is merely one of rediscovering lost data and of building bigger and better reflectors? If so, then the chronicle is the only correct form for his work. But if it is to understand—however one chooses to define the word—then it is to generalize, for every explanation is, or implies, one or more generalizations. (p. 34)

Aydelotte (1963) also states the argument for generalization:

Certainly the impossibility of final proof of any historical generalization must be at once conceded. Our knowledge of the past is both too limited and too extensive. Only a minute fraction of what has happened has been recorded, and only too often the points on which we need most information are those on which our sources are most inadequate. On the other hand, the fragmentary and incomplete information we do have about the past is too abundant to prevent our coming to terms with it; its sheer bulk prevents its being easily manipulated, or even easily assimilated, for historical purposes. Further, historians deal with complex problems, and the pattern of the events they study, even supposing it to exist, seems too intricate to be easily grasped. Doubtless, finality of knowledge is impossible in all areas of study. We have learned through works of popularization how far this holds true even for the natural sciences, and, as Crane Brinton says, the historian no longer needs to feel that "the uncertainties and inaccuracies of his investigation leave him in a position of hopeless inferiority before the glorious certainties of physical science." (pp. 156–157)

The foregoing quotations are presented in support of the position that the activities of the historian are not different from those of the scientist. Historical research as it is defined in this chapter includes delimiting a problem, formulating hypotheses or generalizations to be tested or questions to be answered, gathering and analyzing data, and arriving at probability-type conclusions or at generalizations based upon deductive–inductive reasoning.

THE HISTORICAL HYPOTHESIS

Nevins (1962) illustrates the use of hypotheses in the historical research of Edward Channing in answering the question, "Why did the Confederacy collapse in April 1865?" Channing formulated four hypotheses and tested each one in light of evidence gathered from letters, diaries, and official records of the army and the government of the Confederacy. He hypothesized that the Confederacy collapsed because of

1. The military defeat of the Confederate army
2. The dearth of military supplies
3. The starving condition of the Confederate soldiers and the civilians
4. The disintegration of the will to continue the war

Channing produced evidence that seemed to refute the first three hypotheses. More than 200,000 well-equipped soldiers were under arms at the time of the surrender, the effective production of powder and arms provided sufficient military supplies to continue the war, and enough food was available to sustain fighting men and civilians.

Channing concluded that hypothesis 4, *the disintegration of the will to continue the war*, was substantiated by the excessive number of desertions of enlisted men and officers. Confederate military officials testified that they had intercepted many letters from home urging the soldiers to desert. Although the hypothesis sustained was not specific enough to be particularly helpful, the rejection of the first three did claim to dispose of some commonly held explanations. This example illustrates a historical study in which hypotheses were explicitly stated.

Hypotheses in Educational Historical Research

Hypotheses may be formulated in historical investigations of education. Several examples are listed:

1. The educational innovations of the 1950s and 1960s were based on practices previously tried and discarded.
2. Christian countries whose educational systems required religious instruction have lower church attendance rates than those countries in which religious instruction was not provided in schools.
3. The observation of European school systems by American educators during the 19th century had an important effect on American educational practices.
4. The pay of teachers is low because of the tradition of teachers being primarily women.

Although hypotheses are not always *explicitly* stated in historical investigations, they are usually implied. The historian gathers evidence and carefully evaluates its trustworthiness. If the evidence is compatible with the consequences of the hypothesis, it is confirmed. If the evidence is not compatible, or negative, the hypothesis is not confirmed. It is through such synthesis that historical generalizations are established.

The activities of the historian when education is his or her field of inquiry are no different from those employed in any other field. The sources of evidence may be concerned with schools, educational practices and policies, movements, or individuals, but the historical processes are the same.

Difficulties Encountered in Historical Research

The problems involved in the process of historical research make it a somewhat difficult task. A major difficulty is delimiting the problem so that a satisfactory analysis is possible. Too often beginners state a problem much too broadly; the experienced historian realizes that historical research must involve a penetrating analysis of a limited problem rather than a superficial examination of a broad area. The weapon of research is the target pistol, not the shotgun.

Because historians may not have lived during the time they are studying and may be removed from the events they investigate, they often depend on inference and logical analysis, using the recorded experience of others rather than direct observation. To ensure that their information is as trustworthy as possible, they must rely on primary, or firsthand, accounts. Finding appropriate primary sources of data requires imagination, hard work, and resourcefulness.

Historians must also keep in mind the context in which the events being studied occurred and were recorded. They need to keep in mind the biases and beliefs of those who recorded the events as well as the social and political climate in which they wrote.

SOURCES OF DATA

Historical data are usually classified into two main categories:

1. Primary sources are eyewitness accounts. They are reported by an actual observer or participant in an event. "Finding and assessing primary historical data is an exercise in detective work. It involves logic, intuition, persistence, and common sense. . . ." (Tuchman, 1994, p. 319)
2. Secondary sources are accounts of an event not actually witnessed by the reporter. The reporter may have talked with an actual observer or read an account by an observer, but his or her testimony is not that of an actual participant or observer. Secondary sources may sometimes be used, but because of the distortion in passing on information, the historian uses them only when primary data are not available, which unfortunately is frequently. As Tuchman (1994) points out, finding the secondary source is only the first step. The researcher must then verify the quality of the source material.

Primary Sources of Data

Documents
Documents are the records kept and written by actual participants in, or witnesses of, an event. These sources are produced for transmitting information to be used

in the future. Documents classified as primary sources are constitutions, charters, laws, court decisions, official minutes or records, autobiographies, letters, diaries, genealogies, census information, contracts, deeds, wills, permits, licenses, affidavits, depositions, declarations, proclamations, certificates, lists, handbills, bills, receipts, newspaper and magazine accounts, advertisements, maps, diagrams, books, pamphlets, catalogs, films, pictures, paintings, inscriptions, recordings, transcriptions, and research reports.

Remains or Relics

Remains or relics are objects associated with a person, group, or period. Fossils, skeletons, tools, weapons, food, utensils, clothing, buildings, furniture, pictures, paintings, coins, and art objects are examples of those relics and remains that were not deliberately intended for use in transmitting information or for use as records. However, these sources may provide clear evidence about the past. The contents of an ancient burial place, for instance, may reveal a great deal of information about the way of life of a people, their food, clothing, tools, weapons, art, religious beliefs, means of livelihood, and customs. Similarly, the contents of an institution for the mentally ill or mentally retarded can reveal a good deal of information about the way the clients were treated, including the quality of food, the opportunity for work and recreational activities, and whether abuses occurred regularly.

Oral Testimony

Oral testimony is the spoken account of a witness of, or participant in, an event. This evidence is obtained in a personal interview and may be recorded or transcribed as the witness relates his or her experiences.

Primary Sources of Educational Data

Many of the old materials mentioned in the preceding section provide primary evidence that may be useful specifically in studying the history of education. A number are listed here.

Official Records and Other Documentary Materials

This category includes records and reports of legislative bodies and state departments of public instruction, city superintendents, principals, presidents, deans, department heads, educational committees, minutes of school boards and boards of trustees, surveys, charters, deeds, wills, professional and lay periodicals, school newspapers, annuals, bulletins, catalogs, courses of study, curriculum guides, athletic game records, programs (for graduation, dramatic, musical, and athletic events), licenses, certificates, textbooks, examinations, report cards, pictures, drawings, maps, letters, diaries, autobiographies, teacher and pupil personnel files, samples of student work, and recordings.

Oral Testimony

This category includes interviews with administrators, teachers and other school employees, students and relatives, school patrons or lay citizens, and members of governing bodies.

Relics

This category includes buildings, furniture, teaching materials, equipment, murals, decorative pictures, textbooks, examinations, and samples of student work.

Secondary Sources of Data

Secondary sources are the reports of a person who relates the testimony of an actual witness of, or participant in, an event. The writer of the secondary source was not on the scene of the event but merely reported what the person who *was* there said or wrote. Secondary sources of data are usually of limited worth for research purposes because of the errors that may result when information passes from one person to another.

Most history textbooks and encyclopedias are examples of secondary sources, for they are often several times removed from the original, firsthand account of events. Some material may be a secondary source for some purposes and a primary source for another. For example, a high school textbook in American history is ordinarily a secondary source. But if one were making a study of the changing emphasis on nationalism in high school American history textbooks, the book would be a primary document or source of data.

HISTORICAL CRITICISM

It has been noted that the historian does not often use the method of direct observation. Past events cannot be repeated at will. Because the historian must get much of the data from the reports of those who witnessed or participated in these events, the data must be carefully analyzed to sift the true from the false, irrelevant, or misleading.

Trustworthy, usable data in historical research are known as *historical evidence.* That body of validated information can be accepted as a trustworthy and proper basis for the testing and interpretation of a hypothesis. Historical evidence is derived from historical data by the process of criticism, which is of two types: *external* and *internal.*

External Criticism

External criticism establishes the authenticity or genuineness of data. Is the relic or document a true one rather than a forgery, a counterfeit, or a hoax? Various tests of genuineness may be employed.

Establishing the age or authorship of documents may require intricate tests of signature, handwriting, script, type, spelling, language usage, documentation, knowledge available at the time, and consistency with what is known. It may involve physical and chemical tests of ink, paint, paper, parchment, cloth, stone, metals, or wood. Are these elements consistent with known facts about the person, the knowledge available, and the technology of the period in which the remains or the document originated?

Internal Criticism

After the authenticity of historical documents or relics has been established, there is still the problem of evaluating their accuracy or worth. Although they may be genuine, do they reveal a true picture? What of the writers or creators? Were they competent, honest, unbiased, and actually acquainted with the facts, or were they too antagonistic or too sympathetic to give a true picture? Did they have any motives for distorting the account? Were they subject to pressure, fear, or vanity? How long after the event did they make a record of their testimony, and were they able to remember accurately what happened? Were they in agreement with other competent witnesses?

These questions are often difficult to answer, but the historian must be sure that the data are authentic and accurate. Only then may he or she introduce them as historical evidence, worthy of serious consideration.

The following examples describe ways in which evidence is tested for authenticity. The first is an example of scholarly historical criticism carried on by scientists and biblical scholars in which historic documents were proved to be genuine. Although these examples are neither particularly relevant to education nor recent, they provide excellent illustrations of how various evidence can be tested for authenticity.

The Dead Sea Scrolls

One of the most interesting and significant historical discoveries of the 20th century was the finding of the Dead Sea Scrolls. This collection of ancient manuscripts was discovered in 1947 by a group of Bedouins of the Ta'amere tribe. Five leather scrolls were found sealed in tall earthenware jars in the Qumran caves near Aim Feshkha on the northwest shore of the Dead Sea (Davies, 1956).

The Bedouins took the scrolls to Metropolitan Mar Athanesius Yeshue Samuel, of St. Mark's monastery in Jerusalem, who purchased them after discovering that they were written in ancient Hebrew. A consultation with biblical scholars confirmed the fact that they were very old and possibly valuable. They were later purchased by Professor Sukenik, an archaeologist of Hebrew University at Jerusalem, who began to translate them. He also had portions of the scrolls photographed and sent to other biblical scholars for evaluation. On examining some of the photographs, Dr. William F. Albright of Johns Hopkins University pronounced them "the greatest manuscript discovery of modern times."

A systematic search of the Wadi Qumran area caves in 1952 yielded other leather scrolls, many manuscript fragments, and two additional scrolls of copper so completely oxidized that they could not be unrolled without being destroyed. By 1956 scientists at the University of Manchester, England, had devised a method of passing a spindle through the scrolls, spraying them with aircraft glue, baking them, and then sawing them across their rolled-up length to yield strips which could be photographed.

The origin, the age, and the historic value of the scrolls have been questioned. By careful and systematic external and internal criticism, however, biblical scholars and scientists have generally established and accepted certain facts.

The scrolls are very old, probably dating back to the first century A.D. They are written in ancient Hebrew and probably originated in a pre-Christian monastery of one of the Jewish sects. The writings contain two versions (one complete and one incomplete) of the Book of Isaiah, a commentary, or *Midrash,* on the Book of Habakkuk, a set of rules of the ancient Jewish monastery, a collection of about twenty psalms similar to those of the Old Testament, and several scrolls of apocalyptic writings similar to the Book of Revelation.

The contents of the copper scrolls and other fragments have now been translated. It is possible that more scrolls and writings may be discovered in the area, and it is likely that these ancient documents may throw new light on the Bible and the origins of Christianity.

It is interesting to note how these documents were authenticated, dated, and evaluated by:

1. Paleography, an analysis of the Hebrew alphabet forms. These written characters were similar to those observed in other documents known to have been written in the first century.
2. A radiocarbon test of the age of the linen scroll covering, conducted by the Institute of Nuclear Research at the University of Chicago. All organic matter contains radiocarbon 14, which is introduced by the interaction of cosmic rays from outer space with the nitrogen in the earth's atmosphere. The radioactivity constantly introduced throughout the life of the specimen ceases at death and disintegrates at a constant known rate. At the time of death, all organic matter yields 15.3 disintegrations per minute per gram of carbon content. The number of disintegrations is reduced by one-half after 5,568 years, plus or minus 30 years. By measuring disintegrations with a Geiger-type counter, it is possible to estimate the age of specimens within reasonable limits of accuracy. Through this technique the date of the scrolls was estimated at A.D. 33, plus or minus 200 years.
3. Careful examination of the pottery form in which the scrolls were sealed. These jars, precisely shaped to fit the manuscripts, were the type commonly used during the first century.
4. Examination of coins found in the caves with the scrolls. These dated Roman coins provided convincing evidence of the age of the scrolls.

5. Translation of the scrolls. When translated, the scrolls compared to other writings, both biblical and nonbiblical, of known antiquity.

Although external criticism has now produced convincing evidence of the genuineness and age of the Dead Sea Scrolls, biblical scholars will pursue the internal criticism of their validity and relevance for many years to come and may provide many new hypotheses concerning biblical writings and the early history of Christianity and the pre-Christian Jewish sects.

Modern approaches to historical research have applied advanced technology, emphasizing the usefulness of both qualitative and quantitative data. As we have seen in this example, researchers employed the radiocarbon 14 test to verify the authenticity of the scrolls. The next example illustrates the use of the computer in archaeological and historical research.

Stonehenge (Hanging Stones)

For centuries historians and archaeologists have debated the origin and purpose of Stonehenge, a curious arrangement of stones and archways, each weighing more than 40 tons, located on the Salisbury Plain about 90 miles southwest of London. From the beginning of recorded history, writers have speculated about the stones. Their construction and arrangement have been attributed to many tribes and national groups who invaded or inhabited England. Modern radiocarbon dating of a deer antler found in the stone fill seems to date their erection at about 1900 to 1600 B.C. Their purpose has been explained in many legends—a city of the dead, a place of human sacrifice, a temple of the sun, a pagan cathedral, and a Druid ceremonial place.

More recently some scientists and historians have suggested that Stonehenge was a type of astronomical computer calendar used by early Britons who were apparently sophisticated enough to compute the position of the sun and the moon at their various stages. Using an IBM 704 computer, Gerald S. Hawkins, an astronomer at the Smithsonian Astrophysical Observatory at Cambridge, Massachusetts, entered into the computer 240 stone alignments translated into celestial declinations. Accomplishing in less than a minute a task that would have required more than 4 months of human calculator activity, the computer compared the alignments with the precise sun/moon extreme positions as of 1500 B.C. and indicated that they matched with amazing accuracy.

Hawkins suggests that the stone arrangements may have been created for several possible reasons: They made a calendar that would be useful for planting crops; they helped to create and maintain priestly power by enabling the priest to call out the people to see the rising and setting of the midsummer sun and moon over the heel stone and midwinter sunset through the great trilithon; or possibly they served as an intellectual exercise. Hawkins concludes:

In any case, for whatever reasons those Stonehenge builders built as they did, their final completed creation was a marvel. As intricately aligned as an interlocking series of astronomical instruments (which indeed it was) and yet architecturally

perfectly simple, in function subtle and elaborate, in appearance stark, imposing,
awesome, Stonehenge was a thing of surpassing ingenuity of design, variety of
usefulness and grandeur—in concept and construction an eighth wonder of the
world. (Hawkins & White, 1965, pp. 117–118)

This interesting historical–archaeological controversy illustrates the use of sophisticated computer technology to test a hypothesis.

Examples of Topics for Educational Historical Study

Brickman (1982) provided a number of possible topics by types of historical research in education and an example for each. His list is repeated here:

1. PERIOD. "Education during the First Half of the Fifteenth Century."
2. GEOGRAPHICAL REGION. "German Education under Frederick the Great."
3. EDUCATIONAL LEVEL. "The Secondary Schools of Ancient Rome."
4. INSTITUTION. "Amherst College in the Nineteenth Century."
5. BIOGRAPHY. "Bronson Alcott as an Educator." Biographical detail, as such, is of less importance for term-report purposes than an exposition of the man's educational ideas, work, and influence.
6. INNOVATIONS. "Three Decades of Audio–Visual Education."
7. PHILOSOPHY. "Changing Concepts of American Higher Education in the Nineteenth Century."
8. METHODOLOGY. "Herbartianism in American Educational Practice."
9. CURRICULUM. "The Subject of Rhetoric in Ancient Greece."
10. PERSONNEL. "The Role of the Teacher during the Renaissance."
11. CHILDREN. "Changing Attitudes toward Corporal Punishment of Children in the United States."
12. LEGISLATION. "Compulsory School Attendance Laws in Prussia during the Eighteenth Century."
13. MATERIALS. "The Evolution of American School Readers, 1700–1830."
14. NONSCHOOL AGENCIES. "The Development of the Library in Nineteenth-Century America."
15. ORGANIZATIONS. "History of the Public School Society of New York."
16. FINANCE. "Methods of School Taxation in Pennsylvania, 1820–1880."
17. ARCHITECTURE. "The Evolution of the School Building in Illinois."
18. ADMINISTRATION. "The Rise of the State Superintendency of Schools."
19. LITERATURE. "A Century of Educational Periodicals in the United States."
20. INFLUENCE. "The Influence of Rousseau upon Pestalozzi."
21. REPUTATION. "The Reception of Horace Mann's Educational Ideas in Latin America."
22. COMPARISON. "A Comparative Study of Renaissance Theories of the Education of the Prince."
23. TEXTBOOK ANALYSIS. "A Study of the Treatment of Primitive Education in Textbooks in Educational History" (pp. 5–6)[1]

Obviously these topics are too broad for a student project and in some cases would probably take most of a career. The processes of delimitation and hypothesis formation are needed to make these topics useful.

An example of how a scholar might decide on a topic for historical educational research is provided in the introduction to Whitehead's (1996) interesting book on the academies of Bartholomew Booth in the 18th century. Whitehead first came across Booth's name while conducting research on another 18th century schoolmaster who referred to Booth in one of his advertisements as a former employer of his. Six years passed before Whitehead had the time to answer some questions that this reference had provoked. He quickly discovered that Booth had emigrated from England to North America in 1773 and settled in Maryland. From the few records left by Booth that still existed (15 in all, mostly letters) it became apparent that he had attracted the attention of some of the leaders of the revolution (e.g., Richard Henry Lee, Robert Morris, Benedict Arnold, and members of the Washington family). However, these few papers of Booth led to even more questions than they answered. Through a careful examination of documents left by Booth's known friends, associates, and students' parents, Whitehead was able to recreate Booth's life and contributions and answer the question, "Might Bartholomew Booth's academies have contributed to the formation of leaders first in England and later in America?" (p. xix) Eleven years after he began work on Booth's documents, Whitehead published his book.

WRITING THE HISTORICAL REPORT

No less challenging than the research itself is the writing of the report, which calls for creativity in addition to the already illustrated qualities of imagination and resourcefulness. It is an extremely difficult task to take often seemingly disparate pieces of information and synthesize them into a meaningful whole. Research reports should be written in a dignified and objective style. However, the historian is permitted a little more freedom in reporting. Hockett suggests that "The historian is not condemned to a bald, plain, unattractive style" and that "For the sake of relieving the monotony of statement after statement of bare facts, it is permissible, now and then, to indulge in a bit of color." He concludes, however, by warning that "Above all, embellishments must never become a first aim, or be allowed to hide or distort the truth" (Hockett, 1948, p. 139).

An evaluation of graduate students' historical-research projects demonstrates the difficulty of the task by often revealing one or more of the following faults:

1. Problem too broadly stated
2. Tendency to use easy-to-find secondary sources of data rather than sufficient primary sources, which are harder to locate but usually more trustworthy
3. Inadequate historical criticism of data because of failure to establish authenticity of sources and trustworthiness of data. For example, there is often a tendency to accept the truth of a statement if several observers agree. It is possible

that one may have influenced the other or that all were influenced by the same inaccurate source of information.

4. Poor logical analysis resulting from:

   a. Oversimplification, failure to recognize the fact that causes of events are more often multiple and complex rather than single and simple

   b. Overgeneralization on the basis of insufficient evidence and false reasoning by analogy, basing conclusions on superficial similarities of situations

   c. Failure to interpret words and expressions in the light of their accepted meaning in an earlier period

   d. Failure to distinguish between significant facts in a situation and those that are irrelevant or unimportant

   e. Failure to consider the documents in the context of their time, that is, the existing beliefs, biases, and so forth

5. Expression of personal bias, as revealed by statements lifted out of context for purposes of persuasion, assuming too generous or uncritical an attitude toward a person or idea (or being too unfriendly or critical), excessive admiration for the past (sometimes known as the "old oaken bucket" delusion), or an equally unrealistic admiration for the new or contemporary, assuming that all change represents progress

6. Poor reporting in a style that is dull and colorless, too flowery or flippant, too persuasive or of the "soap-box" type, or improper in usage

It is apparent that historical research is difficult and demanding. The gathering of historical evidence requires long hours of careful examination of such documents as court records, records of legislative bodies, letters, diaries, official minutes of organizations, or other primary sources of data. Historical research may involve traveling to distant places to examine the necessary documents or relics. In fact, any significant historical study would make demands that few students have the time, financial resources, patience, or expertise to meet. For these reasons good historical studies are not often attempted to meet academic degree requirements.

SUMMARY

History, the meaningful record of human achievement, helps us to understand the present and, to some extent, to predict the future. Historical research is the application of scientific method to the description and analysis of past events.

Historians ordinarily draw their data from the observations and experience of others. Because they are not likely to have been at the scene of the event, they must use logical inferences to supplement what is probably an incomplete account.

Primary sources may be "unconscious" testimony, not intended to be left as a record—relics or remains such as bones, fossils, clothing, food, utensils, weapons, coins, and art objects are useful. Conscious testimony, in the form of records or documents, is another primary source of information: constitutions, laws, court decisions, official minutes, autobiographies, letters, contracts, wills, certificates, newspaper and magazine accounts, films, recordings, and research reports.

Historical criticism is the evaluation of primary data. External criticism is concerned with the authenticity or genuineness of remains or documents, and internal criticism is concerned with the trustworthiness or veracity of materials. The accounts of the Dead Sea Scrolls and Stonehenge illustrate the processes of historical criticism.

The historical research studies of graduate students often reveal serious limitations. Frequently encountered are such faults as stating the problem too broadly, inadequate primary sources of data, unskillful historical criticism, poor logical analysis of data, personal bias, and ineffective reporting.

EXERCISES

1. Write a proposal for a historical study in a local setting. You may select a community, school, church, religious or ethnic group, or individual. State an appropriate title, present your hypothesis, indicate the primary sources of data that you would search, and tell how you would evaluate the authenticity and validity of your data.

2. Select a historical thesis from the university library and analyze it in terms of

    a. hypothesis proposed or questions raised
    b. primary and secondary sources of data used
    c. external and internal criticism employed
    d. logical analysis of data relationships
    e. soundness of conclusions
    f. documentation

ENDNOTE

1. Used with the permission of Emeritus, Inc., publisher.

REFERENCES

Abington School District v. Schempp, 374 U.S. 203 (1963).

Aydelotte, W. O. (1963). Notes on the problem of historical generalization. In L. Gottschalk (Ed.), *Generalization in the writing of history.* Chicago: University of Chicago Press.

Best, J. H. (1996). Education in the forming of the American south. *History of Education Quarterly, 36,* 39–51.

Berkhofer, R. F., Jr. (1995). *Beyond the great story: History as test and discourse.* Cambridge, MA: Harvard University Press.

Brickman, W. W. (1982). *Educational historiography: Tradition theory, and technique.* Cherry Hill, NJ: Emeritus.

Cohen, D. W. (1994). *The combing of history.* Chicago: University of Chicago Press.

Cremin, L. (1961). *The transformation of the school: Progressivism in American education.* New York: Alfred A. Knopf.

Davies, A. P. (1956). *The meaning of the Dead Sea Scrolls.* New York: New American Library of World Literature.

Finley, M. I. (1963). Generalizations in ancient history. In L. Gottschalk (Ed.), *Generalization in the writing of history.* Chicago: University of Chicago Press.

Gallop Organization Newsletter Archive. *Http://www.gallop.com/newsletter/july95/7schpryr.html.* Vol. 60, No. 11, July 20, 1995.

Gottschalk, L. R. (1963). Categories of historical generalizations. In L. Gottschalk (Ed.), *Generalization in the writing of history.* Chicago: University of Chicago Press.

Hawkins, C. S., & White, J. B. (1965). *Stonehenge decoded.* Garden City, NY: Doubleday.

Hockett, H. C. (1948). *Introduction to research in American history.* New York: Macmillan.

Lannie, V. L., & Diethorn, B. C. (1968). For the honor and glory of God: The Philadelphia bible riots of 1840. *History of Education Quarterly, 8,* 44–106.

Nevins, A. (1962). *The gateway to history* (rev. ed.). Boston: Raytheon Education Co.

Robenstine, C. (1992). French colonial policy and the education of women and minorities: Louisiana in the early eighteenth century. *History of Education Quarterly, 32,* 193–211.

Search, P. W. (1901). *An ideal school: Looking forward.* New York: Appleton-Century-Crofts.

Seldon, A. (Ed.). (1988). *Contemporary history: Practice and method.* Oxford: Basil Blackwell.

Thursfield, R. E. (1945). *Henry Barnard's American Journal of Education.* Baltimore: Johns Hopkins University Press.

Tuchman, G. (1994). Historical social science: Methodologies, methods, and meanings. In N. K. Denzin & Y. S. Lincoln (Eds.). *Handbook of qualitative research.* Thousand Oaks, CA: Sage.

Weiler, K. (1994). Women and rural school reform: California, 1900–1940. *History of Education Quarterly, 34,* 25–47.

Whitehead, M. (1996). *The academies of the Reverend Bartholomew Booth in Georgian England and revolutionary America.* Lewiston, NY: Edwin Mellon Press.

SAMPLE ARTICLE

Used with permission of the author.

clear and concise

French Colonial Policy and the Education of Women and Minorities: Louisiana in the Early Eighteenth Century *

Clark Robenstine

In speaking of the settlement of America, Lawrence Cremin observed that "it is [the] fact of empire that holds the key to the dynamics of early American education."[1] This was as true of French colonial efforts in the New World as it was for those of the English, though French colonial motivation was tempered by the vague notion of "for the glory of the King," which revolved around defensive military needs while giving lesser consideration to economic imperialism. And with the French, as for the English, education played a significant and necessary role in colonial policy which attempted to achieve social and cultural dominance. Within a scant decade of the establishment of New Orleans as a permanent settlement in the Louisiana Territory in 1718, provisions were made for the education of the females of the area—white and minority. While meager efforts had been made to provide education for the male youth, those efforts were not well received by the small local population and ultimately were short lived. Consequently, the first lasting element of institutionalized education in French colonial Louisiana, the Ursuline school and convent, put a unique emphasis on female and minority education. How this unusual development merged with, and reflected, colonial political goals is the central concern of this essay.

purpose of study

Contrasting the efforts of the French in colonizing America and the role of education in those efforts with the better-known English patterns not only reinforces elements of accepted interpretations of English success in these efforts (for example, those of Cremin), but, more importantly, identifies the reasoning behind French colonial political policy and at the same time contributes to an understanding of why the French failed in the end. That ultimate failure to achieve social and cultural dominance in the New World notwithstanding, the French Louisiana Territory in general and the New Orleans settlement in particular provide an exemplary case of the use of education, especially for females, for social and political purposes. The identification of these social and political factors shed light on the Ursuline effort, specifically on what was taught, who was taught, and why. Furthermore, an analysis of Ursuline education and the impetus behind it helps reconstruct French life in the nascent colony and provides a basis of comparison with English colonial antecedents.

statement of problem or reason for study

statement of problem or reason for study

This contrast yields certain lessons, not the least of which is the vital importance of the family unit and the establishment of viable and stable communities for the ultimate success of colonization. Therein lies the greatest failing of the French in America. It is too facile to point solely to the fact that the majority of the population in colonial America was English. While the French

Clark Robenstine is an assistant professor in educational foundations, University of Southwestern Louisiana, Lafayette.

[1]Lawrence A. Cremin, *Traditions of American Education* (New York, 1977), 4.

were certainly outnumbered, numbers provide only a partial explanation for English success and French failure. The relatively late arrival of the French in America also does not fully explain their failure. While being vastly outnumbered and entering the American colonial picture almost a century after the English certainly could not have helped the French cause, the determining factor was the initial absence of social stability because of a lack of coherent family units in early French colonizing efforts in the Louisiana Territory.

For the English by 1622 it had already become apparent that the success of their colonization in America would be tied "to the development of self-sufficient agricultural and trading communities, that self-sufficiency would sooner or later require the planting of families, and that the planting of families would be facilitated by institutions like those of England." Having come relatively late, the French had no time to waste but at least could benefit from adoption of this English conception of colonization. By 1689, a decade before the French began thinking about a colony in America, there were established English settlements from Maine to the Carolinas. The English conception of colonies had evolved firmly to that of permanent, self-sustaining communities embracing all institutions which would propagate elements of English culture and society.[2]

Though the French learned this lesson from the English, the colonizers did not act quickly enough. While the establishment of the Ursuline school is proof that the French recognized the importance of the English model, they failed in the critical early years of colonial policy to achieve social and cultural stability through strong family structures.

What is so noteworthy about the value of the family unit is the importance it places on the role of women in the colonial context, and in attracting them to and keeping them in the colony. As suggested, the most prominent factors affecting the establishment and success of the Ursuline school were not exclusively educational in nature or even religious, except on the surface. The provision of education for females in the colony was an explicit and intended element of French colonial *political* policy. Women's education was inextricably linked with the development of Louisiana's economic and strategic value.[3]

EARLY FRENCH COLONIAL EDUCATION

The education policies in early colonial Louisiana were intended as the extension of the education policies of eighteenth-century France. To a degree they were.

[2]Lawrence A. Cremin, *American Education: The Colonial Experience, 1607–1783* (New York, 1970), 13, 22. Of utmost importance in the struggle for dominance was the number of households in the English colonies by 1689. For example, Massachusetts had approximately eight thousand households, and Virginia over seven thousand. See ibid., 238–41.

[3]Certain characteristics of the period render extant source material somewhat confusing. Intense and interrelated personal, political, and religious rivalries in the Louisiana colony resulted in a mass of correspondence crossing the Atlantic detailing charges and countercharges of competing factions or individuals against each other. According to one twentieth-century scholar of French Louisiana, these letters and *mémoires* to the home government "were not only written by [colonial] officials, but by anybody who could hold a pen." In the bitter struggle for power in the colony, "all arms were fair: detraction, defamation, calumny, nothing was thought too ugly to satisfy one's spite against a personal enemy, or if by so doing there was the slightest chance of securing one's own advancement." Jean Delanglez, *The French Jesuits in Lower Louisiana, 1700–1763* (Washington, D.C., 1935), 213.

Generally, wherever the Roman Catholic church dominated, it dominated education as well. Therefore, the educators of France in the eighteenth century were predominantly the Catholic religious orders. This pattern had been established early on in New France (Canada) with the arrival of the Jesuits and Ursulines, both teaching orders, in the 1620s and 1639, respectively.[4]

The earliest French involvement in the Louisiana Territory was marked by a notable lack of success in most aspects. Leaving France with the blessing of Louis XIV in 1698, Pierre Le Moyne d'Iberville, his younger brother Jean-Baptiste Le Moyne de Bienville, and an expedition of three hundred colonists and sailors eventually located the mouth of the Mississippi. Iberville selected a site for settlement on the Gulf Coast on the banks of Biloxi Bay. The first few years of the settlement saw little progress, and both colonists and commerce were in short supply. Due largely to the War of the Spanish Succession in Europe during the opening years of the eighteenth century—a critical period for the infant colony—Louisiana was virtually cut off from supplies. Also, importantly, the French were much less given to emigration than their English counterparts.

Although an earlier experience with proprietary ownership under Antoine Crozat had failed, the Louisiana colony was turned over in 1717 to John Law's Company of the West, soon to be merged into the larger Company of the Indes (1719). An immense area, the claimed Louisiana colony included all the land from the Gulf to the English territory on the east, New Spain on the west, and the Great Lakes and New France on the north. The upper colony, Illinois country, was more closely and directly connected with New France than was the lower part. With such a large area and such a small population, lower colonial Louisiana, by and large, consisted of New Orleans and the Gulf Coast, with a few other scattered settlements.

It was under the early control of the Company of the Indes that New Orleans was established in 1718 as a permanent settlement, and then made the colonial capital in 1721. It was under the control of the Company also that the first efforts at providing education for the inhabitants were made. Records indicate that as early as 1725 in New Orleans, a school for boys was organized under the direction of the Capuchin vicar-general, Father Raphael de Luxembourg. In witnessing a marriage, one Pierre Fleurtet signed the register of New Orleans's St. Louis Church as choirmaster on 4 April 1725. On 14 April he signed for the first time as *maitre d'école*—schoolmaster.[5]

With regards to this school, Father Raphael wrote to the ecclesiastical director of the Company of the Indes, Gilles Bernard, Abbé Raguet, on 18 May 1726: "I have the honor, Sir, to notify you by my previous letter that I have established a small college at New Orleans. I have now the honor to assure you that the studies made there are very good. The number of pupils is as yet very small, but there

Clear narrative description of the historical facts (with appropriate interpretation) begins here and continues till the "Conclusion."

[4]T. H. Harris, *The Story of Public Education in Louisiana* (New Orleans, 1924), 1; see Joyce Marshall, trans. and ed., *Word from New France: The Selected Letters of Marie de l'Incarnation* (Toronto, 1967) for a general account of the Jesuits and a particular account of the Ursulines in Canada.

[5]Marriage Register, 1720–30, St. Louis Cathedral Archives, New Orleans, Louisiana. See also, Father Raphael de Luxembourg to Gilles Bernard, Abbé Raguet, 15 Sep. 1725, p. 409, vol. 8, ser. B, General Correspondence, Louisiana, Ministry of the Marine, French National Archives, Paris.

good use of primary sources

are few children in the colony." Few specifics are known about the Capuchin school. Although the Company had been instructed to provide some sort of education, no plot had been reserved for a school in the plan for New Orleans. The colonists themselves showed little interest in such a project, consequently the Capuchin monks took it upon themselves to enter into an agreement with two influential men in the colony to secure a location for the school. They agreed to buy conjointly an available house, with each party promising to pay one-third of the cost. The Capuchins had all but paid their portion when the other two parties to the contract refused to abide by the agreement and even petitioned for the return by the Capuchins of previously advanced monies.[6]

The matter was brought ultimately to the attention of colonial governor Etienne de Périer and *ordonnateur* (administrator of colonial finances) Jacques de la Chaise. They recommended that the Company study the matter and give a decision.[7] According to one history of the Catholic church in America, "the Company turned a deaf ear to his [Father Raphael's] pleadings, and the majority of the colonists looked upon his work with indifference."[8] The case dragged on and was eventually decided against the Capuchins, causing the disestablishment of the school in the very early 1730s. The Company saw little need for, and had no interest in, establishing and financially supporting a formal school for boys. Louisiana was a proprietary venture; thus, unnecessary costs, those perceived as having no explicit profit value; were to be avoided.[9] Boys would receive any required practical knowledge and skills through their apprenticeships.

Contrary to the rather disagreeable experience of the Capuchins in establishing some sort of permanent school for boys, the provision of educational opportunities for the females of the area—regardless of class or race—has a more successful history. With the help of Jesuit Father Nicholas de Beaubois, a contract of twenty-eight articles was entered into on 13 September 1726 between the Company of the Indes and the Ursuline nuns of France—those who had been the first nuns to bring instruction for girls to Quebec in New France.[10]

The preamble of the treaty with the Ursulines reveals that, although they were also "et pourvoir en même temps à l'éducation des jeunes filles" (to provide at the same time for the education of young girls), their primary duty was to be the operation of the colonial hospital in New Orleans. The Company petitioned Louis XV through the Regent Philip, duke of Orleans, to approve the treaty which did occur with a commission dated 18 September 1726. Mother Superior Marie

Good use of secondary sources but this article relies for the most part on primary sources. This use of primary sources allows the reader to have more faith in the accuracy of the information presented. Also, multiple sources are used, which agree on information in common.

[6]Raphael to Raguet, 18 May 1726, pp. 46, 178, vol. 10, sub-ser. 13a, ser. C, General Correspondence, Louisiana, Colonial Archives, French National Archives.

[7]Ibid.

[8]Harold A. Buetow, *Of Singular Benefit: The Story of Catholic Education in the United States* (New York, 1970), 21.

[9]Directors General of the Company of the Indes to Colonial Governor Etienne de Périer, 21 Nov. 1727, p. 80, vol. 11, sub-ser. 13A, ser. C, Colonial Archives.

[10]Diane M. Moore, *Their Adventurous Will: Profiles of Memorable Louisiana Women* (Lafayette, La., 1984), 84. See also Marguerite Aron, *The Ursulines,* trans. M. Angela Griffin, O.S.U. (New York, [1947]) for a general history of the Order.

Tranchepain, seven professed nuns, one novice, and two secular nuns left France on 22 February 1727, arriving at Balize, an outpost near the mouth of the Mississippi, on 23 July 1727.[11]

Much unlike the inhabitants' response to the Capuchin effort, the Ursulines' arrival was met with strong enthusiasm, as evidenced by novice Marie Hachard's account of the nuns' voyage up the Mississippi to New Orleans: "When we were eight or ten leagues from New Orleans, we began to meet some inhabitants who vied with each other as to who could persuade us to enter their homes. Everywhere we were received with acclamations of joy. . . . They promised us some boarders, and several wished already to confide them to us." Arriving in New Orleans on 6 August 1727, they had already received thirty requests from parents in the area to accept their daughters as boarding students.[12]

With their monastery being built on one end of town near the hospital, the nuns moved into temporary quarters rented for them by the Company on the other side of town. From the first moments, Mother Superior Tranchepain stated, "the inhabitants of New Orleans are careful that we lack nothing, it being, who will send us most." Because of the distance across town through difficult terrain and because the Ursulines were a cloistered order, it was some time before they took control of the hospital. Consequently, they directed their total efforts at once toward the school. According to Marie Hachard, "a small apartment in which to teach the day-scholars and lodge the boarders" was being built at the Ursulines' temporary residence.[13]

Unlike the lack of support for the Capuchin school for boys, so important was the arrival of the nuns and the establishment of their school for girls that Marie Hachard reports, "The fathers and mothers are transported with joy to see us, saying that they no longer care to return to France, since they have here the means of procuring an education for their daughters."[14] The Ursulines opened their school for girls, amid this local enthusiasm and support, on 17 November 1727.[15]

[11] Traité de la Compagnie des Indes avec Les Ursulines, 13 Sep. 1726, and "Louis XV Brevet en Faveur des Ursulines de la Louisanne," 18 Sep. 1726, Archival Records, Ursuline Convent, New Orleans; Rev. Mother Marie Tranchepain, *Journal of the Voyage of the First Ursulines to New Orleans, 1727,* trans. Olivia Blanchard (New Orleans, 1940). See also Marie Hachard to her father, 27 Oct. 1727, *Account of the Ursulines' Voyage from L'Orient to New Orleans,* translation in Henry Semple, *The Ursulines in New Orleans and Our Lady of Prompt Succor: A Record of Two Centuries, 1727–1925* (New York, 1925), 201–19. For the names of the nuns embarking for Louisiana, see the letter of Mother Superior Tranchepain to the Directors of the Company, 24 Dec. 1726, p. 69, vol. 10, ser. B, Ministry of the Marine.

[12] Hachard, *Account of the Ursulines' Voyage.* See also Tranchepain, *Journal of the Voyage.*

[13] Tranchepain, *Journal of the Voyage;* Hachard, *Account of the Ursulines' Voyage.*

[14] Hachard, *Account of the Ursulines' Voyage.* Not only had some entire families returned to France for the education of their daughters (an action not conducive to the permanence of the colony), but on occasion provisions were made for sending only the daughter back for formal education. See, for example, the Judicial Records of the French Superior Council, 8 May 1726, Louisiana State Museum, New Orleans, for arrangements to send the minor daughter of M. Des Fontaines to Brittany for that reason.

[15] Letter of Father Nicholas de Beaubois, 17 Nov. 1727, pp. 314–16, vol. 10, sub-ser. 13a, set. C, Colonial Archives.

The following facts about the Ursuline school can be stated briefly. That the sisters instructed not only white females but other girls regardless of race is shown in Marie Hachard's letter to her father dated 1 January 1728. In the letter she reported that the school had nine boarding students with more to come, and a number of day pupils. She goes on to tell her father that they have also "a class for Negro and Indian girls and women."[16] The instruction of the Negro slaves was set apart from that for the French girls and was handled by Sister Marguerite.[17] Further, a letter from Father Beaubois to Abbé Raguet, written 6 May 1728, indicates the growth of the school. By that date the school served sixteen boarders, seven slave girls, who were also boarders, and twenty-five day students. The nuns were commended for "the great good which they do by liberally educating so many children and slaves."[18]

As far as curriculum and instruction were concerned, the Ursulines attempted to follow, as closely as was practical given local conditions, the traditions of the Order. According to the Ursulines' Constitutions, the primary purpose of the Order was to give a good and solid education to young persons according to their condition, with the sisters taking "a special pleasure in teaching poor girls." The curriculum offered initially consisted of practical and basic subjects, such as reading, writing, arithmetic, and manual training. In particular, the black slaves and Indian girls attended class for two hours every day (half as long as French girls attended), save Sunday, and were instructed in reading, writing, sewing, the making of fabric, and the care of silkworms. And of course, most importantly, all were instructed in religion.[19]

Equally important, while the program did contain significant elements of religious instruction, a great deal of time was devoted to manual training as well. The students were first taught to sew and knit, and then how to make their own clothing, as well as many other items useful in the Louisiana colonial household. Knowledge of this kind was considered especially important.[20]

While the exact impact the activities of the nuns had on the New Orleans area is not unequivocally known, what is clear is that they were supported continuously by the Company of the Indes and the local population—even during the period of years in the late 1720s when such support was noticeably lacking for the Capuchin school. Even more curious, *any* support for a school for boys was to be years in the future. French colonial officials came to acknowledge what they perceived to be the moral and intellectual position of the girls schooled by the Ursulines. With a keen appreciation of the disadvantages under which the male youth of the colony were laboring with respect to education, Governor Bienville,

[16]Marie Hachard to her father, 1 Jan. 1728, translation in Semple, *The Ursulines in New Orleans,* 219–24.

[17]Charles Bournigalle, comp., "Annals, Ursuline Convent" (1891), Archival Records, Ursuline Convent, ch. 10, 155.

[18]Beaubois to Raguet, 6 May 1728, p. 256, vol. II, sub-ser. 13A, set. C, Colonial Archives.

[19]*Constitutions of the Ursulines Order* (Paris, 1646), 1: "Rules for the Ursulines in Religion," Second Part: Day School, Paris, 1705, Archival Records, Ursuline Convent; see also Bournigalle, "Annals, Ursuline Convent," ch. 10, 155; Marie Hachard to her father, 24 Apr. 1728, translation in Semple, *The Ursulines in New Orleans,* 224–38.

[20]"Rules for the Ursulines in Religion," Second Part: Day School.

in a letter dated 15 June 1742, pressed the French government to provide education for the boys.[21] He was again turned down.

Neither the establishment and success of the Ursuline school nor the lack of success of the Capuchin school can be explained as a purely educational phenomenon. Such success can be understood only by placing the Ursuline school within the dominant political, economic, and ecclesiastical context.

GALLICANISM, RELIGION, AND COLONIAL POLICY

French colonial policy in Louisiana was driven by three objectives: "the commerce of the goods it [Louisiana] can produce, that which can be carried out with the Spaniards, and the need to limit the English, who are already too powerful in that part of America." Although all three objectives were important, it was the last of these that came to play the most prominent role in determining policy for Louisiana. While commerce was valuable, the greatest fear was that, if left unchecked, "the English would become the masters of all North America."[22] Only a strong establishment in Louisiana could prevent this.

Understanding the role of the church in this undertaking is a fairly specific matter. In their *History of the Catholic Church,* Thomas Neill and Raymond Schmandt observe that the decline in the absolute power of the church through the seventeenth and eighteenth centuries coincided with the growth of absolute power in the dynastic state. Absolute monarchs in Catholic countries viewed religion as a political concern, with both church and state under their jurisdiction. With little "interference" from Rome tolerated, this religious manifestation of nationalism by absolute monarchs of Catholic countries is termed Gallicanism.[23] Specifically, what this meant for the French colonies was that all of French North America was subject to authority shared among the governor, *ordonnateur,* and bishop; but even that jurisdiction was ultimately subject to regulation by the French crown and royal bureaucracy. In particular in Louisiana, the charter granted by the crown placed ecclesiastical jurisdiction under the aegis of the Company of the Indes and its directors.

French political control, through authority granted to the Company, then was predominant in both civil and religious matters since, in Louisiana, even the church and its missionaries were under the authority of the Company alone. The edict for the establishment of the original Company of the West, binding on the Company of the Indes, stated:

> *Since in the settling of the lands granted to the Company of these present letters, We look particularly to the Glory of God, in procuring the salvation of the settlers, the Indians, the Savages and the Negroes, whom We wish to be instructed in the true Religion, the said Company will be obliged to build at its expense the churches of the place of its planta-*

---

[21]Memoir, Jean-Baptiste Le Moyne De Bienville, 15 June 1742, p. 312, vol. 26, sub-ser. 13A, ser. C, Colonial Archives.

[22](Anonymous), "Memoir to Make Known the Necessity of Sending Settlers to the Colony of Louisiana," 1714, p. 655, vol. 3, sub-ser. 13a, ser. C, Colonial Archives.

[23]Thomas P. Neill and Raymond H. Schmandt, History of the Catholic Church (Milwaukee, Wis., 1957), 431–32.

tions, as well as support the numbers of approved churchmen that will be needed, whether in the office of pastor or some other as will be proper, there to preach the Holy Gospel, conduct divine service, and administer the Sacraments, all under the authority of the Bishop of Quebec. The pastors and other churchmen that the Company will support are to be at its nomination and under its patronage.[24]

The last sentence in particular illustrates that, while Catholic Louisiana was responsible to the Bishop of Quebec, Jean-Baptiste La Croix de Chevrières de St. Vallier, allegiance was to the Gallican viewpoint—the viewpoint of the French crown and its regent.

In practical terms, then, this Gallicanism obscured any distinction between the religious and the political within French colonial policy. The Ursuline functioned within this context. While colonial living conditions were often extreme, the more difficult challenges for the Ursulines and the success of their school were consequences of their role in colonial political policy and their position in resulting ecclesiastical disputes.

From very early on in New France, the French had recognized the need to make colonial settlement in North America attractive. There, the lack of tenants to work the land was held out to potential emigrants as especially conducive to social and economic mobility. Also of early concern was the "English threat." Not only was the arrival of the English in North America bad enough strategically, but their presence encroached on French north Atlantic trade as well. Though the last decade of the seventeenth century had witnessed little French activity in colonial North America, rumors of projected English and Dutch settlements in the Gulf region reaching Paris and Versailles prompted the French into action. Of greatest concern was the possibility of English occupation of the Gulf Coast. Thus, as a preventive strike, the Mississippi expedition led by Iberville reached the coast and began building a fort at Biloxi on 8 April 1699.[25]

With the ascension of Philip of Anjou, Louis XIV's grandson, to the Spanish throne in 1700, the Spanish-French American colonies became allies against the English. The string of posts along the Mississippi was not only intended to protect Mexico and the Spanish borderlands, but also to contain the English. Taking a defensive posture, then, the French clearly had little intention to occupy and develop Louisiana unless its usefulness became obvious militarily. Likewise, Iberville had insisted that France establish a strong presence on the Gulf Coast to prevent English intrusion. In a 1699 memoir to the king, he pointed out the

[24]"Letters patent for the Establishment of a Company of Commerce, under the name of Company of the West," Aug. 1717, quoted in Charles E. O'Neill, *Church and State in French Colonial Louisiana: Policy and Politics to 1732* (New Haven, Conn., 1966), 11.

[25]Sigmund Diamond, "An Experiment in Feudalism: French Canada in the Seventeenth Century," *William and Mary Quarterly*, 3d ser., 18 (Jan. 1961): 3–34; Henry P. Biggar, *The Early Trading Companies of New France: A Contribution to the History of Commerce and Discovery in North America* (New York, 1965), 119; Jean Louis Phèlypeaux de Pontchartrain to Dantin, 15 Oct. 1698, p. 253, vol. 136, Memoires and Documents, America, Archives of the Minister of Foreign Affairs, French National Archives; Carl A. Brasseaux, trans. and ed., *A Comparative View of French Louisiana, 1699 and 1762: The Journals of Pierre Le Moyne d'Iberville and Jean-Jacques-Blaise d'Abbadie* (Lafayette, La., 1979).

phenomenal growth of the English colonies which would enable them to drive all other nations from the American continent within ten years.[26]

By the early 1720s Louisiana, in addition to being a military outpost, had attracted at least small numbers of adventurers and fortune seekers—emigrants, but not really settlers. The "English threat" was to be dealt with by the construction in the colony of a viable, stable French culture and society. That had been the approach taken in New France with the early recognition of the necessity of well-planned settlements. Still, the French fell short of this model. In the first half of the seventeenth century, Louis XIV's advisor, Sebastian de Vauban, admitted that only those colonies established by the English and Dutch were designed in such a way as to promote the welfare and prosperity of their colonists.[27]

Two facts—continuing tension with the English colonies and Louisiana's status as a proprietary colony until 1731—account for the establishment of education for the females of the colony. While the latter required the general growth of the colony for the success of trade and commerce, the former required as well the stability of French occupation and the gaining of influence over Indian tribes that might be used in an alliance against the English. Both growth and stability required establishing religion, according to colonial political thinking.

Missionaries came to play an increasing role in colonial politics. By Christianizing the Indians, encouraging them to settle in permanent villages, and teaching them French, the religious were to transform barbarians into good, loyal subjects of the king (for the glory of the King).[28] This would go a long way in making them allies against the English. In this way, wrote Father Beaubois, the Louisiana missionary was seen chiefly as an arm of secular colonization: "The Indians respect a missionary and listen to him, and even should he not succeed in converting them, he does at least win their allegiance to the French."[29]

Under Cardinal Armand Duplessis, Cardinal Richelieu, the French Prime Minister until 1642, social policy had been to create a new French society in New France out of a union of French settlers and "Frenchified" natives. Only through religious conversion could this occur. This social vision of colonization called for a grand scheme for the assimilation of the Indians "into a new half-breed society based on the same ethics, the same social base of the family, the same concept of order, authority and obedience as French society. The conversion of the Indians was therefore a priority since, along with the acquisition of the French lan-

[26]Charles E. O'Neill, ed., *Charlevoix's Louisiana: Selections from the History and the Journal* (Baton Rouge, La., 1977), 12–13; Pontchartrain to Ducasse, 1 July 1699, p. 372, vol. 21, ser. B, Colonial Archives, Orders of the King, French National Archives; Memoir, Pierre Le Moyne d'Iberville, 30 Aug. 1699, p. 188, vol. 1, sub-ser. 13A, set. C, Colonial Archives. Iberville's fears were to be realized when, with the Treaty of Utrecht in 1713, the English took possession of Acadia in New France. Thus, the French had to develop new lines of defense against further English expansion.

[27]David Farrell, "Reluctant Imperialism: Pontchartrain, Vauban, and the Expansion of New France, 1699–1702," in *Proceedings of the Twelfth Meeting of the French Colonial Historical Society, May 1986*, ed. Philip Boucher and Serge Courville (Lanham, Md., 1988), 39.

[28]William J. Eccles, *Frontenac: The Courtier Governor* (Toronto, 1959), 54–55. Evangelization of the natives was an obligation every charter imposed on companies or individuals granted a colonial monopoly; see Allain, *Not Worth a Straw*, 35.

[29]Memoir, Father Beaubois, 1725, p. 260, vol. 12, sub-ser. 13a, set. C, Colonial Archives.

guage, it would transform 'savages' into subjects."[30] Jean-Baptiste Colbert, Richelieu's successor, pursued the same social policy in all settlement colonies by assuming that conversion of the Indians (later policy in Louisiana included blacks) would entice them into civilized (in other words, French) society. Efforts were to be directed especially toward Indian children who were to be drawn into the communities by the clergy so that they all "may evolve into a single nation."[31]

Thus, the legacy brought to Louisiana was that colonies should be extensions of the mother country, very much like old France but improved. The colonies were to have the same administrative institutions as continental provinces, be ministered by the same church, and develop the same social structure. These New French societies which would flourish across the Atlantic would therefore closely resemble their continental model, except that they would blend white settlers, converted Indians, and in Louisiana, contented black laborers, into a harmonious, orderly whole.[32]

While the minority males and females (Indian and black) required conversion, efforts to achieve some semblance of French society were directed toward all *women*, minority and French.[33] Thus, females formed the group requiring the most "attention" in order to accomplish the goals of this social policy. The absence of Frenchwomen and particularly their influence had been part of Iberville's complaint that France lacked the national "colonizing spirit" so characteristic of the English, who sent established families.[34]

In Louisiana as in New France earlier, one of the most serious obstacles to the general growth of the colony was the constant shortage of women. In the early years of the Louisiana colony, French administrators had founded great hopes on marriages between Frenchmen and Indian girls. But these mixed unions were deleterious to Frenchifying goals. The native women did not passively accept Western civilization; instead, their French husbands adopted the Indian lifestyle. Consequently, unions with Indian women, whether legitimate marriages or concubinage, came to be seen as a major impediment to colonial progress. Bienville complained in 1706, "We must bring back all the Frenchmen who are among the

[30]Allain, *Not Worth a Straw,* 11, 7.

[31]Eccles, *Frontenac, 56.* With respect to the work of the missionaries in Louisiana in converting both the Indians and blacks, see Roger Baudier, *The Catholic Church in Louisiana* (New Orleans, 1939), esp. 75–77.

[32]Allain, *Not Worth a Straw,* 70. Of course this scheme did not work out quite so neatly. Transposing European institutions wholesale to the colonies proved more difficult than the French ever thought possible, as evidenced in Louisiana.

[33]French males form the group noticeably missing here. The reasons for this are 1) that they were already Catholic, even if some practiced the faith badly; and 2) that the belief was that "civilization depends more upon the training and education of the feminine sex than the masculine." To the extent that some practiced the faith poorly, French males were to be "helped" by the presence of morally strong, religiously faithful women-to-be-wives who, by their very influence, would set the men back on the "right" path. For evidence of this belief in the civilizing role of women, see Mary Theresa Austin Carroll, *The Ursulines in Louisiana, 1727-1824* (New Orleans, 1886), 4; Vaughan Baker, "Les Louisianaises: A Reconnaissance," and Mathe Allain, "Manon Lescaut et ses Consoeurs: Women in the Early French Period, 1700–1731," *Proceedings of the Fifth Meeting of the French Colonial Historical Society, 1979,* ed. James Cooke (Lanham, Md., 1980), 6–15 and 18–26, respectively; and, Allain, *Not Worth a Straw,* 83–87.

[34]Farrell, "Reluctant Imperialism," 37.

Indians and forbid them to live there as libertines simply because they have wives among them." Indian marriages proved such a disaster that the prevention of these unions was one of the most frequently cited reasons for wanting French-women. One colonial official wrote in 1712 that unless French girls were sent, "it will be difficult to prevent concubinage. The Indian women are easy, the air is stimulating, and the men are young, that is to say, very vigorous."[35]

Thus, attracting and keeping Frenchwomen came to be seen as essential to establishing and maintaining French culture, French society, and French family life in colonial Louisiana. French historian Jean François Saintoyant argued that, because of the stabilizing presence of women and children, an English colony, unlike a French colony, was "effectively a city from the moment of posses-sion."[36] His premise, a reflection of accepted belief and the premise accepted here, is clearly that women were indispensable in the Louisiana context to the development of stability and civilization. Not only were Frenchwomen neces-sary to pull into civilized society the backwoodsmen and adventurers, but a 1709 memoir had suggested even more frankly that French wives would force the men to work in order to maintain family social status: "Once married, they should work to support their families in mutual rivalry."[37]

One early French response to the clamor for Frenchwomen was the policy of forced emigration, though this was a short-lived and mostly unsuccessful pol-icy. A more significant contribution to the colony and its nascent society was made by the *épouseuses,* the marriageable girls. They came in waves, with the first arriving in 1704. While the 1700 census listed only males, the 1706 census listed some families, a few already with one child. The next group arrived in 1713, though they were less successful. Perceiving this group as an unattractive lot, one report suggested that, in the future, it would behoove recruiters "to seek looks rather than virtue," for the men are not too "particular" about the girls' behavior before marriage. Other significant groups arrived in the colony in 1721 and 1728, the latter group under the responsibility of the Ursulines.[38] For what-ever reasons they arrived, these women tried to adapt and, when possible, re-establish the French ways to which they were accustomed. In this way, women and the perceived needs of women so necessary to the existence and survival of the French colony received high priority.

In the urgent necessity of the colonial reconstruction of French life, the civ-ilizing influence of the Ursuline nuns through their education of young girls can-not be underestimated. At least as far as colonial officials were concerned, despite the care supposedly exercised in choosing the *épouseuses,* selection was some-times slovenly. In the year or two prior to the Ursulines' arrival a number of

---

[35]Bienville to Pontchartrain, 28 July 1706, p. 537, vol. I, and Martin d'Artaguiette to Pontchartrain, 8 Sep. 1712, p. 799, vol. 2, sub-ser. 13A, ser. C., Colonial Archives.

[36]Jean François Saintoyant, *La Colonisation française sous l'Ancien Régime (du XVe siècle à 1789)* (Paris, 1929), quoted in Baker, "Les Louisianaises," 8.

[37]Marigny de Mandeville, Memoir on Louisiana, 29 Apr. 1709, p. 475, vol. 2, sub-ser. 13A, ser. C, Colonial Archives.

[38]Antoine de La Mothe Cadillac to Pontchartrain, 26 Oct. 1713, pp. 50–51, and Memoir to Jean-Baptiste du Bois Duclos, 15 July 1713, pp. 138–40, vol. 3, sub-ser. 13A, ser. C, Colo-nial Archives; Bournigalle, "Annals, Ursuline Convent," ch. 11, 155.

reports had been made complaining about the immorality of the colony. Father Raphael found "a frightful indifference for the sacraments and a horrifying acceptance of public concubinage." Colonial governor Périer commented in November 1727 that "there are many women and girls of bad life here." On the other hand, over a short period of time, the women educated by the Ursulines came to be in demand as wives, their tenure with the nuns a kind of seal of approval or guarantee. The Records of the Superior Council, the governing body of the colony, contain numerous references to marriages of women "from the convent of the Ursuline Ladies," and these women continued to be sought after as wives through the period of French domination.[39]

The religious instruction notwithstanding, conceivably the greatest influence the Ursulines had on the colony was the provision of manual training, such as sewing instruction. Survival and growth of the colony depended upon the success of family groups and the establishment of households, goals achieved largely through the efforts of the Ursulines. As a proprietary colony, trade and commerce were increasingly important. As a French colony, limiting English expansion was increasingly important. Neither objective would be met without the general growth of the colony, and the general growth of the colony would not be achieved without the presence of women suitable for the colonial conditions. The securing of Louisiana through the reconstruction of French life, modified by colonial realities, to a large degree was the task of the Ursulines and the education they provided to young girls.[40]

General growth and stability meant also working the land. With colonists always in short supply, requests for slaves were frequent, and the French turned to black slavery to provide Louisiana with a laboring class. The first slaves were

[39]Raphael to Raguet, 15 May 1725, p. 402, vol. 8, and Périer to the Company of the Indes, 2 Nov. 1727, p. 108, Heloise Cruzat, vol. 10, sub-ser. 13A, ser. C, Colonial Archives; "The Ursulines of Louisiana," *Louisiana Historical Quarterly* 2 (Jan. 1919): 5–24.

[40]Mention should be made here of changing European attitudes toward women, and especially young girls, which had some effect on the educational situation in colonial Louisiana. Philippe Ariès chronicles a changing conception of childhood such that in the first half of the seventeenth century, there was a growing concern for the education of young girls. Whereas before they had stayed at home with the women of the house or else in a convent receiving only religious instruction, girls now received a broader (relatively speaking) education from religious orders, such as the Ursulines. As already noted, the education of young girls was the purpose of the Ursuline Order, and the Ursulines had gone to New France in 1639 for that reason. Increasingly then, according to Ariès, in the sixteenth and seventeenth centuries the "great event" in this respect was the revival of an interest in education essentially for children. The traditional apprenticeship for children (especially males) was replaced by the school. And largely, this education was for sociability and civility. See Philippe Ariès, *Centuries of Childhood: A Social History of Family Life,* trans. Robert Baldick (New York, 1962), esp. 298, 383–86, 403–13. I suggest that this changing conception of childhood was, of course, mitigated by the realities of the Louisiana frontier context and resulted in a necessary reemphasis on apprenticeship for boys, while formal education for girls remained. This would account for the noticeable lack of local support for the Capuchin school for boys and the noticeable local enthusiasm for the Ursuline school for girls. On the use of apprenticeship for boys, see Robert B. Holtman and Glenn R. Conrad, eds., *French Louisiana: A Commemoration of the French Revolution Bicentennial* (Lafayette, La., 1989), 122.

imported in 1719.[41] The most common theme within the correspondence request-
ing slaves was the claim of guaranteed prosperity (for the Company one assumes)
if only sufficient numbers of slaves would be sent.[42] By 1724 the number of slaves
in the Louisiana colony had become large enough to warrant legislation. Although
containing numerous articles regulating the relationship between owner and slave,
the Black Code specifically ordered that all slaves in the colony had to be instructed
and baptized in the Catholic religion.[43]

Both the Black Code and the conversion of the Indians fit into the larger colonial goal of Christianizing all those not of the "true" religion. Not only would
God's kingdom be enlarged, but more importantly as far as colonial policy was
concerned, the number of useful, productive inhabitants would be increased. And
it would never hurt to have more subjects loyal to the French crown in staving
off the English. Conversion of the Indians was difficult at best (and not very successful), given the large area involved and the paucity of missionaries to complete
the task, but slaves were much more accessible. The Black Code, in addition to
requiring religious conversion, also enumerated without hesitation what today
would count as cruel and unusual punishment—flogging, branding, ear cropping,
hamstringing. But the Code was an expression of eighteenth-century French jus-
tice, which actually tended to be even more harsh in France—burning at the
stake, breaking on the wheel, as well as drawing and quartering; and military
criminals in Louisiana had their heads crushed between two stones. The Black
Code reflected a part of the transfer of French social patterns to the New World,
another effort at creating New Frances.[44]

Whether Christianizing Indian and slave girls or educating Frenchwomen,
the activities of the Ursulines were religious only on the surface. First and foremost, especially as far as the crown and the Company of the Indes were concerned, they helped serve the purpose of secular political colonization. The
rallying of support for the Ursulines at the time of ecclesiastical controversy in the
late 1720s demonstrated their importance in this political mission.

The Ursulines faced adverse conditions so severe that one eyewitness
account described New Orleans at the time of the Ursulines' arrival as presenting "no better aspect than that of a vast sink or sewer . . . and within a stone's
throw of the church . . . reptiles croaked, and malefactors and wild beasts lurked,
protected by impenetrable jungle."[45] But it was a controversy over religious juris-

[41]Daniel Unser, "From African Captivity to American Slavery: The Introduction of Black
Laborers to Colonial Louisiana," *Louisiana History* 20 (Winter 1979): 25–48. Regarding the
constant requests for slaves for the Louisiana colony see as examples, Pierre Dugué de Bois-
briant to Pontchartrain, 24 Oct. 1725, p. 236, vol. 8, French Superior Council to Pontchartrain, 17 Feb. 1725, p. 51, vol. 9, French Superior Council to Pontchartrain, 28 Aug. 1725,
p. 239, vol. 9, French Superior Council to Pontchartrain, 6 Apr. 1726, p. 251, vol. 9, Périer
to Raguet, 25 Apr. 1727, p. 211, vol. 10, ser. B, Ministry of the Marine.

[42]See, for example, Périer to Raguet, 25 Apr. 1727, p. 211, vol. 10, ser. B, Ministry of the
Marine.

[43]Black Code, art. 2, in *Publications of the Louisiana Historical Society*, vol. 4 (New
Orleans, 1908), n.p. This requirement was a reflection of an added stipulation in the original charter for the Company of the West that all foreign immigrants must be of the Catholic
religion.

[44]Black Code, arts. 3–40; Allain, *Not Worth a Straw*, 83.

[45]Quoted in Carroll, *The Ursulines in Louisiana*, 10.

diction between Jesuit Father Beaubois and Capuchin Father Raphael that most severely threatened the continuing presence of the Ursulines in Louisiana. The controversy escalated as Father Raphael increasingly saw the presence of Father Beaubois as a threat to Capuchin authority. This problem was extended to include the Ursulines because it had been Beaubois who had arranged their selection.[46] The correspondence back and forth in this matter is extensive. De la Chaise and Raphael lodged continual complaint against Beaubois, often supported by the coadjustor of Quebec, Louis François Duplessis de Mornay, up to the time of Beaubois's recall to France. Along the way the Ursulines, having accepted Beaubois as their Superior, suffered guilt by association. In 1728 two letters to the directors of the Company, one from Governor Périer and one from Mother Superior Tranchepain, charged that the nuns suffered because supplies were being withheld by de la Chaise as a result of the latter's quarrels with Beaubois. Ignoring objections by Father Raphael, the Mother Superior also reaffirmed the right of Father Beaubois alone to be the Ursulines' superior.[47]

The pertinent point here is that, fearing the worst for the survival of the colony at the recall of Beaubois, the Company pleaded with, and Raguet exhorted, the nuns not to leave. The purely religious welfare of the inhabitants was not their sole or even primary concern. Abbé Raguet, ecclesiastical director of the Company, went so far as to request that the now-dismissed Beaubois use all his influence to convince the Ursulines to remain in Louisiana, at the same time reminding the nuns of their duty to detach themselves from earthly affections.[48]

While the Ursulines never made good on their threat to leave Louisiana, the Company was concerned enough to acquiesce quickly to the nuns' demands and have the Jesuit Beaubois replaced by another Jesuit, as Mother Superior Tranchepain continued in 1729 to reject the authority of the Capuchins. What became clear to the Company was the social and cultural, thus political, value of the nuns' presence.[49]

[46]Louis François Duplessis de Mornay to Raguet, 3 June 1727, pp. 31–34, vol. 10, sub-ser. 13A, ser. C, Colonial Archives. In November 1727, shortly after the arrival of the Ursulines, Governor Périer wrote to Raguet: "The arrival of the Ursulines here, has almost caused a division in the Church. Father de Beaubois claimed to be their Superior in the quality of vicar-general and wished to direct them which was contrary to the conditions of his agreement with the Company. . . . Father Raphael, on his side, although very good and prudent, would not tolerate that Father de Beaubois should perform the functions of the office of Superior without being stirred by it." See Périer to Raguet, 2 Nov. 1727, p. 191, ibid.

[47]Périer to Directors, Company of the Indes, 14 Aug. 1728, p. 9, and Tranchepain to Directors, Company of the Indes, 28 Apr. 1728, p. 277, vol 11, ser. B, Ministry of the Marine. See also Périer to Raguet, [early 1728?], p. 6, vol. 12, sub-ser. 13A, ser. C, Colonial Archives. Tranchepain to Raguet, 5 Jan. 1728, p. 272, vol. 11, ser. B, Ministry of the Marine.

[48]Raguet to Beaubois, 27 Oct. 1728, p. 241, and Raguet to Tranchepain, 27 Oct. 1728, p. 244, vol. 11, ser. B, Ministry of the Marine. Regarding Gallicanism, it should be noted that this problem was handled directly by the Company and its agents as representatives of the French government, not by the Bishop of Quebec.

[49]Tranchepain to Raguet, 9 Mar. 1729, p. 283, vol. 12, ser. B, Ministry of the Marine. The dispute over Beaubois and the Ursulines, and the pertinent correspondence, between 12 Aug. and 15 Nov. 1728, is chronicled in pp. 236–82, vol. 11, ser. B, Ministry of the Marine. Vols. 8–12, ser. 8, Ministry of the Marine, covering 1725–29, contain additional letters which pertain to the longstanding jurisdictional dispute between the Jesuits and Capuchins.

As the tenure of the Company of the Indes came to an end in 1731, the Ursulines had greatly expanded their social service to the colony by sheltering abused women and taking in large numbers of female orphans.[50] An institution that had come perilously close to abandonment instead gained strength, far outlasting French domination itself. The Ursuline convent and school for girls has operated in New Orleans without interruption since its inception in the colony in 1727.

CONCLUSION

Conclusions appropriate & justified by facts presented earlier.

To say simply that the Ursulines and the Ursuline school played a part in the development of colonial Louisiana is to severely understate their significance. In settling Louisiana, the transposition of European institutions and ideas wholesale to the frontier proved exceedingly difficult. But Louisiana colonists and colonial officials clung to their transplanted views. One dominant aspect of this context was that of Gallicanism—a viewpoint not often shared but grudgingly accepted by those missionaries on the frontlines. The result was that these religious emissaries served political aims conjointly with religious ones. Nowhere is this more evident than in the role the Ursulines exercised in the establishment and maintenance of the family social unit. Although the French monarchy had never intended to invest more in Louisiana than was strictly necessary to keep it out of English hands, the "English threat" soon required the full-fledged development of the colony.

As expressed both in the dominant French social policy for the colony and in the belief in the necessity of women for stability and civility, staving off the English threat required that two conditions be met: 1) the establishment of a viable French society and culture which, in turn, required 2) the strong presence of family units, not just soldiers and adventurers. Both of these conditions required the presence and influence of women. Thus, the primary French political objective of cutting off English expansion westward was heavily dependent upon this presence and influence. While English colonies had been established largely by family groups, which built societies more quickly, French colonies remained, for too many early years, primarily masculine. The growth, stability, and security of the Louisiana colony demanded first and foremost the establishment of households and family units. The knowledge and skills offered by the Ursulines in their school were integral in meeting this objective—a fact certainly clear to the Company of the Indes.

In summary, all *women* were the key to the establishment of French culture and society, and thus to stability. This meant Frenchwomen, obviously, but minority women, as well, who would bear the responsibility of imitating French society and thereby help create, within their own context, a unified social whole. Once the French accepted this view of the role of women, the remaining task was the religious conversion of minority males.

In retrospect, while the French in Louisiana were almost too late from the very beginning, the number of families did increase. The census figures for the

[50]Judicial Records of the French Superior Council, 15 Feb.–4 Sep. 1728; Périer and Edmé-Gatien Salmon to the King, 8 Dec. 1731, p. 571, vol. 14, sub-ser. 13A, ser. C, Colonial Archives.

Louisiana colony identify 96 families present in 1721, increasing substantially to 368 families by 1731.[51] Without claiming a sole cause-effect relationship, it is reasonable to suggest that the Ursulines played a part in that increase. Similar to the earlier realization of the English that colonial stability and success would require the establishment of social and cultural institutions like those of the home country, including the presence of families, the French came to realize the value of pursuing the same goal. The Ursulines' emphasis on the role of women linked them and their schools with French colonial political policy. Within the Louisiana colonial context, while the formal education of males outside of apprenticeship was viewed as frivolous, the education of females was regarded as essential. As with the conversion of minority males by missionaries and slaveholders, in the provision of education for white and minority women, the Ursulines were to serve secular political colonization through Christianizing and acculturating the Indians and slaves, and by advancing the social reconstruction of French life in the infant colony.

[51]Charles R. Maduell, *The Census Tables for the French Colony of Louisiana from 1699 through 1732* (Baltimore, 1972), 17–27, 114–22. My minimum criteria for "family" are husband and wife, with or without children.

5

DESCRIPTIVE STUDIES: ASSESSMENT, EVALUATION, AND RESEARCH

A descriptive study describes and interprets what *is*. It is concerned with conditions or relationships that exist, opinions that are held, processes that are going on, effects that are evident, or trends that are developing. It is primarily concerned with the present, although it often considers past events and influences as they relate to current conditions.

The term *descriptive study* masks an important distinction, for not all descriptive studies fall into the category of research. In fact, of the three kinds of descriptive studies included in this chapter, only one is actually research. Chapter 1 briefly discusses the similarities and differences between assessment, evaluation, and research. This discussion of descriptive studies will restate those similarities and differences. Also, this chapter confines itself to descriptive studies that use quantitative methods. Qualitative studies are discussed in Chapter 8.

Assessment describes the status of a phenomenon at a particular time. It describes without value judgment a prevailing situation; it attempts no explanation of underlying reasons and makes no recommendations for action. It may deal with prevailing opinion, knowledge, practices, or conditions. As it is ordinarily used in education, assessment describes the progress students have made toward educational goals at a particular time. For example, in the National Assessment of Education Progress program, the data are gathered by a testing program and a sampling procedure in such a way that no individual is tested over the entire test battery. It is not designed to determine the effectiveness of a particular process or program but merely to estimate the degree of achievement of a large number of individuals exposed to a great variety of educational and environmental influences. It does not generally provide recommendations, but there may be some implied judgment on the satisfactoriness of the situation or the fulfillment of society's expectations.

Evaluation is a process used to determine what has happened during a given activity or in an institution. The purpose of evaluation is to see if a given program is working, if an institution is successful according to the goals set for it, or if the original intent is being successfully carried out. To assessment, evaluation adds the ingredient of value judgment of the social utility, desirability, or effectiveness of a process, product, or program, and it sometimes includes a recommendation for some course of action. School surveys are usually evaluation studies; educational products and programs are examined to determine their effectiveness in meeting accepted objectives, often with recommendations for constructive action.

Descriptive research deals with the relationships between variables, the testing of hypotheses, and the development of generalizations, principles, or theories that have universal validity. It is concerned with functional relationships. The expectation is that, if variable A is systematically associated with variable B, prediction of future phenomena may be possible, and the results may suggest additional or competing hypotheses to test. Descriptive research is sometimes divided into correlational research, causal–comparative research, and other descriptive research that is neither correlational nor designed to find causation but describes existing conditions. All of these types of descriptive research are included here because they have the same basic components: They are all attempting to find generalizable attributes, and they all deal with present conditions.

In carrying out a descriptive research project, in contrast to an experiment, the researcher does not manipulate the variable, decide who receives the treatment, or arrange for events to happen. In fact, the events that are observed and described would have happened even if there had been no observation or analysis. Descriptive research also involves events that have already taken place and may be related to a present condition.

The method of descriptive research is particularly appropriate in the behavioral sciences because many of the types of behavior that interest the researcher cannot be arranged in a realistic setting. Introducing significant variables may be harmful or threatening to human subjects. Ethical considerations often preclude exposing human subjects to harmful manipulation. For example, it would be unthinkable for an experimenter to randomly decide who should smoke cigarettes and who should not smoke them for the purpose of studying the effect of smoking on cancer, heart disease, or other illnesses thought to be caused by cigarette smoke. Similarly, to deliberately arrange auto accidents, except when mannequins are used, in order to evaluate the effectiveness of seat belts or other restraints in preventing serious injury would be absurd.

Although many experimental studies of human behavior can be appropriately carried out both in the laboratory and in the field, the prevailing research method of the behavioral sciences is descriptive. Under the conditions that naturally occur in the home, the classroom, the recreational center, the office, or the factory, human behavior can be systematically examined and analyzed.

The many similarities between these types of descriptive studies may cloud the distinctions between them. They are all characterized by disciplined inquiry, which requires expertise, objectivity, and careful execution. They all develop knowledge, adding to what is already known. They use similar techniques of observation, description, and analysis. The differences between them lie in the motivation of the investigator, the treatment of the data, the nature of the possible conclusions, and the use of the findings. The critical distinctions are that the three types of studies have different purposes and, therefore, approach the problem differently and that *only descriptive research studies lead to generalizations* beyond the given sample and situation.

A single study may also have multiple purposes. For instance, a study may evaluate the success or failure of an innovative program and also include sufficient controls to qualify as a descriptive research study. Similarly, an assessment study may include elements that result in descriptive research also. Unfortunately, this potential overlap further clouds the distinction. Put simply, in order for a descriptive study to be considered research, it must have sufficient controls to permit generalization of the results.

Examples of these three types of descriptive studies follow. It is important to keep in mind that, although these examples are presented to illustrate each individual type of study (assessment, evaluation, or descriptive research), they are not mutually exclusive. That is, for example, although surveys are used to illustrate assessment and evaluation studies, surveys are also used in descriptive research studies. Similarly, although causal–comparative studies illustrate their major use in descriptive research, this type of design can also be used in an assessment or evaluation study.

ASSESSMENT STUDIES

The Survey

The survey method gathers data from a relatively large number of cases at a particular time. It is not concerned with characteristics of individuals *as* individuals. It is concerned with the statistics that result when data are abstracted from a number of individual cases. It is essentially cross-sectional.

Ninety-four percent of American homes have at least one television set. About three out of five students who enter American secondary schools remain to graduate. Seventy-one percent of Americans say they favor a constitutional amendment to permit school prayer, whereas only 45% would still favor school prayer if it offended a large percentage of parents. In 1990, 4,717,641 children were enrolled in California public schools, whereas slightly more than 10% of that number, 474,194, were enrolled in Iowa's public schools. On an average day, 11,137 babies are born. In both 1987 and 1995, 77% of those polled favored an increase in the minimum wage. The population of Illinois according to the 1980 census was 11,426,518. The Illinois population increased slightly according to the 1990 census figures to 11,430,602. Data like these result from many types of surveys. Each statement pictures a prevailing condition at a particular time. All of the survey data above were obtained from resources on the Internet, which provides a new method of disseminating information much more quickly than through the usual publication channels.

In analyzing political, social, or economic conditions, one of the first steps is to get the facts about the situation or a picture of conditions that prevail or that are developing. These data may be gathered from surveys of the entire population. Others are inferred from a study of a sample group carefully selected from the total population. At times the survey may describe a limited population that is the only group under consideration.

The survey is an important type of study. It must not be confused with the mere clerical routine of gathering and tabulating figures. It involves a clearly defined problem and definite objectives. It requires expert and imaginative planning, careful analysis and interpretation of the data gathered, and logical and skillful reporting of the findings.

Social Surveys

Surveys became a common method of data collection in the first half of this century. In the late 1930s a significant social survey was directed by the Swedish sociologist Gunnar Myrdal and sponsored by the Carnegie Foundation. Myrdal and his staff of researchers made a comprehensive analysis of the social, political, and economic life of African Americans in the United States, yielding a great mass of data on race relations in America (Myrdal, 1944).

The late Alfred Kinsey of Indiana University made a comprehensive survey of the sexual behavior of the human male, based on data gathered from more than 12,000 cases (Kinsey, Pomeroy, & Martin, 1948). His second study (Kinsey, Pomeroy, Martin, & Gebhard, 1953) of the behavior of the human female followed later. Studies of sexual behavior have continued to the present. However, we should note that there are problems with surveys of sensitive topics such as these (Zimmerman & Langer, 1995). The most obvious of the problems with surveys of sensitive behaviors is whether the responses are honest. Because some people may exaggerate and others understate their behaviors, the data from such surveys are often hard to interpret. Zimmerman and Langer suggest ways to optimize the estimates regarding the rates of sensitive behaviors. Although studies on sexual behaviors have raised considerable controversy, they represent a scientific approach to the study of an important social problem and have many implications for jurists, legislators, social workers, and educators.

Witty (1967) studied the television viewing habits of school children and published annual reports on his investigations. These studies were conducted in the Chicago area and indicate the amount of time devoted to viewing and the program preferences of elementary and secondary students, their parents, and their teachers. Witty attempted to relate television viewing to intelligence, reading habits, academic achievement, and other factors. Recent survey data (July,

1996) on television viewing reported by the American Academy of Pediatrics (http://edie.cprost.sfu.ca/gcnet/iss4-21c.html) indicate that American children and adolescents spend between 22 and 28 hours a week watching television, more than any other activity except sleeping. The American Psychological Association estimates that the average American child or teenager views 10,000 murders, rapes, and aggravated assaults on television each year. More than 1,000 studies have indicated that exposure to heavy doses of television violence increases the likelihood of aggressive behavior, particularly in males. Unfortunately, these data and studies of aggressive behavior have not led to changes in the television programming or viewer behavior despite the fact that almost 80% of Americans believe that violence on television contributes to violence in society.

Shaw and McKay (1942) conducted a study of juvenile delinquency in Chicago, yielding significant data on the nature and extent of delinquency in large urban communities. Lang and Kahn (1986) examined special education teacher estimates of their students' criminal acts and crime victimizations. The data indicated that special education students seem to be victimized in the same way as others but to a greater degree. This preliminary study led to Lang's (1987) dissertation, an experiment aimed at reducing the rate of victimization of mentally retarded students.

Many other organizations collect information on behaviors and events of interest to them. The National Safety Council conducts surveys on the nature, extent, and causes of automobile accidents in all parts of the United States; state high school athletic associations conduct surveys on the nature and extent of athletic injuries in member schools; and, of course, the U.S. Census bureau collects information on the shifting U.S. population demographics.

Public Opinion Surveys

In our culture, where so many opinions on controversial subjects are expressed by well-organized special interest groups, it is important to find out what the people think. Without a means of polling public opinion, the views of only the highly organized minorities are effectively presented through the printed page, radio, and television.

How do people feel about legalized abortion, the foreign aid program, busing to achieve racial integration in the public schools, or the adequacy of the public schools? What candidate do they intend to vote for in the next election? Such questions can be partially answered by means of the public opinion survey. Many research agencies carry on these surveys and report their findings in magazines and in syndicated articles in daily newspapers.

Because it would be impracticable or even impossible to get an expression of opinion from every person, sampling techniques are employed in such a way that the resulting opinions of a limited number of people can be used to infer the reactions of the entire population.

The names Gallup, Roper, and Harris are familiar to newspaper readers in connection with public opinion surveys. These surveys of opinion are frequently analyzed and reported by such classifications as age groups, sex, educational level, occupation, income level, political affiliation, or area of residence. Researchers are aware of the existence of many publics, or segments of the public, who may hold conflicting points of view. This further analysis of opinion by subgroups adds meaning to the analysis of public opinion in general.

Those who conduct opinion polls have developed more sophisticated methods of determining public attitudes through more precise sampling procedures and by profiting from errors that plagued early efforts. In prediction of voter behavior several well-known polls have proved to be poor estimators of election results.

As described earlier, in 1936 a prominent poll with a sample of over 2 million voters predicted the election of Alfred Landon over President Roosevelt by nearly 15 percentage points. The primary reason for this failure in prediction was the poll's sampling procedure. The sample was taken from telephone directories and automobile registration lists that did not adequately represent poor persons, who in this election voted in unprecedented numbers. Gallup, on the other hand, correctly predicted that Roosevelt would win, using a new procedure, *quota sampling*, in which various components of the population are included in the sample in the same proportion that they are represented in the population. However, there are problems with this procedure, a fact which resulted in Gallup and others being wrong in 1948 (Babbie, 1989).

In the 1948 election campaign most polls predicted the election of Thomas E. Dewey over President Truman. This time the pollsters were wrong, perhaps partly because of the sampling procedure and partly because the polls were taken too far before the election despite a trend toward Truman throughout the campaign. Had the survey been made just prior to election day, a more accurate prediction might have resulted. In addition, most survey researchers (including pollsters) use *probability sampling* instead of quota sampling. This results in all members of a given population having the same probability of being chosen for the sample. In the 1984 election, Ronald Reagan won with 59% of the vote to Walter Mondale's 41%. The prediction of the Gallup Poll was exactly the percentage of the vote for Reagan with a sample of only about 2,000 voters. Other polls were within a few percentage points of this landslide victory. This accuracy was possible due to the use of probability sampling (Babbie, 1989).

In addition to the limitations suggested, there is a hazard of careless responses, given in an offhand way, that are sometimes at variance with the more serious opinions expressed as actual decisions.

Since 1969 the Gallup organization has conducted an annual nationwide opinion poll of public attitudes toward education. Using a stratified cluster sample of 1,500 or more individuals over 18 years of age, the data have been gathered by personal interviews from seven geographic areas and four size-of-community categories. The responses are analyzed by age, sex, race, occupation, income level, political affiliation, and level of education. A wide range of problem areas has been considered. For instance, in the 1975 poll such problem areas confronting education were the use of drugs and alcohol; programs on drugs or alcohol; behavior standards in the schools; policies on suspension from school; work required of students, including amount of homework; requirements for graduation from high school; federal aid to public schools; the nongraded school program; open education; alternative schools; job training; right of teachers to strike; textbook censorship; and the role of the school principal as part of management (Elam, 1979). The 1982 poll indicated the public's clear support for education. Education was ranked first among 12 funding categories considered in the survey above health care, welfare, and military defense with 55% selecting public education as one of their first three choices (*Nation at Risk*, 1983, p. 17).

Elam (1995) has provided an overview of the polls from 1969 to 1994. He provides a description of how the views of education have changed during this time. In general, people rate their local schools higher than the schools nationwide, probably because of having firsthand knowledge of the local schools but only secondary knowledge (e.g., from the news media) about the schools of the nation as a whole. As we all know, the media is more likely to do a story on school problems than on successes. Thus, it is not surprising that schools would be viewed more negatively in the abstract than those known personally by the respondent. Elam also notes that often the poll reflects concerns that are actually not major problems. For instance, in 1986 poll respondents stated that drug use was the number one problem in schools. At the same time the University of Michigan surveys indicated that drug use among students was declining.

National Center for Education Statistics

The National Center for Education Statistics, part of the U.S. Department of Education, conducts a number of surveys to collect information about the educational programs and children's achievement in the United States. Among these reports one of the most important and enduring is the National Assessment of Educational Progress (NAEP).

The NAEP was the first nationwide, comprehensive survey of educational achievement to be conducted in the United States. Originally financed by the Carnegie Foundation and the Fund for the Advancement of Education, with a supporting grant from the U.S. Office of Education, the Committee on Assessing the Progress of Education (CAPE) began its first survey in the spring of 1969. The agency now conducting the assessment is the National Assessment of Educational Progress (NAEP), financed by the National Center for Educational Statistics, a division of the Department of Education. Periodic reports are provided for educators, interested lay adults, and the general public through press releases to periodicals.

The NAEP gathers achievement test data by a sampling process such that no one individual is tested over the whole test battery or spends too long in the process. Achievement now is assessed every 2 years (but was up to 5 years apart in the past, depending on the area being assessed and the years of the assessment) in four age groups (9, 13, 17) in four geographical areas (Northeast, Southeast, Central, and West), for four types of communities (large city, urban fringe, rural, and small city), and for several socioeconomic levels and ethnic groups. Achievement has been assessed in art, reading, writing, social studies, science, mathematics, literature, citizenship, and music. Comparisons between individuals, schools, or school systems have never been made.

A recent analysis (Mullis et. al., 1994) of trends in the NAEP data (from 1969 to 1992 for science; 1973 to 1992 for mathematics; from 1971 to 1992 in reading; and from 1984 to 1992 in writing) indicates that science and mathematics scores have rebounded to the scores of the early 1970s from the lows of the early 1980s, whereas reading scores have declined slightly during the same period. At all three ages science performance declined in the 1970s but improved during the 1980s. The mathematics data tells a similar story. However, reading performance improved during the 1970s but declined during the 1980s, returning to its initial level. Writing performance was more stable from 1984 (when first measured) to 1992, although there was a significant decrease in 1990, followed by a similar increase in 1992, perhaps indicating a problem with the 1990 data. Other recent reports have been issued on each of the subject areas (e.g., Binkley & Williams, 1996; Mullis, Jenkins, & Johnson, 1994).

Other reports by the National Center for Education Statistics include a profile of schools and students and staffing at them (Choy et al., 1993). These data include such diverse information as ethnic and gender makeup of students and teachers (e.g., 49% of schools in the United States had no minority teachers, 87% of teachers were white, and 73 percent were female); compensation (the basic average full-time salary in 1990–91 was $29,987); teachers' perceptions of school problems (the percentage of teachers who thought student drug abuse was a serious problem declined from 7% to 4% between 1987–88 and 1990–91); attitudes toward teaching (39% said that they would become teachers again if they had it to do over); and various characteristics of schools such as size and student compositions. The Center also has published reports on the 100 largest public school districts (Sietsema & Bose, 1995) and a compendium of educational statistics (Snyder & Hoffman, 1994).

International Assessment

The International Association for the Evaluation of Educational Achievement, headquartered in Stockholm, Sweden, has been carrying on an assessment program in several countries since 1964. The first study, *The International Study of Achievement in Mathematics* (Torsten, 1967), compared achievement in 12 countries: Austria, Belgium, England, Finland, France, West Germany, Israel, Japan, the Netherlands, Scotland, Sweden, and the United States. Short answer and multiple choice tests were administered to 13-year-olds and to students in their last year of the upper secondary schools, before university entrance. More than 132,000 pupils and 5,000 schools were involved in the survey. Japanese students excelled above all others regardless of their socioeconomic status, and United States students ranked near the bottom. The study continues as the International Assessment of Educational Progress and includes other subjects.

Although the purpose of assessment is not to compare school systems, the data leads observers to make such comparisons. Critics of the first assessment pointed out the inappropriateness of comparing 17-year-olds in the United States, in which more than 75% are enrolled in secondary schools, with 17-year-olds in other countries in which those enrolled in upper secondary schools comprise a small, highly selected population.

More recent assessments (Snyder & Hoffman, 1994) reveal that, although the top United States students are equal to or surpass similar groups in other countries, on average, U.S. students placed 9th out of 31 countries participating in reading for 14-year-olds, 12th out of 14 in science for 13-year-olds, and 13th out of 14 for 13-year-olds in mathematics. Data from the survey of countries includes the age at which students begin, the average cost of education in the country, and the number of hours of homework.

Activity Analysis

The analysis of the activities or processes that an individual is called upon to perform is important, both in industry and in various types of social agencies. This process of analysis is appropriate in any field of work and at all levels of responsibility. It is useful in the industrial plant, where needed skills and competencies of thousands of workers are carefully studied in jobs ranging in complexity from unskilled laborer to plant manager.

In school systems the roles of the superintendent, the principal, the teacher, and the custodian have been carefully analyzed to discover what these individuals do and need to do. *The Commonwealth Teacher Training Study* (Charters & Waples, 1929) described and analyzed the activities of several thousand teachers and searched previous studies for opinions of writers on additional activities in which classroom teachers should engage. A study by Morris, Crowson, Porter-Gehrie, & Hurwitz (1984) described and analyzed the activities of school principals. This study is described in some detail later in Chapter 8 as an example of ethnographic research.

This type of analysis may yield valuable information that would prove useful in establishing

1. The requirements for a particular job or position
2. A program for the preparation or training of individuals for various jobs or positions
3. An in-service program for improvement in job competence or for upgrading of individuals already employed
4. Equitable wage or salary schedules for various jobs or positions

Trend Studies

The trend study is an interesting application of the descriptive method. In essence it is based on a longitudinal consideration of recorded data indicating what has been happening in the past, what the present situation reveals, and, on the basis of these data, what is likely to happen in the future. For example, if the population in an area shows consistent growth over time, one might predict that by a certain date the population will reach a given level. These assumptions are based on the likelihood that the factors producing the change or growth will continue to exert their influence in the future. The trend study points to conclusions reached by the combined methods of historical and descriptive analysis and is illustrated by *Problems and Outlook of Small Private Liberal Arts Colleges: Report to the Congress of the United States by the Comptroller General* (1978). In response to a questionnaire sent to 332 institutions, 283 furnished data on facility construction, loan repayments, enrollment, the effectiveness of methods to attract more students, financial aid, and the general financial health of their institutions.

Based on past and present experience, such influences as the growth of the community college, the effect of inflation on operating costs, tuition, living expenses and fees, and the decline in the number of college-age students were projected for the years 1978 to 1985, and their impact upon the financial stability of the small liberal arts college assessed.

The following trend study topics are also appropriate:

1. The Growing Participation of Women in Intercollegiate Sports Programs
2. Trends in the Methods of Financial Support of Public Education
3. The Growth of Black Student Enrollment in Graduate Study Programs
4. The Minimum Competency Requirement Movement in American Secondary Education

EVALUATION STUDIES

School Surveys

What has traditionally been called a school survey is usually an assessment and evaluation study. Its purpose is to gather detailed information for judging the effectiveness of instructional facilities, curriculum, teaching and supervisory personnel, and financial resources in terms of best practices and standards in education. For example, professional and regional accrediting agencies send visitation teams to gather data on the characteristics of the institution seeking accreditation. Usually, following a self-evaluation by the school staff, the visiting educators evaluate the institution's characteristics according to agency guidelines.

Many city, township, and county school systems have been studied by this method to determine status and adequacy. These survey evaluations are sometimes carried on by an agency of a university in the area. Frequently a large part of the data is gathered by local educators, with the university staff providing direction and advisory services. Many states now require each school district to provide a wide range of information to the state's Department of Education. The state then issues reports on the quality and quantity of services for each location and in the aggregate for the state. For instance, in Illinois, each school district is issued a "report card" that can often be further broken down into report cards for each school.

As part of the federal legislation mandating public schools to provide an education to students with disabilities (PL 94–142), the Office of Special Education must provide a yearly report to Congress that includes information on services being provided and the number of students with disabilities served in each state. These annual reports have shown a dramatic increase in students identified with learning disabilities, and a concomitant decline in students identified with mental retardation, between 1975, when the law took first effect, and 1985. This trend became less pronounced in the last decade.

Program Evaluation

The most common use of evaluation is to determine the effectiveness of a program and sometimes the organization. The *school surveys* described above are evaluations only of the organization. Program evaluations, although often including the organization, focus primarily on program effectiveness results. Evaluation of program effectiveness, although focusing on the intended results, may find unintended results as well. Program evaluation attempts to answer the following questions:

1. What are the goals and objectives of the program being evaluated?
2. What are the intended results of the program?
3. Are the intended results of the program achieved?
4. Are there other unintended results of the program, and, if so, were they positive or negative?
5. Are the results of the program sufficient to warrant continuation?

These are basic questions that all program evaluations should answer. They deal with the program activities and the worth of these activities in terms of what they accomplished. Who answers each of these questions may differ, depending on who conducts the evaluation and the degree of involvement of program administrators. For instance a paid outsider may answer questions 3 and 4, get the information about questions 1 and 2 from the staff of the program, and leave question 5 for the funding agency to decide.

Because in many cases of educational program evaluation what is being evaluated is a school-based program, one often implicitly knows the goals and objectives of the organization—student learning. In these cases the focus of the evaluation is on what is taught, how it is taught, whether the subject matter was learned, if appropriate, whether attitudes were modified, and sometimes whether the information learned resulted in changed behavior. For instance, in an evaluation of a drug-free school program, Wiener, Pritchard, Frauenhoffer, and Edmonds (1993) studied whether the program resulted in changes in student attitudes, knowledge, and intentions to use substances. Although these are probably important in predicting drug use, it would have been helpful to include a later anonymous survey of students to determine usage.

Evaluations of this type can be conducted by the school district or outsiders hired to evaluate a specific program. In addition, good teachers continuously evaluate their teaching and whether and how their students are learning. Thus, evaluations of school-based programs are concerned with two aspects of the evaluation process, *formative* and *summative* evaluations.

Summative evaluation is what most people think of when they consider evaluation. Its primary purposes are to determine grades, judge teaching competence, and compare curricula (Bloom, Hastings, & Maldaus, 1971). Teachers use this type of evaluation at regular intervals to give students grades, usually at the end of a set time (e.g., every few weeks or at the end of the semester) or after a certain portion of content has been covered (e.g., at the end of a chapter or set of information such as statistics).

Formative evaluation, on the other hand, is an ongoing continuous process. "The main purpose of formative observations is to determine the degree of mastery of a given learning task and to pinpoint the part of the task not mastered. Perhaps a negative description will be even clearer. The purpose is not to grade or certify the learner; it is to help both the learner and teacher focus on the particular learning necessary for movement toward mastery" (Bloom, Hastings, & Maldaus, 1971, p. 61). Thus, the distinction between formative and summative evaluation has to do with the purpose (e.g., grading or looking for what aspect of a task is not yet mastered) and the portion of the content involved (e.g., an entire course or a single specific skill). These two aspects of evaluation are not mutually exclusive and are often combined.

Evaluators use a number of evaluation models. Some models are actually research approaches to evaluation. Ruttman (1977) used the term *evaluation research* to describe evaluation procedures using rigorous research methodology. To accomplish evaluation with the rigor of research usually requires that the evaluator be involved in designing the evaluation before the program to be evaluated is implemented. Usually, it is only in this way that the necessary controls can be put in place.

More often evaluators are involved after the program is implemented. Although these evaluations are important and useful, they do not have the same degree of rigor required for research. Three factors should be considered when one selects the evaluation model and data collection tools to evaluate a particular program: the purpose of the evaluation, the needs of those for whom the evaluation is being performed (e.g., replication to other sites, modification of the existing program, fiscal decisions), and the objectives of the program being evaluated.

Quantitative methods, qualitative methods, or a combination may be used to collect the pertinent data for a complete evaluation. Benson and Michael (1990) describe four basic designs that can be used effectively to evaluate programs: experimental, quasi-experimental, survey, and naturalistic. These designs are very broad and encompass a number of potential designs. They need a great deal more elaboration before implementation. The reader interested in conducting an evaluation should read more on the subject before designing the evaluation.

An evaluation study of nontraditional training programs for mathematics and science teachers (Kirby, Darling-Hammond, & Hudson, 1989), which used rigorous research methodology, is used here as an illustration of evaluation research. Three programs were compared: nontraditional recruitment techniques to recruit potential teachers from pools not usually tapped but that required the full certification program normally used in that state; alternative certification programs (usually consisting of fewer courses and/or practicum hours); and retraining programs, which focused on helping teachers trained in other fields to obtain certification in science and/or mathematics. Nine programs from a list of 64 were selected for in-depth study. The nontraditional recruitment programs were then further divided into midcareer change and recent BA programs.

Questionnaires were mailed to participants and graduates of these nine programs, and 481 completed responses (77%) were received. The evaluation, and therefore the questionnaire, focused on six questions: What are the recruits' backgrounds? Why did the recruits decide to go into mathematics and science teaching? What are the graduates of the programs currently doing? Are the recruits' actual teaching experiences similar to what they expected? Do the recruits plan to continue teaching as a career? Why did some decide not to teach after graduation from a program? The results of the questionnaires and background information about the nine programs were then analyzed to determine the success of the programs.

Without going into great detail, the findings of Kirby, Darling-Hammond, and Hudson (1989) indicated that not all of the programs were equally effective; the recruits "contain a higher than average representation of minority, female and older candidates" (p. 319); the "quality and intensity of preparation makes a difference in how well prepared recruits feel to teach"; and "for all their promise nontraditional teacher preparation programs cannot fully overcome other attributes of teaching that make recruitment and retention of teachers difficult" (p. 301).

With impending teacher shortages, which already exist in some fields, such as mathematics and science, innovative programs to recruit people into teaching may be needed. This study may be useful in suggesting to teacher certification boards, colleges of education, and policy makers (e.g., legislators) how to most effectively recruit a new cohort of teachers.

ASSESSMENT AND EVALUATION IN PROBLEM SOLVING

In solving a problem or charting a course of action, the researcher may need several sorts of information. These data may be gathered through assessment and evaluation methods.

The first type of information is based on *present conditions*. Where are we now? From what point do we start? These data may be gathered by a systematic description and analysis of all the important aspects of the present situation.

The second type of information involves *what we may want*. In what direction may we go? What conditions are desirable or are considered to represent best practice? This clarification of objectives or goals may come from a study of what we think we want, possibly resulting from a study of conditions existing elsewhere or of what experts consider to be adequate or desirable.

The third type of information is concerned with *how to get there*. This analysis may involve finding out about the experience of others who have been involved in similar situations. It may involve the opinions of experts, who presumably know best how to reach the goal.

Some studies emphasize only one of these aspects of problem solving. Others may deal with two, or even three, of the elements. Although a study does not necessarily embrace all the steps necessary for the solution of a problem, it may make a valuable contribution by clarifying only one of the necessary steps—from description of present status to charting of the path to the goal.

Assessment and evaluation methods may supply some or all of the needed information. An example will illustrate how they can be used to help solve an educational problem. Washington Township has a school building problem. Its present educational facilities seem inadequate, and if present developments continue, conditions may be much worse in the future. The patrons and educational leaders in the community know that a problem exists, but they realize that this vague awareness does not provide a sound basis for action. Three steps are necessary to provide such a basis.

The first step involves a systematic analysis of present conditions. How many school-age children are there in the township? How many children are of preschool age? Where do they live? How many classrooms now exist? How adequate are they? What is the average class size? How are these present buildings located in relation to residential housing? How adequate are the facilities for food, library, health, and recreational services? What is the present annual budget? How is it related to the tax rate and the ability of the community to provide adequate educational facilities?

The second step projects goals for the future. What will the school population be in 5, 10, or 20 years? Where will the children live? How many buildings and classrooms will be needed? What provisions should be made for special school services, for libraries, cafeterias, gymnasiums, and play areas, to take care of expected educational demands?

Step three considers how to reach those goals that have been established by the analysis of step two. Among the questions to be answered are the following: Should existing facilities be expanded or new buildings constructed? If new buildings are needed, what kind should be provided? Should schools be designed for grades 1 through 8, or should 6-year elementary schools and separate 2- or 3-year junior high schools be provided? How will the money be raised? When and how much should the tax rate be increased? When should the construction program get underway?

Many of the answers to the questions raised in step three will be arrived at by analysis of practices of other townships; the expressed opinions of school patrons and local educational leaders; and the opinions of experts in school buildings, school organization, community planning, and public finance. Of course, this analysis of school building needs is but one phase of the larger educational problem of providing an adequate educational program for tomorrow's children. There remain problems of curriculum, pupil transportation, and school personnel, which can also be attacked by similar methods of assessment and evaluation.

THE FOLLOW-UP STUDY

The follow-up study investigates individuals who have left an institution after having completed a program, a treatment, or a course of study. The study concerns what has happened to them and what impact the institution and its program has had on them. By examining their status or seeking their opinions, one may get some idea of the adequacy or inadequacy of the institution's program. Which courses, experiences, or treatments proved to be of value? What proved to be ineffective or of limited value? Studies of this type enable an institution to evaluate various aspects of its program in light of actual results. Researchers also are interested at times in finding out what happened to the participants in an earlier intervention. Follow-up studies may be evaluation studies or descriptive research, depending on their purpose and design. Follow-up studies are distinguished from longitudinal studies by whether they have continual contact with the participants. Those studies that continue to follow their participants throughout the entire study are longitudinal. On the other hand, studies that do not continue to investigate the participants but later conduct a subsequent study of the former participants are follow-up studies.

Follow-up studies are often difficult to accomplish because of problems locating program participants years after completion of the program. At times, however, it may be relatively simple. For instance, a school district may be interested in studying how students from different elementary schools do in the district's high school. In cases in which the program has not been in touch with the participants for some time, it may be more difficult. Because of the difficulty and cost of maintaining contact with participants for long periods of time between participation in the program and later follow-up, or finding them later if no contact was maintained, there are few good follow-up research studies that are not based on longitudinal research or school based and focusing on the participants still in the district's schools. However, many programs attempt to find earlier participants and study them.

One setting in which follow-up studies are frequently attempted for program evaluation is higher education. Many university programs undergo various forms of accreditation. These reviews usually ask about graduates of the programs. Thus, the Special Education Program at the University of Illinois at Chicago periodically surveys its graduates regarding their current positions and their views of the program from which they graduated. Unfortunately, many of the surveys are returned "addressee unknown," and others are not returned at all. This means that a relatively small number of the program's graduates are providing the information that goes into the report to the accrediting agency.

The Carolina Abecedarian Study was designed to study the effectiveness of early intervention (beginning during the child's first year) with children born at risk for mental retardation due to various factors. Ramey and his colleagues (e.g., Ramey & Smith, 1977) began this longitudinal research by first assessing the characteristics that make children not born with a disability more likely to develop mental retardation. They determined that a variety of characteristics, mostly related to economic, educational, and occupational status of the parents, were the best predictors of children becoming mentally retarded. The studies included random assignment to intervention and control groups to permit them to determine the effectiveness of their early intervention.

Ramey and a colleague (Campbell and Ramey, 1994) later conducted an excellent follow-up investigation of the effects of this early intervention program on intellectual and academic achievement of children from low income families. In the original study four groups of children were followed from before their first birthday (average age at entry was 4.4 months) until they were 8 years old. One group received intervention from the beginning until they were 8 years old, a second group received treatment for only the first 5 years (preschool), a third group received no intervention until age 5 and then received the intervention until age 8 (school age intervention only), and the last group received no intervention for any part of the 8 years (control group). Four years later when the children were 12 years old, they were again given the battery of tests to determine the lasting effects of the interventions. Children who received intervention from the beginning, for 5 years or 8 years, did not significantly differ from each other; but both performed higher than the groups receiving no treatment during the first 5 years, whether followed by 3 years of school age intervention or no intervention at all. Thus, the results indicated that the critical time for intervention was during the first 5 years. Although the follow-up sample was somewhat reduced from the original sample (from 111 children at the beginning of the study to 90 for the follow-up), researchers were able to show that the attrition was not related to any characteristics of the sample (i.e., the children in the follow-up sample were similar in characteristics to those who began the study).

Another high quality investigation involved a comparison of first- and fifth-grade American, Japanese, and Taiwanese children and their parents on academic performance and child and parent attitudes regarding school (e.g., the importance of homework) (Stevenson & Lee, 1990). An additional component of the study, pertinent here, involved going back 4 years later and following-up in fifth grade the first graders from the initial study. The findings indicated that the three groups (American, Japanese, and Taiwanese) did not change position on the various measures during this time, although they did change as would be expected. This study, which primarily was a descriptive study of first and fifth graders, will be discussed further later in this chapter in the section titled Other Descriptive Research.

DESCRIPTIVE RESEARCH

The examples discussed up to this point in the chapter (with the exception of Cambell & Ramey, 1994 and Stevenson & Lee, 1990 in the section on follow-up studies) have been designated as assessment studies and/or evaluation studies. Descriptive research studies have all of the following characteristics distinguishing them from the type previously described:

1. They involve hypothesis formulation and testing.
2. They use the logical methods of inductive–deductive reasoning to arrive at generalizations.
3. They often employ methods of randomization so that error may be estimated when population characteristics are inferred from observations of samples.
4. The variables and procedures are described as accurately and completely as possible so that the study can be replicated by other researchers.

These characteristics make descriptive research similar to other kinds of research including those described in Chapter 6. However, descriptive research methods are nonexperimental because they deal with the relationships among nonmanipulated variables. Because the events or conditions have already occurred, the researcher merely selects the relevant variables for an analysis of their relationships.

Descriptive research seeks to find answers to questions through the analysis of variable relationships. What factors seem to be associated with certain occurrences, outcomes, conditions, or types of behaviors? Because it is often impracticable or unethical to arrange occurrences, an analysis of past events or of already existing conditions may be the only feasible way to study causation. This type of research is usually referred to as *ex post facto* or *causal–comparative research* or, when correlational analyses are used, as *correlational research*.

For example, one would not arrange to have people consume alcohol and then drive in order to study automobile accidents and their causes. The automobile industry, police departments, safety commissions, and insurance companies study the conditions associated with the accidents. Such factors as mechanical faults or failures, excessive speed, driving under the influence of alcohol, and others have been identified as causal.

However, although studies of past events may be the only practicable way to investigate certain problems, the researcher needs to be aware of the problems inherent in this type of research. The researcher must be aware that the information used in *ex post facto* studies may be incomplete. That is, the researcher may not have sufficient information about all of the events and variables occurring at the time being studied. This lack of control or even of knowledge regarding what variables were controlled makes causal statements based on this type of research very difficult to make. This problem is the *post hoc* fallacy, the conclusion that because two events occur at the same time or two variables are related to each other one must have caused the other. This is discussed further later in this chapter.

Research on cigarette smoking has had a tremendous effect on society. Laws banning television advertising and cigarette smoking in certain areas resulted from the U.S. Surgeon General's reports (1964, 1979). These reports compiled the research of epidemiologists on the effects of smoking on a person's health. Epidemiological research methods are used to study trends and incidences of disease and are descriptive in nature. The epidemiological research on smoking included two types of descriptive methodology: retrospective studies that relate personal histories with medical and mortality records and prospective studies that follow a group of individuals for an indefinite period or until they die. The early studies, from 1939 to the early 1960s, were primarily retrospective. These studies found that persons who had died of lung cancer were more likely to have been cigarette smokers than nonsmokers.

A number of prospective studies, begun in the 1950s, found a greater likelihood of a variety of health problems among smokers than nonsmokers. As the Surgeon General's report states:

> *The mortality ratio for male cigarette smokers compared with non-smokers, for all causes of death taken together, is 1.68, [this means that on the average, 168 smokers die for every 100 persons who do not smoke of the same age] representing a total death rate nearly 70 percent higher than for non-smokers. (This ratio includes death rates for diseases not listed in the table as well as the 14 disease categories shown.)*
>
> *In the combined results from the seven studies, the mortality ratio of cigarette smokers over non-smokers was particularly high for a number of diseases: cancer of the lung (10.8), bronchitis and emphysema (6.1), cancer of the larynx (5.4), oral cancer (4.1), cancer of the esophagus (3.4), peptic ulcer (2.8), and the group of other circulatory diseases (2.6). For coronary artery disease the mortality ratio was 1.7.*
>
> *Expressed in percentage-form, this is equivalent to a statement that for coronary artery disease, the leading cause of death in this country, the death rate is 70 percent higher for cigarette smokers. For chronic bronchitis and emphysema, which are among the leading causes of severe disability, the death rate for cigarette smokers is 500 percent higher than for non-smokers. For lung cancer, the most frequent site of cancer in men, the death rate is nearly 1,000 percent higher. (pp. 28–29)*

Although this evidence appears overwhelming, it is not totally convincing by itself. Because the researchers could not randomly assign persons to the smoking and nonsmoking groups, it is possible that persons who decide to smoke are particularly nervous individuals and that it is their nervousness, not their smoking, that causes their greater incidence of illness and early death. This argument has been used by the tobacco industry. Of course, this research when added to the animal studies and the chemical analyses indicating carcinogens in cigarette smoke becomes completely convincing and compelling.

More recently the focus has been more on secondhand smoke and its effects on nonsmokers. Lee (1992) reviewed more than 20 descriptive studies comparing persons with lung cancer with those not having lung cancer. The overall conclusion was that those with lung cancer were more likely to have a spouse, or other person they lived with, who smoked than those without lung cancer. This overall effect, however, was not as strong as the evidence about those who are smokers themselves.

Another aspect of smoking and its effects on others was studied by Nicholl and O'Cathain (1990). They examined the data on 998 babies who died between the ages of 1 week and 2 years (303 of whose deaths were from Sudden Infant Death Syndrome [SIDS]) with 773 controls matched for date and place of birth who did not die. The smoking habits of the mother and partner were known for 242 of the SIDS cases and 251 of the control cases matched to the SIDS cases. After adjusting for risk factors, such as birth weight, these researchers concluded that there is an increased risk of SIDS among children living in homes where there are smokers. However, based on this retrospective study, it cannot be stated that SIDS is caused by passive smoke exposure. Still, the authors suggest, based on their own and others' findings, that if maternal smoking could be eliminated, both prenatally and after birth, the SIDS death rate could be reduced by 27% and the overall infant death rate from all causes by 10%.

Sesame Street Studies

Minton (1975) studied the effect of viewing the children's television program "Sesame Street" on the reading readiness of kindergarten children. Of three sample groups, a 1968, a 1969, and a 1970 group, only the 1970 group had viewed the program.

Reading Readiness and "Sesame Street"

Sample Group	N	White	Black	Spanish-Speaking
1968	482	431	51	18
1969	495	434	61	9
1970	524	436	88	25

From "Impact of Sesame Street on Reading Readiness" by I. M. Minton, *Sociology of Education*, 1975, *48*, 141–31. Reprinted by permission.

Scores on the Metropolitan Reading Readiness Test battery, consisting of six subtests (word meaning, listening, matching, alphabet letter recognition, numbers, and copying text) were used to measure readiness. Using pretest–posttest design, the mean gain scores of the 1970 group were compared with those of the 1968 and 1969 groups.

No significant differences at the 0.05 level were observed in total scores. On only one subtest—letter recognition—was a significant difference observed, favoring the 1970 group. In a classification by socioeconomic status, advantaged children watched more and scored higher than disadvantaged children. The hypothesis that viewing "Sesame Street" would help to close the gap between advantaged and disadvantaged children was not supported; rather, the gap was widened.

Anderson and Levin (1976) studied the effect of age on the viewing attention of young children to a 57-minute taped "Sesame Street" program, consisting of 41 bits, each ranging in length from 10 to 453 seconds. Six groups of five boys and five girls, ages 12, 18, 24, 30, 36, 42, and 48 months, were observed by videotape recordings. In a viewing room, in the presence of parents, toys were provided as alternatives to viewing. The following observations were reported:

1. Length of attention increased with age. The younger children appeared to be more interested in the toys and interacting with their mothers.
2. Length of attention decreased as bit length increased.
3. Attention to animals increased to 24 months but dropped thereafter.
4. Children showed more interest in the presence of women, lively music, puppets, peculiar voices, rhyming, repetition, and motion.
5. Children showed less interest in the presence of adult men, animals, inactivity, and still drawings.

Other Descriptive Research

Both the research on smoking described above and the study on "Sesame Street" (Minton, 1975) are *causal comparative studies* because they were interested in suggesting causation for their findings. Other *causal comparative research* includes the study by Frey and Grover (1982). The literature suggests that there are "adverse effects of early father unavailability on the cognitive development of children" (Frey & Grover, 1982, p. 105). Because it is impossible to randomly assign children to father-present and -absent conditions, descriptive research is most common in this area. Frey and Grover (1982) studied the effect of father absence on social problem solving, using a combination of descriptive and experimental procedures. They first used descriptive research to verify the relationship and then followed this with an experimental intervention designed to improve the children's social problem solving. Only the descriptive study will be described here.

Sixty children from father-absent homes were matched with 60 children from father-present homes on socioeconomic factors, sex, and IQ (within 5 points). Children with chronic behavioral and emotional problems were excluded from the study. The children were then assessed individually on two problem-solving measures and a self-rating scale designed to measure self-confidence, self-efficacy, and self-worth. The statistical analysis of the data indicated that the two groups of children, father present and father absent, differed, with the father-present children scoring higher in problem solving and on the measures of self. Because these findings supported their hypothesis, Frey and Grover then carried out the intervention phase of their research.

Another *causal comparative study*, mentioned earlier, was conducted by Stevenson and Lee (1990). They examined the educational and home environments of first- and fifth-grade students in the United States (Minneapolis), Japan (Sendai), and Taiwan (Taipei) as well as their academic achievement. The "major purpose of the study was to attempt to understand some of the reasons for the high academic achievement of Chinese and Japanese children compared to American children" (p. v). The results indicated differences between the American children and the Japanese and Chinese students that might explain the academic achievement differences. Among these differences were

1. Chinese and Japanese parents pay much more attention to the academic achievement of their children than American parents;
2. parental expectations of academic achievement differed significantly in a similar direction;
3. Chinese and Japanese children believe their effort is more related to their academic performance than American children;
4. American parents appeared to be more interested in activities that would enhance their children's general cognitive development than specific academic achievement scores; and
5. American parents overestimated their children's abilities and were more pleased with their children's academic achievement than were Japanese or Chinese parents.

McLaughlin and Owings (1993) conducted a *correlational study* that examined the relationships among the fiscal and demographic characteristics of the 50 states and implementation of P.L. 94–142, the Individuals with Disabilities Education Act (IDEA). Three demographic characteristics, "rural school age population, minority public school enrollments, and percentage of children enrolled in school who are living in poverty" (p. 249), and four state fiscal characteristics—per-capita income, per-pupil expenditures, the state's reliance on federal education aid other than special education funds, and the percentage of all nonfederal education revenues that were from state sources—were studied as they related to the states' percentage of identified children with disabilities (three categories were used: learning disabled, emotionally disturbed, and multiply disabled) and the rate at which children with disabilities are placed in integrated settings. The data were obtained from the annual reports to Congress prepared by the U.S. Department of Education for the years 1976–1977, 1980–1981, and 1983–1984. Although there were a number of significant correlations between the fiscal and demographic variables and the identification and placement rates, most were below .40 and thus low to moderate correlations (see Chapter 10 for an explanation of correlations). Some examples of the significant findings were

1. In 1976 states with high percentages of rural students were more likely to identify fewer students with disabilities ($r = .36$).
2. States with more federal aid for education, not including special education funds, identified fewer learning disabled and emotionally disturbed children (range from $-.32$ to $-.43$).

3. States with higher percentages of children living in poverty were less likely to identify children as learning disabled in 1976 and 1980 ($r = -.43$ and $r = -.40$, respectively).

4. Children with disabilities were more likely to be placed in more restrictive (less integrated) settings in states with more rural students in 1980 and 1983 ($r = -.37$) and in states with greater per capita personal income in 1980 and 1983 ($r = .29$ and $r = .28$, respectively).

The information gathered in this study indicated that the relationships among a state's fiscal and demographic characteristics played some role in the percentage of students identified as disabled and the type of category in which they were likely to be placed. However, the lack of strong correlations left the authors with few firm conclusions or suggestions for modification of public policy in this area.

Finally, we describe two descriptive studies that are neither correlational nor causal comparative. The first was reported by Beckman (1991), who studied the relative stress of 54 mothers and 54 fathers with young children (between 18 and 72 months) half of whom had disabilities. Data collected included measures of stress (*Parenting Stress Index*), support (*Carolina Parent Support Scale*), and caregiving requirements (*Caregiving Questionnaire*). Significant findings indicated that parents (both mothers and fathers) with children with disabilities reported more caregiving requirements and greater stress than those with children without disabilities. She also found a significant relationship between the increased caregiving requirements of having a child with a disability and the stress of the mothers on whom these caregiving needs are more likely to fall. Finally, there was an overall effect in which mothers reported more stress than did fathers. This study, which was descriptive, still has implications for intervention. Because stress differs for mothers and fathers of children with disabilities, it may be important to work with parents in different ways to help them best handle the type of stress they are experiencing. In particular, the added responsibilities of caregiving that falls mostly on mothers needs to be addressed to help with their stress.

The final study described in this section also appears in its entirety at the end of this chapter as the sample article. Porretta, Gillespie, and Jansma (1996) conducted a survey of representatives of agencies and organizations providing a variety of services to persons with disabilities to determine the current status of their organizations (e.g., ages and disabilities served, philosophy of agency/organization), the terminology used (i.e., "What term does your agency/organization use to describe those with mental retardation?"), and their knowledge and beliefs about the Special Olympics (an organization that has provided sports and recreational opportunities for many years). The results of the survey included the following findings.

1. Mental retardation is used by only 62.4% of the respondents, with developmental disability used by 65.8%, mentally challenged by 12.8%, and so on.

2. Most (76.3%) see a trend away from the term *mental retardation*.

3. Persons with a number of disabilities are being served by these agencies in addition to those with mental retardation.
4. Many of the respondents believe that the Special Olympics serves persons with a wide range of disabilities but think that it should be even wider than it currently is.
5. Most of the respondents believe that the Special Olympics should place more emphasis on inclusion (87.8%).

Readers are encouraged to examine this article in more depth at the end of the chapter where it appears in its entirety. As indicated in the title, this is a preliminary study as is a common use for surveys. Subsequent research might use more in-depth interviews or a more comprehensive survey instrument (the one used had only 15 questions).

Still another area that could use more descriptive research is the study of juvenile delinquency, which might compare the social and educational backgrounds of delinquents and nondelinquents. What factors, if any, were common to the nondelinquent group? Any factors common to one group but not to the other might serve as a possible explanation of the underlying causes of delinquency.

REPLICATION AND SECONDARY ANALYSIS

If research is good, it can be replicated.

Replication, a combination of the terms *repetition* and *duplication,* is an important method of challenging or verifying the conclusions of a previous study. Using different subjects at a different time and in a different setting and arriving at conclusions that are consistent with those of the previous study would strengthen its conclusions and justify more confidence in its validity. Replication is essential to the development and verification of new generalizations and theories.

Another useful procedure, known as *secondary analysis,* consists of reanalyzing the data gathered by a previous investigator and may involve different hypotheses, different experimental designs, or different methods of statistical analysis. The subjects are the same, and the data are the same. The differences are purpose of the analyses and alternative methods of analysis.

Secondary analysis has a number of advantages that commend its use:

1. The new investigator may bring an objectivity or a fresh point of view to the investigation and may think of better questions to be raised or hypotheses to be tested. For example, the viewpoint of a psychologist rather than that of a sociologist (or vice versa) may find greater meaning in the data already available.
2. Secondary analysis may bring greater expertise to the area of investigation and greater skill in experimental design and statistical analysis.
3. The reanalysis involves less expense in both time and money. Because the data are already available, a more modest appropriation of funds is possible. It is

not necessary to intrude on the time of subjects (teachers and students) whose primary activities had been diverted in the original investigation.

4. Secondary analysis may provide useful experience for students of research methodology by enabling them to use real data, rather than simulated or inferior data, for the purposes of the exercise.

Secondary analysis has played an important part in educational research. In addition to secondary analyses on research study data, a common characteristic of secondary analyses is using data collected by a governmental organization such as the U.S. Census Bureau of the U.S. Department of Education's National Center for Educational Statistics.

The National Longitudinal Survey of Youth (NLSY) is a very large (more than 12,000 persons when the study began in 1979), nationally representative sample of persons who were between the ages of 14 and 22 when the study began and who have been followed ever since. This longitudinal data collection is conducted by the U.S. Department of Education's National Center for Educational Statistics. These data are made available to scholars who wish to analyze them in their own data analyses, using their own hypotheses. These data are among the most used because they offer a very complete data set on a very large and representative sample.

One recent controversial book used the NLSY extensively (Herrnstein & Murray, 1994). In their book *The Bell Curve*, the authors argue that a variety of outcomes, from academic achievement to unemployment, criminal behavior, and citizenship, is related to and caused by intelligence. That is, people of high intelligence do better in academic achievement and are more likely to be employed, have never been to prison, and are better citizens than persons of low intelligence. The major source of data for these claims is Herrnstein and Murray's analyses of the NLSY data. Unfortunately they bury their analyses in an appendix where few readers will venture, most likely to make their book more palatable to the average reader. As pointed out by many critics of this book (e.g., Carey, 1995; Gardiner, 1995; Holt, 1995; Kamin, 1995), the authors' analyses are flawed and they overstate their findings. These authors, to judge by their previous publications, had a strongly held belief that IQ is the root of all good and evil. Thus, secondary analysis can be used inappropriately to make a case for which one is determined. In this case Herrnstein and Murray manipulated the data to support their hypotheses. One example is their definition of criminal behavior. There is no significant finding relating IQ with criminal behavior, defined as one offense. So they conducted an analysis defining criminal behavior as one jail sentence and a second offense. In this analysis they found a statistically significant but nearly meaningless result. By this we mean that the relationship of IQ with criminal behavior results in less than 2% of criminal behavior being explained by IQ. The statistical significance is more a result of the large sample than a strong relationship. In fact, we describe the correlation they found ($r = 0.123$) between IQ and criminal behavior as negligible in Chapter 10.

The above should not be interpreted as a condemnation of the NLSY or of most of the studies based on it. Another study used the 1988 data from the NLSY self-concept measures, which included some items from the Australian *Self*

Description Questionnaire (SDQ II) (Marsh, 1992) a self-concept measure developed with an Australian sample (Marsh, 1994). The purpose of the study was to examine these data in light of self-concept theory and measurement practices. Marsh used the data from the NLSY as well as from an Australian study using the SDQ II. The results supported the construct validity (see Chapter 9) of the measure of self-concept under study. Many other valuable studies have been conducted using NLSY data.

an effect size = the higher the #, the better it is

Meta-analysis

A relatively recent innovation that allows a researcher to systematically and statistically combine the findings of several previous studies is known as *meta-analysis, research synthesis,* or *research integration.* There are a number of quantitative techniques, ranging from fairly simple to quite complex, by which the data from previously published studies can be combined. Glass (1978) and his colleagues (Glass, Smith, & Barton, 1979) have developed and described some of these techniques. Walberg (1986) discusses the relative advantages of the traditional review of the literature and the statistical research synthesis. He suggests that a combination of these approaches can be useful in estimating the effects of a number of studies. Walberg and his colleagues have conducted several studies using these techniques. The special issue of *Evaluation in Education,* 1980, Vol. 4, pp. 1–142, edited by Walberg and Haertel, is still one of the best selections of these and other research integration efforts.

A recent study (Ijzendoorn & Bus, 1994) used meta-analysis to confirm the conclusions of a typical narrative review of the literature (Rack, Snowling, & Olson, 1992). In the initial paper, the authors reviewed a number of studies comparing dyslexic readers with typical readers on a phonological task that required the children to attempt to sound out nonsense words (this controls for sight word vocabulary differences). The conclusions of the narrative review supported a phonological disorder as a major component of dyslexia. The meta-analysis examined the statistical findings from 18 studies included in the initial review. In this analysis the authors controlled for the effects of age and other pertinent factors. This study found support for the earlier conclusion that "there is extremely strong evidence for the phonological deficit hypothesis" (Ijzendoorn & Bus, 1994, p. 273). The meta-analysis found a significant difference between the dyslexic children and the average readers on the phonologic tasks but no difference in sight word recognition tasks. The similar conclusions of a review of the literature *and* a subsequent statistical analysis of the same studies add tremendously to the strength of the conclusions. This is the sort of combination of traditional review and statistical synthesis suggested by Walberg (1986).

THE POST HOC *FALLACY*

One of the most serious dangers of descriptive research that uses *ex post facto* and causal–comparative procedures is the *post hoc* fallacy, the conclusion that, because two factors go together, one must be the cause and the other the effect. Because there seems to be a high relationship between the number of years of education completed and earned income, many educators have argued that staying in school will add X number of dollars of income over a period of time for each additional year of education completed. Although there may be such a relationship, it is also likely that some of the factors that influence young people to seek additional education are more important than the educational level completed. Such factors as socioeconomic status, persistence, desire, willingness to postpone immediate gratification, and intelligence level are undoubtedly significant factors in vocational success. Staying in school may be a symptom rather than the cause.

Some critics of cigarette-cancer research have advanced a similar argument. The case that they propose follows this line of reasoning: Let us suppose that certain individuals with a type of glandular imbalance have a tendency toward cancer. The imbalance induces a certain amount of nervous tension. Because excessive cigarette smoking is a type of nervous tension release, these individuals tend to be heavy smokers. The cancer could result from the glandular imbalance rather than from the smoking, which is only a symptom. This error of confusing symptoms or merely associated factors with cause could lead researchers to deduce a false cause-and-effect relationship.

This illustration is not presented to discredit this type of cancer research. Substantial evidence does suggest a significant relationship. Laboratory experiments have substantiated the causal relationship between the coal-tar products distilled from cigarette combustion and malignant growth in animals. The association explanation, if not substantiated by the animal and chemical studies, would not be sufficient by itself. Thus, the causal conclusion based on an association is one that should always be examined carefully. *The Bell Curve* (Herrnstein & Murray, 1994), mentioned earlier in the section on secondary analyses, is an example of a study that makes causal claims based on correlations, many of which are weak or moderate at best, and ignores other potential explanations.

Ex post facto and causal–comparative research is widely and appropriately used, particularly in the behavioral sciences. In education, because it is impossible, impracticable, or unthinkable to manipulate such variables as aptitude, intelligence, personality traits, cultural deprivation, teacher competence, and some variables that might present an unacceptable threat to human beings, this method will continue to be used.

However, its limitations should be recognized:

1. The independent variables cannot be manipulated.
2. Subjects cannot be randomly, or otherwise, assigned to treatment groups.
3. Causes are often multiple and complex rather than single and simple.

For these reasons scientists are reluctant to use the expression *cause and effect* in nonexperimental studies in which the variables have not been carefully manipulated. They prefer to observe that when variable A appears, variable B is consistently associated, possibly for reasons not completely understood or explained.

Because there is a danger of confusing symptoms with causes, *ex post facto* research should test not just one hypothesis but other logical alternate or competing hypotheses as well. Properly employed and cautiously interpreted, it will continue to provide a useful methodology for the development of knowledge.

Students who have completed a course in research methods should be sensitive to the operation of extraneous variables that threaten the validity of conclusions. Glass (1968) cautions educators of the need for critical analysis of reported research. He cites a number of interesting examples of carelessly conducted studies that resulted in completely false conclusions. Unfortunately, these conclusions were accepted by gullible readers and widely reported in popular periodicals and some educational psychology textbooks.

The authors trust that the experience of the introductory course in educational research will help students and educators to read research reports more carefully and to apply more rigorous standards of judgment.

SUMMARY

The term *descriptive studies* has been used to classify a number of different types of activity. This chapter points out the distinctions between three major categories: assessment, evaluation, and descriptive research.

Assessment describes the status of a phenomenon at a particular time *without* value judgment, explanation of reasons or underlying causes, or recommendations for action.

Evaluation adds to the description of status the element of value judgment in terms of effectiveness, desirability, or social utility and may suggest a course of action. No generalizations are extended beyond the situation evaluated.

Descriptive research is concerned with the analysis of the relationships between nonmanipulated variables and the development of generalizations, extending its conclusions beyond the sample observed.

Assessment types of studies described are surveys, public opinion polls, the *National Assessment of Educational Progress,* the *International Assessment of Educational Progress,* activity analysis, and trend studies.

Evaluation studies included are school surveys and follow-up studies. The application of evaluation findings to social problem solving is discussed.

Descriptive research studies include *ex post facto* or explanatory observational studies. These methods have been described and examples provided. The hazards of the *post hoc* fallacy have been emphasized.

EXERCISES

1. Why is it sometimes difficult to distinguish between an assessment study, an evaluation study, and a descriptive research project? Illustrate with an example.

2. Public opinion polls base their conclusions on a sample of approximately 1,500 respondents. Is this an adequate sample for a nationwide survey?

3. In a 1974 study the West Virginia State Department of Education reported that counties with the highest per-pupil expenditure were the counties with the highest level of academic achievement and that this "shows for the first time the clearest possible relationship between student achievement and the amount of money invested in the public schools." Can you suggest several competing hypotheses that might account for high academic achievement?

4. What is the difference between a study and a research project?

5. In what ways does conducting longitudinal studies run the risk of the violation of confidentiality of personal information?

6. How can a study of money and investment trends help you provide for your future financial security?

7. Draw up a proposal for a follow-up study of your high school graduating class of 5 years ago. Indicate what information you believe would be helpful in improving the curriculum of the school.

8. Of what value are the findings of the annual Gallup poll of public attitudes toward education?

9. How could the survey-type of study be helpful in arriving at solutions to the crime problem in large cities?

REFERENCES

Anderson, D. B., & Levin, S. B. (1976). Young children's attention to Sesame Street. *Child Development, 47*, 806–811.

Babbie, E. R. (1989). *The practice of social research,* (5th ed.). Belmont, CA: Wadsworth.

Beckman, P. J. (1991). Comparison of mothers' and fathers' perceptions of the effect of young children with and without disabilities. *American Journal of Mental Retardation, 95*, 585–595.

Benson, J., & Michael, W. B. (1990). Basic principles of design and analysis in evaluation research. In H. J. Walberg & G. D. Haertel (Eds.), *The international encyclopedia of educational evaluation.* New York: Pergamon.

Binkley, M., & Williams, T. (1996). *Reading literacy in the United States.* Washington, DC: U.S. Department of Education, National Center for Education Statistics.

Bloom, B. S., Hastings, J. T., & Maldaus, G. F. (1971). *Handbook on formative and summative evaluation of student learning.* New York: McGraw-Hill.

Campbell, F. A., & Ramey, C. T. (1994). Effects of early intervention on intellectual and academic achievement: A follow-up study of children from low-income families. *Child Development, 65*, 684–698.

Carey, J. Clever arguments, atrocious science. In R. Jacoby & N. Glauberman (Eds.), *The bell curve debate.* New York: Random House.

Charters, W. W., & Waples, D. (1929). *The Commonwealth teacher training study.* Chicago: University of Chicago Press.

Choy, S., Henke, R., Alt, M., Medrich, E., & Bobbit, S. (1993). *Schools and staffing in the United States: A statistical profile, 1990–91.* Washington, DC: U.S. Department of Education, National Center for Education Statistics.

Elam, S. M. (1979). *A decade of Gallup polls of attitudes toward education: 1969–1978.* Bloomington, IN: Phi Delta Kappa.

Elam, S. M. (1995). *How America views its schools: The PDK/Gallup polls, 1969–1994.* Bloomington, IN: Phi Delta Kappa.

Frey, P. S., & Grover, S. C. (1982). The relationship between father absence and children's social problem solving competencies. *Journal of Applied Developmental Psychology, 3,* 105–120.

Gardiner, H. (1995). Scholarly brinksmanship. In R. Jacoby & N. Glauberman (Eds.), *The bell curve debate.* New York: Random House.

Glass, G. V. (1968). Educational Piltdown men. *Phi Delta Kappan, 50,* 148–151.

Glass, G. V. (1978). Integrating findings: The meta-analysis of research. In L. Shulman (Ed.), *Review of research in education, 5,* 351–379.

Glass, G. V., Smith, M. L., & Barton, M. (1979). *Methods of integrative analysis.* Annual report on grant NIE-G-78-0148. Boulder, Colorado: University of Colorado.

Herrnstein, R. J., & Murray, C. (1994). *The bell curve.* New York: Free Press.

Holt, J. (1995) Skin-deep science. In R. Jacoby & N. Glauberman (Eds.), *The bell curve debate.* New York: Random House.

Ijzendoorn, M. H. van, & Bus, A. G. (1994). Meta-analytic confirmation of the nonword reading deficit in developmental dyslexia. *Reading Research Quarterly, 29,* 267–275.

Kamin, L. J. (1995). Lies, damned lies, statistics. In R. Jacoby & N. Glauberman (Eds.), *The bell curve debate.* New York: Random House.

Kinsey, A. C., Pomeroy, W. B., & Martin, C. E. (1948). *Sexual behavior in the human male.* Philadelphia: W. B. Saunders.

Kinsey, A. C., Pomeroy, W. B., Martin, C. E., & Gebhard, P. H. (1953). *Sexual behavior in the human female.* Philadelphia: W. B. Saunders.

Kirby, S. N., Darling-Hammond, L., & Hudson, L. (1989). Nontraditional recruits to mathematics and science teaching. *Educational Evaluation and Policy Analysis, 11,* 301–323.

Lang, R. E. (1987). *Crime prevention strategies for educable mentally retarded children and youth in structured and unstructured conditions.* Unpublished doctoral dissertation, University of Illinois, Chicago.

Lang, R. E., & Kahn, J. V. (1986). Special education teacher estimates of crime victimization and delinquency among their students. *Journal of Special Education, 20,* 359–365.

Lee, P. N. (1992). *Environmental tobacco smoke and mortality.* New York: Karger.

Marsh, H. W. (1992*). Self-description Questionnaire II: Manual.* Macarthur, Australia: University of Western Sydney.

Marsh, H. W. (1994). Using the National Longitudinal Study of 1988 to evaluate theoretical models of self concept: The self-description questionnaire. *Journal of Educational Psychology, 86,* 439–455.

McLaughlin, M. J., & Owings, M. F. (1993). Relationships among states' fiscal and demographic data and the implementation of P.L. 94–142. *Exceptional Children, 59,* 247–261.

Minton, J. M. (1975). Impact of Sesame Street on reading readiness. *Sociology of Education, 48,* 141–151.

Morris, V. C., Crowson, R., Porter-Gehrie, C., & Hurwitz, E. (1984). *Principals in action.* Columbus, OH: Charles Merrill.

Mullis, I., Dossey, J., Campbell, J., Gentile, C., O'Sullivan, C., & Latham, A. (1994). *NAEP 1992 trends in academic progress.* Washington, DC: U.S. Department of Education, National Center for Education Statistics.

Mullis, I., Jenkins, F., & Johnson, E. (1994). *Effective schools in mathematics.* Washington, DC: U.S. Department of Education, National Center for Education Statistics.

Myrdal, G. (1944). *An American dilemma.* New York: Harper and Row.

Nation at Risk. (1983). Washington, DC: National Commission on Excellence in Education, U.S. Department of Education.

Nicholl, J., & O'Cathain, A. (1990). Antenatal smoking, postnatal passive smoking, and the sudden infant death syndrome. In D. Poswillo & E. Alberman (Eds.), *Effects of smoking on the fetus, neonate, and child.* New York: Oxford.

Porretta, D. L., Gillespie, M., & Jansma, P. (1996). Perceptions about Special Olympics from service delivery groups in the United States: A preliminary investigation. *Education and Training in Mental Retardation, 31,* 44–54.

Problems and outlook of small private liberal arts colleges: Report to the Congress of the United States by the Comptroller General. (1978). Washington, D.C.: United States General Accounting Office.

Rack, J. P., Snowling, M. J., & Olson, R. K. (1992). The nonword reading deficit in developmental dyslexia: A review. *Reading Research Quarterly,* *27,* 29–53.

Ramey, C. T., & Smith, B. (1977). Assessing intellectual consequences of early intervention with high-risk infants. *American Journal of Mental Deficiency, 81,* 319–324.

Ruttman, L. (Ed.). (1977). *Evaluation research methods: A basic guide.* Beverly Hills, CA: Sage.

Shaw, C. R., & McKay, H. D. (1942). *Juvenile delinquency in urban areas.* Chicago: University of Chicago Press.

Sietsema, J., & Bose, J. (1995). *Characteristics of the 100 largest public elementary and secondary school districts in the United States: 1992–93.* Washington, DC: U.S. Department of Education, National Center for Education Statistics.

Snyder, T., & Hoffman, C. (1994). *Digest of education statistics.* Washington, DC: U.S. Department of Education, National Center for Education Statistics.

Stevenson, H. W., & Lee, S. (1990). Contexts of achievement. *Monographs of the Society for Research in Child Development, 55.*

Torsten, H. (Ed.). (1967). *International study of achievement in mathematics.* New York: John Wiley.

U.S. Surgeon General's Advisory Committee Report. (1964). *Smoking and health.* Washington, DC: Government Printing Office.

U.S. Surgeon General's Report. (1979). *Smoking and health.* Washington, DC: Government Printing Office.

Walberg, H. J. (1986). Synthesis of research on teaching. In M. C. Wittrock (Ed.), *Handbook of research on teaching* (3rd ed.). New York: MacMillan.

Wiener, R. L., Pritchard, C., Frauenhoffer, S. M., & Edmonds, M. (1993). Evaluation of a drug-free schools and community program. *Evaluation Review, 17,* 488–503.

Witty, P. (1967). Children of the T.V. era. *Elementary English, 64,* 528–535.

Zimmerman, R. S., & Langer, L. M. (1995). Improving estimates of prevalence rates of sensitive behaviors: The randomized lists technique and consideration of self-reported honesty. *The Journal of Sex Research, 32,* 107–117.

SAMPLE ARTICLE

*Used with permission of the Council of Exceptional Children Division on Mental Retardation and Developmental Disabilities.

clear & concise

Perceptions About Special Olympics from Service Delivery Groups in the United States: A Preliminary Investigation*

David L. Porretta
Michael Gillespie
and Paul Jansma
Ohio State University

Abstract: Special Olympics has been providing sport/recreation opportunities for individuals with mental retardation for over a quarter of a century. Recent trends such as access, inclusion and the use of the non-categorical approach in identifying individuals with disabilities, however, has led Special Olympics to reevaluate its programs. To this end, a 15 question survey instrument was developed and sent to a total of 232 potential respondents across 9 identified strata. These respondents represented various agencies/organizations throughout the United States that provide a variety of services to individuals with disabilities. Survey questions addressed terminology, philosophy, perceptions and programming. An overall response rate of 50.4 percent was obtained across the 9 strata, with 117 total questionnaires returned. Results indicate that: 1) the mission of Special Olympics should be to place more emphasis on inclusion opportunities, 2) there appears to be a trend away from the term "mental retardation" toward other terms, 3) Special Olympics should provide opportunities to a wider variety of individuals with disabilities, and 4) Special Olympics should examine its mission statement in order to stay abreast with current philosophies being espoused by other agencies/organizations. Future research efforts should extend the efforts of this preliminary investigation in examining Special Olympics' mission and goals.

Current legislation, such as the Individuals with Disabilities Education Act (United States Congress, 1990b) and the Americans with Disabilities Act (United States Congress, 1990a), provides unprecedented access and opportunity for individuals with disabilities in the United States. Laws such as these have led to an increasing trend of including individuals with disabilities into regular community schools and activities (Downs & Williams, 1994). In addition, there is a trend in the literature toward emphasizing the non-categorical approach when identifying individuals with disabilities (Rizzo & Vispoel, 1992).

This research project was partially funded by the National Association of Special Olympics Professionals (NASOP). The contents presented are those of the authors and do not necessarily reflect the position or policy of NASOP and no official endorsement by NASOP should be inferred.

The survey instrument, and a complete list of books and journals used in the literature review, can be obtained upon written request. Correspondence should be addressed to David L. Porretta, Ohio State University, 343 Larkins Hall, 337 West 17th Avenue, Columbus, OH 43210.

Trends such as inclusion and non-categorization have ongoing long term ramifications for personnel in agencies and organizations which provide services for individuals with disabilities. For example, Schalock et al. (1994) noted that with the new American Association on Mental Retardation's (AAMR) definition of mental retardation, there has been a move away from labeling of individuals and a trend toward describing the individual and supports required by that person. In this connection, it is important that all organizations who are involved with these individuals constantly evaluate the way in which they provide services, in order to determine whether or not they are truly providing the most beneficial and meaningful programs possible. An example of such an organization is Special Olympics. Since the time that Special Olympics was founded in 1968 in order to meet the increasing need for expansion of services to individuals with mental retardation (Orelove, Wehman, & Wood, 1982), it has expanded its services to all 50 states and 110 countries worldwide (Klein, Gilman, & Zigler, 1993). With over 1 million athletes participating, "Special Olympics continues to be the largest sports organization in the world for athletes with mental retardation" (Special Olympics, 1991).

statement of problem

During the time which Special Olympics has been in existence, it has provided a number of positive benefits. Hourcade (1989) noted three positive benefits: a) additional attention and social opportunities received by the participants, b) publicity which individuals with mental retardation receive from participating, and c) potential gains in physical fitness and recreation skills. However, as Block & Moon (1992) noted, a number of special education professionals continue to question the value and appropriateness of Special Olympics programs. For example, Orelove et al., (1982) cited four major limitations of Special Olympics: a) grouping persons with mental retardation into one competition is abnormal and not in keeping with the principle of normalization, b) since Special Olympics athletes only train and compete with other individuals who are labeled as mentally retarded, they will not have an opportunity to develop skills or receive instruction on how to relate and to interact with non-disabled peers, c) many of the events in Special Olympics competitions are isolated, non-functional activities which are not as important as other activities in the overall development of the individual, and d) the nature of Special Olympics has become highly competitive. Based on these limitations Orelove et al. (1982), provided the following suggestions for improving the value and quality of Special Olympics programs; including individuals without disabilities, developing a well-balanced recreation program, and including individuals with disabilities in community-based recreation. By adhering to these suggestions, it was felt that Special Olympics will be able to improve the value and quality of its programs.

comprehensive review of pertinent literature

well-organized review

In an attempt to address some of the suggestions outlined by its critics, Special Olympics has made a number of organizational and programmatic changes (Block & Moon, 1992). Key examples include the development of programs such as Unified Sports, Sports Partnerships, Partners Club programs, the introduction of lifetime leisure sports. In addition, Special Olympics has attempted to take an active role in encouraging and assisting community-based recreation facilities and programs to open their services to individuals with mental retardation.

As noted by Downs and Williams (1994), current federal legislation provides the impetus for including individuals with disabilities into regular community schools and activities. In addition, the AAMR has recently adopted a new definition and classification system for mental retardation based on the changing conception of mental retardation (Schalock et al., 1994). This system utilizes a single diagnostic code for mental retardation, describing the individuals' strengths and weaknesses in terms of four dimensions (intellectual functioning and adaptive skills; psychological and emotional well-being; health, physical well-being; and etiology), and provides a profile of supports which are needed.

With new emphases on access, inclusion and the non-categorization of individuals with disabilities, it is important for Special Olympics to again address its service delivery efforts. In order to determine the quality of current services, and the direction and quality of future services, Special Olympics personnel recognize that ongoing feedback from individuals representing various agencies/organizations impacting individuals with disabilities is valuable. In addition, effective communication also will be enhanced and maintained with the general public as to the mission and goals of Special Olympics. It is with these concerns in mind that this preliminary investigation was conducted.

The specific purpose of the study was to address four research questions: a) What is the prevailing overall philosophy of and among agencies, public and private, servicing individuals with mental retardation?, b) How has terminology shifted within agencies, public and private, as it pertains to describing mental retardation?, c) What strategies are being employed by leading agencies (public and private) in the United States to attract people with disabilities (mental retardation) to service delivery systems?, and d) What is the prevailing perception of agency professionals (public and private) of the Special Olympics' mission?

purposes clearly delineated and stated as research questions

METHOD

SURVEY DESIGN AND IMPLEMENTATION

A survey instrument was developed in order to address the four specific research questions cited above. In the development phase, the instrument was analyzed by two Ohio State University faculty members in adapted physical education, as well as two outside experts in the same field, in order to determine whether or not the content of the questions were valid. The final instrument consisted of 15 questions divided into two separate sections. Section I was answered by all respondents, while Section II was answered only by those affiliated with agencies/organizations whose personnel directly serve individuals with disabilities. This distinction was made because not all of the questions within the survey were relevant for all respondents.

clear description of survey development

The respondents were drawn from nine different strata, with a total of 232 agencies/organizations being targeted from across the United States. The nine strata, with the total number of potential respondents in parentheses, are: State Special Olympic Executive Directors (N=25); Parent Organizations (N=59); State Directors of Special Education (N=29); State Directors of Developmental Disability Services (N=26); University Affiliated Programs (N=28); State Vocational Agencies (N=33); Other Disabled Sport Organizations (N=10); Transition Services Organizations (N=9); and Various Agencies/Organizations Providing Services to Individuals with Disabilities (N=13). Respondents for the first six strata listed were selected through a systematic random sample of 50 percent of the total population frame for each individual stratum. For the final three strata, the entire population frame for each stratum was used.

good procedure for selecting respondents

procedure
clear &
properly
done

Due to a short (10 week) time frame, a modified version of the Dillman method (1978) was utilized to obtain data. Postcard follow-ups were mailed to those who had not returned a completed survey instrument. These follow-ups occurred seven and 14 days after the initial survey instrument mailing. In addition, telephone follow-ups were conducted with selected agencies/organizations who had not responded after the two mailed follow-ups.

In addition, relevant literature was surveyed in order to examine whether some of the trends which appear to be occurring in the field are also reflected in journals and textbooks. This review targeted 11 textbooks in adapted physical activity published after 1990 and 11 journals (post-1990 editions) from the fields of adapted physical education and special education. Issues such as environments in which services/programs were provided, and terminology used to describe individuals with cognitive disabilities were addressed in examining the literature.

ANALYSIS OF DATA

appropriate
to answer
research
questions

Data were analyzed through totaling the frequency of responses. The responses were then converted to percentage scores for each of the fifteen questions where appropriate. Further, these responses were divided for each of the nine strata. Responses from the open-ended questions on the instrument were summarized to highlight major trends. With respect to the review of literature, frequency counts were taken from the books and journals summarizing the number of times a selected term was used, the number of pages dealing with a specific topic, and the number of articles which dealt with a given topic or issue.

RESULTS

Relatively high response rates were achieved given the overall 10 week time frame in which the study was to be completed. Out of 232 agencies/organizations, a total of 117 responses were received, giving an overall response rate of 50.4 percent. The response rate for each of the nine strata is presented in Table 1. The results from the survey's 15 questions are grouped below according to which of the four primary research questions they addressed.

results
organized
by research
questions

RESEARCH QUESTION ONE

This primary question asked "What is the prevailing philosophy of and among agencies servicing the population with mental retardation as we approach the mid 1990s?"

Four subquestions contained in the survey addressed this primary research question, and the results are highlighted in Table 2. The first subquestion asked: "What is your agency/organization's philosophy related to servicing people with disabilities?" The results for this subquestion indicate that the majority (77) of agencies/organizations providing services for those individuals with disabilities do so in an environment characterized as least restrictive. This result, when combined with the "full inclusion" respondents (106 total), indicate that services are usually provided in non-segregated environments. This is substantiated by the fact that only two respondents offer services in segregated environments. In contrast, results from the review of current literature indicate that 459 out of 1490 total articles (30.8 percent) discuss individuals with mental retardation in segregated

All 5 tables are easy to read & helpful.

TABLE 1 **Name and Total Number of Each of the Nine Strata Along with Number of Respondents and Return Rate Percentage**

Strata	N	# of Respondents	Return Rate %
Special Olympics Executive Directors	25	16	64.0
Parent Organizations	59	36	61.0
State Directors of Special Education	29	18	62.1
Transition Services Organizations	9	5	55.6
State Directors of Developmental Disabilities	26	14	53.8
Other Disabled Sport Organizations	10	5	50.0
Various Agencies/Organizations Providing Services to Individuals with Disabilities	13	6	46.2
University Affiliated Programs	28	10	35.7
State Vocational Agencies	33	7	21.2

contexts, as opposed to only 82 articles (5.5 percent) which focus on inclusive settings). When divided by strata, 13 of the 17 Special Olympics directors indicated that their programs took place in an inclusive or least restrictive setting.

The second subquestion in this section posed the question: "Has there been a philosophical change within your agency/organization with respect to delivery of services as a result of the movement towards less labeling and inclusion?" The results of this question indicate that the number of respondents whose agencies/organizations have undergone a philosophic change (60) is almost equal to those whose philosophy has remained the same (57). When divided by strata, 81.3 percent of Special Olympics directors indicated that a philosophic shift had occurred within their organization. The narrative responses for this subquestion indicate the nature of these philosophic changes. The major changes with respect to philosophy among these agencies appear to include changing terminology (e.g., away from labeling and categorization), increasing opportunities for individuals with disabilities, and moving toward providing more inclusive situations for individuals with disabilities in the school and community.

The third subquestion asked: "Where do your services take place?" Results indicate that the responding agencies/organizations provide services in a wide variety of settings. There is a fairly even distribution of sites where service delivery occurs, ranging from 38 (32.5 percent) who use schools to 22 (18.8 percent) whose programs are provided in other settings.

The fourth subquestion in this section was divided into two parts. The first section asked: "Has your agency/organization shifted its focus to include individuals with disabilities other than those you have traditionally served?" The results for this subquestion indicate that 35 (61.4 percent) of the respondents felt that there had not been a shift in focus within their agency/organization, while 22 (38.6 percent) of the respondents felt that such a shift had indeed occurred. Among Special Olympics directors, three of the 13 who responded indicated that there had not been a shift in focus. The second part of the subquestion asked: "If you answered "yes" to subquestion 4(a), please indicate each specific disability now served, but

TABLE 2   **Number and Percentage of Responses by Subquestion for Research Question 1: What Is the Prevailing Overall Philosophy of and Among Agencies Servicing Individuals with Mental Retardation?**

Subquestion	Response	N	%
1. What is your agency/organization's philosophy related to servicing people with disabilities?	LRE Based	77	65.8
	Full Inclusion Based	29	24.7
	Other	16	13.7
	Segregation Based	2	1.7
2. Has there been a philosophic change within your agency/ organization with respect to delivery of services as a result of the movement toward less labeling and inclusion?	Yes	60	51.3
	No	57	48.7
3. Where do your services take place?	Schools	38	32.5
	Community	33	28.2
	Training Center	31	26.5
	Home	31	26.5
	Work Site	25	21.4
	Group Home	23	19.7
	Other	22	18.8
4. (a) Has your agency/organization shifted its focus to include individuals with disabilities other than those you have traditionally served?	No	35	61.4
	Yes	22	38.6
(b) If yes, please indicate each specific disability now served, but not traditionally served in the past.	Traumatic Brain Injury	6	10.5
	Specific Learning Disability	6	10.5
	Serious Emotional Disturbance	5	8.8
	Autism	3	5.3
	Orthopedic Impairments	2	3.5
	Other Health Impaired	2	3.5
	Hearing Impairments	2	3.5
	Mental Retardation	1	1.7
	Visual Impairments	1	1.7

not traditionally served in the past." Among the 38.6 percent who had attempted to include other individuals, it appears that those labeled with either traumatic brain injury or a specific learning disability are the most prevalent.

RESEARCH QUESTION TWO

This primary question asked: "How has terminology shifted within agencies, public and private, as it pertains to describing mental retardation?"

Three subquestions addressed this issue, and results are highlighted in Table 3. The first subquestion from this section asked: "What term does your agency/organization use to describe those with mental retardation?" Results indicate that the

TABLE 3 **Number and Percentage of Responses by Subquestion for Research Question 2: How Has Terminology Shifted Within Agencies, Public and Private, as It Pertains to Describing Mental Retardation?**

Subquestion	Response	N	%
1. What term does your agency/ organization use to describe those with mental retardation?	Developmental Disability	77	65.8
	Mental Retardation	73	62.4
	Cognitive Delay	29	24.8
	Mental Disability	18	15.4
	Mentally Challenged	15	12.8
	Other	14	12.0
	Mental Handicap	8	6.8
	Intellectual Disability/ Delay	5	4.3
2. Does your agency/organization see a trend occurring away from the term "mental retardation" toward such terms such as "developmental disabilities" or other common descriptors for cognitive delays?	Yes	87	76.3
	No	27	23.7
3. Is the term "mental retardation" commonly used by your agency/ organization for identification/ classification purposes?	Yes	33	61.1
	No	21	38.9

majority of agencies/organizations responding incorporate either the term "developmental disability" (77) (65.8 percent) or "mental retardation" (73) (62.4 percent) when discussing individuals who are mentally retarded. Results from the literature review, however, indicate that the term "mental retardation" is the most common descriptor used in both current textbooks (primary descriptor in 8 of 11 textbooks reviewed) and journals (360 total articles).

The second subquestion in this section asked: "Does your agency/organization see a trend occurring away from using the term "mental retardation" toward terms such as "developmental disabilities" or other common descriptors for cognitive delays?" The results from this question indicate that 87 (76.3 percent) of respondents believe that there is a trend away from using the term "mental retardation" toward usage of other terms in describing cognitive delays. In contrast, 27 (23.7 percent) of the respondents do not believe that this trend is taking place. Among the Special Olympics chapters responding, 15 (93.8 percent) responded that they believe a shift is occurring, with only one (6.2 percent) responding that it does not believe a terminology shift is in fact occurring.

The third subquestion in this section stated: "Is the term "mental retardation" commonly used by your agency/organization for identification/classification purposes?" The data obtained for this question indicate that 33 (61.1 percent) of those agencies/organizations which provide services for individuals with disabilities continue to utilize the term "mental retardation" for identification/classification purposes, while 21 (38.9 percent) of the respondents did not agree that this term was still utilized. Among Special Olympics chapters responding to this question, 12 (92.3 percent) indicated that they use the term "mental retardation," while only one (7.7 percent) stated that they do not utilize the term.

RESEARCH QUESTION THREE

This primary question asked: "What strategies are being employed to attract people with disabilities (e.g., mental retardation) to service delivery systems by leading agencies (public and private) in the United States?"

Five subquestions addressed this issue, and the results are highlighted in Table 4. The first subquestion asked: "What effect does the terminology now used by your agency have with respect to client outreach efforts in providing services?" Results reveal that the terminology now used by the responding agencies/organizations has a somewhat varied effect on direct service outreach efforts. For example, among Special Olympics executive directors, 64.3 percent of the 16 responding felt that current terminology hindered outreach efforts, compared to only 14.3 percent who felt that it actually enhanced efforts.

The second subquestion in this section asked: "What are the primary disabilities of those individuals served by your agency/organization?" Results indicate that the responding agencies/organizations provide services for diverse groups. Many organizations indicated that they offer program opportunities for more than one group of individuals with disabilities. Stated differently, these agencies/organizations do not tend to provide services exclusively for one specific group of individuals.

Subquestion three in this question asked: "What is the primary age range of those individuals served by your organization?" The results indicate that, as was the case with disability type, all responding agencies/ organizations provide services to individuals in a very diverse and broad manner with respect to age groups. Many agencies provide services to individuals covering a wide range of ages. The most prevalent age range within which services were provided by the respondents was 14–21 years, with 0–2 years (early childhood) being the age range within which the fewest number of respondents were served.

The fourth subquestion asked respondents: "What impact has the trend towards inclusion and less labeling had with respect to the number of individuals your agency serves?" The data indicate that a majority (51.9 percent) of the respondents do not feel that the recent trend toward inclusion and less labeling have had any impact on the number of individuals participating in their programs and services. Data from the Special Olympics executive directors, however, reveal that of those responding to the question (15), nearly 50 percent (7) believe that they have had either a slight or significant decrease in the number of individuals they serve base on these trends.

The final subquestion in this section asked: "What strategies do your agency/ organization use in its effort to attract new clients?" Results indicate that a wide variety of methods are utilized by various agencies/organizations with respect to attracting new clients. Many respondents indicate that they utilize many of these methods in order to procure new members. Direct contact with parents/guardians was reported to be the most prevalent method (43) by those agencies/organizations responding.

RESEARCH QUESTION FOUR

This primary question asked: "What is the prevailing perception of agency professionals (public and private) of the Special Olympics' mission?"

TABLE 4   Number and Percentage of Responses by Subquestion for Research Question 3: What Strategies Are Being Employed to Attract People with Disabilities (e.g., Mental Retardation) to Service Delivery Systems by Leading Agencies (Public and Private) in the United States

Subquestion	Response	N	%
1. What effect does the terminology now used by your agency have with respect to client outreach efforts in providing services?	No Effect	21	38.9
	Enhances Service Efforts	18	33.3
	Hinders Service Efforts	15	27.8
2. What are the primary disabilities of those individuals served by your agency/organization?	Mental Retardation	49	41.9
	Autism	40	34.2
	Specific Learning Disability	32	27.4
	Traumatic Brain Injury	31	26.5
	Orthopedic Impairments	30	25.7
	Speech Impairments	30	25.7
	Hearing Impairments	27	23.1
	Visual Impairments	25	21.4
	Other Health Impaired	25	21.4
	Serious Emotional Disturbance	24	20.5
3. What is the primary age range of those individuals served by your organization?	14–21	46	39.3
	6–13	43	36.8
	22+	41	35.0
	3–5	35	29.9
	0–2	31	26.5
4. What impact has the trend towards inclusion and less labeling had with respect to the number of individuals your agency serves?	No Real Impact	27	51.9
	Slight Increase in Number	9	17.3
	Slight Decrease in Number	6	11.5
	Substantial Increase in Number	5	9.6
	Substantial Decrease in Number	5	9.6
5. What strategies do your agency/organization use in its effort to attract new clients?	Direct Contact with Parents/Guardians	43	79.6
	Publications	41	75.9
	Direct Contact with Related Agencies	41	75.9
	Direct Contact with Potential Clients	30	55.6
	Use Various Media	29	53.7
	Other	11	20.4

Three subquestions addressed this issue, and the results are highlighted in Table 5. The first subquestion asked: "What types of disabilities do you believe Special Olympics addresses now?" Results indicate that all but one of the respondents believe that Special Olympics serves individuals identified as mentally retarded. However, the results also indicate the respondents felt that Special Olympics serves individuals who are identified under each of the other nine disabilities listed.

TABLE 5   Number and Percentage of Responses by Subquestion for Research Question 4: What Is the Prevailing Perception of Agency Professionals (Pubic and Private) of the Special Olympics' Mission?

Subquestion	Response	N	%
1. What types of disabilities do you believe Special Olympics addresses now?	Mental Retardation	116	99.1
	Autism	64	54.7
	Orthopedic Impairments	54	46.2
	Traumatic Brain Injury	35	29.9
	Specific Learning Disability	34	29.1
	Hearing Impairments	30	25.6
	Visual Impairments	28	23.9
	Serious Emotional Disturbance	24	20.5
	Other Health Impairments	23	19.7
	Speech Impairments	18	15.4
2. What types of disabilities do you think Special Olympics should address?	Mental Retardation	101	86.3
	Autism	85	72.6
	Traumatic Brain Injury	70	59.8
	Orthopedic Impairments	66	56.4
	Specific Learning Disability	58	49.6
	Visual Impairments	56	47.9
	Hearing Impairments	55	47.0
	Other Health Impairments	55	47.0
	Serious Emotional Disturbance	55	47.0
	Speech Impairments	43	36.8
3. (a) Do you believe, based on the trends toward less labeling and inclusion, that the mission of Special Olympics needs to remain the same or change?	Change	90	79.6
	Remain the Same	23	20.4
(b) If you chose "change", in what way(s) should Special Olympics change?	Place More Emphasis on Inclusion Opportunities	79	87.8
	Offer Programs that Address More Disabilities	36	40.0
	Offer a Wide Variety of Services	20	22.2
	Other	17	18.9

The second subquestion asked respondents: "What types of disabilities do you think Special Olympics should address?" The results show mental retardation as the most prevalent disability which Special Olympics should serve. These results also illustrate, however, that Special Olympics should be providing programs for individuals across a wide range of disabilities.

The third subquestion in this section was divided into two parts. The first part asked: "Do you believe, based on the trends toward less labeling and inclusion, that the mission of Special Olympics needs to remain the same or change?" The data indicate that 90 (79.6 percent) of the total respondents felt that the mission

results reported in a clear & comprehensive manner—good use of tables

of Special Olympics needs to change. Among the Special Olympics executive directors responding to this question, 10 (63 percent) stated that they felt the mission of Special Olympics needs to change. The second part to this subquestion asked: "If you chose 'change,' in what way(s) should Special Olympics change?" Results indicate recommendations to provide more inclusionary opportunities (87.8 percent) and programs which address individuals with a variety of disabling conditions (40.0 percent).

DISCUSSION

Discussion relates results to research questions and provides reasonable answers for each question.

Based on the results of this preliminary investigation, it appears that Special Olympics needs to further examine its current programs and events. Therefore, a number of primary conclusions can be drawn. First, Special Olympics should consider providing more opportunities for its participants with disabilities to participate with their able-bodied peers in inclusionary-type programs. The concept of offering more integrated programming has been well documented in the literature (Block & Moon, 1992; Hourcade, 1989; Klein et al., 1993; Orelove et al., 1982; Orelove & Moon, 1984; Wehman & Moon, 1985). Data from this project indicate that very few (1.7 percent) agencies/organizations provide services to individuals with disabilities in segregated settings, and that Special Olympics should place more emphasis on inclusive opportunities. Although Special Olympics has attempted to address this issue in the past (Block & Moon, 1992), it appears that further efforts toward integrated programming are necessary. For example, in addition to Unified Sports, Special Olympics should place added emphasis on promoting Sports Partnerships. In this program, individuals with mental retardation train and compete alongside athletes without disabilities in a school setting. As stated by Riggen & Ulrich (1993), "the ideal sport or fitness program for individuals with mental retardation should encourage improvements in physical abilities, with the additional movement toward complete social integration."

Second, Special Olympics should examine further a shift in terminology away from the term "mental retardation." Survey data from this preliminary investigation indicate that more than three out of four agencies/organizations responding identify a trend toward descriptors for cognitive delays other than "mental retardation." In addition, the data indicate that more agencies/organizations utilize the term "developmental disability" (77) (65.8 percent) than the term "mental retardation" (73) (62.4 percent) to describe individuals with cognitive disabilities. This is a significant finding. Through an examination of the terminology used to describe its athletes, Special Olympics may wish to use a different term to describe the population which it serves. For example, if the term "developmental disability" is used as opposed to "mental retardation," a greater number of individuals with disabilities could be eligible to participate in Special Olympics programs.

The two recommendations cited above appear to be in conflict with the findings based on the current literature review (i.e., a greater number of pages in journals and textbooks deal with segregated, as opposed to integrated, settings and the term "mental retardation" is used more often than other descriptors for cognitive delays). This discrepancy may be explained in part by the delay or lag in publication time after a manuscript is submitted for editorial review. As such, some of the material examined in the literature review could have in fact been written in the late 1980s, which would explain the differences found between the survey results and the published literature. It is expected that trends such as those addressed in this project (i.e., inclusion, non-categorization) will become increasingly prevalent in the literature as we approach the end of the 1990s. Another possible explanation for the prevalent use of the term "mental retardation" in the literature has to do with terminology used by professional associations in the field. For example, "mental retardation" is the accepted term used by the American Association on Mental Retardation (AAMR), which is considered to be the authority in the area. Therefore it seems reasonable to expect that the term "mental retardation" is used more often than other descriptors.

Third, Special Olympics should further explore providing opportunities for individuals with a wider variety of disabilities and age groups. Data from this preliminary investigation indicate that agencies/organizations providing services to individuals with disabilities do so across a wide variety of conditions and age groups, and they feel Special Olympics should attempt to do the same. For example, is the cut off of eight years of age for Special Olympics events appropriate? Given this information, it may be appropriate for Special Olympics to examine the feasibility of offering cross-category opportunities for its athletes across all age spans. Such an approach would not allow Special Olympics athletes to participate in integrated programs, but would also provide an arena through which individuals with a variety of disabilities and ages could engage in various sport and recreation activities together.

Fourth, Special Olympics should examine its mission statement in order to stay abreast with current philosophies being espoused by other agencies/organizations providing services to individuals with disabilities. In fact, the results from this preliminary investigation indicate that 79.6 percent (N=90) of those responding feel that the mission of Special Olympics needs to change. However, because of the unique nature of its programs, Special Olympics may not necessarily need to totally change its mission statement. Rather, by reexamining its mission and goals, Special Olympics might then provide programs for its participants which reflect the current philosophies of other related agencies/organizations.

Special Olympics continues to be a leader in the arena of sport for individuals with disabilities. Data from this preliminary investigation, however, indicate that further examination of programs and service delivery systems may be necessary in order for Special Olympics to stay at the forefront of this movement, and to stay abreast of emerging societal trends toward individuals with disabilities. As noted by Storey, Stern, and Parker (1990), the effectiveness of programs for individuals with disabilities depends upon changes in attitudes by their families, professionals, and members of the community at large.

Finally, it is recommended that a more extensive study be completed to examine more comprehensively the questions addressed in this preliminary investigation. A follow-up study should address the research questions used in this current study in a more extensive manner, targeting an expanded frame of respondents which would include physical educators, adapted physical educators, therapeutic recreation specialists, special educators, and individuals who work directly with athletes at the local level. Additionally, Special Olympics athletes (in so far as possible) should also be asked to respond, since their opinions are critical for determining the future dynamics of Special Olympics programs. Continued examination of programs is necessary in order to allow Special Olympics to continue as a valued provider of sport/recreation programs for varied participants well into the 21st century.

REFERENCES

Block, M., & Moon, M. (1992). Orelove, Wehman, and Wood revisited: An evaluative review of Special Olympics ten years later. *Education and Training in Mental Retardation, 27,* 379–386.

Dillman, D. (1978). *Mail and Telephone Surveys: The Total Design Method.* New York: John Wiley and Sons.

Downs, P., & Williams, T. (1994). Student attitudes toward integration of people with disabilities in activity settings: A European comparison. *Adapted Physical Activity Quarterly, 11,* 32–43.

Hourcade, J. (1989). Special Olympics: A review and critical analysis. *Therapeutic Recreation Journal, 23,* 59–65.

Klein, T., Gilman, E., & Zigler, E. (1993). Special Olympics: An evaluation by professionals and parents. *Mental Retardation, 31,* 15–23.

Orelove, F., & Moon, M. (1984). The Special Olympics program: Effects on retarded persons and society. *Arena Review, 8,* 41–45.

Orelove, F., Wehman, P., & Wood, J. (1982). An evaluative review of Special Olympics: Implications for community integration. *Education and Training of the Mentally Retarded, 17,* 325–329.

Riggen, K., & Ulrich, D. (1993). The effects of sport participation on individuals with mental retardation. *Adapted Physical Activity Quarterly, 10,* 42–51.

Rizzo, T., & Vispoel, W. (1992). Changing attitudes about teaching students with handicaps. *Adapted Physical Activity Quarterly, 9,* 54–63.

Schalock, R., Stark, J., Snell, M., Coulter, D., Polloway, E., Luckasson, R., Reiss, S., & Spitalnik, D. (1994). The changing conception of mental retardation: Implications for the field. *Mental Retardation, 32,* 181–193.

Special Olympics (1991). *Special Olympics International Official Media Guide.* Washington, DC: Author.

Storey, K., Stern, R., & Parker, R. (1990). A comparison of attitudes toward typical recreational activities versus the Special Olympics. *Education and Training in Mental Retardation, 25,* 94–99.

United States Congress (1990a). *Americans with Disabilities Act, PL 101-336.* Washington, DC: Author.

United States Congress (1990b). *Individuals with Disabilities Education Act, PL 101-476.* Washington, DC: Author.

Wehman, P., & Moon, M. (1985). Designing and implementing leisure programs for individuals with severe handicaps. In M. P. Brady and P. L. Gunter (Eds.) *Integrating Moderately and Severely Handicapped Learners* (pp. 214–237). Springfield, IL: Charles C. Thomas.

6

EXPERIMENTAL AND QUASI-EXPERIMENTAL RESEARCH

Experimental research provides a systematic and logical method for answering the question, "If this is done under carefully controlled conditions, what will happen?" Experimenters manipulate certain stimuli, treatments, or environmental conditions and observe how the condition or behavior of the subject is affected or changed. Their manipulation is deliberate and systematic. They must be aware of other factors that could influence the outcome and remove or control them so that they can establish a logical association between manipulated factors and observed effects.

Experimentation provides a method of hypothesis testing. After experimenters define a problem, they propose a tentative answer or hypothesis. They test the hypothesis and confirm or refute it in the light of the controlled variable relationship that they have observed. It is important to note that the confirmation or rejection of the hypothesis is stated in terms of probability rather than certainty.

Experimentation is the classic method of the science laboratory where elements manipulated and effects observed can be controlled. It is the most sophisticated, exacting, and powerful method for discovering and developing an organized body of knowledge.

Although the experimental method finds its greatest utility in the laboratory, it has been effectively applied in nonlaboratory settings such as the classroom, where significant factors or variables can be controlled to some degree. The immediate purpose of experimentation is to predict events in the experimental setting. The ultimate purpose is to generalize the variable relationships so that they may be applied outside the laboratory to a wider population of interest.

EARLY EXPERIMENTATION

The earliest assumptions of experimental research were based on what was known as the *law of the single variable.* In 1873 John Stuart Mill provided a definition for this principle. He stated five rules or canons that he believed would include all types of logical procedure required to establish order among controlled events. One of his canons, known as the *method of difference,* states:

> *If an instance in which the phenomenon under investigation occurs, and an instance in which it does not occur have every circumstance in common save one, that one occurring only in the former, the circumstance in which alone the two instances differ is the effect, or the cause, or an indispensable part of the cause of the phenomenon. (Mill, 1873, p. 222)*

In simpler language, if two situations are alike in every respect, and one element is added to one but not the other, any difference that develops is the effect of the added element; or, if two situations are alike in every respect, and one element is removed from one but not from the other, any difference that develops may be attributed to the subtracted element.

The law of the single variable provided the basis for much early laboratory experimentation. In 1662 Robert Boyle, an Irish physicist, used this method in arriving at a principle on which he formulated his law of gases: When temperature is held constant, the volume of an ideal gas is inversely proportional to the pressure exerted on it. In other words, when pressure is raised, volume decreases; when pressure is lowered, volume increases. In Boyle's law, *pressure* is the single variable:

$$\frac{V_1}{V_2} = \frac{P_2}{P_1}$$

A little more than a century later, Jacques A. C. Charles, a French physicist, discovered a companion principle, now known as Charles's law. He observed that when the pressure was held constant, the volume of an ideal gas was directly proportional to the temperature. When temperature is raised, volume increases; when temperature is lowered, volume decreases. In Charles's law, *temperature* is the single variable:

$$\frac{V_1}{V_2} = \frac{T_1}{T_2}$$

Although the concept of the single variable proved useful in some areas of the physical sciences, it failed to provide a sound approach to experimentation in the behavioral sciences. Despite its appealing simplicity and apparent logic, it did not provide an adequate method for studying complex problems. It assumed a highly artificial and restricted relationship between single variables. Rarely, if ever, are human events the result of single causes. They are usually the result of the inter-action of many variables, and an attempt to limit variables so that one can be iso-lated and observed proves impossible.

The contributions of R. A. Fisher, first applied in agricultural experimentation, have provided a much more effective way of conducting realistic experimentation in the behavioral sciences. His concept of achieving pre-experimental equating of conditions through random selection of subjects and random assignment of treat-ments, and his concepts of analysis of variance and analysis of covariance made possible the study of complex interactions through factorial designs in which the influence of more than one independent variable on more than one dependent variable could be observed. Current uses of this type of design will be discussed more fully later in this chapter.

EXPERIMENTAL AND CONTROL GROUPS

An experiment involves the comparison of the effects of a particular treatment with that of a different treatment or of no treatment. In a simple conventional experi-ment, reference is usually made to an *experimental group* and to a *control group*.

These groups are equated as nearly as possible. The experimental group is exposed to the influence of the factor under consideration; the control group is not. Observations are then made to determine what difference appears or what change or modification occurs in the experimental as contrasted with the control group.

Sometimes it is also necessary to control for the effect of actually participat-ing in an experiment. Medical researchers have long recognized that patients who receive any medication, regardless of its real efficacy, tend to feel better or per-form more effectively. In medical experiments a harmless or inert substitute is administered to the control group to offset the psychological effect of medication. These substitutes, or *placebos*, are indistinguishable from the real medication un-der investigation, and neither experimental nor control subjects know whether they are receiving the medication or the placebo. The effectiveness of the true medication is the difference between the effect of the medication and that of the placebo.

What seems to be a similar psychological effect was recognized in a series of experiments at the Hawthorne Plant of the Western Electric Company and origi-nally published in 1933 (Mayo, 1960). The studies concerned the relationships between certain working conditions and worker output efficiency. Illumination was one of these manipulated experimental variables. The researchers found that as light intensity was increased, worker output increased. After a certain peak was apparently reached, it was decided to see what effect the reduction of intensity of illumination would have. To the surprise of the researchers, as intensity was de-creased by stages, output continued to increase. The researchers concluded that the attention given the workers and their awareness of participation in the exper-iment apparently were important motivating factors. From these studies the term *Hawthorne Effect* was introduced into the psychological literature.

It has been commonly believed that this reactive effect of knowledge of participation in an experiment, the Hawthorne Effect, is similar to the medical placebo effect. Researchers have frequently devised nonmedical placebos to counteract this potential effect. One such device, used in connection with experiments involving the comparison of traditional teaching materials with new experimental materials, is to reprint the traditional, or control, materials and label both these and the new, experimental materials "Experimental Method."

A group receiving a placebo is usually known as a "placebo control group" to distinguish it from the more common control group that receives nothing additional as a result of the study.

Even when the subjects of a study are unlikely to know or care that they are participants in an experiment, it may be necessary to utilize a placebo control group. Research with severely and profoundly retarded children may result in increased time spent with the experimental group children over the control group children unless a placebo is introduced. An example is a study in which Kahn (1984) investigated the effect of a cognitive training program on acquisition of language. Rather than have the usual control group, this study made sure that the nonexperimental group children received as much individual instruction as the experimental group children, albeit in areas other than the experimental treatment. Thus, this study used a placebo control group to assure that group differences were a result of the training procedure rather than additional attention.

Experiments are not always characterized by a treatment–nontreatment comparison. Varying types, amounts, or degrees of the experimental factor may be applied to a number of groups. For example, in medical research an experiment to test the effectiveness of a particular medication in reducing body temperature might involve administering a massive dosage to one group, a normal dosage to a second, and a minimal dosage to a third. Because all the groups receive medication, there is no control group in the limited sense of the term, but control of the experimental factors and observation of their effects are essential elements.

In educational research varying types or degrees of an experimental factor might also be used with different groups. For instance, a researcher might compare three different methods of teaching spelling. Or a researcher might wish to study the effect of class size on learning in a high school history course. Such a study might compare three classes of varying size, say 35, 30, and 25, to see which class did better. Of course, the researcher would have to be certain that all other factors (e.g., intelligence, prior knowledge, time of day, and length of instruction) were equated.

VARIABLES

Independent and Dependent Variables

Variables are the conditions or characteristics that the experimenter manipulates, controls, or observes. The *independent* variables are the conditions or characteristics that the experimenter manipulates or controls in his or her attempt to ascertain their relationship to observed phenomena. The *dependent* variables are the conditions or characteristics that appear, disappear, or change as the experimenter introduces, removes, or changes independent variables.

In educational research an independent variable may be a particular teaching method, a type of teaching material, a reward, a period of exposure to a particular condition, or an attribute such as sex or level of intelligence. The dependent variable may be a test score, the number of errors, or measured speed in performing a task. Thus, the dependent variables are the measured changes in pupil performance attributable to the influence of the independent variables.

There are two types of independent variables: *treatment* and *organismic or attribute* variables. Treatment variables are those factors that the experimenter manipulates and to which he or she assigns subjects. Attribute variables are those characteristics that cannot be altered by the experimenter. Such independent variables as age, sex, race, and intelligence level have already been determined, but the experimenter can decide to include them or remove them as variables to be studied. The question of whether 8-year-old girls show greater reading achievement than 8-year-old boys is an example of the use of an organismic variable, sex. The teaching procedure is the same for both groups so there is no treatment-independent variable.

Confounding Variables

Confounding variables are those aspects of a study or sample that might influence the dependent variable (outcome measure) and whose effect may be confused with the effects of the independent variable. Confounding variables are of two types: intervening and extraneous variables.

Intervening Variables

In many types of behavioral research the relationship between the independent and dependent variables is not a simple one of stimulus to response. Certain variables that cannot be controlled or measured directly may have an important effect on the outcome. These modifying variables intervene between the cause and the effect.

In a classroom language experiment a researcher is interested in determining the effect of immediate reinforcement on learning the parts of speech. He or she suspects that certain factors or variables other than the one being studied, immediate reinforcement, may be influencing the results, even though they cannot be observed directly. These factors—anxiety, fatigue, motivation, for example—may be intervening variables. They are difficult to define in operational, observable, terms, but they cannot be ignored. Rather, they must be controlled as much as is feasible through the use of appropriate designs.

Extraneous Variables

Extraneous variables are those uncontrolled variables (i.e., variables not manipulated by the experimenter) that *may* have a significant influence on the results of a study. Many research conclusions are questionable because of the influence of these extraneous variables.

In a widely publicized study, the effectiveness of three methods of social studies teaching was compared. Intact classes were used, and the researchers were unable to randomize or control such variables as teacher competence or enthusiasm or the age, socioeconomic level, or academic ability of the student subjects. The criterion of effectiveness was achievement measured by scores on standardized tests. It would seem clear that the many extraneous variables precluded valid conclusions about the relative effectiveness of the independent variables, which were teaching methods. It should be noted that in order for an extraneous variable to confound the results of a study it must be correlated strongly enough with both the independent and dependent variables so that its influence can be mistaken for that of the independent variable.

Although it is impossible to eliminate all extraneous variables, particularly in classroom research, sound experimental design enables the researcher to largely neutralize their influence.

CONTROLLING EXTRANEOUS VARIABLES

Variables that are of interest to the researcher can be controlled by building them into the study as independent variables. For instance, a researcher comparing two different reading programs may wish to control for the potentially confounding extraneous variable of sex by making it an independent attribute variable and thereby investigating the effect of sex on the two different reading programs.

Variables not of direct interest to the researcher may be removed or their influence minimized by several methods, which are discussed in the following sections.

Removing the Variable
Variables may be controlled by eliminating them completely. Observer distraction may be removed by separating the observer from both experimental and control groups by a one-way glass partition. Some variables between subjects may be eliminated by selecting cases with uniform characteristics. Using only female subjects removes sex as a variable but thereby reduces the generalization from the study to only females.

Randomization
Randomization involves pure chance selection and assignment of subjects to experimental and control groups for a limited supply of available subjects. Random selection was discussed in Chapter 1. Here we are referring to random assignment, the method by which everyone already selected for the sample has an equal chance of being assigned to the various treatment conditions (e.g., experimental and control).

If two groups are involved, randomization can be achieved by tossing a coin, assigning a subject to one group if heads appear, to the other if the toss is tails.

When more than two groups are involved, dice or a table of random numbers can be used.

Randomization provides the most effective method of eliminating systematic bias and of minimizing the effect of extraneous variables. The principle is based on the assumption that through random assignment differences between groups result only from the operation of probability or chance. These differences are known as *sampling error* or *error variance,* and their magnitude can be established by the researcher.

In an experiment differences in the dependent variables that may be attributed to the effect of the independent variables are known as *experimental variance.* The significance of an experiment may be tested by comparing experimental variance with error variance. If at the conclusion of the experiment the differences between the experimental and control groups are too great to attribute to error variance, it may be assumed that these differences are attributable to experimental variance. This process is described in detail in Chapter 11.

Matching Cases

When randomization is not feasible (e.g., there are too few subjects), selecting pairs or sets of individuals with identical or nearly identical characteristics and assigning one of them to the experimental group and the other to the control group provide another method of control. This method is limited by the difficulty of matching on more than one variable. It is also likely that some individuals will be excluded from the experiment if a matching subject is not available. Matching is not considered satisfactory unless the members of the pairs or sets are then randomly assigned to the treatment groups, a method known as *matched randomization.*

Balancing Cases or Group Matching

Balancing cases consists of assigning subjects to experimental and control groups in such a way that the means and the variances of the groups are as nearly equal as possible. Because identical balancing of groups is impossible, the researcher must decide how much departure from equality can be tolerated without loss of satisfactory control. This method also presents a similar difficulty noted in the matching method, namely, the difficulty of equating groups on the basis of more than one characteristic or variable.

Analysis of Covariance

This method permits the experimenter to eliminate initial differences on several variables between the experimental and control groups by statistical methods. The use of pretest mean scores as covariates is considered preferable to the conventional matching of groups. Analysis of covariance is a rather complicated statistical procedure, beyond the scope of this elementary treatment. For a complete discussion readers may wish to consult Glass and Hopkins (1996), Hays (1981), Kerlinger (1986), Kirk (1995), or Shavelson (1996).

EXPERIMENTAL VALIDITY

To make a significant contribution to the development of knowledge, an experiment must be valid. Campbell and Stanley (1966) described two types of experimental validity, *internal validity* and *external validity*. Cook and Campbell (1979) further divided experimental validity, adding two other types, *statistical validity* and *construct validity*. For purposes of this introductory treatment of the issue, the discussion is confined to the two types of experimental validity described by Campbell and Stanley.

Internal Validity

An experiment has internal validity to the extent that the factors that have been manipulated (independent variables) actually have a genuine effect on the observed consequences (dependent variables) in the experimental setting.

External Validity — *Generalization*

The researcher would achieve little of practical value if these observed variable relationships were valid only in the experimental setting and only for those participating. External validity is the extent to which the variable relationships can be generalized to other settings, other treatment variables, other measurement variables, and other populations.

Experimental validity is an ideal to aspire to, for it is unlikely that it can ever be completely achieved. Internal validity is very difficult to achieve in the nonlaboratory setting of the behavioral experiment in which there are so many extraneous variables to attempt to control. When experimental controls are tightened to achieve internal validity, the more artificial, less realistic situation may prevail, reducing the external validity or generalizability of the experiment. Some compromise is inevitable so that a reasonable balance may be established between control and generalizability between internal and external validity.

Threats to Internal Experimental Validity

In educational experiments, or in any behavioral experiments, a number of extraneous variables are present in the situation or are generated by the experimental design and procedures. These variables influence the results of the experiment in ways difficult to evaluate. In a sense they introduce rival hypotheses that could account for experimental change not attributable to the experimental variables under consideration. Although these extraneous variables usually cannot be completely eliminated, many of them can be identified. It is important that behavioral researchers anticipate them and take all possible precautions to minimize their influence through sound experiment design and execution.

A number of factors jeopardize the power of the experimenter to evaluate the effects of independent variables unambiguously. Campbell and Stanley (1966) have discussed these factors in their excellent definitive treatment. They include the following:

Maturation

Subjects change (biologically and psychologically) in many ways over time, and these changes may be confused with the effect of the independent variables under consideration. During the course of a study, the subjects might become more tired, wiser, hungrier, older, and so on. They may be influenced by the incidental learning or experiences encountered through normal maturation. This threat is best controlled by randomly assigning subjects to experimental and control groups. Differences between the groups are then considered to be due to the treatment rather than to maturation.

History

Specific external events occurring between the first and second measurements and beyond the control of the researcher may have a stimulating or disturbing effect on the performance of subjects. The effect of a fire drill, the emotional tirade of a teacher, a pep session, the anxiety produced by a pending examination, or a catastrophic event in the community may significantly affect the test performance of a group of students.

In many experiments these external events will have a similar effect on both experimental and control subjects, in which case this threat is controlled. However, because they are specific events, they may affect one group but not the other. The effect of these uncontrolled external events is one of the hazards inherent in experiments carried on outside the laboratory. In laboratory experiments these extraneous variables can be controlled more effectively.

Testing

The process of pretesting at the beginning of an experiment can produce a change in subjects. Pretesting may produce a practice effect making subjects more proficient in subsequent test performance. Testing presents a threat to internal validity that is common to pretest–posttest experiments. Of course, an equivalent control group would be affected by the test in a similar way as the experimental group. Thus, having experimental and control groups controls for this threat in the same way that it does for the threat of maturation. In the next section on threats to external validity, we will discuss another type of threat related to testing that is not controlled by having an equivalent control group, the interaction effect of testing.

Unstable Instrumentation

Unreliable instruments or techniques used to describe and measure aspects of behavior are threats to the validity of an experiment. If tests used as instruments of observation are not accurate or consistent, a serious element of error is introduced. If observers are used to describe behavior changes in subjects, changes in observers or in their standards due to fatigue, increased insight, or skill or changes in criteria of judgment over a period of time—all these are likely to introduce error. This instability of measurement deals with the topic of test reliability and the measurement of observer reliability, which are discussed in Chapter 9.

Statistical Regression

Statistical regression, also known as *regression to the mean,* is a phenomenon that sometimes operates when subjects are selected on the basis of extremely high or extremely low pretest scores and when the measurement device is not totally reliable, a situation which is common. Subjects who score very high, near the ceiling, on a pretest will most likely score lower (nearer the mean) on a subsequent testing. Subjects who score very low, near the floor, on a pretest will most likely score higher (nearer the mean) on a subsequent testing, with or without anything pertinent to their performance (e.g., instruction) occurring in the meantime. The reader should be aware that this phenomenon occurs only when subjects are selected as a group because of their extreme scores and that the regression referred to is for the group as a whole, not for all individuals. Posttest scores for individuals may go in the opposite direction expected by this phenomenon for the group.

The purpose of a study may require the researcher to select subjects based on their extreme scores. A study of the effects of different remedial reading programs assumes that the subjects must need remedial reading instruction and, therefore, have very low reading scores on the pretest. To control for regression to the mean, the researcher would randomly assign his or her sample of poor readers to the experimental and control groups. Because both groups would be expected to improve equally because of regression to the mean, if the experimental group improved significantly more than the control group, the researcher could conclude that this was because of the experimental treatment rather than statistical regression.

Selection Bias

Selection bias is represented by the nonequivalence of experimental and control groups, and its most effective deterrent is the random assignment of subjects to treatments. Selection bias is likely when, on invitation, volunteers are used as members of an experimental group. Although they may appear to be equated to the nonvolunteers, their characteristics of higher motivation may introduce a bias that would invalidate reasonable comparison. Selection bias may be introduced when intact classes are used as experimental and control groups: Because of scheduling arrangements, an English class meeting during the fourth period may consist of particularly able students who are scheduled at that period because they are also enrolled in an advanced mathematics class. Another example of this effect occurs when students and/or their parents have the opportunity to volunteer for a special program. The volunteers or their parents may be more motivated than the students who did not volunteer. Thus, the only good control group would be a random group of volunteers who were unable to participate because the program had more volunteers than could be enrolled. This control group would usually be on the waiting list and get the special program at a later date.

Interaction of Selection and Maturation

This type of threat to the internal validity of a study is not the same as selection bias. The interaction of selection and maturation may occur whenever the subjects can select which treatment (e.g., which instructional method) they will receive. Even though the groups may be equivalent on the pretest and on other cognitive measures, the reasons some people choose one treatment over another may be related to the outcome measure (dependent variable). Thus, if more motivated students chose method A for learning calculus over method B because method A appears harder and requires greater academic motivation, that differential motivation might be confused for the effects of the experimental variable.

Experimental Mortality

Mortality, or loss of subjects, particularly likely in a long-term experiment, introduces a potentially confounding element. Although experimental and control groups are randomly assigned, the survivors might represent groups that are quite different from the unbiased groups that began the experiment. Those who survive a period of experimentation are likely to be healthier, more able, or more highly motivated than those who are absent frequently or who drop out of school and do not remain for the duration of the experiment. The major concern here is whether the groups experienced different loss rates or reasons for dropouts that might confound the results. Usually a comparison of the pretest scores of those remaining in the study and those who dropped out will help determine if the dropout of the experimental and control subjects was for different reasons and has resulted in significantly different groups than began the study.

Experimenter Bias

This type of bias is introduced when the researcher has some previous knowledge about the subjects in an experiment. This knowledge of subject status may cause the researcher to convey some clue that affects the subjects' reaction or may affect the objectivity of his or her judgment.

In medical research it is common practice to conceal from the subject the knowledge of who is receiving the placebo and who the experimental medication. This is known as a *blind*. Having someone other than the experimenter administer the treatments and record which subjects are receiving the medication and which the placebo provides an additional safeguard. This practice, known as a *double blind*, helps to minimize contamination.

Beginners in educational research have been known to contaminate a study by classifying student performance when they know the nature of the variable to be correlated with that performance. In a simple *ex post facto* study a student proposed to determine the relationship between academic achievement and citizenship grades in her class. Because she proposed to assign the citizenship grades herself, it would seem apparent that an element of contamination would result. Her knowledge of the student's previous academic achievement would tend to precondition her judgment in assigning citizenship grades.

In educational studies of this type, researchers would minimize contamination if outside observers rated the subjects without any knowledge of their academic status.

— Generalization

Threats to External Experimental Validity

Laboratory research has the virtue of permitting the experimenter to carefully avoid threats to internal validity. However, the artificial nature of such a setting greatly reduces the generalizability of the findings from such research. Because educational researchers are primarily concerned with the practical uses of their findings, they frequently conduct their studies in real classroom situations. Although these real-life settings present opportunities for greater generalization, they do not automatically result in externally valid research. Campbell and Stanley (1966) also discussed the factors that may lead to reduced generalizability of research to other settings, persons, variables, and measurement instruments. The factors they discussed include the following:

Interference of Prior Treatment

In some types of experiments the effect of one treatment may carry over to subsequent treatments. In an educational experiment learning produced by the first treatment is not completely erased, and its influence may accrue to the advantage, or disadvantage, of the second treatment. This is one of the major limitations of the single-group, equated-materials experimental design in which the same subjects serve as members of both control and experimental groups. If an equated-materials design is necessary, a counterbalanced design will generally control for this threat.

The Artificiality of the Experimental Setting   — *has nothing to do w/ reality (ex: ADHD)*

In an effort to control extraneous variables the researcher imposes careful controls that may introduce a sterile or artificial atmosphere not at all like the real life situation to which generalization is desired. The reactive effect of the experimental process is a constant threat.

Interaction Effect of Testing

The use of a pretest at the beginning of a study may sensitize individuals by making them more aware of concealed purposes of the researcher and may serve as a stimulus to change. This is a different potential problem than that of testing, discussed earlier as a threat to internal validity.

With testing, the threat is that the pretest will affect the subjects' performance on the posttest in a direct fashion. That is easily controlled by having a control group. In the case of the interaction effect of testing, there is a more difficult problem. Here the pretest may alert the experimental group to some aspect of the interventions that is not present for the control group. That is, the pretest may interact differently with the experimental intervention than it does with the control or placebo conditions. To avoid this threat requires random assignment and either no pretest or the Solomon four-group design discussed in the next section, Experimental Design.

Interaction of Selection and Treatment

Educational researchers are rarely, if ever, able to randomly select samples from the wide population of interest or randomly assign to groups; consequently, generalization from samples to populations is hazardous. Samples used in most classroom experiments are usually composed of intact groups, not of randomly selected individuals. They are based on an accepted invitation to participate. Some school officials agree to participate; others refuse. One cannot assume that samples taken from cooperating schools are necessarily representative of the target population, which includes schools that would not cooperate. Such schools are usually characterized by faculties that have higher morale, less insecurity, greater willingness to try a new approach, and a greater desire to improve their performance.

The Extent of Treatment Verification

Because of the potential threat of experimenter bias, most researchers have research assistants or others who are not directly involved in the formulation of the research hypotheses deliver the treatment. This leads to a potential threat to external validity. Was the treatment administered as intended and described by the researcher? The researcher must have a verification procedure (e.g., direct observation, videotape) to make sure that the treatment was properly administered.

After reading about these threats to experimental validity, the beginner is probably ready to conclude that behavioral research is too hazardous to attempt. Particularly outside of the laboratory, ideal experimental conditions and controls are never likely to prevail. However, an understanding of these threats is important so that the researcher can make every effort to remove or minimize their influence. If one were to wait for a research setting free from all threats, no research would ever be carried out. Knowing the limitations and doing the best that he or she can under the circumstances, the researcher may conduct experiments, reach valid conclusions, provide answers to important questions, and solve significant problems.

EXPERIMENTAL DESIGN

Experimental design is the blueprint of the procedures that enable the researcher to test hypotheses by reaching valid conclusions about relationships between independent and dependent variables. Selection of a particular design is based on the purposes of the experiment, the type of variables to be manipulated, and the conditions or limiting factors under which it is conducted. The design deals with such practical problems as how subjects are to be assigned to experimental and control groups, the way variables are to be manipulated and controlled, the way extraneous variables are to be controlled, how observations are to be made, and the type of statistical analysis to be employed in interpreting data relationships.

The adequacy of experimental designs is judged by the degree to which they eliminate or minimize threats to experimental validity. Three categories are presented here:

1. *Pre-experimental design* is the least effective, for it provides either no control group or no way of equating the groups that are used.
2. *True experimental design* employs randomization to provide for control of the equivalence of groups and exposure to treatment.
3. *Quasi-experimental design* provides a less satisfactory degree of control, used only when randomization is not feasible.

A complete discussion of experimental design would be too lengthy and complex for this introductory treatment. Therefore, only a relatively few designs are described. Readers may wish to refer to Campbell and Stanley's (1966) and Cook and Campbell's (1979) excellent treatments of the subject, in which many more designs are described.

In discussing experimental designs, we have followed Campbell and Stanley's symbol system:

R   random assignment of subjects to groups or treatments
X   exposure of a group to an experimental (treatment) variable
C   exposure of a group to the control or placebo condition
O   observation or test administered

Pre-Experimental Designs

The *least adequate* of designs is characterized by (1) the lack of a control group, or (2) a failure to provide for the equivalence of a control group.

The One-Shot Case Study

$$X \quad O$$

Carefully studied results of a treatment are compared with a general expectation of what would have happened if the treatment had not been applied. This design provides the weakest basis for generalization.

Mr. Jones used a 25-minute film on racial integration in his junior high school history class. In a test administered after the showing of the film, the mean score was 86 (a high score indicated a favorable attitude toward acceptance of all racial groups). Mr. Jones believes that the mean score was higher than it would have been had the film not been viewed and, as he recalls, higher than the mean score of a test that he had administered to a similar class several years before. He concludes that the film has been effective in reducing racial prejudice.

However, Mr. Jones has come to this conclusion on the basis of inadequate data. The reader has no way of knowing if a change has occurred because of the lack of a pretest or if a similar group who had not seen the film (a control group) would have scored differently from the group viewing the film. This design is the poorest available and should not be used.

The One-Group, Pretest–Posttest Design

$$O_1 \quad X \quad O_2$$

O_1 = pretest O_2 = posttest

This design provides some improvement over the first, for the effects of the treatment are judged by the difference between the pretest and the posttest scores. However, no comparison with a control group is provided.

In the same setting Mr. Jones administered a pretest before showing the film and a posttest after the viewing. He computed the mean difference between the pretest and the posttest scores and found that the mean had increased from 52 to 80, a mean gain of 28 score points. He also apparently detected some temporary improvement in attitude toward racial integration. He concludes that there has been a significant improvement in attitude as a result of the students' viewing the film. But what about the sensitizing effect of the pretest items that may have made the students aware of issues that they had not even thought of before? What would the gain have been if the pretest and the posttest had been administered to another class that had not viewed the film? Threats to the internal validity that are not controlled include history, maturation, testing, and so forth. External validity is also poor.

The Static-Group Comparison Design

X O

C O

This design compares the status of a group that has received an experimental treatment with one that has not. There is no provision for establishing the equivalence of the experimental and control groups, a very serious limitation.

A beginning researcher administered the 25-minute racial integration film to a group of elementary teachers in one school. He then administered the attitude scale and computed the mean score. At another elementary school he administered the attitude scale to teachers who had not viewed the film. A comparison of mean scores showed that the teachers who had viewed the film had a higher mean score than those who had not. He concluded that the film was an effective device in reducing racial prejudice.

What evidence did he have that the initial attitudes of the groups were equivalent? Without some evidence of equivalence of the control and experimental groups, attributing the difference to the experimental variable is unwarranted.

Campbell and Stanley (1966) provide a table that quickly describes which threats to the internal and external validity of a study are controlled by each of the pre-experimental and true experimental designs. Table 6.1 presents Campbell and Stanley's Table 1. They refer to two threats to external validity differently in this table than is done in the test. Campbell and Stanley's "reactive arrangements" is the artificiality of experimental setting and their "multiple X [X means treatment] interference" is the interference of prior treatment. They also shorten the names of some threats in the list of internal threats.

True Experimental Designs

In a true experiment the equivalence of the experimental and control groups is provided by random assignment of subjects to experimental and control treatments. Although it is difficult to arrange a true experimental design, particularly in school

TABLE 6.1   Summary Table from Campbell & Stanley (1966).

TABLE 1
SOURCES OF INVALIDITY FOR DESIGNS 1–6

| | Sources of Invalidity | | | | | | | | | | | |
| | Internal | | | | | | | | External | | | |
	History	Maturation	Testing	Instrumentation	Regression	Selection	Mortality	Interaction of Selection and Maturation, etc.	Interaction of Testing and X	Interaction of Selection and X	Reactive Arrangements	Multiple-X Interference
Pre-Experimental Designs:												
1. One-Shot Case Study X O	−	−				−	−			−		
2. One-Group Pretest–Posttest Design O X O	−	−	−	−	?	+	+	−	−	−		?
3. Static-Group Comparison X O O	+	?	+	+	+	−	−	−		−		
True Experimental Designs:												
4. Pretest–Posttest Control Group Design R O X O R O O	+	+	+	+	+	+	+	+	−	?	?	
5. Solomon Four-Group Design R O X O R O O R X O R O	+	+	+	+	+	+	+	+	+	?	?	
6. Posttest–Only Control Group Design R X O R O	+	+	+	+	+	+	+	+	+	?	?	

Note: In the tables, a minus indicates a definite weakness, a plus indicates that the factor is controlled, a question mark indicates a possible source of concern, and a blank indicates that the factor is not relevant.

It is with extreme reluctance that these summary tables are presented because they are apt to be "too helpful," and to be depended upon in place of the more complex and qualified presentation in the text. No + or − indicator should be respected unless the reader comprehends why it is placed there. In particular, it is against the spirit of this presentation to create uncomprehended fears of, or confidence in, specific designs.

classroom research, it is the strongest type of design and should be used whenever possible. Three experimental designs are discussed in the following sections:

The Posttest-Only, Equivalent-Groups Design

$$R \quad X \quad O_1$$

$$R \quad C \quad O_2$$

This design is one of the most effective in minimizing the threats to experimental validity. It differs from the static group comparison design in that experimental and control groups are equated by random assignment. At the conclusion of the experimental period the difference between the mean test scores of the experimental and control groups is subjected to a test of statistical significance, usually a *t* test or an analysis of variance. The assumption is that the means of randomly assigned experimental and control groups from the same population will differ only to the extent that random sample means from the same population will differ as a result of sampling error. If the difference between the means is too great to attribute to sampling error, the difference may be attributed to the treatment variable effect.

The researcher randomly selects 80 students from a school population of 450 sophomores. The 80 students are randomly assigned to experimental and control treatments, using 40 as the experimental group and 40 as the control group. The experimental group is taught the concepts of congruence of triangles by an experimental procedure method X, and the control group is taught the same set of concepts by the usual method, method C. Time of day, treatment length in time, and other factors are equated. At the end of a 3-week period the experimental and control groups are administered a test, and the difference between mean scores is subjected to a test of statistical significance. The difference between mean scores is found to favor the experimental group but not by an amount that is statistically significant. The researcher rightly concludes that the superiority of the X group could well have been the result of sampling error and that there was no evidence of the superiority of the X method. If, on the other hand, the finding was that the difference between the means was sufficient to be statistically significant, the researcher would have rejected the null hypothesis and stated that her research hypothesis was supported.

The Pretest–Posttest Equivalent-Groups Design

$$R \quad O_1 \quad X \quad O_2 \qquad X \text{ gain} = O_2 - O_1 \qquad O_1 \, O_3 = \text{pretests}$$

$$R \quad O_3 \quad C \quad O_4 \qquad C \text{ gain} = O_4 - O_3 \qquad O_2 \, O_4 = \text{posttests}$$

This design is similar to the previously described design, except that pretests are administered before the application of the experimental and control treatments and posttests at the end of the treatment period. Gain scores may be compared and subjected to a test of the significance of the difference between means. Pretest scores can also be used in analysis of covariance to statistically control for any differences between the groups at the beginning of the study. This is a strong design, but there may be a possibility of the influence of the interaction effect of testing with the experimental variable.

Laney (1993) conducted a pretest–posttest true experiment to study the relative impact of two interventions on first graders' understanding of economic concepts. He randomly assigned 31 first-grade students to two groups. Both groups set up and operated a market economy in their classrooms, but one group received economic instruction (referred to as "debriefing") after each "market day," and the other group dictated a story about the experience (a placebo condition). The purposes of the study were to determine what misconceptions first-grade students have about economic concepts and to determine if the debriefing sessions when added to the market experience, were superior to the experience alone, as the theory being studied suggested. The results clearly indicated that the experience with instruction was superior to the experience-only condition. Laney added a third group the following year that did not get the market experience but did get the instruction (debriefing). This group was added to study whether the instruction was the sole critical condition for the learning of economics rather than experience being critical, too. This group was found to be superior to the experience-only group, but the experience and instruction group was found to a have a more advanced understanding of economics than the instruction-only control group. Thus, economic concepts can be learned best by first graders by combining experience with instruction. The complete text of this study appears at the end of this chapter as the sample article.

Watanabe, Hare, and Lomax (1984) also reported on a study that included a pretest–posttest equivalent-groups design. This study compared a procedure for teaching eighth-grade students to be better able to predict the content of newspaper stories from their headlines than a control group of eighth-grade students. A pilot study, reported in their article, indicated that even good middle school readers have difficulty predicting the content of news stories from the headlines but that college students have no trouble with this task. Because the eighth graders they surveyed reported reading primarily comics, movie, and sport sections (a fact which might explain their poor prediction of content from headlines) and because most teachers would prefer that their students read more of the newspaper, the authors felt that it would be useful to determine if a training program could teach eighth graders how to better understand headlines.

Watanabe et al. randomly assigned 46 eighth graders to either headline reading instruction (experimental group) or regular reading instruction (control group). All 46 students were asked to read 20 headlines and predict story content prior to, and after, a 3-week period of instruction. The authors scored each attempt to predict story content on a scale of 0 to 4, with 0 indicating that the students' response explained nothing and 4 indicating an "on-target potential prediction" (pp. 439–440). Thus, each student could receive a score from 0 to 80 on each of the testings.

At the end of the 3 weeks of instruction, the authors compared the two groups using analysis of covariance (ANCOVA) and found that the experimental group was better able to predict story content from headlines after training than the control group. ANCOVA was used because even with random assignment the groups were not exactly equal. ANCOVA permitted the authors to statistically control for differences on the pretest so that posttest differences would not be due to initial differences before training.

The Solomon Four-Group Design

$$R \quad O_1 \quad X \quad O_2$$
$$R \quad O_3 \quad C \quad O_4$$
$$R \quad \quad X \quad O_5$$
$$R \quad \quad C \quad O_6$$

In this design

1. Subjects are randomly assigned to four groups.
2. Two groups receive the experimental treatment (X).
3. One experimental group receives a pretest (O_1).
4. Two groups (control) do not receive treatment (C).
5. One control group receives a pretest (O_3).
6. All four groups receive posttests (O_2 O_4 O_5 O_6).

The design is really a combination of the two two-group designs previously described, the posttest only and the pretest–posttest. The Solomon Four-Group Design permits the evaluation of the effects of testing, history, and maturation. Analysis of variance is used to compare the four posttest scores; analysis of covariance may be used to compare gains in O_2 and O_4.

Because this design provides for two simultaneous experiments, the advantages of a replication are incorporated. A major difficulty is finding enough subjects to assign randomly to four equivalent groups.

Quasi-Experimental Designs

These designs provide control of when and to whom the measurement is applied, but *because random assignment to experimental and control treatments has not been applied,* the equivalence of the groups is not assured. Of the many quasi-experimental designs, only five are described. See Cook and Campbell (1979) for a comprehensive review of quasi-experimental designs. Campbell and Stanley (1966) again provide a table that quickly describes which threats to the internal and external validity of a study are controlled by each of the quasi-experimental designs described. Table 6.2 on page 176 presents Campbell and Stanley's Table 2.

The Pretest–Posttest Nonequivalent-Groups Design

$$O_1 \quad X \quad O_2 \qquad X \text{ Gain} = O_2 - O_1 \qquad O_1 \, O_3 = \text{pretests}$$
$$O_3 \quad C \quad O_4 \qquad C \text{ Gain} = O_4 - O_3 \qquad O_2 \, O_4 = \text{posttests}$$

– No random assignment

This design is often used in classroom experiments when experimental and control groups are such naturally assembled groups as intact classes, which may be

TABLE 6.2   Summary Table from Campbell & Stanley (1966)

TABLE 2
SOURCES OF INVALIDITY FOR QUASI-EXPERIMENTAL DESIGNS 7–12

| | Sources of Validity | | | | | | | | | | | |
| | Internal | | | | | | | | External | | | |
	History	Maturation	Testing	Instrumentation	Regression	Selection	Mortality	Interaction of Selection and Maturation, etc.	Interaction of Testing and X	Interaction of Selection and X	Reactive Arrangements	Multiple-X Interference
Quasi-Experimental Designs:												
7. Time Series $O\ O\ O\ OXO\ O\ O\ O$	−	+	+	?	+	+	+	+	−	?	?	
8. Equivalent Time Samples Design $X_1O\ X_0O\ X_1O\ X_0O$, etc.	+	+	+	+	+	+	+	+	−	?	−	−
9. Equivalent Materials Samples Design $M_aX_1O\ M_bX_0O\ M_cX_1O\ M_dX_0O$, etc.	+	+	+	+	+	+	+	+	−	?	?	−
11. Counterbalanced Design $\underline{X_1O\ X_2O\ X_3O\ X_4O}$ $\underline{X_2O\ X_4O\ X_1O\ X_3O}$ $\underline{X_3O\ X_1O\ X_4O\ X_2O}$ $X_4O\ X_3O\ X_2O\ X_1O$	+	+	+	+	+	+	+	?	?	?	?	−

similar. The difference between the mean of the O_1 and O_2 scores and the difference between the mean of the O_3 and O_4 scores, respectively (mean-gain scores) are tested for statistical significance. Analysis of covariance may be used. Because this design may be the only feasible one, the comparison is justifiable, but the results should be interpreted cautiously.

Two first-grade classes in a school were selected for an experiment. One group was taught by the initial teaching alphabet (ITA) approach to reading, and the other was taught by the traditional alphabet approach. Prior to the introduction of the two reading methods and again at the end of the school year, both groups were administered a standardized reading test, and the mean gain scores of the two groups were compared. The ITA group showed a significant superiority in test scores over the conventional alphabet group. However, without some evidence of the equivalence of the groups in intelligence, maturity, readiness, and other factors at the beginning of the experimental period, conclusions should be cautiously interpreted.

The Follow-Through Planned Variation Study

An interesting example of the pretest–posttest nonequivalent groups design was the *Follow-Through Planned Variation Study* (Abt Associates, 1977), conceived in the late 1960s and initiated and funded by the United States Office of Education. The purpose of the program was to implement and evaluate a variety of compensatory programs extending the services of Project Head Start for disadvantaged children into the primary grades. Head Start was a large-scale enterprise including many innovative instructional models and involving the expenditure of more than a half billion dollars. The study extended over a period of more than 9 years, with more than 79,000 first-, second-, and third-grade children participating. Of the 20 different instructional models and 170 projects, 17 models and 70 projects were selected for evaluation. Approximately 2% of the total number of children in the program were included in the study.

Participation by school districts was voluntary, with each district selecting the particular model that it wished to implement and helping to choose the groups that were to be used as controls. Treatments were not randomly assigned, nor control groups randomly selected.

The unit of analysis was pupil mean gain for groups K–3 and 1–3 growth scores, statistically compared by instructional model and by project, using variants of linear regression and analysis of covariance. Outcome measures were derived from gain scores on the following measuring instruments:

1. *The Metropolitan Achievement Test Battery* covering such basic skills as reading comprehension, spelling, word usage and analysis, and mathematical computation, concepts, and problem solving.
2. *The Raven's Coloured Matrices Test,* a nonverbal test of problem-solving ability, requiring the manipulation of geometric patterns, essentially a measure of intelligence rather than a measure of learning outcomes.
3. *The Coopersmith Self-Image Inventory,* a measure of self-esteem but questioned on the grounds that it required a maturity of judgment beyond the competence of primary-age children.
4. *The Intellectual Achievement Responsibility Scale,* which attempts to assess the child's experience of success or failure, indicating the degree to which the child attributes success to internal or external causes. This instrument was also judged to require insights beyond the maturity level of small children.

There have been many analyses and evaluations of the program by official and independent agencies funded by the United States Office of Education and by private philanthropic foundations. Among the evaluating agencies were the Office of Education; Abt Associates, Inc.; The Stanford Research Institute; The Huron Institute; and The Center for Research and Curriculum Evaluation of the University of Illinois.

It is unlikely that any large-scale study has been scrutinized so extensively concerning research design, procedures employed, and interpretation of the data. There have been critiques of the evaluations and critiques of the critiques, with sharp disagreement on most aspects of the study (Anderson, St. Pierre, Proper, & Stebbins, 1978; House, Glass, McLean, & Walker, 1978; Wisler, Burns, & Iwamoto, 1978).

However, the consensus is that the findings were disappointing because most of the experimental effects were negligible. Only a few of the treatment effects produced as much as a one-quarter standard deviation change. (This concept is discussed in Chapter 10.) Of those that met this criterion, two instructional models with at least one positive effect were structured approaches. Three models with at least one negative effect were unstructured approaches. Few of either cognitive, structured approaches or child-centered, unstructured approaches yielded significant effects.

Much of the disagreement centered around the reasons the study was ineffective. Several explanations have been suggested.

1. The research was deficient in design, implementation, statistical analysis, and interpretation. Because experimental treatments were not randomly selected and control groups were not randomly assigned, mismatching resulted, and comparisons were really made between different populations.
2. There was great inter-site difference in effectiveness within a given instructional model. Most of the within-model differences were greater than the between-models difference. There may have been serious deficiencies in the competence of those who implemented the innovative procedures or in the actual method implemented, even though the teachers and their teacher aides were specially trained and their activities monitored by the project sponsors.
3. The measuring instruments may have been incompatible with the goals of the project because of inadequate identification and definition of appropriate outcome variables. The more effective instruments seemed to focus on basic skills or traditional educational goals rather than on goals ordinarily associated with unstructured approaches to education. Some measured intellectual status rather than achievable learning goals. Others appeared to require a maturity of response too complex for primary-age children.

Not all reactions to the study were negative. Hodges, a member of the Follow Through Task Force, lists a number of reasons for viewing the program as significant and worthwhile. "Just because Follow Through has not proved to be an easy, workable, inexpensive solution for all the educational problems of poor children does not mean it should be dismissed as just another failure in compensatory education" (Hodges, 1978, p. 191).

A more recent study examined the relative effects of age and schooling on the rapid developmental changes that generally occur between 5 and 7 years of age (Morrison, Smith, & Dow-Ehrensberger, 1995). This phenomenon of a major shift in the way children think, cognitively, socially, and even morally, is generally accepted and usually has been thought to be due to maturation. This view is based on Piaget's theory of cognitive development. However, in recent years research has suggested that the experiences children have in schools may play a major role in these changes. Because children are arbitrarily assigned to start school in a given year depending on their birth date (e.g., must be 6 by March 1, December 1, or September 1, depending on the district/state, to enter first grade), it is possible to keep age relatively stable and study only the schooling effect by using children who just made the cutoff date to enter school or who just missed the date. This is what Morrison, Smith, and Dow-Ehrensberger did. The cutoff date in the community they studied was turning 6 by March 1 to enter first grade. Thus, they compared children who turned 6 in January or February and entered 1st grade (young first graders) with those who turned 6 in March or April and entered kindergarten instead (old kindergarten students). The first-grade group of 10 children were, on average, 41 days older than the 10 children in the kindergarten group. The children were tested three times on measures of short-term memory and phonological skill at the beginning of the study in grade 1 or kindergarten (depending on the age group they were in), at the beginning of first or second grade, and at the beginning of second or third grade, again depending on their group. The findings of this study indicated a strong schooling effect in particular for short-term memory. It seems that grade 1 experiences enhanced short-term memory regardless of age in first grade. The phonological measure was affected by both schooling and age. Thus, this design permitted the researchers to support maturational theories (e.g., Piaget) but also demonstrate that experiences in school play an important role in the changes that seem to occur between the ages of 5 and 7.

Most important for readers of this text, this study had to be quasi-experimental. Although a better design would have taken children born between January 1 and April 30 and randomly assigned them to kindergarten or first grade, this was not possible for two reasons. First, the school district would not go along with such random assignment because it would change a basic policy and might have led to parents being very upset and possibly suing the district. Second, random assignment would be unethical because of the unknown effects of having older children in kindergarten and younger children in first grade than would be typical for this district.

In behavioral research the random selection and assignment of subjects to experimental and control groups may be impracticable. Because of administrative difficulties in arranging school experiments, it may be necessary to use the same group as both the experimental and control group. These designs have two apparently attractive features. Three of these designs (time-series, equivalent time-samples, and equivalent materials) are described below. They can be carried out with one intact group without a noticeable reorganization of the classroom schedule. The changes in procedures and testing can be concealed within ordinary classroom routines. Artificiality can be minimized, for the procedures can be introduced without the subjects' awareness of participation in an experiment.

The Time-Series Design
At periodic intervals observations (measurements) are applied to individuals or a group. An experimental variable (X) is introduced, and its effect may be judged

by the change or gain from the measurement immediately before to the one just after its introduction. The purpose of the series of measurements before and after the intervention or treatment is to demonstrate little or no change except from immediately before to just after the intervention.

In the time-series experimental design, a measured change or gain from observation 4 (O_4) to observation 5 (O_5) would indicate that the treatment had an effect. This design is particularly sensitive to the failure to control the extraneous variable, history, for it is possible that some distracting, simultaneous event at the time of the intervention would provide a rival hypothesis for the change.

$$O_1 \quad O_2 \quad O_3 \quad O_4 \quad X \quad O_5 \quad O_6 \quad O_7 \quad O_8$$

The diagram showing one X and several Os does not necessarily represent the relative number of sessions for each. It may be that each O represents one measurement, and the single X represents an intervention of several weeks. Although it is better to have several observations, as shown, it is not always possible to have this many. For instance, a time-series experiment by a student of the second author used only two pre-intervention and two post-intervention measures. Because this study was measuring the effect of a program to reduce the number of criminal victimizations of students with disabilities, it was necessary to have a 2-month period between measurements in order to have a sufficient number of victimizations for each period measured. That is, O_1 in November measured September and October crimes against the subjects; O_2 in January measured crimes in November and December, and so on for O_3 and O_4. In this study the intervention/instruction occurred in January, followed two and four months later with measures of victimizations. The findings showed no changes between O_1 and O_2 or between O_3 and O_4 but a significant reduction in victimizations from O_2 to O_3. Thus, the intervention/instruction appeared successful in reducing crimes committed against persons with disabilities.

The Equivalent Time-Samples Design

Instead of having equivalent samples of persons, it may be necessary to use one group as the experimental and control group. In this design the experimental condition X_1 is present between some observations and not (X_0) between others. This may be diagrammed as shown below, although the number of observations and interventions vary and the alternation of the experimental condition with the control condition is normally random rather than systematic as shown here. This design is the group design that is analogous to the A-B-A-B design for single-subject research discussed in Chapter 7.

$$O_1 \quad X_1 \quad O_2 \quad X_0 \quad O_3 \quad X_1 \quad O_4 \quad X_0 \quad O_5$$

A study by Hall et al. (1973) provides an excellent illustration of the equivalent time-samples design. Five subjects, identified as the most violently aggressive, were selected from a group of 46 boys with mental retardation living in an institution dormitory. Their ages ranged from 12 to 16 (mean = 13.8), and their IQs from 40 to 62 (mean = 50). Each individual was observed for 10 weeks in 10 randomly selected 3-minute periods during which time acts of aggressive behavior were recorded. Acts were classified as motor aggressive (throwing objects, kicking, fighting, scratching) and nonmotor aggressive (verbal abuse, screaming or shouting, insubordination).

The observations were scheduled in four periods:

1. **Observation (baseline)**   session 1
2. **On-reinforcement**   sessions 2, 3, 4, 5
3. **Off-reinforcement**   sessions 6, 7
4. **On-reinforcement**   sessions 8, 9, 10

Positive reinforcement as a reward for nonaggressive behavior consisted of candy, praise, or trips to the canteen. Punishment following aggressive acts consisted of ostracizing from group activities, taking away a favorite toy, or reprimanding verbally. Two observers were employed, one observing motor aggressive acts, the other, nonmotor aggressive acts.

The researchers concluded that reinforcement affected the amount of aggressive output. Motor aggressive behavior was reduced more effectively than nonmotor aggressive behavior (see Figure 6.1 on page 182). To assess the permanence of behavior change after the conclusion of the experiment, a phase-out period of 89 days of observation was scheduled. The only reinforcement used was the posting of stars for nonaggressive behavior. Observations during the phase-out period indicated much more acceptable dormitory behavior.

Designs of this type have a number of limitations. Although they may minimize the effect of history, it is possible that they may increase the influence of maturation, unstable instrumentation, testing, and experimental mortality.

The Equivalent Materials, Pretest, Posttest Design

$$O_1 \quad X_{MA} \quad O_2 \quad O_3 \quad X_{MB} \quad O_4$$

X_{MA} = teaching method A X_{MB} = teaching method B

O_1 and O_3 are pretests O_2 and O_4 are posttests

Another experimental design, using the same group or class for both experimental and control groups, involves two or more cycles. The class may be used as a control group in the first cycle and as an experimental group in the second. The order of exposure to experimental and control can be reversed—experimental first and control following.

Essential to this design is the selection of learning materials different but as nearly equal as possible in interest to the students and in difficulty of comprehension. An example may help to clarify the procedure.

Ms. Smith hypothesized that the students in her class who were used to background music while doing their homework would learn to spell more efficiently

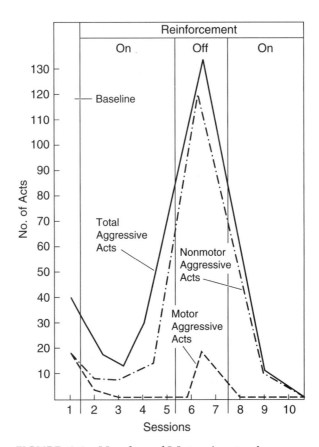

FIGURE 6.1 **Number of Motor Aggressive, Nonmotor Aggressive, and Total Aggressive Acts During On-Reinforcement and Off-Reinforcement Experimental Conditions**

in the classroom if music were provided. Because she was unable to arrange a parallel group experiment, she decided to use her class as both an experimental and a control group.

To equate the words to be learned, she randomly selected 200 words from an appropriate graded word list and randomly assigned 100 words each to list A and list B. For cycle I, the control cycle, she pretested the class on word list A. Then for 20 minutes each day the students studied the words, using drill and the usual spelling rules. At the end of 2 weeks she retested the class and computed the mean gain score in correct spelling.

For cycle II, the experimental cycle, she pretested the class on word list B. Then for 20 minutes each day, with soft, continuous music in the background (the experimental condition), the students studied their word list, using the same drill and spelling rules. At the end of the second 2-week period she retested the class and computed the mean gain score in correct spelling.

The mean gain score for the experimental cycle was significantly greater than the mean gain score for the control cycle. She concluded that the introduction of the experimental variable had indeed improved the effectiveness of the learning experience.

The apparent simplicity and logic of this design are somewhat misleading and when examined in light of the threats of experimental validity, the design's weaknesses become apparent:

1. It is often difficult to select equated materials to be learned. For types of learning other than spelling, finding learning materials that are equally interesting, difficult, and unfamiliar would be a serious problem.
2. As the students enter the second cycle, they are older and more mature (if each instructional method is brief this may not be a problem). They also have more experience.
3. Outside events (history) would be more likely to affect the experience in one cycle than in the other.
4. There would be an influence of prior treatment carrying over from the first cycle to the second.
5. The effects of testing would be more likely to have a greater impact on the measurement of gain in the second cycle.
6. Mortality, or loss of subjects from the experiment, would be more likely in an experimental design spread over a longer period of time.
7. If the experimenter's judgment is a factor in assessment of the students' progress, contamination, the experimenter's knowledge of subject performance in the first cycle could possibly influence evaluation of performance in the second.

Some of the limitations of the equivalent-materials, single-group, pretest–posttest design can be partially minimized by a series of replications in which the order of exposure to experimental and control treatments is reversed. This process, known as *rotation*, is illustrated by this pattern in a four-cycle experiment.

$$\begin{array}{cccc}
\text{I} & \text{II} & \text{III} & \text{IV} \\
O_1 \ X \ O_2 & O_3 \ C \ O_4 & O_5 \ C \ O_6 & O_7 \ X \ O_8
\end{array}$$

$$O_1 \ O_3 \ O_5 \ O_7 = \text{pretests} \qquad O_2 \ O_4 \ O_6 \ O_8 = \text{posttests}$$

If the experimental treatment yielded significantly greater gains regardless of the order of exposure, its effectiveness could be accepted with greater confidence. However, it is apparent that this design is not likely to equate materials, subjects, or experimental conditions.

All single-group experimental designs are sensitive to the influences of many of the threats to validity previously mentioned in this chapter: history, maturation, unstable instrumentation, testing, and experimental mortality. Replication of the studies, using different units as subjects, is an effective way to improve their validity. However, single-group experiments may be performed when randomly equated group designs cannot be arranged.

Counterbalanced Designs

These are designs in which experimental control derives from having all the subjects receive all the treatment conditions. The subjects are placed into, in the case of this example, four groups. Each of the groups then receives all four treatments but in different orders. This may be diagrammed as follows:

Replication	O_1X_1	O_2X_2	O_3X_3	O_4X_4	O_5
1	Group A	B	C	D	
2	Group B	D	A	C	
3	Group C	A	D	B	
4	Group D	C	B	A	

In the first sequence following a pretest (O_1), group A receives Treatment 1, group B receives Treatment 2, group C receives Treatment 3, and group D receives Treatment 4. After a second test (O_2), each group then receives a second treatment, and so on. Thus, each group receives all treatments, and each treatment is first, second, third, or fourth in the order received by one of the groups.

This design has excellent internal validity because history, maturation, regression, selection, and mortality are all generally well controlled. The major limitation is that an order effect could wipe out any potential differences among the treatments. Four randomly assigned groups in which each group receives a different treatment would therefore be preferable. Thus, this design should be used when random assignment is not possible and when it is expected that the different treatments will not interfere too much with each other. This design is particularly useful when the researcher uses preassigned groups (i.e., preexisting classes) and the number of groups is a multiplicand of the number of treatments (e.g., 4 treatments with 4, 8, 12, or 16 groups).

Factorial Designs

When more than one independent variable is included in a study, whether a true experiment or a quasi-experiment, a factorial design is necessary. Because most real-world outcomes are the result of a number of factors acting in combination, most significant experimentation involves the analysis of the interaction of a number of variable relationships. By using factorial designs researchers can determine, for example, if the treatment interacts significantly with gender or age. That is, the experimenter can determine if one treatment is more effective with boys and another with girls, or if older girls do better on the treatment than younger girls, whereas older and younger boys do equally well on the treatment.

Treatment

Experimental   Control

FIGURE 6.2   Factorial Design

The simplest case of a factorial design would be to have two independent variables with two conditions of each, known as a *2 × 2 factorial design*. This design would be used if a researcher decided to compare a new (experimental) method of teaching reading to reading-disabled children with a commonly used (control) method and also wanted to determine if boys and girls would do differently on the two methods. Such a design would look like Figure 6.2.

With this design we have four *cells,* each of which represents a subgroup (experimental females, control females, experimental males, and control males). This design permits the researcher to determine if there is a significant overall effect, known as *main effect,* for treatment and/or gender. It also permits the determination of whether these two variables interact significantly such that boys do best in the experimental condition and girls do best in the control condition. If this were the case, the subjects in Cell 2 would have a higher average score than those in Cell 1, and the subjects in Cell 3 would outperform those in Cell 4.

The study by Morrison, Smith, and Dow-Ehrensberger (1995) that we described earlier in the section on pretest–posttest nonequivalent groups/designs includes a factorial design. In their study the first independent variable, described earlier, was age, with the conditions being young first graders or old kindergarten students determined by the birth date cutoff for admission to first grade. The other independent variable was experience in school, determined by the grades at which they were tested (e.g., the first test was at the beginning of kindergarten for one group but at the beginning of first grade for the second group). Thus, this study was a 2 × 3 design because there were two groups and three levels of experience, with the children being tested three times at one-year intervals. These authors found one significant interaction for the phonological measure (graphically represented in Figure 6.3 on page 186). The interaction effect indicated that young first-grade children at the beginning of second grade were superior in phonic skills to the old kindergarten children at the beginning of first grade (the second

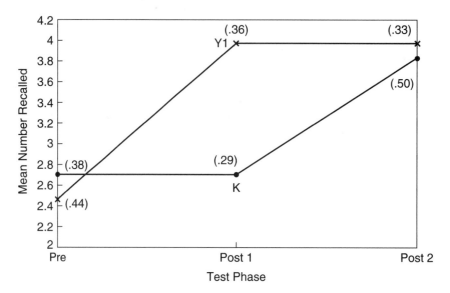

Figure 1 Mean number of pictures recalled by the kindergarten (K) and young grade one (Y1) groups across the three testing intervals (standard deviations in parentheses).

FIGURE 6.3   Interaction Effect from Morrison, Smith, & Dow-Ehrensberger (1995)

Used with permission of the author and the American Psychological Association.

test for each group) but that the two groups did not differ at the initial testing (beginning of first grade and beginning of kindergarten, respectively) or at the final testing (at the beginning of second grade and beginning of first grade, respectively). This finding along with the earlier reported finding of enhanced short-term memory from schooling was interpreted as indicating that schooling adds to the general maturational effect that has been found in children going from 5 to 7 years old. Thus, the belief that this change occurs only because of the so-called laws of cognitive development is no longer supported. Schooling appears to add significantly to this effect. In fact, for phonological skills, Figure 6.3 suggests that the experience of first grade is the critical component. As can be seen in Figure 6.3, it was the first-grade experience that made the difference in the growth curve. Both the young first graders and old kindergarten students showed significant growth during first grade (Post 1 for the first graders and Post 2 for the kindergarten students) and limited or no growth at the other times measured, kindergarten for one group and second grade for the other group.

Another factorial study by Nucci and Nucci (1982) examined the responses of children to the social transgressions (such as spitting on the ground) of their peers. They observed boys and girls between 7 and 10 and between 11 and 14 years of

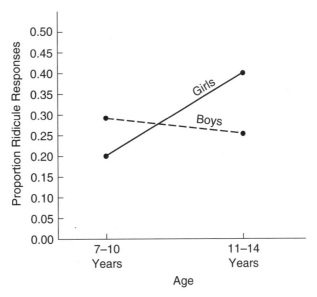

FIGURE 6.4 Interaction Effect

(Based on data from Nucci & Nucci, 1982.)

age and coded their observations of the responses into one of eight categories. They found an interaction effect of gender by age for just one of the categories. This interaction effect could be graphically represented as in Figure 6.4. As can be seen, the two lines actually cross, thus clearly indicating that "With increased age the girls provided greater frequencies of ridicule responses to [social transgressions] while the boys responded with approximately the same frequencies as at the younger age" (Nucci & Nucci, 1982, p. 1341). Figure 6.5 on page 188 shows an example of another type of response, stating the rule being violated, for which Nucci and Nucci found no interaction effect. Here there are two relatively parallel lines.

Of course, factorial designs can have more than two independent variables and more than two conditions of each variable. A study might have three treatment conditions (e.g., three methods of reading instruction), the two genders, three age groups, and three intelligence levels (gifted, average, and mildly retarded) as the independent variables. This would be a 3 × 2 × 3 × 3 design and would have a total of 54 subgroups or cells. Such designs are too complex for this elementary treatment. We mention such a complex design only to point out that these designs exist and that they are frequently appropriate and necessary. Advanced students may wish to refer to such sources as Glass and Hopkins (1996), Kirk (1995), and Winer (1971) for more detailed information.

This discussion, which has examined the many limitations of the experimental method in behavioral research, may convey a sense of futility. As is true in many other areas of significant human endeavor, researchers do not work under

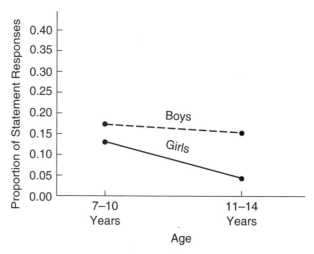

FIGURE 6.5   No Interaction Effect

(Based on data from Nucci & Nucci, 1982.)

ideal conditions. They must do the best they can under existing circumstances. They will find, however, that in spite of its limitations, the well-designed and well-executed experiment provides a legitimate method for testing hypotheses and making probability decisions about the relationships between variables.

Some variables cannot be manipulated. The ethical problems that would be raised if some others were manipulated indicates a place for such nonexperimental methods as *ex post facto* research. The researcher starts with the observation of dependent variables and goes back to the observation of independent variables that have previously occurred under uncontrolled conditions. Such studies are *not* experiments, for the researcher has had no control over the events; they occurred before he or she began the investigation. The description of cigarette-smoking cancer research in Chapter 5 is an example of *ex post facto* research. Qualitative research methods, discussed in Chapter 8, provide other ways of conducting research into areas that would be difficult or impossible to investigate with experimental methods.

SUMMARY

The experimental method provides a logical, systematic way to answer the question, "If this is done under carefully controlled conditions, what will happen?" To provide a precise answer, experimenters manipulate certain influences, or variables, and observe how the condition or behavior of the subject is affected or changed. Experimenters control or isolate the variables in such a way that they can be reasonably sure that the effects they observe can be attributed to the variables they have manipulated rather than to some other uncontrolled influences. In testing hypotheses or evaluating tentative answers to questions, experimenters make decisions based on probability rather than on certainty. Experimentation, the classic method of the laboratory, is the most powerful method for discovering and developing a body of knowledge about the prediction and control of events. The experimental method has been used with some success in the school classroom, where, to some degree, variables can be controlled.

The early applications of experimental method, based on John Stuart Mill's law of the single variable, have been replaced by the more effective applications of factorial designs made possible by the contributions of R. A. Fisher. His concept of equating groups by random selection of subjects and random assignment of treatments and his development of the analysis of variance and the analysis of covariance have made possible the study of complex multivariate relationships that are basic to the understanding of human behavior.

Experimenters must understand and deal with threats to the internal validity of the experiment so that the variable relationships they observe can be interpreted without ambiguity. They must also understand and deal with threats to the external validity of the experiment so that their findings can be extended beyond their experimental subjects and generalized to a wider population of interest.

Experimental design provides a plan, or blueprint, for experimentation. Three pre-experimental, three true-experimental, and five quasi-experimental designs have been presented, and their appropriate use, advantages, and disadvantages have been briefly discussed.

Experimentation is a sophisticated technique for problem solving and may not be an appropriate activity for the beginning researcher. It has been suggested that teachers may make their most effective contribution to educational research by identifying important problems that they encounter in their classrooms and by working cooperatively with research specialists in the conduct and interpretation of classroom experiments.

EXERCISES

1. Why is it more difficult to control extraneous variables in a classroom experiment than in a pharmaceutical laboratory experiment?

2. What significant element distinguishes a quasi-experiment from a true experiment?

3. Why is an *ex post facto* study not an experiment?

4. A researcher proposing a research project defines the dependent variable as "achievement in mathematics." What difficulty does this definition present? How would you improve it?

5. How could a double blind be applied in an educational experiment?

6. Under what circumstances could an independent variable in one study be a dependent variable in another study?

7. Why is randomization the best method for dealing with extraneous variables?

8. How could a high degree of experimental mortality seriously affect the validity of an experiment?

9. Read the report of an experiment in an educational research journal.
   a. Was the problem clearly stated?
   b. Were the variables defined in operational terms?
   c. Was the hypothesis clearly stated?
   d. Were the delimitations stated?
   e. Was the design clearly described?
   f. Were extraneous variables recognized? What provisions were made to control them?
   g. Were the population and the sampling methods described?
   h. Were appropriate methods used to analyze the data?
   i. Were the conclusions clearly presented?
   j. Were the conclusions substantiated by the evidence presented?

REFERENCES

Abt Associates (1977). *Education as experimentation: A planned variation model.* Cambridge, MA: Abt Associates. Also issued as *The follow through planned variation experiment series.* Washington, D. C.: U.S. Office of Education, 1978.

Anderson, R. B., St. Pierre, R. C., Proper, E. C., & Stebbins, L. B. (1978). Pardon us, but what was the question again? A response to the critique of the follow through evaluation. *Harvard Educational Review, 48,* 161–170.

Campbell, D. T., & Stanley, I. C. (1966). *Experimental and quasi-experimental designs for research.* Chicago: Rand McNally.

Cook, T. D., & Campbell, D. T. (1979). *The design and analysis of quasi-experiments for field settings.* Chicago: Rand McNally.

Glass, G. V., & Hopkins, K. D. (1996). *Statistical methods in education and psychology* (3rd ed.). Boston: Allyn & Bacon

Hall, H. V., Price, A. B., Shinedling, M., Peizer, S. B., & Massey, R. H. (1973). Control of aggressive behavior in a group of retardates using positive and negative reinforcement. *Training School Bulletin, 70,* 179–186.

Hays, W. L. (1981). *Statistics* (3rd ed.). New York: Holt, Rinehart, and Winston.

Hodges, W. L. (1978). The worth of the follow through experience. *Harvard Educational Review, 48,* 186–192.

House, E. L., Glass, C. V., McLean, L. D., & Walker, D. F. (1978). No simple answer: Critique of the follow through evaluation. *Harvard Educational Review, 48,* 128–160.

Kahn, J. V. (1984). Cognitive training and initial use of referential speech. *Topics in Language Disorders, 5,* 14–28.

Kerlinger, F. N. (1986). *Foundations of behavioral research* (3rd ed.). New York: Holt, Rinehart, and Winston.

Kirk, R. (1995). *Experimental design: Procedures for the behavioral sciences* (3rd ed.). Pacific Grove, CA: Brooks/Cole.

Laney, J. D. (1993). Experiential versus experience-based learning and instruction. *Journal of Educational Research, 86,* 228–236.

Mayo, E. (1960). *The human problems of an industrial civilization.* New York: Viking Press.

Mill, J. 5. (1873). *A system of logic.* New York: Harper and Row.

Morrison, F. J., Smith, L., & Dow-Ehrensberger, M. (1995). Education and cognitive development: A natural experiment. *Developmental Psychology, 31,* 789–799.

Nucci, L. P., & Nucci, M. 5. (1982). Children's responses to moral and social conventional transgressions in free-play settings. *Child Development, 53,* 1337–1342.

Shavelson, R. J. (1996). *Statistical reasoning for the behavioral sciences* (3rd ed.). Boston: Allyn and Bacon.

Watanabe, P., Hare, V. C., & Lomax, R. C. (1984). Predicting news story content from headlines: An instructional study. *Journal of Reading, 27,* 436–442.

Winer, B. I. (1971). *Statistical principles in experimental design.* New York: McGraw-Hill.

Wisler, C. E., Burns, C. P., & Iwamoto, D. (1978). Follow through redux: A response to the critique by House, Class, McLean, and Walker. *Harvard Educational Review, 48,* 177–185.

SAMPLE ARTICLE

*Journal of Educational Research, 86(4) 228–236, 1993. Reprinted with permission of the Helen Dwight Reid Educational Foundation. Published by Heldref Publications, 1319 Eighteenth St., N.W., Washington, D.C. 20036-1802. Copyright © 1993.

*concise
& clear*

Experiential Versus Experience-Based Learning and Instruction*

James D. Laney

Abstract: This study tested claims about the superiority of experience-based over experiential approaches to teaching economic concepts. Students were randomly assigned to three groups— experience-dictation, experience-debriefing, and debriefing-only. At pretest and posttest students were interviewed to probe their understanding of 10 basic economic concepts and to determine their proclivity to use the concept of cost–benefit analysis in a personal decision-making situation. Planned comparisons revealed the following statistically significant differences on the understanding-of-economic-concepts posttest: (a) the combined means of the experience-debriefing and debriefing-only groups were higher than the mean of the experience-dictation group and (b) the mean of the experience-debriefing group was higher than the mean of the debriefing-only group. No significant differences were found between groups on the use-of-cost benefit analysis measure. Overall, the findings support the superiority of experienced-based instruction.

*Part of
statement
of problem*

Only a few researchers have explored the economic thinking of preschool and primary-grade children. Of those, most (Ajello, Bombi, Pontecorvo, & Zuccermaglio, 1987; Armento, 1982; Berti, Bombi, & De Beni, 1986; Burris, 1976; Fox, 1978; Furth, 1980; Schug, 1981, 1983; Schug & Birkey, 1985; and Strauss, 1952) have undertaken interview studies in which they seek developmental patterns in economic reasoning. The findings of those studies suggest that economic thinking develops in an age-related, stage-like sequence. Summarizing across the aforementioned studies, Armento (1986) described children's concept response patterns as progressing "from egocentric to objective; from tautological, literal, and rule-oriented to generalizable; from concrete to abstract, and from inconsistent and narrow to consistent, flexible, and accurate" (p. 89).

According to Schug (1983), many young children exhibit unreflective economic reasoning characterized by (a) a preoccupation with the physical characteristics of the object or process being discussed, (b) egocentric thinking, (c) confusion in identifying causes and effects, and (d) an inclination to treat variables as interchangeable. Research on economic learning has demonstrated that young children tend to have many misconceptions about basic economic concepts indicative of unreflective economic reasoning. Specifically, young children have problems understanding and using such concepts as wants, scarcity, money, monetary value, exchange, change, profits (and what store owners do with the money received from customers), opportunity cost, and cost–benefit analysis (Armento, 1982; Burris,

1976; Fox, 1978; Furth, 1980; Kourilsky, 1987; Schug, 1981, 1983; Schug & Birkey, 1985; Strauss, 1952; Laney, 1990).

Most of the research on children's economic reasoning cited above has focused on spontaneous concept development that occurs as children experience economics in their daily lives. According to Schug (1981), an important question for future research is to determine whether economics *instruction* fosters the development of economic reasoning ability. Ajello et al. (1987), Berti et al. (1986), Laney (1989), Armento (1986), and Kourilsky (1983) have provided guidance on how to design economic instruction to achieve this end at the elementary school level.

Components of statement of problem

Berti et al. (1986) and Ajello et al. (1987) discovered that economic training changed third graders' conceptions of (a) profit and (b) work and profit, respectively. In the study by Berti et al., progress toward economic understanding was not dramatic, but it occurred when children (a) were given correct information about economic ideas and (b) found discrepancies between predicted and actual outcomes of economic events. In addition, Berti et al. suggested that having children talk about economic concepts may contribute to their progress in mastering those concepts.

Review of literature is well organized around problem & leads to research questions.

Laney's (1989) findings suggested that real-life experiences are better than vicarious experiences for promoting first graders' learning and retention of the economic concept of opportunity cost. Laney explained his results by suggesting that real-life experiences make economic concepts more meaningful and thus more memorable to students.

According to Armento (1986), children experience economic situations and events on a daily basis. She maintains that (a) play provides the best means for young children to explore their economic world and (b) the economic content emphasized during the early years is best taken from happenings in the children's everyday lives (e.g., buying. selling, making goods and services).

Kourilsky (1983) stressed that it is important for elementary school students to participate in economic experiences that are both personal and active. In defining the role of experience in economic concept acquisition, she distinguishes between experiential learning and experience-based learning. Kourilsky stated that experience with economic concepts (i.e., experiential learning) is not sufficient. She also found that substantive acquisition of economic concepts is dependent on experience-based learning; that is, experiences are followed by debriefings and discussions in which situations are analyzed and economic concepts derived. Kourilsky noted that debriefings focus students' attention on relevant ideas. To support her assertion, Kourilsky offered the following analogy: "Most of you played Monopoly as children, but probably few of you learned an extensive amount of economics from participating in the game" (p. 5).

Armento (1986) also downplayed experience, in and of itself, as the cause of a child's direct and predictable learning. She stated that the meanings constructed by a child from his or her economic experiences are most probably attributable to the child's cognitive capabilities at the moment, the value and motivational orientation of the child, the nature of the experience, and the child's prior knowledge.

Kourilsky has authored three experience-based economic education programs for elementary school students—Kinder-Economy (Grades K through 2), Mini-Society (Grades 3 through 6), and the Co-Learner Parent Education Program. Studies by Kourilsky (1977, 1981) and Cassuto (1980) have demonstrated the effectiveness of those programs in increasing participants' economic cognition,

but no previous study has tested Kourilsky's (1983) assertion regarding the superiority of experience-based over experiential approaches to economic education.

*clearly
stated*

RESEARCH QUESTIONS

In this study, I attempted to answer two research questions. The first question was
based on a suggestion for future research from Schug (1981). Does instruction in
economics foster the development of economic reasoning ability? Stated more specifically for the purposes of this study, what misconceptions do transitional first-grade
students have about economic concepts, and can those misconceptions be corrected through economics instruction? The second research question tested the
assertions or Kourilsky (1983) regarding experiential versus experience-based learning. Is experience-based learning superior to experiential learning in promoting the
acquisition and use of economic concepts among transitional first-grade students?

*not
clearly
defined*

METHOD

Transitional first-grade students were chosen as the population of interest for two
reasons. First, because of his or her maturational age level, the transitional first
grader is likely to have many misconceptions about basic economic concepts.
Second, transitional first-grade classrooms make use of developmentally appropriate practices, and the treatment conditions used in this study were designed in
accordance with such practices.

All of the transitional first-grade students in one elementary school in north
central Texas participated as subjects in the study. Thirty-one students made up
the sample, including 25 Caucasians, 5 African-Americans, and 1 Hispanic student. Twenty of the students were boys, and 11 were girls. None of the students
had received instruction in economics prior to the study.

Students' eligibility for placement in transitional first grade was determined
at the end of their kindergarten year. Placement in the program was dependent
on (a) the student's being 6 years of age by September 1 and (b) the student's having an approximate behavior age of 5½ years as indicated by his or her score on
an individually administered readiness test, the Maturational Assessment Test
(Hull House Publishing Company, 1988), given by the school counselor. In addition to the two main selection criteria listed above, parents' and teachers' observations were also taken into account. Parental permission was obtained before a
child's final placement in the program.

Students placed in transitional first grade were randomly assigned to one of
two classrooms at the beginning of the school year. At the start of the spring
semester, I randomly assigned the two treatment conditions to the two randomly
formed classrooms.

I used a pretest–posttest control group design. Subjects were pretested and
posttested on their understanding of economic concepts and on their use of cost–
benefit analysis. The two treatment conditions consisted of an experience–dictation
procedure (experiential learning) group and an experience–debriefing (experience-based
described learning) group. The pretreatment, treatment, and posttreatment phases of the study
adequately are described in detail below.
for possible   In the pretreatment and posttreatment phases of the study, I conducted inter-
replication views with each subject, probing each child's thinking with respect to selected
economic concepts (i.e, wants, scarcity, money, monetary value, exchange, profit,

and how store owners spend their earnings, alternatives/choices, opportunity cost, and cost–benefit analysis). Students' responses were tape recorded and later transcribed to facilitate analysis.

In Table 1, I list the interview questions and the directions followed by the interviewer. Questions 1 through 8 and 10 through 14 comprised the 13-item, *good use* understanding-of-economic-concepts measure, and Question 9 comprised the *of table* one-item, use-of-cost–benefit-analysis measure.

Items for the understanding-of-economic-concepts measure were based on queries used by Burris (1976), Fox (1978), Furth (1980), Schug (1983), and Strauss (1952). With respect to Items 1 through 6, 8, and 10 through 14, subjects received 1 point for each correct, misconception-free response and 0 points for each incorrect, misconception-driven response (or no response). Item 7 was worth from 0 to 3 points, depending on the number of correct responses given out of the three possible correct responses. Across all items, use of traditional economic concepts labels was not required for a response to be considered correct. I, along with another judge and a classroom teacher whom I trained, scored each student response independently and blindly. The points awarded for each test item reflected the average of the two judges' scores. Decision consistency between the two judges' scores was 95%.

A decision–consistency approach was also used to establish the test–retest reliability of the understanding-of-economic-concepts measure. After receiving their respective treatments, I tested and retested a random selection of half of the subjects participating in this study (after an appropriate time delay), using the understanding-of-economic-concepts measure. With the cut-off score for mastery set at 80% correct, consistent mastery/nonmastery decisions were made 100% of the time; thus, I found that the test had a high test–retest reliability.

With respect to the use-of-cost–benefit-analysis measure (Item 9), I used an economic dilemma from Schug (1983) to reveal students' proclivity to use the cost–benefit analysis way of thinking in their day-to-day decision making. Students' responses to this *real-life* dilemma (i.e., a decision-making situation in which each student made and *implemented* his or her decision) were evaluated by the same two judges described above in terms of a three-level hierarchy of economic reasoning. The judges scored subjects' responses independently and blindly. A response to the dilemma was worth between 0 and 3 points, and the judges scored each response at the highest level of economic reasoning exhibited. The mean of the two judges' scores served as the indicator of a student's level of economic reasoning. Decision consistency for the two judges was 100%; thus, interjudge reliability was high.

The point allocation criteria for the students' responses are given below, along with sample responses to the real-life "allowance" dilemma— deciding what store item to buy with one's allowance.

0 points = no recognition or use of economic reasoning ("I'll buy the pencil. I like pencils.")

1 point = recognition of the existence of scarce resources and identification of scarcity as a relevant decision-making issue ("I'll buy the pencil. It costs 5¢ and I only have 5¢.)

2 points = ability to identify specific alternative uses for scarce resources ("I could buy the pencil, or the eraser, or the pad of paper. There are many nice things from which to choose.")

TABLE 1   Pretest/Posttest Questions and Directions to Interviewer

*clear &
helpful*

Pretest/posttest questions	Directions to interviewer
1. Do people have everything they want?	1.
2. Why do/don't people have everything they want?	2.
3. Which dollar would you prefer/like to have? Why would you prefer/like to have that dollar?	3. Present the student with two bills—one genuine and one play.
4. Why does this dollar have value/worth?	4. Point to the genuine dollar bill.
5. Why does this dollar have no real value/worth?	5. Point to the play dollar bill.
6. Why do customers give money to store owners?	6. Show a picture of a person purchasing something in a store. Point to the customer (standing behind a shopping cart). Point to the store owner (standing behind a cash register).
7. What happens next with the money? What does the store owner do with the money she or he gets from the customer? What does she or he use the money for?	7. Show the same picture as in question No. 6. Point to the store owner. Point to the customer.
8. Why do store owners give change/money back to customers?	8. Show the same picture as in question No. 6. Point to the store owner. Point to the customer. After the student answers the question, remove the picture.
9. You are at a store and have 5 cents in your pocket. Pick out three things you would like to have from the store. Remember you have 5 cents in your pocket. The ( ) costs 5 cents; the ( ) costs 5 cents; and the ( ) costs 5 cents. What will you do with your money? Talk out loud as you think about what to do. Tell me everything you are thinking about to help you decide.	9. Give the student an "allowance" of 5 cents. Show the student a box labelled "store" and containing five items, each priced at 5 cents. After the student indicates his or her three wants, remove all other items from the student's view. Point to each item/want as you talk about it.
10. Let's start over and pretend you have not made a decision about what to do with your money. You have 5 cents. The ( ) costs 5 cents; the ( ) costs 5 cents; and the ( ) costs 5 cents. What is your problem?	10. Give the student an "allowance" of 5 cents. She or he is shown the same three items/wants from question No. 9. Point to each item/want as you talk about it.

TABLE 1   *Continued*

Pretest/posttest questions	Directions to interviewer
11. What are your alternatives/possible choices of what to do with your money?	11. After the student answers this question, have him or her (a) list reasons why she or he would like to have each item, (b) select one item to keep, (c) pay for the item, and (d) tell why she or he selected that item over the others.
12. When you selected the ( ) over the ( ), was there anything that you were giving up? Can you explain how?	12. Point to each item/want as you talk about it. Remove all items after the student answers the question.
13. I'd like to tell you a short story about a girl named Susan. Susan is 15 years old. Last Friday night, some of Susan's friends asked her if she wanted to go to a movie. But, Susan's father said that if she stayed home and babysat on Friday, he'd pay her $3. Does Susan give up anything if she chooses to babysit on Friday night? Can you explain how?	13.
14. The leaders of our country, like the President, sometimes must decide how our country's money should be spent. Imagine that the President can use $5 million of our country's money to make our schools better, or he can use the $5 million to improve our highways by widening and building new roads. In this case, does our country give up anything if the President uses the money to make the schools better? How?	14.

3 points = ability to identify those alternative uses that are realistically within one's consideration set and prioritize them in terms of anticipated benefits ("I could buy the pencil, which I like. It is a pretty color and has pictures on it. I also like the eraser because I could erase big mistakes with it. But I think I would choose the pad of paper. It is good for writing notes, and I can use the pencil I already have.")

The economic reasoning scale described above was developed by Kourilsky and Murray (1981). The scale distinguishes between three levels of explicitness in the application of cost–benefit analysis to personal decision making and has been used in several previous studies (Kourilsky, 1985; Kourilsky & Graff, 1986; Kourilsky & Kehret-Ward, 1983; Kourilsky & O'Neill, 1985; Laney, 1988; Laney, 1990).

During the treatment phase and with my guidance, the subjects in each of the two treatment groups created a market economy within their respective classrooms. Development of these classroom economies was accomplished using a three-step process.

First, play money in the form of $1 and $5 bills was infused into the economy by paying students on a daily basis for attending school and for cleaning the classroom at the end of the school day. The payments were discontinued after 1 week.

Second, in order to set up their own stores, students were allowed to purchase a limited number of items (five of a kind for $5) from a "factory warehouse" located in the classroom and operated by me. Products and raw materials for sale at the factory warehouse included pencils, markers, erasers, pads of paper, toys, children's costume jewelry, and miniature play groceries.

Third, the subjects in both treatment groups engaged in dramatic play activities within their classroom marketplaces. In all, students experienced 12 "market days"—two 20-min market days a week across a 6-week period. During each market day, students were free to buy, sell, and produce goods and services. To prevent students from using the factory warehouse as just another store, I opened the factory warehouse every other market day, and students were limited to one purchase (five of a kind for $5) a day from the factory warehouse.

Post-market-day learning activities differed for the two treatment conditions. For both groups, the activities were limited to 20 min. Activity descriptions for the experience-debriefing (experience-based learning) group and the experience–dictation (experiential learning) group are provided in the next two paragraphs.

I led students in the experience–debriefing (experience based learning) group in instructional intervention in the form of post-market-day debriefings. Through role playing and guided discussion, the debriefings addressed mistakes in play and misconceptions about economic concepts identified during the pretreatment interviews. Topics for the 12 debriefing sessions were as follows: money and exchange, monetary value, review, and change; wants and scarcity; review, choice/alternatives, opportunity cost, and review; and cost–benefit analysis, profit (and how store owners spend their earnings), and review.

Each debriefing session followed a four-step sequence suggested by Kourilsky (1983). First, the students verbally described and role played an instructor-selected economic event from their classroom marketplace. Second, the students, with the instructor's help, identified the central issue, problem, or question associated with the event. Third, the instructor provided the students with new information about the economic concept(s) relevant to resolving the issue, solving the problem, or answering the question. Fourth, the instructor aided the students in relating the new information to their past experiences and in applying the new information to the current issue, problem, or question.

Students in the experience–dictation (experiential learning) group did not participate in any post-market-day debriefings. Instead, at the close of each market day, students independently dictated language experience stories about their ongoing activities in the classroom marketplace. During each dictation session, students were free to dictate stories about a market-day-related topic of their own choosing or to dictate stories about the "topic of the day" (e.g., money, customers, store owners, stores, decisions, what they liked/disliked about their classroom marketplace). Each student's language experience story was recorded in writing by one of three adults—

the regular classroom teacher, a student teacher, or me. When a student was not dictating, she or he was busy drawing a picture to illustrate her or his story.

A possible rival hypothesis to this study as described above is that any learning gains made by the experience–debriefing (experience-based learning) group would be attributable to the instructional debriefing alone rather than the market day experience *plus* the instructional debriefing. To test this rival hypothesis, I added a debriefing-only control group to this study during the following school year. This group was drawn from the same elementary school as the other two groups and consisted of 17 first graders from one randomly formed classroom. There were 11 boys and 6 girls. Thirteen were Caucasian; 2 were African-American; and 2 were Hispanic. These students were given the equivalent of the 12 debriefing sessions described previously, but they did not participate in any classroom market days.

Because I served as instructor, interviewer, and one of two judges in this study, experimenter bias represented a potential threat to external validity. Several steps were taken to minimize this threat. First, the transcribed pretest and posttest responses of each subject were scored by two judges—myself and a classroom teacher whom I had trained. The second judge was unaware of my outcome expectations and thus served as an unbiased evaluator. As noted previously, interjudge reliability was high on both instruments used in this study. Second, a time delay of several months occurred between the transcribing of the interview responses and the scoring of those responses; consequently, I had time to forget which subjects gave which responses. Third, a subject's name and classroom membership was recorded on the back of the transcriptions to ensure blind evaluation by both judges.

good use of control group

RESULTS

The percentage of correct responses (or response types) on each pretest/posttest question achieved by students in the experience–dictation (experiential learning) and experience–debriefing (experience-based learning) groups are listed in Table 2. With respect to the percentage of correct responses at pretest, the two treatment groups were fairly comparable on each question. By posttest, the experience–debriefing group was outperforming the experience–dictation group on every question.

Analysis of students' incorrect pretest responses revealed that the economic misconceptions evident among transitional first-grade subjects participating in this study matched those found in earlier studies of young children's economic reasoning (Armento, 1982; Burris, 1976; Fox, 1978; Furth, 1980; Kourilsky, 1987; Schug, 1981, 1983; Schug & Birkey, 1985; Strauss, 1952). At posttest, the number of students giving incorrect responses (and thus the number of students with misconceptions about economic concepts) dropped dramatically in the experience-debriefing group. In contrast, the number of students giving misconception-driven, incorrect responses in the experience-dictation group changed little from pretest to posttest. In a few instances (i.e., Questions 1, 2, 4, and 10), students in the experience–dictation group actually lost ground.

Table 3 contains the pretest–posttest score means and standard deviations for the experience-dictation and experience-debriefing groups on the understanding-of-economic-concepts measure. Pretest means ranged from 4.8 for the experience-debriefing group to 5.4 for the experience-dictation group, whereas posttest means

TABLE 2   Percentage of Correct Responses (or Response Types) for Each Pretest/Posttest Question by Treatment Group

good use of table to present descriptive data

Question	Experience-dictation group (%)		Experience-debriefing group (%)	
	Pretest	Posttest	Pretest	Posttest
1. Do people have everything they want?	87	80	75	100
2. Why do/don't people have everything they want?	60	53	38	100
3. Which dollar would you prefer/like to have? Why would you prefer/like to have that dollar?	7	7	13	88
4. Why does this dollar have value/worth?	27	13	25	100
5. Why does this dollar have no real value/worth?	13	13	25	100
6. Why do customers give money to store owners?	80	93	72	100
7. What happens next with the money? What does the store owner do with the money she or he gets from the customer? What does she or he use the money for?	33 (to live on) 7 (to run his/her business) 60 (for change)	47 (to live on) 40 (to run his/her business) 27 (for change)	50 (to live on) 13 (to run his/her business) 13 (for change)	100 (to live on) 81 (to run his/her business) 75 (for change)
8. Why do store owners give change/money back to customers?	13	20	0	69
9. Real-life "allowance" dilemma: What will you do with your 5 cents?	87 (Level 0) 13 (Level 1) 0 (Level 2) 0 (Level 3)	67 (Level 0) 33 (Level 1) 0 (Level 2) 0 (Level 3)	94 (Level 0) 6 (Level 1) 0 (Level 2) 0 (Level 3)	63 (Level 0) 13 (Level 1) 13 (Level 2) 13 (Level 3)
10. What is your problem?	60	53	38	100
11. What are your alternatives/ possible choices of what to do with your money?	33	33	25	100
12. When you selected the ( ) over the ( ), was there anything that you were giving up? Can you explain how?	0	7	6	75
13. Opportunity cost story: "Susan's Dilemma."	33	47	56	100
14. Opportunity cost story: "Presidential Dilemma"	27	33	31	81

Note. Questions 10 through 12 were posed in conjunction with the same real-life "allowance" dilemma used in Question 9.

TABLE 3   Score Means and Standard Deviations on the Understanding-of-Economic-Concepts Measure

Treatment group	Pretest		Posttest	
	M	*SD*	*M*	*SD*
Experience-dictation group (*n* = 15)	5.4	2.2	5.7	1.9
Experience-debriefing group (*n* = 16)	4.8	2.2	13.7	1.3

ranged from 5.7 for the experience-dictation group to 13.7 for the experience-debriefing group. A one-tailed *t* test for independent samples showed no statistically significant difference between group means at pretest test, *t* observed = − .77, *t* critical = 1.7, *df* = 29, *p* < .05, indicating that the two groups were comparable prior to instruction. A second one-tailed *t* test for independent samples at posttest indicated that the mean of the experience-debriefing group was significantly greater than the mean of the experience-dictation group, *t* observed = 13.72, *t* critical = 1.7, *df* = 29, *p* < .05.

appropriate use of t test

The percentage of students in the experience-dictation and the experience-debriefing groups performing at mastery level (80 to 100% correct) on the understanding-of-economic-concepts measure are listed in Table 4. At pretest, no student in either group was performing at mastery level. By posttest, 94% of the students in the experience-debriefing group had readied mastery level, compared with 0% in the experience-dictation group.

Means and standard deviations of the experience-dictation and experience-debriefing groups on the use-of-cost–benefit-analysis measure are contained in Table 5. Pretest means ranged from .06 for the experience-debriefing group to .13 for the experience-dictation group. At posttest, means ranged from .33 for the experience-dictation group to .75 for the experience-debriefing group. Posttest scores ranged from 0 to 1 in the experience-dictation (experiential learning) group and from 0 to 3 in the experience-debriefing group. There was no significant difference between group means at pretest, as indicated by a one-tailed *t* test for independent samples, *t* observed = − .65, *t* critical = 1.7, *df* = 29, *p* < .05;

TABLE 4   Percentage of Students in Each Treatment Group Performing at Mastery Level (80–100% Correct) on the Understanding-of-Economic-Concepts Measure

Treatment group	Pretest (in %)	Posttest (in %)
Experience-dictation group (*n* = 15)	0	0
Experience-debriefing group (*n* = 16)	0	94

TABLE 5   Score Means and Standard Deviations on the Use-of-Cost-Benefit-Analysis Measure

	Pretest		Posttest	
Treatment group	***M***	***SD***	***M***	***SD***
Experience-dictation group (*n* = 15)	.13	.35	.33	.49
Experience-debriefing group (*n* = 16)	.06	.25	.75	1.13

thus, the two groups were comparable prior to instruction. Results at posttest were in the expected direction but did not reach statistical significance. A one-tailed *t* test for independent samples showed that the mean of the experience-debriefing (experience-based) learning group was not significantly greater than the mean of the experience-dictation group (*t* observed = 1.32, *t* critical = 1.7, *df* = 29, *p* < .05.

Additional data were collected and analyzed to test the rival hypothesis that the learning gains made by the experience-debriefing group were attributable to the debriefing alone, rather than the experience *plus* the debriefing. Table 6 contains the pretest–posttest means and standard deviations for the debriefing-only control group on the understanding-of-economic-concepts and the use-of-cost–benefit-analysis measures, and Tables 7 and 8 the results of 2 one-way analyses of variance used to compare the pretest means of the experience-dictation, experience-debriefing and debriefing-only groups on the understanding-of-economic-concepts and use-of-cost–benefit-analysis measures, respectively. The 2 one-way ANOVAs indicated that the three groups were comparable at pretest in terms of their understanding of economic concepts and use of cost–benefit analysis.

On both the understanding-of-economic-concepts and the use-of-cost–benefit-analysis posttests, the mean score of the debriefing-only group fell above the

TABLE 6   Pretest-Posttest Means and Standard Deviations for the Debriefing-Only Control Group

	Pretest		Posttest	
Instrument	***M***	***SD***	***M***	***SD***
Understanding-of-economic-concepts measure	4.71	1.05	7.94	2.25
Use-of-cost–benefit-analysis measure	.24	.66	.71	1.05

Note. n = 17.

TABLE 7 **Analysis of Variance Summary Table for the Understanding-of-Economic-Concepts Pretest**

Source of variation	SS	df	MS	F
Between groups	4.51	2	2.25	.62*
Within groups	163.11	45	3.62	
Total	167.62	47		

*p < .05; F critical: 3.21.

mean score of the experience-dictation (experiential learning) group and below the mean score of the experience-debriefing group. Only 6% of the students in the debriefing-only group reached mastery level (80 to 100% correct) on the understanding-of-economic-concepts posttest. In conjunction with each posttest measure, two planned (a priori) comparisons were used to compare (a) the combined means of the experience-debriefing and debriefing-only groups versus the mean of the experience-dictation group and (b) the mean of the experience-debriefing group versus the mean of the debriefing-only group.

With respect to the understanding-of-economic-concepts posttest, both planned comparisons revealed statistically significant differences between the means and combinations of means tested. The first planned comparison showed that the average of the means of the experience-debriefing and debriefing-only groups was greater than the mean of the experience dictation (experiential learning), group, t observed = 8.83, t critical = 1.68, df = 45, p < .05. The second planned comparison indicated that the mean of the experience-debriefing group was greater than the mean of the debriefing-only group, (t observed = 8.81, t critical = 1.68, df = 45, p < .05.

With respect to the use-of-cost–benefit-analysis posttest, the two planned comparisons failed to reveal any statistically significant differences. The average of the means of the experience-debriefing and debriefing-only groups was not greater than the mean of the experience-dictation group, t observed = 1.35, t critical = 1.68, df = 45 p < .05. Similarly, the mean of the experience-debriefing (experience-based learning) group was not greater than the mean of the debriefing-only group, t observed = .12, t critical = 1.68, df = 45, p < .05.

TABLE 8 **Analysis of Variance Summary Table for the Use-of-Cost–Benefit-Analysis Pretest**

Source of variation	SS	df	MS	F
Between groups	.25	2	.12	.58*
Within groups	9.73	45	.21	
Total	9.98	47		

*p < .05; F critical: 3.21.

appropriate use of ANOVA

Used a total of 6 t tests and 2 ANOVAs. Should mention experiment-wide error rate.

DISCUSSION

Schug (1981) asked whether economic instruction could foster the development of economic reasoning ability. The results cited above suggest that many of the misconceptions that young children have about economic concepts can be overcome through experience-based economics instruction featuring (a) real-life experiences with economic concepts and (b) instructor-led debriefing sessions that focus students' attention on the economic concepts hidden within these experiences. Experience-based learning seems to help young children reject misconceptions indicative of a lower level of economic reasoning and embrace accurate conceptions indicative of a higher level of economic reasoning. As in Ajello et al. (1987) and Berti et al. (1986), giving primary-grade students correct information about economic concepts appears to cause them to relinquish more primitive conceptions and to adopt more sophisticated conceptions.

This study provides support for Kourilsky's (1983) assertion regarding the superiority of experience-based learning over experiential learning. It is not sufficient for young children to simply participate in economic experiences. To make substantive gains in their understanding of economic concepts, young children must also have their attention focused on the economic concepts that can be distilled from those experiences. Debriefing sessions featuring instructor-led, inquiry-oriented discussions and role playing provide the needed focus. As evinced by the experience-dictation group's gaining little ground (and even losing ground) from pretest to posttest on their understanding of economic concepts, experiential learning appears to focus students' attention on surface–level social interactions and the physical characteristics of objects or processes rather than the economic concepts hidden below the surface. When students' attention is directed to irrelevant ideas, misconceptions are likely to be reinforced rather than replaced.

According to Amento (1987), learning theory recognizes attention as an important factor affecting knowledge acquisition. Some techniques that can be used to focus students' attention include pointing out the purpose and most important ideas in a lesson, reviewing main ideas, and having students state ideas in their own words. In addition, helping students make connections between new ideas and what they already know is a way of directing their attention. All of the aforementioned techniques, were used with the experience-debriefing group in this study.

Vygotsky (1978) noted that language development tends to lag behind conceptual development. Perhaps another explanation for the superiority of the experience-based approach is that it simultaneously enhances both conceptual development and language development. Through instructor-led debriefings using role playing and class discussion, children learn to describe economic events accurately and to attach labels to experiences. This language-related learning, in turn, may deepen children's understanding and thinking about economic concepts. Such thinking is in line with that of Berti et al. (1986)—the notion that children make progress toward concept mastery by talking about economic concepts they have not yet mastered.

One wonders what would have happened in this study if market-day experiences, instructor-led debriefings, and language-experience story dictation had been combined into a single treatment condition. The addition of language-experience story dictation to the experience-debriefing treatment condition would have provided students with a further means of (a) growing in the area of language development and (b) reinforcing their knowledge of economic events and concept labels introduced during debriefing sessions.

Experience-based learning does not appear to have an advantage over experiential learning in promoting young children's proclivity to use cost–benefit analysis in their personal decision making. Mean posttest scores on the use-of-cost–benefit-analysis measure (i.e., interview Item 9, the real-life "allowance" dilemma) were low for both treatment groups. Laney's (1990) explanation that young children may not be developmentally ready to profit from instruction on the cost–benefit analysis way of thinking seems unsatisfactory. Interview Items 10 through 12 of the understanding-of-economic-concepts measure consisted of the same real-life "allowance" dilemma used for the use-of-cost–benefit-analysis measure. The only difference was that the dilemma was broken down into three parts, with each part cuing students to use the cost–benefit analysis way of thinking. As indicated by the high percentage of correct responses at posttest on those three items, children in the experience-debriefing group demonstrated an understanding of the subconcepts inherent in the cost–benefit analysis process (i.e., scarcity, alternatives/ choice, and opportunity cost).

In other words, when cued to do so, the students successfully used cost–benefit analysis. Why, then, were posttest scores so low on the real-life allowance dilemma (interview Item 9) that constituted the use-of-cost–benefit analysis measure? Perhaps students were using cost– benefit analysis but were not verbalizing the steps of the process in an effective manner, because they were not cued to do so. Or perhaps the students had the capacity, but not the proclivity, to use cost–benefit analysis in their personal decision making. For young children, development of this proclivity may require instruction on economic decision making over an extended period of time. *True, but research needed to confirm this hypothesis.*

The performance of the debriefing-only control group provides some evidence to discount the rival hypothesis that the learning gains made by the experience-debriefing group are attributable to the instructional debriefing alone, rather than the market day experience *plus* the instructional debriefing. On the understanding-of-economic-concepts posttest, the mean of the debriefing-only group fell above the mean of the experience-dictation group, but was well below the mean of the experience-debriefing group. Just as experience alone is not the best teacher, neither is economics instruction alone sufficient to produce substantive learning, at least with respect to young children's understanding of economic concepts. As in Laney (1989), economic concepts appear to be more meaningful and memorable when real-life experiences with these concepts are provided.

Why? This is over-generalization. The implications of this study extend beyond early economic education to concept teaching and early childhood education in general. It seems likely that the benefits of experience-based approaches can be extended to other disciplines and a variety of concept types. Katz and Chard (1990) called for a developmentally appropriate early childhood curriculum focusing on intellectual goals. They stressed the importance of engaging children's minds so that children better understand their experiences and environment. Experience-based approaches, by connecting experiences with inquiry-oriented debriefing sessions, have the potential to engage children's intellects to a greater extent than either spontaneous play or systematic academic instruction (i.e., teaching a sequence of interrelated subskills to individual children). As noted by Katz and Chard, what is needed is a balanced usage of current early childhood practices.

REFERENCES

Ajello, A. M., Bombi, A. S., Ponte-corvo, C., & Zucchermaglio, C. (1987). Teaching economics in primary school: The concepts of work and profit. *The International Journal of Behavioral Development, 10*(1), 51–69.

Armento, B. J. (1982, March). *Awareness of economic knowledge: A developmental study.* Paper presented at the annual meeting of the American Educational Research Association, New York.

Armento, B. J. (1986). Learning about the economic world. In Virginia Atwood (Ed.), *Elementary social studies: Research as a guide to practice,* Bulletin No. 79 (pp. 85–101). Washington, DC: National Council for the Social Studies.

Armento, B. J. (1987). Ideas for teaching economics derived from learning theory. *Theory Into Practice, 26*(3), 176–182.

Berti, A. E., Bombi, A. S., & De Beni, R. (1986). Acquiring economic notions: Profit. *The International Journal of Behavioral Development, 9,* 15–29.

Burris, V. I. (1976). *The child's conception of economic relations: A genetic approach to the sociology of knowledge.* Unpublished doctoral dissertation, Princeton University.

Cassuto, A. (1980). The effectiveness of the elementary school Mini-Society program. *The Journal of Economic Education 11*(2), 59–61.

Fox, K. F. A. (1978). What children bring to school: The beginnings of economic education. *Social Education, 42*(6), 478–481.

Furth, H. G. (1980). *The world of grown-ups: Children's conceptions of society.* New York: Elsevier North Holland.

Hull House Publishing Company. (1988). *Maturational assessment test for determining behavior, age, and school readiness: 3 to 7.*

Katz, L. G., & Chard, S. C. (1990). *Engaging children's minds: The project approach.* Norwood, NJ: Ablex.

Kourilsky, M. L. (1977). The Kinder-Economy: A case study of kindergarten pupils' acquisition of economic concepts. *The Elementary School Journal, 77*(3), 182–191.

Kourilsky, M. L. (1981). Co-learners approach to parent/child economic education: An empirical investigation. *NABTE Review, 8,* 40–45.

Kourilsky, M. L. (1983). *Mini-Society: Experiencing real-world economics in the elementary school classroom.* Menlo Park, CA: Addison-Wesley.

Kourilsky, M. L. (1985). Economic reasoning and decision making by high school students: An empirical investigation. *The Social Studies 76*(2), 69–75.

Kourilsky, M, L. (1987). Children's learning of economics: The imperative and the hurdles. *Theory Into Practice, 26*(3), 198–205.

Kourilsky. M. L., & Graff, E. (1986). Children's use of cost-benefit analysis: Developmental or nonexistent. In S. Hodkinson & D. Whitehead (Eds.), *Economic education: Research and development issues* (pp. 127–139). Essex, England: Longman.

Kourilsky, M. L., & Kehret-Ward, T. (1983). Determinants of economic reasoning in monetary and time-allocation decisions: An exploratory study. *Journal of Economic Education, 14*(4), 23–31.

Kourilsky, M. L., & Murray, T. (1981. September). The use of economic reasoning to increase satisfaction with family decision making, *Journal of Consumer Research, 8,* 183–188.

Kourilsky, M. L., & O'Neill, J. B. (1985). The perceived importance of time in economic decision making. *Journal of Private Enterprise, 1*(1), 88–94.

Laney, J. D. (1988). The impact of perceived familiarity and perceived importance on economic reasoning in time-allocation decisions. *Journal of Economic Education, 19*(3), 209–216.

Laney. J. D. (1989). Experience- and concept-label-type effects on first graders' learning, retention of economic concepts. *The Journal of Educational Research, 82*(4), 231–236.

Laney, J. D. (1990). Generative teaching and learning of cost-benefit analysis: An empirical investigation. *Journal of Research and Development in Education, 23*(3), 136–144.

Schug, M. C. (1981). What educational research says about the development of economic thinking. *Theory and Research in Social Education, 9*(3), 25–36.

Schug, M. C. (1983). The development of economic thinking in children and adolescents. *Social Education, 47*(2), 141–145.

Schug, M. C., & Birkey. J. (1985). The development of children's economic reasoning. *Theory and Research in Social Education, 13*(1), 31–42.

Strauss, A. L. (1952). The development and transformation of monetary meanings in the child. *American Sociological Review, 17,* 275–286.

Vygotsky, L. S. (1978). *Mind in society. The development of higher psychological processes.* Cambridge, MA: Harvard University Press.

7

SINGLE-SUBJECT EXPERIMENTAL RESEARCH

Diane Browder

Kazdin

The research designs just described in Chapter 6 all have one common characteristic: They all are used to study group behavior and change. Single-subject research, also sometimes referred to as *single-case* or *N of one* research, is a particular type of experimental research. Its distinguishing feature is the rigorous study of the effect of interventions on an individual. Although the focus of this type of study is the individual subject, most of these studies include more than one subject. When there are multiple subjects, the data are still analyzed separately for each subject rather than as a group as would be done in the designs described in Chapter 6.

Although there are many fine books on the topic of single-subject research, two, which the authors find particularly useful, are Barlow and Hersen (1984) and Kazdin (1982). The structure of this chapter and, where indicated, the content were influenced by these two superb texts. Although there are more recent books on the topic, these texts are recommended to anyone wishing an in-depth coverage of single-subject research.

As with experimental research in general, single-subject research is a method of testing hypotheses. It also is prone to many of the same threats to internal and external validity to which other research designs are subject. In particular, many critics of single-subject research question its external validity, in particular its ability to generalize to other subjects. Proponents point out that this is a problem of most research. They question whether group analyses are useful for determining an individual's treatment. They argue that just because the experimental group outgained the control group on the average does not mean that every person receiving the experimental treatment outgained every person in the control group or even that everyone in the experimental group improved.

The decision to use a single-subject research design depends, as does the selection of any research design, on the purpose of the study, the population of interest, and the situation in which the study is to be conducted. Single-subject research designs are particularly useful in the study of behavior modification. Most, if not all, behavior modification research uses single-subject designs. In fact, this type of research and the methodology are so often used together that many people confuse the two. Behavior modification research studies the effect of a certain type of intervention, operant conditioning, on individuals. Single-subject research is a methodology that can be applied to a variety of research topics.

The case study method described in Chapter 8 is the clinical, descriptive foundation from which the experimental study of single-subjects developed. "The development of single-case research, as currently practiced, can be traced to the work of B. F. Skinner (b. 1904), who developed programmatic animal laboratory research to elaborate operant conditioning" (Kazdin, 1982, p. 10).[1] Skinner's (1938, 1953) research methodology, known as the *experimental analysis of behavior,* included certain features that are characteristic of single-subject research today. He included only one or a few subjects in each of his studies. He used the subject as its own control by changing the intervention presented to the subject and studied the impact of the changes on the subject. Skinner was also very interested in the frequency with which a behavior occurred under various conditions (Kazdin, 1982).

Beginning in the 1950s, a number of investigators adapted Skinner's operant approach and methodology of the experimental analysis of behavior to humans. The early laboratory research produced findings that indicated the clinical utility of operant conditioning with a variety of populations (e.g., autistic children, mentally retarded persons, psychiatric patients). Thus was born the field of *applied behavior analysis* with its own journal, the *Journal of Applied Behavior Analysis,* first published in 1968. Most of the research published in this journal uses single-subject research methods. In the last two decades, an increasing number of studies using this methodology for operant conditioning and other research topics has appeared in a variety of journals. A recent edited book by Neuman and McCormick (1995) provides an overview of single-subject research as well as a number of examples of the use of these designs in reading and literacy.

Single-subject designs are similar to three of the quasi-experimental designs described in Chapter 6, the time-series design, the equivalent samples design, and the equivalent materials pretest–posttest design. Each of these designs includes some change in the conditions applied to the subjects with repeated observations or measurements. The major difference between these designs and single-subject research designs is that these quasi-experimental designs are used with a group of subjects and the data are analyzed accordingly, whereas single-subject research is concerned with individuals.

Single-subject research requires careful assessment, repeated observations or measurements, and careful control and applications of the experimental treatment. This chapter will address these issues and describe the most common designs.

GENERAL PROCEDURES

Repeated Measurement

One aspect of single-subject research is the repeated measurement or observation of the individual. The purpose is obvious: to determine if changes in the experimental conditions effect changes in the subject. The careful, systematic use of these repeated observations is critical to assure reliable and valid data.

The measurement used must be clearly defined. If, as is common, the procedure is observation, the behaviors to be observed must be carefully defined and observable. The researcher must also be careful in selecting the behaviors to be observed. In particular, the behaviors must be ones that the subject would normally be expected to exhibit with a reasonable degree of frequency.

If the measurement procedure includes tests, surveys, or attitude scales, the researcher must select instruments that can be used repeatedly without the contamination of test or test-interaction effects. Because elimination of the test and test-interaction effects is often impossible, observation is the primary measurement tool in single-subject research studies.

The measurements also must be used under completely standardized conditions. The researcher needs to use the same measurements, or observation procedures, for each replication of the measurement. Where possible, the same observers or test givers should be used for all measurements. When this is not possible, the researcher should demonstrate reliability of the measurements across the various personnel used. The measurements should take place under the same conditions each time they are conducted. Conditions that should be standardized across measurements include the time of day, the circumstances (e.g., during a certain lesson such as spelling), and the general surroundings (e.g., location, others present) in where the measurements take place.

Baselines

The baseline in single-subject research is analogous to a pretest in group research designs. Baseline data generally are collected by observing the aspect of the individual's behavior that is under study at several times prior to intervention. Because a baseline is used to determine the status of the subject's behavior prior to the intervention and to predict what the immediate future behavior would be if no intervention was implemented, the baseline must be long enough to determine the trend in the data. That is, the baseline should demonstrate a stable rate, an increasing rate, or a decreasing rate of the behavior to be modified. Figure 7.1 on page 212 provides hypothetical data showing a stable, an improving (increasing), and a worsening (decreasing) rate of appropriate behavior. Because the purpose of the intervention would be to increase the rate of appropriate behavior, only the baseline showing an increasing trend (the middle panel) would present a serious problem in evaluating the effectiveness of the intervention. This trend would be a problem because the baseline is already showing a trend in the desired direction.

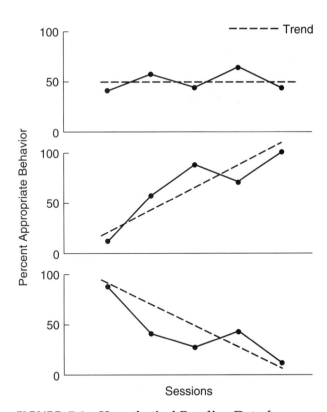

FIGURE 7.1   **Hypothetical Baseline Data for Attending Behavior. The Top Panel Shows Stable, Middle Panel Increasing, and Bottom Panel Decreasing Trend in the Behavior**

A baseline must include a minimum of three separate observations but will often include from five to eight, or even more, observations. The length of the baseline is determined by a number of factors. Ideally for research purposes, the baseline will continue until a stable trend, with a minimum of variability, is established. However, ethical considerations may shorten the baseline from the optimal to the minimum acceptable. For instance, the researcher working on correcting the self-abusive behavior of an autistic child cannot withhold treatment indefinitely until a satisfactory baseline is established.

Manipulating Variables

A fundamental principle of any type of research, particularly true of single-subject research, is that only one variable should be manipulated, or changed, at any given time. When two or more variables are manipulated during the same phase of a single-subject study, the effect of each cannot be separated.

For instance, in dealing with a hyperactive child, a researcher might want to study the effects of medication and of operant conditioning. To do such a study properly, the researcher should follow the baseline with one of the interventions or treatments, let us say the medication. After a period of time with the medication, the treatment should be removed and the baseline repeated. Following the second baseline, the researcher would introduce the second intervention, operant conditioning. The second baseline period is commonly known as *withdrawal.* This design will permit a comparison of the effectiveness of the two interventions. (Ideally, two subjects should be used, with the order of treatments reversed so as to control for any possible order effect.) This design would be an A-B-A-B design ("A" represents baseline or no intervention, and "B" represents an intervention).

If the researcher in the above study had introduced both treatments, medication and operant conditioning, at the same time, with a baseline before and after, the relative effect of each treatment would not be discernible. Although the design looks appropriate on the surface, an A-B-A design (baseline, intervention, baseline), the manipulation of two variables in the same phase, makes it uninterpretable.

Length of Phases

> *When considering the individual length of phases independently of other factors (e.g., time limitations, ethical considerations, relative length of phases), most experimenters would agree that baseline and experimental conditions should be continued until some semblance of stability in the data is apparent. (Barlow & Hersen, 1984, p. 96)*[2]

That is, the data collection in each phase should continue until there is no upward or downward trend and a fairly constant level of variability between data collection points. This would obviously result in the phases of a typical study—baseline, intervention, baseline, intervention (A-B-A-B)—being radically different in length (Barlow & Hersen, 1984).

On the other hand Barlow and Hersen (1973) have pointed out problems with having unequal phase and "cited the advantages of obtaining a relatively equal number of data points for each phase" (Barlow & Hersen, 1984, p. 96). Obviously, some compromises must be made between these two often competing ideals, stability of each phase, and equal phase length. For instance, in some cases it may be necessary for the first intervention to be longer than the initial baseline to demonstrate a behavioral change. In such a case the subsequent phases, second baseline and intervention, should be the same length as the first intervention to replicate the changes in behavior. "Where possible, the relative equivalence of phase lengths is desirable" (Barlow & Hersen, 1984, p. 97).

A potential problem, which is sometimes related to the length of the intervention phase, is a carryover effect. A *carryover effect* is found when the effect of the intervention continues into the next phase, withdrawal. The purpose of the withdrawal phase is to support the effectiveness of the intervention by demonstrating that the effect disappears (or is at least reduced) when the treatment is removed. In the typical A-B-A-B design, the treatment is then reintroduced and the effect reappears, thus clearly demonstrating the effectiveness of the treatment. If the intervention effect carries over to the withdrawal phase (second baseline), there are plausible alternative hypotheses for the behavioral improvement that occurred during the intervention phase (e.g., maturation, history, and so on).

Bijou, Peterson, Harris, Allen, and Johnston (1969) recommend short interventions to prevent carryover effects "since long ones might allow enough time for the establishment of new conditioned reinforcers" (p. 202). Thus, once an effect has been demonstrated, the withdrawal phase should be introduced right away. Barlow and Hersen (1984) suggest alternating treatment designs (discussed later in this chapter) and counterbalancing procedures as ways to prevent carryover effects from obscuring the results.

Transfer of Training and Response Maintenance

Transfer of training to other situations, settings, or behaviors is of obvious importance in applied behavior analysis. If a teacher eliminates an undesirable behavior in his or her classroom but the behavior continues elsewhere, the instructional program has limited success. Barlow and Hersen (1984) and Kazdin (1982) suggest a number of design options that are useful in providing for, and studying, the transfer of intervention effects.

Similarly, keeping the undesirable behavior from recurring as soon as the reinforcement schedule is eliminated or changed is also relevant. A child must learn to behave acceptably without receiving tangible reinforcements for the rest of his or her life. Thus, maintenance of positive behavioral responses or of the elimination of undesirable responses is a prime purpose of the practitioner. Various reinforcement schedules result in more or less maintenance of the intervention effect. The reader should consult one of several fine texts (e.g., Alberto & Troutman, 1990; Cooper, Heron, & Heward, 1987; Schloss & Smith, 1994) for a detailed discussion of reinforcement schedules and response maintenance. Barlow and Hersen (1984) describe design strategies that also are useful in studying and effecting response maintenance.

ASSESSMENT

Assessment of the effect of the intervention(s) in single-subject research is usually accomplished by observing the behaviors under study. Chapter 9 includes a section on the use of observation as a method of data collection. However, the assessment of behavioral change is so central to the issue of single-subject research that certain aspects primarily relevant to this topic will be briefly described here. The texts by Barlow and Hersen (1984) and Kazdin (1982) contain a great deal more detail than can be covered in this introductory treatment.

Target Behavior

The target behavior or focus of the research is usually determined by the research or real problem. If the problem involves the elimination of inappropriate (e.g., violent, disruptive) behaviors in the classroom, then the target behaviors will obviously be the inappropriate behaviors displayed. The researcher may need to observe the situation for a period of time prior to implementing the study in order to determine the precise nature of the behaviors (e.g., hitting other children, calling out, throwing spitballs).

Once the researcher fully understands the behavior(s) to be changed, the target behavior needs to be operationally defined. The definition should refer only to observable aspects of the behavior. References to intent or other unobservable components should be avoided. The definition should be clearly worded for easy, unambiguous, nonsubjective understanding. The definition also needs to completely define the outer boundaries of the behavior under study (Barlow & Hersen, 1984).

The purpose of assessing the target behavior is

> *[first to determine] the extent to which the target behavior is performed before the program [intervention] begins. The rate of preprogram behavior is referred to as the baseline or operant rate. Second, assessment is required to reflect behavior change after the intervention is begun. Since the major purpose of the program is to alter behavior, behavior during the program must be compared with behavior during baseline. (Kazdin, 1982, pp. 23–24)*

Data Collection Strategies

As stated earlier, the major data collection procedure used in single-subject research is observation of overt behaviors. There are a number of ways to measure such behaviors.

A *frequency measure* is simply a count of the number of occurrences of the behavior observed during a given period. If a teacher wants to know how frequently a particular student talks without permission, he or she may simply count the number of occurrences during a given class period. This type of measure is relatively easy and is most useful when the occurrences of the behavior are all about the same length of time. More than one behavior are sometimes counted in this procedure (e.g., talking to other children *and* on-task behavior).

A time-based measure of overt behavior is *duration*. In this method the actual amount of time during which the individual performs the behavior is determined. If an instructional program is designed to teach a mentally retarded student to perform an already mastered task more rapidly, the teacher would want a measure of the duration of the task performance.

Another time-based measure is *time sampling* or *interval recording*. In this method the observation period, such as a class period, is divided into brief observation/nonobservation intervals. In a study designed to decrease inappropriate behavior, the observer might observe the child every 30 seconds for a 15-second interval followed by a 15-second nonobservation period for recording the observed behaviors. This method is frequently used but is considered to have serious flaws (Barlow & Hersen, 1984).

The final method to be described here is *real-time observation*. In this procedure behaviors are recorded in their actual frequency, duration, and order. This is an excellent method, but it is rarely used because of the need for expensive recording equipment.

The strategies mentioned thus far are useful for overt behavior. For research on behaviors that are not overt, other measures are needed. For a study on weight reduction, the data might include a count of calories consumed and of distance walked in a day. These data could be the totals for each day derived from a calorie counter and a pedometer. These types of measures are called *response-specific measures* by Kazdin (1982). Other types of measures used in single-subject research include psychophysiological (e.g., pulse, skin temperature) and self-reports.

In single-subject research the researcher must be able to demonstrate the *reliability* and *validity* of the measures used. For instance, do two observers count the same overt behavior in the same way? What of the effect of the observer's presence on the person(s) being observed? These issues are addressed in Chapter 9.

BASIC DESIGNS

There are two fundamental types of designs that are used in single-subject research, *A-B-A* and *multiple baseline.* Each of these design types will be described, and an example of each will be presented. Other designs that are too complex for this elementary discussion will be mentioned and texts suggested for those interested in more detail.

A-B-A Designs

As with all single-subject designs, "A" represents a series of baseline measurements, and "B" represents a series of measurements occurring during the treatment. Thus, A-B-A includes three phases, baseline, intervention, and withdrawal (baseline), each of which represents a series of measurements. Most research studies of this type are more complex than the most basic A-B-A design. More often than not, the intervention is reintroduced after the withdrawal phase, resulting in an A-B-A-B design. Although additional baselines and/or treatment phases may be added, further complicating the design, the most common of these designs is the A-B-A-B.

The A-B-A-B design is analogous to the equivalent time-samples design described in Chapter 6. The primary difference is that the A-B-A-B design assumes continuous measurement of the behavior(s) being studied and the analysis of individual subjects' data. The equivalent time-samples design has specific times for the measurements, and the data are analyzed for the group of subjects.

The A-B-A-B design permits a careful examination of the effects of intervention. Kazdin (1982) puts it quite well:

The A-B-A-B design examines the effects of an intervention by alternating the baseline condition (A phase), when no intervention is in effect, with the intervention condition (B phase). The A and B phases are repeated again to complete the four phases. The effects of the intervention are clear if performance improves during the first intervention phase, reverts to or approaches original baseline levels of performance when treatment is withdrawn, and improves when treatment is reinstated in the second intervention phase. (p. 110)

A critical aspect of the expected events described above is that the direction of the behavior changes each time the intervention is introduced or withdrawn. Thus, the actual behavior differs from what would have been expected if the conditions were not changed. Figure 7.2 shows what the graph of such data might look like. Clearly the intervention was effective in this hypothetical example.

Fantuzzo and Clement (1981) used an A-B-A-B design to study the effect of the reinforcement given to one student upon other students. Although the study included a number of conditions and subjects, for the purposes of this discussion we will concentrate on just one aspect of the study. In this situation "Al" was to reinforce himself every 60 seconds if he was attending to his assigned task. "Ed"

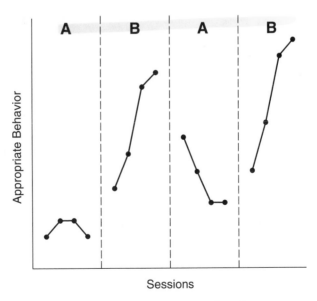

FIGURE 7.2   Hypothetical Data Showing an Effective Intervention for Increasing Appropriate Behavior in an A-B-A-B Design

was able to observe Al and to behave similarly. At the end of each session Al was able to select edible rewards based on the number of points he had awarded himself. Ed was not offered the edible reward regardless of his behavior or the number of points he awarded himself. The actual percentages of attentive behavior for Al and Ed are given in Figure 7.3. As can be seen, the treatment was effective with both students even though only Al received the edibles. The withdrawal and second intervention were also successful in effecting behavior in the directions expected. Each time the conditions changed, A to B, B to A, and A to B again, the direction of the behaviors changed. Thus, the study demonstrated successful generalization of reinforcement from one student to another.

Gardner, Heward, and Grossi (1994) used the A-B-A-B design to alternate and compare two different approaches in teaching science to 22 fifth-grade inner-city students. In the first and third phases (A) students raised their hands to be called. In the second and fourth phases (B) students were provided with a laminated board (response cards) on which to write one or two word answers in response to the teacher's questions. Five of the students were further selected for observation in consultation with the teacher, who indicated that they were representative of the class as a whole. There were five dependent variables measured in this study: teacher presentation rate, number of student responses, accuracy of student responses, next-day quiz scores, and biweekly review test scores. Figure 7.4 provides a description of the number of student responses (academic responses and hand raises for those phases) in the typical A-B-A-B format. As can be seen, the overall

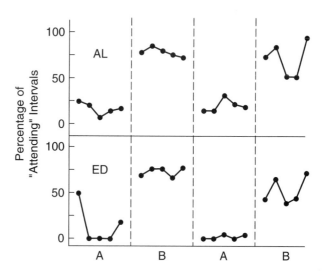

FIGURE 7.3   Percentage of Attentive Behavior Across Experimental Phases for Al and Ed

(Adapted from Fantuzzo & Clements [1981] with permission of the authors. Copyright © by the Society for the Experimental Analysis of Behavior, Inc.)

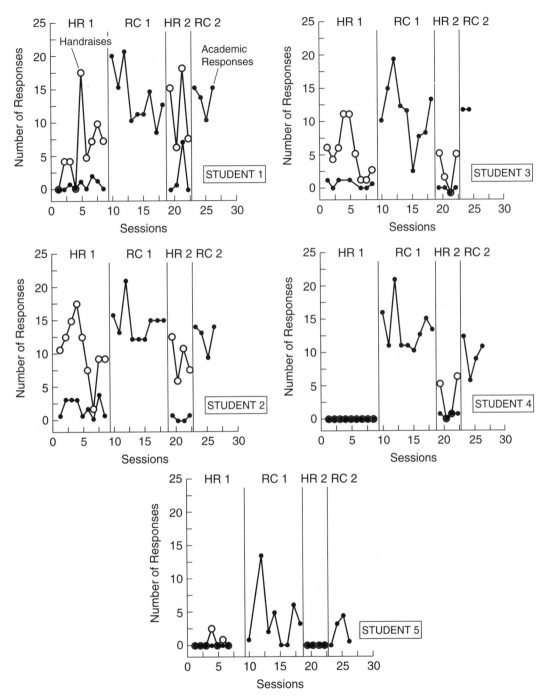

Figure 1. Number of academic responses and hand raises by students 1 through 5 during science lessons in which students participated by hand raising (HR) or response cards (RC). Breaks in data paths indicate student absences.

FIGURE 7.4 **Example of A-B-A-B Design from Gardner, Heward, & Grossi, 1994**

(Used with permission of the first author. Copyright © the Society for the Experimental Analysis of Behavior, Inc.)

level of academic responses was higher for the response card phases. For the five students the average number of times a student raised his/her hand in those phases was 9.9 times with a range of 0.7 to 21.3 across students. The average number of academic responses during the hand raising phases was 1.5 per session with a range of 0 to 2.8. When response cards were used, each target student responded to teacher questions an average of 21.8 times per session (range, 5.8 to 28.3), a 14-fold increase. The other dependent variable data supported the effectiveness of the response cards versus the hand raising conditions. For example, 21 of the 22 students scored higher on next day quiz scores during the first response card session than they had scored during the hand raising in the preceding phase. It should be noted that this article might have been improved, although only slightly, by alternating the order of the two conditions with different children. However, this would have complicated the study because another class and, possibly, teacher would have been necessary. Because both conditions in the third and fourth phases are repeated, any concern over all of the children having the interventions applied in the same order is only slight. The complete Gardner, Heward, and Grossi (1994) article appears at the end of this chapter as a sample.

Multiple Baseline Designs

The designs described in this section are quite different from the A-B-A designs just considered. In A-B-A designs the intervention effect is demonstrated by withdrawal and by, usually, reintroduction of the intervention. In multiple baseline designs the intervention effect is demonstrated by having more than one baseline. Here each baseline represents a different person, setting, or behavior, which are the three principal variations of this type of design. The subsequent baselines (e.g., for the second and third behaviors) are longer than the previous baselines and extend into the previous ones' interventions. Figure 7.5 provides an example, using hypothetical data, of a typical multiple baseline design with three subjects. As can be seen, each subject shows improvement only after the intervention is introduced to that subject.

Multiple baseline designs are actually replication designs. If each subject or behavior shows the same pattern of response to the treatment only when the treatment is applied to that subject or behavior, there is strong evidence of a true treatment effect. By extending the second subject's baseline until after an intervention effect is demonstrated for the first subject, the researcher controls for maturation, history, and other threats to the internal validity of the study. In addition, by demonstrating the treatment effect with more than one subject, the researcher demonstrates generalizability to other subjects. Likewise, multiple baseline designs that use multiple behaviors or multiple settings also control for various threats to internal validity and demonstrate generalizability of the treatment to other behaviors or settings.

McGee, Krantz, and McClannahan (1986) studied the effect of a particular teaching approach, incidental teaching, on the learning of sight words by an autistic child. They used a multiple baseline design across three sets of words and added

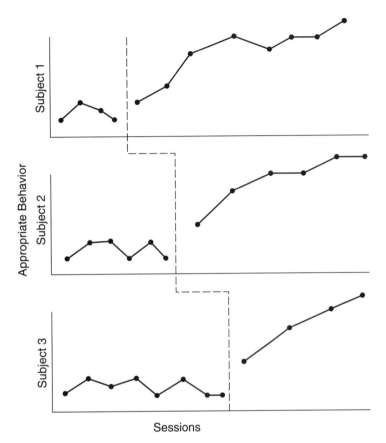

**FIGURE 7.5 Hypothetical Data Showing an Effective
Intervention to Increase Appropriate
Behavior Using a Multiple Baseline Design**

a follow-up phase to check for longer-term effects. As can be seen in Figure 7.6, for each set of words the percentage of correct responses began to improve only when the treatment was implemented on that set of words. The follow-up at 15 and 25 days also indicated retention of the learned material. Clearly the treatment was effective, and threats to the internal validity of the study were well controlled.

Other Designs

In addition to A-B-A and multiple baseline designs, a number of additional options are available to the researcher. *Alternating treatment* or *multiple treatment* designs permit the researcher to compare two or more treatments while controlling for possible order effects. In these designs the researcher alternates treatments for each session or randomly assigns the sessions to each treatment. In the first

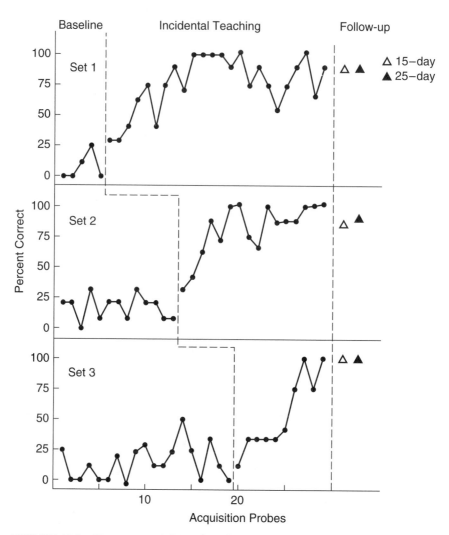

FIGURE 7.6   Percentage of Correct Responses on Acquisition Probes During Baseline Incidental Teaching and at 15- and 25-day Follow-ups

(Adapted from McGee, Krantz, & McClannahan [1986] with permission of the authors. Copyright © the Society for the Experimental Analysis of Behavior, Inc.)

case, with two treatments, the researcher simply uses Treatment 1 in the session following the first baseline, Treatment 2 after the second baseline, and so on. With random assignment the researcher decides on the number of intervention sessions and randomly assigns each session to a treatment. Thus, with two treatments and ten sessions, the order of treatment might be 1-1-2-1-2-2-1-2-2-1. These procedures permit a clear comparison of two, or more, treatments. Those wishing more details regarding this type of design should refer to Barlow and Hersen (1984) or Kazdin (1982).

Researchers also combine these various designs into even more intricate designs. Kazdin (1982) describes a number of options for doing this. Barlow and Hersen (1984) suggest the use of replication in applied research and describe a number of strategies for carrying out replications appropriately.

Miller and Kelley (1994) conducted a study that demonstrates a combination of the two basic designs, A-B-A-B and multiple baseline. In this study there were four parent–child dyads in which the children, ages 9 to 11, had demonstrated problems with their homework. "A combination of reversal (A-B-A-B) and multiple baseline designs was used to evaluate the effects of goal setting and contingency contracting on subjects' homework performance" (p. 77). Each of the four dyads in the study had initial baselines followed by the intervention and subsequent baseline and intervention phases, the standard A-B-A-B design. However, the number of sessions of baseline varied as in the multiple baseline design, thus, a combination design. Two of the measures used to determine if goal setting and contingency contracting were beneficial were on-task behavior and percentage of homework completed accurately. Figure 7.7 on page 224 presents the data from the accuracy of homework measure. As can be seen, each of the four dyads had better accuracy in the intervention phases of the study than in the baseline phases. Although the standard A-B-A-B reversal design alone would probably have provided convincing data, by combining this design with the multiple baseline design, the authors have provided an even more convincing argument for the success of the intervention.

EVALUATING DATA

In studies comparing the performances of two or more groups of subjects, a statistical test of the differences between the groups is the usual method for analyzing the effects of the experimental condition. In single-subject research, however, statistical analyses are rarely used. Visual inspection of the data is the most common method used to evaluate the effect of the treatment in single-subject studies.

In single-subject designs the approach is to see if the effect is replicated at the appropriate point. In an A-B-A-B design the effect should replicate at the beginning of each new phase, the change from A to B, from B to A, and from A to B again. In a multiple baseline design, the effect should replicate across subjects, behaviors, or settings by occurring at each point that the treatment is applied (Kazdin, 1982).

Visual inspection is relatively easy in cases in which there are major changes in the behavior. For instance, if the behavior never occurs during baseline and occurs frequently during the intervention, an effect is obvious. However, this is not the usual case, so we must have predetermined characteristics of the data to use in evaluating whether an effect occurred. Kazdin (1982) suggests two types of change, *magnitude* and *rate*, that can be judged. He further suggests using changes in the *average rate* of performance and in the *level* at the change point to assess the

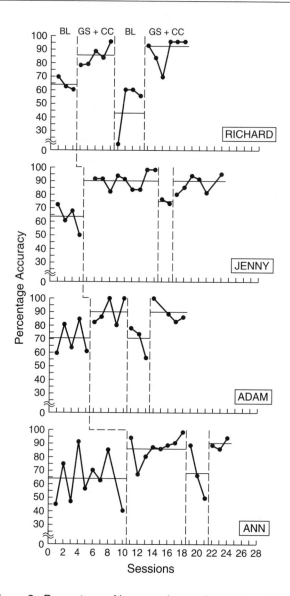

Figure 2. Percentage of homework completed accurately during baseline and treatment conditions across subjects. Sessions correspond to sequential school days (i.e., Mondays through Thursdays) on which subjects were assigned homework. Data were not collected on days on which homework was not assigned.

FIGURE 7.7   Example of Combined Multiple Baseline and A-B-A-B Designs from Miller & Kelley, 1994

(Used with permission of the Society for the Experimental Analysis of Behavior, Inc.)

magnitude of the change. The average rate of performance is simply the number of occurrences divided by the number of sessions. A line can be superimposed on the graph of the data to show any changes. A change in the level refers "to the shift or discontinuity of performance from the end of one phase to the beginning of the next phase" (Kazdin, 1981, p. 234).

Kazdin (1982) proposes to use changes in *trend* and *latency* to assess changes in the rate of the behavior under study. The trend of the data can be measured by the slope and is the "tendency for the data to show systematic increases or decreases over time" (p. 235) or to show no change at all (preferable for baseline data). The latency of the changes refers to how quickly the change occurs after beginning the intervention or withdrawal phase. Obviously, the more rapidly a change occurs, the better evidence for the treatment having caused the change.

Thus, in evaluating a subject's data, the researcher looks to see if the average performance changes between phases, if a shift in the rate of the behavior occurs between the phases, if the slopes of the data lines are in different directions for the different phases, and how quickly a change occurs after the intervention or withdrawal is introduced. These and other characteristics discussed by Kazdin (1982) are used to determine if the treatment was effective in changing behavior.

Another approach to evaluating the data is a statistical analysis. Although the statistical analysis of single-subject data is a relatively recent phenomenon, it can be quite useful in convincing readers of the importance of the data beyond what merely looking at graphs can do. Kratochwill and Levin (1992) edited a book on advance single-subject designs and analyses. Included are two important chapters on statistical analysis of single case data (Busk & Marascuilo, 1992; Edgington, 1992). Unfortunately, this topic is too advanced for this introductory treatise.

SUMMARY

Single-subject experimental research differs from other experimental research in that the focus of the research is on the individual rather than on a group. The procedures used in single-subject research are just as rigorous as in other types of experimental research. Single-subject research is used to test hypotheses. In general, this type of research is used to test the hypothesis that a particular treatment will have an overt effect on one or more behaviors. Because most research on behavior modification has used single-subject research methods, the two are often confused and thought to be the same. Although single-subject methodology is appropriate and useful in research on behavior modification, it is also appropriate and used for other research topics.

This chapter has emphasized the need to collect data repeatedly and carefully. The most commonly used method to collect data in this type of research is observation. Thus, the method of observation, also described in Chapter 9, was considered in some detail here.

The need for baseline data and the careful manipulation of variables were described. Assessment of the effects of a single-subject study depend upon having carefully collected baseline and treatment data. The length of these phases should be kept as similar as possible.

Two fundamental designs, A-B-A and multiple baseline, were described in detail, and an actual study of each was presented. A-B-A designs usually include a second intervention, A-B-A-B, and are sometimes referred to as withdrawal designs. Multiple baseline designs include two or more replications across persons, behaviors, or settings. The baseline for later replications is longer than the earlier ones, thereby controlling for threats to the internal validity of such studies.

The data in single-subject research is usually evaluated through visual inspection. Statistical analysis is rare. Visual inspection considers such factors as changes in the magnitude and rate of the behaviors studied.

EXERCISES

1. What distinguishes single-subject research from other forms of experimental research?

2. Single-subject research is similar to certain quasi-experimental designs. Discuss these similarities and how they are dissimilar.

3. Why is single-subject research confused with behavior modification? In what ways are they different?

4. What is a baseline? How does the initial baseline differ from a subsequent one in an A-B-A design?

5. A researcher's baseline stabilizes after four sessions, and she begins the intervention. If there is no effect after four sessions, should she continue the treatment or reintroduce the baseline? Why?

6. Most single-subject studies are of overt behavior. What other types of research might use single-subject methods?

7. How does an A-B-A-B design control for threats to the internal validity of the study?

8. How does a multiple baseline design control for threats to the external validity of the study?

9. Read the report of a single-subject experiment in a journal.
   a. What design was used?
   b. Were the variables clearly defined?
   c. Was the hypothesis clearly stated?
   d. Would a group design (Chapter 6) have been better? Why or why not?
   e. Were the phase lengths appropriate?
   f. What method was used to collect the data? If observation, how were the data recorded?
   g. How were the data evaluated? Was the evaluation appropriate?
   h. Were the conclusions clearly stated?
   i. Were the conclusions substantiated by the data presented?

ENDNOTES

1. All quotes from Kazdin (1982) used with permission of Oxford University Press.

2. All quotes from Barlow and Hersen, 1984 used with permission of Pergamon Press, Ltd.

REFERENCES

Alberto, P. A., & Troutman, A. C. (1990). *Applied behavior analysis for teachers* (3rd ed.). Columbus, OH: Merrill.

Barlow, D. H., & Hersen, M. (1984). *Single case experimental designs* (2nd ed.). New York: Pergamon.

Bijou, S. W., Peterson, R. F., Harris, F. R., Allen, K. E., & Johnston, M. S. (1969). Methodologies for experimental studies of young children in natural settings. *Psychological Record, 19,* 177–210.

Busk, P. L., & Marascuilo, L. A. (1992). Statistical analysis in single-case research: Issues, procedures, and recommendations, with applications to multiple behaviors. In T. R. Kratochwill & J. R. Levin (Eds.), *Single-case research designs and analysis.* Hillsdale, NJ: Lawrence Erlbaum.

Cooper, J. O., Heron, T. E., & Heward, W. L. (1987). *Applied behavior analysis.* Columbus, OH: Merrill.

Edgington, E. S. (1992). Nonparametric tests for single-case experiments. In T. R. Kratochwill & J. R. Levin (Eds.), *Single-case research designs and analysis.* Hillsdale, NJ: Lawrence Erlbaum.

Fantuzzo, J. W., & Clement, P. W. (1981). Generalization of the effects of teacher- and self-administered token reinforcers to nontreated students. *Journal of Applied Behavior Analysis, 14,* 435–447.

Gardner, R., Heward, W. L., & Grossi, T. A. (1994). Effects of response cards on student partici-pation and academic achievement: A systematic replication with inner-city students during whole-class science instruction. *Journal of Applied Behavior Analysis, 27,* 63–71.

Kazdin, A. E. (1982). *Single-case research designs.* New York: Oxford.

Kratochwill, T. R., & Levin, J. R. (Eds.). (1992). *Single-case research designs and analysis.* Hillsdale, NJ: Lawrence Erlbaum.

McGee, C. C., Krantz, P. J., & McClannahan, L. E. (1986). An extension of incidental teaching procedures to reading instruction for autistic children. *Journal of Applied Behavior Analysis, 19,* 147–157.

Miller, D. L., & Kelley, M. L. (1994). The use of goal setting and contingency contracting for improving children's homework performance. *Journal of Applied Behavior Analysis, 27,* 73–84.

Neuman, S. B., & McCormick, S. (Eds.). (1995). *Single-subject experimental research: Applications for literacy.* Newark, DE: International Reading Association.

Skinner, B. F. (1938). *The behavior of organisms.* New York: Appleton-Century-Crofts.

Skinner, B. F. (1953). *Science and human behavior.* New York: Macmillan.

Schloss, P. J., & Smith, M. A. (1994). *Applied behavior analysis in the classroom.* Needham Heights, MA: Allyn and Bacon.

SAMPLE ARTICLE

*Used with permission of the first author and the Society for the Experimental Analysis of Behaviors, Inc.

*good
clear,
concise
title*

Effects of Response Cards on Student Participation and Academic Achievement: A Systematic Replication with Inner-City Students During Whole-Class Science Instruction*

Ralph Gardner, III
William L. Heward
Teresa A. Grossi

We evaluated the use of response cards during science instruction in a fifth-grade inner-city classroom. The experiment consisted of two methods of student participation—hand raising and write-on response cards—alternated in an ABAB design. During hand raising, the teacher called upon 1 student who had raised his or her hand in response to the teacher's question. During the response-card condition, each student was provided with a laminated board on which to write one- or two-word answers in response to each question asked by the teacher. Frequency of active student response was 14 times higher with response cards than with hand raising. All 22 students scored higher on next-day quizzes and on 2-week review tests that followed instruction with response cards than they did on quizzes and tests that covered facts and concepts taught with the hand-raising procedure.

DESCRIPTORS: academic behavior, classroom, education, teaching, response cards

*statement
of problem
clear &
important*

A significant and growing body of behavioral and educational research is providing empirical support for John Dewey's (1916) contention that students learn by doing. Researchers using single-subject or group-comparison experimental methods have arrived at the same conclusion: Learning is enhanced when the frequency with which student actively respond during instruction is increased (e.g., Brophy, 1986; Delquadri, Greenwood, Stretton, & Hall, 1983; Greenwood, Delquadri, & Hall, 1984; Narayan, Heward, Gardner, Courson, & Omness, 1990; Pratton & Hales, 1986; Rosenshine, 1980; Rosenshine & Berliner, 1978; Sindelar, Bursuck, & Halle, 1986). Too often, however, classroom instructional activities allow students to be passive observers rather than active participants (Hall, Delquadri, Greenwood, & Thurston, 1982; Stanley & Greenwood, 1983). In fact, Graden, Thurlow, and Ysseldyke (1982) reported that the amount of time that students engage in actively responding occupied the smallest portion of time allocated for instruction.

This report is based on a dissertation submitted by the first author in partial fulfillment of the requirements for the Doctor of Philosophy degree at The Ohio State University. The research was supported in part by a leadership training grant (G008715568–88) from the Office of Special Education and Rehabilitation Services, U.S. Department of Education.

Correspondence and reprint requests may be sent to Ralph Gardner, III, Applied Behavior Analysis Program, The Ohio State University, 356 Arps Hall, 1945 N. High St., Columbus, Ohio 43210–1172.

Although Carta and Greenwood (1988) found that the quality and amount of instruction were the most important factors in improving the level of academic achievement by inner-city youth, these students may receive fewer opportunities to respond than their suburban counterparts do (Greenwood, Delquadri, Stanley, Terry, & Hall, 1986). Carta and Greenwood (1988) reported that deficits in academic behavior were independent of the students' levels of intelligence or socioeconomic status, but were dependent on how instruction was presented by the teacher. The variable most consistently related to increases in achievement was the extent to which students were academically engaged during instruction.

review of literature—comprehensive and related to both problem and research question.

One of the most commonly used methods of whole-class instruction is lecture by the teacher (Brophy, 1988); however, this method has been found to be less effective than alternative strategies such as one-on-one tutoring (Bloom, 1984). One likely reason for the relative ineffectiveness of the lecture method is that students have few, if any, opportunities to respond during the lesson. A common strategy used by teachers for generating student participation during whole-class instruction is to pose a question to the entire class and then call one student to answer (Brophy & Evertson, 76). This strategy often results in more frequent responses by high-achieving students and few or no responses by low-achieving students (Maheady, Mallette, Harper, & Sacca, 1991).

The use of response cards is one strategy that has shown promising initial results for increasing the frequency of active student response and subsequent academic achievement during large-group instruction (Narayan et al., 1990). Response cards are reusable signs or cards held up simultaneously by each student in the class to indicate his or her answer. Narayan et al. compared response cards and hand raising during whole-class social studies instruction in an inner-city fourth-grade classroom. During lessons in which response cards were used, individual students actively responded to 15 times more teacher-posed questions than during lessons in which students raised their hands. In addition, most students scored higher on daily quizzes following lessons with which response cards than on quizzes following lessons with hand raising.

The present study was designed as a systematic replication of the study by Narayan et al. (1990). We sought to extend the findings of the earlier study by (a) increasing the time between instruction and quiz to determine if the positive effects of response cards found in the earlier study could be extended to the next school day, (b) administering biweekly review tests to determine if any differential effects on achievement would be maintained, and (c) analyzing student performance on recall and recognition quiz and test questions.

research purpose & question

The purposes of the study were to compare the effects of hand raising (HR) and response cards (RC) on (a) the frequency of active student responding during instruction, (b) the accuracy of student responses during instruction, (c) student performance on next-day quizzes and biweekly review tests, and (d) student performance on recall and recognition test questions. We also assessed which method of responding the students preferred.

METHOD

SUBJECTS AND SETTING

The study took place in a fifth-grade classroom in an elementary school located in a low socioeconomic area of a large midwestern city. There were 13 boys and 11 *teacher selection could bias findings*

could bias results regarding attention to task

girls in the class, ranging in age from 10 to 12 years. Because of frequent absences by 2 of the students, data are presented for only 22 students. Five students were selected for observation after consultation with their regular teacher, who indicated that they were representative of the range of participation and academic performance of the class. The 5 target students were divided into two groups of 3 and 2 students each, and the students in each group were observed on alternating trials. Students in each group sat at adjacent desks, enabling the observers to record the occurrence and accuracy of each student's response on the same trial.

good procedure

The classroom was equipped with an overhead projector and screen. Students' desks and chairs were arranged in standard rows and columns, providing each student with an unobstructed view of the screen. The first author served as the teacher during the study. The third author served as the primary observer and sat to the right of the teacher, facing the students.

DEPENDENT VARIABLES

Five dependent variables were measured during the study: (a) teacher presentation rate, (b) number of student responses, (c) accuracy of student responses, (d) next-day quiz scores, and (e) biweekly review test scores. In addition, students' preferences and opinions concerning the two response methods used in the study were obtained in a two-question interview with each student at the conclusion of the study. Definitions and observation and measurement tactics for the first three dependent variables (a, b, and c above) were identical to those used by Narayan et al. (1990).

clear

Next-day quiz scores. Beginning with Session 2, a 16-question quiz was administered at the start of each session. The quizzes tested students on science concepts and facts from the most recent session. Each quiz consisted of eight recognition questions (multiple choice and true or false) and eight recall questions (requiring one- or two-word short answers or fill-in-the-blank).

Review tests. A 40-question review test was given every 2 weeks during the study. Each of the four review tests covered an equal amount of material selected randomly from each of the six to nine lessons conducted during the preceding 2 weeks. Each review test consisted of 20 recognition questions and 20 recall questions in an alternating sequence.

INTEROBSERVER AGREEMENT

good reliability of observation

A second observer independently recorded the teacher's presentation of each instructional trial and the responses of the target students during at least two sessions of each of the four experimental phases. Procedures for obtaining and calculating interobserver agreement data were identical to those used by Narayan et al. (1990). During the two HR phases, interobserver agreement for hand raises across the 5 target students ranged from 82% to 100%. Agreement for number of student responses and accuracy of student responses during the HR phases across students ranged from 94% to 100% and from 92% to 100%, respectively. During the two RC phases, interobserver agreement for number of student responses ranged from 92% to 100%, and agreement for accuracy of student responses ranged from 82% to 100%. Interobserver agreement for next-day quiz scores across all 22 students ranged from 94% to 100% ($M = 97\%$). Interobserver agreement on the two review tests scored by the second observer across all 22 students ranged from 95% to 100% ($M = 98.4\%$).

EXPERIMENTAL DESIGN AND PROCEDURE

An ABAB reversal design was used to analyze the effects of both experimental conditions. Each 45- to 55-min session consisted of three parts. Except for the first session, each session began with a quiz over the previous lesson. Each student was provided with an answer sheet and a yellow cover sheet to conceal his or her answers. To control for the students' wide range of reading abilities, the teacher read each question aloud twice while displaying the questions one at a time on the overhead projector. The teacher waited 10 s after reading a recall question for the second time and 5 s after reading a recognition question for the second time before displaying the next question. After all 16 questions had been presented, students were allowed to request the rereading of specific questions. Quiz scores counted toward the students' science grades.

very clearly stated procedure

During the second part of each session, the teacher used the overhead projector to present new science information to the students. To ensure treatment fidelity, the teacher followed a script for each lesson. The scripted lessons specified the content to be presented, questions to be asked, and all responses that would be scored correctly. The script also indicated the student response mode (HR or RC) to be used and ensured that the number of concepts presented remained constant across all sessions. Lessons on meteorology, climates, plants, and the solar system were developed for the study, using the fifth-grade text and activity book *Accent on Science* (Sund, Adams, & Hackett, 1982) and the *Silver Burdett Science Teacher Resource Book* (Mallinson, Mallinson, Smallwood, & Valentino, 1987). After each new fact or concept was presented, the teacher covered the information on the overhead projector and asked a question about the just-presented fact or concept. The students responded to all teacher-posed questions using the response method in use for that session. During the third and final part of each session, the teacher asked a series of review questions over the facts and concepts from that day's lesson.

Hand raising. On the school day preceding Session 1, the teacher used a geography lesson to provide the students with practice on the procedure for raising their hands and responding to questions. During HR sessions, the teacher waited 3 s after asking each question before calling upon an individual student whose hand was raised. As in the Narayan et al. (1990) study, a list of randomly ordered names of all students in the class was used to determine which student was called upon after each question.

The teacher provided praise for each correct student response (e.g., "Excellent [student's name]! The *sun* is a star.") and corrective feedback for each incorrect answer (e.g., "No, the answer is the *sun*. The *sun* is a star."). Feedback statements were controlled so that all students heard the correct answer (e.g., *sun*) twice on every instructional trial.

Response cards. Presentation and question-asking procedures during the RC sessions were identical to those used during the HR sessions. Each student was provided with a white laminated particle board (22.9 cm by 30.5 cm) on which to write his or her responses to the teacher's questions with a dry-erase marker. On the school day prior to the first RC session, a 10-min practice session with response cards was conducted using a geography lesson. Procedures for using the response cards were the same as described by Narayan et al. (1990).

After visually scanning all of the response cards held up by the students on each trial, the teacher provided praise and/or corrective feedback. If everyone in the class had the right answer, the teacher addressed the feedback to the whole class (e.g., "Good class, water vapor in the atmosphere is a *gas*."). If some of the students' responses were incorrect, the teacher said, for example, "I see that many of you have *gas* as the answer. That is correct, water vapor in the air is in the form of a *gas*." If no student had the correct answer, the teacher said, for example, "I don't see any correct answers. The correct answer is *gas*. Water vapor in the atmosphere is a *gas*." As in the HR phases, the feedback procedure controlled the number of times (twice) students wrote and/or heard the correct answer to each question during instruction.

RESULTS

TEACHER PRESENTATION RATE

clear presentation of data

Mean teacher presentation rate during hand raising was 1.54 questions asked per minute, with a range of 1.00 to 2.16 across sessions. Mean teacher presentation rate when response cards were used was 0.99 questions per minute, ranging from 0.95 to 1.24 across sessions.

STUDENT RESPONSES DURING INSTRUCTION

The number of academic responses emitted by each of the 5 target students during each session is shown in Figure 1. Also shown is the number of times each student raised his or her hand during the two HR phases. During HR, the average number of times a target student raised his or her hand was 9.9, with a range of 0.7 to 21.3 across students. The number of academic responses by the target students during HR averaged 1.5 per session, with a range of 0 to 2.8. When response cards were used, each target student responded to teacher questions an average of 21.8 times per session (range, 5.8 to 28.3), a 14-fold increase.

Overall, the target students as a group orally responded 53 times to 1,103 teacher-posed questions during HR sessions, a participation level of 4% (see Table 1). During RC, these same students responded to 678, or 68%, of the 1,015 questions asked by the reacher. Data for several of the individual students are even more dramatic. For example, Student 5 made no responses during any of the 11 HR sessions for which he was present, but he answered teacher questions during 9 of the 12 RC sessions he attended, with a high of 13 responses during one session. Student 4 made only one response in each of three HR sessions and no responses in the other 10 HR sessions. In contrast, Student 4 averaged 12.7 responses per session when response cards were used.

Accuracy of student responses during instruction was high under both experimental methods, averaging 92% overall during HR sessions and 93% during RC sessions.

NEXT-DAY QUIZ SCORES

The mean quiz scores for 21 of the 22 students during the first RC session were higher than the scores they obtained during the first HR session. Withdrawal of response cards during the second HR session resulted in a decrease in those students' mean quiz scores, and their quiz scores increased again during the second

RESPONSE CARDS

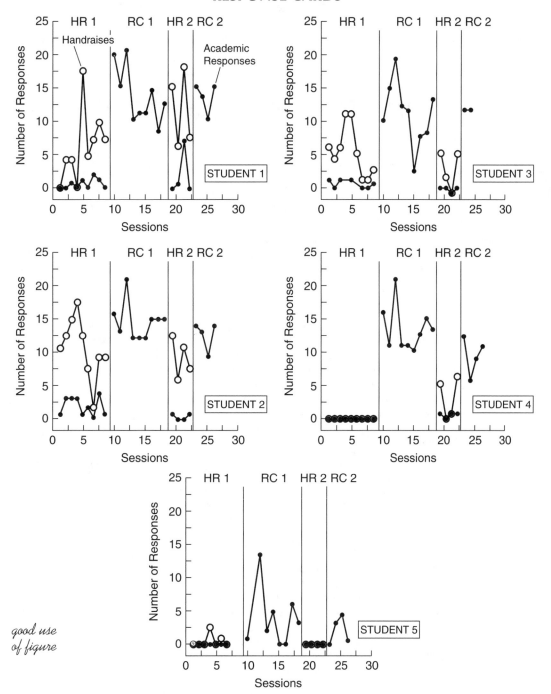

Figure 1. Number of academic responses and hand raises by students 1 through 5 during science lessons in which students participated by hand raising (HR) or response cards (RC). Breaks in data paths indicate student absences.

good use of figure

TABLE 1   Student Participation During Both Experimental Conditions

	Hand Raising (13)[a]				Response cards (13)[a]			
Student	Responses	Response opportu- nities[b]	Partici- pation[c] (%)	Accuracy (%)	Responses	Response opportu- nities[b]	Partici- pation[c] (%)	Accuracy (%)
1	16	230	6.9	93.7	178	189	94.1	91.5
2	22	230	9.6	90.9	183	189	96.8	97.8
3	0	193	0.0	—	40	169	23.6	87.5
4	12	225	5.3	83.3	113	273	41.4	92.9
5	3	225	1.3	100.0	164	195	84.1	96.3
Group	53	1,103	4.0	91.9	678	1,015	68.0	93.2

[a]Numbers in parentheses indicate number of sessions in each condition.
[b]Differences in response opportunities across students are a function of absences.
[c]Percentage of response opportunities answered.

good use of table

RC session. The mean quiz score for the 22 students increased from 59% during the first HR session to 70% during the first RC session, decreased to 51% when response cards were withdrawn, and increased again to 70% when response cards were reinstated. The overall mean score for the entire class during all HR sessions was 57% correct, compared to an overall mean score of 70% correct during RC sessions. (Results of individual students' next-day and review test scores can be obtained from the first author.)

REVIEW TESTS

Each student's accuracy on review test questions covering content initially instructed during RC was higher than his or her performance on test questions taught using HR. The class mean on review rest items instructed during HR was 49% (range, 6% to 81%) across students. The mean percentage of RC-instructed items answered correctly on the review tests was 70%, (range, 32% to 95%).

RECALL AND RECOGNITION ITEMS

Next-day quizzes. The mean percentage of recall items correctly answered on next-day quizzes covering content presented during HR was 39%, compared to 62% on recall questions taught using RC. Overall accuracy on recognition items instructed during HR was 64%, compared to 78% for RC-instructed recognition items.

Review tests. The mean percentage correct recall test questions was 39% during HR, compared to 65% during RC. For recognition questions, the mean percentages were 60% for HR and 74% for RC.

STUDENT PREFERENCES

During the end-of-study interview, 16 of the 22 students said they preferred response cards over hand raising; 19 students said response cards helped them during instruction more than hand raising, and 20 students indicated that response cards helped them receive better grades than did hand raising.

DISCUSSION

good job of discussing results in context of replication of earlier study—the major purpose of study

This study replicated the findings of Narayan et al. (1990) in that response cards increased the frequency of active student response during whole-class instruction, improved students' scores on quizzes over the instructed content, and a majority of the students preferred response cards over hand raising. The results of this study also yielded new information on the use of response cards. First, positive effects of response cards were extended to science instruction, as compared to social studies in the Narayan et al. study. Although we agree with the current advocacy for more hands-on learning in science (Brandwein & Glass, 1991), there is a multitude of facts and definitions that students must master to be successful in science. Response cards allow the teacher to teach facts and definitions more effectively in conjunction with hands-on experiences in which students apply those concepts. Second, the next-day quizzes offered a more significant measure of learning than did the same-day tests used by Narayan et al. Teachers typically do not test students until some time has passed after instruction. It was important to determine if the initial superior effects of response cards found by Narayan et al. could be sustained over time. We found that not only was improved achievement sustained when the students were quizzed the next day, but that improved performance on RC-instructed material was maintained on the biweekly review tests. These maintenance effects suggest that response cards might help students to be more successful in their school careers. The study also demonstrated a relationship between the method of student responding and the type of test question asked. Teachers were provided with information that allowed them to determine the most effective instructional strategy based on the type of test question the student is most likely to encounter.

As reported by Narayan et al. (1990), in the current study the teacher presented questions at a higher rate with the hand-raising procedure than when response cards were used. However, because only one student at a time could actively respond to each question during HR, a total of approximately 45 active instructional trials occurred during each session (1.5 questions presented × 30 min × 1 student). When response cards were used, an average of 660 potential instructional trials were presented each session (1 question presented × 30 min × 22 students). Using the participation level of the 5 target students during RC as representative of the whole class, it can be estimated that an average of 448 active learning trials actually took place during each 30-min lesson (660 × .68 × 100). Based on these data, if response cards were used instead of hand raising during a single 30-min lesson each school day, each student would make approximately 3,700 additional academic responses over the course of a 180-day school year.

In addition to increasing each student's opportunity to respond during instruction, response cards offered an important advantage for the teacher—visual access to each student's response on each learning trial. This direct and ongoing assessment of each student's performance enables the teacher to modify instruction as it is delivered.

Although the increases in quiz scores were relatively small and significant variability was observed within and across the HR and RC phases, a functional relation between use of response cards and improved quiz performance is suggested by the fact that the mean quiz score for all but 1 student increased from the first HR session to the first RC session, decreased during the second HR session. and improved again during the second RC session. These small increases and variability in quiz scores may have been influenced by the large number of questions (16 items) on each quiz, the difficulty of the subject matter, and/or the students' prior exposure to the various topics covered. In an effort to reduce the possibility of a ceiling effect on daily quiz scores, the number of quiz items was increased to 16 in the present study (from the 10 items used by Narayan et al., 1990). This change required more concepts to be presented each day, perhaps too many for the students to master in a single lesson. Despite these limitations, if letter grades had been assigned during HR based on the average quiz score earned by each student, only 2 students would have earned a "B" or better (80% correct and above), and 14 of the 22 students would have received a failing grade (below 60% correct). By contrast, 7 students earned a "B" or better during RC, and 5 students would have failed with RC.

Evidence that the effects of response cards were maintained is provided by the students' superior performance on RC-instructed items on the biweekly review tests. The mean performance for the class on review tests improved from a failing grade under HR to a "C" average during RC. Increasing students' ability to retain greater amounts of academic information over time has important implications in terms of curriculum-based assessment and, depending on the curriculum, on standardized achievement tests as well. Although these maintenance data are based on only four review tests, the results are promising and suggest the importance of further research in this area.

Although accuracy of student responding to both recall and recognition questions improved with RC, the greater increase in accuracy on recall questions taught with RC suggests that the type of responses students make during instruction may be related to their ability to respond correctly to similar test questions later. Additional research is needed to determine if the write-on response cards used in this study, which required a recall response, may have positively influenced student performance on recall questions on the quizzes and review tests.

authors did NOT over-generalize findings

Most of the students preferred response cards over hand raising, stating that they were more fun to use. Students also felt that they learned more when response cards were used. In fact, during HR some students appeared frustrated at times when they were not called on: Some students stopped raising their hands at all, others put their heads down on their desks, and still others complained about not being called on. These behaviors were not observed during RC sessions. Subjective observation during this study showed that the students were less disruptive and stayed more on task when response cards were used than they were when the hand-raising method was used. These anecdotal results suggest that analyses of the effects of response cards on the social behavior of students during instruction are warranted. Finally, because experimenters implemented the response-card procedure in both this study and that of Narayan et al. (1990), future research must demonstrate that classroom teachers can use response cards effectively with their students.

REFERENCES

Bloom, B. S. (1984). The search for methods of group instruction as effective as one-to-one tutoring. *Educational Leadership, 41*(8), 4–17.

Brandwein, P. F., & Glass, L. W. (1991). A permanent agenda for science teachers. Part II: What is good science teaching? *The Science Teacher, 58*(4), 36–39.

Brophy, J. E. (1986). Teacher influences on student achievement. *American Psychologist, 41,* 1069–1077.

Brophy, J. E. (1988). Research linking teacher behavior to student achievement: Potential implications for instruction of chapter 1 students. *Educational Psychologist, 23,* 235–86.

Brophy, J. E., & Evertson, C. M. (1976). *Learning from teaching: A developmental approach.* Boston: Allyn and Bacon.

Carta. J. J., & Greenwood, C. R. (1988). Reducing academic risks in inner-city classrooms. *Youth Policy, 10,* 16–18.

Delquadri, J., Greenwood. C. R., Stretton, K., & Hall, R. V. (1983). The peer tutoring spelling game: A classroom procedure for increasing opportunity to respond and spelling performance. *Education and Treatment of Children, 6,* 225–239.

Dewey, J. (1916). *Democracy and education.* New York: Macmillan.

Graden, J., Thurlow. M. L., & Ysseldyke. J. E. (1982). *Academic engaged time and its relationship to learning: A review of the literature* (Monograph 17). Minneapolis, MN: University of Minnesota Institute for Research on Learning Disabilities.

Greenwood, C. R., Delquadri, J., & Hall, R. V. (1984) Opportunity to respond and student academic performance. In W. L. Heward, T. E. Heron, D. S. Hill, & J. Trap-Porter (Eds.). *Focus on behavior analysis in education* (pp. 58–88). Columbus, OH: Merrill.

Greenwood. C. R., Delquadri, J., Stanley. S., Terry, B., Hall. R. V. (1986). Observational assessment of ecobehavioral interaction during academic instruction. In S. E. Newstead. S. H. Irvine, & P. D. Dan (Eds.), *Human assessment: Cognition and motivation* (pp. 319–40). Dordrecht, The Netherlands: Nijhoff Press.

Hall, R. V., Delquadri, J., Greenwood, C. R., & Thurston, L. (1982). The importance of opportunity to respond in children's academic success. In E. B. Edgar, N. G. Haring, J. R. Jenkins. & C. G. Pios (Eds.), *Mentally handicapped children: Education and training* (pp. 107–140). Baltimore, MD: University Park Press.

Maheady, L., Mallette, B., Harper, G. F., & Sacca, K. (1991). Heads together: A peer-mediated option for improving the academic achievement of heterogeneous learning groups. *Remedial and Special Education, 12*(2), 25–33.

Mallinson, G. G.. Mallinson, J. B., Smallwood, W. L., & Valentino, C. (1987). *Silver Burdett science: Teacher resource book.* Morristown, NJ: Silver Burdett Company.

Narayan, J. S., Heward, W. L., Gardner, R., III, Courson, F. H.. & Omness. C. (1990). Using response cards to increase student participation in an elementary classroom. *Journal of Applied Behavior Analysis, 23,* 483–490.

Pratton, J., & Hales, L. W. (1986). The effects of active participation on student learning. *Journal of Educational Research, 79*(4), 210–215.

Rosenshine, B. (1980). How time is spent in elementary classrooms. In C. Denham & A. Lieberman (Eds.), *The appraisal of teaching: Concepts, findings, and implications* (pp. 28–56). Berkeley, CA: McCutchan.

Rosenshine, B., & Berliner, D. C. (1978). Academic engaged time.

British Journal of Teacher Education, 4, 3–16.

Sindelar, P. T., Bursuck, W. D., & Halle, J. W. (1986). The effects of two variations of teacher questioning on student performance. *Education and Treatment of Children, 20,* 195–207.

Stanley, S. O., & Greenwood, C. R. (1983). Assessing opportunity to respond in classroom environments through direct observations: How much opportunity to respond does the minority, disadvantaged student receive in school? *Exceptional Children, 49,* 370–373.

Sund, R. B., Adams, D. K., & Hackett, J. K. (1982). *Accent on science.* Columbus, OH: Merrill.

8

QUALITATIVE RESEARCH

As alluded to in the introduction to Part II, research methodologies can be divided into two major paradigms, logical-positivism and phenomenological inquiry. Logical-positivism has dominated educational research and is based on the assumptions of the natural sciences. This is the paradigm elaborated on in the description of the scientific method, hypothesis testing, and others in Chapter 1. Chapters 5, 6, and 7 also describe research methodologies based on this paradigm. This chapter elaborates on the other paradigm, phenomenological inquiry as broadly defined. In recent years this paradigm has become increasingly common in educational research.

There has been much confusion over just what qualitative research is. One of the problems is that qualitative research is often described by a negative. That is, it is research that is nonquantitative. This is a problem for two reasons. First, some qualitative research results in some quantification (e.g., counting the number of occurrences of a particular behavior). Second, it represents a negative connotation; the issue might be more accurately put that quantitative research is based on the logical-positive paradigm, which utilizes experimental research methodologies, whereas qualitative research is based on the phenomenological paradigm, which uses a variety of interpretive research methodologies.

Another problem in understanding qualitative research methods lies with the misconception that qualitative research is a unitary approach when in reality qualitative research is a variety of alternative approaches to the traditional, positivistic research most often found in the literature. A variety of terms have been used for the various forms of qualitative methods, including *ethnographic, case study, phenomenological, constructivist, participant observational,* and others.

Erickson (1985) uses "the term *interpretive* to refer to the whole family of approaches to participant observational research" (p. 119), one of the most common types of qualitative research methods. He uses this term, which could be used for all qualitative methods, because it avoids the suggestion that the approaches are simply nonquantitative, it is more inclusive than some other terms (e.g., *ethnography*), and a key feature of this "family" of approaches is that the researcher plays a more central role in the elucidation and interpretation of the behaviors observed. Lincoln and Guba (1985) refer to this type of research as *naturalistic inquiry,* which implies that participant observational techniques result in a more natural approach than the tests, surveys, and the like used in the more traditional quantitative approaches. Marshall and Rossman (1995) suggest that qualitative research offers opportunities for conducting exploratory and descriptive research "that assumes the value of context and setting, and that searches for a deeper understanding of the participants' . . . experiences . . ." (p. 39).

Qualitative research uses different forms of data from those used in traditional research methods. As Patton (1990) sets forth:

> *Qualitative methods consist of three kinds of data collection: (1) in-depth, open-ended interviews; (2) direct observation; and (3) written documents. The data from interviews consist of direct quotations from people about their experiences, opinions, feelings, and knowledge. The data from observations consist of detailed descriptions of people's activities, actions, and the full range of interpersonal interactions and organizational processes that are part of observable human experience. Document analysis in qualitative inquiry yields excerpts, quotations, or entire passages from organizational clinical or program records; memoranda and correspondence; official publications and reports; personal diaries; and open-ended written responses to questionnaires and surveys.*[1]

Qualitative research studies use these techniques in isolation or in combination.

Finally, six assumptions of qualitative research (Merriam, 1988) include the following: it is descriptive; it involves fieldwork; it is "concerned primarily with process rather than outcomes or products" (p. 19); it is inductive in that researchers build abstractions, concepts, theory, and hypotheses from details; the "researcher is the primary instrument for data collection and analysis"; and it is primarily "interested in meaning—how people make sense of their lives, experiences, and their structures of the world" (p. 19).

THEMES OF QUALITATIVE RESEARCH

Patton (1990) proposes 10 themes that inculcate qualitative research. These themes are summarized in Table 8.1 and are what make the various qualitative research methods both distinct from quantitative methods and similar to each other. Although not all qualitative methods are consistent with all 10 themes, they all have most of these themes in common. At the same time quantitative methods, based on the logical-positivistic paradigm, do not adhere to any of these themes.

All qualitative research methods have in common the use of *qualitative data, context sensitivity, emphatic neutrality,* and *inductive analysis* as well as other themes. At the same time although most qualitative studies make use of *naturalistic inquiry,* it is possible for research to be qualitative and not use this theme. For instance, philosophical research may not include observations of real-world situations. On

TABLE 8.1   Themes of Qualitative Inquiry

1. Naturalistic inquiry	Studying real-world situations as they unfold naturally; nonmanipulative, unobtrusive, and noncontrolling; openness to whatever emerges—lack of predetermined constraints on outcomes
2. Inductive analysis	Immersion in the details and specifics of the data to discover important categories, dimensions and interrelationships; begin by exploring genuinely open questions rather than testing theoretically derived (deductive) hypotheses
3. Holistic perspective	The *whole* phenomenon under study is understood as a complex system that is more than the sum of its parts; focus on complex interdependencies not meaningfully reduced to a few discrete variables and linear, cause–effect relationships
4. Qualitative data	Detailed, thick description; inquiry in depth; direct quotations capturing people's personal perspectives and experiences
5. Personal contact and insight	The researcher has direct contact with and gets close to the people, situation, and phenomenon under study; researcher's personal experiences and insights are an important part of the inquiry and critical to understanding the phenomenon
6. Dynamic systems	Attention to process; assumes change is constant and ongoing whether the focus is on an individual or an entire culture
7. Unique case orientation	Assumes each case is special and unique; the first level of inquiry is being true to, respecting, and capturing the details of the individual cases being studied; cross-case analysis follows from and depends on the quality of individual case studies
8. Context sensitivity	Places findings in a social, historical, and temporal context; dubious of the possibility or meaningfulness of generalizations across time and space
9. Empathic neutrality	Complete objectivity is impossible; pure subjectivity undermines credibility; the researcher's passion is understanding the world in all its complexity—not proving something, not advocating, not advancing personal agendas, but understanding; the researcher includes personal experience and empathic insight as part of the relevant data, while taking a neutral nonjudgmental stance toward whatever content may emerge
10. Design flexibility	Open to adapting inquiry as understanding deepens and/or situations change; avoids getting locked into rigid designs that eliminate responsiveness; pursues new paths of discovery as they emerge

Source: M. Q. Patton. *Qualitative Evaluation and Research Methods* (Newbury Park, Calif.: Sage Publications, © 1990), Table 2.1, pp. 40–41. Used with permission of Sage Publications.

the other hand, these themes are the antithesis of the logical-positivistic, quantitative paradigm. For instance, the use of hypotheses in quantitative research precludes *inductive analysis.* Quantitative research is designed to test hypotheses that are theoretically derived. Whether the hypotheses are supported or refuted, the researcher reports the results objectively. Qualitative researchers, on the other hand, do not bring such hypotheses to their research.

Perhaps the most relevant of Patton's themes for this discussion are three of the ones specifically mentioned in the previous paragraph, *qualitative data, context sensitivity,* and *inductive analysis.* That qualitative research methods rely on qualitative data probably seems obvious. Yet this point cannot be emphasized too much. The very nature of the in-depth, detailed descriptions of events, interviews, and the like is what makes qualitative research so powerful. The richness of the data permits a fuller understanding of what is being studied than could be derived from the experimental research methods described in the previous chapters. Although those methods are important for their careful control of confounding variables, they do not permit the type of in-depth study of individuals that is the essence of qualitative research.

Context sensitivity cannot be completely separated from the theme of qualitative data. The reason that qualitative data are so powerful is that they are sensitive to the social, historical, and temporal context in which the data were collected. The particular importance of context sensitivity is that the data are not generalized to other contexts, socially, spatially, or temporally. Because something occurs in one classroom at a particular school and at a particular time does not mean that similar occurrences should be expected elsewhere or even in the same classroom at another time. The logical-positivistic paradigm, on the other hand, purposefully pursues research findings that can be generalized to other settings, persons, and times.

Inductive analysis enables the researcher to explore the data without prior hypotheses. This openness to find whatever there is to find is unique to qualitative research. It permits the researcher to discover reality without having to fit it into a preconceived theoretical perspective. This is obviously the antithesis of the logical-positivistic approach, which insists that research be based on hypotheses generated from theory, prior research, or experience.

Two other of Patton's themes deserve special mention. The *holistic perspective* taken by qualitative researchers is important for understanding the complex nature of many aspects of human and organizational behavior. Two examples of research issues that could benefit from the holistic approach are the study of student characteristics that are relevant to learning and the study of qualities that make for successful schools. *Design flexibility* is critical for qualitative research. Whereas experimental research is carefully planned prior to commencing data collection, with no possibility of change once started, qualitative research is open to change throughout the data collection process. This permits the researcher to adjust the direction of the inquiry based on the ongoing experience of collecting and thinking about the data.

RESEARCH QUESTIONS

"Initial questions should be linked to the problem and significance. . . . Questions may be theoretical ones, which can be researched in any number of different sites or with different samples. Or they may be focused on a particular population or class of individuals; these too can be studied in various places. Finally, the questions may be site-specific because of the uniqueness of a specific program or organization" (Marshall & Rossman, 1995, p. 27). Marshall and Rossman go on to suggest a number of questions that fit each of the types described above.

The theoretical questions include:

"How does play affect reading readiness? Through what cognitive and affective process? Do children who take certain roles—for example, play leadership roles—learn faster? If so, what makes the difference?" (Marshall & Rossman, 1995, p. 27).

"How does the sponsor–protégé socialization process function in school administration careers? Does it work differently for women? For minorities? What processes are operating?" (Marshall & Rossman, 1995, p. 27).

Questions focused on particular populations would include:

"What are the various techniques used by lobbying groups as they try to influence education policy? Which are perceived to be the most effective?" (Marshall & Rossman, 1989, p. 28).

"How do school superintendents manage relations with school board members? What influence processes do they use?" (Marshall & Rossman, 1995, p. 27).

Site-specific questions would include:

"Why is the program working well in this school but not in others? What is special about the people? The plan? The support? The context?" (Marshall & Rossman, 1989, p. 28).

"How do school–parent community relations of private and parochial schools differ from those of public schools? How are the differences connected with differences in educational philosophies and outcomes?" (Marshall & Rossman, 1995, p. 28).[2]

Other research questions that best could be answered with qualitative research methods include:

How do school principals spend their time?

What do teachers think the principal's role is and/or should be?

What actually takes place at school board meetings in a particular school district based on observations and school board minutes?

How do young children react to standardized testing situations?

How do state legislators view the state affiliates of the National Education Association and the American Federation of Teachers?

These are but a few possible questions that would use qualitative methods. Others can be found in any school, school district, or governmental agency. All one needs to do is to look for areas undergoing change. These "new" curricula, administrative arrangements, reform movements, and the like are ripe for qualitative inquiry.

THEORETICAL TRADITIONS

There are a number of different ways to view the theoretical perspectives of the various methodologies subsumed under the term *qualitative* research. Jacob (1987) describes six perspectives from ecological psychology (behavioral settings and specimen records), anthropology (holistic ethnography, ethnography of communication, and cognitive anthropology), and social psychology (symbolic interactionism). Although this is a useful system, it is not comprehensive, and it complicates the issue by fragmenting some fields of study (e.g., two types of ethnography and two areas of ecological psychology). Thus, rather than use Jacob's categories, we will refer again to Patton (1990), who provides a wider, yet simpler, system of categorizing the theoretical traditions on which most qualitative research is based.

Patton (1990) provides a description of 10 theoretical perspectives of qualitative research. These perspectives, their disciplinary roots, and the questions they pose are summarized in Table 8.2.

We will provide a brief description of those perspectives that have the most relevance to educational research. The reader interested in a more comprehensive analysis of any of these methods should refer to the references and suggested additional readings at the end of this chapter. Which method is "best" will depend upon the research question to be answered and the perspective of the researcher.

Ethnography, in addition to being a theoretical perspective, is also is a method for carrying out qualitative observational research. The basic purpose of ethnographic research is to determine the physical and social environment in which the individuals under study live, go to school, and work. The roots for ethnography are in anthropology, which includes the study of cultural phenomena. In educational research, ethnography has been used to study the culture of schools and the people who inhabit them. A study will be described later in this chapter that used ethnography to study school principals.

Symbolic interactionism stems from social psychology and has been used to a great extent in linguistics as well. A premise of symbolic interactionism is the belief that people act according to how they understand the meanings of words, things, and acts in their environment. It is important for teachers in our multicultural society to understand that students coming from different cultural backgrounds will understand the world differently. Test performance, motivation to please the teacher or do well in school, and the like will differ depending upon the students' cultural history. Research using a symbolic interactionism perspective might investigate how different children from different backgrounds perceive and comprehend the school environment.

TABLE 8.2   Variety in Qualitative Inquiry: Theoretical Traditions

Perspective	Disciplinary Roots	Central Questions
1. Ethnography	Anthropology	What is the culture of this group of people?
2. Phenomenology	Philosophy	What is the structure and essence of experience of this phenomenon for these people?
3. Heuristics	Humanistic psychology	What is *my* experience of this phenomenon and the essential experience of others who also experience this phenomenon intensely?
4. Ethnomethodology	Sociology	How do people make sense of their everyday activities so as to behave in socially acceptable ways?
5. Symbolic interactionism	Social psychology	What common sets of symbols and understandings have emerged to give meaning to people's interactions?
6. Ecological psychology	Ecology, psychology	How do individuals attempt to accomplish their goals through specific behaviors in specific environments?
7. Systems theory	Interdisciplinary	How and why does this system function as a whole?
8. Chaos theory: nonlinear dynamics	Theoretical physics, natural sciences	What is the underlying order, if any, of disorderly phenomenon?
9. Hermeneutics	Theology, philosophy, literary criticism	What are the conditions under which a human act took place or a product was produced that makes it possible to interpret its meanings?
10. Orientational, qualitative	Ideologies, political economy	How is x ideological perspective manifest in this phenomenon?

Source: Patton, *Qualitative Evaluation and Research Methods* (© 1990), Table 3.2, p. 88. Used with permission of Sage Publications.

The *ecological psychology* perspective attempts to understand the connection between persons' behavior and their environment. Ecological psychologists believe that behavior is goal directed. Thus, when a child misbehaves in class, the ecological psychologist looks for the reason. The behavior's goal may be to receive attention, or it may be something not as obvious. For instance, a child who is asked to perform a task (e.g., read a passage from a book) that he or she cannot do may misbehave rather than demonstrate the inability (to read). This perspective assumes that the behavior is related to the individual's needs as well as the context or environment in which the behavior occurs. Ecological psychologists collect data through observing the individual and the environment. They keep detailed descriptions of both and then code these descriptions for numerical analysis. Thus, the methodology is qualitative whereas the data analysis is quantitative. The reader should note that it is possible for "one to go from the thick description of qualitative data to quantitative analysis, but not vice versa. One cannot generate thick description and qualitative narrative from original quantitative data" (Patton, 1990, p. 78).

Research studies using a systems theory perspective are often large, interdisciplinary studies. They are attempts to find out how a system or organization functions, what works and what does not work. For instance, studies that attempt to determine the characteristics of successful schools will need to examine a variety of issues about the school itself (e.g., administration, teacher characteristics, student characteristics), the environment in which the school exists including the family structure of the students, and the interaction of these various factors. Such a large-scale study could involve a range of disciplines, including a variety of departments in colleges of education as well as in nursing, psychology, sociology, public health, and social work.

RESEARCH STRATEGIES

Marshall and Rossman (1989) suggest three primary strategies to assist the researcher in designing appropriate data collection procedures. The choice of strategy "depends on the focus of the research and the desired time frame for the study. Examples of strategies include life histories, case studies, and field studies" (pp. 75–75). Ethnography falls within the more general category of field studies. Other strategies include experimental methods from the logical-positivistic paradigm, surveys, in-depth interviewing, and document analyses.

In selecting the most appropriate strategy, the researcher must first determine what is to be studied. If one is interested in studying the ways in which teachers organize their days at work, some form of field study is probably most suitable. On the other hand, if one wished to study a person with mental retardation who has a particular ability in music (i.e., a *savant*), the life history approach would be more relevant.

Another factor in determining the most appropriate strategy is the time period under study; is the study about something contemporary or from the past? Obviously field studies would not be possible if the event to be studied was historical in nature. In such a case some other strategy would be needed such as a life history or document analysis. Three strategies—document and content analysis, case studies, and ethnography—will be described in greater detail.

Document or Content Analysis

Documents are an important source of data in many areas of investigation, and the methods of analysis are similar to those used by historians. The major difference between this type of research and historical research is that, whereas historical research often uses document analysis, it deals solely with past events. When document analysis is used as descriptive research, current documents and issues are the foci. The analysis is concerned with the explanation of the status of some phenomenon at a particular time or its development over a period of time. It serves a useful purpose in adding knowledge to fields of inquiry and in explaining certain social events. Its application to educational research is suggested in some of the studies listed as examples.

In documentary analysis the following may be used as sources of data: records, reports, printed forms, letters, autobiographies, diaries, compositions, themes or other academic work, books, periodicals, bulletins or catalogues, syllabi, court decisions, pictures, films, and cartoons.

When using documentary sources, one must bear in mind that data appearing in print are not necessarily trustworthy. Documents used in descriptive research must be subjected to the same careful types of criticism employed by the historian. Not only is the authenticity of the document important, but the validity of its contents is crucial. It is the researcher's obligation to establish the trustworthiness of all data that he or she draws from documentary sources.

The following purposes may be served through documentary analysis (examples of actual studies are given as illustrations). The first five purposes are of a descriptive research nature, whereas the subsequent three are historical in nature:

1. To describe prevailing practices or conditions.

   Entrance Requirements of Ohio Colleges as Revealed by an Analysis of College Bulletins
   Criteria for Primary Pupil Evaluation Used on Marion County Report Cards

2. To discover the relative importance of, or interest in, certain topics or problems.

   Public Information on Education as Measured by Newspaper Coverage in Three Indianapolis Daily Newspapers during the Month of December, 1958
   Statistical Concepts Presented in College Textbooks in Educational Research Published since 1940

3. To discover the level of difficulty of presentation in textbooks or in other publications.

   The Vocabulary Level of Intermediate Science Textbooks Abstract Concepts Found in First-Grade Readers

4. To evaluate bias, prejudice, or propaganda in textbook presentation.

   The Soviet Union as Presented in High School History Textbooks
   The Free Enterprise System as Pictured in High School Social Problems Textbooks
   Racial and Religious Stereotypes in Junior High School Literature Textbooks

5. To analyze types of errors in students' work.

   Typing Errors of First Semester Typing Students at Shortridge High School
   Errors in English Usage Found in Letters of Application for Admission to the University of Wisconsin

6. To analyze the use of symbols representing persons, political parties or institutions, countries, or points of view.

> *Great Britain as a Symbol, as Represented in New York City Newspaper Cartoons in the Decade, 1930–1940*
> *The New Dealer as Depicted in the American Press from 1932 to 1942*

7. To identify the literary style, concepts, or beliefs of a writer.

> *Shakespeare's Use of the Metaphor*
> *Alexander Campbell's Concept of the Trinity, as Revealed in His Sermons*
> *John Dewey's Interpretation of Education as Growth*

8. To explain the possible causal factors related to some outcome, action, or event.

> *The Effect of Media Coverage upon the Outcome of the 1976 Presidential Election*
> *The Influence of Newspaper Editorials upon the Action of the State Assembly on Sales Tax Legislation*

Content or document analysis should serve a useful purpose in yielding information helpful in evaluating or explaining social or educational practices. Because there are so many significant areas to be investigated, setting up studies for the pure joy of counting and tabulating has little justification. "The Uses of Shall and Will in the Spectator Papers" or "The Use of Too, Meaning Also, in the Works of Keats" would seem to add little useful knowledge to the field of literature.

✳ The Case Study

The case study is a way of organizing social data for the purpose of viewing social reality. It examines a social unit as a whole. The unit may be a person, a family, a social group, a social institution, or a community. The purpose is to understand the life cycle or an important part of the life cycle of the unit. The case study probes deeply and analyzes interactions between the factors that explain present status or that influence change or growth. It is a longitudinal approach, showing development over a period of time.

The element of typicalness rather than uniqueness is the focus of attention, for an emphasis on uniqueness would preclude scientific abstraction. As Bromley (1986) notes, "A 'case' is not only about a 'person' but also about that 'kind of person.' A case is an exemplar of, perhaps even a prototype for, a category of individuals" (p. 295). Thus, the selection of the subject of the case study needs to be done carefully to assure that he or she is typical of those to whom we wish to generalize.

Data may be gathered by a wide variety of methods, including

1. Observation by the researcher or his or her informants of physical characteristics, social qualities, or behavior

2. Interviews with the subject(s), relatives, friends, teachers, counselors, and others

3. Questionnaires, opinionnaires, psychological tests, and inventories
4. Recorded data from newspapers, schools, courts, clinics, government agencies, or other sources.

A single case study emphasizes analysis in depth. Although it may be fruitful in developing hypotheses to be tested, it is not directed toward broad generalizations. One cannot generalize from a number (*N*) of 1. To the extent that a single case may represent an atypical situation, the observation is sound. But if the objective analysis of an adequate sample of cases leads researchers to consistent observations of significant variable relationships, hypotheses may be confirmed, leading to valid generalizations.

The individual case study has been a time-honored procedure in the field of medicine and medical research. Sigmund Freud was a pioneer in using case study methods in the field of psychiatry. In an effort to treat his psychoneurotic patients, he began to discover consistent patterns of experience. Under his careful probing, patients recalled long-forgotten, traumatic incidents in their childhood and youth. Freud hypothesized that these incidents probably explained their neurotic behavior (Strachey, 1964).

His famous case history of Sergei Petrov, "the Wolf Man," published in 1918 under the title *From the History of an Infantile Neurosis,* is one of the classic examples of Freud's use of the case study. He believed that these case studies confirmed his hypotheses, leading to psychoanalysis as a method of treatment. He also used them to demonstrate how theoretical models could be used to provide concrete examples.

Case studies are not confined to the study of individuals and their behavioral characteristics. Case studies have been made of all types of communities, from hamlet to great metropolis, and of all types of individuals—alcoholics, drug addicts, juvenile delinquents, migratory workers, sharecroppers, industrial workers, members of professions, executives, army wives, trailer court residents, members of social classes, Quakers, Amish, members of other religious sects and denominations, African Americans, American Indians, Chinese Americans, Hispanics, and many other social and ethnic groups. Such institutions as colleges, churches, corrective institutions, welfare agencies, fraternal organizations, and business groups have been studied as cases. These studies have been conducted for the purpose of understanding the culture and the development of variable relationships.

For example, a community study is a thorough observation and analysis of a group of people living together in a particular geographic location in a corporate way. The study deals with such elements of community life as location, appearance, prevailing economic activity, climate and natural resources, historical development, mode of life, social structure, goals or life values and patterns, the individuals or power groups that exert the dominant influence, and the impact of the outside world. It also evaluates the social institutions that meet the basic human needs of health, protection, making a living, education, religious expression, and recreation.

The early community studies of Lynd and Lynd are well known. The first, *Middletown* (1929), and the second, *Middletown in Transition* (1937), described the way of life in Muncie, Indiana, a typical Midwestern, average-size city, tracing its development from the gas boom of the 1890s through World War I, the prosperity of the 1920s, and the depression of the 1930s. West (1945) described the nature of a very small community in the Ozark region in *Plainville, USA*. Sherman and Henry (1933) studied the way of life in five "hollow" communities, hidden in the Blue Ridge Mountains, in *Hollow Folk*.

Some community studies have singled out particular aspects for special investigation. Drake and Cayton (1945) described life in the black section of Chicago in *Black Metropolis*. Hollingshead (1949) portrayed the life of adolescents in a small Illinois community in *Elmtown's Youth*. Warner and Lunt (1941) developed a hypothesis of social class structure in a New England community in their study of Newburyport, Massachusetts, in *Social Life of a Modern Community*. Lucas (1970) compared the way of life in three Canadian communities in *Minetown, Milltown, Railtown: Life in Canadian Communities of Single Industry*.

Although the case study is a useful method of organizing research observations, certain precautions should be considered:

1. The method may look deceptively simple. To use it effectively, the researcher must be thoroughly familiar with existing theoretical knowledge of the field of inquiry and skillful in isolating the significant variables from many that are irrelevant. There is a tendency to select variables because of their spectacular nature rather than for their crucial significance.
2. Subjective bias is a constant threat to objective data-gathering and analysis. The danger of selecting variable relationships based upon preconceived convictions and the apparent consistency of a too limited sample of observations may lead the researcher to an unwarranted feeling of certainty about the validity of his or her conclusions.
3. Effects may be wrongly attributed to factors that are merely associated rather than cause-and-effect related.

Those wishing to conduct research on, and read further about, case studies should consult Yin (1994) and Stake (1994, 1995). In particular, Stake's (1995) quite readable book takes the reader through the entire process from selecting cases and research questions to data collection and the analysis and interpretation of the data. Also included are issues of the case researcher's role, validity (triangulation of data), and writing the report.

Ethnographic Studies

Ethnography, sometimes known as cultural anthropology or more recently as *naturalistic inquiry*, is a method of field study observation that became popular in the latter part of the 19th century. It has continued to show significant development, suggesting promising techniques for the study of behavior in an educational situation. In its early application it consisted of participant observation, conversation, and the use of informants to study the cultural characteristics of primitive people: African, South Sea Island, and American Indian tribes. These groups were small, geographically and culturally isolated, with little specialization in social function, and with simple economies and technology. Such cultural features as language, marriage and family life, child-rearing practices, religious beliefs and practices, social relations and rules of conduct, political institutions, and methods of production were analyzed.

The data gathered consisted of observation of patterns of action, verbal and nonverbal interaction between members of the tribe as well as between the subjects and the researcher and his or her informants, and the examination of whatever records or artifacts were available.

Many early studies were subsequently criticized on the grounds that the anthropologist spent too little time among the people of the tribe to get more than a superficial view, did not learn the native language and had to depend too much on the reports of poorly trained informants, and relied too much on his or her own cultural perspective, reaching ethnocentric, judgmental conclusions that resulted in stereotyped theories of the development of the primitive society.

Later investigators realized that studies of this type would be invalid unless the observer

1. Lived for a much more extensive period of time among the tribe and became an integrated member of the social group
2. Learned the native language, enabling him or her to develop the sensitivity to think, feel, and interpret observations in terms of the tribe's concepts, feelings, and values while at the same time supplementing his or her own objective judgment in interpreting observations
3. Trained his or her informants to systematically record field data in their own language and cultural perspective.

This refinement of participant observation resulted in more objective and valid observation and analysis. Some studies were directed toward the examination of the total way of life of a group. Other studies singled out a particular phase of the culture for intensive analysis, taking into account those elements relevant to the problem.

In her classic study *Coming of Age in Samoa,* Mead (1928) observed the development of 53 adolescent girls in a permissive Samoan society. She concluded that there were no differences in the physical processes of adolescent growth between Samoan and American girls: The differences were differences in response. The difficulties of this period of development, a troublesome feature of American life, do not occur in Samoa. She attributed the difference to Samoa's more homogeneous culture, a single set of religious and moral beliefs, and a wider kinship network that conferred authority and affection. The difficulties of American girls were attributed to cultural restraints, not nature.

Many of the time-honored techniques of the ethnographic study involving integration into the group and observation are being applied to psychology and education as well as to anthropology and sociology. An excellent example of this methodology applied to an educational issue is a study of school principals. Morris, Crowson, Porter-Gehrie, and Hurwitz (1984) were interested in determining exactly what principals actually do and how much time is spent on those activities. Their procedure was to have each principal observed for up to 12 full work days. The observers followed the principal wherever he or she went. The authors "were interested in whom the principal interacted with and by what means (verbal face to face, written word, telephone). We wanted to know which party initiated each interchange, whether it was planned or spontaneous, how long it lasted, and where it took place. Most important, we wanted to follow the changing subject matters of these conversations, not only to see what topics consumed the principal's time but also to trace the rhythm of the principal's working hours" (Morris et al., 1984, p. v).[3] One of the conclusions of this study was that principals usually spend less than half their workday in their offices, that they have a good deal of discretion in their decision-making, and that the principal's behavior "affects four distinct 'constituencies' ": teachers and students, parents and others in the community, superiors, and the principal himself or herself (Morris et al., 1984, p. v).

A recent ethnographic study (Lopez-Reyna, Boldman, and Kahn, 1996) examined the perceptions of various professionals (teachers, occupational therapists, physical therapists, speech language pathologists, teacher aides, and nurses) toward a child with HIV in an early childhood special education setting. The speech language pathologist was the second author. She conducted the interviews and collected extensive field notes from her observations. An interesting finding was the inconsistency of two of the professionals' statements with their behaviors. For example, one person believed the little girl with HIV had every right to be in the classroom but, based on observations, did not want to come in physical contact with her, whereas another person did not believe school was appropriate but engaged in frequent physical contact. This article appears at the end of the chapter as an example of qualitative research.

Using the method of observation, the researcher observes, listens to, and sometimes converses with the subjects in as free and natural an atmosphere as possible. The assumption is that the most important behavior of individuals in groups is a dynamic process of complex interactions and consists of more than a set of facts, statistics, or even discrete incidents. The strength of this kind of study lies in the observation of natural behavior in a real-life setting, free from the constraints of more conventional research procedures.

Another assumption is that human behavior is influenced by the setting in which it occurs. The researcher must understand that setting and the nature of the social structure and its traditions, values, and norms of behavior. It is important to observe and interpret as an outside observer but also to observe and interpret in terms of the subjects—how they view the situation, how they interpret their own thoughts, words, and activities as well as those of others in the group. The researcher gets inside the minds of the subjects, at the same time interpreting the behavior from his or her own perspective.

The relationship of researchers to their subjects is based on trust and confidence. Researchers do not allow themselves to be aligned with either the authority figures or the subjects. A position of neutrality is essential to objective participant observation.

Unlike conventional deductive quantitative research, participant observers begin without preconceptions and hypotheses. Using inductive logic, they build their hypotheses as they are suggested by observations. They periodically reevaluate them on the basis of new observations, modifying them when they appear to be inconsistent with the evidence. They look for negative evidence to challenge their temporary hypotheses. In a sense this type of research has the characteristics of a series of consecutive studies. The interpretation is not deferred to the conclusion but is a constant ongoing process of testing tentative hypotheses against additional observations in a real situation.

Ethnographic methods of research have been used to investigate such problems as

1. Student Leadership Roles in an Urban, Racially Integrated High School
2. Pupil–Teacher Relationships in a Suburban Junior High School
3. Social Relationships in a Class of Emotionally Disturbed Children
4. Changes in Attitudes and Behavior in a Drug Abuse Rehabilitation Center
5. The Social Class Structure of a Florida, Cuban–American Community
6. Staff–Parent Interactions in an Individualized Education Plan (IEP) Staffing

DATA COLLECTION TECHNIQUES

Chapter 9 covers a wide variety of data collection procedures, including tests, observation, and interviews, although can be used to collect either quantitative or qualitative data. However, although qualitative methods are included, the major focus of that chapter is on the way that various tools can be used in quantitative studies. Thus, this section will review some of the most useful techniques in qualitative research.

Marshall and Rossman (1995) point to three techniques that are the critical procedures for collecting qualitative data: observation (which they separate into direct observation and participant observation), document review, and in-depth interviewing. Although a number of other approaches exist and will be mentioned later, it appears that most qualitative research studies in education utilize observation, interviews, or a combination of the two as all or part of their data collection procedures.

Observations

When observation is used in qualitative research, it usually consists of *detailed notation* of behaviors, events, and the contexts surrounding the events and behaviors. On the other hand, in quantitative research, observation is usually employed to collect data regarding the number of occurrences in a specific period of time, or the duration, of very specific behaviors or events (see Chapter 7). The detailed descriptions collected in qualitative research can be converted later to numerical data and analyzed quantitatively, but the reverse is not possible.

Patton (1990) proposes five dimensions along which observations vary. First, the observer's role may vary from full participant to complete outsider. A teacher observing in his or her own class would be a participant observer, whereas a research assistant sitting unobtrusively in the back of an auditorium would not. Second, the observer may conduct the observations covertly (e.g., from behind a one-way mirror or casually "hanging around" the halls), with the full knowledge of those being observed or with only some of those being observed aware of the observation (e.g., the teacher knows but the students do not). Third, those being observed may be given full explanations, partial explanations, no explanations, or given a false explanation. The fourth dimension is duration. The observations may take place over the course of an entire school year (or even longer) or could be as brief as an hour. The final dimension is the breadth of focus. The observations may vary from quite broad (e.g., an entire elementary school's curriculum) to quite narrow (e.g., how students in a particular class respond to a substitute mathematics teacher).

Observations can be of the setting or physical environment, social interactions, physical activities, nonverbal communications, planned and unplanned activities and interactions, and unobtrusive indicators (e.g., dust on equipment may indicate a lack of use). The observer also should be alert for nonoccurrences, things that should have happened but did not. The second author and a colleague conducted a quantitative study some years ago on the percentage of time that students were spending "on task" (performing the assigned activity) versus "off task." The most intriguing finding was that for a large percentage of the time (over 40% of the average class period) no task was assigned. The nonoccurrence of the teacher's assigning work to students partially explained the finding that students were on task less than 50% of the class period. Thus, what was not occurring was the most interesting aspect of the results.

An excellent source on observational techniques is the chapter by Adler and Adler (1994).

Interviews

"The purpose of interviewing is to find out what is in or on someone else's mind. The purpose of open-ended interviewing is not to put things in someone's mind (for example, the interviewer's preconceived categories for organizing the world) but to access the perspective of the person being interviewed" (Patton, 1990, p. 278). In conducting interviews it is important for researchers to keep this quote from Patton in mind. Interview data can easily become biased and misleading if the person being interviewed is aware of the perspective of the interviewer. Too often interviewees provide information based on what they think the interviewer wants to hear. Therefore it is critical for the interviewer to make sure the person being interviewed understands that the researcher does not hold any preconceived notions regarding the outcome of the study.

Interviews range from quite informal and completely open-ended to very formal with the questions predetermined and asked in a standard manner (e.g., the questions may be read to the interviewee to assure the same wording with all those being interviewed). Table 8.3 on page 256 summarizes the characteristics of four types of interviews along a continuum from very informal to very formal and provides the strengths and weaknesses of each.

Interviews are used to gather information regarding an individual's experiences and knowledge; his or her opinions, beliefs, and feelings; and demographic data. Interview questions can be asked so as to determine past or current information as well as predictions for the future. The preferred method for data collection is to tape record the interview if the respondent is willing. Otherwise, the interviewer must keep notes contemporaneously and expand on them as necessary immediately following the interview while the information is still fresh in the interviewer's mind. An excellent source for readers who want more depth on interviewing is Fontana and Frey, 1994).

Review of Documents

Document analysis may be for a study that utilizes only this technique or as part of a study that includes observation, interviews, or other techniques. Documents may include primary or secondary sources as described in Chapter 4 on historical research. In fact, most of the description of sources and analysis of data in that chapter pertains here as well. Types of documents useful here include minutes of meetings attended by a participant observer (e.g., how minutes match the events observed by the researcher), formal policy statements (e.g., do people select health insurance based on a complete understanding of the options available?), and various types of archival data. An excellent chapter on interpreting documents can be found in Hodder (1994).

Other Qualitative Data Collection Techniques

Marshall and Rossman (1995) provide descriptions of nine categories of "supplemental data collection techniques" (p. 83) following their delineation of the two "basic" ones, observation and in-depth interviewing. Although all of the nine are worthy of use, this discussion includes only the most pertinent. One technique they describe, *questionnaires* and *surveys,* can be used to gather either quantitative or qualitative data. This category, along with *opinionnaires,* is covered in Chapter 9 and needs no further description here. Similarly, *projective techniques* and *psychological tests* can be used quantitatively or qualitatively and are covered adequately in Chapter 9.

"*Proxemics* is the study of people's use of space and its relationship to culture" (Marshall & Rossman, 1989, p. 89). Studies have been conducted in a variety of environments using this technique. Uses in education would include studies of "the effect of seating arrangements on student behavior" (Marshall & Rossman, 1989, p. 89) or the effect of organizing classrooms into various work areas on student learning, student behavior, and/or teacher behavior.

TABLE 8.3   Variations in Interview Instrumentation

Type of Interview	Characteristics	Strengths	Weaknesses
(1) Informal conversational interview	Questions emerge from the immediate context and are asked in the natural course of things; there is no predetermination of question topic or wording.	Increases the salience and relevances of questions; interviews are built on and emerge from observations; the interview can be matched to individuals and circumstances.	Different information collected from different people with different questions. Less systematic and comprehensive if certain questions do not arise "naturally." Data organization and analysis can be quite difficult.
(2) Interview guide approach	Topics and issues to be covered are specified in advance, in outline form; interviewer decides sequence and wording of questions in the course of the interview.	The outline increases the comprehensiveness of the data and makes data collection somewhat systematic for each respondent. Logical gaps in data can be anticipated and closed. Interviews remain fairly conversational and situational.	Important and salient topics may be inadvertently omitted. Interviewer flexibility in sequencing and wording questions can result in substantially different responses from different perspectives, thus reducing the comparability of responses.
(3) Standardized open-ended interview	The exact wording and sequence of questions are determined in advance. all interviewees are asked the same basic questions in the same order. Questions are worded in a *completely* open-ended format.	Respondents answer the same questions, thus increasing comparability of responses; data are complete for each person on the topics addressed in the interview. Reduces interviewer effects and bias when several interviewers are used. Permits evaluation users to see and review the instrumentation used in the evaluation. Facilitates organization and analysis of the data.	Little flexibility in relating the interview to particular individuals and circumstances; standardized wording of questions may constrain and limit naturalness and relevance of questions and answers.
(4) Closed, fixed response interview	Questions and response categories are determined in advance. Responses are fixed; respondent chooses from among these fixed responses.	Data analysis is simple; responses can be directly compared and easily aggregated; many questions can be asked in a short time.	Respondents must fit their experiences and feelings into the researcher's categories; may be perceived as impersonal, irrelevant, and mechanistic. Can distort what respondents really mean or experienced by so completely limiting their response choices.

Source: Patton, *Qualitative Evaluation and Research Methods* (© 1990), Table 7.1, pp. 288–289. Used with permission of Sage Publications.

Kinesics is the study of body movements. People communicate nonverbally in many situations. This communication is often at a subconscious level and can provide insights into the individual's current state or mood. Kinesics can also be useful in combination with interviews. A person's posture, and facial expressions, for example, can provide additional information beyond her or his answers to the interviewer's questions.

Street ethnography could be adapted to studies of schools. This form of ethnography concentrates on the person's becoming a part of the place under study. To study the homeless might mean spending a great deal of time with them on the street. Similarly to understand the perspective of the members of a local school council in a Chicago public school might require becoming a member so as to be a full participant on that "street."

Narratives are used to study people's individual life stories. This form of inquiry requires a great deal of understanding and sensitivity between the researcher and the person(s) being studied. In fact, narrative analysis can be viewed as a collaborative effort by the researcher and person studied. A good source for those wishing to pursue this approach is Riessman's (1993) short book.

All the data collection techniques described in this chapter, and for that matter in the next chapter, have strengths and weaknesses. One way to emphasize the strengths and minimize the weaknesses is to use more than one method in a study. By selecting complementary methods, a researcher can cover the weaknesses of one method with the strengths of another. Thus, good qualitative research will often include multiple methods of data collection. For instance, a research strategy described earlier, ethnography, most often includes observation and interviews. This permits the researcher to verify interview information with observed events and to better understand what is observed through interview responses. The use of multiple data collection techniques is known as *triangulation.* Triangulation of data permits the verification and validation of qualitative data.

Data Analysis and Interpretation

The data analyses described in Part III of this book deal entirely with quantitative, statistical analyses. Thus, a brief description of qualitative data analysis is provided here. For a more detailed discussion on the subject, the source relied most heavily on for this brief analysis of the topic, Patton's splendid book (1990, pp. 369–506) is suggested. In addition to Patton there are a number of other recent sources for data analysis and interpretation procedures (e.g., Altheide & Johnson, 1994; Huberman & Miles, 1994; Miles & Huberman, 1994; Richards & Richards, 1994) that include the use of computer software. One such program, called QSR NUD*IST (*Non-Numerical Unstructured Data Indexing Searching and Theory-Building*), is designed to be used to organize and analyze qualitative data such as text from interviews, historical or legal documents, or nontextual documentary material such as videotapes.

"The challenge is to make sense of massive amounts of data, reduce the volume of information, identify significant patterns, and construct a framework for communicating the essence of what the data reveal" (Patton, 1990, pp. 371–372). The problems are myriad. Replication of the researcher's thought processes is impossible. There are no tests of reliability and validity. There are no commonly agreed-upon procedures for this task.

The first step in analyzing qualitative research involves *organizing the data*. Qualitative research often results in voluminous notes from observations, interviews, and/or documents. The method of organizing these data will differ, depending on the research strategy and data collection technique(s) used. Interview data, for instance, may be organized according to individual respondents or, if a standard interview format is used with a number of individuals, by grouping answers together across respondents. Similarly observations may be considered individually or by grouping similar types of occurrences together while also looking for differences among individuals, settings, or times. Which approach is taken will depend on the purpose of the research; the number of individuals, settings, and/or times observed or interviewed; and whether the focus is on the particular person, setting, or time under study or on similarities and differences among the persons, settings, or times under study.

Once the data have been organized, the researcher can move to the second stage in data analysis, *description*. The researcher describes the various pertinent aspects of the study including the setting, both temporally and physically; the individuals being studied; the purpose of any activities examined; the viewpoints of participants; and the effects of any activities on the participants.

Only after the data have been organized and described does the researcher begin the final and most critical phase of the analysis process, *interpretation*.

> *Interpretation involves explaining the findings, answering "why" questions, attaching significance to particular results, and putting patterns into an analytic framework. It is tempting to rush into the creative work of interpreting the data before doing the detailed, hard work of putting together coherent answers to major descriptive questions. But description comes first. The discipline and rigor of qualitative analysis depend on presenting solid descriptive data . . . in such a way that others reading the results can understand and draw their own interpretations.*[4]

Patton's last point is crucial. The *interpretation* of qualitative research data is more dependent on the researcher's background, skills, biases, and knowledge than on conclusions drawn from quantitative research, that are derived more directly from the numerical analyses of the data. Thus, it is critical that the reader of qualitative research have access to the descriptive information on which the researcher's interpretations are based. Only in this manner can the reader fully comprehend how the researcher reached her or his conclusions and interpretations and agree or disagree with them.

Finally, the researcher needs to keep in mind the issues of internal validity and external validity of qualitative research just as this was done in experimental research. Just as these issues of validity had specific applications in Chapter 6 on experimental research, they also have meaning here in qualitative research. Internal validity is concerned with the accuracy of the information and how it matches reality. Most qualitative researchers try to to enhance their internal validity through triangulation. This is the process by which data are verified by agreement with other data obtained from other sources, different researchers/data collectors, or different procedures of collecting the data. The issue of external validity means that the researcher needs to discuss the limited generalizabiltiy of the findings and the need, if possible, to replicate the study and its findings. Of course, many qualitative researchers are unconcerned about generalizabiltiy, but the readers must be made aware of this limitation.

SUMMARY

Qualitative research differs from the traditional logical-positivistic, quantitative research in a variety of ways. Qualitative research focuses on in-depth interviews, observations, and document analysis. A holistic perspective permits a broader view of the complex issues facing educational researchers. In addition, although some qualitative research includes limited quantification (e.g., counting the number of occurrences of an event), in general, qualitative research interprets data without numerical analysis.

This chapter has provided an overview of qualitative research and how it differs from the quantitative research methods described elsewhere in this book. A number of themes of qualitative research were related to assist in describing the common elements of the various forms of qualitative methods. Three of the most common forms of qualitative research were also presented: document and content analysis, case studies, and ethnography.

This chapter also includes a brief overview of qualitative data analysis. Three steps in this process were described. The first is data organization. This is critical becasue of the often voluminous data collected in a qualitative study. The second step is description of the data, the setting in which they were collected, and the participants in the study. Finally, the data must be interpreted.

EXERCISES

1. What distinguishes qualitative research from quantitative research? Describe three distinguishing characteristics.

2. Suggest a research topic that could be answered best by using:
   a. case study
   b. ethnography
   c. content and document analysis

3. System theory is an interdisciplinary approach to qualitative research. Propose a research question that would use this perspective, and name the appropriate disciplines that should participate in the study.

4. There are five dimensions on which observations vary from one another. What are these dimensions, and how do they affect the process of observational data collection?

5. What are the strengths and weaknesses of each of the following types of interviews?

   a. informal conversational interview
   b. interview guide approach
   c. standardized open-ended interview
   d. closed, fixed-response interview

6. Suggest an appropriate research topic for each of the types of interviews listed in question 5.

ENDNOTES

1. From Patton, *Qualitative Evaluation and Research Methods* (Newbury Park, CA: Sage Publications, © 1990), p. 12. Used with permission of Sage Publications.

2. From C. Marshal and G. Rossman, *Designing Quantitative Research* (1st and 2nd editions) (Thousand Oaks, CA: Sage Publications, © 1995, 1989). Used with permission of Sage Publications.

3. Used with the permission of the authors and of Charles E. Merrill Publishing Co.

4. Patton, *Qualitative and Research Methods* (© 1990), p. 375. Used with permission of Sage Publications.

REFERENCES

Adler, P. A., & Adler, P. (1994). Observational techniques. In N. K. Denzin & Y. S. Lincoln (Eds.), *Handbook of qualitative research.* Thousand Oaks, CA: Sage.

Altheide, D. L., & Johnson, J. M. (1994). Criteria for assessing interpretive validity in qualitative research. In N. K. Denzin & Y. S. Lincoln (Eds.), *Handbook of qualitative research.* Thousand Oaks, CA: Sage.

Bromley, D. B. (1986). *The case study method in psychology and related disciplines.* New York: John Wiley.

Drake, S. C., & Cayton, H. R. (1945). *Black metropolis.* New York: Harcourt Brace, and World.

Erickson, F. (1985). Qualitative methods in research on teaching. In M. C. Wittrock (Ed.), *Handbook of research on teaching* (3rd ed.). New York: Macmillan, 119–161.

Fontana, A., & Frey, J. H. (1994). Interviewing: The art of science. In N. K. Denzin & Y. S. Lincoln (Eds.), *Handbook of qualitative research.* Thousand Oaks, CA: Sage.

Hodder, I. (1994). The interpretation of documents and material culture. In N. K. Denzin & Y. S. Lincoln (Eds.), *Handbook of qualitative research.* Thousand Oaks, CA: Sage.

Hollingshead, A. B. (1949). *Elmstown's youth.* New York: John Wiley.

Huberman, A. M., & Miles, M. B. (1994). Data management and analysis methods. In N. K. Denzin & Y. S. Lincoln (Eds.), *Handbook of qualitative research.* Thousand Oaks, CA: Sage.

Jacob, E. (1987). Traditions of qualitative research: A review. *Review of Educational Research, 51,* 1–50.

Lincoln, Y. S., & Guba, E. C. (1985). *Naturalistic inquiry.* Beverly Hills, CA: Sage.

Lopez-Reyna, N. Boldman, R. F., & Kahn, J. V. (1996). Professionals' perceptions of HIV in an early childhood developmental center. *Infant-Toddler Intervention, 6,* 105–116.

Lucas, R. A. (1970). *Minetown, milltown, railtown: Life in Canadian communities of single industry.* Toronto, Canada: University of Toronto Press.

Lynd, R. S., & Lynd, H. M. (1929). *Middletown.* New York: Harcourt Brace.

Lynd, R. S., & Lynd, H. M. (1937). *Middletown in transition.* New York: Harcourt, Brace, and World.

Marshall, C., & Rossman, C. B. (1989). *Designing qualitative research.* Newbury Park, CA: Sage.

Marshall, C., & Rossman, C. B. (1995). *Designing qualitative research* (2nd ed.). Thousand Oaks, CA: Sage.

Mead, M. (1928). *Coming of age in Samoa.* New York: William Morrow.

Merriam, S. B. (1988). *Case study research in education: A qualitative approach.* San Francisco: Jossey-Bass.

Miles, M. B., & Huberman, A. M. (1994). *Qualitative data analysis.* Thousand Oaks, CA: Sage.

Morris, V. C., Crowson, R., Porter-Gehrie, C., & Hurwitz, E. (1984). *Principals in action.* Columbus, OH: Charles Merrill.

Patton, M. Q. (1990). *Qualitative evaluation and research methods* (2nd ed.). Thousand Oaks, CA: Sage.

QSR NUD*IST 3.0 [Computer software]. Thousand Oaks, CA: Scolari.

Riessman, C. K. (1993). *Narrative analysis.* Thousand Oaks, CA: Sage.

Richards, T. J., & Richards, L. (1994). Using computers in qualitative research. In N. K. Denzin & Y. S. Lincoln (Eds.), *Handbook of qualitative research.* Thousand Oaks, CA: Sage.

Stake, R. E. (1994) Case studies. In N. K. Denzin & Y. S. Lincoln (Eds.), *Handbook of qualitative research.* Thousand Oaks, CA: Sage.

Stake, R. E. (1995). *The art of case study research.* Thousand Oaks, CA: Sage.

Sherman, M., & Henry, T. R. (1933). *Hollow folk.* New York: Thomas Y. Crowell.

Strachey, I. (Ed.). (1964). *The complete psychological works of Sigmund Freud, Vol. XVII.* London: Hogarth.

Warner, W. L., & Lunt, P. S. (1941). *Social life in a modern community* (Vol. 1). New Haven, CT: Yale University Press.

West, J. (1945). *Plainville, USA.* New York: Columbia University Press.

Yin, R. K. (1994). *Case study research: Design and methods* (2nd ed.). Thousand Oaks, CA: Sage.

SAMPLE ARTICLE

*Reprinted with permission by Singular Publishing Group, Inc. 401 West "A" St., Suite 325, San Diego, CA 92101-7904 (1-800-521-8545). © 1996. *Infant Toddler Intervention: The Transdisciplinary Journal, 6,* 105–116.

clear and concise

Professionals' Perceptions of HIV in an Early Childhood Developmental Center*

Norma A. Lopez-Reyna, Ph.D.
Rhea F. Boldman, M.A.
James V. Kahn, Ph.D.

Children with HIV exhibit mild to severe cognitive disabilities that qualify them for early childhood special education services in the public school system. In this study, we explored the perceptions of the early childhood teaching staff in a developmental center regarding the appropriateness of educational placement of children with HIV. Formal and informal interviews were conducted with the teachers, occupational therapist, physical therapist, speech-language pathologist, teacher aide, and nurse regarding the placement of 3-year-old "Jeannie," who was HIV positive, in their early childhood program for 3- to 5-year-old children with developmental disabilities. Extensive field notes on interactions with her were also collected. Most of the staff accepted Jeannie's placement, though there were some inconsistencies between what they said and how they interacted with her. Implications for teacher preparation and the appropriateness of educational programs for children who are HIV positive are presented.

clearly stated

The purpose of this study was to explore the perceptions of the early childhood staff at a developmental school regarding the education of children who are infected with the human immunodeficiency virus (HIV) and the possible relationship of their perceptions and teaching behaviors to their knowledge of HIV and acquired immunodeficiency syndrome (AIDS).

Rosen and Granger (1992) reported that children with HIV are clearly in need of developmental and educational supports. Children who are HIV infected suffer neurological insult, and most have developmental disabilities that entitle them to special education and/or early intervention services within the public school system in the least restrictive environment appropriate to their needs (Meyers & Weitzman, 1991). Denying educational or developmental services to children with HIV would be an infringement of their basic right to a free and appropriate education within the least restrictive environment (Crocker, 1989).

Section 504 of the Rehabilitation Act also addresses the rights of children with HIV: "No otherwise qualified handicapped individual in the United States . . . shall solely by reason of his handicap, be excluded from participation in, be denied the benefits of, or be subjected to discrimination under any program or activity receiving federal financial assistance." This universal educational protection is extended to children with HIV due to the developmental disabilities usually associated with the infection (Klindworth, Dokecki, Baumeister, & Kupstas, 1989; Meyers & Weitzman, 1991).

As children with HIV enter early intervention programs, teachers and other *statement of problem—could have come earlier in article* professionals will encounter not only children with developmental delays, but children with developmental delays infected with HIV. These early childhood professionals are faced with a series of concerns which likely include an emotional reaction regarding HIV infection and the placement of children with HIV in early intervention and early childhood school programs.

We became interested in the educational services provided to preschool children with HIV following the enrollment of two children who were HIV positive at a developmental center in a large urban school system. This developmental school provides service to children 3 to 5 years of age who exhibit cognitive and physical disabilities ranging from mild/moderate to severe/profound. The majority of these children are functioning cognitively 2 or more years below their chronological age level, with some children exhibiting infantile oral behaviors such as mouthing objects, drooling, and biting. These oral behaviors (and specifically biting) could possibly present a health concern (Baker & Moore, 1987; Dagan & Hall, 1983; Garrard, Leland, & Smith, 1988) when considering the placement of a child diagnosed as HIV positive who engages in injurious behaviors and exhibits severe/profound developmental delays. The second author, who was the speech–language pathologist at the Developmental Center, was able to "view" firsthand the professional staff's reactions, interactions, and perceptions regarding HIV. She discussed her ongoing observations with the other authors. The study emerged from open discussions and inquiries among the staff and among the three authors around the issue of what is fact or fiction regarding HIV and transmission of the virus, as well as questions about appropriateness of educational placement for a child with severe cognitive impairments who is infected with HIV.

somewhat brief review of literature but in keeping with problem and research question

Are children with HIV appropriately placed in developmental programs with *clear research question* other children who are not infected? Staff members at the Developmental Center were asked this question regarding "Jeannie," a 3-year-old child with severe/profound cognitive and physical delays diagnosed as HIV positive. Using qualitative inquiry, these interviews were combined with extensive field notes to identify themes, particularly congruence among knowledge about HIV, beliefs about placement, and teacher-child interactions.

METHOD

clear description

SETTING

This study took place in a public Developmental Center that served approximately 100 children between the ages of 3 and 5, with developmental disabilities ranging from mild/moderate to severe/profound cognitive and/or physical delays. The majority of children were bussed to the Center except for the 10 to 15 neighborhood preschool children who attended the State Pre-kindergarten Program at the Center that included children with developmental delays. The children were of African–American (83%), Hispanic (10%), and Anglo–American (7%) backgrounds and came from homes representing a range of socioeconomic levels from low income to upper middle class.

All of the children at the Center participated in a gross motor program (adaptive PE) and free play in which they could ride bikes and scooters, play on swing/slide set equipment, and have the opportunity to interact with children from other classrooms. The children were all toileted in a general bathroom area where the aides and attendants also diapered the children who were not toilet trained. A hot lunch program was provided, and the children ate in their respective classrooms.

Most activities in the classrooms were geared toward lower developmental levels within the sensorimotor stage of development with a considerable amount of physical interaction with adults. The children with developmental delays received occupational therapy (OT), physical therapy (PT), and speech and language pathology therapy (SLP) in an integrated format in the classroom. The integrated therapies were accomplished in a group language activity called "Circle Time" on the classroom rug. During this time, the classroom teacher and therapists determined the daily activities while the OT addressed fine motor and upper trunk stability. The PT set an optimal position for each child as well as suggesting gross motor activities, and the SLP provided the language concepts and accompanying manual signs.

Each adult involved in the Circle Time activities was involved in a one-on-one interaction with a child. At any given time, specific interactions could change, dependent on the child's current level of interest and motivation and/or movement to another adult. Therefore, all the professionals within the group were involved, hands-on, during most of the Circle Time.

good description

PARTICIPANTS

Jeannie, one of the children enrolled at the Center, was medically diagnosed as HIV positive within the first year of life. Jeannie exhibited open mouth posture, drooling, "raspberries," and spitting behaviors which appeared indiscriminately and, at times, were directed toward other children or adults. She displayed self-injurious physical behavior of stabbing her thumb into her face that resulted in the frequent presence of blood and/or scabs on her forehead and checks. Due to her depressed immune system, Jeannie was constantly congested with a cold, including symptoms such as a runny nose. Her clothing (shirt and pants) was typically wet with saliva from drooling. Jeannie was nonverbal and nonambulatory, functioning at approximately the 12-month level and requiring assistance for all of her daily living activities, for example, feeding, dressing, and diaper changing.

Laura, one of the classroom teachers, had worked in the field of special education for over 19 years. She had a master's degree in early childhood special education and held state certification in the areas of elementary education, physically handicapped, early childhood, and educable mentally handicapped. Before teaching at the Developmental Center, Laura taught primary-level children with physical and mental disabilities. Laura attended a medically based inservice workshop on the topic of HIV/AIDS provided by the Board of Education during the course of this study.

Laura's team teacher, Beth, had worked at the Center for 4 years and had prior teaching experience at a parochial school system in general education classrooms. Beth was certified in early childhood and physically handicapped education and was currently pursuing her master's degree in the area of early childhood special education. Beth had attended a similar medically based inservice workshop on HIV/AIDS 3 years prior to the study. The teacher aide was a full-time "cadre" (substitute teacher) with a bachelor's degree in general education and was pursuing her master's degree in special education. The teacher aide had not attended any inservice classes regarding HIV/AIDS.

The occupational thrapist was on contract to the Center from one of the city's major hospitals. She had past experience working with individuals with AIDS during her therapy practicum. She was state licensed and certified in the field of occupational therapy. The physical therapist also worked on a contractual basis to the Center and had prior experiences providing therapy to individuals with AIDS. In addition to her degree, licenses, and certification in physical therapy, she was also certified in neuro-developmental treatment.

The nurse was a licensed practical nurse (LPN) who was responsible for responding to the medical needs of the trachea and medically fragile children on the buses to and from school. She had been with the school system for over 35 years and was approaching retirement. The nurse had not attended any inservice classes regarding HIV/AIDS.

clear statement of procedure

PROCEDURE

The second author was the speech and pathologist (SLP) for the Developmental Center, and as such, worked closely with the staff in an integrated therapy approach. This position afforded her the opportunity, as a nonthreatening individual and "insider," to gather information which we believe would not have been shared under other circumstances. Within the course of the study, the SLP observed and participated in group activities with all of the participants. Information regarding each individual's perceptions and reactions to Jeannie was readily expressed in an informal atmosphere. The SLP kept field notes after each of her observations and informal interviews.

Data were collected through direct observations of classroom activities, group language activities, and interactions between the aforementioned professionals and Jeannie in the playroom at least weekly during one academic school year. The interactions between Jeannie and the six professional staff members who dominated her school day were observed and recorded as field notes. Other field notes consisted of discussions occurring during team meetings, ongoing comments within the classroom, and conversations during lunch. The focus of the initial observations was on obtaining a general understanding of the staff's perceptions of Jeannie in terms of her educational and health needs and the extent to which they believed that she was appropriately placed. Upon reviewing the transcripts and field notes, we noted an interplay occurring between two factors and the manner in which professionals perceived and interacted with Jeannie. The two factors were the individuals' levels of knowledge regarding HIV and AIDS and their levels of fear in working with children like Jeannie. To explore this possible interplay, a more formal data collection procedure was used.

Systematic audiotaped formal interviews with each of the staff members were conducted to obtain more information from each of them regarding their perceptions of Jeannie and the appropriateness of her placement in a developmental program, their knowledge regarding HIV and AIDS, and their personal concerns associated with working with a child who is HIV positive. Each staff member was interviewed two to four times, with each interview averaging 50 minutes. These interviews were conducted in October, January, April, and June. The nurse was interviewed only in October and June. Table 1 provides the guiding questions used in the initial formal interviews. During the subsequent interviews,

*good use
of table*

TABLE 1. Guiding Questions Used for Initial Formal Interviews

1. Do you feel that a child with HIV is appropriately placed in this type of program for children with developmental delays?

2. Do you participate in any safety precautions when working with a child who is HIV positive that are different from when you work with a child who is not?

3. Have you had any past experience working with individuals with AIDS?

4. Do you have any concerns of contracting HIV from working with a child who is HIV positive?

5. Are the biting, scratching, spitting, and drooling behaviors a health issue or of concern to you?

issues similar to those addressed in the initial set of questions were explored through other questions. Repeated interviews were conducted across the school year to document the consistency or changes in the feelings, perceptions, knowledge, and concerns of the individuals regarding HIV and AIDS and program placement. During these interviews, we also shared our observations with the individuals and asked them to respond regarding the accuracy of *our* perceptions of their opinions and behaviors. Thus, our interviews served to validate and "triangulate" (Lancy, 1993) our impressions from observations and informal interviews.

DATA ANALYSIS

*good
description
of data
analysis
process*

Data analysis was directed at identifying and describing salient issues and concerns of the staff members regarding their work with Jeannie and the appropriateness of her placement, as well as their general perceptions regarding children who are infected with HIV and are being served in a group setting. We focused primarily on the congruence between the nature of the interactions with Jeannie (vis-à-vis their interactions with other students) and their voiced perceptions and knowledge of HIV and AIDS. We coded the themes from interviews and observations by tagging the transcripts and field notes (Bogdan & Biklen, 1992). When this first phase of coding of transcripts was completed, we proceeded by clustering the ideas around the most salient and recurring themes regarding their knowledge, perceptions, and interactions with Jeannie. Our analysis was ongoing during subsequent interviews and observations, and we shared the themes with the participants for verification and further elaboration.

*good
organization
—3 parts*

RESULTS

Our guiding questions served as a starting point for understanding the staff members' perceptions. However, more enlightening were the themes that emerged as each of the staff members was observed and interviewed over an extended period of time. In the following sections, we present the participants' perceptions with respect to the appropriateness of Jeannie's placement and outline related issues we believe played a role in their decisions regarding the issue of placement of children who are HIV positive.

PERCEPTIONS AND BELIEFS

Initial interviews with staff members, for the most part, revealed clear opinions regarding the appropriateness of Jeannie's placement. Laura, one of the classroom teachers, expressed her disagreement with Jeannie's placement in a single statement without further explanation, "I don't think this is an appropriate placement at all." Beth, her classroom team teacher stated, "I had initial concerns about her placement. However, her cognitive level and overall functioning is in concert with the levels that we have in this room." She elaborated no further regarding this point.

The teacher aide who interacted physically on a daily basis with Jeannie appeared hesitant in her response, "I think . . . it's a . . . I'm a little for and against it. I think she should be able to receive an education but in a more limited structure." The nurse also appeared reluctant in her response, "In some instances I feel . . . I feel that these children are inappropriately placed not only [because] of HIV but the low functioning of the other children who cannot protect themselves."

Both the occupational (OT) and physical therapists (PT) were in agreement that Jeannie's placement was appropriate and felt similarly about children infected with HIV in general. The OT stated this belief emphatically, "Should they have the right to be in the system? Yes, they have the right to be here and if you don't agree, move on to something else [find another job]." The PT echoed the same sentiments reflecting her view of the child, not the virus. "The child should be here as much as any other severely or profoundly delayed child in a school setting. Every child should have the opportunity to learn and be in school . . . that is their job when they're kids. They need the exposure. I wouldn't want them kept at home and treated as sick kids. That would be a great travesty."

The PT and the OT verbalized Jeannie's right to a free and appropriate education and seemed to clearly separate Jeannie as a child with developmental disabilities and Jeannie as a child infected with HIV. The other staff members did not articulate this distinction. It was evident, however, that their hesitations regarding accepting her placement as the most appropriate were because Jeannie was HIV positive and could perhaps endanger the other children.

It became evident as we analyzed our data that the major issue in each professional's decisions about whether she thought placement was appropriate or not was the extent to which she believed there was a risk of HIV transmission to other adults and the extent to which a staff member believed it was Jeannie's "right" that was in question. Those who believed there was no real risk of others being infected believed that Jeannie was appropriately placed and had a right to a free and public education. They referred to their knowledge of how HIV is transmitted and to educational codes and regulations. On the other hand, those who elaborated on the various risk factors to others believed that Jeannie was inappropriately placed.

Beth expressed that she took safety precautions by physically restricting Jeannie within the classroom to protect the other children from contracting HIV, "The safety of *all* children should be [of] concern, not just one. She has aggressive behavior which has to be addressed. She has to be monitored constantly or restrained in a chair so she can't harm the other children." To control Jeannie's behavior, Beth confined Jeannie to a chair, tying her in, thus limiting her interactions with the other children. Beth said she feared Jeannie would or could bite one of the other children and subsequently infect another child with HIV.

The PT, in her endeavors to provide Jeannie with more opportunities to explore her environment, disputed Beth's concerns regarding Jeannie's interactions with others. Despite providing Beth with ideas for initiating appropriate interactions with Jeannie, the PT expressed concern that Beth was being resistant to her input. She described an example of a typical conversation with Beth: "I would say to Beth, 'Isn't this good she [Jeannie] likes to be bounced an your lap or if you give her [Jeannie] input to the trunk she sits much nicer.' I've tried to give her [Beth] hand on hand [modeling] and have been interrupted [by Beth] 'No, you see, cognitively we are working on something different.' So anytime I [PT] go into the classroom to challenge what she says, like letting Jeannie explore, I get 'No, you see right now we're working on a table top activity.' So she's [Jeannie] not being able to explore."

Another major concern was that Jeannie herself was medically fragile and that her depressed immune system left Jeannie a likely host for many childhood infections that might result in her death. The risk was primarily expressed by the PT: "She herself is at a very great risk, because of being immune depressed, of being severely ill with a virus, so the fact that she is putting things in her mouth that other children have handled, concerns me."

DELIVERY OF SERVICES

How HIV is transmitted or how some of the Developmental Center's staff believed it was transmitted directly influenced their interactions with Jeannie. The mouthing of toys was developmentally appropriate behavior for Jeannie who was functioning at approximately a 12-month cognitive level and did not exhibit intentional biting behaviors. Also, as noted previously, Jeannie displays self-injurious behaviors of stabbing her thumb into her face, resulting in the presence of blood and/or scabs on her forehead and cheeks.

Four of the staff members showed congruence in their beliefs and knowledge about AIDS transmission and their interactions with Jeannie. The OT, PT, and teacher aide were consistent in their accepting physical interactions and reported beliefs that Jeannie was appropriately placed within the classroom setting, but the nurse was consistent in her disagreement regarding placement and her interactions with Jeannie, which were minimal.

The nurse expressed a concern regarding the need for protecting the other children from contracting HIV, particularly given Jeannie's aggressive behaviors of biting, scratching, and drooling which posed a potential threat. In her words, "The biting could become a problem and because some of our children have other medical problems it could become something serious." Beth concurred, "There is a lot of biting, spitting, and drooling and we just can't allow this with the other children. We can't have this sharing of toys that other children have mouthed or that she [Jeannie] has mouthed and other children pick up and mouth."

The teacher aide, who worked with Jeannie in a manner similar to how she worked with other children, explained that her behaviors were based on information regarding HIV, "For instance, she does bite a lot; she doesn't mean to; she spits and I was just reading some information Laura brought back from the AIDS convention and they say there's still a lot of things they're not sure about. But, she likes to spit a lot, but the doctors said that once the saliva hits the air, the cells are dead and she's not salivating in my mouth, so I don't think there's anything to be afraid of there." Although she related "facts" that she had read, the teacher aide seemed not to be convinced of the absence of danger of contracting HIV.

The OT expressed little concern for the aggressive behaviors of biting and scratching, "I don't think it's [biting, scratching, drooling] any more serious than any other child who bites or scratches who might be a carrier of TB [tuberculosis] or meningitis. So these behaviors shouldn't be looked at with an HIV child as any more dangerous. Our job is the same for an HIV child or the child sitting right next to him or her who bites or spits. Personally, I feel no threat from it. On a[n] emotional level [I feel that] there's more of a threat to the other children than I do for myself. Other children are not aware [of the biting] but if we carry out the same precautions, there should be no threat."

From a stance of inclusion of all children, the PT responded to Jeannie's oral behaviors, "The biting, scratching, and drooling behaviors in any child must be addressed. We need to set up a safety level of restriction of behavior until we can teach them a more adaptive form of behavior, and I think that's what our job is here." The PT appeared to be acknowledging these unacceptable behaviors of biting and scratching as containing meaningful and communicative intent for the child. In her opinion, Jeannie's aggressive behaviors were characteristic of her developmental level and could have been a result of her own frustration and inability to have her needs met.

Inconsistency in reported beliefs and behavior was evident in both the classroom teachers, but in opposite directions. Laura viewed Jeannie's placement as inappropriate, yet she physically interacted with Jeannie in classroom activities in the same way as with other children. In contrast, Beth verbally accepted Jeannie's placement, but physically limited her interactions with her.

Laura was bitten by Jeannie during our study while holding her during a group language activity. She was understandably shaken, yet she responded calmly to the bite, exhibiting control, "I'm not as upset as I would have been had I not attended that inservice on AIDS, and besides the bite didn't break the skin and there was no blood." Laura's colleagues believed that she reacted in a calm manner, particularly given that she disagreed with Jeannie's current placement.

When physically interacting with Jeannie, Beth wore a lab coat and surgical gloves as a safety precaution. During an interview she stated, "Absolutely, I still feel to a certain degree that I'm not an expert in the field of AIDS; but the experts state that you must be concerned with the viral infection contained within cells. I'm not sure that mucousy substances, when the child has a very bad cold or congestion or coughs up mucousy substance, that these cells are not contained within a bodily secretion. And I feel just a little bit safer with the gloves and sometimes lab coat on."

AN EMOTIONAL/INTELLECTUAL STRUGGLE

Toward the latter part of our study, Beth became the focus as we sought to understand her apparent concerns. Verbally, Beth expressed her understanding of Jeannie's educational needs and her acceptance of Jeannie in the classroom, but she physically interacted at a minimal level with her. Beth's inconsistencies were noted by her colleagues, who commented on and referred to them as a "verbal/physical contradiction." Her lab coat and surgical gloves were constant reminders of how *different* Jeannie was from her peers.

By bringing this to Beth's attention, the inconsistency between Beth's stated beliefs and her practices became a topic of discussion among the staff. We were able to begin to more fully explore the nature of the apparent fears that were raised and to more openly discuss and educate ourselves and the staff about the actual, documented modes of transmission of HIV in order to make informed decisions about our own beliefs and practices. While the school staff held informal discussions during lunch and other school settings, the authors reviewed the extant research on the topic.

good description of data— reader can see for self (through quotes, etc.) how the results were analyzed

The nurse supported Beth's concerns and acknowledged that Beth was acting primarily out of her fear of contracting HIV, "I think it [lab coat] is an overreaction. But, if people are afraid it's terminal . . . can't say oops, I should have had, but it's too late. I can see why people overprotect themselves in fear."

The PT believed that Beth's belief/behavior mismatch was basically because she was unaware that she exhibited any fear, "Intellectually, she [Beth] wants to agree with us, but emotionally it hasn't sunken in yet and she has some deep-seated fears. There's an emotional/intellectual fight going on. Other people think that she's changed because they hear her repeat information that has been given to her. I have seen some change, but it is very superficial. I see change in that this staff member is becoming strong[er] in [her] reasons why we don't need to fear interacting with this child while at the same time, or on a messy day when the child is congested, I see rubber gloves and even the lab coat."

This emotional/intellectual battle was also noted by the OT. "I think it really is a fear and that we all have been through it before. On an intellectual level we know a certain thing, but on an emotional level, when we have to work with someone [with HIV] it's a whole lot different, and I think an individual struggles emotionally with this."

Beth acknowledged the struggle she was experiencing and the effect it had on her interactions with Jeannie and openly discussed her feelings. "I don't have the same kind of initial reactions that I had which were probably fear-based on my part as well as lack of knowledge of HIV and, having obtained some more information, I feel more comfortable having *the pupil* [emphasis, ours] here." The struggle regarding knowledge of HIV and fear of the infection and AIDS, regardless of her knowledge base, appeared to cause great emotional turmoil for her. She was unable to fully interact with Jeannie in the manner she required and appeared to fear, not only the virus, but Jeannie herself. Beth continued to take the full range of precautions.

DISCUSSION AND IMPLICATIONS

This study is the first qualitative research that addresses the complex relations among professionals' beliefs, knowledge, and practices in the design of educational programs for young children with disabilities infected with HIV. For four of the six professionals, there seemed to be a clear link between their fears about the likelihood of HIV transmission and their willingness to interact with Jeannie. This supports models of teacher education that endorse enabling preservice and inservice teachers to acknowledge and reflect on their own beliefs and practices (Calderhead, 1989; Pope, 1993).

The apparent presence of an emotional/intellectual struggle is noted in the literature regarding nurses, medical students, and drug treatment staff and their interactions with individuals with AIDS (Alexander & Fitzpatrick, 1991; Connors,

Lewis, Russo, & Baker, 1991; Simon, Weyant, Asabigi, Zucker, & Koopman, 1991). Although our study involved only one team of professionals at a developmental school, we believe that we can use the medical research as a basis for understanding the beliefs, fears, and emotions that some educators face. However, Jeannie was a child with developmental delays who was also physically challenged and required educational intervention of similar quality to that of her peers. In the school setting, her educational needs should be the priority and emphasis within the context of ensuring the safety of the other children. It cannot be ignored, however, that some professionals' levels of knowledge regarding an individual with AIDS and transmission of HIV bear directly on their beliefs and corresponding interactions with infected individuals.

Are teachers justified in their concerns and in the precautions they may take in an effort to protect themselves and other children from becoming infected with HIV? It is well documented that HIV infects the white blood cells, brain, bowel, skin, and other tissues of an individual and manifests itself, in its most severe form, as AIDS (Simonds & Rogers, 1992). HIV has also been found to be associated with certain symptoms and opportunistic diseases and has been described as a progressive, degenerative condition that ultimately results in AIDS and death (Meyers & Weitzman, 1991). Furthermore, despite the vast amount of medical research being conducted, no cure has been found for AIDS nor has an effective means of containing the effects of HIV been developed (Rogers, Ou, Kilbourne, & Schochetman, 1991; Rubinstein, 1983). Thus, fear of being infected is quite justified and more serious than fear of contracting tuberculosis which, although more likely, does not have fatal implications. The question remains, however, as to the degree of vulnerability of becoming infected with HIV that educators actually face.

What the medical research community knows about how HIV is transmitted is incomplete. Basically, there are four forms of transmission of pediatric HIV that have been documented: receipt of Factor VIII treatment for hemophilia, blood transfusion with infected blood, sexual abuse from an infected abuser, or perinatal exposure from an infected mother (Prose, 1990). Since 1987, 80% of all pediatric AIDS cases have been reported to be directly related to maternal factors (Diamond & Cohen, 1992); that is, the child was infected with HIV in utero (Bennett & Rogers, 1991; Canosa, 1991). More directly related to public school contexts and concerns of teachers, however, is the possibility of contracting HIV from saliva or blood that is secreted by drooling or from open wounds.

Studies regarding the transmission of HIV through saliva are inconclusive. Although HIV transmission is evident only when there is the presence of blood, there still exists a fear of transmission of the virus through human bites and saliva. While HIV can be isolated in saliva and has received attention as a possible form of transmission, there is no evidence that saliva can transmit the disease, due to the low level of infectious particles (Freidland, 1990). On the other hand, oral transmission cannot be completely ruled out in the presence of oral cuts and possible presence of blood (Sears, 1989), since bodily fluids that are tinged with blood and that contain a high level of infectious particles may contain HIV (Friedland, 1990; Friedland & Klein, 1987). Based on our review of the literature, there are no known cases of oral transmission.

As medical researchers continue to investigate the issues of transmission and search for treatments to contain the effects of HIV, educational professionals need to continue developing policies for a growing number of children infected with HIV who are entering our schools. Sicklick and Rubinstein (1992) estimate that

90% of all children infected with HIV in utero will develop symptoms of the disease by 4 years of age. Others have stated that although many children infected with HIV are asymptomatic at birth, most begin to develop symptoms and/or signs of HIV infection during the first year of life (Meyers & Weitzman, 1991), whereas a small proportion of children infected in utero may remain asymptomatic for 7 years or more (Prose, 1990). In short, we can expect increasing numbers of children with HIV in our schools, particularly in early intervention and early childhood programs that serve children with special needs.

Medical research has linked the congenital HIV infection with neurological dysfunction and subsequent developmental disabilities (e.g., Caldwell & Rogers, 1991; Diamond & Cohen, 1992; Spiegel & Mayers, 1991; Ultmann et al., 1987). Given the difficulties that many of these children face, programs that coordinate children's services will be necessary to effectively address their educational needs.

Most special educators have been trained in teacher preparation programs based on premises and assumptions regarding the rights of all children to a free and appropriate education. Course and practicum content do not typically involve working with children who present potentially life-threatening situations to themselves, their peers, and their teachers. The relative newness of children with HIV in our schools has brought about new issues for consideration when making decisions about the most appropriate education and especially regarding the most appropriate setting. In our study, educators' stated beliefs appeared to be largely affected by this situation, and it did not seem to suffice to quote Public Laws 99–457 and 101–476 (Individuals with Disabilities Education Act [IDEA]).

not over-generalized In the case of a few professionals, their actions reflected a level of uncertainty about the safety and rights of all involved and, therefore, they posed the question, "Is this the most appropriate setting?" The balance of how best to protect the rights of a child infected with HIV to a free and appropriate education and how best to protect the same child, the other children in the classroom, and the educators seemed to be affected by the stated levels of knowledge about how HIV was transmitted and the extent to which the individual felt convinced that she or he was safe.

discussion & conclusions clear & come directly from results as they relate to research questions In this article, we have described the perceptions of a professional staff in a Developmental Center regarding the educational placement of a child who was HIV positive. Additionally, we provided current research information about the risk of transmission to assist educators in making informed decisions regarding their beliefs and subsequent practices with children who are HIV positive. It was evident during our study that educators are exposed to a range of information and misinformation that can lead to fear and discrepancies between their stated beliefs and practices. We hope this article will assist in opening dialogue among early childhood educators regarding the most appropriate education for children who are HIV positive and symptomatic. Further, it is clear that personnel preparation programs and school administrators must address effective ways to provide preservice and inservice education for their early childhood educators.

REFERENCES

Alexander, R., & Fitzpatrick, J. (1991). Variables influencing nurses' attitudes toward AIDS and AIDS patients. *AIDS Patient Care,* 315–320.

Baker, S., & Moore, S. (1987). Human bites in children. *American Journal of Diseases of Children, 141,* 1285–1290.

Bennett, J., & Rogers, M. (1991). Child survival and perinatal infections with human immunodeficiency virus. *American Journal of Diseases in Children, 145,* 1242–1247.

Bogdan, R. C., & Biklen, S. K. (1992). *Qualitative research for education: An introduction to theory and methods.* Boston, MA: Allyn and Bacon.

Calderhead, J. (1989). *Exploring teacher thinking.* London: Cassell Education.

Caldwell, M., & Rogers, M. (1991). Epidemiology of pediatric HIV infection. *Pediatric Clinics of North America, 38,* 1–16.

Canosa, C. (1991). HIV infection in children. *AIDS Care, 3,* 303–309.

Connors, M., Lewis, B., Russo, J., & Baker, L. (1991). Drug treatment staff's attitudes toward AIDS and work place transmission of HIV: A survey and follow-up Spectrum House, Inc. *Journal of Substance Abuse Treatment, 8,* 297–302.

Crocker, A. (1989). Developmental services for children with HIV infection. *Mental Retardation, 27,* 223–225.

Dagan, R., & Hall C. (1983). Serious infections induced by specific oral habits. *American Journal of Diseases of Children. 137,* 1021.

Diamond G., & Cohen, H. (1992). Developmental disabilities in children with HIV infection. In A. Crocker, H. Cohen. & A. Kastner, (Eds.), *HIV infection and developmental disabilities: A resource for service providers.* Baltimore: Paul H. Brookes.

Friedland, G. (1990). Risk of transmission of HIV to home care and health care workers. *Journal of the American Academy of Dermatology, 320,* 1171–1174.

Friedland, G., & Klein R. (1987). Transmission of the human immunodeficiency virus. *New England Journal of Medicine, 317,* 1125–1135.

Garrard, J., Leland. N., & Smith, D. (1988). Epidemiology of human bites to children in a day-care center. *American Journal of Diseases in Children, 142,* 643–650.

Klindworth, L., Dokecki, P., Baumeister, A., & Kupstas, F. (1989). Pediatric AIDS, developmental disabilities, and education: A review. *AIDS Education and Prevention, 4,* 291–302.

Lancy, D. F. (1993). *Qualitative research in education: An introduction to the major traditions.* New York: Longman Publishing Group.

Meyers, A., & Weitzman M. (1991). Pediatric HIV disease. The newest chronic illness of childhood. *Pediatric Clinics of North America, 38,* 169–194.

Pope, M. (1993). Anticipating teacher thinking. In C. Day, J. Caiderhead, & P. Denicolo (Eds.), *Research on teacher thinking: Understanding professional development.* Washington, DC: The Falmer Press.

Prose, N. (1990). HIV infection in children. *Journal of the American Academy of Dermatology, 22,* 1223–131.

Rogers, M., Ou, C., Kilbourne, B., & Schochetman, G. (1991). Advances and problems in the diagnosis of human immunodeficiency virus infection in infants. *The Pediatric Infectious Disease Journal, 10,* 523–531.

Rosen, S., & Granger, M. (1992). Early intervention and school programs. In A. Crocker, H. Cohen, & A. Kastner, (Eds.), *HIV infection and developmental disabilities: A resource for service providers.* Baltimore: Paul H. Brookes.

Rubinstein, A. (1983). Acquired immunodeficiency syndrome in infants. *American Journal of Diseases in Children, 137,* 825–827.

Sears, C. (1989). The oral manifestations of AIDS. *AIDS Patient Care,* 8–10.

Sicklick, M., & Rubinstein, A. (1992). Types of HIV infection and the course of the disease. In A. Crocker, H. Cohen, & A. Kastner, (Eds.), *HIV infection and developmental disabilities: A resource for service providers.* Baltimore: Paul H. Brookes.

Simonds, R., & Rogers, M. (1992). Epidemiology of HIV infection in children and other populations. In A. Crocker, H. Cohen, & A. Kastner, (Eds.), *HIV infection and developmental disabilities: A resource for service providers.* Baltimore: Paul H. Brookes.

Simon, M., Weyant, R., Asabigi, K., Zucker, L., & Koopman, J. (1991). Medical students' attitudes toward the treatment of HIV infected patients. *AIDS Education and Prevention, 3,* 124–132.

Spiegel, L., & Mayers, A. (1991). Psychosocial aspects of AIDS in children and adolescents. *Pediatric Clinics of North America, 38,* 153–167.

Ultmann, M., Diamond, G., Ruff, H., Belman, A., Novick, B., Rubinstein, A., & Cohen, H. (1987). Developmental abnormalities in children with acquired immunodeficiency syndrome (AIDS). A follow-up study. *International Journal of Neuroscience, 32,* 661–667.

9

METHODS AND TOOLS
OF RESEARCH

To carry out the types of research investigation described in the preceding chapters, the researchers must gather data with which to test the hypotheses or answer the questions. Many different methods and procedures have been developed to aid in the acquisition of data. These tools employ distinctive ways of describing and quantifying the data. Each is particularly appropriate for certain sources of data, yielding information of the kind and in the form that can be most effectively used.

Many writers have argued the superiority of the interview over the questionnaire or the use of the psychological test over the interview. The late Arvil S. Barr, University of Wisconsin teacher and researcher, resolved discussions of this sort by asking, "Which is better, a hammer or a handsaw?" Like the tools in the carpenter's chest, each is appropriate in a given situation.

Some researchers become preoccupied with one method of inquiry and neglect the potential of others. Examining the publications of some authors shows that many studies use the same method applied to many different problems, possibly indicating that the authors have become attached to one particular method and choose problems that are appropriate to its use.

There is probably too much dependence upon single methods of inquiry. Because each data-gathering procedure or device has its own particular weakness or bias, there is merit in using multiple methods, supplementing one with others to counteract bias and generate more adequate data. Students of research should familiarize themselves with each of these research tools and attempt to develop skill in their use and sensitivity to their effectiveness in specific situations.

RELIABILITY AND VALIDITY OF RESEARCH TOOLS

Reliability and *validity* are essential to the effectiveness of any data-gathering procedure. These terms are defined here in the most general way. A more detailed discussion is presented later in the chapter.

Reliability is the degree of consistency that the instrument or procedure demonstrates: Whatever it is measuring, it does so consistently. *Validity* is that quality of a data-gathering instrument or procedure that enables it to measure what it is supposed to measure. Reliability is a necessary but not sufficient condition for validity. That is, a test must be reliable for it to be valid, but a test can be reliable and still not be valid.

It is feasible through a variety of statistical treatments to quantify the reliability and validity of psychological tests and inventories. It is more difficult, though usually possible, to determine these qualities for some other data-gathering instruments or procedures, such as observation, interview, or the use of the questionnaire, in which responses are more qualitative and yield data that are not always readily quantifiable. One should attempt to improve the reliability and validity of the procedures, but precise determination of the degree to which they are achieved is often elusive, particularly in the case of validity.

A brief consideration of the problems of validity and reliability follows the discussion of each type of data-gathering procedure.

QUANTITATIVE STUDIES

Quantification has been defined as a numerical method of describing observations of materials or characteristics. When a defined portion of the material or characteristic is used as a standard for measuring any sample, a valid and precise method of data description is provided. Scientists distinguish among four levels of measurement, listed and described in the following.

A Nominal Scale

A nominal scale is the least precise method of quantification. A nominal scale describes differences between things by assigning them to categories—such as professors, associate professors, assistant professors, instructors, or lecturers—and to subsets such as males or females (see Table 9.1).

Nominal data are counted data. Each individual can be a member of only one set, and all other members of the set have the same defined characteristic. Such

TABLE 9.1   **Academic Rank of Members of the Instructional Staff of Southland College**

	Male	Female	Total
Professors	20	4	24
Associate professors	34	22	56
Assistant professors	44	30	74
Instructors	26	14	40
Lecturers	17	5	22
Totals	141	75	216

categories as nationality, gender, socioeconomic status, race, occupation, or religious affiliation provide examples. Nominal scales are nonorderable, but in some situations this simple enumeration or counting is the only feasible method of quantification and may provide an acceptable basis for statistical analysis.

An Ordinal Scale

Sometimes it is possible to indicate not only that things differ but that they differ in amount or degree. Ordinal scales permit the ranking of items or individuals from highest to lowest. The criterion for highest to lowest ordering is expressed as relative position or rank in a group: 1st, 2nd, 3rd, 4th, 5th, . . . nth. Ordinal measures have no absolute values, and the real differences between adjacent ranks may not be equal. Ranking spaces them equally, although they may not actually be equally spaced. The following example illustrates this limitation:

Subject	Height in Inches	Difference in Inches	Rank
Jones	76		1st
Smith	68	8	2nd
Brown	66	2	3rd
Porter	59	7	4th
Taylor	58	1	5th

An Interval Scale

An arbitrary scale based on equal units of measurements indicates how much of a given characteristic is present. The difference in amount of the characteristic possessed by persons with scores of 90 and 91 is assumed to be equivalent to that between persons with scores of 60 and 61.

The interval scale represents a decided advantage over nominal and ordinal scales because it indicates the relative amount of a trait or characteristic. Its primary limitation is the lack of a true zero. It does not have the capacity to measure the complete absence of the trait, and a measure of 90 does not mean that a person has twice as much of the trait as someone with a score of 45. Psychological tests and inventories are interval scales and have this limitation, although they can be added, subtracted, multiplied, and divided.

A Ratio Scale

A ratio scale has the equal interval properties of an interval scale but has two additional features:

1. The ratio scale has a true zero. It is possible to indicate the complete absence of a property. For example, the zero point on a centimeter scale indicates the complete absence of length or height.
2. The numerals of the ratio scale have the qualities of real numbers and can be added, subtracted, multiplied, and divided and expressed in ratio relation-

ships. For example, 5 grams is one-half of 10 grams, 15 grams is three times 5 grams, and on a laboratory weighing scale two 1-gram weights will balance a 2-gram weight. One of the advantages enjoyed by practitioners in the physical sciences is the ability to describe variables in ratio scale form. The behavioral sciences are generally limited to describing variables in interval scale form, a less precise type of measurement.

Proceeding from the nominal scale (the least precise type) to ratio scale (the most precise), increasingly relevant information is provided. If the nature of the variables permits, the scale that provides the most precise description should be used.

In behavioral research many of the qualities or variables of interest are abstractions and cannot be observed directly. It is necessary to define them in terms of observable acts from which the existence and amount of the variables are inferred. This operational definition tells what the researcher must do to measure the variable. For example, intelligence is an abstract quality that cannot be observed directly, however intelligence may be defined operationally as scores achieved on a particular intelligence test.

Operational definitions have limited meaning. Their interpretation is somewhat subjective, a fact which may lead experts to disagree about their validity. The fact that numerical data are generated does not insure valid observation and description, for ambiguities and inconsistencies are often represented quantitatively.

Some behavioral scientists feel that excessive emphasis on quantification may result in the measurement of fragmentary qualities not relevant to real behavior. The temptation to imitate the descriptive measures of the physical scientist has led some behavioral researchers to focus their attention on trivial, easy-to-measure elements of behavior, resulting in pretentious studies of little value.

The limitations mentioned are not intended to minimize the significance of quantitative methods. Progress is being made in developing more valid operational definitions and better observation techniques. The quantitative approach is not only useful but also may be considered indispensable in most types of research. It has played an essential role in the history and development of science as it progressed from pure philosophical speculation to modern empirical, verifiable observation.

QUALITATIVE STUDIES — *No manipulation; strictly observation*

As discussed in Chapter 8, qualitative studies are those in which the description of observations is not ordinarily expressed in quantitative terms. It is not that numerical measures are never used but that other means of description are emphasized. For example, in the studies described in Chapter 8, when the researcher gathers data by participant observation, interviews, and the examination of documentary materials, little measurement may be involved. However, observations may be classified into discrete categories, yielding nominal level data.

Piaget, a scientist who had a distinguished research career of more than 60 years, came to the conclusion that a nonquantitative search for explanations would be fruitful in the study of human development. His qualitative approach, known as *genetic epistemology,* has suggested another method of observing behavior and the nature of human growth and development. He built his logic of operations on what he observed when children of different age levels were confronted with tasks that required reasoning for their solution.

In some types of investigation, events and characteristics are appropriately described qualitatively. Chapter 8 gives some examples of research questions for which qualitative data are appropriate. This chapter focuses on methods of collecting quantitative data. However, some of the techniques described in this chapter are also appropriate for qualitative data. In particular, projective tests, observation, open-ended questionnaires and opinionnaires, and interviews are used in qualitative research. Chapter 8 also covers some of these data collection techniques from a qualitative research perspective.

To conclude this discussion on quantitative and qualitative studies, several observations may be appropriate. It may be unwise to try to draw a hard-and-fast distinction between qualitative and quantitative studies. The difference is not absolute; it is one of emphasis. One emphasis should not be considered superior to the other. The appropriate approach depends on the nature of the questions under consideration and the objectives of the researchers.

PSYCHOLOGICAL AND EDUCATIONAL TESTS AND INVENTORIES

As data-gathering devices, psychological tests are among the most useful tools of educational research, for they provide the data for most experimental and descriptive studies in education. Because here we are able to examine only limited aspects of the nature of psychological testing, students of educational research should consult other volumes for a more complete discussion (e.g., Aiken, 1991; Anastasi, 1988; Cronbach, 1984; Mehrens & Lehmann, 1991; Thorndike, 1997).

A psychological test is an instrument designed to describe and measure a sample of certain aspects of human behavior. Tests may be used to compare the behavior of two or more persons at a particular time or of one or more persons at different times. Psychological tests yield objective and standardized descriptions of behavior, quantified by numerical scores. Under ideal conditions achievement or aptitude tests measure the best performance of which individuals are capable. Under ideal conditions inventories attempt to measure typical behavior. Tests and inventories are used to describe status (or a prevailing condition at a particular time), to measure changes in status produced by modifying factors, or to predict future behavior on the basis of present performance.

In the simple experiment on reading headlines (Watanabe, Hare, & Lomax, 1984) described in Chapter 6, test scores were used to equate the experimental and control groups, to describe relative skill at this task prior to the application of the teaching methods, to measure student gains resulting from the application of the experimental and control teaching methods, and to evaluate the relative effectiveness of teaching methods. This example of classroom experimentation illustrates how experimental data may be gathered through the administration of tests.

In descriptive research studies tests are frequently used to describe prevailing conditions at a particular time. How does a student compare with those of his or her own age or grade in school achievement? How does a particular group compare with groups in other schools or cities? As described in Chapter 5, achievement tests were used in the study comparing American, Japanese, and Taiwanese students (Stevenson & Lee, 1990).

In school surveys for the past several decades, achievement tests have been used extensively in the appraisal of instruction. Because tests yield quantitative descriptions or measure, they make possible more precise analysis than can be achieved through subjective judgment alone.

There are many ways of classifying psychological tests. One distinction is made between *performance tests* and *paper-and-pencil tests*. Performance tests, usually administered individually, require that the subjects manipulate objects or mechanical apparatus while their actions are observed and recorded by the examiner. Paper-and-pencil tests, usually administered in groups, require the subjects to mark their response on a prepared sheet.

Two other classes of tests are *power* versus *timed* or *speed* tests. Power tests have no time limit, and the subjects attempt progressively more difficult tasks until they are unable to continue successfully. Timed or speed tests usually involve the element of power, but in addition they limit the time the subjects have to complete certain tasks.

Another distinction is that made between *nonstandardized,* teacher-made tests and *standardized* tests. The test that the classroom teacher constructs is likely to be less expertly designed than that of the professional, although it is based on the best logic and skill that the teacher can command and is usually "tailor-made" for a particular group of pupils.

Which type of test is used depends on the test's intended purpose. The standardized test is designed for general use. The items and the total scores have been carefully analyzed, and validity and reliability have been established by careful statistical controls. Norms have been established based on the performance of many subjects of various ages living in many different types of communities and geographic areas. Not only has the content of the test been standardized, but the administration and scoring have been set in one pattern so that those subsequently taking the tests will take them under similar conditions. As far as possible, the interpretation has also been standardized. Although it would be inaccurate to claim that all standardized tests meet optimum standards of excellence, the test authors have attempted to make them as sound as possible in the light of the best that is known by experts in test construction, administration, and interpretation. One relatively new area of concern is the use of standardized tests with persons for whom English is not their first language. The American Psychological Association has published a volume that deals with test issues of Hispanics (Geisinger, 1992).

Nonstandardized or teacher-made tests are designed for use with a specific group of persons. Reliability and validity are not usually established. However, more practical information may be derived from a teacher-made test than from a standardized test because the test is given to the group for whom it was designed and is interpreted by the teacher or test maker. Psychological tests may also be classified in terms of their purpose—that is, what types of psychological traits they describe and measure.

QUALITIES OF A GOOD TEST AND INVENTORY

Validity

In general, a test is valid if it measures what it claims to measure. Validity can also be thought of as utility. Is the test useful for the tester's particular purpose? The overall purpose of educational and psychological testing is to draw an inference about the individual (Popham, 1990). These inferences may include the following: Joey knows the important dates associated with the American revolution; Kathleen has a positive self-concept whereas Fred has a negative one; Emily is among the most knowledgeable students in third grade mathematics in her school district; only half of the students entering first grade in this school are "ready" to learn to read; or Gabriel, because of his high IQ score, is likely to do well academically in first grade. Because these inferences are made on the basis of test scores and because they play an important role in class placement, instructional program offered to an individual, and promotion, the tests on which they are based must be valid measures.

There are three broad types of validity: content, criterion-related, and construct. Not all tests must meet all three types. Different types of tests need different types of validity. In other words, because different tests are used for different purposes, they have different validity issues. For example, tests of intelligence are designed to predict academic achievement and are based on a psychological theory or construct. Thus, this type of test needs to demonstrate construct and predictive validity but not necessarily demonstrate content validity. On the other hand, most achievement tests need only demonstrate content validity.

Content Validity

Content validity refers to the degree to which the test items actually measure, or are specifically related to, the traits for which the test was designed. It shows how adequately the test samples the universe of knowledge and skills a student is expected to master. Content validity is based on careful examination of course textbooks, syllabi, objectives, and the judgments of subject matter specialists. The criterion of content validity is often assessed by a panel of experts in the field who judge its adequacy, but there is no numerical way to express it. Content validity is particularly important for achievement tests but not very important for aptitude tests.

Face validity is frequently referred to as a form of content validity, but it is actually different. Basically, face validity asks the question, Does the test look as if it is measuring what it is supposed to measure? This may seem important but is not when compared to the question, Is the test measuring the content that it is supposed to measure? So called face validity is an appearance issue that we view as relatively unimportant because a test may measure what it says it is without appearing on the surface to do so.

In order to demonstrate content validity, the test maker needs to first define the universe of content that could be included in the test. Next the test's items should be shown to be representative of this universe. These two steps in demonstrating content validity can be done in the test development stage or by using a panel of experts after the test has been developed.

However, for users of tests there is still the issue of whether the test's content is appropriate for the persons to be tested. For instance a reading test that relies heavily on phonic skills may have good content validity for schools where that approach is emphasized but not for schools taking a different approach to teaching reading.

Criterion-Related Validity

Criterion-related validity is a broad term that actually refers to two different types of validity with different time frames:

1. *Predictive validity* refers to the usefulness of a test in predicting some future performance, such as the usefulness of the high school Scholastic Aptitude Test in predicting college grade-point averages. If a test is designed to pick out good candidates for appointment as shop foremen and test scores show a high positive correlation with later actual success on the job, the test has a high degree of predictive validity, whatever factors it actually measures. It predicts well. It serves a useful purpose.

   But before a test can be evaluated on the basis of predictive validity, success on the job must be accurately described and measured. The criteria of the production of the department, the judgment of supervisors, or measures of employee morale might serve as evidence. Because these criteria might not be entirely satisfactory, however, predictive validity is not easy to assess. It is often difficult to discover whether the faults of prediction lie in the test, in the criteria of success, or in both.

2. *Concurrent validity* refers to whether a test is closely related to other measures, such as present academic grades, teacher ratings, or scores on another test of known validity. That is, it is possible to demonstrate validity of a new measure by demonstrating that it is highly related to another measure of known validity or other important criteria that are known.

   An example is the well-known scale of personal adjustment, the Minnesota Multiphasic Personality Inventory, which required sorting nearly 500 cards into three categories, *yes, no,* and *cannot say.* The equipment was expensive, and it could not be easily administered to large groups at the same time. A paper-and-pencil form was devised using the simple process of checking responses to printed items on a form. This form could be administered to a large group at one time and then scored by machine, all with little expense.

The results were so similar to the more time-consuming expensive card-sorting process that the latter has been almost completely replaced. This is the process of establishing *concurrent validity,* in this case by comparing an expensive individual device with an easy-to-administer group instrument.

In like manner performance tests have been validated against paper-and-pencil tests, and short tests against longer tests. Through this process more convenient and more appropriate tests can be devised to accomplish the measurement of behavior more effectively.

Criterion-related validity is expressed as the coefficient of correlation between test scores and some measure of future performance or between test scores and scores on another test or measure of known validity. The subject of correlation is explained in detail in Chapter 10.

Construct Validity

Construct validity is the degree to which scores on a test can be accounted for by the explanatory constructs of a sound theory. A construct is a trait that cannot be observed. If one were to study a construct such as dominance, one would hypothesize that people who have this characteristic will perform differently from those who do not. Theories can be built describing how dominant people behave in a distinctive way. If this is done, people of high and low dominance can be identified by observation of their behavior, rating or classifying them in terms of the theory. A device could then be designed to have construct validity to the degree that the instrument's scores are systematically related to the judgments made by observation of behavior identified by the theory as dominant. Note that dominance was not observed in this example. Rather the test was compared to behaviors suggested as common among persons of high and low dominance by a theory of dominance.

Intelligence tests are a good example of tests that require adequate construct validity. Because different intelligent tests are based on different theories, each test should be shown to measure what the appropriate theory defines as intelligence. Construct validity is particularly important for personality and aptitude tests.

Reliability

A test is *reliable* to the extent that it measures whatever it is measuring consistently. In tests that have a high coefficient of reliability, errors of measurement have been reduced to a minimum. Reliable tests are stable in whatever they measure and yield comparable scores on repeated administration. An unreliable test is comparable to a stretchable rubber yardstick that yields different measurements each time it is applied. One way a test maker can reduce the probability of measurement error and increase reliability is to increase the number of items in a test. An example will help to show why this is so. Let's say that the instructor of this course gives a final examination with just two multiple choice items. Some students with a great deal of knowledge may do poorly because the test didn't sample their knowledge; that is, they knew a lot but not the answers to those two items. Others with only a partial understanding of the course content may guess and get the answers right whereas still others may guess and get both wrong or only one right. Thus, a test with only a few items has a great deal of measurement error. If the number of items is increased to, say, 40, a great deal more of the course content will be sampled so guessing will not play such a great role in determining grades, and the measurement error that existed with just two items will be reduced.

The reliability or stability of a test is usually expressed as a correlation coefficient. There are a number of types of reliability:

1. Stability over time (test–retest). The scores on a test will be highly correlated with scores on a second administration of the test to the same subjects at a later date if the test has good test–retest reliability. Because individual scores may change due to having taken the test before, we are interested here in the relative position of the individual's score. That is, does everyone's score change in the same direction and about the same amount from test one to test two?

2. Stability over item samples (equivalent or parallel forms). Some tests have two or more forms that may be used interchangeably. In these cases the scores on one version will be very similar with scores on the alternative form of the test (for example, scores on form A will be very close with scores on form B) if the test has this type of reliability. Correlation is not as important here as is equal results on the two versions. Time and testers are not factors because the two versions will usually be combined and given as one longer test with the items separated later for separate scoring of the two versions.

3. Stability of items (internal consistency). Test items should be highly related to other test items. This is important because the test, or in some cases the subtest, needs to measure a single construct. For instance, if some test items measure reading readiness and others measure musical ability, the test will not measure either construct consistently. Thus, each test or subtest, if the subtests are to be used individually, must demonstrate item consistency. There are two methods of measuring for internal consistency:

   a. Split halves. This can be accomplished in two different ways. Scores on the odd-numbered items can be correlated with the scores on the even-numbered items. Second, on some but not on most tests, the scores on the first half of the test can be correlated with scores on the second half of the test. (This only works if the test items are equally difficult throughout the test). Because the correlations resulting from the above splits would be for only half a test and because generally the longer a test is, the more internal consistency it has, the correlation coefficient is modified by using the *Spearman-Brown formula.*

   b. Coefficient of consistency. The Kuder-Richardson formula is a mathematical test that results in the average correlation of all possible split half correlations (Cronbach, 1951).

4. Stability over scorers (inter-scorer). Certain types of tests, in particular projective tests, leave a good deal to the judgment of the person scoring the test.

Scorer reliability can be determined by having two persons independently score the same set of test papers or videotapes of the test and then calculate a correlation between their scores, determined by the scores.

5. Stability over testers. It also may be important to demonstrate that two different trained testers can administer the same test to the same people and not have their personality or other attributes affect the results. In this case the same procedure is used as for test–retest reliability, but two different testers administer the two testings, with each one giving the test first half of the time.

6. Standard error of measurement. This statistic permits the interpretation of individual scores obtained on a test. Because no tests are perfectly reliable, we know that the score an individual receives on a given test is not necessarily a *true* measure of the trait being measured. The standard error of measurement tells us how much we can expect an *obtained* score to differ from the individual's *true* score. Test makers usually provide this statistic in the test manual.

The reliability of a test may be raised by increasing the number of items of equal quality to the other items. Carefully designed directions for the administration of the test with no variation from group to group, providing an atmosphere free from distractions and one that minimizes boredom and fatigue, will also improve the reliability of the testing instrument.

A test may be reliable even though it is not valid. However, for a test to be valid, it must be reliable. That is, a test can consistently measure (reliability) nothing of interest (be invalid), but if a test measures what it is designed to measure (validity), it must do so consistently (reliably).

Economy

Tests that can be given in a short period of time are likely to gain the cooperation of the subject and to conserve the time of all those involved in test administration. The expense of administering a test is often a significant factor if the testing program is being operated on a limited budget.

Ease of administration, scoring, and interpretation are important factors in selecting a test, particularly when expert personnel or an adequate budget is not available. Many good tests are easily and effectively administered, scored, and interpreted by the classroom teacher, who may not be an expert.

Interest

Tests that are interesting and enjoyable help to gain the cooperation of the subject. Those that are dull or seem silly may discourage or antagonize the subject. Under these unfavorable conditions the test is not likely to yield useful results.

In selecting a test the researchers must recognize that a good test does not necessarily possess all the desirable qualities for all subjects on all levels of performance. A test may be suitable within a certain range of age, maturity, or ability.

For other individuals outside that range, the test may be quite unsatisfactory and a more appropriate one needed.

The selection should be made after careful examination of the standardizing data contained in the test manual and extensive analysis of published evaluations of the instrument. Research workers should select the most appropriate standardized tests available. Detailed reports of their usefulness and limitations are usually supplied in the manual furnished by the publisher. The considered judgments of outside experts are also available. The 11th *Mental Measurements Yearbook* (Kramer & Conoley, 1992) and its predecessors, along with its supplements, are the best references on psychological tests. These volumes contains many critical evaluations of published tests, each contributed by an expert in the field of psychological measurement. Usually several different evaluations are included for each test. The yearbook is published every few years with supplements (e.g., Conoley & Impara, 1994) between major new editions. Because the reports are not duplicated from one volume to another, it is advisable to consult *Tests in Print* (Murphy, Conoley, & Impara, 1994) or previous *Yearbooks* for additional reports not included in the current volume. In addition to the reviews and evaluations, the names of test publishers, prices, forms, and appropriate uses are included. Readers are also urged to consult the listings and reviews of newly published psychological tests in the *Journal of Educational Measurement*.

When psychological tests are used in educational research, one should remember that standardized test scores are only approximate measures of the traits under consideration. This limitation is inevitable and may be ascribed to a number of possible factors:

1. Errors inherent in any psychological test—no test is completely valid or reliable
2. Errors that result from poor test conditions, inexpert or careless administration or scoring of the test, or faulty tabulation of test score
3. Inexpert interpretation of test results
4. The choice of an inappropriate test for the specific purpose in mind

TYPES OF TESTS AND INVENTORIES

Keeping in mind the issues related to validity and reliability just described, we will now discuss some commonly used types of tests. At the end of each section describing that type of test, we will suggest the most important aspects of validity and reliability needed for that type of test. However, depending on the specific form of the test (e.g., multiple choice, essay, or interview) and the purpose for which it is being used (e.g., prediction of future performance, understanding of current status, or theory building), different types of validity and reliability become more important. Thus, any and all forms of reliability and validity may be needed for each of the tests described below. The description of which forms are most important are only for the typical test use for that type of test and must be used cautiously.

Achievement Tests

Achievement tests attempt to measure what an individual has learned–his or her present level of performance. Most tests used in schools are achievement tests. They are particularly helpful in determining individual or group status in academic learning. Achievement test scores are used in placing, advancing, or retaining students at particular grade levels. They are used in diagnosing strengths and weaknesses and as a basis for awarding prizes, scholarships, or degrees. Many of the achievement tests used in schools are nonstandardized, teacher-designed tests. School districts, however, often use standardized tests to compare schools and school districts. These include tests developed by individual states (e.g., Illinois has developed and mandates the use of the IGAP for certain grades in all Illinois public schools) as well as those long-published tests that have been used for decades (e.g., California and Iowa achievement test batteries). There is a national movement to have standards that would be measured by standardized tests, some in existence but others that would need to be developed.

In research, achievement test scores are used frequently in evaluating the influences of courses of study, teachers, teaching methods, and other factors considered to be significant in educational practice. In using tests for evaluative purposes, researchers must remember not to generalize beyond the specific elements measured. For example, to identify effective teaching exclusively with the limited products measured by the ordinary achievement test would be to define effective teaching too narrowly. It is essential that researchers recognize that the elements of a situation under appraisal need to be evaluated on the basis of a number of criteria, not merely on a few limited aspects.

Content validity is critical for this type of test. Concurrent validity might be used to help establish a new achievement test's validity. Other forms of validity are probably not necessary but would only be important if relevant for the test use. For standardized tests, and assuming the test is group-administered paper and pencil with multiple choice items, the only forms of reliability that are critical are test–retest, stability over test items, and the standard error of measurement. If multiple forms are available, one should add the need for stability over item samples. For tests that also have items requiring some degree of subjectivity (e.g., essay answers), interscorer reliability is needed.

Aptitude Tests

Aptitude tests attempt to predict the degree of achievement that may be expected from individuals in a particular activity. To the extent that they measure past learning, they are similar to achievement tests. To the extent that they measure nondeliberate or unplanned learning, they are different. Aptitude tests attempt to predict an individual's capacity to acquire improved performance with additional training.

Actually capacity (or aptitude) cannot be measured directly. Aptitude can only be inferred on the basis of present performance, particularly in areas where there has been no deliberate attempt to teach the behaviors to be predicted.

Intelligence is a good example of a trait that cannot be measured directly. An individual's intelligence quotient (IQ) is derived from comparing his or her current knowledge with a group of persons of equal chronological age who were administered the test by the author or the author's employees. If a person scores relatively high, average, or low, one assumes the score to be a measure of how effectively a person has profited from both formal and informal opportunities for learning. To the extent that others have had similar opportunities, an individual's ability for future learning can be predicted. This is a matter of inference rather than of direct measurement. Because it has proved useful in predicting future achievement, particularly in academic pursuits, this concept of intelligence measurement is considered a valid application.

Intelligence tests include individual tests such as the *Stanford-Binet Intelligence Scale* and the three Wechsler scales (the *Wechsler Preschool and Primary Scale of Intelligence: WPPSI*; the *Wechsler Intelligence Scale for Children-Revised: WISC-R*; and the *Wechsler Adult Intelligence Scale: WAIS*), as well as some group administered tests of general aptitude. One general aptitude test that is designed to be administered to groups of children or adults is the *California Test of Mental Maturity*, which has five subtests: logical reasoning, spatial relations, numerical reasoning, verbal concepts, and memory.

Aptitude tests have also been designed to predict improved performance with further training in many areas. These inferred measurements have been applied to mechanical and manipulative skills, musical and artistic pursuits, and many professional areas involving many types of predicted ability.

In music, for example, the ability to remember and discriminate between differences in pitch, rhythm pattern, intensity, and timbre seems to be closely related to future levels of development in musicianship. Present proficiency in these tasks provides a fair predictive index of an individual's ability to profit from advanced instruction, particularly when the individual has had little formal training in music prior to the test.

Aptitude tests may be used to divide students into relatively homogeneous groups for instructional purposes, identify students for scholarship grants, screen individuals for particular educational programs, or guide individuals into areas where they are most likely to succeed. The *Metropolitan Reading Readiness Test* is often used by schools to group students for reading instruction.

Aptitude tests, particularly those that deal with academic aptitude, that are used for purposes of placement and classification have become highly controversial, and their use has been prohibited in many communities. The fact that some individuals with culturally different backgrounds do not score well on these tests has led to charges of discrimination against members of minority groups. The case has been made that most of these tests do not accurately predict academic achievement because their contents are culturally biased. Efforts are being made to develop culture-free tests that eliminate this undesirable quality. However, it is extremely difficult to eliminate culture totally and develop one test that is equally fair for all.

Content validity is not critical for this type of test. Predictive validity and construct validity are usually important here. For standardized tests that are group-administered paper and pencil with multiple choice items (e.g., a group intelligence test), the only forms of reliability that are critical are test–retest, stability over test items, and the standard error of measurement. If multiple forms are available, then one adds the need for stability over item samples. For tests that also have items that require some degree of subjectivity (e.g., individual intelligence tests in which the tester interacts individually with the person taking the test), inter-scorer and inter-tester reliability are needed.

Interest Inventories

Interest inventories attempt to yield a measure of the types of activities that an individual has a tendency to like and to choose. One kind of instrument has compared the subject's pattern of interest to the interest patterns of successful practitioners in a number of vocational fields. A distinctive pattern has been discovered to be characteristic of each field. The assumption is that an individual is happiest and most successful working in a field most like his or her own measured profile of interest.

Another inventory is based on the correlation between a number of activities from the areas of school, recreation, and work. These related activities have been identified by careful analysis with mechanical, computational, scientific, persuasive, artistic, literary, musical, social service, and clerical areas of interest. By sorting the subject's stated likes and dislikes into various interest areas, a percentile score for each area is obtained. It is then assumed that the subject will find his or her area of greatest interest where the percentile scores are relatively high.

Interest blanks or inventories are examples of self-report instruments in which individuals note their own likes and dislikes. These self-report instruments are really standardized interviews in which the subjects, through introspection, indicate feelings that may be interpreted in terms of what is known about interest patterns. Two commonly used interest inventories used to help individuals decide on the type of jobs they might want to pursue are the *Kuder Preference Record* and the *Strong-Campbell Interest Inventory.*

Content validity is usually important here as are predictive and construct validity. However, the actual purpose of the test user will determine the types of validity needed. Test–retest, stability over items, and standard error of measurement are the relevant forms of reliability here as may be stability over scores and inter-tester, depending on the nature of the specific test.

Personality Inventories

Personality scales are usually self-report instruments. The individual checks responses to certain questions or statements. These instruments yield scores that are assumed or have been shown to measure certain personality traits or tendencies.

Because of individuals' inability or unwillingness to report their own reactions accurately or objectively, these instruments may be of limited value. Part of this limitation may be due to the inadequate theories of personality on which some of these inventories have been based. At best they provide data that are useful in suggesting the need for further analysis. Some have reasonable empirical validity with particular groups of individuals but prove to be invalid when applied to others. For example, one personality inventory has proved valuable in yielding scores that correlate highly with the diagnoses of psychiatrists in clinical situations. But when applied to college students, its diagnostic value has proved disappointing.

The development of instruments of personality description and measurement is relatively recent, and it is likely that continued research in this important area will yield better theories of personality and better instruments for describing and measuring its various aspects.

The Mooney Problems Check List (1941) is an inventory used by students to report their own problems of adjustment. The subjects are asked to indicate on the checklist the things that trouble them. From a list of these items, classified into different categories, a picture of the students' problems, from their own viewpoint, is drawn. Although the most useful interpretation may result from an item analysis of personal problems, the device does yield a quantitative score that may indicate the degree of difficulty that students feel they are experiencing in their adjustment. This instrument has been used as a research device to identify and describe the nature of the problems facing individuals and groups in a school.

The tendency to withhold embarrassing responses and to express those that are socially acceptable, emotional involvement of individuals with their own problems, lack of insight—all these limit the effectiveness of personal and social-adjustment scales. Some psychologists believe that the projective type of instrument offers greater promise, for these devices attempt to disguise their purpose so completely that the subject does not know how to appear in the best light.

The types of validity and reliability needed for this type of test depends greatly on the nature of the test and its intended use. Any of the forms of validity may or may not be critical. How the test is to be used will determine this. As to reliability, we can assume test–retest, stability of items, and standard error of measurement. Other forms depend on the type of test, multiple choice, interview, and so on.

Projective Devices

A projective instrument enables subjects to project their internal feelings, attitudes, needs, values, or wishes to an external object. Thus the subjects may unconsciously reveal themselves as they react to the external object. The use of projective devices is particularly helpful in counteracting the tendency of subjects to try to appear in their best light, to respond as they believe they should. Projection tests include the *Rorschach,* the *Thematic Apperception Test,* and the *Children's Apperception Test.*

Projection may be accomplished through a number of techniques:

1. *Association.* The respondent is asked to indicate what he or she sees, feels, or thinks when presented with a picture, cartoon, ink blot, word, or phrase. The Thematic Apperception Test, the Rorschach Ink Blot Test, and various word-association tests are familiar examples.

2. *Completion.* The respondent is asked to complete an incomplete sentence or task. A sentence-completion instrument may include such items as

My greatest ambition is
My greatest fear is
I most enjoy
I dream a great deal about
I get very angry when
If I could do anything I wanted, it would be to

3. *Role-playing.* Subjects are asked to improvise or act out a situation in which they have been assigned various roles. The researcher may observe such traits as hostility, frustration, dominance, sympathy insecurity, prejudice—or the absence of such traits.
4. *Creative or constructive.* Permitting subjects to model clay, finger paint, play with dolls, play with toys, or draw or write imaginative stories about assigned situations may be revealing. The choice of color, form, words, the sense of orderliness, evidence of tensions, and other reactions may provide opportunities to infer deep-seated feelings.

Construct validity is critical here as is inter-scorer and inter-tester forms of reliability. Predictive validity also is probably important, whereas content validity is most likely not relevant. Test–retest reliability may also be pertinent.

OBSERVATION

From the earliest history of scientific activity, observation has been the prevailing method of inquiry. Observation of natural phenomena, aided by systematic classification and measurement, led to the development of theories and laws of nature's forces. Observation continues to characterize all research: experimental, descriptive, and qualitative. The use of the technique of participant observation in ethnological research was described in Chapter 8. The importance of observational techniques for single-subject research and some aspects of the methodology involved in using them were discussed in Chapter 7. Most of the discussion here focuses on quantitative research. The use of observation in qualitative research is covered in Chapter 8.

A reason observation is most often used in single-subject experimental research is that it is very costly to observe a sufficient sample of behavior for a large number of subjects. Observation must occur during a number of baseline and intervention sessions in this type of research. In a study described in Chapter 7, Fantuzzo and Clement (1981) observed the attending behavior of their subjects. This is an example of the type of observation technique known as *time sampling* (see Chapter 7 for a description). Every 60 seconds, the subjects were observed to see if they were attending to their task.

In Chapter 6 a study by Hall et al. (1973) was used as an example of an equivalent time-samples design. Observation was used to collect the data in this study also. The observers counted the number of occurrences of aggressive behavior, the technique known as *frequency count* (described in Chapter 7).

In experimental research, observation is most frequently the method of choice for behavior modification studies that use single-subject research designs (e.g., Fantuzzo & Clement, 1981). It is rare to see observation used in group designs (those described in Chapters 5 and 6), unfortunately more because of the cost than because it is less appropriate than the other measures used in its place.

As a data-gathering device, direct observation may also make an important contribution to descriptive research. Certain information can best be obtained through direct examination by the researcher. When the information concerns aspects of material objects or specimens, the process is relatively simple and may consist of classifying, measuring, or counting. But when the process involves the study of a human subject in action, it is much more complex.

One may study the characteristics of a school building by observing and recording aspects such as materials of construction, number of rooms for various purposes, size of rooms, amount of furniture and equipment, presence or absence of certain facilities, and other relevant aspects. Adequacy could then be determined by comparing these facilities with reasonable standards previously determined by expert judgment and research.

In university athletic departments or professional sports organizations, observation has been used effectively to scout the performance of opposing teams. For instance, in football, careful observation and recording of the skills and procedures of both team and individual players are made, and defenses and offenses are planned to cope with them. What formations or patterns of attack or defense are employed? Who carries the ball? Who does the passing, and where and with what hand does he pass? Who are the likely receivers, and how do they pivot and cut?

During a game a coaching assistant may sit high in the stands, relaying strategic observations by phone to the coach on the bench. At the same time every minute of play is being recorded on film for careful study by the coaching staff and players. Who missed his tackle when that play went through for 20 yards? Who missed his block when play number two lost 6 yards? Careful study of these films provides valuable data on weaknesses to be corrected before the following game. Through the use of binoculars, the phone, the motion picture camera, and the video tape recorder, observations can be carefully made and recorded.

Although this example may seem inappropriate in a discussion of observation as a research technique, improving the performance of a football team is not altogether different from analyzing learning behavior in a classroom. The difference is one of degree of complexity. The objectives of the football team are more concretely identifiable than are the more complex purposes of the classroom. Yet some of the procedures of observation so effective in football coaching may also be systematically employed to study classroom performance. In some schools teachers make short periodic classroom or playground observations of pupil behavior, which are filed in the cumulative folder. These recorded observations, known as *anecdotal reports,* may provide useful data for research studies.

Laboratory experimentation seeks to describe action or behavior that will take place under carefully arranged and controlled conditions. But many important aspects of human behavior cannot be observed under the contrived conditions of the laboratory. Educational research seeks to describe behavior under less rigid controls and more natural conditions. The behavior of children in a classroom situation cannot be effectively analyzed by observing their behavior in a laboratory. It is necessary to observe what they actually do in a real classroom.

This does not suggest that observation is haphazard or unplanned. On the contrary, observation as a research technique must always be systematic, directed by a specific purpose, carefully focused, and thoroughly recorded. Like other research procedures it must be subject to the usual checks for accuracy, validity, and reliability.

The observer must know just what to look for. He or she must be able to distinguish between the significant and insignificant aspects of the situation. Of course, objectivity is essential, and careful and accurate methods of measuring and recording must be employed.

Because human behavior is complex and many important traits and characteristics are difficult or impossible to observe directly, they must be carefully defined in precise operational form. Perhaps students' interests can be operationally defined by the number of times they volunteer to participate in discussion by raising their hand within a time sample period. Lack of concentration during a study period can be operationally defined by the number of times students look around, talk to other students, fiddle with books, pens, or papers, or engage in other distracting acts within a time sample period. These examples of operational definitions may be unsatisfactory, but they do illustrate the kinds of behavior that can be directly observed.

Behaviors that might mean different things to different observers must also be carefully defined. Acting-out behavior may mean very disruptive acts such as fighting or, at the other extreme, any behavior for which the child did not first obtain permission, such as getting up to sharpen a pencil. In defining which behaviors meet the meaning of acting out, the researcher would need first to determine the class rules to avoid labeling permissible behavior as "acting out."

Instruments such as stopwatches, mechanical counters, audio and videotape recordings, notebook computers, and other devices make possible observations that are more precise than mere sense observations. Having a permanent record on videotape also permits the researcher to start and stop the action for more accurate recording of data (especially when more than one subject is to be observed), to collect interobserver reliability data (see next section) without having two or more observers at the observation site, and to reexamine his or her ideas and decide on a new format for coding behaviors. Where feasible, the video recording of the behaviors under study is recommended.

Computers can be used to record continuous data streams. A given key is assigned to each behavior under study, and, when pressed, it continuously records that behavior as occurring until it is pressed again. In some cases, the researcher may record multiple behaviors at the same time by pressing a second or third key, or the computer can be programmed to stop recording the initial behavior when the next key is pressed. Which way to program the computer depends on the purpose of the study. After the data are all entered into the computer, they can be printed out or further analyzed.

Systematic observation of human behavior in natural settings (e.g., classrooms) is to some degree an intrusion into the dynamics of the situation. This intrusion may be reactive, that is, it may affect the behavior of the person(s) being observed. These potential confounding effects cannot be ignored. It is widely believed that individuals do not behave naturally when they know that they are being observed. The situation may become too artificial, too unnatural, to provide for a valid series of observations.

Concealing the observer has been used to minimize this reactive effect. Cameras and one-way screens were used by Gesell (1948) to make unobtrusive observations of infant behavior. One-way glass and concealed microphones and videotape recorders have been used in observing the behavior of children in natural group activities so that the observers could see and hear without being seen and heard.

Some authorities believe that the presence of an outside observer in the classroom over a period of time will be taken for granted, viewed as a part of the natural setting, and have little effect on the behavior observed. Others feel that introducing observers as active participants in the activities of the group will minimize the reactive effect more efficiently.

Should the participant observers make their purposes known to the members of the group observed? Some feel that concealing the intentions of the participant observers raises ethical questions of invasion of privacy and establishes a false, hypocritical, interpersonal relationship with the individuals in the group. However, in some cases informing those observed of the complete purpose of the study may affect behaviors so as to make the study meaningless. Do the ends of science justify the means of deception? In a society that increasingly questions the ethics of science, this issue must be confronted. In any case, deception should be minimized.

Validity and Reliability of Observation

For the researcher's observations to achieve a satisfactory degree of content validity, the truly significant incidents of behavior must be identified and sampled. Supplementing the knowledge and skill of the researcher, the judgment of experts in the field may help in selecting a limited number of observable incidents whose relationship to the qualities of interest is based on sound, established theories.

Criterion-related and construct validity may also be necessary, depending on the purpose of the study and inferences made regarding behaviors. For instance, if certain behaviors were considered to be evidence of shyness, construct validity is needed to demonstrate a relationship between the behaviors and the underlying construct.

The reactive effect of the intrusion of the observer as a threat to the reliability of the process has been mentioned. In addition, when researchers are sole observers, they unconsciously tend to see what they expect to see and to overlook those incidents that do not fit their theory. Their own values, feelings, and attitudes, based upon past experience, may distort their observations. It may be desirable to engage others who are then well-prepared as observers, restricting the researchers' role to that of interpreters of the observations. Kazdin (1982) recommends that the researchers not be the observers. To further reduce the possibility of bias, the observers should be kept as ignorant as possible regarding the purposes and hypotheses of the study. This is called a blind. If the persons being observed are also unaware that they are participants in an experiment, thereby reducing the chances of a placebo effect, this becomes a double-blind.

Independent observers should be prepared by participation in

1. The development of the procedures for observing and recording observations
2. The try-out or dry-run phase of the procedure
3. The critique of the results of the try-out phase.

If more than one observer is necessary (as is usually the case), reliability among the observers should be demonstrated. This is done by having each participant observe with at least one other participant for a period of time and comparing their recorded observations. Percentage of agreement among observers should be quite high (usually 90% or higher) if the observations are to be considered reliable. High interobserver reliability is most likely when the behaviors to be observed are well defined and the observers well trained.

Recording Observations

If it does not distract or create a barrier between observer and those observed, simultaneous recording of observations is recommended. This practice minimizes the errors resulting from faulty memory. There are other occasions when recording would more appropriately be done after observation. The recording of observations should be done as soon as possible, while the details are still fresh in the mind of the observer. But many authorities agree that objectivity is more likely when the interpretation of the meaning of the behavior described is deferred until a later time, for simultaneous recording and interpretation often interfere with objectivity. Obviously, a video record permits later viewing of the tape and coding of the observed behaviors.

Systematizing Data Collection

To aid in the recording of information gained through observation, a number of devices have been extensively used. Checklists, rating scales, scorecards, and scaled specimens provide systematic means of summarizing or quantifying data collected by observation or examination.

Checklist

The checklist, the simplest of the devices, is a prepared list of behaviors or items. The presence or absence of the behavior may be indicated by checking *yes* or *no*, the type or number of items may be indicated by inserting the appropriate word or number, or a mark may be made each time a behavior is observed in the space for that behavior (these marks are counted later for the total number of times each behavior occurred). This simple "laundry-list" device systematizes and facilitates the recording of observations and helps to ensure the consideration of the important aspects of the object or act observed. Readers are familiar with checklists prepared to help buyers purchase a used car, choose a home site, or buy an insurance policy, which indicate characteristics or features that one should bear in mind before making a decision. Appendix H illustrates a checklist of this type for the evaluation of a research report.

As indicated above, checklists are also used to count the number of times each behavior occurs in a given period. This is the most common use in single-subject research. In Chapter 7, we described a study by Fantuzzo and Clement (1981) in which they observed whether each child was attentive every 60 seconds during a class period. They most likely used a checklist to mark, and later count, the number of times each child was and was not attending to the task.

Rating Scale

The rating scale involves qualitative description of a limited number of aspects of a thing or of traits of a person. The classifications may be set up in five to seven categories in such terms as

1. superior	above average	average	fair	inferior
2. excellent	good	average	below average	poor
3. always	frequently	occasionally	rarely	never

Another procedure establishes positions in terms of behavioral or situational descriptions. These statements may be much more specific and may enable the judge to identify more clearly the characteristic to be rated. Instead of deciding whether the individual's leadership qualities are superior or above average, the judge may find it easier to decide between "Always exerts a strong influence on his associates," and "Sometimes is able to move others to action."

One of the problems of constructing a rating scale is conveying to the rater exactly which quality one wishes evaluated. It is likely that a brief behavioral statement is more objective than an adjective that may have no universal meaning in the abstract. For this to be considered an effective method in observational research, the traits and categories must be very carefully defined in observable (behavioral) terms.

Rating scales have several limitations. In addition to the difficulty of clearly defining the trait or characteristic to be evaluated, the halo effect causes raters to carry qualitative judgment from one aspect to another. Thus, there is a tendency to rate a person who has a pleasing personality high on other traits such as intelligence or professional interest. This halo effect is likely to appear when the rater is asked to rate many factors on a number of which he has no evidence for judgment. This suggests the advisability of keeping at a minimum the number of characteristics to be rated.

Another limitation of rating is the raters' tendency to be too generous. A number of studies have verified the tendency to rate 60% to 80% of an unselected group above average in all traits. Rating scales should carry the suggestion that raters omit the rating of characteristics that they have had no opportunity to observe.

Scorecard

The scorecard, similar in some respects to both the checklist and the rating scale, usually provides for the appraisal of a relatively large number of aspects. In addition, the presence of each characteristic or aspect, or the rating assigned to each, has a predetermined point value. Thus, the scorecard rating may yield a total weighted score that can be used in the evaluation of the object observed. Scorecards are frequently used in evaluating communities, building sites, schools, or textbooks. Accrediting agencies sometimes use the scorecard to arrive at an overall evaluation of a school.

Scorecards have been designed to help estimate the socioeconomic status of a family. Such aspects as type of neighborhood, home ownership, number of rooms, ownership of a piano, number of books in the library, number and type of periodicals subscribed to, presence of a telephone, occupations of parents, and organizational membership of the adults are all considered significant and have appropriate point values assigned.

The limitations of the scorecard are similar to those of the rating scale. In addition to the difficulty of choosing, identifying, and quantifying the significant aspects of the factor to be observed, there is the suspicion that the whole of a thing may be greater than the sum of its parts.

Colleges and universities are frequently evaluated in terms of such elements as size of endowment, proportion of faculty members holding the earned doctoral degree, pupil–teacher ratio, and number of volumes in the library. Although these aspects are important, the effectiveness of an institution may not be accurately appraised by their summation, for certain important intangibles do not lend themselves to scorecard ratings.

The Scaled Specimen

The scaled specimen, although not frequently encountered in observational research, provides a method for evaluating certain observed levels of performance or measures of a quality in question. Testing a solution for acidity in a chemistry laboratory involves a pH test. A drop of color indicator is introduced into a sample of the solution. The resulting color of the solution is matched with the color of one of a set of display vials, indicating the percentage of acidity in the solution.

One of the early scaled specimens developed in the field of education was the handwriting scale developed by Thorndike. From a large sample of handwriting exhibits taken at different ages and grade levels, norms were established. The handwriting to be evaluated was then matched with the exhibit sample, yielding a measure of handwriting quality.

The Goodenough-Harris Drawing Test (Harris, 1963) provides a 71-point scale with examples for comparing various details of a child's drawing of a man, a woman, or a self-portrait. Each point is scored + or 0, indicating the presence or absence of a part of body detail in the figure drawn. The total of + scores is equated with separate age norms established for boys and girls. The scale is based on the assumption that as individuals mature intellectually they perceive greater detail in the human figure that they reveal in their drawings. Variations of the test include *Draw a Man, Draw a Woman,* and *Draw Yourself.* Studies have reported correlations (see Chapter 10) as high as +.60 to +.72 with the Stanford-Binet Intelligence Scale.

Characteristics of Good Observation

Observation, as a research data-gathering process, demands rigorous adherence to the spirit of scientific inquiry. The following standards should characterize observers and their observations:

Observation is carefully planned, systematic, and perceptive. Observers know what they are looking for and what is irrelevant in a situation. They are not distracted by the dramatic or the spectacular.

Observers are aware of the wholeness of what is observed. Although they are alert to significant details, they know that the whole is often greater than the sum of its parts.

Observers are objective. They recognize their likely biases, and they strive to eliminate their influence on what they see and report.

Observers separate the facts from the interpretation of the facts. They observe the facts and make their interpretation at a later time.

Observations are checked and verified, whenever possible by repetition or by comparison with those of other competent observers.

Observations are carefully and expertly recorded. Observers use appropriate instruments to systematize, quantify, and preserve the results of their observations.

Observations are collected in such a way as to make sure that they are valid and reliable.

INQUIRY FORMS: THE QUESTIONNAIRE

The general category of inquiry forms includes data-gathering instruments through which respondents answer questions or respond to statements in writing. A *questionnaire* is used when factual information is desired. When opinions rather than facts are desired, an *opinionnaire* or *attitude scale* is used. Of course these two purposes can be combined into one form that is usually referred to as a questionnaire.

Questionnaires administered personally to groups of individuals have a number of advantages. The person administering the instrument has an opportunity to establish rapport, explain the purpose of the study, and explain the meaning of items that may not be clear. The availability of a number of respondents in one place makes possible an economy of time and expense and provides a high proportion of usable responses. It is likely that a principal would get completely usable responses from teachers in the building or a teacher from students in the classroom. However, individuals who have the desired information cannot always be contacted personally without the expenditure of a great deal of time and money in travel. It is in such situations that the mailed questionnaire may be useful. The mailed questionnaire is one of the most used and probably most criticized data-gathering devices. It has been referred to as the lazy person's way of gaining information, although the careful preparation of a good questionnaire takes a great deal of time, ingenuity, and hard work. There is little doubt that the poorly constructed questionnaires that flood the mails have created a certain amount of contempt. This is particularly true when the accompanying letter pleads that the sender needs the information to complete the requirements for a graduate course, thesis, or dissertation. The recipient's reaction may be, "Why should I go to all this trouble to help this person get a degree?"

Filling out lengthy questionnaires takes a great deal of time and effort, a favor that few senders have any right to expect of strangers. The unfavorable reaction is intensified when the questionnaire is long, the subject trivial, the items vaguely worded, and the form poorly organized. The poor quality of so many mailed questionnaires helps to explain why so small a proportion is returned. As a result of low response rates, often less than 40%, the data obtained are often of limited validity. The information in the unreturned questionnaires might have changed the results of the investigation dramatically. The very fact of no response might imply certain types of reactions, reactions that can never be included in the summary of data.

Unless one is dealing with a group of respondents who have a genuine interest in the problem under investigation, know the sender, or have some common bond of loyalty to a sponsoring institution or organization, the rate of returns is frequently disappointing and provides a flimsy basis for generalization.

Although the foregoing discussion may seem to discredit the questionnaire as a respectable research technique, we have tried to consider the abuse or misuse of the device. Actually the questionnaire has unique advantages, and, properly constructed and administered, it may serve as a most appropriate and useful data-gathering device in a research project.

Closed Form

Questionnaires that call for short, check-mark responses are known as the *restricted*, or *closed-form*, type. Here mark a *yes* or *no*, write a short response, or check an item from a list of suggested responses. The following example illustrates the closed-form item:

Why did you choose to do your graduate work at this university? Kindly indicate three reasons in order of importance, using the number 1 for the most important, 2 for the second most important, and 3 for the third most important.

	Rank
(a) Convenience of transportation	_____
(b) Advice of a friend	_____
(c) Reputation of institution	_____
(d) Expense factor	_____
(e) Scholarship aid	_____
(f) Other _____	_____
(kindly indicate)	

Even when using the closed form, it is advisable to provide for unanticipated responses. Providing an "other" category permits respondents to indicate what might be their most important reason, one that the questionnaire builder had not anticipated. One should note the instruction to rank choices in order of importance, a fact which enables the tabulator to properly classify all responses.

For certain types of information the closed-form questionnaire is entirely satisfactory. It is easy to fill out, takes little time, keeps the respondent on the subject, is relatively objective, and is fairly easy to tabulate and analyze.

The Open Form

The *open-form*, or *unrestricted*, questionnaire calls for a free response in the respondent's own words. The following open-form item seeks the same type of information as did the closed-form item:

Why did you choose to do your graduate work at this university?

Note that no clues are given. The open form probably provides for greater depth of response. The respondents reveal their frame of reference and possibly the reasons for their responses. But because it requires greater effort on the part of the respondents, returns are often meager. Also, the open-form item can sometimes be difficult to interpret, tabulate, and summarize in the research report.

Many questionnaires include both open- and closed-type items. Each type has its merits and limitations, and the questionnaire builder must decide which type is more likely to supply the information wanted.

Improving Questionnaire Items

Inexperienced questionnaire makers are likely to be naive about the clarity of their questions. One author of this book recalls a brilliant graduate student who submitted a questionnaire for his approval. She was somewhat irritated by his subsequent questions and suggestions, remarking that anyone with any degree of intelligence should know what she meant. At the advisor's suggestion she duplicated some copies and personally administered the questionnaire to a graduate class in research.

She was swamped with questions of interpretation, many of which she could not answer clearly. There was considerable evidence of confusion about what she wanted to know. After she had collected the completed copies and had tried to tabulate the responses, she began to see the questionnaire's faults. Even her directions and explanation in class had failed to clarify the ambiguous intent of her questionnaire. Her second version was much improved.

Many beginning researchers are not really sure what they want to know. They use a shotgun approach, attempting to cover their field broadly in the hope that some of the responses will provide the answers for which they are groping. Unless researchers know exactly what they want, however, they are not likely to ask the right questions or to phrase them properly.

In addition to the problem of knowing what one wants, there is the difficulty of wording the questionnaire clearly. The limitations of words are particular hazards in the questionnaire. The same words mean different things to different people. After all, even questionnaire makers have their own interpretation, and the respondents may have many different interpretations. In the interview, as in conversation, we are able to clear up misunderstandings by restating our question, by inflection of the voice, by suggestions, and by a number of other devices. But the written question stands by itself, often ambiguous and misunderstood.

A simple example illustrates the influence of voice inflection alone. Consider the following question. Read it over, each time emphasizing the underlined word, noting how the change in inflection alters the meaning.

<u>Were</u> you there last night?

Were <u>you</u> there last night?

Were you <u>there</u> last night?

Were you there <u>last</u> night?

Were you there last <u>night</u>?

Questionnaire makers must depend on written language alone. Obviously they cannot be too careful in phrasing questions to insure their clarity of purpose. Although there are no certain ways of producing foolproof questions, certain principles can be employed to make questionnaire items more precise. A few are suggested here with the hope that students constructing questionnaires and opinionnaires will become critical of their first efforts and strive to make each item as clear as possible.

Define or qualify terms that could easily be misinterpreted. What is the value of your house? The meaning of the term *value* is not clear. It could imply several different meanings: the assessed value for tax purposes, what it would sell for on the present market, what you would be willing to sell it for, what it would cost to replace, or what you paid for it. These values may differ considerably. It is essential to frame questions specifically, such as, "What is the present market value of your house?"

As simple a term as *age* is often misunderstood. When is an individual 21? Most people would say that a person is 21 from the day of the 21st birthday until the day of the 22nd birthday. But an insurance company considers a person 21 from age 20 and 6 months until age 21 and 6 months. Perhaps this question could be clarified by asking *age at last birthday* or *date of birth.*

Hundreds of words are ambiguous because of their many interpretations. One has only to think of such words and phrases as *curriculum, democracy, progressive education, cooperation,* and *integration* and even such simple words as *how much* and *now.* To the question, "What work are you doing now?" the respondent might be tempted to answer, "Filling out your foolish questionnaire."

Be careful in using descriptive adjectives and adverbs that have no agreed-upon meaning. This fault is frequently found in rating scales as well as in questionnaires. *Frequently, occasionally,* and *rarely* do not have the same meanings to different persons (Hakel, 1968). One respondent's *occasionally* may be another's *rarely.* Perhaps a stated frequency—*times per week* or *times per month*—would make this classification more precise.

Beware of double negatives. Below are two questions with double negatives that could easily be reworded so as to avoid this mistake.

"Are you opposed to *not* requiring students to take showers after gym class?"

This could be changed to read:

"Are you in favor of requiring students to take showers after gym class?"

"Federal aid should *not* be granted to those states in which education is *not* equal regardless or race, creed, or religion."

This could be reworded to read:

"Federal aid should only be granted to those states in which education is equal regardless of race, creed, or religion."

Be careful of inadequate alternatives.

Married?   Yes _____   No _____

Does this question refer to present or former marital status? How would the person answer who is widowed, separated, or divorced?

"How late at night do you permit your children to watch television?"

There may be no established family policy. If there is a policy, it may differ for children of different ages. It may be different for school nights or for Friday and Saturday nights, when watching a late movie may be permitted.

Avoid the double-barreled question.

"Do you believe that gifted students should be placed in separate groups for instructional purposes and assigned to special schools?"

One might agree on the advisability of separate groups for instructional purposes but be very much opposed to the assignment of gifted students to special schools. Two separate questions are needed.

Underline a word to indicate special emphasis.

"A parent should <u>not</u> be told his child's IQ score."

"Should all schools offer a <u>modern</u> foreign language?"

When asking for ratings or comparisons, provide a point of reference.

"How would you rate this student teacher's classroom demeanor?"

Superior _____   Average _____   Below average _____

With whom is the student teacher to be compared—an experienced teacher, other student teachers, former student teachers—or should the criterion be what a student teacher is expected to be able to do?

Avoid unwanted assumptions.

"Are you satisfied with the salary raise that you received last year?"

A *no* answer might mean either "I did not get a raise" or "I *did* get a raise but am not satisfied."

"Do you feel that you benefited from the spankings that you received as a child?"

A *no* response could mean either that the spankings did not help or that the parents did not administer corporal punishment. These unwarranted assumptions are nearly as bad as the classic, "When did you stop beating your wife?"

Phrase questions so that they are appropriate for all respondents.

"What is your monthly teaching salary?"

Some teachers are paid on a 9-month basis, some on 10, some on 11, and some on 12. Three questions would be needed.

Your salary per month? _____

Number of months in school term? _____

Number of salary payments per year? _____

Or the question might refer to annual salary and number of months worked for that salary.

If your answer is *Yes*, kindly check *how often* and *what sections* of the *Star* you read.

Section	Always	Usually	Seldom	Never
National and inter- national news				
State and local news				
Editorial				
Sports				
Comic				
Society				
Financial				
Advertising				
Want ad				
Syndicated features				
Special features				
Other (specify)				

FIGURE 9.1   Sample Questionnaire Item

Design questions that will give a complete response.

Do you read the *Indianapolis Star*? Yes _____ No _____

A *yes* or *no* answer would not reveal much information about the reading habits of the respondent. The question might be followed with an additional item, as in Figure 9.1.

Provide for the systematic quantification of responses. The type of question that asks respondents to check a number of items from a list is difficult to summarize, especially if not all respondents check the same number. One solution is to ask respondents to rank, in order of preference, a specific number of responses.

"What are your favorite television programs? Rank in order of preference your first, second, third, fourth, and fifth choices."

The items can then be tabulated by inverse weightings.

1st choice	5 points
2nd choice	4 points
3rd choice	3 points
4th choice	2 points
5th choice	1 point

The relative popularity of the programs could be described for a group in terms of total weighted scores, the most popular having the largest total.

Consider the possibility of classifying the responses yourself rather than having the respondent choose categories. If students were asked to classify their fathers' occupation in one of the following categories, the results might be quite unsatisfactory.

Unskilled labor	_____
Skilled labor	_____
Clerical work	_____
Managerial work	_____
Profession	_____
Proprietorship	_____

It is likely that by asking the children one or two short questions about their fathers' work, it could be classified more accurately.

1. At what place does your father work?
2. What kind of work does he do?

Very often a researcher wants to gather information (facts) and attitudes (opinions). This allows later analyses to determine if attitudes are related to personal characteristics such as age, gender, or race. Figure 9.2 is an example of just such a combination. This questionnaire collects information about the individual and then asks for the opinion of the person regarding factors that contribute to teacher morale.

---

1. Male _____ Female _____
2. Age _____
3. Marital status: single _____ married _____ divorced/separated _____
4. Number of dependent children _____; their ages _____
5. Number of other dependents _____
6. Highest degree held _____
7. Years of teaching experience _____
8. Years of teaching at present school _____
9. Teaching level; primary _____ intermediate _____ upper grades _____
   Jr. H.S. _____ Sr. H.S. _____; If secondary, your major teaching area _____
10. Enrollment of your school _____
11. Your average class size _____
12. Population of your community or school district _____
13. Your principal is: male _____ female _____

(continued)

FIGURE 9.2   Teacher Morale Questionnaire–Opinionnaire

FIGURE 9.2 continued

	Excellent	Good	Fair	Poor
14. How does your salary schedule compare with those of similar school districts?				
15. How would you rate your principal on these traits?				
competence				
friendliness				
helpfulness				
ability to inspire				
16. How would you rate the consulting or advisory services that you receive?				
encourage creativity				
availability				
17. Provision made for teacher free time				
relaxation				
preparation				
lunch				
conferences				
18. How would you rate your faculty lounge?				
19. How would you rate your faculty professional library?				
books				
periodicals				
references				
20. How would you evaluate the adequacy of teaching materials and supplies?				
textbooks				
references				
AV aids				
supplies				
21. How would you evaluate the assignment of your nonteaching duties? (leave blank if item *does not apply*)				
reports				
meetings				
halls				
lunchroom				
supervision of playground				
study hall				
extra class				
organizations				
22. How would you rate the compatibility of your faculty?				
23. How would you rate the parent support of your school?				
24. How would you rate your morale as a teacher?				

FIGURE 9.2   continued

25. Kindly *rank in order of importance to you* at least *five* factors that you would consider most important in increasing your morale or satisfaction with your working conditions: Rank 1, most important, 2 next in importance, etc.

_____ a. higher salary

_____ b. smaller class size

_____ c. more free time

_____ d. more adequate faculty lounge

_____ e. more compatible faculty

_____ f. more adequate teaching materials

_____ g. more effective principal

_____ h. better consulting services

_____ i. more effective faculty meetings

_____ j. assistance of a teacher aide

_____ k. more attractive classroom/building

_____ l. fewer reports to make out

_____ m. fewer nonteaching duties

_____ n. better provision for atypical students

_____ o. more participation in policy making

_____ p. fewer committee meetings

_____ q. teaching in a higher socioeconomic area

_____ r. teaching in a lower socioeconomic area

_____ s. other (kindly specify)

On the back of this sheet kindly add any comments that you believe would more adequately express your feelings of satisfaction or dissatisfaction with teaching.

Characteristics of a Good Questionnaire

1. It deals with a significant topic, one the respondent will recognize as important enough to warrant spending one's time on. The significance should be clearly and carefully stated on the questionnaire or in the letter that accompanies it.

2. It only seeks information that cannot be obtained from other sources such as school reports or census data.

3. It is as short as possible and only long enough to get the essential data. Long questionnaires frequently find their way into the wastebasket. Keep the writing required of the respondent to a minimum and make the response system clear and easy to complete.

4. It is attractive in appearance, neatly arranged, and clearly duplicated or printed.

5. Directions for a good questionnaire are clear and complete. Important terms are defined. Each question deals with a single idea and is worded as simply and clearly as possible. Avoid asking two questions in one. The categories provide an opportunity for easy, accurate, and unambiguous responses.

6. The questions are objective with no leading suggestions as to the responses desired. Leading questions are just as inappropriate on a questionnaire as they are in a court of law.

7. Questions are presented in good psychological order, proceeding from general to more specific responses. This order helps respondents to organize their own thinking so that their answers are logical and objective. It may be well to present questions that create a favorable attitude before proceeding to those that may be a bit delicate or intimate. If possible, avoid annoying or embarrassing questions. When questions of a delicate nature are necessary, the questionnaire should be anonymous.

8. It is easy to tabulate and interpret. It is advisable to preconstruct a tabulation sheet, anticipating how the data will be tabulated and interpreted, before the final form of the questionnaire is decided on. This working backward from a visualization of the final analysis of data is an important step for avoiding ambiguity in questionnaire form. If computer tabulation is to be used, it is important to designate code numbers for all possible responses to permit easy transference to a computer program's format.

Preparing and Administering the Questionnaire

One should get all the help possible in planning and constructing the questionnaire. Other questionnaires should be studied, and items should be submitted for criticism to other members of the class or to the faculty, especially to those who have had experience in questionnaire construction.

If a computer is not readily available for easily modifying questions and rearranging the items, it is advisable to use a separate card or slip for each item. As the instrument is being developed, items can be refined, revised, or replaced by better items without recopying the entire instrument. This procedure also provides flexibility in arranging items in the most appropriate psychological order before the instrument is put into its final form.

The questionnaire should be tried on a few friends and acquaintances. If this is done personally, one may find that a number of items are ambiguous. What may seem perfectly clear to the researcher may be confusing to a person who does not have the frame of reference that the researcher has gained from living with and thinking about an idea over a long period. It is also a good idea to "pilot test" the instrument with a small group of persons similar to those who will be used in the study. These dry runs will be well worth the time and effort. They may reveal defects that can be corrected before the final form is printed and committed to the mails. Once the instrument has been sent out, it is too late to remedy its defects.

One should choose respondents carefully. It is important that questionnaires be sent only to those who possess the desired information and are likely to be sufficiently interested to respond conscientiously and objectively. A preliminary card asking whether the individual would be willing to participate in the proposed study is recommended by some research authorities. This is not only a courteous approach but a practical way of discovering those who will cooperate in furnishing the desired information. It also is critical should the questions be offensive to some individuals (e.g., items of a sexual nature).

In a study on questionnaire returns, See (1957) discovered that a better return was obtained when the original request was sent to the administrative head of an organization rather than directly to the person who had the desired information. It is likely that when a superior officer gives a staff member a questionnaire to fill out, there is an implied feeling of obligation.

Getting Permission

If the questionnaire is to be used in a public school, it is essential that approval of the project be secured from the principal, who may then wish to secure approval from the superintendent of schools. Schools are understandably sensitive to public relations. One can imagine the unfavorable publicity that might result from certain types of studies conducted by individuals not officially designated to conduct the research. School officials may also want to prevent the exploitation of teachers and pupils by amateur researchers whose activities require an excessive amount of time and effort not related to the purposes of the school.

Parental permission also may need to be secured. Students should be informed that participation is voluntary. Particularly if sensitive questions (e.g., about drug use) are to be asked, parental and student consent is essential.

If the desired information is delicate or intimate in nature, the possibility of providing for anonymous responses should be considered. The anonymous instrument is most likely to produce objective and honest responses. There are occasions, however, for purposes of classification or for a possible follow-up meeting, when it might be necessary to identify the respondents. If identification is needed, it is essential to convince the respondents that their responses will be held in strict confidence and that their answers will in no way jeopardize the status and security of their position. After all of the data have been collected, the data should be coded to make it impossible to identify the individual respondents.

The aid of sponsorship should be enlisted. Recipients are more likely to answer if a person, organization, or institution of prestige has endorsed the project. Of course, it is unethical to claim sponsorship unless it has been expressly given.

The Cover Letter

A courteous, carefully constructed cover letter should be included to explain the purpose of the study. The letter should promise some sort of inducement to the respondent for compliance with the request. Commercial agencies furnish rewards in goods or money. In educational circles a summary of questionnaire results is considered an appropriate reward, a promise that should be scrupulously honored after the study has been completed.

The cover letter should assure the respondent that all information will be held in strict confidence or that the questionnaire is anonymous. The matter of sponsorship also might well be mentioned. Of course, a stamped, addressed return envelope should be included. To omit this virtually guarantees that many of the questionnaires will go into the wastebasket. Some researchers suggest that two copies of the questionnaire be sent, one to be returned when completed and the other to be placed in the respondent's own file.

Follow-Up Procedures

Recipients are often slow to return completed questionnaires. To increase the number of returns, a vigorous follow-up procedure may be necessary. A courteous postcard reminding the recipient that the completed questionnaire has not been received may bring in some additional responses. This reminder will be effective with those who have put off filling out the document or have forgotten to mail it. A further step in the follow-up process may involve a personal letter of reminder. In extreme cases a phone call or personal visit may bring additional responses. In some cases it may be appropriate to send another copy of the questionnaire with the follow-up letter. However, the researcher must know who has already responded so as not to receive potential duplicates.

It is difficult to estimate, in the abstract, what percentage of questionnaire responses is considered adequate. The importance of the project, the quality of the questionnaire, the care in selecting recipients, the time of year, and many other factors may be significant in determining the proportion of responses. In general, the smaller the percentage of responses, the smaller the degree of confidence one may place in the data collected. Of course, objectivity of reporting requires that the proportion of responses received should always be included in the research report. Babbie (1989) suggests that a response rate of 50% is adequate, 60% good, and 70% very good.

A Sample Questionnaire

Figure 9.3 provides a questionnaire that has been used with teachers in Texas every 2 years since 1980 by David Henderson of Sam Houston State University. The data from these questionnaires are reported in Figure 9.4 on page 312. As can be seen, the questionnaire is short (one page) and easy to understand, complete, and tabulate.

Validity and Reliability of Questionnaires

Questionnaire designers rarely deal consciously with the degree of validity or reliability of their instrument. Perhaps this is one reason why so many questionnaires are lacking in these qualities. It must be recognized, however, that questionnaires, unlike psychological tests and inventories, have a very limited purpose. They are often one-time data-gathering devices with a very short life, administered to a limited population. There are ways, however, to improve both validity and reliability of questionnaires.

Basic to the validity of a questionnaire is asking the right questions phrased in the least ambiguous way. In other words, do the items sample a significant aspect of the purpose of the investigation?

The meaning of all terms must be clearly defined so that they have the same meaning to all respondents. Researchers need all the help they can get; suggestions from colleagues and experts in the field of inquiry may reveal ambiguities that can be removed or items that do not contribute to a questionnaire's purpose. The panel of experts may rate the instrument in terms of how effectively it samples significant aspects of its purpose, providing estimates of content validity.

Teachers, Moonlighting, and Morale—1996

DIRECTIONS: Please circle or answer *all* items that apply to you. Add comments on the back if you wish.

1. What is your age? — Years _____
2. What is your sex? — Male — Female
3. What is your marital status? — Married — Single — Other
4. If married, does your spouse work? — Yes — No — NA
5. What is your highest degree? — Bachelor — Master — Doctor
6. Are you the major bread winner in your household? — Yes — No — Equal
7. Are you pleased with the *changes* in the No Pass/No Play rule? — Yes — No
8. Are you seriously considering leaving the teaching profession? — Yes — No
   If yes, why are you considering leaving? _____
9. In what type of district do you teach? — Urban — Suburban — Rural
10. What grade level do you *primarily* teach? — K-5 — 6-8 — 9-12
11. How many years have you taught in the public schools? — Years _____
12. What is your current teaching salary *per year*? — $ _____
13. Do you have adequate time to prepare and teach? — Yes — No
    If No, what changes could be made in the regular instructional day to provide more time to prepare and teach? (please write on the back)
14. How many *hours per week* spent outside of class on school related work? — Hours _____
15. Do you have health insurance with the school district? — Yes — No
16. How much do you pay *per month* out-of-pocket for the health insurance? — $ _____ — None
17. How is the quality of teaching at my school compared to *five* years ago? — Better — Worse — Same
18. Is social promotion a serious problem at your school? — Yes — No
    If Yes, circle on 1–10 scale (1=no problem, 10=very serious problem) — 1 2 3 4 5 6 7 8 9 10
19. Do you have an extra job during the *summer*? — Yes — No
20. How much *extra* do you earn during the summer? — $ _____ — None
21. Do you have an *extra* (moonlighting) job during the *regular school year* to supplement your teaching salary? — Yes — No
    *** If your answer to Question #21 is yes, please answer the following questions. ***
22. Do you feel that the quality of your teaching would improve if you did *not* have a second job during the regular school year? — Yes — No
23. How much *extra* money do you earn during the *regular school year*? $ _____
24. How many *hours per week* during the regular school year do you spend working at the *moonlighting* job? — Hours _____
25. Would you quit the second job if your teaching salary would enable you to give up moonlighting during the school year? — Yes — No
26. How large a raise in your teaching salary would you require to enable you to give up moonlighting during the regular school year? $ _____
27. What is your *extra* job during the school year? (Please give a job title such as bookkeeper, sales clerk, coach, bus driver, rancher, etc.) _____

FIGURE 9.3 Questionnaire

(Used with the permission of the author, David L. Henderson.)

Survey of Texas Public School Teachers

Characteristics	1980	1982	1984	1986
Average Salary	$14,113	$17,351	$20,259	$24,601
Average Age	38.6	39.2	41.2	41.3
Sex: Male	20%	20%	15%	18%
Female	80%	80%	85%	83%
Married	77%	75%	75%	77%
Spouse Works	70%	70%	66%	72%
Degree: Bachelor	64%	63%	55%	50%
Master	36%	37%	44%	49%
Doctorate	0%	0%	1%	1%
Major Breadwinner	40%	40%	40%	39%
Consider Leaving	38%	37%	40%	42%
Districts: Urban	41%	43%	43%	46%
Suburban	33%	37%	39%	37%
Rural	27%	20%	18%	17%
Grade Taught: K-5	51%	50%	46%	52%
6-8	20%	20%	24%	23%
9-12	29%	30%	30%	26%
Years Experience	11.8	12.1	13.7	14.3
Extra Job in Summer	30%	36%	34%	31%
Summer Earnings	$1252	$2076	$2205	$1891
Moonlight	22%	29%	26%	23%
Moonlight Detrimental	64%	69%	70%	50%
Moonlight Earnings	$2799	$3189	$3615	$3522
Moonlight Hours Weekly	13.6	11.9	14.4	12.8
Quit Moonlighting	75%	75%	82%	61%
Raise to Quit Moonlighting	$3399	$4750	$5000	$3921
No Pass–No Play (Changes)	*	*	*	55%
Quality of Teaching: Better	*	*	*	*
(Compared to Worse	*	*	*	*
Five Years Ago) Same	*	*	*	*
Health Insurance	*	*	*	*
Average Pay for Insurance	*	*	*	*
Social Promotion a Problem	*	*	*	*
Hours Outside Classroom	*	*	*	*
Adequate Time to Prepare	*	*	*	*

FIGURE 9.4   **Data from Teachers, Moonlighting and Morale—1996 Questionnaire**

1988	1990	1992	1994	1996
$26,161	$26,838	$28,444	$30,395	$33,134
43.0	42.5	43.6	43.0	45.5
16%	15%	17%	16%	14%
84%	85%	83%	84%	86%
73%	74%	73%	73%	76%
67%	70%	73%	68%	76%
53%	53%	60%	57%	56%
47%	47%	39%	42%	43%
0%	0%	1%	1%	1%
43%	41%	46%	42%	42%
38%	45%	35%	38%	44%
38%	42%	41%	40%	40%
40%	40%	37%	41%	39%
22%	18%	22%	19%	21%
52%	51%	53%	47%	50%
23%	25%	27%	29%	21%
25%	24%	21%	24%	29%
15.4	14.9	14.4	14.8	16.7
29%	32%	30%	33%	36%
$2480	$2087	$2221	$2391	$3035
20%	21%	22%	23%	30%
66%	61%	65%	73%	63%
$4627	$4329	$3552	$3533	$4504
10.4	11.6	11.1	12.0	10.8
78%	73%	72%	78%	64%
$4914	$4891	$5167	$5597	$5893
70%	78%	79%	77%	64%
37%	39%	43%	43%	39%
14%	28%	28%	34%	30%
49%	33%	29%	23%	31%
*	82%	82%	78%	84%
*	$108.22	$144.00	$149.90	$125.90
*	*	*	*	54%
*	*	*	*	12.1
*	*	*	*	41%

(Used with the permission of the author, David L. Henderson.)
Note: Responses in percentages are a "YES" answer.
State Survey by: Dr. David L. Henderson (Sam Houston State University) and
    Travis W. Henderson (Windham School District) for the TSTA.

It is possible to estimate the predictive validity of some types of questionnaires by follow-up observations of respondent behavior at the present time or at some time in the future. In some situations overt behavior can be observed without invading the privacy of respondents. A comparison of questionnaire responses with voting data on a campus or community election may provide a basis for estimating predictive validity.

Reliability of questionnaires may be inferred by a second administration of the instrument, comparing the responses with those of the first. Reliability may also be estimated by comparing responses of an alternate form with the original form.

INQUIRY FORMS: THE OPINIONNAIRE

An information form that attempts to measure the attitude or belief of an individual is known as an *opinionnaire,* or *attitude scale.* Because the terms *opinion* and *attitude* are not synonymous, clarification is necessary.

How people feel, or what they believe, is their attitude. But it is difficult, if not impossible, to describe and measure attitude. Researchers must depend on what people *say* are their beliefs and feelings. This is the area of opinion. Through the use of questions, or by getting people's expressed reaction to statements, a sample of their opinions is obtained. From this statement of opinion, one may infer or estimate their attitude—what they *really* believe.

Inferring attitude from expressed opinion has many limitations. People may conceal their attitudes and express socially acceptable opinions. They may not really know how they feel about a social issue, never having given the idea serious consideration. People may be unaware of their attitude about a situation in the abstract. Until confronted with a real situation, they may be unable to accurately predict their reaction or behavior.

Even behavior itself is not always a true indication of attitude. When politicians kiss babies, their behavior may not be a true expression of affection toward infants. Social custom or the desire for social approval makes many overt expressions of behavior mere formalities, quite unrelated to people's inward feelings. Even though there is no sure method of describing and measuring attitude, the description and measurement of opinion may, in many instances, be closely related to people's real feelings or attitudes.

With these limitations in mind, psychologists and sociologists have explored an interesting area of research, basing their data on people's expressed opinions. Several methods have been employed:

1. Asking people directly how they feel about a subject. This technique may employ a schedule or questionnaire of the open or closed form. It may employ the interview process in which the respondents express their opinions orally.
2. Asking people to check on a list the statements with which they agree.
3. Asking people to indicate their degree of agreement or disagreement with a series of statements about a controversial subject.

4. Inferring their attitudes from reactions to projective devices through which they may reveal attitudes unconsciously. (A *projective device* is a data-gathering instrument that conceals its purpose so that the subjects cannot guess how they should respond to appear in their best light. Thus their real characteristics are revealed.)

Three procedures for eliciting opinions and attitudes have been used extensively in opinion research, and they warrant a brief description.

Thurstone Technique

The first method of attitude assessment is known as the Thurstone Technique of Scaled Values (Thurstone & Chave, 1929). A number of statements, usually 20 or more, are gathered that express various points of view toward a group, institution, idea, or practice. They are then submitted to a panel of judges, each of whom arranges them in 11 groups ranging from one extreme to another in position. This sorting by each judge yields a composite position for each of the items. When there has been marked disagreement among the judges in assigning a position to an item, that item is discarded. For items that are retained, each is given its median scale value (see Chapter 10) between 1 and 11 as established by the panel.

The list of statements is then given to the subjects, who are asked to check the statements with which they agree. The median value of the statements that they check establishes their score or quantifies their opinion.

Likert Method

The second method—the Likert Method of Summated Ratings—can be performed without a panel of judges and has yielded scores very similar to those obtained by the Thurstone method. The coefficient of correlation (see Chapter 10) between the two scales was reported as high as $+0.92$ in one study (Edwards & Kenney, 1946). Because the Likert-type scale takes much less time to construct, it offers an interesting possibility for the student of opinion research.

The first step in constructing a Likert-type scale is to collect a number of statements about a subject. The correctness of the statements is not important as long as they express opinions held by a substantial number of people. It is important that they express definite favorableness or unfavorableness to a particular point of view and that the number of favorable and unfavorable statements is approximately equal.

After the statements have been gathered, a trial test should be administered to a number of subjects. Only those items that correlate with the total test should be retained. This testing for internal consistency will help to eliminate statements that are ambiguous or that are not of the same type as the rest of the scale.

The attitude or opinion scale may be analyzed in several ways. The simplest way to describe opinion is to indicate percentage responses for each individual statement. For this type of analysis by item, three responses—"agree," "undecided," and "disagree"—are preferable to the usual five. If a Likert-type scale is used, it may be possible to report percentage responses by combining the two outside categories: "strongly agree" and "agree," "disagree" and "strongly disagree."

Strongly agree   Undecided   Disagree
   Agree   Strongly disagree

For example, 70% of the male respondents agree with the statement, "Merit rating will tend to encourage conformity and discourage initiative."

The Likert scaling technique assigns a scale value to each of the five responses. Thus, the instrument yields a total score for each respondent, and a discussion of each individual item, although possible, is not necessary. Starting with a particular point of view, all statements favoring the above position are scored:

	Scale Value
Strongly agree	5
Agree	4
Undecided	3
Disagree	2
Strongly disagree	1

For statements opposing this point of view, the items are scored in the opposite order:

	Scale Value
Strongly agree	1
Agree	2
Undecided	3
Disagree	4
Strongly disagree	5

The opinionnaire illustrated in Figure 9.5 attempts to measure Christian religious orthodoxy or conservatism. It is apparent that this type of instrument could be used to measure opinion in many controversial areas: racial integration, merit rating of teachers, universal military training, and many others. The test scores obtained on all the items would then measure the respondent's favorableness toward the given point of view.

Figure 9.6 on page 318 illustrates an instrument that was used to seek the opinions of a group of classroom teachers toward merit rating.

If an opinionnaire consisted of 30 statements or items, the following score values would be revealing:

$30 \times 5 = 150$ Most favorable response possible

$30 \times 3 = 90$ A neutral attitude

$30 \times 1 = 30$ Most unfavorable attitude

The following statements represent opinions, and your agreement or disagreement will be determined on the basis of your particular beliefs. Kindly check your position on the scale as the statement first impresses you. Indicate what you believe, rather than what you think you should believe.

	Strongly Agree	Agree	Undecided	Disagree	Strongly Disagree
1. Heaven does *not* exist as an actual place or location.					
2. God sometimes sets aside natural law, performing miracles.					
3. Jesus was born of a virgin, without a human father.					
4. Hell does *not* exist as an actual place or location.					
5. The inspiration that resulted in the writing of the Bible was no different from that of any other great religious literature.					
6. There is a final day of judgment for all who have lived on earth.					
7. The devil exists as an actual person.					
8. Prayer directly affects the lives of persons, whether or not they know that such prayer has been offered.					
9. There is another life after the end of organic life on earth.					
10. When on earth, Jesus possessed and used the power to restore the dead to life.					
11. God is a cosmic force, rather than an actual person.					
12. Prayer does *not* have the power to change such conditions as a drought.					
13. The creation of the world did *not* literally occur in the way described in the Old Testament.					
14. After Jesus was dead and buried, he actually rose from the dead, leaving an empty tomb.					
15. Everything in the Bible should be interpreted as literally true.					

FIGURE 9.5   A Likert-Type Opinionnaire

The scores for any individual would fall between 30 and 150—above 90 if opinions tended to be favorable to the given point of view and below 90 if opinions tended to be unfavorable.

It would be wise to conclude this discussion with a recognition of the limitations of this type of opinion measure. Obviously it is somewhat inexact and fails to measure opinion with the precision one would desire. There is no basis for belief that the five positions indicated on the scale are equally spaced. The interval between "strongly agree" and "agree" may not be equal to the interval between "agree" and "undecided." It is also unlikely that the statements are of equal value in "for-ness" or "against-ness." It is unlikely that the respondent can validly react to a short statement on a printed form in the absence of real-life qualifying situations. It is doubtful whether equal scores obtained by several individuals indicate equal favorableness toward the given position: Actually, different combinations of positions can yield equal score values without necessarily indicating

Merit Rating Opinionnaire

Male _____ Female _____ Age _____

Teaching level: elementary _____ secondary _____

Marital status: single _____ married _____ divorced/separated _____
    widowed _____

Years of teaching experience _____ years.

The following statements represent opinions, and your agreement or disagreement will be determined on the basis of your particular convictions. Kindly check your position on the scale as the statement first impresses you. Indicate what you believe, rather than what you think you should believe.

	Strongly Agree	Agree	Undecided	Disagree	Strongly Disagree
1. It is possible to determine what constitutes merit, or effective teaching.					
2. A valid and reliable instrument can be developed to measure varying degrees of teaching effectiveness.					
3. Additional remuneration will *not* result in improved teaching.					
4. Merit rating destroys the morale of the teaching force by creating jealousy, suspicion, and distrust.					
5. Mutual confidence between teachers and administrators is impossible if administrators rate teachers for salary purposes.					
6. Merit salary schedules will attract more high-quality young people to the teaching profession.					
7. Merit salary schedules will hold quality teachers in the profession.					
8. Parents will object to having their children taught by nonmerit teachers.					
9. Merit rating can be as successful in teaching as it is in industry.					
10. The hidden purpose of merit rating is to hold down salaries paid to most teachers by paying only a few teachers well.					
11. There is no justification for paying poor teachers as well as good teachers are paid.					
12. Apple-polishers will profit more than superior teachers from merit rating.					
13. Merit rating will encourage conformity and discourage initiative.					
14. The way to make teaching attractive is to reward excellence in the classroom.					
15. Most administrators *do not* know enough about teaching to rate their faculty members fairly.					
16. Salary schedules based on education and experience only encourage mediocre teaching.					

FIGURE 9.6   A Likert-Type Opinionnaire on Merit Rating

equivalent positions of attitude or opinion. Although the opinionnaire provides for anonymous response, there is a possibility that people may answer according to what they think they *should* feel rather than how they *do* feel.

Semantic Differential

The third method of attitude assessment was developed by Osgood, Suci, and Tannenbaum (1957). The semantic differential is similar to the Likert method in that the respondent indicates an attitude or opinion between two extreme choices. This method usually provides the individual with a 7-point scale with two adjectives at either end of the scale, such as good–bad, unhealthy–healthy, clean–dirty. The respondent is asked to rate a group, individual, or object on each of these bipolar scales.

One author of this book had a student who used the semantic differential method to compare the attitudes of regular teachers and special education teachers toward children with mental retardation, learning disabilities, or behavior disorders. The results of the semantic differential can be graphically displayed as profiles. Figure 9.7 shows a partial profile of the regular and special-education teachers when asked about children with mental retardation.

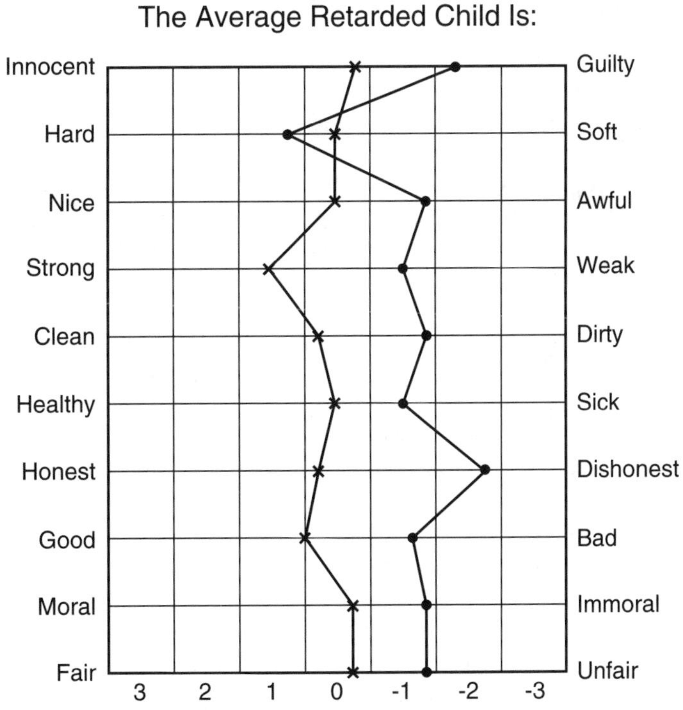

FIGURE 9.7 **Semantic Profiles for Regular Class and Special Class Teachers**

(Dots represent regular class teachers and Xs represent special class teachers.)

The semantic differential has limitations similar to those of the Thurstone and Likert approaches. In spite of these limitations, however, the process of opinion measurement has merit. Until more precise measures of attitude are developed, these techniques can serve a useful purpose in social research.

THE INTERVIEW

The interview is in a sense an oral questionnaire. Instead of writing the response, the subject or interviewee gives the needed information orally and face-to-face (or via the telephone). The discussion here includes using interviews in quantitative research. The use of interviews in qualitative research is covered in Chapter 8.

With a skillful interviewer, the interview is often superior to other data-gathering devices. One reason is that people are usually more willing to talk than to write. After the interviewer gains rapport or establishes a friendly, secure relationship with the subject, certain types of confidential information may be obtained that an individual might be reluctant to put into writing. To establish sufficient rapport, however, it may be necessary to consider the gender, race, and possibly other characteristics of the interviewer in relation to the interviewee. For instance, a woman should probably interview rape victims, and an African American should interview other African Americans regarding instances of discrimination that they have experienced.

Another advantage of interviewing is that the interviewer can explain more explicitly the investigation's purpose and just what information he or she wants. If the subject misinterprets the question, the interviewer may follow it with a clarifying question. At the same time he or she may evaluate the sincerity and insight of the interviewee. It is also possible to seek the same information in several ways at various stages of the interview, thus checking the truthfulness of the responses. Through the interview technique the researcher may stimulate the subject's insight into his or her own experiences, thereby exploring significant areas not anticipated in the original plan of investigation.

The interview is also particularly appropriate when dealing with young children. If one were to study what junior high school students like and dislike in teachers, some sort of written schedule would probably be satisfactory. To conduct a similar study with first-grade pupils, the interview would be the only feasible method of getting responses. The interview is also well suited for a person with reading or other language difficulties.

Preparation for the interview is a critical step in the procedure. Interviewers must have a clear conception of just what information they need. They must clearly outline the best sequence of questions and stimulating comments that will systematically bring out the desired responses. A written outline, schedule, or checklist will provide a set plan for the interview, precluding the possibility that the interviewer will fail to get important and needed data.

An open-form question in which the subject is encouraged to answer in his or her own words at some length is likely to provide greater depth of response. In fact, this penetration exploits the advantage of the interview in getting beneath-the-surface reactions. However, distilling the essence of the reaction is difficult, and interviewer bias may be a hazard. The closed-form question (in the pattern of a multiple-choice response) is easier to record but may yield more superficial information.

Avoid leading questions that unconsciously imply a specific answer. The question "Do you think that the United Nations has failed in its peace-keeping function?" illustrates the danger of eliciting agreement to an idea implanted in the question. It would be preferable to phrase it, "How effective do you feel the United Nations has been in its peace-keeping function?" This form is neutral and does not suggest a particular response. A question of this type would appropriately be followed by "Could you explain how you reached this conclusion?"

The relationship between interviewer and subject requires an expertness and sensitivity that might well be called an art. The initial task of securing the confidence and cooperation of the subject is crucial. Talking in a friendly way about a topic of interest to the subject will often dispel hostility or suspicion, and before he or she realizes it, the subject is freely giving the desired information. As in the use of the questionnaire, the interviewer must be able to assure the subject that responses will be held in strict confidence. When interviews are not tape recorded, it is necessary for the interviewer to take written notes, either during the interview or immediately thereafter. The actual wording of the responses should be retained. It is advisable to make the interpretation later, separating this phase of analysis from the actual recording of responses.

Recording interviews on tape is preferred because they are convenient and inexpensive and obviate the necessity of writing during the interview, which may be distracting to both interviewer and subject. Interviews recorded on tape may be replayed as often as necessary for complete and objective analysis at a later time. In addition to the words, the tone of voice and emotional impact of the response are preserved by the tapes. It is unethical to record interviews without the knowledge and permission of the subject.

To obtain reliable and objective data, interviewers must be carefully trained. This training should include skills in developing rapport, asking probing questions, preparing for the interview, and a host of other details. The Institute for Social Research at the University of Michigan has published an excellent interview-training manual that includes a 90-minute audio cassette of a model interview and some exercises (Guenzel, Berkmans, & Cannell, 1983).

Validity and Reliability of the Interview

The key to effective interviewing is establishing rapport. This skill is somewhat intangible, including both a personality quality and a developed ability. Researchers have studied the relationship of interviewer status to the achievement of this confidence. Many studies have been conducted in which interviewers of different status have interviewed the same respondents. The responses were often significantly different both in how much the subject was willing to reveal and in the nature of the attitudes expressed.

Ethnic origin seems to be important. Interviewers of the same ethnic background as their subjects seem to be more successful in establishing rapport. When there is an ethnic difference, a certain amount of suspicion and even resentment may be encountered. The same relationship seems to prevail when the social status of the interviewer and respondent is different. Even the interviewer's clothing may have an inhibiting effect. Younger interviewers seem to be more successful than older, particularly when middle-aged respondents are involved. Women seem to have a slight advantage over men in getting candid responses, although, depending on the topic (e.g., male impotence), male interviewers might be more successful. Of course, experience tends to improve interviewing skill.

Validity is greater when the interview is based on a carefully designed structure, thus ensuring that the significant information is elicited (content validity). The critical judgment of experts in the field of inquiry is helpful in selecting the essential questions.

Reliability, or the consistency of response, may be evaluated by restating a question in slightly different form at a later time in the interview. Repeating the interview at another time may provide another estimate of the consistency of response. If more than one interviewer is used, the researcher must demonstrate reliability of technique and scoring among the interviewers. This can be done through observing the interviews and having more than one interviewer score each tape or transcript.

As a data-gathering technique, the interview has unique advantages. In areas where human motivation is revealed through actions, feelings, and attitudes, the interview can be most effective. In the hands of a skillful interviewer, a depth of response is possible that is quite unlikely to be achieved through any other means.

This technique is time-consuming, however, and one of the most difficult to employ successfully. The danger of interview bias is constant. Because the objectivity, sensitivity, and insight of the interviewer are crucial, this procedure is one that requires a level of expertness not ordinarily possessed by inexperienced researchers.

Q METHODOLOGY

Q methodology, devised by Stephenson (1953), is a technique for scaling objects or statements. It is a method of ranking attitudes or judgments (similar to the first step in the Thurstone technique) and is particularly effective when the number of items to be ranked is large. The procedure is known as a Q-sort, in which cards or slips bearing the statements or items are arranged in a series of numbered piles. Usually 9 or 11 piles are established, representing relative positions on a standard scale. Some examples of simple polarized scales are illustrated:

most important	least important
most approve	least approve
most liberal	least liberal

most favorable	least favorable
most admired	least admired
most like me	least like me

The respondent is asked to place a specified number of items on each pile, usually on the basis of an approximately normal or symmetrical distribution. From 50 to 100 items should be used.

Most Like Me							Least Like Me	
Pile 1	2	3	4	5	6	7	8	9
% 4	7	12	17	20	17	12	7	4

Self-Concept Q-Sort

Let us assume that a Q-sort has been designed to measure the before-and-after therapy status of a subject. A few examples of appropriate traits are presented to be placed on the scale.

afraid	ignored	discouraged
suspicious	admired	energetic
successful	disliked	loved
enthusiastic	cheerful	hated
friendly	happy	stupid

A change in position of items from before-therapy to after-therapy would indicate possible change or improvement in self-esteem. Computing the coefficient of correlation (see Chapter 10 for a description of this concept) between the pile positions of items before and after therapy would provide a measure of change. If no change in item placement had occurred, the coefficient of correlation would be $+1.00$. If a completely opposite profile appeared, the coefficient would be -1.00. Although a perfect $+1.00$ or -1.00 coefficient is improbable, a high positive coefficient would indicate little change, whereas a high negative coefficient would indicate significant change.

Another type of Q-sort solicits the composite judgment of a selected panel of experts (in this case professors of educational research). The criterion of judgment involves the relative importance of research concepts that should be included in the introductory course in educational research. One hundred slips, each listing a concept, were to be sorted into nine piles, ranging from most important to least important. A few of the concepts that were considered are listed:

hypothesis
probability
dependent variable
coefficient of correlation
sources of reference materials

preparing the research report
randomization
post hoc fallacy
experimental method
interviewing
level of significance
the research proposal
attitude studies
historical method
survey
null hypothesis
preparing a questionnaire
deductive method
descriptive method
sampling
intervening variables
independent variable
Q-sorts
standard deviation
nonparametric statistics
action research

The mean value of the positions assigned to each item indicates the composite judgment of the panel as to its relative importance.

Two applications of the Q-sort technique have been illustrated in this simplified discussion. The first attempted to measure change in the attitude of an individual toward himself or herself, the second the composite judgment of a group of individuals. Many types of analysis may be carried on in the area of attitudes by the use of Q methodology. Researchers contemplating the use of this technique should carefully consider the theoretical assumptions underlying the criteria and the items selected.

SOCIAL SCALING

Sociometry

Sociometry is a technique for describing the social relationships among individuals in a group. In an indirect way it attempts to describe attraction or repulsion between individuals by asking them to indicate whom they would choose or reject in various situations. Children in a school classroom may be asked to name in order of preference (usually two or three) the child or children that they would invite to a party, eat lunch with, sit next to, work on a class project with, or have as a close friend. Although some researchers object to the method, it is also common to ask the children to name the children, again in order of preference, that they would *least* like to invite to a party, eat lunch with, sit next to, and so forth.

There is an extensive body of sociometric research on classroom groups from kindergarten through college, fraternities and sororities, dormitory residents, camp groups, factory and office workers, military combat units, and entire communities. The United States Air Force has used sociometry to study the nature of leadership in various situations. For example, the following question was used in a study of air combat crews: "What member of the crew would you select, disregarding rank, as the most effective leader if your plane were forced down in a remote and primitive area? Name three in order of your preference."

Scoring Sociometric Choices

One widely used procedure is to count the number of times an individual is chosen, disregarding the order of choice. This is the simplest method, and it is widely used. The objection has been raised that it is insensitive, for it does not distinguish between a first and third choice.

Another procedure is to score a first choice three points, a second choice two points, and a third choice one point. This plan's weakness is that it suggests that the difference between a third choice and no choice at all is identical to the differences between third, second, and first choices. This assumption is difficult to defend.

A third scoring procedure is based on the concept of the normal curve standard score distribution (see Chapter 10 for a discussion of this topic). However, this method is more complex and seldom used.

Once obtained, the scores for each individual in the group can be related to such measures as intelligence or other traits that can be measured by tests or to such categories as sex, race, nationality, religious affiliation, economic status, birth order, family size, grade-point average, teacher, employer, or other characteristics that may be of interest to the researcher.

The Sociogram

Sociometric choices may be represented graphically on a chart known as a *sociogram*. There are many versions of the sociogram pattern, and the reader is urged to consult specialized references on sociometry. A few observations will illustrate the nature of the sociogram.

In consulting a sociogram, boys may be represented by triangles and girls by circles. A choice may be represented by a single-pointed arrow and a mutual choice by an arrow pointing in opposite directions. Those chosen most often are referred to as *stars*, those not chosen by others as *isolates*. Small groups made up of individuals who choose one another are *cliques*.

Identifying numbers are placed within the symbols. Numbers of those chosen most often are placed nearest the center of the diagram, and numbers of those chosen less often are placed further outward. Those not chosen are, literally, on the

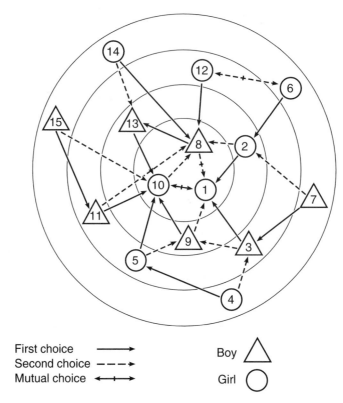

First choice   ⟶   Boy △
Second choice   ‐ ‐ ‐ ▸
Mutual choice   ◂‐+‐▸   Girl ○

**FIGURE 9.8   Sociogram Showing First and Second
Choices in a Third Grade Class**

outside (see Figure 9.8), but remember, however, that relationships among individuals in a group are changeable. Children's choices are mostly temporary because
stability tends to develop only with age.

Students of group relationships and classroom teachers may construct a number of sociograms over a period of time to measure changes that may have resulted
from efforts to bring isolates into closer group relationships or to transform cliques
into more general group membership. The effectiveness of socializing or status-
building procedures can thus be measured by the changes revealed in the sociogram. Because sociometry is a peer rating rather than a rating by superiors, it adds
another dimension to the understanding of members of a group.

"Guess-Who" Technique

A process of description closely related to sociometry is the "guess-who" technique.
Developed by Hartshorne and May (1929), the process consists of descriptions of
the various roles played by children in a group.

Children are asked to name the individuals who fit certain verbal descriptions.

This one is always happy.
This one is always picking on others.
This one is always worried.
This one never likes to do anything.
This one will always help you.

Items of this type yield interesting and significant peer judgments and are useful in the study of individual roles. Of course, the names of children chosen should not be revealed.

Social-Distance Scale

Another approach to the description and measurement of social relationships is the social-distance scale developed by Bogardus (1933). This device attempts to measure to what degree an individual or group of individuals is accepted or rejected by another individual or group.

Various scaled situations, with score values ranging from acceptance to rejection, are established. The individual checks his or her position by choosing one of the points on the scale. For example, in judging acceptance of different minority groups, the choices might range between these extremes:

Complete acceptance	I wouldn't object to having a member of this group become a member of my family by marriage.
Partial acceptance	I wouldn't mind sitting next to a member of this group on a bus.
Rejection	I don't think that members of this group should be admitted into our country.

When applied to an individual in a classroom situation, the choices might range between these extremes:

Complete acceptance	I'd like to have this student as my best friend.
Partial acceptance	I wouldn't mind sitting near this student.
Rejection	I wish this student weren't in my room.

Of course, in the real social-distance scale, illustrated by the sample items above, there would be a larger number of evenly spaced scaled positions (usually seven), giving a more precise measure of acceptance or rejection.

Devices of the type described here have many possibilities for the description and measurement of social relationships and, in this important area of social research, may yield interesting and useful data.

ORGANIZATION OF DATA COLLECTION

The following discussion is directed to the beginner and does not suggest appropriate procedures for the advanced researcher. Theses, dissertations, and advanced research projects usually involve sophisticated experimental designs and statistical analysis. The use of the computer is standard procedure. Because it can effectively process complex variable relationships, it has become a necessary tool in the conduct of research. Chapter 12 discusses computers and their uses for organizing and analyzing data.

When the results of an observation, interview, questionnaire, opinionnaire, or test are to be analyzed, problems of organization confront the researcher. Even with computers, the first problem is to designate appropriate, logical, and mutually exclusive categories for tabulation of the data. At times the hypothesis or question to be answered may suggest the type of organization. If the hypothesis involved the difference between the attitudes of men and women toward teacher merit rating, the categories *male* and *female* are clearly indicated. In other instances the categories are not determined by the hypothesis, and other subdivisions of the group under investigation may be desirable. The researcher should keep these issues in mind when selecting, or designing, the data collection procedure. Proper attention given to this matter of organization early in the research process can save a great deal of time at the data analysis phase. In addition, once the data have been collected, it is difficult if not impossible to go back and get additional information, such as gender or income, if not asked initially.

All information collected should be assigned codes and entered into whatever computer program is being used to keep the data. For instance, let us say that we have just collected a questionnaire from a group of 100 education students. Each of the 100 questionnaires is assigned an identification number (ID) from 001 to 100. Because we are interested in gender, socioeconomic level, and the students' major, we will assign codes for each of these variables. For gender we will assign a 1 for males and a 2 for females; for socioeconomic level we will use a 7-point scale and assign a 1 to 7 to each student; and because there are four majors available in the college under study, we will assign a 1 for elementary education, a 2 for secondary education, a 3 for special education, and a 4 for early childhood education. In each of these cases these codes represent nominal data in that we are establishing categories. Thus, each of these variables—gender, socioeconomic level, and major—will be in separate columns plus a column for ID. Other columns will be used for other variables including additional demographic information, if available, and the answers to each question on the questionnaire. Because there are 100 questionnaires, there will be 100 rows, one for each student. Once the data are entered, the computer program used to analyze the data will be able to assign individuals to the different groups by the codes in the column for that variable.

When the responses or characteristics of a group are analyzed, it is sometimes satisfactory to describe the group as a whole. In simple types of analyses, when the group is sufficiently homogeneous, no breakdown into subgroups is necessary. But in many situations the picture of the whole group is not clear. The heterogeneity of the group may yield data that have little meaning. One tends to get an unreal picture of a group of subjects that are actually very different from one another, and the differences are concealed by a description of a nonexistent or unreal average. In such cases it may be helpful to divide the group into more homogeneous subgroups that have in common some distinctive characteristics that may be significant for the purpose of the analysis. Distinguishing between the response of men and women, between elementary and secondary teachers, or between gifted and average-learning children may reveal significant relationships. If all the information collected initially is entered into the data set, it is fairly simple to use computer programs to analyze the data first for the entire group and then for the subgroups separately.

For example, a new type of classroom organization may seem to have little impact on a group of students. But after one divides the group into two subgroups, the gifted and the average learners, some interesting relationships may become clear. The grouping may be effective for the bright students but most ineffective for the average learners.

Many studies employ the classification of data into dichotomous, or twofold, categories. When the categories are established on the basis of test scores, rankings, or some other quantitative measure, it may be advisable to compare those at the top with those at the bottom, omitting from the analysis those near the middle of the distribution. It is possible to compare the top third with the bottom third, or the top 25% with the bottom 25%. This eliminates those cases near the midpoint that tend to obscure the differences that may exist. Through elimination of the middle portion, sharper contrast is achieved, but the risk of the regression to the mean effect is increased.

Comparisons are not always dichotomous. At times it is desirable to divide a sample into more than two categories, depending on the nature of the variables that are to be considered. Chapter 12, Computer Data Analysis, describes these processes further.

Outside Criteria for Comparison

In addition to the comparisons that may be made between subgroups *within* the larger group, the group may be analyzed in terms of some *outside criteria*. Of course, it must be assumed that reasonably valid and reliable measuring devices are available for making such comparisons. These "measuring sticks" may consist of standardized tests, scorecards, frequency counts, and physical as well as psychological measuring devices. Some of these outside criteria include the following:

1. *Prevailing conditions, practices, or performance of comparable units.* Comparison may be made with other communities, schools, and classes. Comparisons may be made with groups that represent best conditions or practices or typical or average status or with equated groups that have been matched in terms of certain variables, leaving one variable or a limited number of variables for comparison.

2. *What experts believe to constitute best conditions or practices.* These experts may comprise a panel specially chosen for the purpose. A group of practitioners in the field who are assumed to be most familiar with the characteristics under consideration, or the survey staff itself, may constitute the body of experts. The judgments of recognized authorities who publish their opinions are frequently selected as criteria.

3. *What a professional group, a commission, an accrediting agency, or another scholarly deliberative body establishes as appropriate standards.* These standards may be expressed as lists of objectives or may be quantitative measures of status for accreditation or approval. The American Medical Association's standards for accreditation of medical schools, the accreditation standards of the North Central Association of Secondary Schools and Colleges, or the standards of the National Council for the Accreditation of Teacher Education for programs of teacher education are examples of evaluative criteria.

4. *Laws or rules that have been enacted or promulgated by a legislative or quasi-legislative body.* Teacher certification regulations, school-building standards, or health and safety regulations provide appropriate criteria for comparison.

5. *Research evidence.* The factors to be analyzed may be examined in the light of principles confirmed by published scholarly research.

6. *Public opinion.* Although not always appropriate as a criterion of what should be, the opinions or views of "the man on the street" are sometimes appropriate as a basis for comparison.

LIMITATIONS AND SOURCES OF ERROR

A number of limitations and sources of error in the *analysis* and *interpretation* of data can jeopardize the success of an investigation. New researchers in particular need to be aware of these potential pitfalls. Some of these problems include

1. *Confusing statements with facts.* A common fault is the acceptance of statements as facts. What individuals report may be a sincere expression of what they believe to be the facts in a case, but these statements are not necessarily true. Few people observe skillfully, and many forget quickly. It is the researcher's responsibility to verify all statements as completely as possible before they are accepted as facts.

2. *Failure to recognize limitations.* The very nature of research implies certain restrictions or limitations about the group or the situation described—its size, its representativeness, and its distinctive composition. Failure to recognize these limitations may lead to the formulation of generalizations that are not warranted by the data collected.

3. *Careless or incompetent data entry.* When one is confronted with a mass of data, it is easy to make simple mechanical errors. Placing a tally in the wrong cell or incorrectly totaling a set of scores can easily invalidate carefully gathered

data. Errors sometimes may be attributed to clerical helpers with limited ability and little interest in the research project.

4. *Faulty logic.* This rather inclusive category embraces a number of errors in the thought processes of the researcher. Invalid assumptions, inappropriate analogies, inversion of cause and effect, confusion of a simple relationship with causation, failure to recognize that group phenomena may not be used indiscriminately to predict individual occurrences or behavior, failure to realize that the whole may be greater than the sum of its parts, belief that frequency of appearance is always a measure of importance, and many other errors are limitations to accurate interpretation.

5. *The researcher's unconscious bias.* Although objectivity is the ideal of research, few individuals achieve it completely. There is great temptation to omit evidence unfavorable to the hypothesis and to overemphasize favorable data. Effective researchers are aware of their feelings and the likely areas of their bias and constantly endeavor to maintain the objectivity that is essential.

SUMMARY

The researcher chooses the most appropriate instruments and procedures that provide for the collection and analysis of data on which hypotheses may be tested. The data-gathering devices that have proved useful in educational research include psychological tests and inventories, questionnaires, opinionnaires, Q methodology, observation, checklists, rating scales, scorecards, scaled specimens, document or content analyses, interviews, sociograms, "guess-who" techniques, and social-distance scales.

Some research investigations use only one of these devices. Others employ a number of them in combination. Students of educational research should make an effort to familiarize themselves with the strengths and limitations of these tools and should attempt to develop skill in constructing and using them effectively.

The analysis and interpretation of data represent the application of deductive and inductive logic to the research process. The data are often classified by division into subgroups and then analyzed and synthesized in such a way that hypotheses may be verified or rejected. The final result may be a new principle or generalization. Data are examined in terms of comparisons between the more homogeneous segments within the whole group and by comparison with some outside criteria.

The processes of classification, sorting, and tabulation of data are important parts of the research process. In extensive studies mechanical and/or computer methods of sorting and tabulating are used to save time and effort and to minimize error. In smaller projects hand-sorting and hand-tabulating processes are still often employed.

The researcher must guard against the limitations and sources of error inherent in the processes of analysis and interpretation of data.

EXERCISES

1. For what type of problem and under what circumstances would you find the following data-gathering techniques most appropriate?

   a. Likert scale
   b. Questionnaire
   c. Interview
   d. Observation
   e. Q-sort

2. Construct a short questionnaire that could be administered in class. The following topics are suggested:

   a. Leisure Interests and Activities
   b. Reasons for Selecting Teaching As a Profession
   c. Methods of Dealing with School Discipline
   d. Political Interests and Activities

3. Construct a Likert-type opinionnaire dealing with a controversial problem. One of the following topics may be appropriate:

   a. Teacher Affiliation with Professional Organizations
   b. Teacher Strikes and Sanctions
   c. Religious Activities in the School Program
   d. The Nongraded School

4. Construct a short rating scale to be used for the evaluation of the teaching performance of a probationary teacher.

5. To what extent is the administration of personal and social adjustment inventories an invasion of a student's privacy?

REFERENCES

Aiken, L. R. (1991). *Psychological testing and assessment* (7th ed.). Boston: Allyn and Bacon.

Anastasi, A. (1988). *Psychological testing* (6th ed.). New York: Macmillan.

Babbie, E. R. (1989). *The practice of social research.* Belmont, CA: Wadsworth.

Bogardus, E. S. (1933). A social distance scale. *Sociology and Social Research, 17,* 265–271.

Conoley, J. C., & Impara, J. C. (1994). *Supplement to the eleventh mental measurement yearbook.* Lincoln, NE: University of Nebraska Press.

Cronbach, L. J. (1951). Coefficient alpha and the internal structure of tests. *Psychometrika, 16,* 297–334.

Cronbach, L. J. (1984). *Essentials of psychological testing* (4th ed.). New York: Harper and Row.

Edwards, A. L., & Kenney, K. C. (1946). A comparison of the Thurstone and Likert techniques of attitude scale construction. *Journal of Applied Psychology, 30,* 72–83.

Fantuzzo, I. W., & Clement, P. W. (1981). Generalization of the effects of teacher- and self-administered token reinforcements to nontreated students. *Journal of Applied Behavior Analysis, 14,* 435–447.

Geisinger, K. F. (Ed.). (1992). *Psychological testing of Hispanics.* Washington, DC: American Psychological Association.

Gesell, A. (1948). *Studies in child development.* New York: Harper and Brothers.

Guenzel, P. J., Berkmans, T. R., & Cannell, C. F. (1983). *General interviewing techniques: A self-*

instructional workbook for telephone and personal interviewer training. Ann Arbor, MI: Institute of Social Research, University of Michigan.

Hakel, M. (1968). How often is often? *American Psychologist, 23,* 533–534.

Hall, H. V., Price, A. B., Shinedling, M., Peizer, S. B., & Massey, R. H. (1973). Control of aggressive behavior in a group of retardates, using positive and negative reinforcement. *Training School Bulletin, 70,* 179–186.

Harris, D. B. (1963). *Children's drawings as measures of intellectual maturity.* New York: Harcourt, Brace and World.

Hartshorne, H., & May, M. A. (1929). *Studies in deceit.* New York: Macmillan.

Kazdin, A. F. (1982). *Single-case research designs.* New York: Oxford.

Kramer, J. J., & Conoley, J. C. (1992). *Eleventh mental measurements yearbook.* Lincoln, NE: University of Nebraska Press.

Mehrens, W. A., & Lehmann, I. J. (1991). *Measurement and evaluation in education and psychology.* Chicago: Holt, Rinehart & Winston.

Murphy, L. L., Conoley, J. C., & Impara, J. C. (Eds.). (1994). *Tests in print, IV.* Lincoln, NE: University of Nebraska Press.

Mooney, R. L. (1941). *Problem checklist, high school form.* Columbus, OH: Bureau of Educational Research, Ohio State University.

Osgood, C. F., Suci, G. I., & Tannenbaum, P. H. (1957). *The measurement of meaning.* Urbana, IL: University of Illinois Press.

Popham, W. J. (1990). *Modern educational measurement* (2nd ed.). Englewood Cliffs, NJ: Prentice Hall.

See, H. W. (1957). Send it to the President. *Phi Delta Kappan, 38,* 129–130.

Stephenson, W. (1953). *The study of behavior.* Chicago: University of Chicago Press.

Stevenson, H. W., & Lee, S. (1990). Contexts of achievement. *Monographs of the Society for Research in Child Development, 55.*

Thorndike, R. M. (1997). *Measurement and evaluation in psychology and education* (6th ed.). Columbus, OH: Merrill.

Thurstone, L. L., & Chave, F. J. (1929). *The measurement of attitudes.* Chicago: University of Chicago Press.

Watanabe, P., Hare, V. C., & Lomax, R. C. (1984). Predicting news story content from headlines: An instructional study. *Journal of Reading, 27,* 436–442.

PART III

DATA ANALYSIS

The final three chapters of this book deal with quantitative analysis of data utilizing statistical procedures. The purpose is to give an overview of commonly used statistical procedures and enough information to calculate many of them by hand (using a calculator, it is to be hoped) or with the aid of a computer.

Chapter 10, Descriptive Data Analysis, provides a general depiction of the types of statistics used in educational research (descriptive versus inferential; parametric versus nonparametric), a brief description of data organization methods, and a variety of statistical procedures for describing a group of subjects. The statistical procedures in Chapter 10 include measures of central tendency, measures of dispersion or variability, the normal distribution, standard scores, correlation, and the standard error of estimate.

Chapter 11, Inferential Data Analysis, explains the concepts of statistical inference and the central limit theorem and includes a number of common inferential statistical procedures. Among the statistical procedures are various forms of the *t* test, analysis of variance, the test for homogeneity of variance, partial correlation, multiple regression, chi square, and the Mann–Whitney test.

Chapter 12, Computer Data Analysis, demonstrates how computers are used to calculate the statistical procedures described in Chapters 10 and 11. This chapter describes how data can be organized for easy entry into a computer program and provides several examples of computer analyses. The computer analyses include two programs and their outputs, run on a university mainframe computer using the SAS package of programs. These examples consist of a program for descriptive statistics, including correlation, and a program for charting data. Also included are the programs and their outputs from a mainframe SPSS multiple regression program and an SPSS for personal computer analysis of variance program. Finally, the outputs of six SPSS for Windows programs are given: two *t* tests; descriptive statistics, including correlations; ANOVA; partial correlation; and multiple regression.

10

DESCRIPTIVE
DATA ANALYSIS

Because this textbook concentrates on educational research methods, the following discussion of statistical analysis is in no sense complete or exhaustive. Only some of the most simple and basic concepts are presented. Students whose mathematical experience includes high school algebra should be able to understand the logic and the computational processes involved and should be able to follow the examples without difficulty.

The purpose of this discussion is threefold:

1. To help the student, as a consumer, develop an understanding of statistical terminology and the concepts necessary to read with understanding some of the professional literature in educational research.
2. To help the student develop enough competence and know-how to carry on research studies using simple types of analysis.
3. To prepare the student for more advanced coursework in statistics.

The emphasis is on intuitive understanding and practical application rather than on the derivation of mathematical formulas. Those who expect and need to develop real competence in educational research will have to take some of the following steps:

1. Take one or more courses in behavioral statistics and experimental design.
2. Study more specialized textbooks in statistics, particularly those dealing with statistical inference (e.g., Glass & Hopkins, 1996; Hays, 1981; Heiman, 1996; Kerlinger, 1986; Kirk, 1995; Siegel, 1956; Shavelson, 1996; Winer, 1971).
3. Read research studies in professional journals extensively and critically.
4. Carry on research studies involving some serious use of statistical procedures.

WHAT IS STATISTICS?

Statistics is a body of mathematical techniques or processes for gathering, organizing, analyzing, and interpreting numerical data. Because most research yields such quantitative data, statistics is a basic tool of measurement, evaluation, and research.

The word *statistics* is sometimes used to describe the numerical data gathered. Statistical data describe group behavior or group characteristics abstracted from a number of individual observations that are combined to make generalizations possible.

Everyone is familiar with such expressions as "the average family income," "the typical white-collar worker," or "the representative city." These are statistical concepts and, as group characteristics, may be expressed in measurement of age, size, or any other traits that can be described quantitatively. When one says that "the average fifth-grade boy is 10 years old," one is generalizing about all fifth-grade boys, not any particular boy. Thus, the statistical measurement is an abstraction that may be used in place of a great mass of individual measures.

The research worker who uses statistics is concerned with more than the manipulation of data. The statistical method serves the fundamental purposes of description and analysis, and its proper application involves answering the following questions:

1. What facts need to be gathered to provide the information necessary to answer the question or to test the hypothesis?
2. How are these data to be selected, gathered, organized, and analyzed?
3. What assumptions underlie the statistical methodology to be employed?
4. What conclusions can be validly drawn from the analysis of the data?

Research consists of systematic observation and description of the characteristics or properties of objects or events for the purpose of discovering relationships between variables. The ultimate purpose is to develop generalizations that may be used to explain phenomena and to predict future occurrences. To conduct research, one must establish principles so that the observation and description have a commonly understood meaning. Measurement is the most precise and universally accepted process of description, assigning quantitative values to the properties of objects and events.

PARAMETRIC AND NONPARAMETRIC DATA

In the application of statistical treatments, two types of data are recognized:

1. *Parametric data.* Data of this type are measured data, and parametric statistical tests assume that the data are normally, or nearly normally, distributed. Parametric tests are applied to both interval- and ratio-scaled data.
2. *Nonparametric* data. Data of this type are either counted (nominal) or ranked (ordinal). Nonparametric tests, sometimes known as distribution-free tests, do not rest on the more stringent assumption of normally distributed populations.

TABLE 10.1   Levels of Quantitative Description[1]

Level	Scale	Process	Data Treatment	Some Appropriate Tests
4	Ratio	measured equal intervals true zero ratio relationship	parametric	*t* test analysis of variance analysis of covariance factor analysis Pearson's *r*
3	Interval	measured equal intervals no true zero		
2	Ordinal	ranked in order	nonparametric	Spearman's *rho* (ρ) Mann-Whitney Wilcoxon
1	Nominal	classified and counted		chi square median sign

[1]Refer to Chapter 9 for a discussion of the four levels of measurements.

Table 10.1 presents a graphic summary of the levels of quantitative description and the types of statistical analysis appropriate for each level. These concepts will be developed later in the discussion.

However, one should be aware that many of the parametric statistics (*t* test, analysis of variance, and Pearson's *r* in particular) are still appropriate even when the assumption of normality is violated. This robustness has been demonstrated for the *t* test, analysis of variance, and, to a lesser extent, analysis of covariance by a number of researchers including Glass, Peckham, and Sanders (1972), Lunney (1970), and Mandeville (1972). Thus, with ordinal data and even with dichotomous data (two choices such as pass–fail), these statistical procedures, which were designed for use with interval and ratio data, may be appropriate and useful. Pearson's *r*, which can also be used with any type of data, will be discussed later in this chapter.

DESCRIPTIVE AND INFERENTIAL ANALYSIS

Until now we have not discussed the limits to which statistical analysis may be generalized. Two types of statistical application are relevant:

Descriptive Analysis
Descriptive statistical analysis limits generalization to the particular group of individuals observed. No conclusions are extended beyond this group, and any

similarity to those outside the group cannot be assumed. The data describe one group and that group only. Much simple action research involves descriptive analysis and provides valuable information about the nature of a particular group of individuals. Assessment studies (see Chapter 5) also often rely solely or heavily on descriptive statistics.

Inferential Analysis

Inferential statistical analysis always involves the process of sampling and the selection of a small group assumed to be related to the population from which it is drawn. The small group is known as the *sample,* and the large group is the *population.* Drawing conclusions about populations based on observations of samples is the purpose of inferential analysis.

A *statistic* is a measure based on observations of the characteristics of a sample. A statistic computed from a sample may be used to estimate a *parameter,* the corresponding value in the population from which the sample is selected. Statistics are usually represented by letters of our Roman alphabet such as X, S, and r. Parameters, on the other hand, are usually represented by letters of the Greek alphabet such as μ, σ, or ρ.

Before any assumptions can be made, it is essential that the individuals selected be chosen in such a way that the small group, or sample, approximates the larger group, or population. Within a margin of error, which is always present, and by the use of appropriate statistical techniques, this approximation can be assumed, making possible the estimation of population characteristics by an analysis of the characteristics of the sample.

It should be emphasized that when data are derived from a group without careful sampling procedures, the researcher should carefully state that findings apply only to the group observed and may not apply to or describe other individuals or groups. The statistical theory of sampling is complex and involves the estimation of error of inferred measurements, error that is inherent in estimating the relationship between a random sample and the population from which it is drawn. Inferential data analysis is presented in Chapter 11.

THE ORGANIZATION OF DATA

The list of test scores in a teacher's grade book provides an example of unorganized data. Because the usual method of listing is alphabetical, the scores are difficult to interpret without some other type of organization.

Alberts, James	60
Brown, John	78
Davis, Mary	90
Smith, Helen	70
Williams, Paul	88

**TABLE 10.2   Scores of 37 Students on a
Semester Algebra Test**

98	85	80	76	67
97	85	80	76	67
95	85	80	75	64
93	84	80	73	60
90	82	78	72	57
88	82	78	70	
87	82	78	70	
87	80	77	70	

Range = 98 − 57 + 1 = 41 + 1 = 42

The Ordered Array or Set

Arranging the same scores in descending order of magnitude produces what is known as an *ordered array*.

90
88
78
70
60

The ordered array provides a more convenient arrangement. The highest score (90), the lowest score (60), and the middle score (78) are easily identified. Thus, the range (the difference between the highest and lowest scores, plus one) can easily be determined.

Illustrated in Table 10.2 is a data arrangement of 37 students' scores on an algebra test in ordered array form.

Grouped Data Distributions

Data are often more clearly presented when scores are grouped and a frequency column is included. Data can be presented in frequency tables (see Table 10.3 on page 342) with different class intervals, depending on the number and range of the scores.

A score interval with an odd number of units may be preferable because its midpoint is a whole number rather than a fraction. Because all scores are assumed to fall at the midpoint of the interval (for purposes of computing the mean), the computation is less complicated:

Even interval of four: 8 9 10 11 (midpoint 9.5)

Odd interval of five: 8 9 10 11 12 (midpoint 10)

There is no rule that rigidly determines the proper score interval, and intervals of 10 are frequently used.

TABLE 10.3   Scores on Algebra Test Grouped in Intervals of Five

Score Interval	Tallies	Frequency (f)	Includes
96–100	11	2	(96 97 98 99 100)
91–95	11	2	(91 92 93 94 95)
86–90	1111	4	etc.
81–85	1111 11	7	
76–80	1111 1111 1	11	
71–75	111	3	
66–70	1111	5	
61–65	1	1	
56–60	11	2	
		$N = 37$	

STATISTICAL MEASURES

Several basic types of statistical measures are appropriate in describing and analyzing data in a meaningful way:

Measures of central tendency or averages

Mean
Median
Mode

Measures of spread or dispersion

Range
Variance
Standard deviation

Measures of relative position

Standard scores
Percentile rank
Percentile score

Measures of relationship

Coefficient of correlation

Measures of Central Tendency

Nonstatisticians use *averages* to describe the characteristics of groups in a general way. The climate of an area is often noted by average temperature or average amount of rainfall. We may describe students by grade-point averages or by average age. Socioeconomic status of groups is indicated by average income, and the return on an investment portfolio may be judged in terms of average income return. But to the statistician the term *average* is unsatisfactory, for there are a number of types of averages, only one of which may be appropriate to use in describing given characteristics of a group. Of the many averages that may be used, three have been selected as most useful in educational research: the mean, the median, and the mode.

The Mean ($\overline{X}$)

The mean of a distribution is commonly understood as the arithmetic average. The term *grade-point average*, familiar to students, is a mean value. It is computed by dividing the sum of all the scores by the number of scores. In formula form

$$\overline{X} = \frac{\Sigma X}{N}$$

where $\overline{X}$ = mean
Σ = sum of
X = scores in a distribution
N = number of scores

Example

X
6
5
4
3
2
1
‾
$\Sigma X = 21$
$N = 6$
$\overline{X} = 21/6 = 3.50$

The mean is probably the most useful of all statistical measures, for, in addition to the information that it provides, it is the base from which many other important measures are computed.

Appendix B contains a data set from a population of 100 children (one set in Microsoft Excel and one in SPSS format). The data for each child includes an ID number, the method of teaching reading that was received, the gender, the category of special education in which the child has been classified (LD = learning disabilities; BD = behavior disordered; MR = mild mental retardation), and both pre- and posttest scores. The reader may wish to randomly select a sample of 25 children (or 15 children if recommended by the professor) from the appendix for use in a variety of calculations throughout this chapter. Now calculate the mean for this sample of 25 children's IQ. The mean of the population given in the appendix is 86.12. How does the sample mean compare to the population mean?

The Median (Md)

The median is a point (not necessarily a score) in an array, above and below which one-half of the scores fall. It is a measure of position rather than of magnitude and is frequently found by inspection rather than by calculation. When there are an odd number of untied scores, the median is the middle score, as in the example below:

7

6   3 scores above

5

4 — median

3

2   3 scores below

1

When there are an even number of untied scores, the median is the midpoint between the two middle scores, as in the example below:

6

5   3 scores above

4

    — median = 3.50

3

2   3 scores below

1

If the data include tied scores at the median point, interpolation within the tied scores is necessary. Each integer would represent the interval from halfway between it and the next lower score to halfway between it and the next higher score. When ties occur at the midpoint of a set of scores, this interval is portioned out into the number of tied scores and the midpoint or median is found. Consider the set of scores in Figure 10.1.

Because there are four scores tied (75), the interval from 74.5 to 75.5 is divided into four equal parts. Each of the scores is then considered to occupy 0.25 of the interval, and the median is calculated.

One purpose of the mean and the median is to represent the "typical" score; most of the time it is satisfactory to use the mean for this purpose. However, when the distribution of scores is such that most scores are at one end and relatively few are at the other (known as a *skewed distribution*), the median is preferable because it is not influenced by extreme scores at either end of the distribution. In the following examples the medians are identical. However, the mean of Group A is 4,

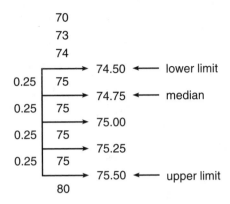

FIGURE 10.1   Median Calculation

and the mean of Group B is 10. The mean and median are both representative of Group A, but the median better represents the "typical" score of Group B.

Group A	Group B
7	50
6	6
5	5
4 — Md	4 — Md
3	3
2	2
1	0

Thus, in skewed data distributions the median is a more realistic measure of central tendency than the mean.

In a small school with five faculty members, the salaries might be

$$
\begin{array}{lll}
\text{Teacher A} & \$36,000 & \\
\text{B} & 22,000 & \\
\text{C} & 21,400 & \text{Median} \\
\text{D} & 21,000 & \\
\text{E} & \underline{19,600} & \\
\end{array}
$$

Total Salaries = \$120,000

$$\overline{X} = \frac{120,000}{5} = 24,000$$

The average salary of the group is represented with a different emphasis by the median salary (\$21,400) than by the mean salary (\$24,000), which is substantially higher than that of four of the five faculty members. Thus, we see again that the median is less sensitive than the mean to extreme values at either end of a distribution.

Using the same 25 children selected from Appendix B to calculate a mean, now calculate the median. How do the two compare? Which is more useful? The median for the population of 100 children is 89.0 (5 scores of 89 fall below the midpoint and 5 above it). How does the sample median compare?

The Mode (Mo)

6
5
4 ⎫
4 ⎬ Mode
3
2
1

The mode is the score that occurs most frequently in a distribution. It is located by inspection rather than by computation. In grouped data distributions the mode is assumed to be the midscore of the interval in which the greatest frequency occurs.

For example, if the modal age of fifth-grade children is 10 years, it follows that there are more 10-year-old fifth-graders than any other age. Or a menswear salesman might verify the fact that there are more sales of size 40 suits than of any other size; consequently, a larger number of size 40 suits are ordered and stocked, size 40 being the mode.

In some distributions there may be more than one mode. A two-mode distribution is referred to as bimodal, more than two, multimodal. If the number of auto accidents on the streets of a city were tabulated by hours of occurrence, it is likely that two modal periods would become apparent—between 7 A.M. and 8 A.M. and between 5 P.M. and 6 P.M., the hours when traffic to and from stores and offices is heaviest and when drivers are in the greatest hurry. In a normal distribution of data there is one mode, and it falls at the midpoint, just as the mean and median do. In some unusual distributions, however, the mode may fall at some other point. When the mode or modes reveal such unusual behavior, they do not serve as measures of central tendency, but they do reveal useful information about the nature of the distribution.

Using the data set in Appendix B, the mode of the categories of disability can be determined. Because 50 of the 100 children have learning disabilities (28 have behavior disorders and 22 have mental retardation) as their classification, this is the mode. Now using the data from the 25 children selected for the mean and median calculations above, determine the mode of the sample for disability category. Now determine the mode for IQ of the sample. The mode for the population is 89. How does the sample mode compare?

Measures of Spread or Dispersion

Measures of central tendency describe location along an ordered scale. There are characteristics of data distributions calling for additional types of statistical analysis. The scores in Table 10.4 were made by a group of students on two different tests, one in reading and one in arithmetic.

The mean and the median are identical for both tests. It is apparent that averages do not fully describe the differences in achievement between students' scores on the two tests. To contrast their performance, it is necessary to use a measure of score spread or dispersion. The arithmetic test scores are homogeneous, with little difference between adjacent scores. The reading test scores are decidedly heterogeneous, with performances ranging from superior to very poor.

The Range

The range, the simplest measure of dispersion, is the difference between the highest and lowest scores plus one. For reading scores the range is 41 (95 − 55 + 1). For arithmetic scores the range is 9 (79 − 71 + 1).

The Deviation from the Mean (x)

A score expressed as its distance from the mean is called a *deviation score*. Its formula is

$$x = (X - \overline{X})$$

TABLE 10.4   Sample Data

Reading			Arithmetic	
Pupil	**Score**	**Academic Grade**	**Score**	**Academic Grade**
Arthur	95	A	76	C
Betty	90	A	78	C
John	85	B	77	C
Katherine	80	B	71	C
Charles	75	C	75	C
Larry	70	C	79	C
Donna	65	D	73	C
Edward	60	D	72	C
Mary	55	F	74	C
	$\Sigma X = 675$		$\Sigma X = 675$	
	$N = 9$		$N = 9$	
	$\overline{X} = \dfrac{675}{9} = 75$		$\overline{X} = \dfrac{675}{9} = 75$	
	$Md = 75$		$Md = 75$	

If the score falls above the mean, the deviation score is positive (+); if it falls below the mean, the deviation score is negative (−).

Using the same example, compare two sets of scores:

Reading		Arithmetic	
X	$(X - \overline{X})$	X	$(X - \overline{X})$
95	+20	76	+1
90	+15	78	+3
85	+10	77	+2
80	+ 5	71	−4
75	0	75	0
70	− 5	79	+4
65	−10	73	−2
60	−15	72	−3
55	−20	74	−1
$\Sigma X = 675$	$\Sigma x = 0$	$\Sigma X = 675$	$\Sigma x = 0$
$N = 9$		$N = 9$	
$\overline{X} = 75$		$\overline{X} = 75$	

It is interesting to note that the sum of the score deviations from the mean equals zero.

$$\Sigma (X - \overline{X}) = 0$$
$$\Sigma x = 0$$

In fact, we can give an alternative definition of the mean: The mean is that value in a distribution around which the sum of the deviation score equals zero.

The Variance (σ^2)

The sum of the squared deviations from the mean, divided by N, is known as the variance. We have noted that the sum of the deviations from the mean equals zero ($\Sigma x = 0$). From a mathematical point of view it would be impossible to find a mean value to describe these deviations (unless the signs were ignored). Squaring each deviation score yields a positive score. The scores can then be summed, divided by N, and the mean of the squared deviations computed. The variance formula is

$$\sigma^2 = \frac{\Sigma(X - \overline{X})^2}{N} \quad \text{or} \quad \frac{\Sigma x^2}{N}$$

Thus, the variance is a value that describes how all of the scores in a distribution are dispersed or spread about the mean. This value is very useful in describing the characteristics of a distribution and will be employed in a number of very important statistical tests. However, because all of the deviations from the mean have been squared to find the variance, it is much too large to represent the spread of scores.

The Standard Deviation (σ)

The *standard deviation*, the square root of the variance, is most frequently used as a measure of spread or dispersion of scores in a distribution. The formula for standard deviation of a population is

$$\sigma = \sqrt{\frac{\Sigma(X - \overline{X})^2}{N}} \quad \text{or} \quad \sqrt{\frac{\Sigma x^2}{N}}$$

In the following example, using the reading scores from Table 10.4, the variance and the standard deviation are computed.

X	x	x^2
95	+20	+400
90	+15	+225
85	+10	+100
80	+ 5	+25
75	0	0
70	− 5	+25
65	−10	+100
60	−15	+225
55	−20	+400
		$\Sigma x^2 = 1500$

Variance $\sigma^2 = 1500/9 = 166.67$

Standard deviation $\sigma = \sqrt{1500/9} = \sqrt{166.67} = 12.91$

As can clearly be seen, a variance of 166.67 cannot represent, for most purposes, a spread of scores with a total range of only 41, but the standard deviation of 12.91 does make sense.

Although the deviation approach (just used in the previous calculation) provides a clear example of the meaning of variance and standard deviation, in actual practice the deviation method can be awkward to use in computing the variances or standard deviations for a large number of scores. A less complicated method, which results in the same answer, uses the raw scores instead of the deviation scores. The number values tend to be large, but the use of a calculator facilitates the computation.

$$\text{Variance } \sigma^2 = \frac{N\Sigma X^2 - (\Sigma X)^2}{N^2}$$

$$\text{Standard deviation } \sigma = \sqrt{\frac{N\Sigma X^2 - (\Sigma X)^2}{N^2}}$$

The following example demonstrates the process of computation, using the raw score method:

X	X^2
95	9025
90	8100
85	7225
80	6400
75	5625
70	4900
65	4225
60	3600
55	3025
$\Sigma X = 675$	$\Sigma X^2 = 52{,}125$
$N = 9$	

$$\sigma^2 = \frac{9\,(51{,}125) - (675)^2}{9\,(9)} = \frac{469{,}125 - 455{,}624}{81}$$

$$\sigma^2 = \frac{13{,}500}{81} = 166.67$$

$$\sigma = \sqrt{166.67} = 12.91$$

Standard Deviation for Samples (S)

The variance and standard deviation for a population have just been described. Because most of the time researchers use samples selected from the population, it is necessary to introduce the formulas for the variance S^2 and the standard deviation (S) of a sample. The sample formulas differ only slightly from the population formulas. As will be seen, instead of dividing by N in the deviation formula and by N^2 in the raw score formula, the sample formulas divide by $n - 1$ and $n(n - 1)$, respectively.[1] This is done to correct for the probability that the smaller the sample the less likely it is that extreme scores will be included. Thus the formula for σ, if used with a sample, would underestimate the standard deviation of the population because a randomly selected sample would probably not include the most extreme scores that exist in the population simply because there are so few of them. Dividing by $n - 1$ or $n(n - 1)$ corrects for this bias, more or less depending upon the sample's size. This makes the standard deviation of the sample more representative of the population. In a small sample, say $n = 5$, the correction is rather large, dividing by 4 instead of 5—a reduction of 20% in the denominator. In a large sample, say $n = 100$, the correction is insignificant, dividing by 99 instead of 100—a reduction of 1% in the denominator. Again, this difference in the percent correction is due to the fact that smaller the sample the less likely are extreme scores to be represented.

We should note that these formulas for the standard deviation of the sample are actually inferential statistics and would normally be in the next chapter. However, because these are the formulas used to describe a sample and because samples are what one normally has to calculate the standard deviation, we believe this is the better place for them.

The two formulas for sample standard deviation with the deviation and the raw score methods of computation, respectively, are

$$S = \sqrt{\frac{(X - \bar{X})^2}{n - 1}} \quad \text{or} \quad \sqrt{\frac{x^2}{n - 1}} \quad \text{and} \quad S = \sqrt{\frac{N\Sigma X^2 - (X)^2}{n(n - 1)}}$$

No doubt the reader can see that the only changes are in the denominator. Thus, if we substitute $n(n - 1)$ for N^2 and calculate S^2 and S using the data from page 350, we would find the following:

$$S^2 = \frac{9(52,125) - (675)^2}{9(8)} = \frac{469,125 - 455,625}{72}$$

$$= \frac{13,500}{72} = 187.50$$

$$S = \sqrt{187.50} = 13.69$$

These results are quite a change from $\sigma^2 = 166.67$ (change of $+20.83$) and $\sigma = 12.91$ (change of $+.78$). These relatively large differences from the population formula to the sample formula are due to the small sample size ($n = 9$), which made a relatively large correction necessary. The correction for calculating the variance and standard deviation is important because, unless the loss of a degree of freedom (discussed in Chapter 11) is considered, the calculated sample variance or standard deviation is likely to underestimate the population variance or standard deviation. This is true because the mean of the squared deviations from the mean of any distribution is the smallest possible value and probably would be smaller than the mean of the squared deviation from any other point in the distribution. Because the mean of the sample is not likely to be identical to the population mean (because of sampling error), the use of $N - 1$ (the number of degrees of freedom) rather than N in the denominator tends to correct for this underestimation of the population variance or standard deviation.

The strength of a prediction or the accuracy of an inferred value increases as the number of independent observations (sample size) is increased. Because large samples may be biased, sample size is not the only important determinant, but if unbiased samples are selected randomly from a population, large samples will provide a more accurate basis than will smaller samples for inferring population values.

The standard deviation for IQ of the population in Appendix B is 11.55, using the formula for the population (it would be 11.61 if the sample formula were used). The reader should calculate the standard deviation (using the formula for a sample) for the sample. How does it compare with the standard deviation of this population?

The standard deviation is a very useful device for comparing characteristics that may be quite different or may be expressed in different units of measurement.

The following discussion shows that when the normality of distributions can be assumed it is possible to compare the proverbial apples and oranges. The standard deviation is independent of the magnitude of the mean and provides a common unit of measurement. To use a rather farfetched example, imagine a man whose height is one standard deviation below the mean and whose weight is one standard deviation above the mean. Because we assume that there is a normal relationship between height and weight (or that both characteristics are normally distributed), a picture emerges of a short, overweight individual. His height, expressed in inches, is in the lowest 16% of the population, and his weight, expressed in pounds, is in the highest 16%. In this chapter only the standard deviation of a population is discussed.

But before using the standard deviation to describe status or position in a group is discussed, the normal distribution needs to be examined.

NORMAL DISTRIBUTION

The earliest mathematical analysis of the theory of probability dates to the 18th century. Abraham DeMoivre, a French mathematician, discovered that a mathematical relationship explained the probabilities associated with various games of chance. He developed the equation and the graphic pattern that describes it. During the 19th century a French astronomer, LaPlace, and a German mathematician, Gauss, independently arrived at the same principle and applied it more broadly to areas of measurement in the physical sciences. From the limited applications made by these early mathematicians and astronomers, the theory of probability, or the curve of distribution of error, has been applied to data gathered in the areas of biology, psychology, sociology, and other sciences. The theory describes the fluctuations of chance errors of observation and measurement. It is necessary to understand the theory of probability and the nature of the curve of normal distribution to comprehend many important statistical concepts, particularly in the area of standard scores, the theory of sampling, and inferential statistics.

We should keep in mind that "the normal distribution does not actually exist. It is not a fact of nature. Rather, it is a mathematical model—an idealization—that can be used to represent data collected in behavioral research" (Shavelson, 1996, p. 120). The law of probability and the normal curve that illustrates it are based on the law of chance or the probable occurrence of certain events. When any body of observations conforms to this mathematical form, it can be represented by a bell-shaped curve with definite characteristics (see Figure 10.2).

1. The curve is symmetrical around its vertical axis—50% of the scores are above the mean and 50% below the mean.
2. The mean, median, and the mode of the distribution have the same value.
3. The terms cluster around the center—most scores are near the mean, median, and mode with fewer scores as the score is further from the center.
4. The curve has no boundaries in either direction, for the curve never touches the base line, no matter how far it is extended. The curve is a curve of probability, not of certainty.

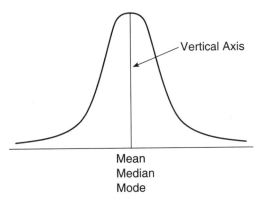

FIGURE 10.2   The Normal Curve

5. One way to think of the normal curve (or the nonnormal curves described shortly) is to view it "as a solid geometric figure made up of all the subjects and their different scores" (Heiman, 1996, p. 53). That is, the curve is a smoothed, curved version of a bar graph that represents each possible score and the number of persons who got that score.

Researchers often consider one standard deviation from the mean to be a particularly important point on the normal curve. This is for both a practical and a mathematical reason. The practical reason is that this results in approximately 68% (slightly over two-thirds) of the population falling between one standard deviation above and one standard deviation below the mean. Perhaps more important, this is the point at which the curve changes from a downward convex shape to an upward convex shape. Thus, mathematically, this is the point at which the direction of the curve changes. As will be discussed later, ±1.96 standard deviations from the mean will result in 95% of the population. This is another critical point in the curve, which is often rounded to 2 standard deviations from the mean.

The operation of chance prevails in the tossing of coins or dice. It is believed that many human characteristics respond to the influence of chance. For example, if certain limits of age, race, and gender were kept constant, such measures as height, weight, intelligence, and longevity would approximate the normal distribution pattern. But the normal distribution does not appear in data based on observations of samples. There just are not enough observations. The normal distribution is based on an infinite number of observations beyond the capability of any observer; thus, there is usually some observed deviation from the symmetrical pattern. But for purposes of statistical analysis, it is assumed that many characteristics do conform to this mathematical form within certain limits, providing a convenient reference.

The concept of measured intelligence is based on the assumption that intelligence is normally distributed throughout limited segments of the population. Tests are so constructed (standardized) that scores are normally distributed in the large group that is used for the determination of norms or standards. Insurance companies determine their premium rates by the application of the curve of probability.

Basing their expectation on observations of past experience, they can estimate the probabilities of survival of a man from age 45 to 46. They do not purport to predict the survival of a particular individual, but from a large group they can predict the mortality rate of all insured risks.

The total area under the normal curve may be considered to approach 100% probability. Interpreted in terms of standard deviations, areas between the mean and the various standard deviations from the mean under the curve show these percentage relationships (see Figure 10.3).

Note the graphic conformation of the characteristics of the normal curve:

1. It is symmetrical—the percentage of frequencies is the same for equal intervals below or above the mean.
2. The terms or scores "cluster" or "crowd around the mean"—note how the percentages in a given standard deviation are greatest around the mean and decrease as one moves away from the mean.

$\overline{X}$ to ±1.00z	34.13%
±1.00 to ±2.00z	13.59%
±2.00 to ±3.00z	2.15%

3. The curve is highest at the mean—the mean, median, and mode have the same value.
4. The curve has no boundaries—a small fraction of 1% of the space falls outside of ±3.00 standard deviations from the mean.

The normal curve is a curve that also describes probabilities. For example, if height is normally distributed for a given segment of the population, the chances are

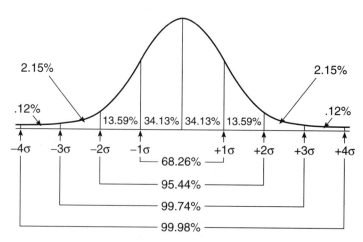

FIGURE 10.3   Percentage of Frequencies in a Normal Distribution Falling within a Range of a Given Number of Standard Deviations from the Mean

$\frac{34.13}{100}$ that a person selected at random will be between the mean and one standard deviation above the mean in height, and $\frac{34.13}{100}$ that the person selected will be between the mean and one standard deviation below the mean in height—or $\frac{68.26}{100}$ that the selected person will be within one standard deviation (above or below) the mean in height. Another interpretation is that 68.26% of this population segment will be between the mean and one standard deviation above or below the mean in height.

An example may help the reader understand this concept. IQ (intelligence quotient) is assumed to be normally distributed. The Wechsler Intelligence Scale for Children-Revised (WISC-R) has a mean of 100 and a standard deviation of 15. Thus, a WISC-R IQ score that is one standard deviation above the mean is 115, and a score of 85 is one standard deviation below the mean. From this information it is known that approximately 68% of the population should have WISC-R scores between 85 and 115.

For practical purposes the curve is usually extended to ±3 standard deviations from the mean (±3z). Most events or occurrences (or probabilities) will fall between these limits. The probability is $\frac{99.74}{100}$ that these limits account for observed or predicted occurrences. This statement does not suggest that events or measures could not fall more than three standard deviations from the mean but that the likelihood would be too small to consider when making predictions or estimates based on probability. Statisticians deal with probabilities, not certainty, and there is always a degree of reservation in making any prediction. Statisticians deal with the probabilities that cover the normal course of events, not the events that are outside the normal range of experience.

Nonnormal Distributions

As mentioned earlier in the discussions of parametric and nonparametric data and the relative usefulness of the mean and median, not all distributions, particularly of sample data, are identical to or even close to a normal curve. There are two other types of distributions that can occur: *skewed* and *bimodal*. In skewed distributions the majority of scores are near the high or low end of the range with relatively few scores at the other end. The distribution is considered skewed in the direction of the tail (fewest scores). In Figure 10.4 on page 356 distribution A is skewed positively, and distribution B is skewed negatively. Skewed distributions can be caused by a number of factors, including a test that is too easy or hard or an atypical sample (very bright or very low intelligence).

Bimodal distributions have two modes (see distribution C in Figure 10.4) rather than the single mode of normal or skewed distributions. This often results from a sample that consists of persons from two populations. For instance, the height of American adults would be bimodally distributed, females clustering around a mode of about 5 feet 4 inches and males around a mode of about 5 feet 10 inches.

Interpreting the Normal Probability Distribution

When scores are normally or near normally distributed, a normal probability table is useful. The values presented in the normal probability table in Appendix B are

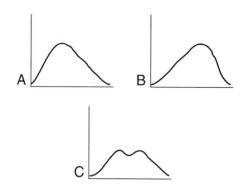

FIGURE 10.4   Nonnormal Distributions

critical because they provide data for normal distributions that may be interpreted in the following ways:

1. The percentage of total space included between the mean and a given standard deviation (z) distance from the mean
2. The percentage of cases, or the number when N is known, that fall between the mean and a given standard deviation (z) distance from the mean
3. The probability that an event will occur between the mean and a given standard deviation (z) distance from the mean

z = number of standard deviations from the mean

$$z = \frac{X - \overline{X}}{\sigma}$$

Figure 10.5 demonstrates how the area under the normal curve can be divided. In a normal distribution the following characteristics hold true:

1. The space included between the mean and +1.00z is .3413 of the total area under the curve.
2. The percentage of cases that fall between the mean and +1.00z is .3413.
3. The probability of an event's occurring (observation) between the mean and +1.00z is .3413.
4. The distribution is divided into two equal parts, one half above the mean and the other half below the mean.
5. Because one half of the curve is above the mean and .3413 of the total area is between the mean and +1.00z, the area of the curve that is above +1.00z is .1587.

Because the normal probability curve is symmetrical, the shape of the right side (above the mean) is identical to the shape of the left side (below the mean). Because the values for each side of the curve are identical, only one set of values is presented in the probability table, expressed to one-hundredth of a sigma (standard deviation) unit.

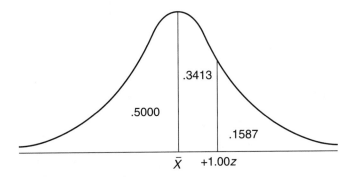

**FIGURE 10.5   The Space Included Under the Normal
Curve Between the Mean and ±1.00z**

The normal probability table in Appendix C provides the proportion of the curve that is between the mean and a given sigma (z) value. The remainder of that half of the curve is beyond the sigma value.

		Probability
Above the mean	.5000	50/100
Below the mean	.5000	50/100
Above +1.96z	.5000 − .4750 = .0250	2.5/100
Below +.32z	.5000 + .1255 = .6255	62.5/100
Below −.32z	.5000 − .1255 = .3745	37.5/100

Practical Applications of the Normal Curve

In the field of educational research the normal curve has a number of practical applications:

1. To calculate the percentile rank of scores in a normal distribution.
2. To normalize a frequency distribution, an important process in standardizing a psychological test or inventory.
3. To test the significance of observed measures in experiments, relating them to the chance fluctuations or errors inherent in the process of sampling and generalizing about populations from which the samples are drawn.

Measures of Relative Position: Standard Scores

Standard scores provide a method of expressing any score in a distribution in terms of its distance from the mean in standard deviation units. The utility of this conversion of a raw score to a standard score will become clear as each type is introduced and illustrated. Three types of standard scores are considered.

1. Z score (Sigma)
2. T score (T)
3. College board score (Z_{cb})

Remember that the distribution is assumed to be normal when using any type of standard score.

The Z Score (Sigma)

In describing a score in a distribution, its deviation from the mean—expressed in standard deviation units—is often more meaningful than the score itself. The unit of measurement is the standard deviation.

$$z = \frac{X - \overline{X}}{\sigma} \quad \text{or} \quad \frac{x}{\sigma}$$

where X = raw score
$\overline{X}$ = mean
σ = standard deviation
$x = (X - \overline{X})$ score deviation from the mean

Example A	Example B
$X = 76$	$X = 67$
$\overline{X} = 82$	$\overline{X} = 62$
$\sigma = 4$	$\sigma = 5$
$z = \dfrac{76 - 82}{4} = \dfrac{-6}{4} = -1.50$	$z = \dfrac{67 - 62}{5} = \dfrac{5}{5} = +1.00$

The raw score of 76 in Example A may be expressed as a Z score of -1.50, indicating that 76 is 1.5 standard deviations below the mean. The score of 67 in Example B may be expressed as a sigma score of $+1.00$, indicating that 67 is one standard deviation above the mean.

In comparing or averaging scores on distributions where total points may differ, the researcher using raw scores may create a false impression of a basis for comparison. A Z score makes possible a realistic comparison of scores and may provide a basis for equal weighting of the scores. On the sigma scale the mean of any distribution is converted to zero, and the standard deviation is equal to 1.

For example, a teacher wishes to determine a student's equally weighted average (mean) achievement on an algebra test and on an English test.

Subject	Test Score	Mean	Highest Possible Score	Standard Deviation
Algebra	40	47	60	5
English	84	110	180	20

It is apparent that the mean of the two raw test scores would not provide a valid summary of the student's performance, for the mean would be weighted overwhelmingly in favor of the English test score. The conversion of each test score to a sigma score makes them equally weighted and comparable, for both test scores have been expressed on a scale with a mean of zero and a standard deviation of one.

$$z = \frac{X - \overline{X}}{\sigma}$$

$$\text{Algebra } z \text{ score} = \frac{40 - 47}{5} = \frac{-7}{5} = -1.40$$

$$\text{English } z \text{ score} = \frac{84 - 110}{20} = \frac{-26}{20} = -1.30$$

On an equally weighted basis, the performance of the student was fairly consistent: 1.40 standard deviations below the mean in algebra and 1.30 standard deviations below the mean in English.

Because the normal probability table describes the percentage of area lying between the mean and successive deviation units under the normal curve (see Appendix C), the use of sigma scores has many other useful applications to hypothesis testing, determination of percentile ranks, and probability judgments.

The reader may wish to select one score from the sample of 25 children selected earlier and calculate the z score for that person in relation to the sample. The population mean (86.12) and standard deviation (11.55) in the formula could then be used to calculate the z for the same child. How do these two z scores compare?

The T *Score (T)*

$$T = 50 + 10 \frac{(X - \overline{X})}{\sigma} \quad \text{or} \quad 50 + 10z$$

Although the z score is most frequently used, it is sometimes awkward to have negatives or scores with decimals. Therefore, another version of a standard score, the T score, has been devised to avoid some confusion resulting from negative z scores (below the mean) and also to eliminate decimal values.

Multiplying the z score by 10 and adding 50 results in a scale of positive whole number values. Using the scores in the previous example, $T = 50 + 10z$:

Algebra $T = 50 + 10(-1.40) = 50 + (-14) = 36$
English $T = 50 + 10(-1.30) = 50 + (-13) = 37$

T scores are always rounded to the nearest whole number. A z score of $+1.27$ would be converted to a T score of 63.

$$T = 50 + 10(+1.27) = 50 + (+12.70) = 62.70 = 63$$

Convert the z scores just calculated for the person selected from the sample into T scores.

The College Board Score (Z_{cb})

The College Entrance Examination Board and several other testing agencies use another conversion that provides a more precise measure by spreading out the scale (see Figure 10.6).

$$Z_{cb} = 500 + 100 \frac{(X - \overline{X})}{\sigma} = 500 + 100z$$

The mean of this scale is 500.
The standard deviation is 100.
The range is 200–800.

Stanines

A stanine is a standard score that divides the normal curve into nine parts, thus the term *stanine* from *sta* of *standard* and *nine*. The 2nd to 8th stanines are each equal to one-half standard deviation unit. Thus, stanine 5 includes the center of the curve and goes one-quarter (.25) standard deviations above and below the mean. Stanine 6 goes from the top of stanine 5 to .75 standard deviations above the mean, whereas stanine 4 goes from the bottom of stanine 5 to .75 standard deviations below the mean and so on. Stanine 1 encompasses all scores below stanine 2, and stanine 9 encompasses all scores above stanine 8. Figure 10.6 demonstrates the stanine distribution and compares it to the other standard scores.

Percentile Rank

Although the percentile rank is not usually considered a standard score, it is pertinent to this discussion. It is often useful to describe a score in relation to other scores; the percentile rank is the point in the distribution below which a given percentage of scores fall. If the 80th percentile rank is a score of 65, 80% of the scores fall below 65. The median is the 50th percentile rank, for 50% of the scores fall below it.

When N is small, the definition needs an added refinement. To be completely accurate, the percentile rank is the score in the distribution below which a given percentage of the scores falls, plus one half the percentage of space occupied by the given score.

Scores
50
47
<u>43</u>
39
30

On inspection it is apparent that 43 is the median, or occupies the 50th percentile rank. Fifty % of the scores should fall below it, but in fact only two out of

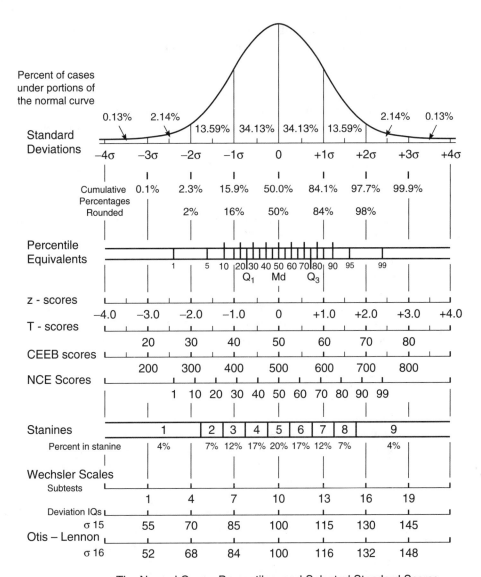

The Normal Curve, Percentiles, and Selected Standard Scores

FIGURE 10.6   Illustration of Various Standard Score Scales

(Test Service Notebook 148, The Psychological Corporation, NY.)

five scores fall below 43. That would indicate 43 has a percentile rank of 40. But by adding the phrase "plus one half the percentage of space occupied by the score," the calculation is reconciled:

40% of scores fall below 43; each score occupies 20% of the total space

40% + 10% = 50 (true percentile rank)

When N is large, this qualification is unimportant because percentile ranks are rounded to the nearest whole number, ranging from the highest percentile rank of 99 to the lowest of zero.

High schools frequently rate their graduating seniors in terms of rank in class. Because schools vary so much in size, colleges find these rankings of limited value unless they are converted to some common basis for comparison. The percentile rank provides this basis by converting class rank into a percentile rank.

$$\text{Percentile rank} = 100 - \frac{(100RK - 50)}{N}$$

where RK = rank from the top.

Jones ranks 27th in his senior class of 139 students. Twenty-six students rank above him, 112 below him. His percentile rank is

$$100 - \frac{(2700 - 50)}{139} = 100 - 19 = 81$$

In this formula 50 is subtracted from $100RK$ to account for half the space occupied by the individual's score. What is the percentile rank of the person you selected in order to calculate z and T scores?

MEASURES OF RELATIONSHIP

Correlation

Correlation is the relationship between two or more paired variables or two or more sets of data. The degree of relationship is measured and represented by the coefficient of correlation. This coefficient may be identified by either the letter r, the Greek letter rho (ρ), or other symbols, depending on the data distributions and the way the coefficient has been calculated.

Students who have high intelligence quotients tend to receive high scores in mathematics tests, whereas those with low IQs tend to score low. When this type of relationship is obtained, the factors of measured intelligence and scores on mathematics tests are said to be positively correlated.

Sometimes variables are negatively correlated when a large amount of one variable is associated with a small amount of the other. As one increases, the other tends to decrease.

When the relationship between two sets of variables is a pure chance relationship, we say that there is no correlation.

These pairs of variables are usually positively correlated: As one increases, the other tends to increase.

1. Intelligence   Academic achievement
2. Productivity per acre   Value of farm land
3. Height   Shoe size
4. Family income   Value of family home

These variables are usually negatively correlated: As one increases, the other tends to decrease.

1. Academic achievement   Hours per week of TV watching
2. Total corn production   Price per bushel
3. Time spent in practice   Number of typing errors
4. Age of an automobile   Trade-in value

There are other traits that probably have no correlation.

1. Body weight   Intelligence
2. Shoe size   Monthly salary

The degree of linear correlation can be represented quantitatively by the coefficient of correlation. A perfect positive correlation is +1.00. A perfect negative correlation is −1.00. A complete lack of relationship is zero (0). Rarely, if ever, are perfect coefficients of correlations of +1.00 or −1.00 encountered, particularly in relating human traits. Although some relationships tend to appear fairly consistently, there are variations or exceptions that reduce the measured coefficient from either a −1.00 or a +1.00 toward zero.

A definition of perfect positive correlation specifies that for every unit increase in one variable there is a proportional unit increase in the other. The perfect negative correlation specifies that for every unit increase in one variable there is a proportional unit decrease in the other. That there can be no exceptions explains why coefficients of correlation of +1.00 or −1.00 are not encountered in relating human traits. The sign of the coefficient indicates the direction of the relationship, and the numerical value its strength.

The Scattergram and Linear Regression Line
When the relationship between two variables is plotted graphically, paired variable values are plotted against each other on the X and Y axis.

The line drawn through, or near, the coordinate points is known as the "line of best fit," or the *regression line.* On this line the sum of the deviations of all the coordinate points has the smallest possible value. As the coefficient approaches zero (0), the coordinate points fall further from the regression line (see Figure 10.7 on page 364 for examples of different correlations' scattergrams).

When the coefficient of correlation is either +1.00 or −1.00, all of the coordinate points fall on the regression line, indicating that, when $r = +1.00$, for every increase in X there is a proportional increase in Y; and when $r = -1.00$, for every increase in X there is a proportional decrease in Y. There are no individual exceptions. If we know a person's score on one measure, we can determine his or her exact score on the other measure.

The slope of the regression line, or line of best fit, is not determined by guess or estimation but by a geometric process that will be described later.

There are actually two regression lines. When $r = +1.00$ or -1.00, the lines are superimposed and appear as one line. As r approaches zero, the lines separate further.

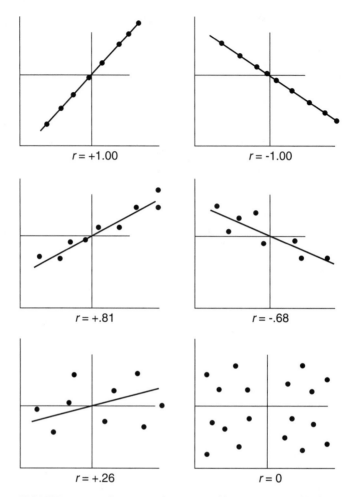

FIGURE 10.7   Scatter Diagrams Illustrating Different Coefficients of Correlation

Only one of the regression lines is described in this discussion, the Y on X (or Y from X) line. It is used to predict unknown Y values from known X values. The X values are known as the predictor variable, and the Y values, the predicted variable. The other regression line (not described here) would be used to predict X from Y.

Plotting the Slope of the Regression Line
The slope of the regression (Y from X) line is a geometric representation of the coefficient of correlation and is expressed as a ratio of the magnitude of the *rise* (if r is $+$) to the run, or as a ratio of the *fall* (if r is $-$) to the run, expressed in standard

deviation units. The geometric relationship between the two legs of the right triangle determines the slope of the hypotenuse, or the regression line.

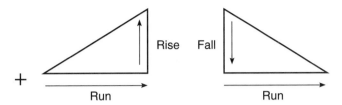

For example, if $r = +.60$, for every sigma unit increase (run) in X, there is a .60 sigma unit increase (rise) in Y.

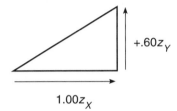

If $r = -.60$, for every sigma unit increase (run) in X, there is a .60 sigma unit decrease (fall) in Y.

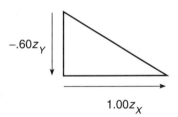

Because all regression lines pass through the intersection of the mean of X and the mean of Y lines, only one other point is necessary to determine the slope. By measuring one standard deviation of the X distribution on the X axis and a .60 standard deviation of the Y distribution on the Y axis, the second point is established (see Figures 10.8 and 10.9 on page 366).

The regression line (r) involves one awkward feature: all values must be expressed in sigma scores (z) or standard deviation units. It would be more practical to use actual scores to determine the slope of the regression line. This can be done by converting to a slope known as b. The slope of the b regression line Y on X is determined by the formula

$$b = r\,\frac{\sigma_Y}{\sigma_X}$$

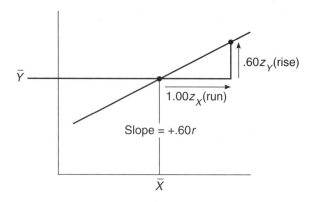

FIGURE 10.8   A Positive Regression Line, $r = +.60$

For example, if $r = +.60$

and $\sigma_y = 6$

               $\sigma_x = 5$

$$b = +.60\ \frac{6}{5} = \frac{3.60}{5} = +.72$$

Thus an r of $+.60$ becomes $b = +.72$. Now the ratio run has another value and indicates a different slope line (Figure 10.10).

Pearson's Product-Moment Coefficient of Correlation (r)

The most often used and most precise coefficient of correlation is known as the *Pearson's Product-Moment coefficient (r)*. This coefficient may be calculated by

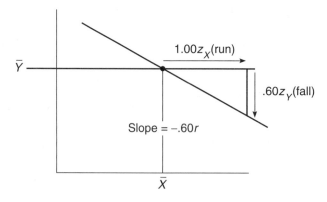

FIGURE 10.9   A Negative Regression Line, $r = -.60$

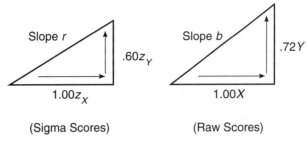

(Sigma Scores)   (Raw Scores)

FIGURE 10.10   Two Regression Lines, *r* and *b*
An *r* of +.60 is converted to a *b* of
+.72 by the formula

$$b = -r\frac{\sigma_Y}{\sigma_X}$$

converting the raw scores to sigma scores and finding the mean value of their cross-products.

$$r = \frac{\Sigma(z_x)(z_y)}{N}$$

z_x	z_y	$(z_x)(z_y)$
+1.50	+1.20	+1.80
+2.00	+1.04	+2.08
−.75	−.90	+.68
+.20	+.70	+.14
−1.00	+.20	−.20
−.40	+.30	−.12
+1.40	+.70	+.98
+.55	+.64	+.35
−.04	+.10	−.00
−.10	+.30	−.03

$$\Sigma\,(z_x)(z_y) = 5.68$$

$$r = \frac{+5.68}{10} = +.568$$

If most of the negative values of X are associated with negative z values of Y, and positive values of X with positive values of Y, the correlation coefficient will be positive. If most of the paired values are of opposite signs, the coefficient will be negative.

positive correlation (+)(+) = + high on X, high on Y
(−)(−) = + low on X, low on Y
negative correlation (+)(−) = − high on X, low on Y
(−)(+) = − low on X, high on Y

The z score method is not often used in actual computation because it involves the conversion of each score into a sigma score. Two other methods, a deviation method and a raw score method, are more convenient, more often used, and yield the same result.

The deviation method uses the following formula and requires the setting up of a table with seven columns.

$$r = \frac{\Sigma xy}{\sqrt{\left(\Sigma x^2\right)\left(\Sigma y^2\right)}}$$

where Σx^2 = the sum of the $\overline{X}$ subtracted from each X score squared
$(X - \overline{X})^2$

Σy^2 = the sum of the $\overline{Y}$ subtracted from each Y score squared
$(Y - \overline{Y})^2$

Σxy = the cross product of the mean subtracted from that score
$(X - \overline{X})(Y - \overline{Y})$

Using the data from Table 10.4, with reading scores being the X variable and arithmetic scores being the Y variable, the researcher calculates r like this:

			Variables			
X	Y	x	x^2	y	y^2	xy
95	76	20	400	1	1	+20
90	78	15	225	3	9	+45
85	77	10	100	2	4	+20
80	71	5	25	−4	16	−20
75	75	0	0	0	0	0
70	79	−5	25	4	16	−20
65	73	−10	100	−2	4	+20
60	72	−15	225	−3	9	+45
55	74	−20	400	−1	1	+20
$\Sigma X = 675$	$\Sigma Y = 675$		$\Sigma x^2 = 1500$		$\Sigma y^2 = 60$	$\Sigma xy = 130$
$\overline{X} = 75$	$\overline{Y} = 75$					

$$r = \frac{130}{\sqrt{(1500)(60)}} = \frac{130}{\sqrt{90{,}000}} = \frac{130}{300} = .433$$

The raw score method requires the use of five columns, as illustrated below using the same data.

$$r = \frac{N\Sigma XY - (\Sigma X)(\Sigma Y)}{\sqrt{N\Sigma X^2 - (\Sigma X)^2}\sqrt{N\Sigma Y^2 - (\Sigma Y)^2}}$$

where ΣX = sum of the X scores
ΣY = sum of the Y scores
ΣX^2 = sum of the squared X scores
ΣY^2 = sum of the squared Y scores
ΣXY = sum of the products of paired X and Y scores
N = number of paired scores

		Variables		
X	Y	X^2	Y^2	XY
95	76	9025	5776	7220
90	78	8100	6084	7020
85	77	7225	5929	6545
80	71	6400	5041	5680
75	75	5625	5625	5625
70	79	4900	6241	5530
65	73	4225	5329	4745
60	72	3600	5184	4320
55	74	3025	5476	4070
$\Sigma X = 675$	$\Sigma Y = 675$	$\Sigma X^2 = 52{,}125$	$\Sigma Y^2 = 50{,}685$	$\Sigma XY = 50{,}755$

$$r = \frac{9(50{,}755) - (675)(675)}{\sqrt{9(52{,}125) - (675)^2}\sqrt{9(50{,}685) - (675)^2}}$$

$$= \frac{456{,}795 - 455{,}625}{\sqrt{469{,}125 - 455{,}625}\sqrt{456{,}165 - 455{,}625}}$$

$$= \frac{1170}{\sqrt{13{,}500}\sqrt{540}}$$

$$= \frac{1170}{(116.19)(23.24)}$$

$$= \frac{1170}{2700.26} = .433$$

Now take the 25 children selected earlier and calculate the correlation of IQ with pretest scores. The correlation for IQ with pretest scores for the entire population of 100 children is +.552. How does the sample's correlation relate to the correlation for the population? Now calculate the correlation of the pretest and posttest scores. The correlation for the population of 100 children between their pretest scores and their posttest scores is +.834. How does the sample's correlation relate to the correlation for the population?

Rank Order Correlation (ρ)

A particular form of the Pearson product-moment correlation that can be used with ordinal data is known as the *Spearman rank order coefficient* of correlation. The symbol ρ (rho) is used to represent this correlation coefficient. The paired variables are expressed as ordinal values (ranked) rather than as interval or ratio values. The correction lends itself to an interesting graphic demonstration.

In the following example, the students ranking highest in IQ rank highest in mathematics, and those lowest in IQ, lowest in mathematics.

Pupil	IQ Rank	Achievement in Mathematics Rank
A	1 ——————— 1	
B	2 ——————— 2	
C	3 ——————— 3	
D	4 ——————— 4	
E	5 ——————— 5	

Perfect positive coefficient of correlation

$\rho = +1.00$

In the following example the students ranking highest in time spent in practice rank lowest in number of errors.

Pupil	Time Spent in Practice Rank	Number of Typing Errors Rank
A	1	5
B	2	4
C	3	3
D	4	2
E	5	1

Perfect negative coefficient of correlation

$\rho = -1.00$

In the following example, there is probably little more than a pure chance relationship (due to sampling error) between height and intelligence.

Pupil	Height Rank	IQ Rank
A	1	3
B	2	4
C	3	2
D	4	1
E	5	5

Very low coefficient of correlation

$\rho = +.10$

To compute the Spearman rank order coefficient of correlation, this rather simple formula is used:

$$\rho = 1 - \frac{6 \, \Sigma D^2}{N(N^2 - 1)}$$

where D = the difference between paired ranks
ΣD^2 = the sum of the squared differences between ranks
N = number of paired ranks

If the previously used data were converted to ranks and calculated Spearman's ρ, it would look like this:

Pupil	Rank in Reading	Rank in Arithmetic	D	D²
Arthur	1	4	−3	9
Betty	2	2	0	0
John	3	3	0	0
Katherine	4	9	−5	25
Charles	5	5	0	0
Larry	6	1	5	25
Donna	7	7	0	0
Edward	8	8	0	0
Mary	9	6	3	9
				$\Sigma D^2 = 68$

$$\rho = 1 - \frac{6(68)}{9(81 - 1)} = 1 - \frac{408}{9(80)}$$

$$= 1 - \frac{408}{720} = 1 - .567$$

$$= +.433$$

As has been just demonstrated, Spearman's ρ and Pearson's r yielded the same result. This occurs when there are no ties. When there are ties, the results will not be identical, but the difference will be insignificant.

The Spearman rank order coefficient of correlation computation is quick and easy. It is an acceptable method if data are available only in ordinal form. Teachers may find this computation method useful when conducting studies using a single class of students as subjects.

Phi Correlation Coefficient (φ)

The data are considered dichotomous when there are only two choices for scoring a variable (e.g., pass–fail or female–male). In these cases each person's score usually would be represented by a 0 or 1, although sometimes 1 and 2 are used instead.

The Pearson product-moment correlation, when both variables are dichotomous, is known as the phi (ϕ) coefficient. The formula for ϕ is simpler than for Pearson's r but algebraically identical. Because there are rarely two dichotomous variables of interest of which the researcher wants to know the relationship, the formula will not be presented here. This brief mention of ϕ is to make the reader aware of it. Those wishing more detail should refer to one of the many statistics texts available (e.g., Heiman, 1996; Glass & Hopkins, 1996).

INTERPRETATION OF A CORRELATION COEFFICIENT

Two circumstances can cause a higher or lower correlation than usual. First, when one person or relatively few people have a pair of scores differing markedly from the rest of the sample's scores, the resulting r may be spuriously high. When this occurs, the researcher needs to decide whether to remove this individual's pair of scores (known as an *outlier*) from the data analyzed. Second, when all other things are equal, the more homogeneous a group of scores, the lower their correlation will be. That is, the smaller the range of scores, the smaller r will be. Researchers need to consider this potential problem when selecting samples that may be highly homogeneous. However, if the researcher knows the standard deviation of the heterogeneous group from which the homogeneous group was selected, Glass and Hopkins (1984) and others describe a formula that corrects for the restricted range and provides the correlation for the heterogeneous group.

There are a number of ways to interpret a correlation coefficient or adjusted correlation coefficient, depending on the researcher's purpose and the circumstances that may influence the correlation's magnitude. One method that is frequently presented is to use a crude criterion for evaluating the magnitude of a correlation:

Coefficient (r)	Relationship
.00 to .20	Negligible
.20 to .40	Low
.40 to .60	Moderate
.60 to .80	Substantial
.80 to 1.00	High to very high

Another interpretative approach is a test of statistical significance of the correlation, based on the concepts of sampling error and tests of significance described in Chapter 11.

Still another way of interpreting a correlation coefficient is in terms of variance. The variance of the measure that the researcher wants to predict can be divided into the part that is explained by, or due to, the predictor variable and the part that is explained by other factors (generally unknown) including sampling error. The researcher finds this percentage of explained variance by calculating r^2, known as the *coefficient of determination*. The percentage of variance not explained by the predictor variable is then $1 - r^2$.

An example may help the reader understand this important concept. In combining studies using IQ to predict general academic achievement, Walberg (1984) found the overall correlation between these variables to be .71. We can use this correlation to find r^2 = .50. This means that 50% of the variance in academic achievement (how well or poorly different students do) is predictable from the variance of IQ. This also obviously means that 50% of the variance of academic achievement is due to factors other than IQ, such as motivation, home environment, school attended, and test error. Walberg also found that the correlation of IQ with science achievement was .48. This means that only 23% (r^2) of variance in science achievement is predictable by IQ and that 77% is due to other factors, some known and some unknown. Finally, the correlation of IQ and posttest scores reported earlier for the 100 children in our data set in Appendix B is +.638 and between the pre- and posttests +.894. Thus, 41% ($.638^2$) of the variance in posttest scores is predicted by IQ while 80% ($.894^2$) is predicted by pretest scores.

There are additional techniques, some too advanced for this introductory text, that allow researchers to use more than one variable. Thus, it is possible, for example, to use a combination of IQ, pretest scores, and other measures such as motivation and a socioeconomic scale to predict academic achievement (posttest scores). This multiple correlation would increase the correlation, which would, in turn, increase the percent of variance of academic achievement that is explained by known factors. The next chapter (11) discusses how multiple regression results in multiple correlations.

Misinterpretation of the Coefficient of Correlation

Several fallacies and limitations should be considered in interpreting the meaning of a coefficient of correlation. The coefficient does not imply a cause-and-effect relationship between variables. High positive correlations have been observed between the number of storks' nests and the number of human births in northwestern Europe and between the number of ordinations of ministers in the New England colonies and the consumption of gallons of rum. These high correlations obviously do not imply causality. As population increases, both good and bad things are likely to increase in frequency.

Similarly, a zero (or even negative) correlation does not necessarily mean that no causation is possible. Glass and Hopkins (1996) point out, "Some studies with college students have found no correlation between hours of study for an examination and test performance. . . . [This is likely due to the fact that] some bright students study little and still achieve average scores, whereas some of their less gifted classmates study diligently but still achieve an average performance. A controlled experimental study would almost certainly show some causal relationship" (p. 139).

Prediction

An important use of the coefficient of correlation and the Y on X regression line is for prediction of unknown Y values from known X values. Because it is a method for estimating future performance of individuals on the basis of past performance of a sample, prediction is an inferential application of correlational analysis. It has been included in this chapter to illustrate one of the most useful applications of correlation.

Let us assume that a college's admissions officers wish to predict the likely academic performance of students considered for admission or for scholarship grants. They have built up a body of data based on the past records of a substantial number of admitted college students over a period of several years. They have calculated the coefficient of correlation between their high school grade-point averages and their college freshman grade-point averages. They can now construct a regression line and predict the future college freshman GPA for any prospective student, based on his or her high school GPA.

Let us assume that the admissions officers found the coefficient of correlation to be +.52. The slope of the line could be used to determine any Y values for any X value. This process would be quite inconvenient, however, for all grade-point averages would have to be entered as sigma (z) values.

A more practicable procedure would be to construct a regression line with a slope of b so that any college grade-point average (Y) could be predicted directly from any high school grade-point average. The b regression line and a carefully drawn graph would provide a quick method for prediction. For example

$$\text{If } r = +.52, \qquad \text{then } \quad b = r \frac{(S_Y)}{(S_X)}$$

$$S_Y = .50 \qquad\qquad b = +.52 \frac{(.50)}{(.60)}$$

$$S_X = .60 \qquad\qquad b = +.43$$

X_A is student A's high school GPA, Y_A his predicted college GPA.
X_B is student B's high school GPA, Y_B her predicted college GPA.

Figure 10.11 uses these data to predict college GPA from high school GPA.

Another, and perhaps more accurate, alternative for predicting unknown Vs from known Ks is to use the regression equation rather than the graph. The formula for predicting Y from X is

$$\hat{Y} = a + bX$$

where $\hat{Y}$ = the predicted score (e.g., college freshman GPA)
$\quad\quad\ X$ = the predictor score (e.g., high school GPA)
$\quad\quad\ b$ = slope
$\quad\quad\ a$ = constant, or Y intercept

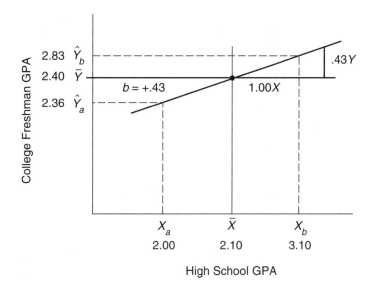

FIGURE 10.11   A Regression Line Used to Predict College Freshman GPA from High School GPA

We have already seen that $b = S_Y/S_X$. We can find a by $a = \overline{Y} - b\overline{X}$. Given the following data, we can then find the most likely freshman GPA for two students.

$b = .43$ (found earlier)

$\overline{X} = 2.10$

$\overline{Y} = 2.40$

$a = 2.40 - 2.10(.43) = 2.40 - .90 = 1.50$

X_a (student A's high school GPA) $= 2.00$

X_b (student B's high school GPA) $= 3.10$

$$\hat{Y}_a = 1.50 + .43(X_a)$$
$$= 1.50 + .43(2.00)$$
$$= 1.50 + .86$$
$$= 2.36$$

$$\hat{Y}_b = 1.50 + .43(X_a)$$
$$= 1.50 + .43(3.10)$$
$$= 1.50 + 1.33$$
$$= 2.83$$

For student A, whose high school GPA was below the mean, the predicted college GPA was also below the mean. For student B, whose high school GPA was well above the mean, the predicted GPA was substantially above the mean. These results are consistent with a positive coefficient of correlation in general: high in X, high in Y; low in X, low in Y.

STANDARD ERROR OF ESTIMATE

When the coefficient of correlation based on a sufficient body of data has been determined as ~ 1.00, there will be no error of prediction. Perfect correlation indicates that for every increase in X, there is a proportional increase (when $+$) or proportional decrease (when $-$) in Y. There are no exceptions. But when the magnitude of r is less than $+1.00$ or -1.00, error of prediction is inherent because there have been exceptions to a consistent, orderly relationship. The regression line does not coincide or pass through all of the coordinate values used in determining the slope.

A measure for estimating this prediction error is known as the standard *error of estimate* (S_{est}).

$$S_{est\,Y} = S_Y\sqrt{1 - r^2}$$

As the coefficient of correlation increases, the prediction error decreases. When $r = \pm 1.00$

$$S_{est\,Y} = S_Y\sqrt{1 - r^2} = S_Y\sqrt{1 - (1)^2} = S_Y(0) = 0$$

When $r = 0$

$$S_{est\,Y} = S_Y\sqrt{1 - (0)^2} = S_Y(1) = S_Y$$

When $r = 0$ (or when the coefficient of correlation is unknown), the best blind prediction of any Y from any X is the mean of Y. This is true because we know that most of the scores in a normal distribution cluster around the mean and that about 68% of them would probably fall within one standard deviation from the mean. In this situation the standard deviation of Y may be thought of as the standard error of estimate. When $r = 0$, $S_{est\,Y} = S_Y$.

If the coefficient of correlation is more than zero, this blind prediction can be improved on in these ways:

1. By plotting Y from a particular X from the regression line (see Figure 10.12)
2. By reducing the error of prediction of Y by calculating how much S_Y is reduced by the coefficient of correlation

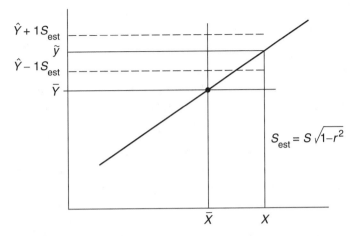

FIGURE 10.12   **A Predicted *Y* Score from a Given *X* Score, Showing the Standard Error of Estimate**

For example, when $r = \pm.60$

$$S_{est\,Y} = S_Y\sqrt{1 - (r)^2} = S_Y\sqrt{1 - (.60)^2} = S_Y\sqrt{1 - .36}$$
$$= S_Y\sqrt{.64} = .80S_Y$$

Thus the estimate error of *Y* has been reduced from S_Y to $.80S_Y$. Interpretation of the standard error of estimate is similar to the interpretation of the standard deviation. If $r = +.60S_Y$, the standard error of estimate of *Y* will be $.80S_Y$. An actual performance score of *Y* would probably fall within a band of $+.80S_Y$ from the predicted *Y* in about 68 of 100 predictions. In other words, the probability is that the predicted score would not be more than one standard error of estimate from the actual score in about 68% of the predictions.

In addition to the applications described, the coefficient of correlation is indispensable to psychologists who construct and standardize psychological tests and inventories. A few of the basic procedures are briefly described.

Computing the coefficient of correlation is the usual procedure used to evaluate the degree of validity and reliability of psychological tests and inventories (see Chapter 9 for a more detailed description of these concepts).

The Coefficient of Validity
A test is said to be valid to the degree that it measures what it claims to measure, or, in the case of predictive validity, to the extent that it predicts accurately such types of behavior as academic success or failure, job success or failure, or stability

or instability under stress. Tests are often validated by correlating test scores against some outside criteria, which may be scores on tests of accepted validity, successful performance or behavior, or the expert judgment of recognized authorities.

The Coefficient of Reliability

A test is said to be reliable to the degree that it measures accurately and consistently, yielding comparable results when administered a number of times. There are a number of ways of using the process of correlation to evaluate reliability:

1. Test–retest—correlating the scores on two or more successive administrations of the test (administration number 1 versus administration number 2)
2. Equivalent forms—correlating the scores when groups of individuals take equivalent forms of the test (form L versus form N)
3. Split halves—correlating the scores on the odd items of the test (numbers 1, 3, 5, 7, and so forth) against the even items (numbers 2, 4, 6, 8, and so forth). This method yields lower correlations because of the reduction in size to two tests of half the number of items. This may be corrected by the application of the *Spearman–Brown prophecy formula*.

$$r = \frac{2r}{1 + r}$$

If $r = \pm.60$,

$$r = \frac{1.20}{1 + .60} = +.75$$

A NOTE OF CAUTION

Statistics is an important tool of the research worker, and an understanding of statistical terminology, methodology, and logic is important for the consumer of research. A number of limitations, however, should be recognized in using statistical processes and in drawing conclusions from statistical evidence:

1. Statistical process, a servant of logic, has value only if it verifies, clarifies, and measures relationships that have been established by clear, logical analysis. Statistics is a means, never an end, of research.
2. A statistical process should not be employed in the analysis of data unless it adds clarity or meaning to the analysis of data. It should not be used as window dressing to impress the reader.
3. The conclusions derived from statistical analysis will be no more accurate or valid than the original data. To use an analogy, no matter how elaborate the mixer, a cake made of poor ingredients will be a poor cake. All the refinement of elaborate statistical manipulation will not yield significant truths if the data

result from crude or inexact measurement. In computer terminology this is known as GI–GO, "garbage in–garbage out."

4. All treatment of data must be checked and double-checked frequently to minimize the likelihood of errors in measurement, recording, tabulation, and analysis.

5. There is a constant margin of error wherever measurement of human beings is involved. The error is increased when qualities or characteristics of human personality are subjected to measurement or when inferences about the population are made from measurements derived from statistical samples.

   When comparisons or contrasts are made, a mere number difference is not in itself a valid basis for any conclusion. A test of statistical significance should be employed to weigh the possibility that chance in sample selection could have yielded the apparent difference. To apply these measures of statistical significance is to remove some of the doubt from the conclusions.

6. Statisticians and liars are often equated in humorous quips. There is little doubt that statistical processes can be used to prove nearly anything that one sets out to prove if the procedures used are inappropriate. Starting with false assumptions, using inappropriate procedures, or omitting relevant data, the biased investigator can arrive at false conclusions. These conclusions are often particularly dangerous because of the authenticity that the statistical treatment seems to confer. Of course, intentionally using inappropriate procedures or omitting relevant data constitutes unethical behavior and is quite rare.

Distortion may be deliberate or unintentional. In research, omitting certain facts or choosing only those facts favorable to one's position is as culpable as actual distortion, which has no place in research. The reader must always try to evaluate the manipulation of data, particularly when the report seems to be persuasive.

SUMMARY

This chapter deals with only the most elementary descriptive statistical concepts. For a more complete treatment the reader is urged to consult one or more of the references listed.

Statistical analysis is the mathematical process of gathering, organizing, analyzing, and interpreting numerical data and is one of the basic phases of the research process. Descriptive statistical analysis involves the description of a particular group. Inferential statistical analysis leads to judgments about the whole population, to which the sample at hand is presumed to be related.

Data are often organized in arrays in ascending or descending numerical order. Data are often grouped into class intervals so that analysis is simplified and characteristics more readily noted.

Measures of central tendency (mean, median, and mode) describe data in terms of some sort of average. Measures of position, spread, or dispersion describe data in terms of relationship to a point of central tendency. The range, deviation, variances, standard deviation, percentile, and Z (sigma) score are useful measures of position, spread, or dispersion.

Measures of relationship describe the relationship of paired variables, quantified by a coefficient of correlation. The coefficient is useful in educational research in standardizing tests and in making predictions when only some of the data are available. Note that a high coefficient does not imply a cause-and-effect relationship but merely quantifies a relationship that has been logically established prior to its measurement.

Statistics is the servant, not the master, of logic; it is a means rather than an end of research. Unless basic assumptions are valid; unless the right data are carefully gathered, recorded, and tabulated; and unless the analysis and interpretations are logical, statistics can make no contribution to the search for truth.

EXERCISES (ANSWERS IN APPENDIX I)

1. More than half the families in a community can have an annual income that is lower than the mean income for that community. Do you agree or disagree? Why?

2. The median is the midpoint between the highest and the lowest scores in a distribution. Do you agree or disagree? Why?

3. Compute the mean and the median of this distribution:

    74
    72
    70
    65
    63
    61
    56
    51
    42
    40
    37
    33

4. Determine the mean, the median, and the range of this distribution:

    88
    86
    85
    80
    80
    77
    75
    71
    65
    60
    58

5. Compute the variance (σ^2) and the standard deviation (σ) using the formula for the population (as indicated by the Greek letters) and then for a sample (S and S^2, respectively) for this set of scores:

    27
    27
    25
    24
    20
    18
    16
    16
    14
    12
    10
    7

6. The distribution with the larger range is the distribution with the larger standard deviation. Do you agree or disagree? Why?

7. If five points were added to each score in a distribution, how would this change each of the following:

    a. the range
    b. the mean
    c. the median
    d. the mode
    e. the variance
    f. the standard deviation

8. Joan Brown ranked 27th in a graduating class of 367. What was her percentile rank?

9. In a coin-tossing experiment where $N = 144$ and P (probability) = .50, draw the curve depicting the distribution of probable outcomes of heads appearing for an infinite number of repetitions of this experiment. Indicate the number of heads for the mean, and at 1, 2, and 3 standard deviations from the mean, both positive and negative.

10. Assuming the distribution to be normal with a mean of 61 and a standard deviation of 5, calculate the following standard score equivalents:

X	x	z	T
66			
58			
70			
61			
52			

11. Using the normal probability table in Appendix C, calculate the following values:

    a. below $-1.25z$ _____%
    b. above $-1.25z$ _____%
    c. between $-1.40z$ and $+1.67z$ _____%

d. between $+1.50z$ and $+2.50z$ _____%

e. 65th percentile rank _____z

f. 43rd percentile rank _____z

g. top 1% of scores _____z

h. middle 50% of scores _____z to _____z

i. not included between $-1.00z$ and $+1.00z$ _____%

j. 50th percentile rank _____z

12. Assuming a normal distribution of scores, a test has a mean score of 100 and a standard deviation of 15. Compute the following scores:

    a. score that cuts off the top 10% _____

    b. score that cuts off the lower 40% _____

    c. percentage of scores above 90 _____%

    d. score that occupies the 68th percentile rank _____

    e. score limits of the middle 68% _____ to _____

13. Consider the following table showing the performance of three students in algebra and history:

	Mean	σ	Tom	Donna	Harry
Algebra	90	30	60	100	85
History	20	4	25	22	19

Who had:

    a. the poorest score on either test? _____

    b. the best score on either test? _____

    c. the most consistent scores on both tests? _____

    d. the least consistent scores on both tests? _____

    e. the best mean score on both tests? _____

    f. the poorest mean score on both tests? _____

14. The coefficient of correlation measures the magnitude of the cause-and-effect relationship between paired variables. Do you agree or disagree? Why?

15. Using the Spearman rank order coefficient of correlation method, compute ρ.

	X Variable	Y Variable
Mary	1	3
Peter	2	4
Paul	3	1
Helen	4	2
Ruth	5	7
Edward	6	5
John	7	6

16. Two sets of paired variables are expressed in z (sigma) scores. Compute the coefficient of correlation between them.

z_X	z_Y
+.70	+.55
−.20	−.32
+1.50	+2.00
+1.33	+1.20
−.88	−1.06
+.32	−.40
−1.00	+.50
+.67	+.80
−.30	−.10
+1.25	+1.10
+.50	−.20

17. Using the Pearson product-moment raw score method, compute the coefficient of correlation between these paired variables:

X	Y	X^2	Y^2	XY
66	42			
50	55			
43	60			
8	24			
12	30			
35	18			
24	48			
20	35			
16	22			
54	38			

18. A class took a statistics test. The students completed all of the questions. The coefficient of correlation between the number of correct and the number of incorrect responses for the class was _____.

19. There is a significant difference between the slope of the regression line r and that of the regression line b. Do you agree? Why?

20. Compute the standard error of estimate of Y from X when:

$S_Y = 6.20$

$r = +.60$

21. Given the following information, predict the Y score from the given X, when $X = 90$, and:

a. $r = +.60$

$X = 80$ $S_X = 12$

$Y = 40$ $S_Y = 8$

b. $r = −.60$

ENDNOTE

1. N represents the number of subjects in the population; n represents the number of subjects in a sample.

REFERENCES

Glass, G. V., & Hopkins, K. D. (1996). *Statistical methods in education and psychology* (3rd ed.). Boston: Allyn and Bacon.

Glass, C. V., Peckham, P. D., & Sanders, I. R. (1972). Consequences of failure to meet assumptions underlying the fixed effects analysis of variance and covariance. *Review of Educational Research, 42,* 237–288.

Hays, W. L. (1981). *Statistics* (3rd ed.). New York: Holt, Rinehart & Winston.

Heiman, G. W. (1996). Basic statistics for the behavioral sciences. (2nd ed.). Boston: Houghton Mifflin.

Kerlinger, F. N. (1986). *Foundations of behavioral research.* (3rd ed.). New York: Holt, Rinehart, and Winston.

Kirk, R. (1995). *Experimental design: Procedures for the behavioral sciences* (3rd ed.). Pacific Grove, CA: Brooks/Cole.

Lunney, G. H. (1970). Using analysis of variance with a dichotomous dependent variable: An empirical study. *Journal of Educational Measurement, 7,* 263–269.

Mandeville, G. K. (1972). A new look at treatment differences. *American Educational Research Journal, 9,* 311–321.

Shavelson, R. J. (1996). *Statistical reasoning for the behavioral sciences* (3rd ed.). Boston: Allyn and Bacon.

Siegel, S. (1956). *Nonparametric statistics for the behavioral sciences.* New York: McGraw-Hill.

Walberg, H. J. (1984). Improving the productivity of America's schools. *Educational Leadership, 41,* 19–30.

Winer, B. J. (1971). *Statistical principles in experimental design* (2nd ed.). New York: McGraw-Hill.

11

INFERENTIAL
DATA ANALYSIS

In Chapter 1 the ultimate purpose of research was described as the discovery of general principles based on observed relationships between variables. If it were necessary to observe all of the individuals in the population about which one wished to generalize, the process would be never-ending and prohibitively expensive. The practical solution is to select samples that are representative of the population of interest; then, through observations and analysis of the sample data, the researcher may infer characteristics of the population. (The reader may wish to refer to the discussion of types of samples and sampling procedures presented in Chapter 1.)

STATISTICAL INFERENCE

Many laypersons share the misconception that an adequate sample must be a miniature carbon copy, or have the identical characteristics, of the population under study. If a large number of researchers selected random samples of 100 teachers from the population of all teachers in California, the mean weight of the samples would not be identical. A few would be relatively high, a few relatively low, but most would tend to cluster around the population mean. This variation of sample means is due to what is known as *sampling error*. The term does not suggest any fault or mistake in the *sampling process* but merely describes the chance variations that are inevitable when a number of randomly selected sample means are computed.

Estimating or inferring a population characteristic (parameter) from a random sample (statistic) is not an exact process. It has been noted that successive means of randomly selected samples from the same population are not identical. Thus, if these means are not identical, it would be logical to assume that any one of them probably differs from the population mean. This would seem to present an insurmountable obstacle to statisticians, for they have only a sample to use as a basis for generalizations about a population. Fortunately, an advantage of random selection is that the sample statistic will be an unbiased estimate of the population parameter. Because the nature of the variations of random sample means is known, it is possible to estimate the degree or variation of sample means on a probability basis.

THE CENTRAL LIMIT THEOREM

An important principle, known as the *central limit theorem,* describes the characteristics of sample means.

If a large number of equal-sized samples (greater than 30 subjects) is selected at random from an infinite population

1. The means of the samples will be normally distributed.
2. The mean value of the sample means will be the same as the mean of the population.
3. The distribution of sample means will have its own standard deviation. This is in actuality the distribution of the expected sampling error. Known as the *standard error of the mean,* it is computed from this formula:

$$S_{\overline{X}} = \frac{S}{\sqrt{N}}$$

where S = the standard deviation of individual scores
$\quad\quad N$ = the size of the sample
$\quad\quad S_{\overline{X}}$ = the standard error of the mean

To illustrate the operation of the central limit theorem, let us assume that the mean of a sample is 180 and the standard deviation is 12. Figure 11.1 illustrates the relationship between the distribution of individual scores and the distribution of sample means when the sample size is 36. If $\overline{X} = 180$, $N = 36$, and $S = 12$:

$$S_{\overline{X}} = \frac{S}{\sqrt{N}} = \frac{12}{\sqrt{36}} = \frac{12}{6} = 2$$

The standard error of the mean has a smaller value than the standard deviation of individual scores. This is understandable because in computing the means of samples the extreme scores are not represented; means are middle score values. Note the difference between the range and standard deviation of individual scores and those of the sample means.

From the formula

$$S_{\overline{X}} = \frac{S}{\sqrt{N}}$$

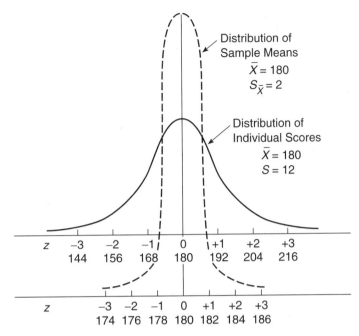

FIGURE 11.1 **Normal Distribution of Individual Scores and of Sample Means when $N = 36$**

it is apparent that as the size of the sample increases, the standard error of the mean decreases. To cite extreme cases as illustrations, as the sample N approaches infinity, the mean approaches the population mean and the standard error of the mean approaches zero.

$$S_{\overline{X}} = \frac{S}{\sqrt{\infty}} = \frac{S}{\infty} = 0$$

As the sample is reduced in size and approaches one, the standard error of the mean approaches the standard deviation of the individual scores.

$$S_{\overline{X}} = \frac{S}{\sqrt{1}} = \frac{S}{1} = S$$

As sample size increases, the magnitude of the error decreases. Sample size and sampling error are negatively correlated (see Figure 11.2 on page 388).

It may be generalized that, as the number of independent observations increases, the error involved in generalizing from sample values to population values decreases and accuracy of prediction increases.

To the statisticians who must estimate the population mean from a sample mean, their obtained sample mean would not be too far away from the unknown

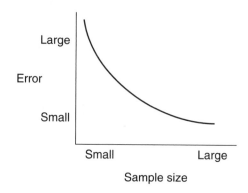

**FIGURE 11.2   The Relationship between
Sample Size and the Magnitude
of Sampling Error**

population mean. One might say that the population mean is "known only to God," but a particular mean calculated from a randomly selected sample can be related to the population mean in the same way as an individual's score is related to the mean, by using the normal curve table in Appendix C.

The chances or probabilities are approximately

$\frac{68}{100}$ that the sample mean will not be farther than 1 $S_{\overline{X}}$ from the population mean

$\frac{95}{100}$ that the sample mean will not be farther than 1.96 $S_{\overline{X}}$ from the population mean

$\frac{99}{100}$ that the sample mean will not be farther than 2.58 $S_{\overline{X}}$ from the population mean

Thus the value of a population mean, inferred from a randomly selected sample mean, can be estimated on a probability basis. In the example presented in Figure 11.1, since $S_{\overline{X}} = 2$ points, there is approximately a $\frac{68}{100}$ probability that the mean of any randomly selected sample of $N = 36$ and $S = 12$ would not be more than 2 points away from the population mean, and $\frac{95}{100}$ probability that the sample mean would not be more than 3.92 points away ($\pm 1.96 S_{\overline{X}}$).

Knowing the mean and the standard error of the mean of a sample, we can easily determine the confidence interval, within which the "true" mean of the population most likely will be. To find the 95% confidence interval, the standard error of the mean is multiplied by 1.96 and the result is added to and subtracted from the mean. To find the 99% confidence interval, the standard error of the mean is multiplied by 2.58 and the result is added to and subtracted from the mean. Thus if we had a sample with a mean of 93, and a standard error of the mean ($S_{\overline{X}}$) of 3.2, the 95% confidence interval would be

$$\mu_{95\%} \text{ (the population mean)} = 93 \pm (1.96)\, S_{\overline{X}}$$
$$= 93 \pm (1.96)\, 3.2 = 93 \pm 6.27$$
$$\mu_{95\%} = \text{between 86.73 and 99.27}$$

The 99% confidence interval would be

$$\mu_{99\%} = 93 \pm (2.58)\, S_{\overline{X}} = 93 \pm (2.58)\, 3.2 = 93 \pm 8.26$$
$$= \text{between 84.7 and 101.26}$$

We could then say that 95 times out of 100 we would probably be correct in stating that the mean of the population is between 86.73 and 99.27; and correct 99 times out of 100 in stating that the mean of the population is between 84.74 and 101.86.

PARAMETRIC TESTS

Parametric tests are considered to be the most powerful tests and should be used if their basic assumptions can be met. These assumptions are based on the nature of the population distribution and on the way the type of scale is used to quantify the data observations. However, as we mentioned in Chapter 10, some parametric tests (the *t* test and analysis of variance, in particular) are quite robust and are appropriate even when some assumptions are violated (see Glass & Hopkins, 1984, for a more complete explanation). The assumptions for most parametric tests are the following:

1. The observations are independent. The selection of one case is not dependent on the selection of any other case (there are specific parametric tests for non-independent samples).
2. The samples have equal, or nearly equal, variances. This condition is particularly important to determine when samples are small.
3. The variables described are expressed in interval or ratio scales. Nominal measures (frequency counts) and ordinal measures (ranking) do not qualify for parametric treatment.

TESTING STATISTICAL SIGNIFICANCE

The Significance of the Difference between the Means of Two Independent Groups

Because a mean is probably the most satisfactory measure for characterizing a group, researchers find it important to determine whether the difference between means of samples is significant. To illustrate the point, an example might be helpful.

Let us assume that an experiment is set up to compare the relative effectiveness of two methods of teaching reading. A sample is randomly selected, and the subjects are randomly assigned to either the experimental group or the control group.

The experimental group is taught by the initial teaching alphabet method and the control group by the traditional alphabet. At the end of a year a standardized reading test is administered, and the mean score of each group is computed. The effectiveness of the experimental group method as compared to the effectiveness of the control group method is the issue, with the end-of-year mean scores of each group the basis for comparison.

A mere quantitative superiority of the experimental group mean score over the control group mean score is not conclusive proof of its superiority. Because we know that the means of two groups randomly drawn from the same population are not necessarily identical, any difference that appeared at the end of the experimental cycle could possibly be attributed to sampling error or chance. To be statistically significant, the difference must be greater than that reasonably attributed to sampling error. Determining whether a difference is significant always involves discrediting a sampling error explanation. The test of the significance of the difference between two means is known as a *t test*. It involves the computation of the ratio between experimental variance (observed difference between two sample means) and error variance (the sampling error factor).

$$t = \frac{\overline{X}_1 - \overline{X}_2}{\sqrt{\dfrac{S_1^2}{N_1} + \dfrac{S_2^2}{N_2}}}$$

where $\overline{X}_1$ = mean of experimental sample
$\overline{X}_2$ = mean of control sample
N_1 = number of cases in experimental sample
N_2 = number of cases in control sample
S_1^2 = variance of experimental sample
S_2^2 = variance of control sample

If the value of the numerator in this ratio is not significantly greater than the denominator, it is likely that sampling error—not the effect of the treatment or experimental variable—is indicated. But before we discuss the quantitative criteria that determine the statistical significance of the difference between means, two additional concepts should be considered:

1. The null hypothesis (H_0)
2. The level of significance

The Null Hypothesis (H_0)

A null hypothesis states that there is no significant difference or relationship between two or more parameters. It concerns a judgment as to whether apparent differences or relationships are true differences or relationships or whether they merely result from sampling error. The experimenter formulates for statistical purposes a null hypothesis, a no-difference or relationship hypothesis. The experimenter hypothesizes that any apparent difference between the mean achievement of the experimental and control sample groups at the end of the experimental cycle is simply the result of sampling error, as explained by the operation of the central limit theorem. It should be noted that, although the null hypothesis is needed for statistical purposes, most actual hypotheses are alternatives to the null, that is, hypotheses that propose that differences will exist.

The use of the null hypothesis is not restricted to experimental studies. It may be used when generalizations are inferred about populations from sample data in descriptive research studies.

Students have complained that the statement of a null hypothesis sounds like double-talk. They are understandably puzzled about the reasons for the negative statement that the researcher attempts to reject. The explanation is somewhat involved, but the logic is sound. Verification of one consequence of a positive hypothesis does not prove it to be true. Observed consequences that may be consistent with a positive hypothesis may also be compatible with equally plausible but competing hypotheses. Verifying a positive hypothesis provides a rather inconclusive test.

Rejecting a null or negative hypothesis provides a stronger test of logic. Evidence that is inconsistent with a particular negative hypothesis provides a strong basis for its rejection. Before a court of law, a defendant is assumed to be not guilty until the not-guilty assumption is discredited or rejected. In a sense the not-guilty assumption is comparable to the null hypothesis.

If the difference between the mean achievement of the experimental and the control groups is too great to attribute to the normal fluctuations that result from sampling error, the experimenter may reject the null hypothesis, saying in effect that it is probably not true that the difference is merely the result of sampling error. The means no longer behave as random sample means from the same population. Something has happened to, or affected, the experimental group in such a way that it behaves like a random sample from a different or changed population. Thus, the researcher may conclude that the experimental variable or treatment probably accounted for the difference in performance, as measured by the mean test scores. The experimenter is using a statistical test to discount chance or sampling error as an explanation for the difference.

If the difference between means was not great enough to reject the null hypothesis, the researcher fails to reject it. He or she concludes that there was no significant difference and that chance or sampling error may have accounted for any observed difference.

The Level of Significance

The rejection or acceptance of a null hypothesis is based on some level of significance (alpha level) as a criterion. In psychological and educational circles, the 5% (.05) alpha (α) level of significance is often used as a standard for rejection. Rejecting a null hypothesis at the .05 level indicates that a difference in means as large as that found between the experimental and control groups would have resulted from sampling error in less than 5 out of 100 replications of the experiment. This suggests a 95% probability that the difference was due to the experimental treatment rather than to sampling error.

A more rigorous test of significance is the 1% (.01) α level. Rejecting a null hypothesis at the .01 level would suggest that a difference in means as large as that found between the experimental and control groups would have resulted from sampling error in less than 1 in 100 replications of the experiment.

When samples are large (more than 30 in size) the t critical value approaches the z (sigma) score. In these cases if the z value equals or exceeds 1.96, the researcher may conclude that the difference between means is significant at the .05 level. If the z value equals or exceeds 2.58, the researcher may conclude that the difference between means is significant at the .01 level. Determining the exact t critical value is discussed later in this chapter.

Using the example of the reading experiment previously described, let us supply the data and test the null hypothesis that there was no significant difference between the mean reading achievement of the initial teaching alphabet experimental group and the traditional alphabet control group.

Experimental ITA Group	Control Traditional Alphabet Group
$N_1 = 32$	$N_2 = 34$
$\overline{X}_1 = 87.43$	$\overline{X}_2 = 82.58$
$S_1^2 = 39.40$	$S_2^2 = 40.80$

$$t = \frac{\overline{X}_1 - \overline{X}_2}{\sqrt{\dfrac{S_1^2}{N_1} + \dfrac{S_2^2}{N_2}}} = \frac{87.43 - 82.58}{\sqrt{\dfrac{39.40}{32} + \dfrac{40.80}{34}}}$$

$$= \frac{4.85}{\sqrt{1.23 + 1.20}} = \frac{4.85}{\sqrt{2.43}} = \frac{4.85}{1.56} \qquad t = 3.11$$

Because a t value of 3.11 exceeds 2.58, the null hypothesis may be rejected at the .01 level of significance. If this experiment were replicated with random samples from the same population, the probability is that a difference between mean performance as great as that observed would result from sampling error in fewer than 1 out of 100 replications. This test would indicate rather strong evidence that the treatment would probably make a difference in the teaching of reading when applied to similar populations of pupils.

DECISION MAKING

Statistical decisions about parameters based on evidence observed in samples always involve the possibility of error. Statisticians do not deal with decisions based on certainty. They merely estimate the probability or improbability of occurrences of events.

Rejection of a null hypothesis when it is really true is known as a *Type I error.* The level of significance (alpha) selected determines the probability of a Type I error. For example, when the researcher rejects a null hypothesis at the .05 level, he or she is taking a 5% risk of rejecting what should be a sampling error explanation when it is probably true.

Not rejecting a null hypothesis when it is really false is known as a *Type II error.* This decision errs in accepting a sampling error explanation when it is probably false.

Setting a level of significance as high as the .01 level minimizes the risk of a Type I error. But this high level of significance is more conservative and increases the risk of a Type II error. The researcher sets the level of significance based on the relative seriousness of making a Type I or a Type II error.

Two-Tailed and One-Tailed Tests of Significance

If a null hypothesis were proposed that there was no difference (other than in sampling error) between the mean IQs of athletes and nonathletes, the researcher would be concerned only with a difference and not with the superiority or inferiority of either group.

> There is no difference between the mean IQs of athletes and nonathletes. In this situation a two-tailed test is applied.

If the null hypothesis were changed to indicate the superiority or inferiority of either group, it might be stated thus:

> Athletes do not have higher IQs than nonathletes.

or

> Athletes do not have lower IQs than nonathletes.

Each of these hypotheses indicates a direction of difference. When researchers are hypothesizing a direction of difference rather than the mere existence of a difference they can sometimes use a one-tailed test.

For a large sample two-tailed test, the 5% area of rejection is divided between the upper and lower tails of the curve (2.5% at each end), and it is necessary to go out to ±1.96 on the sigma (z) scale to reach the area of rejection (see Figure 11.3 on page 394).

For a one-tailed test, because the 5% area of rejection is either at the upper tail or at the lower tail of the curve, the *t* critical value is lower because it is not necessary to go as far out on the sigma scale to reach the area of rejection (see Figure 11.4 on page 394). The *t* critical value in such a case is ±1.645.

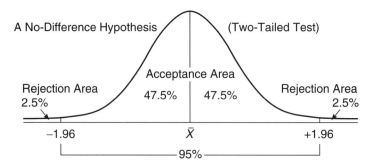

FIGURE 11.3   **A Two-Tailed Test at the .05 Level (2.5% at Each End)**

Large Sample *t* Critical Values for Rejection of the Null Hypothesis

	.05 level	.01 level
Two-tailed test	1.96	2.58
One-tailed test	1.64	2.33

A similar pair of curves would illustrate the difference between *t* critical areas of rejection at the 1% level of significance. The *t* values must equal or exceed these *t* critical values for the rejection of a null hypothesis.

Because the *t* values needed to reject a null hypothesis are smaller for a one-tailed test and because most researchers would like to reject the null hypothesis, it is tempting always to propose a directional hypothesis so as to be able to use a one-tailed test. However, a one-tailed test should be used only when a directional hypothesis is actually proposed for logical and/or theoretical reasons prior to the

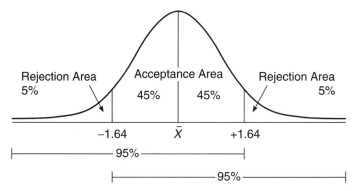

FIGURE 11.4   **A One-Tailed Test at the .05 Level (5% at One End or 5% at the Other End)**

collection of even preliminary data. If a reasonable alternative hypothesis could be proposed in the opposite direction, then, even if a directional hypothesis is to be tested, a two-tailed test should be used. Hypotheses that athletes have higher or lower IQs than nonathletes are probably inappropriate for one-tailed tests. A better example of a directional hypothesis, for which a one-tailed test would be appropriate, would be

> Children will score higher on a reading achievement test after first grade than they did prior to first grade.

In this case, although no difference might be found, it is very unlikely that findings would be in the opposite direction, reading being lower after first grade.

The test of the significance of the difference between two independent means to this point has concerned large samples, and the critical t values for rejection of the null hypothesis have been found in the normal probability table.

When small samples are used to infer population differences, a different set of t critical values is used. But before discussing small sample tests, an important concept known as degrees of freedom should be considered.

Degrees of Freedom

The number of degrees of freedom in a distribution is the number of observations or values that are independent of each other, that cannot be deduced from each other. Although this concept has been puzzling to students of statistics, several analogies and their application to estimation or prediction may help to clarify it.

1. Let us assume that a coin is tossed in the air. The statistician predicts that a head will turn up. If a head comes up, he or she has made one correct, independent prediction. But if the statistician predicted that a head would turn up and a tail would face down, he or she has made two predictions. Only one prediction, however, is an independent prediction, for the other can be deduced from the first. The second added no new information. In this case there was 1 degree of freedom, not 2. The strength of a prediction is increased as the number of independent observations or degrees of freedom is increased.
2. When a mean is computed from a number of terms in a distribution, the sum is calculated and divided by N.

$$\bar{X} = \frac{\Sigma X}{N}$$

But in computing a mean, 1 degree of freedom is used up or lost, and subsequent calculations of the variance and the standard deviation will be based on $N - 1$ independent observations or $N - 1$ degrees of freedom. An example of the loss of a degree of freedom follows.

A Original Distribution	B Altered Distribution	
+5	15 ⎫	
+4	8 ⎪	These four terms can be
+3	5 ⎬	altered in any way.
+2	7 ⎭	
+1	−20 ◄───	This term is dependent on,
$\Sigma X = +15$	$\Sigma X = +15$	or determined by, the other
$N = 5$	$N = 5$	four terms.
$\overline{X} = +3$	$\overline{X} = +3$	

In the altered distribution the fifth term must have a value of -20 for the sum to equal $+15$, the mean to be $+3$, and the sum of the deviations from the mean to equal zero. Thus, four terms are independent and can be altered, but one is dependent or fixed and is deduced from the other four. There are $N - 1$ $(5 - 1)$ or 4 degrees of freedom.

STUDENT'S DISTRIBUTION (t)

When small samples are involved, the t table is used to determine statistical significance rather than the normal probability table. This concept of small sample size was developed around 1915 by William Sealy Gosset, a consulting statistician for Guinness Breweries of Dublin, Ireland. Because his employer's rules prohibited publication under the researcher's name, he signed the name "Student" when he published his findings.

Gosset determined that the distribution curves of small sample means were somewhat different from the normal curve. Small sample distributions were observed to be lower at the means and higher at the tails, or ends, of the distributions.

Gosset's t critical values, carefully calculated for small samples, are reproduced in the t distribution table in Appendix E. The critical values necessary for rejection of a null hypothesis are higher for small samples at a given level of significance (see Figure 11.5). Each t critical value for rejection is based on the appropriate number of degrees of freedom.

As the sample sizes increase, the t critical values necessary for rejection of a null hypothesis diminish and approach the z values of the normal probability table.

Significance of the Difference between Two Small Sample Independent Means

When the samples are small and their variances are equal or nearly equal, the method of pooled variances provides the appropriate test of the significance of the difference between two independent means.

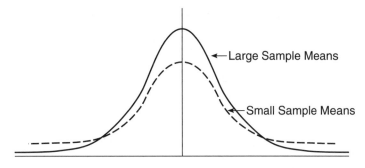

FIGURE 11.5   Distribution of Large and Small Sample Means

The formula is a bit more involved than the one previously illustrated, but it provides a more precise test of significance. The appropriate t critical value for rejection of the null hypothesis would be found for $N + N - 2$ degrees of freedom, using the t distribution table.

$$t = \frac{\overline{X}_1 - \overline{X}_2}{\sqrt{\dfrac{(N_1 - 1)S_1^2 + (N_2 - 1)S_2^2}{N_1 + N_2 - 2}\left(\dfrac{1}{N_1} + \dfrac{1}{N_2}\right)}}$$

For example, in comparing the significance of the mean IQ difference between samples of 8 athletes and 10 nonathletes, the number of degrees of freedom would be $N + N - 2 = 8 + 10 - 2 = 16$. From the t distribution table at 16 degrees of freedom, the t critical values necessary for the rejection of the null hypothesis would be

16 Degrees of Freedom	Level of Significance	
	.05	.01
Two-tailed test	2.120	2.921
One-tailed test	1.746	2.583

HOMOGENEITY OF VARIANCES

In t tests for small samples, one condition must be met to justify the method of pool variances. This condition is known as equality or *homogeneity of variance.* It does not literally mean that the variances of the samples to be compared must be identical but only that they do not differ by an amount that is statistically significant. Differences that would be attributed to sampling error do not impair the validity of the process.

To determine whether the samples meet the criterion of equality of variances, an F_{max} test is used:

$$F = \frac{S^2 \text{ (largest variance)}}{S^2 \text{ (smallest variance)}}$$

This F ratio is never less than 1, for the largest variance is always divided by the smallest. To test for homogeneity of variance, an F distribution table is used in much the same way as the t distribution table. F critical values are presented for determining the statistical significance of the calculated F critical ratio, based on the appropriate rows and columns, each at $N - 1$ degrees of freedom.

A few .05-level-of-significance values from the F_{max} distribution table are presented in Table 11.1. The degrees of freedom for the largest group is used if the samples differ in size. With t tests there will be only two variances. For analysis of variance (discussed later in this chapter), there usually will be more than two variances.

Unless the calculated F equals or exceeds the appropriate F critical value, it may be assumed that the variances are homogeneous and the difference is not significant.

For example, if two samples with 10 degrees of freedom (greater variance 38.40) and 12 degrees of freedom (smaller variance 18.06) were subjected to the test of homogeneity, then

$$F = \frac{38.40}{18.06} = 2.13$$

An F critical value of 3.28 must be equaled or exceeded to determine that the difference between variances is significant at the .05 level. In this example, because $2.13 < 3.28$, the researcher would conclude that the variances fulfilled the condition of homogeneity and that the method of pooled variances is appropriate. An example using small samples illustrates the process of calculating the F ratio to test homogeneity of variance and then calculating the appropriate t test.

The mean score of 10 delinquent boys on a personal adjustment inventory was compared with the mean score of 12 nondelinquent boys, both groups selected at random. Test the null hypothesis that there is no statistically significant difference between the mean test scores at the .01 level of significance.

TABLE 11.1   Distribution of *F* (.05 level)

Number of Variances

		2	3	4
Degrees of	9	4.03	5.34	6.31
freedom for	10	3.72	4.85	5.67
largest group	12	3.28	4.16	4.79
$(N-1)$	15	2.86	3.54	4.01

Delinquent Boys	Nondeliquent Boys
$\overline{X}_2 = 9$	$\overline{X}_1 = 14$
$S_2^2 = 20.44$	$S_1^2 = 19.60$
$N_2 = 10$	$N_1 = 12$

$$F = \frac{20.44}{19.60} = 1.04 \ \text{(the variances are homogeneous)}$$

$$df = 10 + 12 - 2 = 20$$

$$t = \frac{\overline{X}_1 - \overline{X}_2}{\sqrt{\dfrac{(N_1 - 1)S_1^2 + (N_2 - 1)S_2^2}{N_1 + N_2 - 2}\left(\dfrac{1}{N_1} + \dfrac{1}{N_2}\right)}}$$

$$= \frac{14 - 9}{\sqrt{\dfrac{11(19.60) + 9(20.44)}{12 + 10 - 2}\left(\dfrac{1}{12} + \dfrac{1}{10}\right)}}$$

$$= \frac{5}{\sqrt{\dfrac{215.60 + 183.96}{20}\left(\dfrac{11}{60}\right)}}$$

$$= \frac{5}{\sqrt{19.98\left(\frac{11}{60}\right)}} = \frac{5}{\sqrt{3.66}}$$

$$= \frac{5}{1.91} = 2.62$$

Because the calculated value is 2.62, it does not equal or exceed the *t* critical value necessary for rejection of the null hypothesis at the .01 level for 20 degrees of freedom; the hypothesis is not rejected, and the conclusion is that there is no significant difference.

Had the .05 level of significance for 20 degrees of freedom been used, the *t* critical value necessary for rejection would be 2.086, and the null hypothesis could have been rejected, for the calculated *t* critical ratio of 2.62 exceeds the 2.086 *t* table value.

By using the data from a previous example, comparing reading achievement of a group using the ITA reading method with that of the control group, one can see that this formula gives the same result as did the formula used in that example:

ITA	Control
$N_1 = 32$	$N_2 = 34$
$\overline{X}_1 = 87.43$	$\overline{X}_2 = 82.58$
$S_1^2 = 39.40$	$S_2^2 = 40.80$

$$F = \frac{40.80}{39.40} = 1.04 \ \text{(the variances are homogeneous)}$$

$$df = 32 + 34 - 2 = 64$$

$$t = \frac{\overline{X}_1 - \overline{X}_2}{\sqrt{\dfrac{(N_1 - 1)S_1^2 + (N_2 - 1)S_2^2}{N_1 + N_2 - 2}\left(\dfrac{1}{N_1} + \dfrac{1}{N_2}\right)}}$$

$$= \frac{87.43 - 82.58}{\sqrt{\dfrac{31\,(39.4) + 33\,(40.8)}{64}\left(\dfrac{1}{32} + \dfrac{1}{34}\right)}}$$

$$= \frac{4.85}{\sqrt{\dfrac{1221.4 + 1346.4}{64}\left(\dfrac{34}{1088} + \dfrac{32}{1088}\right)}}$$

$$= \frac{4.85}{\sqrt{40.12\left(\dfrac{66}{1088}\right)}}$$

$$= \frac{4.85}{\sqrt{2.43}} = \frac{4.85}{1.56}$$

$$= 3.11$$

Thus, the two formulas presented in this chapter for comparing the means of two independent samples are actually equivalent.

Now take the 25 children selected from Appendix B for analyses in the previous chapter (Chapter 10) and compare those in Method 1 with those in Method 2 on their posttest scores using a t test. If most of the sample received one method, select a sample of 12 children from each of Methods 1 and 2. For the entire population of 100 children the results are $t = .68$, $df = 98$, $p > .49$.

Significance of the Difference between the Means of Two Matched or Correlated Groups (Nonindependent Samples)

The two previous examples of testing the significance of the difference between two independent means assume that the individuals were randomly assigned to the control and experimental groups. There are situations in which it is appropriate to determine the significance of the difference between means of groups that are not randomly assigned. Two such situations are

1. When the pairs of individuals who make up the groups have been matched on one or more characteristics—IQ, reading achievement, identical twins, or on some other basis for equating the individuals.
2. When the same group of individuals takes a pretest, is exposed to a treatment, and then is retested to determine whether the influence of the treatment has been statistically significant, as determined by mean gain scores.

Because the groups are not independent samples, it is necessary to calculate the coefficient of correlation between

1. the posttest scores of the matched pairs sample, or
2. the pretest and posttest scores of the participants in the experiment.

If the coefficient of correlation is used, the appropriate t test would be based on this formula:

$$t = \frac{\overline{X}_1 - \overline{X}_2}{\sqrt{\frac{S_1^2}{N_1} + \frac{S_2^2}{N_2} - 2r\left(\frac{S_1}{\sqrt{N_1}}\right)\left(\frac{S_2}{\sqrt{N_2}}\right)}}$$

The number of degrees of freedom would be the number of pairs minus one. Two examples illustrate situations A and B:

Example A

Two groups, each made up of 20 fifth-grade students, were matched on the basis of IQs. Filmstrips were used to teach the experimental group; the control group was exposed to a conventional "read and discuss" method.

The researcher wished to test the null hypothesis that there was no difference between the mean achievement of the two groups (a two-tailed test) at the .05 level.

X	C
$N_1 = 20$	$N_2 = 20$
$S_1^2 = 54.76$	$S_2^2 = 42.25$
$\overline{X}_1 = 53.20$	$\overline{X}_2 = 49.80$
$r = +.60$	$df = 19$

$$F = \frac{54.76}{42.25} = 1.30 \ \ (\text{variances are homogeneous})$$

$$t = \frac{53.20 - 49.80}{\sqrt{\frac{54.76}{20} + \frac{42.85}{20} - 2(+.60)\left(\frac{7.40}{4.47}\right)\left(\frac{6.50}{4.47}\right)}}$$

$$= \frac{3.40}{\sqrt{2.74 + 2.14 - 1.20(1.66)(1.45)}}$$

$$= \frac{3.40}{\sqrt{4.84 - 2.89}}$$

$$= \frac{3.40}{\sqrt{1.95}} = \frac{3.40}{1.40} = 2.43$$

Because the t value of 2.43 exceeds the t critical value of 2.093 for a two-tailed test at the .05 level at 19 degrees of freedom, the null hypothesis may be rejected.

Example B

A typing teacher wished to determine the effectiveness of 10 minutes of transcendental meditation on the speed and accuracy of his class of 30 students. He administered a timed speed/accuracy test and recorded the score for each student. The next day, after 10 minutes of class participation in a TM exercise, he administered a similar timed speed/accuracy test.

He computed the mean scores for the pretest and the scores obtained after the TM experience and calculated the coefficient of correlation between the pairs of scores to be +.84.

He then tested the null hypothesis that the TM experience would not improve the proficiency in speed and accuracy of typing of his class. He chose the .01 level of significance, using a one-tailed test.

Pretest	Test after TM
$N_2 = 30$	$N_1 = 30$
$S_2^2 = 37.21$	$S_1^2 = 36.10$
$\overline{X}_2 = 44.80$	$\overline{X}_1 = 49.10$
$r = +.84$	$df = 29$

$$F = \frac{37.21}{36.10} = 1.03 \ \text{(variances are homogeneous)}$$

$$t = \frac{49.10 - 44.80}{\sqrt{\dfrac{37.21}{30} + \dfrac{36.10}{30} - 2(+.84)\left(\dfrac{6.10}{5.48}\right)\left(\dfrac{6.01}{5.48}\right)}}$$

$$= \frac{4.30}{\sqrt{1.24 + 1.20 - 1.68(1.11)(1.10)}}$$

$$= \frac{4.30}{\sqrt{2.44 - 2.05}} = \frac{4.30}{\sqrt{.39}}$$

$$= \frac{4.30}{.62} = 6.94$$

Because the *t* value of 6.94 exceeds the *t* critical value of 2.462 for a one-tailed test at the .01 level for 29 degrees of freedom, he rejected the null hypothesis, concluding that the meditation experience did improve performance proficiency.

The reader can now compare the pretest and posttest scores for the sample of 25 children using the *t* test for nonindependent samples. Because there is good reason to think that posttest scores should always be higher than pretest scores (at least under normal conditions), a one-tailed test of significance can be used. For the entire population of 100 children the results are $t = 12.82$, $df = 99$, $p < .001$.

Statistical Significance of a Coefficient of Correlation

Throughout this chapter on inferential data analysis, the idea of statistical significance and its relationship to the null hypothesis have been emphasized. An observed coefficient of correlation may result from chance or sampling error, and a test to determine its statistical significance is appropriate. In small sample correlations chance could yield what might appear to be evidence of a genuine relationship.

The null hypothesis (H_0) states that the coefficient of correlation is zero. Only when chance or sampling error has been discredited on a probability basis can a coefficient of correlation be accepted as statistically significant. One test of the significance of r is determined by the use of the formula

$$t_r = \frac{r\sqrt{N-2}}{\sqrt{1-r^2}}$$

With $N - 2$ degrees of freedom, a coefficient of correlation is judged as statistically significant when the t value equals or exceeds the t critical value in the t distribution table. If

$r = .40$

$N = 25$

$$t = \frac{.40\sqrt{23}}{\sqrt{1-(.40)^2}} = \frac{1.92}{.92} = 2.09$$

Using a two-tailed test at the .05 level with 23 degrees of freedom, the null hypothesis is rejected, exceeding the t critical value of 2.07. As sample size is decreased, the probability of sampling error increases. For a smaller sample, the coefficient must be larger to be statistically significant. If

$r = .40$

$N = 18$

$$t = \frac{.40\sqrt{16}}{\sqrt{1-(.40)^2}} = \frac{1.60}{.92} = 1.74$$

At 16 degrees of freedom the observed value of 1.74 fails to equal or exceed the t critical value of 2.12 at the .05 level of significance, and the null hypothesis would not be rejected. Thus, with a sample N of 18, a coefficient of correlation of .40 would not be large enough for the rejection of the null hypothesis, a sampling error explanation.

There is a more direct and simple way to evaluate the statistical significance of the coefficient of correlation. Instead of computing the t value and using the table in Appendix E, critical values of r can be read directly from the table in Appendix D at the .10, .05, .02, and .01 levels.

Determine whether the correlations for IQ with pretest and pretest with posttest that you calculated in Chapter 10 with the sample of 25 children are statistically significant. The correlation for IQ with pretest for the population reported in the last chapter was .552, and for pretest with posttest .834. With 100 subjects these correlations are both easily significant at $p < .01$. Even if there were only 25 children for these correlations, as there are here, both correlations would be significant at $p < .01$. Are either or both of these correlations significant?

Statistical significance merely indicates the probable influence of chance or sampling error on an observed coefficient of correlation between sample variables. It is related to sample size. When sample size decreases, sampling error increases. When samples are small, what may appear to be a large coefficient of correlation may not pass the test of statistical significance. When samples are large enough, almost any coefficient, however small, may prove to be significant. At the .05 level, when $N = 18$, an r of .468 would be necessary for statistical significance, but when $N = 500$ an r of .088 would be sufficient.

It is apparent that statistical significance is not a measure of the magnitude of a variable relationship. It is only an estimate of the probable influence of sampling error in the observed coefficient of correlation. Statistical significance may be of great importance to the researcher who conducts small sample studies but of less importance in large sample research.

The reader should remember from Chapter 10 that the interpretation of a correlation involves more than just its statistical significance. A low correlation, for example $r = .20$, is statistically significant if a large sample, 200 subjects, was used. Despite its statistical significance this correlation, .20, is still a low correlation with the two variables having only .04 of their variance in common.

The values presented in the table in Chapter 10 provide guidelines for evaluating the magnitude of r, but they should be interpreted cautiously in terms of several criteria:

1. The magnitude and statistical significance of the coefficient of correlation
2. The nature of the variables
3. The design of the study
4. The reported findings of other respected investigators in the field of inquiry

ANALYSIS OF VARIANCE (ANOVA)

We have noted that the t test is employed to determine, after treatment, whether the means of two random samples were too different to attribute to chance or sampling error. The analysis of variance is an effective way to determine whether the means of *more than two samples* are too different to attribute to sampling error.

It would be possible to use a number of t tests to determine the significance of the difference between five means, two at a time, but it would involve 10 separate tests. The number of necessary pair-wise comparisons of N things is determined by the formula:

$$\frac{N(N-1)}{2}$$

If $N = 5$,

$$\frac{5(5-1)}{2} = \frac{20}{2} = 10$$

Analysis of variance makes it possible to determine whether the five means differ significantly with a single test rather than 10. Another advantage lies in the fact that computing a number of separate t tests will increase the overall Type I error rate for the experiment. For instance, if we calculated 10 t tests (for comparing five means) and accepted .05 as our significance level, we would have 10 times .05, or .50, as the probability that we would reject at least one null hypothesis when it is really true (Type I error). Thus, we would have an unacceptably high error rate for the total experiment. Analysis of variance takes care of this by comparing all five means simultaneously in a single test.

In *single classification,* or *one-way analysis of variance, the relationship between one independent and one dependent variable is examined.* For example

A test of abstract reasoning is administered to three randomly selected groups of students majoring in mathematics, philosophy, and chemistry in a large state university. Are the mean test scores of each of the three groups significantly different from one another?

The analysis of variance consists of these operations:

1. The variance of the scores for three groups is combined into one composite group known as the *total groups variance* (V_t).
2. The mean value of the variances of each of the three groups, computed separately, is known as the *within-groups variance* (V_w).
3. The difference between the total groups variance and the within-groups variance is known as the *between-groups variance* $(V_t - V_w = V_b)$.
4. The F ratio is computed

$$F = \frac{V_b}{V_w} = \frac{\text{(between-groups variance)}}{\text{(within-groups variance)}}$$

The logic of the F ratio is as follows: The within-groups variance represents the sampling error in the distributions and is also referred to as the *error variance* or *residual.* The between-groups variance represents the influence of the variable of interest or the experimental variable. If the *between-groups variance* is not substantially greater than the *within-groups variance,* the researcher would conclude that the difference between the means is probably only a reflection of sampling error. If the F ratio were substantially greater than 1, it would seem that the ratio of the *between-groups variance* and the *within-groups variance* was probably too great to attribute to sampling error.

The critical values of the F ratio (named for Sir Ronald Fisher) are found in an F table (different from the F_{max} table referred to earlier), which indicates the critical values necessary to test the null hypothesis at selected levels of significance.

As can be seen in the F table presented in Appendix G, there are two different degrees of freedom, one for V_b (the numerator) and one for V_w (the denominator). The degrees of freedom for the within-groups variance (V_w) is determined in the same way as it is for the t test—that is, the sum of the subjects for all of the groups minus the number of groups. We can use K to represent the number of groups and $N_1 + N_2 + \ldots - K$ to represent the degrees of freedom for the within-groups variance. In the above example, if there were 10 students in each of the three groups, there would be $10 + 10 + 10 - 3$, or 27, degrees of freedom for the within-groups variance. The degrees of freedom for the between-groups variance (V_b) is determined by the number of groups minus 1 ($K - 1$). In the above example there are three groups, thus, 2 degrees of freedom. The above example then has 2 degrees of freedom for the numerator and 27 for the denominator for a total of 29, one less than the total number of subjects.

The calculation of F involves finding the mean of the deviations from the mean, squared. Thus, the between-groups variance (V_b) is more commonly referred to as the mean squared between (MS_b), and the within-groups variance (V_w) is more commonly referred to as the mean squared within (MS_w). The formula then becomes

$$F = \frac{MS_b}{MS_w}$$

TABLE 11.2   Sample Data for Calculating Analysis of Variance

Group 1 Mathematics Majors		Group 2 Philosophy Majors		Group 3 Chemistry Majors	
X_1	X_1^2	X_2	X_2^2	X_3	X_3^2
18	324	26	676	18	324
22	484	27	729	14	196
18	324	18	324	15	225
23	529	22	484	14	196
19	361	23	529	19	361
24	576	19	361	21	441
20	400	27	729	17	289
21	441	26	676	17	289
19	361	24	576	18	324
25	625	26	676	19	361
$\Sigma X_1 = 209$	$\Sigma X_1^2 = 4425$	$\Sigma X_2 = 238$	$\Sigma X_2^2 = 5760$	$\Sigma X_3 = 172$	$\Sigma X_3^2 = 3006$
$\overline{X}_1 = 20.9$		$\overline{X}_2 = 23.8$		$\overline{X}_3 = 17.2$	

$\overline{\overline{X}} = 20.63$ $\Sigma X^2 = \Sigma X_1^2 + \Sigma X_2^2 + \Sigma X_3^2 = 13{,}191$

Given the data in Table 11.2, F is calculated as follows. The first step is to find the sum of the squared deviations of each person's score for the mean of all of the subjects. This is known as the total sum of squares (SS_t) and can be found by using the following formula:

$$SS_t = \Sigma X^2 - \frac{(\Sigma X)^2}{N}$$

In our example this would be

$$SS_t = 13,191 - \frac{(619)^2}{30} = 13,191 - 12,772.03 = 418.97$$

The next step is to divide the total sum of squares into the between-groups sum of squares (SS_b) and the within-groups sum of squares (SS_w). We determine SS_b using the formula:

$$SS_b = \frac{(\Sigma X_1)^2}{n_1} + \frac{(\Sigma X_2)^2}{n_2} + \cdots - \frac{(\Sigma X)^2}{N}$$

n = the number of subjects in a group
N = the number of subjects for all the groups combined

In our example this would be

$$SS_b = \frac{(209)^2}{10} + \frac{(238)^2}{10} + \frac{(172)^2}{10} - \frac{(619)^2}{30}$$
$$= 4368.1 + 5664.4 + 2958.4 - 12,772.03$$
$$= 218.87$$

The within-groups sum of squares (SS_w) can be calculated in two ways. First, we can calculate it directly, using the formula:

$$SS_w = \Sigma X_1^2 - \frac{(\Sigma X_1)^2}{n_1} + \Sigma X_2^2 - \frac{(\Sigma X_2)^2}{n_2} \cdots + \Sigma X_i^2 - \frac{(\Sigma X_i)^2}{n_i}$$

In our example this would be

$$SS_w = 4425 - 4368.1 + 5760 - 5664.4 + 3006 - 2958.4$$
$$= 200.1$$

SS_w can also be found by subtracting SS_b from SS_t:

$$SS_w = SS_t - SS_b$$
$$= 418.97 - 218.87 = 200.1$$

By using both methods of calculating SS_w, we can check our results for computational errors.

To find the mean square between (MS_b) and the mean square within (MS_w), we divide the sum of squares between (SS_b) and the sum of squares within (SS_w) by the respective degrees of freedom (df).

$$F = \frac{MS_b}{MS_w} = \frac{SS_b/df_b}{SS_w/df_w}$$

$$= \frac{MS_b}{MS_w} = \frac{218.87/2}{200.1/27}$$

$$= \frac{109.44}{7.41} = 14.77$$

Table 11.3 shows what a typical summary table for this analysis of variance would look like. The F of 14.77 is statistically significant at the .01 level. That is, there is less than 1 chance in 100 that the observed differences among these three group means is due to sampling error. We can reject the null hypothesis with this degree of confidence.

However, this significant F does not pinpoint exactly where the differences are in a pair-wise way. That is, the three groups differ significantly, but does Group 1 differ from Group 2 and/or Group 3? Does Group 2 differ from Group 3? These questions can be answered by still further analysis of the data using one of the several *post hoc* analyses available (e.g., Scheffe, Tukey, Neuman–Keuls, Duncan). The reader should consult one of several fine texts (e.g., Glass & Hopkins, 1996; Kirk, 1995; Winer, 1971) for more information regarding the use and calculation of these *post hoc* tests.

Using the data in Appendix B, randomly select eight children from each of the three groups—learning disabled (LD), behavior disordered (BD), and mentally retarded (MR)—and then calculate an ANOVA to determine if there is a difference on the posttest scores among the groups. For the entire sample there are 50 LD, 28 BD, and 22 MR students. The ANOVA results indicate a significant difference among these groups on the posttest scores ($F = 34.99$, $df = 2/97$, $p < .001$).

TABLE 11.3   Summary of Three Group Analysis of Variance

Source of Variance	SS	df	MS	F
Between groups (major)	218.87	2	109.44	14.77*
Within groups (error)	200.10	27	7.41	
Total	418.97			

*$p < .01$

In *multiple classification* or *factorial analysis of variance, both the independent and interactive effects of two or more independent variables on one dependent variable may be analyzed.* Not only may the effect of several independent variables be tested, but their interaction (how they may combine in a significant way) may be examined. Because human behavior and the factors influencing it are complex and can rarely be explained by single independent variable influences, this method of analysis is a powerful statistical tool of the behavioral researcher.

With computers so readily available, it is rarely necessary to calculate a factorial analysis of variance by hand. An example of a computer printout from such an analysis is included in Chapter 12.

In factorial designs the total variance is divided into more than two parts. It is divided into one part for each independent variable (main effect), one part for each interaction of two or more independent variables, and one part for the residual, or within-group, variance. Thus, in a design with two independent variables, the variance is divided into four parts. For example, in the previous example comparing the performance of mathematics, philosophy, and chemistry majors on a test of abstract reasoning, each of the three groups could also be divided into males and females. There is then a factorial design with two independent variables, students' major and sex. Because there are three conditions of student major and two conditions of sex, this is a 3 × 2 design. As shown in Chapter 12, this results in the variance being divided into four parts: the main effect of students' major, the main effect of students' sex, the interaction effect of students' major with sex, and residual. From this, three separate *F*s are derived: one to test the difference among the three majors, one to test the difference between males and females, and one to test the interaction of students' sex and major. An example of a significant interaction was presented in Chapter 6 (see Figure 6.3).

With the aid of computers, analysis of variance can be used with any number of independent variables. The only limitations are in controlling for potentially confounding variables and interpreting complex interaction effects. Glass and Hopkins (1996), Kirk (1995), and Winer (1971) are excellent resources for the student wanting more information about analysis of variance designs and computation.

ANALYSIS OF COVARIANCE (ANCOVA) AND PARTIAL CORRELATION

Analysis of covariance and partial correlation are statistical techniques that can remove the effect of a confounding variable's influence from a study. *Partial correlation* is used to remove the effect of one variable on the correlation between two other variables. For example, if a correlation is desired between IQ and academic achievement and the subjects have a range of ages, the researcher would not want the variable of chronological age to affect the correlation. Thus, the researcher would partial out its effect on the other two variables, IQ and academic achievement. This is symbolized by $r_{12.3}$, the correlation of variables 1 and 2 with 3 removed. The partial correlation can be calculated using the following formula:

$$r_{12.3} = \frac{r_{12} - (r_{13})(r_{23})}{\sqrt{(1 - r_{13}^2)(1 - r_{23}^2)}}$$

An example from Glass and Hopkins (1984) may help to further clarify this concept. In this example a correlation between visual perception (X_1) and reading performance (X_2) is found to be .64 for children ranging in age (X_3) from 6 to 15 years. Because of the wide age range, and because children's reading and visual perception both generally improve with age, it seems appropriate to partial out the effect of age. Given the following correlation coefficients, the researcher can calculate the partial correlation of visual perception and reading performance with age removed.

r_{12} [correlation of visual perception (X_1) and reading performance (X_2)] = .64
r_{13} [correlation of X_1 and age (X_3)] = .80
r_{23} (correlation of X_2 and X_3) = .80

$$r_{12.3} = \frac{.64 - (.80)(.80)}{\sqrt{(1 - .80^2)(1 - .80^2)}} = \frac{.64 - .64}{.36} = .00$$

As Glass and Hopkins (1984) point out:

> . . . one would estimate the value of r_{12} for children of the same chronological age to be zero. If enough children of the same chronological age were available, r could be calculated for them alone to check the previous result. The partial correlation coefficient serves the purpose of estimating r_{12} for a single level of chronological age even when there is an insufficient number of persons at any single chronological age to do the estimating by direct calculation. (p. 131)

Once again using the data in Appendix B, one can calculate the correlation of IQ with pretest scores and then partial out the effect of pretest scores. The correlation of IQ with posttest (r_{12} = .638) and pretest with posttest (r_{12} = .834) has already been calculated for the population (and has been done so for the sample). The correlation of IQ with posttest is r_{13} = .552. Thus,

$$r_{12.3} = \frac{.638 - (.552)(.834)}{\sqrt{(1 - .552^2)(1 - .834^2)}} = \frac{.638 - .460}{.459} = .388$$

Thus, when the variable pretest scores is partialled out, the correlation of .638 between IQ and posttest becomes only .388. What was found for the partial correlation with the sample of 25 children?

Analysis of covariance (ANCOVA) uses the principles of partial correlation with analysis of variance. It is particularly appropriate when the subjects in two or more groups are found to differ on a pretest or other initial variable. In this case the effects of the pretest and/or other relevant variables are partialled out, and the resulting adjusted means of the posttest scores are compared. Analysis of covariance is a method of analysis that enables the researcher to equate the pre-experimental status of the groups in terms of relevant known variables. The initial status of the groups may be determined by pretest scores in a pretest–posttest study or in posttest only studies by such measures as intelligence, reading scores, grade-point average, or previous knowledge of subject matter. Differences in the initial status of the groups can be removed statistically so that they can be compared as though their initial status had been equated. The scores that have been corrected by this procedure are known as *residuals*, for they are what remain after the inequalities have been removed.

Analysis of covariance, used with one or more independent variables and one dependent variable, is an important method of analyzing experiments carried on under conditions that otherwise would be unacceptable. The mathematical procedures are rather complicated, and there are many steps in computing their values. However, with the use of standard computer programs, the analysis of complex studies can be processed almost instantaneously.

It should be noted that analysis of covariance is not as robust as analysis of variance. That is, violation of the assumptions on which analysis of covariance is based may make its use inappropriate. In addition, as Glass and Hopkins (1996) point out, ANCOVA does not transform a quasi-experiment into a true (randomized) experiment. There is no substitute for randomization.

MULTIPLE REGRESSION AND CORRELATION

In Chapter 10 we discussed correlation and linear regression when only two variables are involved. We demonstrated the prediction (regression) equation for estimating the value of one variable from another: $\hat{Y} = a + bX$.

In many cases it is better to use more than one predictor variable to predict an outcome, or dependent, variable. For example, a university may use a number of variables to predict college GPA in its admission process. High school grades and SAT or ACT scores may be used. Ranks in high school graduating class could also be included.

Multiple regression is the term used for predicting $\hat{Y}$ (in the example above, college GPA) from two or more independent variables combined. The formula for multiple regression is just an extension of that for linear regression:

$$\hat{Y} = a + b_1X_1 + b_2X_2 + \ldots$$

where $\hat{Y}$ = the variable to be predicted
a = the constant or intercept
b_1 = the slope of the first predictor
b_2 = the slope of the second predictor
X_1 = the score of the first predictor
X_2 = the score of the second predictor

An example may further clarify the procedure. In Chapter 10 we gave an example of predicting college GPA from high school GPA. We will use the data given in that example and add SAT score (combined verbal and quantitative).

$\hat{Y}$ = college GPA

X_1 = high school GPA

X_2 = SAT scores

r_{12} = correlation of high school GPA and SAT score

r_{y1} = correlation of college GPA and high school GPA

r_{y2} = correlation of college GPA and SAT score

The data are as follows:

$\overline{Y} = 2.40$

$S_y = 0.50$

$\overline{X}_1 = 2.10$

$S_{x1} = 0.60$

$\overline{X}_2 = 930.00$

$S_{x2} = 80.00$

$r_{12} = 0.22$

$r_{y1} = 0.52$

$r_{y2} = 0.66$

The first step in finding b is to calculate the standardized beta weight (β):

$$\beta_1 = \frac{r_{y1} - (r_{y2})(r_{12})}{1 - r_{12}^2}$$

$$= \frac{.52 - (.66)(.22)}{1 - (.22)^2} = \frac{.375}{.952} = .394$$

$$\beta_2 = \frac{r_{y2} - (r_{y1})(r_{12})}{1 - r_{12}^2}$$

$$= \frac{.66 - (.52)(.22)}{1 - (.22)^2} = \frac{.546}{.952} = .574$$

Using the standardized beta weights and the standard deviations, we can calculate the raw score beta weights (b):

$$b_1 = \beta_1 \frac{(S_y)}{S_{x1}} = .394 \left(\frac{.50}{.60} \right) = .328$$

$$b_2 = \beta_2 \frac{(S_y)}{S_{x2}} = .574\left(\frac{.50}{80}\right) = .004$$

The next step is to calculate the intercept, a, from the formula:

$$a = \overline{Y} - b_1\overline{X}_1 - b_2\overline{X}_2 - \ldots$$

In this case:

$$a = 2.4 - .328(2.1) - .004(930)$$
$$= 2.4 - .689 - 3.72 = -2.01$$

Finally, we can calculate the predicted college GPA for the two students in the example from Chapter 10:

$$X_{a1} = \text{(student A's high school GPA)} = \quad 2.00$$
$$X_{a2} = \text{(student A's SAT score)} \quad = \quad 900.00$$
$$X_{b1} = \text{(student B's high school GPA)} = \quad 3.10$$
$$X_{b2} = \text{(student B's SAT score)} \quad = 1100.00$$

$$\hat{Y} = a + b_1 X_1 + b_2 X_2 \ldots$$

$$\hat{Y}_a = -2.01 + .328(2.00) + .004(900)$$
$$= -2.01 + .656 + 3.6 = 2.25$$

$$\hat{Y}_b = -2.01 + .328(3.10) + .004(1100)$$
$$= -2.01 + 1.02 + 4.4 = 3.41$$

Student A with the below-average high school GPA and SAT score is predicted to have a below-average college GPA, and student B with the above-average high school GPA and SAT score is expected to have an above-average college GPA. When one compares these findings with the regression results in Chapter 10, one sees that the addition of a confirming score resulted in a prediction further above or below the average. That is, when an SAT score was included for student A that was to the same side of (below) the means as his or her high school GPA, the result was a predicted college GPA further below the average than the one predicted by high school GPA alone (2.25 versus 2.36). Conversely, when an SAT score was included for student B that was above the mean, as was his or her high school GPA, the result was a predicted college GPA further above the average than the one predicted by high school GPA alone (3.41 versus 2.83).

If a disconfirming SAT score had been added to high school GPA, it would have the opposite effect described above. For example, if student A had an SAT of

1080 instead of 900, his or her predicted college GPA would be higher than that predicted with high school GPA alone.

$$\hat{Y}_a = -2.01 + .328(2.00) + .004(1080)$$
$$= -2.01 + .656 + 4.32 = 2.97$$

In either case, confirming the addition of related variables to a prediction equation will result in more accurate predictions.

We should point out that when we write of "adding" a variable to the equation, we do not mean that the amount of the prediction from one variable is just added to by the amount of prediction from a second, and/or subsequent, variable. The multiple regression equation controls for the overlap (relatedness) of the predictor variables. The result is that the second variable only "adds" the amount of prediction that it has independent of the first variable. This is necessary because other attributes (variables) may directly influence more than one of the predictor variables. For instance, in the previous example high school grades and SAT scores are probably both influenced by IQ. Multiple regression controls for that part that SAT scores and high school grades have in common due to other factors such as IQ. This has the same effect as partial correlation.

Once again using the data in Appendix B, one can calculate the regression equation for predicting posttest scores using IQ and pretest scores. Do this with the sample of 25 children, then select an additional child from the other 75 children in the population, and see how close the prediction equation comes. In the case of the population, a b for IQ of .215 and a b for pretest of .722 with the constant being 7.26 were found. Thus, if child number 26 is selected from this population who had an IQ of 98 and a pretest of 55, his or her predicted posttest score would be 68.04. The actual posttest score was 66—not too far off.

Multiple correlation (R) is the correlation between the actual scores (Y) and the scores predicted (Ŷ) by two or more independent variables. It is most useful for determining the percentage of the variance of the predicted scores that can be explained by the predictors. This was discussed as the coefficient of determination (r^2) in relation to the simple, bivariate correlation (r) in Chapter 10. For multiple correlation, R^2 is the percentage of the variance of the predicted (dependent) variable that is due to, or explained by, the combined predictor (independent) variables. Conversely, $1 - R^2$ is the percentage of the variance of the predicted variable that is due to factors other than the predictor variables.

In the previous multiple regression example, the multiple correlation (the correlation between actual college GPA and predicted college GPA) is $R = .583$. The percentage of college GPA that is due to a combination of high school GPA and SAT scores is then $R^2 = .340$. Thirty-four percent of the variance of college GPA is explained by high school grades and SAT scores. Because $1 - R^2$ is .660, 66% of college GPA is due to other factors such as motivation, involvement in extracurricular activities, measurement error, and so on. This gives a good idea of just how accurate we can expect individual predictions to be. Given this data, we would expect to be able to predict broad categories such as "probable fail," "borderline," "probable pass," and probable high GPA. To expect to accurately predict a person's college GPA would be unrealistic.

For greater detail, the reader should consult a more advanced text that specializes on this topic (e.g., Cohen & Cohen, 1983; Neter, Wasserman, & Kutner, 1985). A computer analysis of a more intricate multiple regression is presented in Chapter 12.

NONPARAMETRIC TESTS

The parametric tests presented in this chapter are generally quite robust; that is, they are useful even when some of their mathematical assumptions are violated. However, sometimes it is necessary, or preferable, to use a nonparametric or distribution-free test.

Nonparametric tests are appropriate when

1. The nature of the population distribution from which samples are drawn is not known to be normal.
2. The variables are expressed in nominal form (classified in categories and represented by frequency counts).
3. The variables are expressed in ordinal form (ranked in order, expressed as first, second, third, etc.).

Nonparametric tests, because they are based on counted or ranked data rather than on measured values, are less precise, have less power than parametric tests, and are not as likely to reject a null hypothesis when it is false.

Many statisticians suggest that parametric tests be used, if possible, and that nonparametric tests be used only when parametric assumptions cannot be met. Others argue that nonparametric tests have greater merit than is often attributed to them because their validity is not based on assumptions about the nature of the population distribution, assumptions that are so frequently ignored or violated by researchers employing parametric tests.

Of the many nonparametric tests, two of the most frequently used are described and illustrated here: the chi square (χ^2) test, and the Mann–Whitney test.

The Chi Square Test (χ^2)

The χ^2 test applies only to discrete data, counted rather than measured values. It is a test of independence, the idea that one variable is not affected by, or related to, another variable. The χ^2 is not a measure of the degree of relationship. It is merely used to estimate the likelihood that some factor other than chance (sampling error) accounts for the apparent relationship. Because the null hypothesis states that there is no relationship (the variables are independent), the test merely evaluates the probability that the observed relationship results from chance. As in other tests of statistical significance, it is assumed that the sample observations have been randomly selected.

The computed χ^2 value must equal or exceed the appropriate table's (see Appendix F) critical value to justify rejection of the null hypothesis or the assumption of independence at the .05 or the .01 level of significance.

A finding of a statistically significant χ^2 value doesn't necessarily indicate a cause-and-effect relationship, a limitation that was observed when a coefficient of correlation was interpreted. A significant χ^2 finding indicates that the variables probably do not exhibit the quality of independence, that they tend to be systematically related, and that the relationship transcends pure chance or sampling error.

There are situations in which the theoretical or expected frequencies must be computed from the distribution. Let us assume that 200 residents of a college dormitory major in business, liberal arts, or engineering. Is the variable, major, related to the number of cigarettes smoked per day on the average for a 3-week period? The null hypothesis would state that major is not related to the number of cigarettes smoked, that the variables major and frequency of cigarette smoking are independent.

Chi square observations should be organized in crossbreak form. In each category the expected frequencies (f_e) as contrasted to the observed frequencies (f_o), is the number of cases that would appear if there were no systematic relationship between the variables, a pure chance relationship.

Number of Cigarettes Smoked per Day

Major	None	1–15	More than 15	Total
Business	6 (12)	60 (56)	14 (12)	80*
Liberal Arts	14 (12)	58 (56)	8 (12)	80*
Engineering	10 (6)	22 (28)	8 (6)	40*
Total	30**	140**	30**	200
				Grand Total

*Σf row
**Σf column

Numbers represent the actual observed frequencies f_o
Numbers in parentheses represent the expected frequencies f_e

The expected frequency for each of the 9 cells is computed by the formula

$$f_e = \frac{(\Sigma f \text{ column})(\Sigma f \text{ row})}{\text{grand total}}$$

Computation of expected frequencies (f_e):

$$\frac{(30)(80)}{200} = (12) \qquad \frac{(140)(80)}{200} = (56) \qquad \frac{(30)(80)}{200} = (12)$$

$$\frac{(30)(80)}{200} = (12) \qquad \frac{(140)(80)}{200} = (56) \qquad \frac{(30)(80)}{200} = (12)$$

$$\frac{(30)(40)}{200} = (6) \qquad \frac{(140)(40)}{200} = (28) \qquad \frac{(30)(40)}{200} = (6)$$

Computation of the χ^2 value:

$$\chi^2 = \Sigma \left(\frac{(f_o - f_e)^2}{f_e} \right)$$

$$\frac{(6-12)^2}{12} = 3 \qquad \frac{(60-56)^2}{56} = .29 \qquad \frac{(14-12)^2}{12} = .33$$

$$\frac{(14-12)^2}{12} = .33 \qquad \frac{(58-56)^2}{56} = 0.07 \qquad \frac{(8-12)^2}{12} = 1.33$$

$$\frac{(10-6)^2}{6} = 2.67 \qquad \frac{(22-28)^2}{28} = 1.29 \qquad \frac{(8-6)^2}{6} = .67$$

$$\chi^2 = 3 + .29 + .33 + .33 + 0.07 + 1.33 + 2.67 + 1.29 + .67 = 9.98$$

$$\text{degrees of freedom} = (\text{rows} - 1)(\text{columns} - 1)$$
$$= (3-1)(3-1) = (2)(2) = 4$$

χ^2 critical values for 4 degrees of freedom (see Appendix E).

.01	.05
13.28	9.49

$\chi^2 = 9.98$

The test indicates that there is a significant relationship between major and number of cigarettes smoked at the .05 but not at the .01 level of significance. If we wished to answer the question, "Is there a relationship between being a business major and number of cigarettes smoked?" we would combine the liberal arts and engineering categories and use a χ^2 table with 6 rather than 9 cells.

Number of Cigarettes Smoked per Day

Major	None	1–15	More than 15	Total
Business	6 (12)	6 (56)	14 (12)	80
Nonbusiness	24 (18)	80 (84)	16 (18)	120
Total	30	140	30	200

$$\frac{(30)(80)}{200} = (12) \qquad \frac{(140)(80)}{200} = (56) \qquad \frac{(30)(80)}{200} = (12)$$

$$\frac{(30)(120)}{200} = (18) \qquad \frac{(140)(120)}{200} = (84) \qquad \frac{(30)(120)}{200} = (18)$$

$$\frac{(6-12)^2}{12} = 3.00 \qquad \frac{(60-56)^2}{56} = .29 \qquad \frac{(14-12)^2}{12} = .33$$

$$\frac{(24-18)^2}{18} = 2.00 \qquad \frac{(80-84)^2}{84} = .19 \qquad \frac{(16-18)^2}{18} = .22$$

$$\chi^2 = 3.00 + .29 + .33 + 2.00 + .19 + .22 = 6.03 \quad \text{at } 2df:$$

.01	9.21
.05	5.99

The null hypothesis may be rejected at the .05 but not at the .01 level of significance.

In a 2 × 2 table (4 cells) with 1 degree of freedom, there is a simple formula that eliminates the need to calculate the theoretical frequencies for each cell.

$$\chi^2 = \frac{N[\,|AD-BC|\,]^2}{(A+B)(C+D)(A+C)(B+D)}$$

Terms in a 2 × 2 table

A	B
C	D

Let us use an example employing this formula. A random sample of auto drivers revealed the relationship between experiences of those who had taken a course in driver education and those who had not.

	Reported Accident	No Accident	Total
Had driver's education	44A	10B	54
No driver's education	81C	35D	116
Total	125	45	170

This is a 2 × 2 table with one degree of freedom.

$$\chi^2 = \frac{170[\,|(44 \times 35) - (10 \times 81)|\,]^2}{(54+10)(81+35)(44+81)(10+35)}$$

$$= \frac{170[\,|1540 - 810|\,]^2}{(64)(116)(125)(45)}$$

$$= \frac{170(730)^2}{41{,}760{,}000} = \frac{90{,}593{,}000}{41{,}760{,}000} = 2.17$$

The χ^2 value does not equal or exceed the critical χ^2 value (3.84) necessary to reject the null hypothesis at the .05 level of significance. There seems to be no significant relationship between completing the course in driver education and the number of individuals who had recorded auto accidents.

Yates's Correction for Continuity

In computing a *chi* square value for a 2 × 2 table with one degree of freedom, the formula is modified when any cell has a frequency count of fewer than 10. This formula differs from the previous formula.

$$\chi^2 = \frac{N\left[\;|AD-BC|-\dfrac{N}{2}\;\right]^2}{(A+B)(C+D)(A+C)(B+D)}$$

Example: A pharmaceutical company wished to evaluate the effectiveness of X-40, a recently developed headache relief pill.

Two randomly selected and assigned samples of patients who complained of headaches were given pills. The experimental group was given six X-40 pills daily and the control group was given six placebos (or sugar pills) daily, although they thought that they were receiving medication. After a week they repeated their experience.

	X-40 X	Placebo C	Total
Headaches relieved	30_A	40_B	70
Headaches continued	4_C	10_D	14
Total	34	50	84

A χ^2 test using a 2 × 2 table at 1 degree of freedom was applied, with Yate's correction. Was the effectiveness of the X-40 medication significant at the .05 level?

$$\chi^2 = \frac{84\,[\;|\,(30\times10)-(40\times4)\,|-42]^2}{(30+40)(4+10)(30+4)(40+10)} = \frac{84\,[\;|\,300-160\,|-42]^2}{(70)(14)(34)(50)}$$

$$= \frac{84\,(98)^2}{1{,}666{,}000} = \frac{84\,(9604)}{1{,}666{,}000} = \frac{806{,}736}{1{,}666{,}000}$$

$$\chi^2 = \frac{806{,}736}{1{,}666{,}000} = .48$$

The computed χ^2 is far below the χ^2 critical value (3.84) necessary for the rejection of the null hypothesis at the .05 level. The researcher concludes that the null hypothesis is not rejected: there is no significant relationship between the use of X-40 pills at this dosage and headache relief. Any apparent effectiveness was probably the result of sampling error.

The Mann–Whitney Test

The Mann–Whitney U test is designed to test the significance of the difference between two populations, using random samples drawn from the same population. It is a nonparametric equivalent of the parametric t test. It may be considered a useful alternative to the t test when the parametric assumptions cannot be met and when the observations are expressed in at least ordinal scale values.

The basic computation is U_1, and in experiments using small samples, the significance of an observed U may be determined by the U critical values of the Mann–Whitney tables.

When the size of either of the groups is more than 20, the sampling distribution of U rapidly approaches the normal distribution, and the null hypothesis may be tested with the reference to the z critical values of the normal probability table.

The values of the combined samples, N_1 and N_2, are ranked from the lowest to the highest rank, irrespective of groups, rank 1 to the lowest score, rank 2 to the next lowest, and so forth. Then the ranks of each sample group are summed individually and represented as ΣR_1 and ΣR_2.

There are two Us calculated for the formulas

a. $\quad U_1 = N_1 N_2 + \dfrac{N_1(N_1 + 1)}{2} - \Sigma R_1$

b. $\quad U_2 = N_1 N_2 + \dfrac{N_2(N_2 + 1)}{2} - \Sigma R_2$

N_1 = number in one group ΣR_1 = sum of ranks in one group
N_2 = number in second group ΣR_2 = sum of ranks in second group

Only one U need be calculated, for the other can be easily computed by the formula

$$U_1 = N_1 N_2 - U_2$$

It is the smaller value of U that is used when consulting the Mann–Whitney U table.

The z value of U can be determined by the formula

$$z = \frac{U - \dfrac{N_1 N_2}{2}}{\sqrt{\dfrac{(N_1)(N_2)(N_1 + N_2 + 1)}{12}}}$$

It does not matter which U (the larger or the smaller) is used in the computation of z. The sign of z will depend on which is used, but the numerical value will identical.

TABLE 11.4   Performance Scores of Students Taught by Method A or by Method B

A	Rank	B	Rank
50	3	49	2
60	8	90	36
89	35	88	33.5
94	38	76	21
82	28	92	37
75	20	81	27
63	10	55	7
52	5	64	11
97	40	84	30
95	39	51	4
83	29	47	1
80	25.5	70	15
77	22	66	12
80	25.5	69	14
88	33.5	87	32
78	23	74	19
85	31	71	16
79	24	61	9
72	17	55	6
68	13	73	18
$N_1 = 20$	$\Sigma R_1 = 469.5$	$N_2 = 20$	$\Sigma R_2 = 350.5$

$$U_1 = N_1 N_2 + \frac{N_1(N_1 + 1)}{2} - \Sigma R_1$$

For example, a teacher wishes to evaluate the effect of two methods of teaching reading to two groups of 20 randomly assigned students, drawn from the same population (see Table 11.4).

The null hypothesis proposed is that there is no significant difference between the performance of the students taught by Method A and the students taught by Method B.

After a period of four month's exposure to the two teaching methods, the score of the students on a standardized achievement test were recorded. All scores were ranked from lowest to highest and the Mann–Whitney test was used to test the null hypothesis at the .05 level of significance.

$$U_1 = N_1 N_2 + \frac{N_1(N_1 + 1)}{2} - \Sigma R_1$$

$$= (20)(20) + \frac{20(21)}{2} - 469.50$$

$$= 400 + 210 - 469.50$$

$$= 140.50$$

$$U_2 = N_1 N_2 + \frac{N_2(N_2 + 1)}{2} - \Sigma R_2$$

$$= (20)(20) + \frac{20(21)}{2} - 350.50$$

$$= 400 + 210 - 350.50$$

$$= 259.50$$

Check: $U_1 = N_1 N_2 - U_2$

$$140.50 = 400 - 259.50$$

$$140.50 = 140.50$$

$$z = \frac{U_1 - \dfrac{N_1 N_2}{2}}{\sqrt{\dfrac{N_1 N_2 (N_1 + N_2 + 1)}{12}}}$$

$$= \frac{140.50 - \dfrac{400}{2}}{\sqrt{\dfrac{(20)(20)(41)}{12}}} = \frac{-59.50}{\sqrt{1366.67}} = \frac{-59.50}{36.97}$$

$$= -1.61$$

Because the observed z value of -1.61 did not equal or exceed the z critical value of 1.96 for a two-tailed test at the .05 level, the null hypothesis was not rejected. The difference was not significant, and the apparent superior performance of the Method A group could well have resulted from sampling error.

For further information on these and other nonparametric tests, we recommend Hollander and Wolfe (1973) and Siegel (1956).

SUMMARY

Statistics is an indispensable tool for researchers that enables them to make inferences or generalizations about populations from their observations of the characteristics of samples. Although samples do not duplicate the characteristics of populations and although samples from the same population will differ from one another, the nature of their variation is reasonably predictable. The central limit theorem describes the nature of sample means and enables the researcher to make estimates about population means (parameters) with known probabilities of error.

The pioneering contributions of Sir Ronald Fisher and Karl Pearson to statistics and scientific method and of William Sealy Gosset to small-sampling theory have made practical the analysis of many of the types of problems encountered in psychology and education as well as in agricultural and biological research, where they were first applied.

Parametric statistical treatment of data is based on certain assumptions about the nature of distributions and the types of measures used. Nonparametric statistical treatment makes possible useful inferences without assumptions about the nature of data distributions. Each type makes a significant contribution to the analysis of data relationships.

Statistical decisions are not made with certainty but are based on probability estimates. The central limit theorem, sampling error, variance, the null hypothesis, levels of significance, and one-tailed and two-tailed tests have been explained and illustrated. Although this treatment has been brief and necessarily incomplete, the presentation of concepts may help the consumer of research to understand many simple research reports. Those who aspire to significant research activity or who wish to interpret complex research studies with understanding will need additional background in statistics and experimental design. They will find it helpful to participate in research seminars and to acquire competence through apprenticeship with scholars who are making contributions to knowledge through their own research activities.

EXERCISES (ANSWERS IN APPENDIX I)

1. Why is it stronger logic to be able to reject a negative hypothesis than to try an confirm a positive one?

2. A statistical test of significance would have no useful purpose in a purely descriptive study in which sampling was not involved. Do you agree? Why?

3. When a statistical test determines that a finding is significant at the .05 level, it indicates that there is $\frac{5}{100}$ probability that the relationship was merely the result of sampling error. Do you agree? Why?

4. Any hypothesis that can be rejected at the .05 level of significance can surely be rejected at the .01 level. Do you agree?

5. The t critical value necessary for the rejection of the null hypothesis (at a given level of significance and for a given number of degrees of freedom) is higher for a one-tailed test than it is for a two-tailed test. Do you agree? Why?

6. A manufacturer guaranteed that a particular type of steel cable had a mean tensile strength of 2,000 pounds with a standard deviation of 200 pounds. In a shipment, 16 lengths of the cable were submitted to a test for breaking strength. The mean breaking strength was 1,900 pounds. Using a one-tailed test at the .05 level of significance, determine whether the shipment met the manufacturer's specifications.

7. Two samples of mathematics students took a standardized engineering aptitude test. Using a two-tailed test at the .05 level of significance, determine whether the two groups were random samples from the same population.

Group A	Group B
$N = 25$	$N = 30$
$\overline{X} = 80$	$\overline{X} = 88$
$S = 8$	$S = 9$

8. An achievement test in spelling was administered to two randomly selected fifth-grade groups of students from two schools. Test the null hypothesis that there was no significant difference in achievement between the two fifth-grade populations from which the samples were selected at the .05 level of significance. Use the method of separate variances.

School A	School B
$N = 40$	$N = 45$
$\overline{X} = 82$	$\overline{X} = 86$
$S = 12.60$	$S = 14.15$

9. One group of rats was given a vitamin supplement and the other group received a conventional diet. The rats were randomly assigned. Test the hypothesis that the vitamin supplement did not result in increased weight gain for the experimental group. Use a one-tailed test at the .05 level.

X	C
$N = 12$	$N = 16$
$S = 15.50$ g	$S = 12.20$ g
$\overline{X} = 140$ g	$\overline{X} = 120$ g

10. A consumer research agency tested two popular makes of automobiles with similar weight and horsepower. Eleven car As provided a mean miles per gallon of 24.20 with an S of 1.40, and 11 car Bs provided a mean miles per gallon of 26.30 with an S of 1.74. Using a two-tailed test at the .05 level, test the null hypothesis that there was no significant difference between the mean gasoline milege of the two makes of cars.

11. Calculate the number of degrees of freedom when

   a. computing the statistical significance of a coefficient of correlation.
   b. determining the significance between two means.
   c. a 2 × 2 χ^2 table computation is involved.
   d. a 3 × 5 χ^2 table computation is involved.

12. In a survey to determine high school students' preference for a soft drink, the results were

	Brand A	Brand B	Brand C
Boys	25	30	52
Girls	46	22	28

Was there any relationship between the brand preference and the gender of the consumers?

13. A group of 50 college freshman was randomly assigned to experimental and control groups to determine the effectiveness of a counseling program upon academic averages. Use the Mann–Whitney test to test the null hypothesis that there was no difference between the academic performance of the experimental and control groups at the .05 level of significance. Use the data in the following table.

Experimental	Control
2.10	2.01
3.00	2.69
1.96	3.07
2.04	2.14
3.27	2.82
3.60	2.57
3.80	3.44
2.75	4.00
1.98	3.01
2.00	2.55
2.98	2.77
3.10	3.09
3.69	2.72
2.66	3.34
2.56	2.81
2.50	3.05
3.77	2.67
2.40	1.90
3.20	1.70
1.71	1.57
3.04	1.39
2.06	2.09
2.86	3.68
3.02	2.11
1.88	2.83

14. Compute the t value of the coefficient of correlation:

$r = +.30$

$N = 18$

15. Calculate $\hat{Y}$, given the following information:

$a = 11.2$

$b_1 = .2$

$b_2 = .4$

$b_3 = .3$

$X_1 = 70$

$X_2 = 60$

$X_3 = 82$

REFERENCES

Cohen, J. & Cohen, P. (1983). *Applied multiple regression correlation analysis for the behavioral sciences* (2nd ed.). Hillsdale, NJ: Lawrence Erlbaum.

Glass, G. V., & Hopkins, K. D. (1984). *Statistical methods in education and psychology* (2nd ed.). Englewood Cliffs, NJ: Prentice-Hall.

Glass, G. V., & Hopkins, K. D. (1996). *Statistical methods ineducation and psychology* (3rd ed.). Englewood Cliffs, NJ: Prentice-Hall.

Hollander, M. & Wolfe, D. A. (1973). *Nonparametric statistical methods.* New York: John Wiley.

Kirk, R. E. (1995). *Experimental design: Procedures for the behavioral sciences* (3rd ed.). Belmont, CA: Brooks/Cole.

Neter, I., Wasserman, W., & Kutner, M. H. (1985). *Applied linear statistical models* (2nd ed.). Homewood, IL: Richard D. Irwin, Inc.

Siegel, S. (1956). *Nonparametric statistics for the behavioral sciences.* New York: McGraw-Hill.

Winer, B. J. (1971). *Statistical principles in experimental design* (2nd ed.). New York: McGraw-Hill.

12

COMPUTER
DATA ANALYSIS

The purpose of this chapter is to show how computers can be used in analyzing data. Computers can perform calculations in just a few seconds that human beings would need weeks to do by hand. Although computers, as we know them today, have been in existence only for approximately 45 years, all of our daily lives are affected by them.

The microchip has made possible small computers that are within the financial reach of many Americans. As the price of these small computers comes down and their capabilities increase, more homes and small businesses will have computers. Three of the computer programs presented later in this chapter were run using a large university "main frame" computer. However, comparable programs are already available for microcomputers, and we have included examples of one set of control statements and output from SPSS-PC+ and six "printouts" of the results from SPSS for Windows™ .[1]

THE COMPUTER

The electronic digital computer is one of the most versatile and ingenious developments of the technological age. It is unlikely that complex modern institutions of business, finance, and government would have developed so rapidly without the contributions of the computer.

To the researcher the use of the computer to analyze complex data has made complicated research designs practical. Performing calculations almost at the speed of light, the computer has become one of the most useful research tools in the physical and behavioral sciences as well as in the humanities.

An early predecessor of the modern computer was a mechanical device developed by Charles Babbage, a 19th-century English mathematician. Late in that century

Herman Hollerith, a director of the U.S. Census Bureau, devised a hole-punched card to aid in the more efficient processing of census data. The punched card was a significant development, for it was a very important part of modern computer data processing.

In the mid-1940s an electrical impulse computer was devised with circuits employing thousands of vacuum tubes. These computers, which were very large and cumbersome, required a great deal of space. The heat generated by the vacuum tubes required extensive air-conditioning equipment to prevent heat damage, and the uncertain life of the vacuum tubes caused frequent malfunction.

With the development of transistorized components, replacement of the vacuum tubes, miniaturization, increased component reliability, elimination of heat dissipation problems, and other improvements, the computer became a much more effective device for the storage, processing, and retrieval of information.

The most advanced current models have incorporated microcircuitry of even more compact size, improved storage capacity, and greater processing speed. Functions can be processed in nanoseconds, or billionths of a second. These "supercomputers," which are available at only a relatively few universities and governmental and private research centers but can be accessed from other sites, are really only necessary for the most complex types of data processing involving models for future predictions Such predictions as which direction a hurricane may move next require complex formulas with large amounts of data. Often multiple models are determined with differing degrees of probability for each. Your TV weatherman uses information distilled from supercomputer models to predict tomorrow's and the next week's weather. In educational research a supercomputer would most likely be overkill because our computations are more modest and can be processed by a Pentium or 486 processor in a desktop (or PC) in a matter of a few seconds.

Computer technology includes four basic functions: input, storage, processing, and output. *Input* entails entering information or data into the computer. This is generally done through the keyboard at a computer terminal that is connected to and interacts with the shared computer or at a desktop computer. Other possible input methods include the use of optical scanning readers that translate printed page information or magnetic tape or CD-ROM, which are often the method with extremely large data sets such as the *National Longitudinal Survey of Youth (NLSY)* referred to in Chapter 5. Once information is inputted, it is *stored* for eventual use on the central computers disk, tapes, or either the hard disk or floppy disk of the desktop computer. Processing of the stored data as well as new input is achieved through programs written in one of several possible computer languages that are translated by the computer. Computer centers have many "canned" or preprepared programs that are available through the central computer or for use on one's own personal computer to perform a variety of statistical procedures. The *output,* or retrieval process, transfers the processed information or data from the computer to the researcher, using one of a number of devices to communicate the results. The output may be displayed on the computer screen, printed on paper, or recorded on the hard or floppy disk.

The computer can perform many statistical calculations easily and quickly. Computation of means, standard deviations, correlation coefficients, *t* tests, analysis of variance, analysis of covariance, multiple regression, factor analysis, and various nonparametric analyses are just a few of the programs and subprograms that are available.

It has been said that the computer makes no mistakes, but those entering data or directions to the computer do make mistakes. The computer doesn't think; it can only execute the directions of a thinking person. If poor data or faulty programs or directions are introduced into the computer, the data analysis will be meaningless. The expression "garbage in, garbage out" describes the problem quite well. It is critical when one is using canned programs to carefully follow the appropriate program syntax. If a comma or slash is missing, the program may stop processing the data or, worse yet, process the data incorrectly. The newest programs for Microsoft Windows and Macintosh computers, developed by the same publishers of the major programs on central computers, only require using a mouse to point and click to tell the computer what program to use, the variables desired in the formulas, and the statistical analyses to calculate.

With the large "main frame" computers of university and large business and governmental computer centers, hundreds of users at different terminals or computers can communicate with the computer at a single time. Computer programs (software) are available at these centers for many purposes, including statistical analyses. The canned programs include the *Statistical Package for the Social Sciences* (SPSS), *Statistical Analysis System*[2] (SAS®), and others. Though the actual programs, input procedures (syntax), and output (printouts) differ for these package programs, they are similar in their capabilities and the variety of statistical analyses that can be performed using them. Perhaps the most widely used are those programs published by SPSS. Which set of programs is used, however, depends on the user's needs and preference. Examples of programs from the SPSS-X™ and SAS systems—using the computer facilities of the University of Illinois at Chicago—will be presented later in this chapter.

Desktop or personal computers (PCs) include a wide range of equipment from small, low-cost computers for games and other purposes to computers that cost several thousands of dollars and can perform a variety of functions. Depending on the model and storage capabilities, there are programs available, SPSS and SAS among them, that can calculate any of the statistical analyses presented in this text, and many more. Examples of programs from SPSS-PC+™ and SPSS for Windows™—using a personal computer—also will be presented later in this chapter.

DATA ORGANIZATION

Prior to the input stage of data analysis comes the organizing of data for proper input into the computer system. Regardless of the type of computer or program to be used, if data are poorly organized, the researcher will have trouble analyzing their meaning.

The data must first be coded. Categorical data, such as a person's sex or occupation, need to be given a number to represent them. For instance in the data set in Appendix B, we show the way it looks for two different programs, Microsoft Excel and SPSS for Windows™. In the Excel file the data include letters (M or F) for the individual's gender, words (phonic or whole word) for the teaching method, and letters (LD for learning disabled, BD for behavior disordered, or MR for mentally retarded) for the individual's category. When these data were converted to the SPSS file, we modified these variables to numbers as indicated below:

Gender	Teaching Method	Category
1 = Male	1 = Phonic	1 = LD
2 = Female	2 = Whole Word	2 = BD
		3 = MR

The researcher may also want to convert interval or ratio data into categories and code them. For instance,

IQ Level	Income
1 = 120 to 139	1 = 40,000 and over
2 = 100 to 119	2 = 30,000 to 39,999
3 = 80 to 99	3 = 20,000 to 29,999
4 = 60 to 79	4 = below 20,000

The next step is to assign each variable to the spaces in which it will always be placed. Some mainframe systems call for a maximum of 80 columns per line. Once the researcher knows how many spaces each variable will occupy, the variables can be assigned to their column numbers (from 1 to 80). If more than 80 spaces are needed for each subject, then two or more lines will need to be assigned. The first columns will usually be the individual subject identity (ID) number. If fewer than 100 subjects are included, two spaces starting with 01 will be needed. Sometimes a researcher may include one or more attributes into the ID number, thereby increasing the number of columns needed. For instance, in the data set used in the SPSS-PC+ version of the analysis of variance presented in this chapter, we use a four-digit ID. The first digit represents the student's major, the second the student's sex, and the third and fourth digits the distinctive ID number. Thus, subject number 2113 was a philosophy major, male, and the thirteenth subject coded. When a large number of variables are used in a study, separating the variables with spaces will make the data easier to comprehend and easier to use with some programs. In any case, the researcher needs to have a list that shows which variables are represented in which column numbers.

In the sample data set in Appendix B, we provide the data in two different MS Windows formats, Excel and SPSS for Windows. In each of these formats, the data for each variable is in a separate column. In the SPSS for Windows format, the column has a title, which is the variable name.

Figure 12.1 shows how one page of actual data used in a study by Kahn (1992) looked when coded on a form. Note how the variables are separated from each

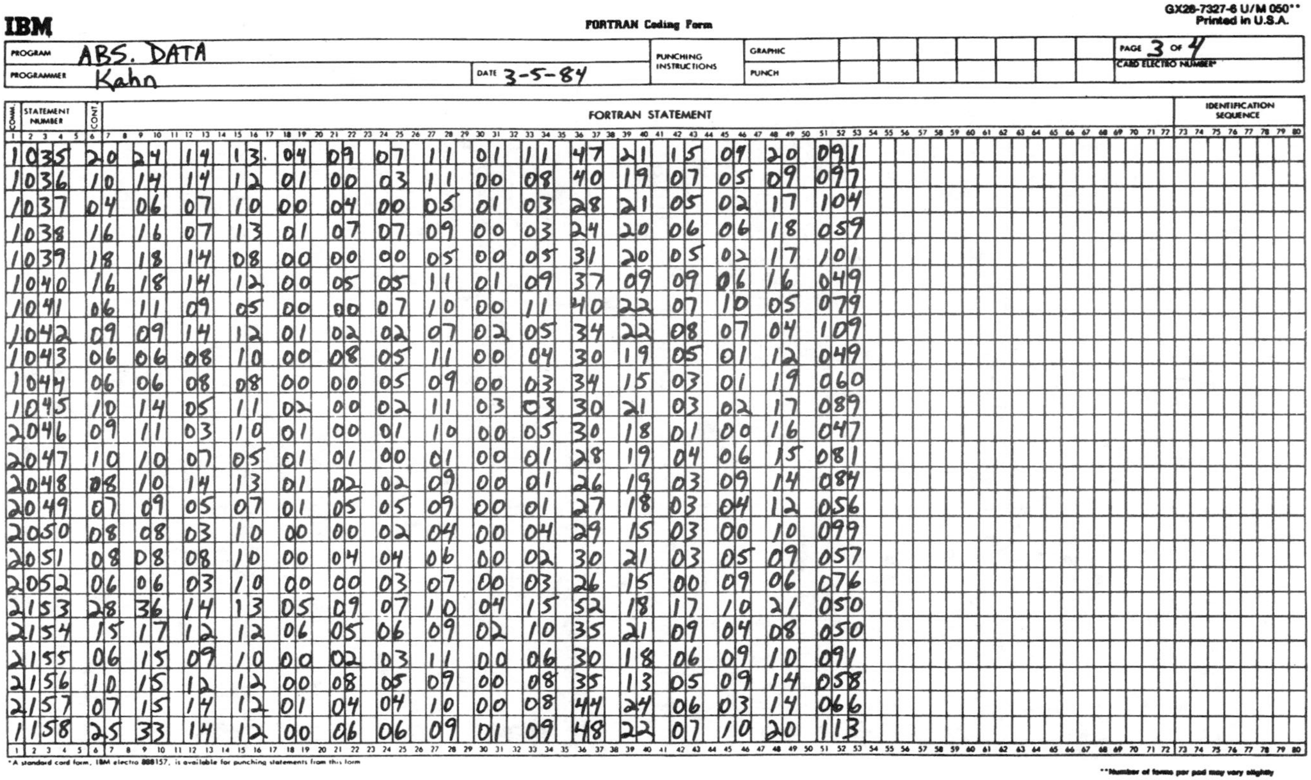

IBM FORTRAN Coding Form GX28-7327-6 U/M 050** Printed in U.S.A.

PROGRAM ABS. DATA | PUNCHING INSTRUCTIONS | GRAPHIC | PUNCH | PAGE 3 OF 4 | CARD ELECTRO NUMBER*

PROGRAMMER Kahn | DATE 3-5-84

STATEMENT NUMBER	FORTRAN STATEMENT															
1035	20	24	14	13.	04	09	07	11	01	11	47	21	15	09	20	091
1036	10	14	14	12	01	00	03	11	00	08	40	19	07	05	09	097
1037	04	06	07	10	00	04	00	05	01	03	28	21	05	02	17	104
1038	16	16	07	13	01	07	07	09	00	03	24	20	06	06	18	059
1039	18	18	14	08	00	00	00	05	00	05	31	20	05	02	17	101
1040	16	18	14	12	00	05	05	11	01	09	37	09	09	06	16	049
1041	06	11	09	05	00	00	07	10	00	11	40	22	07	10	05	079
1042	09	09	14	12	01	02	02	07	02	05	34	22	08	07	04	109
1043	06	06	08	10	00	08	05	11	00	04	30	19	05	01	12	049
1044	06	06	08	08	00	00	05	09	00	03	34	15	03	01	19	060
1045	10	14	05	11	02	00	02	11	03	03	30	21	03	02	17	089
2046	09	11	03	10	01	00	01	10	00	05	30	18	01	00	16	047
2047	10	10	07	05	01	01	00	01	00	01	28	19	04	06	15	081
2048	08	10	14	13	01	02	02	09	00	01	26	19	03	09	14	084
2049	07	09	05	07	01	05	05	09	00	01	27	18	03	04	12	056
2050	08	08	03	10	00	00	02	04	00	04	29	15	03	00	10	099
2051	08	08	08	10	00	04	04	06	00	02	30	21	03	05	09	057
2052	06	06	03	10	00	00	03	07	00	03	26	15	00	09	06	076
2153	28	36	14	13	05	09	07	10	04	15	52	18	17	10	21	050
2154	15	17	12	12	06	05	06	09	02	10	35	21	09	04	08	050
2155	06	15	09	10	00	02	03	11	00	06	30	18	06	09	10	091
2156	10	15	12	12	00	08	05	09	00	08	35	13	05	09	14	058
2157	07	15	14	12	01	04	04	10	00	08	44	24	06	03	14	066
1158	25	33	14	12	00	06	06	09	01	09	48	22	07	10	20	113

*A standard card form, IBM electro 888157, is available for punching statements from this form

**Number of forms per pad may vary slightly

FIGURE 12.1 Coded Data

TABLE 12.1 Variable List for Coded Data

Column Number		Column Number	
1–4	ID Number	33–34	Socialization (ABS10)
6–7	Expressive Language (EL)	36–37	Independent Functioning
9–10	Receptive Language (RL)		(ABS1)
12–13	Object Permanence (OP)	39–40	Physical Development
15–16	Means-End (ME)		(ABS2)
18–19	Vocal Imitation (VI)	42–43	Language (ABS4)
21–22	Gestural Imitation (GI)	45–46	Self-direction (ABS8)
24–25	Causality	48–49	Mental Age (MA)
27–28	Spatial Relations	51–53	Chronological Age (CA)
30–31	Responsibility (ABS9)		

other by a space left between them. Table 12.1 is the list used to determine which columns contained the different variables.

Survey researchers frequently have a system for coding and recording their data prior to distributing the questionnaires. For example, the questionnaire may ask for the sex of the respondent, "1" for male or "2" for female. If data are pre-coded for all questions and the researcher knows into which columns each answer will be placed, the data may be inputted to the computer directly from the returned survey forms, thereby saving the time of transferring the data to coding forms.

COMPUTER ANALYSIS OF DATA

Once the data are coded, they are ready to be stored on the computer's hard disk or on a floppy disk. The researcher then must decide on the descriptive and inferential statistics desired and the program(s) that he or she will use to analyze the data. The selection of appropriate statistics will generally depend on the design of the study, and the specific program(s) to be used will depend on the researcher's preference. Some researchers prefer one of the canned program packages and almost always use just that one. Others use different statistical programs from different packages. In the following we introduce two of the more popular statistical systems, presenting the control statements and output for two analyses from each. Control statements are used to tell the mainframe and non-windows or Macintosh personal computer systems what analyses to compute.

A large main-frame computer at the University of Illinois at Chicago (UIC) was used in the first three analyses. For the fourth analysis, the ANOVA example, a personal computer was used. In each of these analyses, the data may be presented with the control statements or can be retrieved by appropriate statements from another location (e.g., disk or tape). In three of the sample programs, the data are imbedded within the control statements. In the second analysis we provide an example of control statements that retrieve the data from a disk.

Example 1: Descriptive Statistics—SAS:CORR

SAS offers a number of descriptive statistics programs. The one presented here is called CORR because it includes correlations as a major component. This program was run on the UIC mainframe computer. The control statements are presented in Figure 12.2 on page 434.

SAS statements are separated from each other by semicolons (;). Thus, TITLE tells the program that the following words in single quotes (') comprise the title of this program, and DATA tells the program to read the data into an SAS data set created by and for this program. The INPUT statement tells the program the names of the variables and where they are. Because the variables in the data set are separated by spaces, we inform the program where they are simply by naming them in the order they appear in the file. When the input statement is used in this way, missing data must be represented by a period (.) rather than a blank space because a blank space cannot represent a missing data point *and* a space between variables. The next statement, LABEL, gives longer labels to the previously listed variables. CARDS merely informs the programs that the data are imbedded in the program, rather than in a separate file, and follow this statement. A semicolon follows the last subject's data to inform the program that all of the data have been read. PROC CORR tells the SAS system that the procedure known as "correlation" is to be used. The next two statements request correlation coefficients to be calculated and printed for only certain combinations. The VAR statement lists the variables desired on the top of the printed correlation matrix, and the WITH statement lists the variables desired on the side of the correlation matrix.

Figure 12.3 on page 434 shows that output produced by this program. The number of subjects, mean, standard deviation, sum of the scores, the lowest score and the highest score for each of the variables is presented first. Below that is the correlation matrix—with the significance level below each correlation—for the VAR variables with the WITH variables. If the VAR and WITH statements had not been included, a correlation matrix consisting of all of the possible combinations (all 13 variables by all 13 variables) would have resulted.

Example 2: Charting—SAS:CHART

Both SPSS and SAS systems have very sophisticated graphing programs including three-dimensional and, if the printer is capable, color graphics. The present example demonstrates the Chart procedure from SAS, a relatively simple one. The UIC mainframe version of SAS was used here.

The first two lines of control statements in Figure 12.4 on page 434 tell the SAS program where to look for the data, in a separate file called absdata. The next six lines present a series of "IF . . . THEN" statements. These statements convert two of the variables to categories. The first four statements deal with chronological age in months (CA). Those children with CAs from 36 to 59 months are assigned a score of 1; those with CAs from 60 to 83 months are assigned a score of 2; those with CAs from 84 to 107 months are assigned a score of 3; and those with CAs

```
TITLE 'SAS CORRELATION EXAMPLE';
DATA:
INPUT ID EL RL OP ME VI GI CAUS SPA ABS9 ABS10 ABS1 ABS2 ABS4
      ABS8 MA CA;
LABEL EL= EXPRESSIVE LANGUAGE RL = RECEPTIVE LANGUAGE
      OP = OBJECT PERMANENCE  ME = MEANS-END
      VI = VOCAL IMITATION    GI = GESTURAL IMITATION
      CAUS = CAUSALITY   ABS1 = INDEPENDENT FUNCTIONING
      ABS4 = LANGUAGE  ABS8 = SELF DIRECTION
      ABS10 = SOCIALIZATION  CA = CHRONOLOGICAL AGE
      MA = MENTAL AGE;
CARDS;
111 31 36 14 13   7  9   7 11   4 24 66   7 15 17 14   80
112 22 26 14 13   9  9   2 11   0 18 56 19 15 17 16   75
113 23 26 14 13   1  9   7 11   3 18 55 23 13 11 20   90
114 17 21 14 13   5  9   6 11   1  5 31 17   5 11 15   40
115 19 24 14 13   2  9   7 11   4  4 35 22   3 11 19   50
116 20 26 14 13   4  9   7 11   4 17 58 24 17 15 21   41
117 17 22 14 13   5  9   6 11   1 13 48 20   9 10 21   57
118 14 25 14 13   7  9   4 10   3 22 64 24   9 14 20   65
119 25 36 14 13   8  9   7 11   3 15 52 24 17 16 21   84
120 22 31 14 13   1  9   7 11   4 16 56 24 11 13 21   92
121 12 22 14 13   6  9   7 11   3 19 64 24   8 10 19   41
122 14 24 14 13   5  9   7 11   2  9 35 19   7  7 17   47
123 14 24 14 13   6  9   6 11   0 16 54 21 14 11 16   48
124 11 18 14 13   6  9   7 11   1 17 56 22   9  9 15   49
125 15 24  8 10   0  8   5  8   2 14 51 17   3  8 14   50
126 15 21 14 13   0  8   4 11   2  4 32 23   7  5 20   60
127 12 18 14 10   0  8   3  9   0  6 37 16   7 11 21   70
128 20 28 14 11   2  9   6 11   1 11 47 24 10   9 20 118
129 14 19 14 10   1  8   7  9   1 14 44 21   7  7 17   31
130  6 11 14 13   0  8   1 11   0 11 47 18   6 10 17   42
131 11 22 14 13   4  8   4 11   1 17 56 19   3  4 16   47
132 12 20 14 13   4  9   7 11   2 15 52 24 11   7 14   64
133 12 18 14 13   0  8   7 11   1  5 32 24   6  8 10   67
134  9 12 14 13   0  7   5 11   3 14 52 24 11 14 18   82
135 24 29 14 13   4  9   7 11   2 14 52 24 17   6 20   91
136 12 17 14 12   1  0   3 11   0  8 41 17   6  8  9   97
137  4  6  7 10   0  4   0  5   1  3 27 22   5  3 17 104
138 22 28  7 13   1  7   7  9   0  3 24 20   7  7 18   59
139 19 21 14  8   0  0   0  5   0  5 33 24   7  4 17 101
140 16 18 14 12   0  5   5 11   2 12 44 24   7  8 16   49
141 14 17  9  5   0  0   7 10   0 11 40 22   7 14  5   79
142 10  9 14 12   1  2   2  7   2  6 37 22   9  8  4 109
143  7  9  8 10   0  8   5 11   0  6 32 19   7  2 12   49
144  8 10  8  8   0  0   5  9   1  4 36 17   3  1 19   60
145 11 15  5 11   2  0   2 11   0  4 32 23   4  4 17   89
146 10 14  3 10   1  0   1 10   0  7 30 16   2  1 16   47
147 11 14  7  5   1  1   0  1   1  1 30 22   6  8 15   81
148  9 14 14 13   1  2   2  9   0  2 29 19   3  9 14   84
149  8 10  5  7   1  5   5  9   2  6 38 21   7  7 12   56
150  9  9  3 10   0  0   2  4   0 14 17 15   5  0 10   99
151  9 11  8 10   0  4   4  6   0  2 30 21   3  5  9   57
152  7  8  3 10   0  0   3  7   0  5 31 17   4 10  6   76
201 30 36 14 13   5  9   7 10   4 17 64 23 19 12 21   50
202 17 19 12 12   6  5   6  9   2 12 37 24   8  5  8   50
203  8 17  9 10   0  2   3 11   0  7 31 16   7  9  9   91
;
PROC CORR;
VAR OP ME VI CAUS MA CA;
WITH EL RL ABS1 ABS4 ABS8 ABS10
```

FIGURE 12.2 Control Statements and Data for Descriptive Statistics Example using SAS

```
SAS CORRELATION EXAMPLE

VARIABLE      N      MEAN     STD DEV       SUM     MINIMUM    MAXIMUM

OP           45   11.60000   3.72583    522.000    3.00000    14.0000
ME           45   11.44444   2.16958    515.000    5.00000    13.0000
VI           45    2.37778   2.69080    107.000    0.00000     9.0000
GI           45    6.00000   3.59292    270.000    0.00000     9.0000
CAUS         45    4.71111   2.32205    212.000    0.00000     7.0000
MA           45   15.46667   4.66418    696.000    4.00000    21.0000
CA           45   68.17778  21.94755   3068.000   31.00000   118.0000
EL           45   14.48889   6.29077    652.000    4.00000    31.0000
RL           45   19.66667   7.70478    885.000    6.00000    36.0000
ABS1         45   42.55556  12.42350   1915.000   17.00000    66.0000
ABS4         45    8.13333   4.34114    366.000    2.00000    19.0000
ABS8         45    8.57778   4.21301    386.000    0.00000    17.0000
ABS10        45   10.51111   6.01748    473.000    1.00000    24.0000
```

PEARSON CORRELATION COEFFICIENTS / PROB > |R| UNDER HO:RHO=0 / N = 45

```
                             OP       ME       VI       GI     CAUS       MA       CA

EL                        0.45652  0.38170  0.51784  0.48869  0.52799  0.43898  0.04397
EXPRESSIVE LANGUAGE       0.0016   0.0097   0.0003   0.0007   0.0002   0.0026   0.7743

RL                        0.54628  0.48900  0.61572  0.63134  0.59282  0.54136 -0.05985
RECEPTIVE LANGUAGE        0.0001   0.0007   0.0001   0.0001   0.0001   0.0001   0.6961

ABS1                      0.59804  0.45439  0.62313  0.63238  0.47839  0.42373 -0.18458
INDEPENDENT FUNCTIONING   0.0001   0.0017   0.0001   0.0001   0.0009   0.0037   0.2248

ABS4                      0.49236  0.39896  0.58317  0.53185  0.45032  0.36614  0.10995
LANGUAGE                  0.0006   0.0066   0.0001   0.0002   0.0019   0.0134   0.4721

ABS8                      0.52037  0.33429  0.49153  0.47595  0.37290  0.20341  0.00550
SELF-DIRECTION            0.0002   0.0248   0.0006   0.0010   0.0116   0.1802   0.9714

ABS10                     0.44623  0.44701  0.63768  0.55503  0.46135  0.28849 -0.14336
SOCIALIZATION             0.0021   0.0021   0.0001   0.0001   0.0014   0.0546   0.3475
```

FIGURE 12.3   Sample SAS PROC CORR Output

```
cms filedef absdata disk abs3rd script a;
DATA;
infile absdata;
INPUT ID A B C D E F G H I J K L M N Q CA;
IF CA>35 <60 THEN AGE=1;
IF CA>59 <84 THEN AGE=2;
IF CA>83 <108 THEN AGE=3;
IF CA>107 THEN AGE=4;
IF ID <200 THEN SEX ='M';
IF ID >200 THEN SEX ='F';
PUT AGE SEX;
PROC FORMAT;
     VALUE AGE 1='3 to 4'
               2='5 to 6'
               3='7 to 8'
               4='9 to 10';
PROC CHART; VBAR AGE/DISCRETE SUBGROUP=SEX;
            FORMAT AGE AGE.;
PROC CHART; PIE AGE/DISCRETE;
            FORMAT AGE AGE.;
```

**FIGURE 12.4   Control Statements for
Charting Example using SAS**

above 107 are assigned a score of 4. Because the first digit of the three-digit ID number represents the subject's sex, those children with IDs over 200 are female (F) and those with IDs below 200 are male (M). The next line (PUT AGE SEX) creates the computer space for the variables of age and sex created in the previous six statements. The PROC FORMAT and VALUE statements assign more meaningful values to the variable age. Thus, those children assigned a 1 for CAs from 36 to 59 months are 3 to 4 years old; those children assigned a 2 for CAs from 60 to 83 months are 5 to 6 years old; and so on.

The next two lines request the SAS procedure CHART, a vertical bar graph (VBAR) to be created using the variable age, and the number of children of each sex to be included in the bars of the graph. The next two lines request another graph using the same SAS procedure. This time a pie or circular graph in sections is to be created using the variable age. This output is shown in Figure 12.5.

Example 3: Multiple Regression—SPSS

The current example uses data collected by the second author and computed using SPSS on the UIC mainframe. The multiple regression presented uses three Piagetian independent variables (object permanence, means-end, and vocal imitation) to predict a receptive language score (presented as an age in months) of 45 profoundly retarded children.

The first SPSS control card in Figure 12.6 on page 438, TITLE, is used to name the program (SPSS REGRESSION EXAMPLE). The DATA LIST statements (two lines are used) tell the program that the data are presented in such a way that each variable is always in the same column (FIXED) and gives the short name and column numbers for each variable (e.g., RL is in columns 9 and 10, OP in columns 12 and 13). The VARIABLE LABELS statement assigns more complete labels to the initially short names. Next comes the REGRESSION command and its options on the next five lines. The first of these lines instructs SPSS to do a regression analysis and identifies the *descriptive statistics* that are desired (those automatically calculated plus significance levels). The second and third lines present the variables to be used in the regression equation and the *regression statistics* to be calculated (R requests the multiple correlation and COEF requests the regression coefficients and beta weights). The fourth and fifth lines specify the dependent variable (RL) and request that all of the other variables—the remaining variables are the independent variables—be entered simultaneously into the prediction equation. Finally, the program is told to read the data (BEGIN DATA), followed by the data set and two statements informing the program to stop reading data (END DATA) and that there are no more statements (FINISH).

Figure 12.7 on page 439 presents two pages of output produced by the above example. The first page shows the descriptive statistics requested. The mean and standard deviation of each variable and a correlation matrix—showing the Pearson *r* and its significance level for each pair of variables—are presented. The second page of output shows the multiple correlation coefficient (MULTIPLE *R*), its square (*R* SQUARE), the adjusted *R* square (which corrects *R* for sampling error),

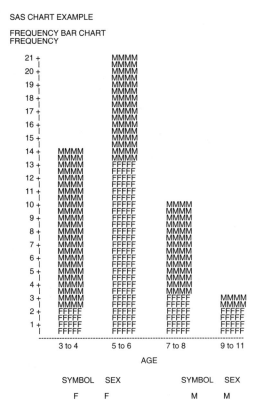

SAS CHART EXAMPLE

FREQUENCY BAR CHART
FREQUENCY

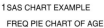

1 SAS CHART EXAMPLE

FREQ PIE CHART OF AGE

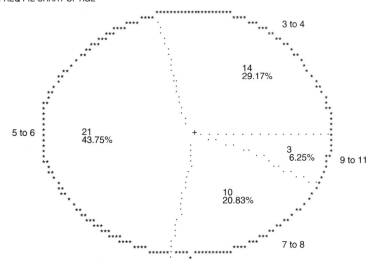

FIGURE 12.5   Sample SAS PROC CHART Output

```
TITLE SPSSX REGRESSION EXAMPLE
DATA LIST           FIXED
 /RL 9-10 OP 12-13 ME 15-16 VI 18-19
VARIABLE LABELS   RL 'RECEPTIVE LANGUAGE'
                  OP 'OBJECT PERMANENCE'
                  ME 'MEANS-END'
                  VI 'VOCAL IMITATION'
REGRESSION    DESCRIPTIVES=DEFAULTS SIG/
              VARIABLES=RL OP ME VI/
              STATISTICS= R COEF/
              DEPENDENT=RL/
              ENTER/
BEGIN DATA
 111 30 36 14 13 07 09 07 11 03 22 64 06 13 14
 112 20 24 14 13 07 09 07 11 03 22 64 06 13 14
 113 22 27 14 13 01 09 07 11 03 16 54 24 13 10
 114 15 20 14 13 05 09 06 11 00 05 30 16 05 11
 115 18 24 14 13 02 09 07 11 02 03 31 22 02 07
 116 21 27 14 13 04 09 07 11 02 16 52 23 16 14
 117 14 20 14 13 05 09 06 11 00 12 48 20 08 07
 118 14 24 14 13 07 09 04 10 02 20 60 22 09 12
 119 24 36 14 13 08 09 07 11 02 14 52 23 16 15
 120 20 30 14 13 01 09 07 11 03 15 54 24 10 13
 121 12 22 14 13 06 09 07 11 03 18 60 22 08 08
 122 14 24 14 13 05 09 07 11 01 07 34 19 07 07
 123 14 22 14 13 06 09 06 11 00 15 56 20 15 12
 124 10 18 14 13 06 09 07 11 01 16 54 19 08 07
 125 16 24 08 10 00 08 05 08 02 12 48 15 03 08
 126 14 20 14 13 00 08 04 11 01 03 30 22 07 01
 127 12 18 14 10 00 08 03 09 00 06 31 14 06 10
 128 18 27 14 11 02 09 06 11 00 10 45 23 09 10
 129 13 18 14 10 01 08 07 09 01 10 43 21 07 07
 130 05 10 14 13 00 08 01 11 00 11 47 18 05 10
 131 10 20 14 13 04 08 04 11 00 16 54 19 04 05
 132 12 20 14 13 04 09 07 11 01 15 55 24 10 05
 133 12 18 14 13 00 08 07 11 00 04 33 23 07 06
 134 08 12 14 13 00 07 05 11 03 12 49 23 07 11
 135 20 24 14 13 04 09 07 11 01 11 47 21 15 04
 136 10 14 14 12 01 00 03 11 00 08 40 19 07 05
 137 04 06 07 10 00 04 00 05 01 03 28 21 05 02
 138 16 16 07 13 01 07 07 09 00 03 24 20 06 06
 139 18 18 14 08 00 00 00 05 00 05 31 20 05 02
 140 16 18 14 12 00 05 05 11 01 09 37 23 07 09
 141 06 11 09 05 00 00 07 10 00 11 40 22 07 10
 142 09 09 14 12 01 02 02 07 02 05 34 22 08 07
 143 06 06 08 10 00 08 05 11 00 04 30 19 05 00
 144 06 06 08 08 00 00 05 09 00 03 34 15 03 01
 145 10 14 05 11 02 00 02 11 00 03 30 21 03 02
 146 09 11 03 10 01 00 01 10 00 05 30 18 01 00
 147 10 10 07 05 01 01 00 01 00 01 28 19 04 06
 148 08 10 14 13 01 02 02 09 00 01 26 19 03 09
 149 07 09 05 07 01 05 05 09 00 01 27 18 03 04
 150 08 08 03 10 00 00 02 04 00 04 29 15 03 00
 151 08 08 08 10 00 04 04 06 00 02 30 21 03 05
 152 06 06 03 10 00 00 03 07 00 03 26 15 00 09
 201 28 36 14 13 05 09 07 10 04 15 52 18 17 10
 202 15 17 12 12 06 05 06 09 02 10 35 21 09 04
 203 06 15 09 10 00 02 03 11 00 06 30 18 06 08
END DATA
FINISH
```

FIGURE 12.6   Control Statements and Data for Regression Example Using SPSS

```
                        * * * *   M U L T I P L E   R E G R E S S I O N   * * *
-Listwise Deletion of Missing Data

            Mean   Std Dev  Label

RL       18.067    8.170    RECEPTIVE LANGUAGE
OP       11.600    3.726    OBJECT PERMANENCE
ME       11.444    2.170    MEANS-END
VI        2.378    2.691    VOCAL IMITATION

N of Cases =     45

Correlation, 1-tailed Sig:

                 RL          OP          ME          VI

RL            1.000        .610        .542        .634
               .999        .000        .000        .000

OP             .610       1.000        .621        .437
               .000        .999        .000        .001

ME             .542        .621       1.000        .508
               .000        .000        .999        .000

VI             .634        .437        .508       1.000
               .000        .001        .000        .999

                        * * * *   M U L T I P L E   R E G R E S S I O N   * * *
Equation Number 1    Dependent Variable..   RL   RECEPTIVE LANGUAGE
   Descriptive Statistics are printed on Page    2

Beginning Block Number   1.  Method:  Enter

Variable(s) Entered on Step Number  1..    VI        VOCAL IMITATION
                                    2..    OP        OBJECT PERMANENCE
                                    3..    ME        MEANS-END

Multiple R            .73784
R Square              .54441
Adjusted R Square     .51107
Standard Error       5.71260

F =      16.33089        Signif F =   .0000
------------------ Variables in the Equation -----------------
Variable            B          SE B        Beta        T    Sig T

VI             1.286557     .377700     .423740     3.406    .0015
OP              .792628     .299906     .361478     2.643    .0116
ME              .384680     .537731     .102156      .715    .4784
(Constant)     1.410578    4.960245                  .284    .7776
-End Block Number    1   All requested variables entered.
        END OF JOB.
```

FIGURE 12.7   Sample Regression Output

and the standard error of estimate for predicting a score using the regression equation. This page also contains a table that shows *B*, standard error of *B*, and *Beta* for each independent variable. The table also presents the constant or intercept and a *T* and its significance level for the importance of each variable to the prediction of the dependent variable. These *t* tests show that only object-permanence and vocal imitation add significantly to the prediction of receptive language.

We could use the information regarding the B weights and the constant in a multiple regression equation to predict a profoundly retarded person's receptive language age given his or her vocal imitation, object-permanence, and means-end scores.

$$\hat{Y} = a + b_1 X_1 + b_2 X_2 \ldots$$

$$\hat{Y}(\text{RL}) = 1.411 + 1.287\,(\text{VI}) + .793\,(\text{OP}) + .385\,(\text{ME})$$

The resulting prediction of receptive language would have a standard error of estimate of 5.713.

Example 4: Analysis of Variance—SPSS-PC+

The data used in this example are identical to the data used in Chapter 11 on the analysis of variance (ANOVA), with one important difference. In the current example, the 10 students in each college major are evenly divided into males and females. Thus, instead of the simple one-way analysis of variance presented in Chapter 11, the current example is a two-way analysis of variance.

The SPSS-PC+ control statements are quire similar to the SPSS-X statements (see Figure 12.8). TITLE is again used to name the program, in this case SPSSPC ANOVA EXAMPLE. The next two lines (DATA LIST) inform the program that each variable is always presented in the same column (FIXED) and gives the name and location of each variable (i.e., MAJOR in column 1, SEX in column 2, and ABSTR in columns 6 and 7). VALUE LABELS give names to the categories of each variable. For instance, a subject with a 1 for major and a 1 for sex is a female mathematics major. While in SPSS-X the command to execute a particular statistic (e.g., regression or ANOVA) would appear next, with SPSS-PC+, the data precede this command. Thus, the next several lines consist of the BEGIN DATA statement, the data themselves, and the END DATA statement. After the data, the ANOVA command, indicating that we want to calculate an analysis of variance, is presented. This line also specifies abstract reasoning (ABSTR) as the dependent variable, major as an independent variable with three levels, sex as another independent variable with two levels, and that we wish certain statistics produced (STATISTICS=3)—the means for each category. Finally, FINISH tells the program that there are no further commands.

Figure 12.9 on page 442 shows two pages of output from the analysis of variance program just described. The first page lists the means (and in parentheses the number of subjects) for the total sample ("population" on the printout), each major, each sex, and the six cells of the major by sex table. The second page of output presents the analysis of variance table. The sources of variation include the total for the two main effects, each of the two main effects (major and sex), the interaction effect of the two independent variables, the total of the main effects and interaction effect (EXPLAINED), the within-groups or error (RESIDUAL), and the

```
TITLE SPSSPC ANOVA EXAMPLE
DATA LIST       FIXED
   /MAJOR 1 SEX 2 ABSTR 6-7
VALUE LABELS    MAJOR 1 'MATHEMATICS'
                      2 'PHILOSOPHY'
                      3 'CHEMISTRY'
                /SEX  1 'FEMALE'
                      2 'MALE'
BEGIN DATA.
1101 18
1102 22
1103 18
1104 23
1105 19
1206 24
1207 20
1208 21
1209 19
1210 25
2111 26
2112 27
2113 18
2114 22
2115 23
2116 19
2117 27
2218 26
2119 24
2220 26
3121 18
3122 14
3123 15
3124 14
3125 19
3226 21
3227 17
3228 17
3229 18
3230 19
END DATA.
ANOVA     ABSTR BY MAJOR (1,3) SEX (1,2)/STATISTICS=3.
FINISH
```

**FIGURE 12.8   Control Cards for Analysis of
Variance Example Using SPSS-PC+**

total. The sum of squares, degrees of freedom (*df*), and mean squared are presented for each of these sources of variation. *F*'s and the significance of each *F* are presented for each of the effects.

Of interest are the *F*'s for the three effects: college major, sex, and the major by sex interaction. The *F* for major was found to be 15.094. Significance levels are carried out to three decimal places. Thus a significance of 0.000 is less than 0.001—less than one chance in a thousand that the three groups of students with different majors were observed to differ because of sampling error. The *F* for sex was found to be 3.352. The significance level of 0.080 is not low enough (.05 being the highest acceptable error rate) for us to reject the null hypothesis for the main effect of sex.

```
                SPSSPC ANOVA EXAMPLE                           9/7/87
                      * * *  C E L L   M E A N S  * * *
                    ABSTR
                 BY MAJOR
                    SEX

TOTAL POPULATION

       20.63
     (   30)

   MAJOR
           1          2          3

       20.90      23.80      17.20
     (   10)  (    10)  (    10)

                SPSSPC ANOVA EXAMPLE                           9/7/87
     SEX
           1          2

       19.73      21.53
     (   15)  (    15)

             SEX
                    1          2
   MAJOR
           1     20.00      21.80
                (    5)  (     5)

           2     23.20      24.40
                (    5)  (     5)

           3     16.00      18.40
                (    5)  (     5)

                SPSSPC ANOVA EXAMPLE                           9/7/87
                  * * *  A N A L Y S I S   O F   V A R I A N C E  * * *

                    ABSTR
                 BY  MAJOR
                    SEX
```

Source of Variation	Sum of Squares	DF	Mean Square	F	Signif of F
Main Effects	243.167	3	81.056	11.180	.000
MAJOR	218.867	2	109.433	15.094	.000
SEX	24.300	1	24.300	3.352	.080
2-way Interactions	1.800	2	.900	.124	.884
MAJOR SEX	1.800	2	.900	.124	.884
Explained	244.967	5	48.993	6.758	.000
Residual	174.000	24	7.250		
Total	418.967	29	14.447		

```
                SPSSPC ANOVA EXAMPLE                           9/7/87

     30 Cases were processed.
      0 CASES (   .0 PCT) were missing.
                SPSSPC ANOVA EXAMPLE                           9/7/87
```

FIGURE 12.9   Sample Analysis of Variance Output

That is, any observed difference between females and males should be considered due to sampling error. Finally the F for the interaction of major and sex was found to be 0.124 with a significance level of 0.884. Obviously, the null hypothesis for the interaction of these variables is also not rejected.

The reader may be interested in comparing the results of this 3 by 2 (major by sex) analysis of variance with the one-way analysis of variance (major) performed in Chapter 11 on the same data. The reader should note that the toal sum of squares and the sum of squares for major are identical. However, because this example included an additional main effect and an interaction effect, the residual (within-groups) sum of squares is reduced by the amount explained by these two effect. Similarly, the degrees of freedom of the residual changes from 27 to 24, with sex (1) and the interaction of sex and major (2) taking up these three degrees of freedom. Finally, due to the changes in the residual, the F for the major (the only one that could be calculated using a one-way ANOVA) was changed slightly from 14.77 to 15.99.

SPSS for Windows Used with Appendix B Data in Chapters 10 and 11 Examples

In Chapters 10 and 11 we provided some results from the data presented in Appendix B and suggested that the reader select a sample and calculate the same statistics that we were reporting on for the entire population of 100. We used SPSS for Windows, version 6.1, for all of these analyses. Below are the printouts of the output from these analyses. There are no control statements as such because this program is designed for use with a mouse. The user merely points to the statistics menu and selects the statistical procedure (e.g., ANOVA, regression, correlation) wanted. Then a series of dialogue boxes leads the user through the process of selecting variables and any additional options.

In Figure 12.10 on page 444 are the results from a correlation analysis. We requested that additional statistics be calculated, including the mean and standard deviation (of a sample) and a correlation matrix of the three variables IQ, pretest, and posttest. Thus, the figure provides the means and standard deviations and correlations for these three variables.

Figure 12.11 on page 444 presents the output from the t test for independent samples analysis comparing the two reading methods on posttest scores and the t test for paired samples comparing the pretest and posttest scores for the entire population. In each case the means, standard deviations (sample formula), and the standard errors of the mean (needed to calculate the t test) for each variable (method 1 and method 2 in the first t test and pretest and posttest in the second t test) are provided. The t value ($-.68$ in the independent samples t test and 12.82 for the paired samples t test) and the degrees of freedom and probability of significance (two-tailed test) are provided.

Figure 12.12 on page 445 provides the output from two analyses, the ANOVA in which we compared the three category groups (LD, BD, and MR) on their posttest

```
         Variable       Cases        Mean      Std Dev

         IQ              100      86.1200      11.6109
         PRETEST         100      66.0400      12.9505
         POSTTEST        100      73.5000      12.0097

               - Correlation Coefficients -

                        IQ         PRETEST     POSTTEST

         IQ            1.0000        .5523        .6383
                      ( 100)       ( 100)       ( 100)
                      P=.          P=.000       P=.000

         PRETEST       .5523       1.0000        .8939
                      ( 100)       ( 100)       ( 100)
                      P=.000       P=.          P=.000

         POSTTEST      .6383        .8939       1.0000
                      ( 100)       ( 100)       ( 100)
                      P=.000       P=.          P=.000
```

(Coefficient / (Cases) / 2-tailed Significance)

"." is printed if a coefficient cannot be computed.

FIGURE 12.10   SAMPLE Descriptive Statistics— Appendix B Data

```
t-test for Independent Samples of METHOD

              Number
Variable     of cases        Mean        SD     SE of Mean
*****************************************************************
POSTTEST

METHOD 1          50       72.6800     12.338       1.745
METHOD 2          50       74.3200     11.739       1.660
*****************************************************************

    Mean Difference=-1.6400

t-test for Equality of Means
                                                   95%
Variances   t-value    df    2-Tail Sig    SE of Diff
*****************************************************************
Equal         -.68     98       .498         2.408
*****************************************************************

t-test for Paired Samples

             Number          2-Tail
Variable    of pairs  Corr    Sig     Mean       SD    SE of Mean
*****************************************************************
POSTTEST                             73.5000   12.010     1.201
              100    .894    .000
PRETEST                              66.0400   12.951     1.295
*****************************************************************

Paired Differences
  Mean     SD    SE of Mean    t-value    df    2-Tail Sig
*****************************************************************
7.4600   5.821      .582        12.82      99       .000
```

FIGURE 12.11   *t* tests Using Appendix B Data

```
          ----- ONEWAY -----

      Variable POSTTEST
   BY Variable CATEGORY

           Analysis of Variance

                           Sum of        Mean         F         F
   Source           DF     Squares      Squares     Ratio      Prob

   Between groups    2    5983.8729    2991.9364   34.9865    .0000
   Within groups    97    8295.1271      85.5168
   Total            99   14279.0000

       --- Partial Correlation Coefficients ---

   Controlling for..   PRETEST

                  IQ          POSTTEST

   IQ          1.0000           .3868
               (    0)         (   97)
               P=.             P=.000

   POSTTEST      .3868         1.0000
               (   97)         (    0)
               P=.000          P=.

   (Coefficient / (DF) / 2-tailed Significance)

   "." is printed if a coefficient cannot be computed.
```

FIGURE 12.12   Sample ANOVA and Partial Correlation—Appendix B Data

scores and the partial correlation in which we partialed out the effect of pretest on the correlation between IQ and posttest. The ANOVA table provides the between groups, within groups, and total degrees of freedom, sum of squares and mean squares and the *F* ratio (34.99) and probability of significance. The partial correlation analysis results in a correlation matrix of the two variables.

Finally, Figure 12.13 on page 446 provides the results from the multiple regression analysis in which we used pretest and IQ as predictors of posttest. The information provided is very similar to that in the SPSS mainframe version of the regression analysis presented earlier in this chapter. In this case an ANOVA table that determines the significance of the model is also presented.

Finally, we present a new analysis using SPSS for Windows, a 3-way ANOVA using the data in Appendix B. We selected as the three independent variables category of disability, method of teaching, and gender to determine if they showed differences on the posttest scores. As can be seen in Figure 12.14 on page 446, the only significant main effect was for category of disability (which also was found significant in the one way ANOVA reported in Figure 12.12). None of the interaction effects were significant. Thus, gender, reading method, and their interactions with category of disability and each other were not significant. Figure 12.14 shows the sum of squares, degrees of freedom, and means squares for each main effect and interaction effect (as well as the totals for the main effects and both types of interaction effects). Also shown are the *F* for each effect and the significance level for the *F*.

```
                         * * * *  M U L T I P L E   R E G R E S S I O N  * * *
-Listwise Deletion of Missing Data

  Equation Number 1     Dependent Variable..   POSTTEST

  Block Number  1.  Method:  Enter    PRETEST IQ

  Variable(s) Entered on Step Number  1..    IQ
                                      2..    PRETEST

  Multiple R           .91057
  R Square             .82914
  Adjusted R Square    .82561
  Standard Error      5.01520

  Analysis of Variance

                    DF      Sum of Squares      Mean Square
  Regression         2         11839.23649       5919.61825
  Residual          97          2439.76351         25.15220

  F =     235.35190      Signif F =  .0000
------------------ Variables in the Equation ------------------
  Variable           B        SE B       Beta        T     Sig T

  PRETEST         .722432    .046687    .779026    15.474    .0000
  IQ              .215150    .052073    .208007     4.132    .0001
  (Constant)     7.261888   3.820515   1.901                 .0603

-End Block Number   1   All requested variables entered.
```

FIGURE 12.13   Sample Multiple Regression—Appendix B Data

```
                    * * *  A N A L Y S I S   O F   V A R I A N C E  * * *

                    POSTTEST
             by     GENDER
                    METHOD
                    CATEGORY

                    UNIQUE sums of squares
                    All effects entered simultaneously
```

Source of Variation	Sum of Squares	DF	Mean Square	F	Sig of F
Main Effects	6204.616	4	1551.154	19.560	.00
GENDER	120.268	1	120.268	1.517	.221
METHOD	93.864	1	93.864	1.184	.280
CATEGORY	5998.925	2	2999.462	37.824	.00
2-Way Interactions	800.664	5	160.133	2.019	.084
GENDER METHOD	4.530	1	4.530	.057	.812
GENDER CATEGORY	268.405	2	134.202	1.692	.190
METHOD CATEGORY	479.865	2	239.933	3.026	.054
3-Way Interactions	63.169	2	31.584	.398	.673
GENDER METHOD CATEGORY	63.169	2	31.584	.398	.673
Explained	7300.491	11	633.681	8.369	.000
Residual	6978.509	88	79.301		
Total	14279.000	99	144.232		

```
100 cases were processed.
0 cases (.0 pct) were missing.
```

FIGURE 12.14   Sample 3-Way ANOVA—Appendix B Data

The purpose of this chapter has been to present an introduction to the use of computers in the analyses of data. We have presented four examples of programs from SAS and SPSS that require control statements (with their output) and several other examples from SPSS for Windows. These are relatively simple, and we hope they have helped to make the capabilities of computer analyses understandable. These programs required less than 3 seconds each of computer time.

We suggest that students wishing to develop skills in computer data analysis consult their university computer center and the most recent editions of the manuals for the statistical program package that they intend to use and that should be available in the university bookstore, at the computer center, or from the publisher directly.

SUMMARY

Technological advances in the past 25 years have made computers an integral part of the functioning of our society. Computers and sophisticated "canned" computer programs have become widely available.

The steps in using a computer to calculate statistical analyses are (1) organization and coding of data, (2) inputting the data into the computer or onto disk, (3) selection of appropriate descriptive and inferential statistics, (4) selection of appropriate programs for the desired statistics, (5) writing of control statements if needed, and (6) execution of the computer program.

This chapter has presented four examples of control statements and output from "canned" programs. The statistics requested in these examples are relatively simple: a two-way analysis of variance, a multiple regression analysis, a descriptive statistics program, and two relatively simple graphics. Also presented were the output from a series of analyses using SPSS for Windows used to provide sample results in Chapters 10 and 11.

ENDNOTES

1. SPSS, SPSS-X, SPSS-PC+, and SPSS for Windows are trademarks of SPSS, Inc. of Chicago, IL, for its proprietary software.

2. SAS is the registered trademark of SAS Institute, Inc., Cary, NC.

REFERENCE

Kahn, J. V. (1992). Predicting adaptive behavior of severely and profoundly mentally retarded children with early cognitive measures. *Journal of Intellectual Deficiency Research, 36,* 101–114.

Appendix A

STATISTICAL FORMULAS AND SYMBOLS

Statistical Formulas

1. $>$ is greater than
   $<$ is less than

2. Mean $\overline{X}$

   $$\overline{X} = \frac{\Sigma X}{N}$$

3. Mode M_o

4. Percentile rank P_r

   $$P_r - 100 - \frac{(100R - 50)}{N}$$

5. Variance σ^2
   Standard deviation σ

   $$\sigma^2 = \frac{\Sigma x^2}{N} \qquad x = (X - \overline{X})$$

   $$\sigma = \sqrt{\frac{\Sigma x^2}{N}}$$

   (deviation computation)

   $$\sigma = \frac{N\Sigma X^2 - (\Sigma X)^2}{N^2}$$

   $$\sigma = \sqrt{\frac{N\Sigma X^2 - (\Sigma X)^2}{N^2}}$$

   (raw score computation)

Glossary of Statistical Symbols

$a > b$ a is greater than b
$b < a$ b is less than a

$\overline{X}$ arithmetic average
Σ sum of
     X, Y scores
     N number of scores

M_o mode: score that occurs most frequently in a distribution

P_r percentage of scores that fall below a given value, plus $\frac{1}{2}$ the percentage of space occupied by that score

R rank from the top of a distribution

σ^2 population variance: mean value of the squared deviations from the mean

σ population standard deviation: positive square root of the variance $x = (X - M)$ deviation from the mean

Statistical Formulas

6. Variance S^2
Standard deviation S

$$S^2 = \frac{\Sigma x^2}{N-1}$$

$$S = \sqrt{\frac{\Sigma x^2}{N-1}}$$

(deviation computation)

$$S^2 = \frac{N\Sigma X^2 - (\Sigma X)^2}{N(N-1)}$$

$$S = \sqrt{\frac{N\Sigma X^2 - (\Sigma X)^2}{N(N-1)}}$$

(raw score computation)

Variance (S_{DV}^2) or standard deviation (S_{DV}) of a dichotomous variable

$$S_{DV}^2 = NP(1-P)$$
$$S_{DV} = \sqrt{NP(1-P)}$$
$$S_{DV}^2 = \frac{N}{4}$$

(general formula)

$$S_{DV} = \sqrt{\frac{N}{4}} \text{ (when } P = .50)$$

7. Standard error of the mean ($S_{\overline{X}}$)

$$S_{\overline{X}} = \frac{S}{\sqrt{N}} \qquad \sigma_{\overline{X}} = \frac{\sigma}{\sqrt{N}}$$

8. Standard scores z, T, Z_{cb}

$$z = \frac{X - \overline{X}}{\sigma} \text{ or } \frac{x}{\sigma}$$

$$T = 50 + 10\frac{(X - \overline{X})}{\sigma}$$

or $T = 50 + 10z$

$$Z_{cb} = 500 + 100z$$

Glossary of Statistical Symbols

S^2 variance of a population estimated from a sample

S standard deviation of population estimated from a sample

Dichotomous variable
an outcome is either-or; plus or minus, true or false, heads or tails

N number of events
P probability of an outcome

z sigma score
T standard score
Z_{cb} College Board standard score

Statistical Formulas

9. Coefficient of correlation (r)

$$r = \frac{\Sigma(z_X)(z_Y)}{N}$$

$$r = \frac{N\Sigma XY - (\Sigma X)(\Sigma Y)}{\sqrt{N\Sigma X^2 - (\Sigma X)^2}\sqrt{N\Sigma Y^2 - (\Sigma Y)^2}}$$

$$\rho\ (\text{rho}) = 1 - \frac{6\Sigma D^2}{N(N^2 - 1)}$$

10. Statistical significance of r/ρ

$$t = \frac{r\sqrt{N-2}}{\sqrt{1-r^2}}$$

$$t = \frac{\rho\sqrt{N-2}}{\sqrt{1-\rho^2}}$$

11. Regression line slope

$$r = \frac{\text{rise}}{\text{run}} = \frac{z_Y}{z_X}$$

$$r = \frac{\text{rise}}{\text{run}} = \frac{Y}{X} \qquad b_Y = r\left(\frac{z_Y}{z_X}\right)$$

$$b_X = r\left(\frac{z_X}{z_Y}\right)$$

12. Regression equations

$$\hat{Y} = a + bX$$
$$\hat{Y} = a + b_1X_1 + b_2X_2 \ldots$$

13. Standard error of estimate S_{est}

$$S_{\text{est}} = S\sqrt{1-r^2}$$

Glossary of Statistical Symbols

r Pearson product-moment coefficient of correlation

ρ (rho)   Spearman difference in ranks coefficient of correlation

D difference between each pair of ranks

Test of the statistical significance of a coefficient of correlation

r the slope expressed in sigma (z) units

b the slope of the line expressed in raw scores.

Predicting a Y from a known X when the coefficient of correlation is known

Statistical Formulas   *Glossary of Statistical Symbols*

14. Standard error of the difference between two means (independent variances; when variances are not equal)

$$S_{\overline{X}_1 - \overline{X}_2} = \sqrt{\frac{S_1^2}{N_1} + \frac{S_2^2}{N_2}}$$

(pooled variances; when variances are equal)

$$S_{\overline{X}_1 - \overline{X}_2} = \sqrt{\frac{(N_1 - 1)S_1^2 + (N_2 - 1)S_2^2}{N_1 + N_2 - 2}\left(\frac{1}{N_1} + \frac{1}{N_2}\right)}$$

15. Significance of the difference between two means

$$t = \frac{\text{difference between means}}{\text{standard error of the difference}}$$

$$t = \frac{\overline{X}_1 - \overline{X}_2}{\sqrt{\frac{(N_1 - 1)S_1^2 + (N_2 - 1)S_2^2}{N_1 + N_2 - 2}\left(\frac{1}{N_1} + \frac{1}{N_2}\right)}}$$

(uncorrelated or unmatched groups)

$$t = \frac{\overline{X}_1 - \overline{X}_2}{\sqrt{\frac{S_1^2}{N_1} + \frac{S_2^2}{N_2} - 2r\left(\frac{S_1}{\sqrt{N_1}}\right)\left(\frac{S_2}{\sqrt{N_2}}\right)}}$$

16. Analysis of variance

$$F = \frac{MS_b}{MS_w}$$

$$MS_b = \frac{SS_b}{df_b}$$

$$SS_b = \frac{(\Sigma X_1)^2}{n_1} + \frac{(\Sigma X_2)^2}{n_2} + \ldots - \frac{(\Sigma X)^2}{N}$$

$$MS_w = \frac{SS_w}{df_w}$$

$$SS_w = \Sigma X_1^2 - \frac{(\Sigma X_1)^2}{n_1} + \Sigma X_2^2 - \frac{(\Sigma X_2)^2}{n_2} \ldots$$

17. Partial correlation

$$r_{12.3} = \frac{r_{12} - (r_{13})(r_{23})}{\sqrt{(1 - r_{13}^2)(1 - r_{23}^2)}}$$

Statistical Formulas   *Glossary of Statistical Symbols*

18. Chi square χ^2

$$\chi^2 = \Sigma \frac{(f_o - f_e)^2}{f_e}$$

f_o observed frequencies
f_e expected frequencies
df degrees of freedom

$$df = (f\,\text{rows} - 1)(f\,\text{columns} - 1)$$

A	B
C	D

$$\chi^2 = \frac{N\left[\,|AD - BC| - \dfrac{N}{2}\right]^2}{(A + B)(C + D)(A + C)(B + D)}$$

Computation for a 2×2 table

19. Mann–Whitney test $(N > 20)$

$$U_1 = (N_1)(N_2) + \frac{N_1(N_1 + 1)}{2} - \Sigma R_1$$

$$U_2 = (N_1)(N_2) + \frac{N_2(N_2 + 1)}{2} - \Sigma R_2$$

$$z = \frac{U - \dfrac{(N_1)(N_2)}{2}}{\sqrt{\dfrac{(N_1)(N_2)(N_1 + N_2 + 1)}{12}}}$$

N_1 number in one group
N_2 number in second group
ΣR_1 sum of ranks of one group
ΣR_2 sum of ranks of second group

The significance of U is read from the U critical table. When $N > 20$, the z computation may be used with the normal probability table values.

SAMPLE DATA
MICROSOFT EXCEL FORMAT

ID	GENDER	METHOD	CATEGORY	IQ	PRETEST	POSTEST
1	M	Phonic	LD	94	77	82
2	M	Phonic	MR	84	37	54
3	M	Phonic	LD	90	55	66
4	F	Phonic	MR	91	56	55
5	F	Phonic	BD	96	84	85
6	M	Phonic	BD	95	77	79
7	M	Phonic	LD	85	56	66
8	F	Phonic	LD	96	92	95
9	M	Phonic	LD	82	33	55
10	M	Phonic	BD	105	56	65
11	M	Phonic	BD	89	46	58
12	F	Phonic	MR	72	42	56
13	F	Phonic	BD	98	88	89
14	M	Phonic	LD	88	55	60
15	M	Phonic	LD	91	67	72
16	F	Phonic	LD	92	66	72
17	M	Phonic	LD	90	55	73
18	M	Phonic	LD	89	59	66
19	M	Phonic	BD	102	87	72
20	F	Phonic	BD	99	77	91
21	M	Phonic	LD	86	55	62
22	M	Phonic	LD	95	85	92
23	M	Phonic	MR	68	57	62
24	F	Phonic	MR	65	66	63
25	M	Phonic	LD	110	95	93
26	M	Phonic	BD	98	55	66
27	F	Phonic	LD	89	55	72
28	M	Phonic	MR	67	56	59
29	M	Phonic	LD	102	84	91
30	M	Phonic	LD	93	77	85
31	F	Phonic	BD	105	56	62
32	M	Phonic	BD	106	72	78
33	M	Phonic	MR	64	62	72
34	M	Phonic	LD	87	66	80
35	M	Phonic	LD	88	72	77
36	M	Phonic	LD	95	91	90
37	F	Phonic	MR	68	64	62
38	M	Phonic	BD	103	66	77
39	M	Phonic	BD	96	55	62
40	F	Phonic	LD	83	59	69

ID	GENDER	METHOD	CATEGORY	IQ	PRETEST	POSTEST
41	F	Phonic	LD	94	87	88
42	F	Phonic	LD	84	55	59
43	M	Phonic	LD	85	65	79
44	M	Phonic	BD	98	64	92
45	M	Phonic	MR	68	63	68
46	M	Phonic	LD	81	57	66
47	F	Phonic	LD	93	81	89
48	F	Phonic	MR	64	42	52
49	M	Phonic	LD	89	62	77
50	M	Phonic	BD	92	63	79
51	F	Whole Word	MR	64	49	58
52	F	Whole Word	LD	92	69	82
53	F	Whole Word	LD	93	72	83
54	F	Whole Word	LD	89	55	68
55	M	Whole Word	BD	98	57	68
56	M	Whole Word	LD	87	58	69
57	F	Whole Word	MR	67	59	63
58	M	Whole Word	MR	65	48	52
59	F	Whole Word	LD	92	81	88
60	M	Whole Word	BD	93	84	92
61	F	Whole Word	BD	93	89	92
62	M	Whole Word	LD	88	77	86
63	F	Whole Word	LD	88	75	81
64	M	Whole Word	LD	84	64	73
65	F	Whole Word	MR	68	55	62
66	F	Whole Word	BD	89	82	86
67	M	Whole Word	MR	66	55	60
68	M	Whole Word	MR	65	54	58
69	F	Whole Word	BD	93	87	94
70	M	Whole Word	LD	90	64	79
71	M	Whole Word	LD	89	68	78
72	M	Whole Word	LD	89	72	82
73	F	Whole Word	LD	87	67	82
74	M	Whole Word	BD	93	82	82
75	F	Whole Word	BD	91	82	91
76	M	Whole Word	MR	67	55	62
77	F	Whole Word	LD	89	71	88
78	M	Whole Word	LD	88	68	72
79	M	Whole Word	BD	90	82	91
80	M	Whole Word	LD	85	64	68
81	M	Whole Word	LD	85	62	69
82	M	Whole Word	MR	66	52	58
83	F	Whole Word	BD	91	77	87
84	M	Whole Word	BD	92	78	82
85	M	Whole Word	LD	89	65	69
86	M	Whole Word	LD	82	62	71
87	F	Whole Word	LD	85	61	73
88	F	Whole Word	LD	86	63	71
89	M	Whole Word	MR	62	59	62
90	M	Whole Word	LD	86	64	71
91	M	Whole Word	BD	90	77	82
92	M	Whole Word	BD	90	77	88
93	M	Whole Word	BD	92	83	86
94	F	Whole Word	LD	81	54	62
95	F	Whole Word	LD	90	68	73
96	M	Whole Word	LD	88	62	68
97	F	Whole Word	MR	67	60	52
98	M	Whole Word	MR	61	52	58
99	F	Whole Word	BD	93	76	83
100	M	Whole Word	MR	60	55	61

c:\spsswin\sample.sav

	id	gender	method	category	iq	pretest	postest
1	1	1	1	1	94	77	82
2	2	1	1	3	84	37	54
3	3	1	1	1	90	55	66
4	4	2	1	3	91	56	55
5	5	2	1	2	96	84	85
6	6	1	1	2	95	77	79
7	7	1	1	1	85	56	66
8	8	2	1	1	96	92	95
9	9	1	1	1	82	33	55
10	10	1	1	2	105	56	65
11	11	1	1	2	89	46	58
12	12	2	1	3	72	42	56
13	13	2	1	2	98	88	89
14	14	1	1	1	88	55	60
15	15	1	1	1	91	67	72
16	16	2	1	1	92	66	72
17	17	1	1	1	90	55	73
18	18	1	1	1	89	59	66
19	19	1	1	2	102	87	72
20	20	2	1	2	99	77	91
21	21	1	1	1	86	55	62
22	22	1	1	1	95	85	92
23	23	1	1	3	68	57	62
24	24	2	1	3	65	66	63
25	25	1	1	1	110	95	93
26	26	1	1	2	98	55	66
27	27	2	1	1	89	55	72
28	28	1	1	3	67	56	59
29	29	1	1	1	102	84	91
30	30	1	1	1	93	77	85
31	31	2	1	2	105	56	62
32	32	1	1	2	106	72	78
33	33	1	1	3	64	62	72
34	34	1	1	1	87	66	80
35	35	1	1	1	88	72	77
36	36	1	1	1	95	91	90
37	37	2	1	3	68	64	62
38	38	1	1	2	103	66	77
39	39	1	1	2	96	55	62
40	40	2	1	1	83	59	69
41	41	2	1	1	94	87	88
42	42	2	1	1	84	55	59
43	43	1	1	1	85	65	79
44	44	1	1	2	98	64	92
45	45	1	1	3	68	63	68
46	46	1	1	1	81	57	66
47	47	2	1	1	93	81	89
48	48	2	1	3	64	42	52
49	49	1	1	1	89	62	77
50	50	1	1	2	92	63	79

c:\spsswin\sample.sav

	id	gender	method	category	iq	pretest	postest
51	51	2	2	3	64	49	58
52	52	2	2	1	92	69	82
53	53	2	2	1	93	72	83
54	54	2	2	1	89	55	68
55	55	1	2	2	98	57	68
56	56	1	2	1	87	58	69
57	57	2	2	3	67	59	63
58	58	1	2	3	65	48	52
59	59	2	2	1	92	81	88
60	60	1	2	2	93	84	92
61	61	2	2	2	93	89	92
62	62	1	2	1	88	77	86
63	63	2	2	1	88	75	81
64	64	1	2	1	84	64	73
65	65	2	2	3	68	55	62
66	66	2	2	2	89	82	86
67	67	1	2	3	66	55	60
68	68	1	2	3	65	54	58
69	69	2	2	2	93	87	94
70	70	1	2	1	90	64	79
71	71	1	2	1	89	68	78
72	72	1	2	1	89	72	82
73	73	2	2	1	87	67	82
74	74	1	2	2	93	82	82
75	75	2	2	2	91	82	91
76	76	1	2	3	67	55	62
77	77	2	2	1	89	71	88
78	78	1	2	1	88	68	72
79	79	1	2	2	90	82	91
80	80	1	2	1	85	64	68
81	81	1	2	1	85	62	69
82	82	1	2	3	66	52	58
83	83	2	2	2	91	77	87
84	84	1	2	2	92	78	82
85	85	1	2	1	89	65	69
86	86	1	2	1	82	62	71
87	87	2	2	1	85	61	73
88	88	2	2	1	86	63	71
89	89	1	2	3	62	59	62
90	90	1	2	1	86	64	71
91	91	1	2	2	90	77	82
92	92	1	2	2	90	77	88
93	93	1	2	2	92	83	86
94	94	2	2	1	81	54	62
95	95	2	2	1	90	68	73
96	96	1	2	1	88	62	68
97	97	2	2	3	67	60	52
98	98	1	2	3	61	52	58
99	99	2	2	2	93	76	83
100	100	1	2	3	60	55	61

Appendix C

PERCENTAGE OF AREA LYING BETWEEN THE MEAN AND SUCCESSIVE STANDARD DEVIATION UNITS UNDER THE NORMAL CURVE

Example: Between the mean and $+1.00z$ is 34.13% of the area.
Between the mean and $-.50z$ is 19.15% of the area.

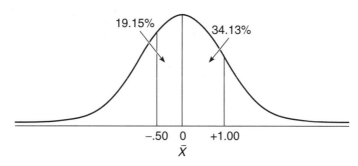

$z\left(\dfrac{x}{\sigma}\right)$	.00	.01	.02	.03	.04	.05	.06	.07	.08	.09
.0	.0000	.0040	.0080	.0120	.0160	.0199	.0239	.0279	.0319	.0359
.1	.0398	.0438	.0478	.0517	.0557	.0596	.0636	.0675	.0714	.0753
.2	.0793	.0832	.0871	.0910	.0948	.0987	.1026	.1064	.1103	.1141
.3	.1179	.1217	.1255	.1293	.1331	.1368	.1406	.1443	.1480	.1517
.4	.1554	.1591	.1628	.1664	.1700	.1736	.1772	.1808	.1844	.1879
.5	.1915	.1950	.1985	.2019	.2054	.2088	.2123	.2157	.2190	.2224
.6	.2257	.2291	.2324	.2357	.2389	.2422	.2454	.2486	.2517	.2549
.7	.2580	.2611	.2642	.2673	.2704	.2734	.2764	.2794	.2823	.2852
.8	.2881	.2910	.2939	.2967	.2995	.3023	.3051	.3078	.3106	.3133
.9	.3159	.3186	.3212	.3238	.3264	.3290	.3314	.3340	.3365	.3389
1.0	.3413	.3438	.3461	.3485	.3508	.3531	.3554	.3577	.3599	.3621
1.1	.3643	.3665	.3686	.3708	.3729	.3749	.3770	.3790	.3810	.3830
1.2	.3849	.3869	.3888	.3907	.3925	.3944	.3962	.3980	.3997	.4015
1.3	.4032	.4049	.4066	.4082	.4099	.4115	.4131	.4147	.4162	.4177
1.4	.4192	.4207	.4222	.4236	.4251	.4265	.4279	.4292	.4306	.4319
1.5	.4332	.4345	.4357	.4370	.4383	.4394	.4406	.4418	.4429	.4441
1.6	.4452	.4463	.4474	.4484	.4495	.4505	.4515	.4525	.4535	.4545
1.7	.4554	.4564	.4573	.4582	.4591	.4599	.4608	.4616	.4625	.4633
1.8	.4641	.4649	.4656	.4664	.4671	.4678	.4686	.4693	.4699	.4706
1.9	.4713	.4719	.4726	.4732	.4738	.4744	.4750	.4756	.4761	.4767
2.0	.4772	.4778	.4783	.4788	.4793	.4798	.4803	.4808	.4812	.4817
2.1	.4821	.4826	.4830	.4834	.4838	.4842	.4846	.4850	.4854	.4857
2.2	.4861	.4864	.4868	.4871	.4875	.4878	.4881	.4884	.4887	.4890
2.3	.4893	.4896	.4898	.4901	.4904	.4906	.4909	.4911	.4913	.4916
2.4	.4918	.4920	.4922	.4925	.4927	.4929	.4931	.4932	.4934	.4936
2.5	.4938	.4940	.4941	.4943	.4945	.4946	.4948	.4949	.4951	.4952
2.6	.4953	.4955	.4956	.4957	.4959	.4960	.4961	.4962	.4963	.4964
2.7	.4965	.4966	.4967	.4968	.4969	.4970	.4971	.4972	.4973	.4974
2.8	.4974	.4975	.4976	.4977	.4977	.4978	.4979	.4979	.4980	.4981
2.9	.4981	.4982	.4982	.4983	.4984	.4984	.4985	.4985	.4986	.4986
3.0	.4987									

CRITICAL VALUES FOR PEARSON'S PRODUCT-MOMENT CORRELATION (r)

n	$\alpha = .10$	$\alpha = .05$	$\alpha = .02$	$\alpha = .01$	df
3	.988	.997	.9995	.9999	1
4	.900	.950	.980	.990	2
5	.805	.878	.934	.959	3
6	.729	.811	.882	.917	4
7	.669	.754	.833	.874	5
8	.622	.707	.789	.834	6
9	.582	.666	.750	.798	7
10	.549	.632	.716	.765	8
11	.521	.602	.685	.735	9
12	.497	.576	.658	.708	10
13	.476	.553	.634	.684	11
14	.458	.532	.612	.661	12
15	.441	.514	.592	.641	13
16	.426	.497	.574	.623	14
17	.412	.482	.558	.606	15
18	.400	.468	.542	.590	16
19	.389	.456	.528	.575	17
20	.378	.444	.516	.561	18
21	.369	.433	.503	.549	19
22	.360	.423	.492	.537	20
23	.352	.413	.482	.526	21
24	.344	.404	.472	.515	22
25	.337	.396	.462	.505	23
26	.330	.388	.453	.496	24
27	.323	.381	.445	.487	25
28	.317	.374	.437	.479	26
29	.311	.367	.430	.471	27
30	.306	.361	.423	.463	28
35	.282	.333	.391	.428	33
40	.264	.312	.366	.402	38
50	.235	.276	.328	.361	48
60	.214	.254	.300	.330	58
70	.198	.235	.277	.305	68
80	.185	.220	.260	.286	78
90	.174	.208	.245	.270	88
100	.165	.196	.232	.256	98
200	.117	.139	.164	.182	198
500	.074	.088	.104	.115	498
1,000	.052	.062	.074	.081	998
10,000	.0164	.0196	.0233	.0258	9,998

Appendix E

CRITICAL VALUES OF STUDENT'S DISTRIBUTION (t)

df	Two-tailed test level of significance		One-tailed test level of significance	
	.05	.01	.05	.01
1	12.706	63.557	6.314	31.821
2	4.303	9.925	2.920	6.965
3	3.182	5.841	2.353	4.541
4	2.776	4.604	2.132	3.747
5	2.571	4.032	2.015	3.365
6	2.447	3.707	1.943	3.143
7	2.365	3.499	1.895	2.998
8	2.306	3.355	1.860	2.896
9	2.262	3.250	1.833	2.821
10	2.228	3.169	1.812	2.764
11	2.201	3.106	1.796	2.718
12	2.179	3.055	1.782	2.681
13	2.160	3.012	1.771	2.650
14	2.145	2.977	1.761	2.624
15	2.131	2.947	1.753	2.602
16	2.120	2.921	1.746	2.583
17	2.110	2.898	1.740	2.567
18	2.101	2.878	1.734	2.552
19	2.093	2.861	1.729	2.539
20	2.086	2.845	1.725	2.528
21	2.080	2.831	1.721	2.518
22	2.074	2.819	1.717	2.508
23	2.069	2.807	1.714	2.500
24	2.064	2.797	1.711	2.492
25	2.060	2.787	1.708	2.485
26	2.056	2.779	1.706	2.479
27	2.052	2.771	1.703	2.473
28	2.048	2.763	1.701	2.467
29	2.045	2.756	1.699	2.462
30	2.042	2.750	1.697	2.457
40	2.021	2.704	1.684	2.423
60	2.000	2.660	1.671	2.390
120	1.980	2.617	1.658	2.358
∞	1.960	2.576	1.645	2.326

Appendix F

ABRIDGED TABLE OF CRITICAL VALUES FOR CHI SQUARE

df	Level of significance	
	.05	.01
1	3.84	6.64
2	5.99	9.21
3	7.82	11.34
4	9.49	13.28
5	11.07	15.09
6	12.59	16.81
7	14.07	18.48
8	15.51	20.09
9	16.92	21.67
10	18.31	23.21
11	19.68	24.72
12	21.03	26.22
13	22.36	27.69
14	23.68	29.14
15	25.00	30.58
16	26.30	32.00
17	27.59	33.41
18	28.87	34.80
19	30.14	36.19
20	31.41	37.57
21	32.67	38.93
22	33.92	40.29
23	35.17	41.64
24	36.42	42.98
25	37.65	44.31
26	38.88	45.64
27	40.11	46.96
28	41.34	48.28
29	42.56	49.59
30	43.77	50.89

Appendix G

CRITICAL VALUES OF THE *F* DISTRIBUTION

The Table presented in this Appendix is used to determine if the *F* ratio resulting from ANOVA, ANCOVA, or homogeneity of variance is statistically significant. As can be seen there are two different degrees of freedom needed to fit the critical value of *F*, one for the numerator and one for the denominator of the formula. If the *F* calculated is equal to or greater than the critical value in the Table for the appropriate degrees of freedom, the finding is considered statistically significant at that probability (α) level.

The formula for the basic ANOVA and homogeneity of variance (*F*) and for the degrees of freedom (*df*) are:

$$F = \frac{MS_b}{MS_w}$$

$$df_b = K - 1$$

$$df_w = N - K$$

MS_b = mean square between

MS_w = mean square within

df_b = degrees of freedom between

df_w = degrees of freedom within

N = total number of subjects in all groups

K = number of groups

df for denominator	α	\multicolumn{12}{c}{df for numerator}
		1	**2**	**3**	**4**	**5**	**6**	**7**	**8**	**9**	**10**	**11**	**12**
1	.10	39.9	49.5	53.6	55.8	57.2	58.2	58.9	59.4	59.9	60.2	60.5	60.7
	.05	161	200	216	225	230	234	237	239	241	242	243	244
2	.10	8.53	9.00	9.16	9.24	9.29	9.33	9.35	9.37	9.38	9.39	9.40	9.41
	.05	18.5	19.0	19.2	19.2	19.3	19.3	19.4	19.4	19.4	19.4	19.4	19.4
	.01	98.5	99.0	99.2	99.2	99.3	99.3	99.4	99.4	99.4	99.4	99.4	99.4
3	.10	5.54	5.46	5.39	5.34	5.31	5.28	5.27	5.25	5.24	5.23	5.22	5.22
	.05	10.1	9.55	9.28	9.12	9.01	8.94	8.89	8.85	8.81	8.79	8.76	8.74
	.01	34.1	30.8	29.5	28.7	28.2	27.9	27.9	27.5	27.3	27.2	27.1	27.1
4	.10	4.54	4.32	4.19	4.11	4.05	4.01	3.98	3.95	3.94	3.92	3.91	3.90
	.05	7.71	6.94	6.59	6.39	6.26	6.16	6.09	6.04	6.00	5.96	5.94	5.91
	.01	21.2	18.0	16.7	16.0	15.5	15.2	15.0	14.8	14.7	14.5	14.4	14.4
5	.10	4.06	3.78	3.62	3.52	3.45	3.40	3.37	3.34	3.32	3.30	3.28	3.27
	.05	6.61	5.79	5.41	5.19	5.05	4.95	4.88	4.82	4.77	4.74	4.71	4.68
	.01	16.3	13.3	12.1	11.4	11.0	10.7	10.5	10.3	10.2	10.1	9.96	9.89
6	.10	3.78	3.46	3.29	3.18	3.11	3.05	3.01	2.98	2.96	2.94	2.92	2.90
	.05	5.99	5.14	4.76	4.53	4.39	4.28	4.21	4.15	4.10	4.06	4.03	4.00
	.01	13.7	10.9	9.78	9.15	8.75	8.47	8.26	8.10	7.98	7.87	7.79	7.72
7	.10	3.59	3.26	3.07	2.96	2.88	2.83	2.78	2.75	2.72	2.70	2.68	2.67
	.05	5.59	4.74	4.35	4.12	3.97	3.87	3.79	3.73	3.68	3.64	3.60	3.57
	.01	12.2	9.55	8.45	7.85	7.46	7.19	6.99	6.84	6.72	6.62	6.54	6.47
8	.10	3.46	3.11	2.92	2.81	2.73	2.67	2.62	2.59	2.56	2.54	2.52	2.50
	.05	5.32	4.46	4.07	3.84	3.69	3.58	3.50	3.44	3.39	3.35	3.31	3.28
	.01	11.3	8.65	7.59	7.01	6.63	6.37	6.18	6.03	5.91	5.81	5.73	5.67
9	.10	3.36	3.01	2.81	2.69	2.61	2.55	2.51	2.47	2.44	2.42	2.40	2.38
	.05	5.12	4.26	3.86	3.63	3.48	3.37	3.29	3.23	3.18	3.14	3.10	3.07
	.01	10.6	8.02	6.99	6.42	6.06	5.80	5.61	5.47	5.35	5.26	5.18	5.11
10	.10	3.29	2.92	2.73	2.61	2.52	2.46	2.41	2.38	2.35	2.32	2.30	2.28
	.05	4.96	4.10	3.71	3.48	3.33	3.22	3.14	3.07	3.02	2.98	2.94	2.91
	.01	10.0	7.56	6.55	5.99	5.64	5.39	5.20	5.06	4.94	4.85	4.77	4.71
11	.10	3.23	2.86	2.66	2.54	2.45	2.39	2.34	2.30	2.27	2.25	2.23	2.21
	.05	4.84	3.98	3.59	3.36	3.20	3.09	3.01	2.95	2.90	2.85	2.82	2.79
	.01	9.65	7.21	6.22	5.67	5.32	5.07	4.89	4.74	4.63	4.54	4.46	4.40
12	.10	3.18	2.81	2.61	2.48	2.39	2.33	2.28	2.24	2.21	2.19	2.17	2.15
	.05	4.75	3.89	3.49	3.26	3.11	3.00	2.91	2.85	2.80	2.75	2.72	2.69
	.01	9.33	6.93	5.95	5.41	5.06	4.82	4.64	4.50	4.39	4.30	4.22	4.16
13	.10	3.14	2.76	2.56	2.43	2.35	2.28	2.23	2.20	2.16	2.14	2.12	2.10
	.05	4.67	3.81	3.41	3.18	3.03	2.92	2.83	2.77	2.71	2.67	2.63	2.60
	.01	9.07	6.70	5.74	5.21	4.86	4.62	4.44	4.30	4.19	4.10	4.02	3.96
14	.10	3.10	2.73	2.52	2.39	2.31	2.24	2.19	2.15	2.12	2.10	2.08	2.05
	.05	4.60	3.74	3.34	3.11	2.96	2.85	2.76	2.70	2.65	2.60	2.57	2.53
	.01	8.86	6.51	5.56	5.04	4.69	4.46	4.28	4.14	4.03	3.94	3.86	3.80
15	.10	3.07	2.70	2.49	2.36	2.27	2.21	2.16	2.12	2.09	2.06	2.04	2.02
	.05	4.54	3.68	3.29	3.06	2.90	2.79	2.71	2.64	2.59	2.54	2.51	2.48
	.01	8.68	6.36	5.42	4.89	4.56	4.32	4.14	4.00	3.89	3.80	3.73	3.67
16	.10	3.05	2.67	2.46	2.33	2.24	2.18	2.13	2.09	2.06	2.03	2.01	1.99
	.05	4.49	3.63	3.24	3.01	2.85	2.74	2.66	2.59	2.54	2.49	2.46	2.42
	.01	8.53	6.23	5.29	4.77	4.44	4.20	4.03	3.89	3.78	3.69	3.62	3.55

15	20	24	30	40	50	60	100	120	200	500	∞	α	*df* for denom- inator
					df for numerator								
61.2	61.7	62.0	62.3	62.5	62.7	62.8	63.0	63.1	63.2	63.3	63.3	.10	1
246	248	249	250	251	252	252	253	253	254	254	254	.05	
9.42	9.44	9.45	9.46	9.47	9.47	9.47	9.48	9.48	9.49	9.49	9.49	.10	2
19.4	19.4	19.5	19.5	19.5	19.5	19.5	19.5	19.5	19.5	19.5	19.5	.05	
99.4	99.4	99.5	99.5	99.5	99.5	99.5	99.5	99.5	99.5	99.5	99.5	.01	
5.20	5.18	5.18	5.17	5.16	5.15	5.15	5.14	5.14	5.14	5.14	5.13	.10	3
8.70	8.66	8.64	8.62	8.59	8.58	8.57	8.55	8.55	8.54	8.53	8.53	.05	
26.9	26.7	26.6	26.5	26.4	26.4	26.3	26.2	26.2	26.2	26.1	26.1	.01	
3.87	3.84	3.83	3.82	3.80	3.80	3.79	3.78	3.78	3.77	3.76	3.76	.10	4
5.86	5.80	5.77	5.75	5.72	5.70	5.69	5.66	5.66	5.65	5.64	5.63	.05	
14.2	14.0	13.9	13.8	13.7	13.7	13.7	13.6	13.6	13.5	13.5	13.5	.01	
3.24	3.21	3.19	3.17	3.16	3.15	3.14	3.13	3.12	3.12	3.11	3.10	.10	5
4.62	4.56	4.53	4.50	4.46	4.44	4.43	4.41	4.40	4.39	4.37	4.36	.05	
9.72	9.55	9.47	9.38	9.29	9.24	9.20	9.13	9.11	9.08	9.04	9.02	.01	
2.87	2.84	2.82	2.80	2.78	2.77	2.76	2.75	2.74	2.73	2.73	2.72	.10	6
3.94	3.87	3.84	3.81	3.77	3.75	3.74	3.71	3.70	3.69	3.68	3.67	.05	
7.56	7.40	7.31	7.23	7.14	7.09	7.06	6.99	6.97	6.93	6.90	6.88	.01	
2.63	2.59	2.58	2.56	2.54	2.52	2.51	2.50	2.49	2.48	2.48	2.47	.10	7
3.51	3.44	3.41	3.38	3.34	3.32	3.30	3.27	3.27	3.25	3.24	3.23	.05	
6.31	6.16	6.07	5.99	5.91	5.86	5.82	5.75	5.74	5.7	5.67	5.65	.01	
2.46	2.42	2.40	2.38	2.36	2.35	2.34	2.32	2.32	2.31	2.30	2.29	.10	8
3.22	3.15	3.12	3.08	3.04	3.02	3.01	2.97	2.97	2.95	2.94	2.93	.05	
5.52	5.36	5.28	5.20	5.12	5.07	5.03	4.96	4.95	4.91	4.88	4.86	.01	
2.34	2.30	2.28	2.25	2.23	2.22	2.21	2.19	2.18	2.17	2.17	2.16	.10	9
3.01	2.94	2.90	2.86	2.83	2.80	2.79	2.76	2.75	2.73	2.72	2.71	.05	
4.96	4.81	4.73	4.65	4.57	4.52	4.48	4.42	4.40	4.36	4.33	4.31	.01	
2.24	2.20	2.18	2.16	2.13	2.12	2.11	2.09	2.08	2.07	2.06	2.06	.10	10
2.85	2.77	2.74	2.70	2.66	2.64	2.62	2.59	2.58	2.56	2.55	2.54	.05	
4.56	4.41	4.33	4.25	4.17	4.12	4.08	4.01	4.00	3.96	3.93	3.91	.01	
2.17	2.12	2.10	2.08	2.05	2.04	2.03	2.00	2.00	1.99	1.98	1.97	.10	11
2.72	2.65	2.61	2.57	2.53	2.51	2.49	2.46	2.45	2.43	2.42	2.40	.05	
4.25	4.10	4.02	3.94	3.86	3.81	3.78	3.71	3.69	3.66	3.62	3.6	.01	
2.10	2.06	2.04	2.01	1.99	1.97	1.96	1.94	1.93	1.92	1.91	1.90	.10	12
2.62	2.54	2.51	2.47	2.43	2.40	2.38	2.35	2.34	2.32	2.31	2.30	.05	
4.01	3.86	3.78	3.70	3.62	3.57	3.54	3.47	3.45	3.41	3.38	3.36	.01	
2.05	2.01	1.98	1.96	1.93	1.92	1.90	1.88	1.88	1.86	1.85	1.85	.10	13
2.53	2.46	2.42	2.38	2.34	2.31	2.30	2.26	2.25	2.23	2.22	2.21	.05	
3.82	3.66	3.59	3.51	3.43	3.38	3.34	3.27	3.25	3.22	3.19	3.17	.01	
2.01	1.96	1.94	1.91	1.89	1.87	1.86	1.83	1.83	1.83	1.80	1.80	.10	14
2.46	2.39	2.35	2.31	2.27	2.24	2.22	2.19	2.18	2.18	2.14	2.13	.05	
3.66	3.51	3.43	3.35	3.27	3.22	3.18	3.11	3.09	3.09	3.03	3.00	.01	
1.97	1.92	1.90	1.87	1.85	1.83	1.82	1.79	1.79	1.77	1.76	1.76	.10	15
2.40	2.33	2.29	2.25	2.20	2.18	2.16	2.12	2.11	2.10	2.08	2.07	.05	
3.52	3.37	3.29	3.21	3.13	3.08	3.05	2.98	2.96	2.92	2.89	2.87	.01	
1.94	1.89	1.87	1.84	1.81	1.79	1.78	1.76	1.75	1.74	1.73	1.72	.10	16
2.35	2.28	2.24	2.19	2.15	2.12	2.11	2.07	2.06	2.04	2.02	2.01	.05	
3.41	3.26	3.18	3.10	3.02	2.97	2.93	2.86	2.84	2.81	2.78	2.75	.01	

| *df* for denom-inator | α | \multicolumn{12}{c}{*df* for numerator} |
		1	2	3	4	5	6	7	8	9	10	11	12
17	.10	3.03	2.64	2.44	2.31	2.22	2.15	2.10	2.06	2.03	2.00	1.98	1.96
	.05	4.45	3.59	3.20	2.96	2.81	2.70	2.61	2.55	2.49	2.45	2.41	2.38
	.01	8.40	6.11	5.18	4.67	4.34	4.10	3.93	3.79	3.68	3.59	3.52	3.46
18	.10	3.01	2.62	2.42	2.29	2.20	2.13	2.08	2.04	2.00	1.98	1.96	1.93
	.05	4.41	3.55	3.16	2.93	2.77	2.66	2.58	2.51	2.46	2.41	2.37	2.34
	.01	8.29	6.01	5.09	4.58	4.25	4.01	3.84	3.71	3.60	3.51	3.43	3.37
19	.10	2.99	2.61	2.40	2.27	2.18	2.11	2.06	2.02	1.98	1.96	1.94	1.91
	.05	4.38	3.52	3.13	2.90	2.74	2.63	2.54	2.48	2.42	2.38	2.34	2.31
	.01	8.18	5.93	5.01	4.50	4.17	3.94	3.77	3.63	3.52	3.43	3.36	3.30
20	.10	2.97	2.59	2.38	2.25	2.16	2.09	2.04	2.00	1.96	1.94	1.92	1.89
	.05	4.35	3.49	3.10	2.87	2.71	2.60	2.51	2.45	2.39	2.35	2.31	2.28
	.01	8.10	5.85	4.94	4.43	4.10	3.87	3.70	3.56	3.46	3.37	3.29	3.23
22	.10	2.95	2.56	2.35	2.22	2.13	2.06	2.01	1.97	1.93	1.90	1.88	1.86
	.05	4.30	3.44	3.05	2.82	2.66	2.55	2.46	2.40	2.34	2.30	2.26	2.23
	.01	7.95	5.72	4.82	4.31	3.99	3.76	3.59	3.45	3.35	3.26	3.18	3.12
24	.10	2.93	2.54	2.33	2.19	2.10	2.04	1.98	1.94	1.91	1.88	1.85	1.83
	.05	4.26	3.40	3.01	2.78	2.62	2.51	2.42	2.36	2.30	2.25	2.21	2.18
	.01	7.82	5.61	4.72	4.22	3.90	3.67	3.50	3.36	3.26	3.17	3.09	3.03
26	.10	2.91	2.52	2.31	2.17	2.08	2.01	1.96	1.92	1.88	1.86	1.84	1.81
	.05	4.23	3.37	2.98	2.74	2.59	2.47	2.39	2.32	2.27	2.22	2.18	2.15
	.01	7.72	5.53	4.64	4.14	3.82	3.59	3.42	3.29	3.18	3.09	3.02	2.96
28	.10	2.89	2.50	2.29	2.16	2.06	2.00	1.94	1.90	1.87	1.84	1.81	1.79
	.05	4.20	3.34	2.95	2.71	2.56	2.45	2.36	2.29	2.24	2.19	2.15	2.12
	.01	7.64	5.45	4.57	4.07	3.75	3.53	3.36	3.23	3.12	3.03	2.96	2.90
30	.10	2.88	2.49	2.28	2.14	2.05	1.98	1.93	1.88	1.85	1.82	1.79	1.77
	.05	4.17	3.32	2.92	2.69	2.53	2.42	2.33	2.27	2.21	2.16	2.13	2.09
	.01	7.56	5.39	4.51	4.02	3.70	3.47	3.30	3.17	3.07	2.98	2.91	2.84
40	.10	2.84	2.44	2.23	2.09	2.00	1.93	1.87	1.83	1.79	1.76	1.73	1.71
	.05	4.08	3.23	2.84	2.61	2.45	2.34	2.25	2.18	2.12	2.08	2.04	2.00
	.01	7.31	5.18	4.31	3.83	3.51	3.29	3.12	2.99	2.89	2.80	2.73	2.66
60	.10	2.79	2.39	2.18	2.04	1.95	1.87	1.82	1.77	1.74	1.71	1.68	1.66
	.05	4.00	3.15	2.76	2.53	2.37	2.25	2.17	2.10	2.04	1.99	1.95	1.92
	.01	7.08	4.98	4.13	3.65	3.34	3.12	2.95	2.82	2.72	2.63	2.56	2.50
120	.10	2.75	2.35	2.13	1.99	1.90	1.82	1.77	1.72	1.68	1.65	1.62	1.60
	.05	3.92	3.07	2.68	2.45	2.29	2.17	2.09	2.02	1.96	1.91	1.87	1.83
	.01	6.85	4.79	3.95	3.51	3.17	2.96	2.79	2.66	2.56	2.47	2.40	2.34
200	.10	2.73	2.33	2.11	1.97	1.88	1.80	1.75	1.70	1.66	1.63	1.60	1.57
	.05	3.89	3.04	2.65	2.42	2.26	2.14	2.06	1.98	1.93	1.88	1.84	1.80
	.01	6.76	4.71	3.88	3.41	3.11	2.89	2.73	2.60	2.50	2.41	2.34	2.27
∞	.10	2.71	2.30	2.08	1.94	1.85	1.77	1.72	1.67	1.63	1.60	1.57	1.55
	.05	3.84	3.00	2.60	2.37	2.21	2.10	2.01	1.94	1.88	1.83	1.79	1.75
	.01	6.63	4.61	3.78	3.32	3.02	2.80	2.64	2.51	2.41	2.32	2.25	2.18

\multicolumn{12}{c}{*df* for numerator}		*df* for denominator
15	20	24	30	40	50	60	100	120	200	500	∞	α	
1.91	1.86	1.84	1.81	1.78	1.76	1.75	1.73	1.72	1.71	1.69	1.69	.10	17
2.31	2.23	2.19	2.15	2.10	2.08	2.06	2.02	2.01	1.99	1.97	1.96	.05	
3.31	3.16	3.08	3.00	2.92	2.87	2.83	2.76	2.75	2.71	2.68	2.65	.01	
1.89	1.84	1.81	1.78	1.75	1.74	1.72	1.70	1.69	1.68	1.67	1.66	.10	18
2.27	2.19	2.15	2.11	2.06	2.04	2.02	1.98	1.97	1.95	1.93	1.92	.05	
3.23	3.08	3.00	2.92	2.84	2.78	2.75	2.68	2.66	2.62	2.59	2.57	.01	
1.86	1.81	1.79	1.76	1.73	1.71	1.70	1.67	1.67	1.65	1.64	1.63	.10	19
2.23	2.16	2.11	2.07	2.03	2.00	1.98	1.94	1.93	1.91	1.89	1.88	.05	
3.15	3.00	2.92	2.84	2.76	2.71	2.67	2.60	2.58	2.55	2.51	2.49	.01	
1.84	1.79	1.77	1.74	1.71	1.69	1.68	1.65	1.64	1.63	1.62	1.61	.10	20
2.20	2.12	2.08	2.04	1.99	1.97	1.95	1.91	1.90	1.88	1.86	1.84	.05	
3.09	2.94	2.86	2.78	2.69	2.64	2.61	2.54	2.52	2.48	2.44	2.42	.01	
1.81	1.76	1.73	1.70	1.67	1.65	1.64	1.61	1.60	1.59	1.58	1.57	.10	22
2.15	2.07	2.03	1.98	1.94	1.91	1.89	1.85	1.84	1.82	1.80	1.78	.05	
2.98	2.83	2.75	2.67	2.58	2.53	2.50	2.42	2.40	2.36	2.33	2.31	.01	
1.78	1.73	1.70	1.67	1.64	1.62	1.61	1.58	1.57	1.56	1.54	1.53	.10	24
2.11	2.03	1.98	1.94	1.89	1.86	1.84	1.80	1.79	1.77	1.75	1.73	.05	
2.89	2.74	2.66	2.58	2.49	2.44	2.40	2.33	2.31	2.27	2.24	2.21	.01	
1.76	1.71	1.68	1.65	1.61	1.59	1.58	1.55	1.54	1.53	1.51	1.50	.10	26
2.07	1.99	1.95	1.90	1.85	1.82	1.80	1.76	1.75	1.73	1.71	1.69	.05	
2.81	2.66	2.58	2.50	2.42	2.36	2.33	2.25	2.23	2.19	2.16	2.13	.01	
1.74	1.69	1.66	1.63	1.59	1.57	1.56	1.53	1.52	1.50	1.49	1.48	.10	28
2.04	1.96	1.91	1.87	1.82	1.79	1.77	1.73	1.71	1.69	1.67	1.65	.05	
2.75	2.60	2.52	2.44	2.35	2.30	2.26	2.19	2.17	2.13	2.09	2.06	.01	
1.72	1.67	1.64	1.61	1.57	1.55	1.54	1.51	1.50	1.48	1.47	1.46	.10	30
2.01	1.93	1.89	1.84	1.79	1.76	1.74	1.70	1.68	1.66	1.64	1.62	.05	
2.70	2.55	2.47	2.39	2.30	2.25	2.21	2.13	2.11	2.07	2.03	2.01	.01	
1.66	1.61	1.57	1.54	1.51	1.48	1.47	1.43	1.42	1.41	1.39	1.38	.10	40
1.92	1.84	1.79	1.74	1.69	1.66	1.64	1.59	1.58	1.55	1.53	1.51	.05	
2.52	2.37	2.29	2.20	2.11	2.06	2.02	1.94	1.92	1.87	1.83	1.80	.01	
1.60	1.54	1.51	1.48	1.44	1.41	1.40	1.36	1.35	1.33	1.31	1.29	.10	60
1.84	1.75	1.70	1.65	1.59	1.56	1.53	1.48	1.47	1.44	1.41	1.39	.05	
2.35	2.20	2.12	2.03	1.94	1.88	1.84	1.75	1.73	1.68	1.63	1.60	.01	
1.55	1.48	1.45	1.41	1.37	1.34	1.32	1.27	1.26	1.24	1.21	1.19	.10	120
1.75	1.66	1.61	1.55	1.50	1.46	1.43	1.37	1.35	1.32	1.28	1.25	.05	
2.19	2.03	1.95	1.86	1.76	1.70	1.66	1.56	1.53	1.48	1.42	1.38	.01	
1.52	1.46	1.42	1.38	1.34	1.31	1.28	1.24	1.22	1.20	1.17	1.14	.10	200
1.72	1.62	1.57	1.52	1.46	1.41	1.39	1.32	1.29	1.26	1.22	1.19	.05	
2.13	1.97	1.89	1.79	1.69	1.63	1.58	1.48	1.44	1.39	1.33	1.28	.01	
1.49	1.42	1.38	1.34	1.30	1.26	1.24	1.18	1.17	1.13	1.08	1.00	.10	∞
1.67	1.57	1.52	1.46	1.39	1.35	1.32	1.24	1.22	1.17	1.11	1.00	.05	
2.04	1.88	1.79	1.70	1.59	1.52	1.47	1.36	1.32	1.25	1.15	1.00	.01	

RESEARCH REPORT EVALUATION[1]

Title:
clear and concise _____

Problem and Hypotheses:
clearly stated _____
significance of problem _____
specific question raised _____
clear statement of hypothesis or
    research question _____
testable hypothesis _____
assumptions stated _____
important terms defined _____

Review of Literature:
adequate coverage _____
well organized _____
important findings noted _____
studies critically examined _____
related to problem and hypothesis _____

Procedures:
subjects and methodology described in
    detail _____
adequate sample _____
appropriate design _____
variables controlled _____
appropriate data gathering
    instruments _____

Data Analysis/Results:
effective use of tables _____
effective use of figures _____
concise but complete report of findings __
appropriate statistical or other treatment
    of data _____
logical analysis _____

Discussion/Conclusions:
problem restated or addressed _____
hypotheses restated or addressed _____
clear and concise _____
conclusions based on results _____
statement of practical or theoretical
    implications _____
appropriate generalizations _____

Overall Form and Style of Paper:
clear and concise _____
appropriate degree of objectivity _____
all parts of the paper are properly related
    to each other _____
Referencing according to appropriate
    style _____

[1]This form can be completed as a checklist in which a + indicates adequate and a - indicates inadequate or as a rating scale in which a 5 represents superior, 4 above average, 3 average, 2 below average, and 1 poor.

Appendix I

ANSWERS TO STATISTICS EXERCISES

CHAPTER 10

1. Agree. The median could be lower than the mean if a large proportion of the families had low incomes.
2. Disagree. The median is that point in the distribution above and below which half of the scores fall. It may not be the midpoint between the highest and the lowest scores.
3. $M = 55.33$
   $Md = 58.50$
4. $M = 75$ Range $= 31$
   $Md = 77$
5. $\sigma^2 = 41.33$ $\sigma = 6.43$
   $S^2 = 45.09$ $S = 6.71$
6. Disagree. The range does not determine the magnitude of the variance or the standard deviation. These values indicate how all of the scores, not the most extreme, are clustered about the mean.
7. a. no change   d. +5
   b. +5   e. no change
   c. +5   f. no change
8. Percentile rank $= 93$.
9. $M = 72$ standard deviation $= 6$

z	-3	-2	-1	0	$+1$	$+2$	$+3$
heads	54	60	66	72	78	84	90

10.

X	x	z	Z
66	+5	+1.00	60
58	−3	−.60	44
70	+9	+1.80	68
61	0	0	50
52	−9	−1.80	32

11. a. 11%   f. $-.18_z$
     b. 89%   g. $+2.33_z$
     c. 87%   h. $-.67_z$ to $+.67_z$
     d. 6%   i. 32%
     e. $+39_z$ j. 0_z
12. a. 119   d. 107
     b. 96   e. 85 to 115
     c. 75%

13.

	Tom	Donna	Harry
algebra z	−1.00	+.33	−.17
history z	+1.25	+.50	−.25

     a. Tom   d. Tom
     b. Tom   e. Donna
     c. Harry   f. Harry

14. Disagree. The coefficient of correlation is an indication of the magnitude of the relationship, but does not necessarily indicate a cause-and-effect relationship.
15. rho $= +.61$
16. $r = +.65$
17. $r = +.53$
18. $r = -1.00$ most correct   most correct
                      least correct   least incorrect
19. Agree. $r = \dfrac{\text{rise}}{\text{run}}$ expressed in sigma units

                 $b = \dfrac{\text{rise}}{\text{run}}$ expressed in raw scores

     The value of r cannot exceed ±1.00
     The value of b can exceed ±1.00
20. $S_{est} = 4.96$
21. a. $\hat{Y} = 44$
     b. $\hat{Y} = 36$

CHAPTER 11

1. Confirming a positive hypothesis provides a weak argument, for the conclusion may be true for other reasons. It does not preclude the validity of alternative or rival hypotheses. Rejecting a negative hypothesis employs stronger logic.
2. Agree. A test of statistical significance provides a basis for accepting or rejecting a sampling error explanation on a probability basis. Only when a sampling process is involved is a test of significance appropriate.
3. Agree. The level of significance determines the probability of a sampling error, rather than a treatment variable explanation. When a researcher finds

an observation significant at the .05 level, he or she is admitting that there is a 5/100 chance of a sampling error explanation.

4. Disagree. The .01 alpha level is a much more rigorous criterion than the .05 level. However, any hypothesis that can be rejected at the .01 level can surely be rejected at the .05 level of significance.

5. Disagree. The *t* critical value for a one-tailed test is lower. The area of rejection is one side of the normal curve and it is not necessary to go out as far to reach it.

t **Critical Values for Rejection**

	2*t*	1*t*
.05 level	1.96	1.64
.01 level	2.58	2.33

6. $t = -2.00$ Reject the null hypothesis. The cable did not meet the manufacturer's specifications.

7. $t = 3.49$ Reject the null hypothesis. The means do not behave as sample means from the same population.

8. $t = 1.38$ Do not reject the null hypothesis. There was no significant difference between the achievement of the two groups.

9. $t = 3.77$ Reject the null hypothesis. The weight gain for the experimental group was significant.

10. $t = 3.13$ Reject the null hypothesis. The difference in gasoline mileage was significant.

11. a. $N - 1$
    b. $N - 2$
    c. $N + N - 2$
    d. 1
    e. 8

12. $\chi^2 = 14.06$ Reject the null hypothesis. There seems to be a significant relationship between gender and brand preference.

13. $z = .28$ Do not reject the null hypothesis. The effect of the counseling program did not seem to be statistically significant.

14. $t = 1.26$ Do not reject the null hypothesis. The coefficient of correlation was not statistically significant.

15. $\hat{Y} = 24.6$

Appendix J

SELECTED INDEXES, ABSTRACTS, AND REFERENCE MATERIALS

REFERENCES ABOUT REFERENCES

There are a number of publications that identify specific references that cover particular areas of knowledge.

American Reference Books Annual. **Bodham S. Wynar, ed. Littleton, CO.: Libraries Unlimited, 1970–date.**

Most reference books published or distributed in the United States are reviewed. Reviews, written by more than 200 library specialists, vary in length from 75 to 300 words, and are not cumulated from year to year. This is probably the most complete and up-to-date reference on references available.

A Guide to Reference Books **(10th ed.). Eugene P. Sheehy, compiler. Chicago: American Library Association, 1986.**

This comprehensive work lists, without evaluation, by subject area, by type, and by author or editor, the most important reference books printed in a number of languages. A section is devoted to education. Supplements appear every two or three years.

Wynar, Christine L. *Guide to Reference Books for School Media Centers.* **Littleton, CO.: Libraries Unlimited, 1976. 475 pp.**

This guide includes 2575 entries with evaluative comments on reference books and selection tools for use in elementary schools, junior and senior high schools, and community and junior colleges. It is indexed by author, subject, and title.

Reference Books Review Index. **Ann Arbor, MI.: Pierian Press, 1978.**

This annotated listing of references issues supplements quarterly.

Booklist. **Chicago: American Library Association, 1905–date.**

Published biweekly and cumulated every two years, this reference presents an unbiased critical analysis by expert librarians of atlases, encyclopedias, biographical works, dictionaries, and other reference materials in terms of their usefulness and reliability for libraries or homes.

Cumulative Book Index. **New York: H. W. Wilson Co., 1898–date.**

This monthly publication, cumulated semiannually and in one- and two-year cumulations, indexes all books published in the English language by author, title, and subject. It is helpful in assuring the student that all pertinent books have been covered in his or her searches.

Books in Print
Subject Guide to Books in Print. **R. R. Bowker Co., 1948–date. 6 vols.**
Vols. 1–3 Authors
Vols. 4–6 Titles and Publishers

These multivolume comprehensive listings of in-print titles list names of publishers and other publication information.

The Standard Periodicals Directory. **New York: Oxbridge Publishing Co., 1964–date.**

Published every other year, this directory of over 30,000 entries covers every type of periodical, with the exception of local newspapers. Periodicals are defined as publications appearing at least once every two years. Two hundred classifications are arranged by subject. An alphabetical index is provided.

Ulrich's International Periodicals Directory. **New York: R. R. Bowker Co., 1966–date. 2 vols.**

This classified list of more than 57,000 foreign and domestic periodicals is arranged by subject and title. Publication information is provided.

Irregular Serials and Annuals. An International Directory: Excepting Periodicals Issued More Frequently than Once a Year. **R. R. Bowker Co., 1972–date.**

Published biennially, this directory includes more than 20,000 publications.

Sources of Information in the Social Sciences **(3rd ed.). Chicago: American Library Association, 1986.**

Organized by subject area and indexed by author and title, this work contains a comprehensive listing and brief description of reference books, monographs, and scholarly journals.

Schorr, Alan E. *Government Reference Books: A Biennial Guide to United States Publications.* **Littleton, CO.: Libraries Unlimited, 1968/69–date.**

This guide describes more than 1300 publications.

INDEXES

A periodical index serves much the same purpose as the index of a book or the card file of a library. Usually listing articles alphabetically under subject, title, and author headings, the sources of periodical articles are indicated. Readers should read the directions for the use of an index before trying to locate references. Most indexes provide complete directions, as well as a list of the periodicals covered, the issue dates included, and a key to all abbreviations used.

Education Index. **New York: H. W. Wilson Co., 1929–date.**

Published monthly (September through June), and cumulated annually.

Canadian Education Index. **Ottawa, Ontario: Canadian Council for Educational Research, 1965–date.**

Issued quarterly, this publication indexes periodicals, books, pamphlets, and reports published in Canada.

Current Contents: Education. **Philadelphia: Institute for Scientific Information and Encyclopedia Britannica Educational Corporation, 1969–date.**

Issued weekly, this publication reproduces the table of contents of more than 500 foreign and domestic educational periodicals. It contains an author index and address directory to facilitate writing for reprints of the articles and to identify the author's organization. Reprints are available directly from the Institute for Scientific Information.

Current Index to Journals in Education. **Phoenix, AZ.: Oryx Press, 1969–date.**

This index is issued monthly and cumulated semiannually and annually, and indexes approximately 20,000 articles each year from more than 700 education and education-related journals, a joint venture with the National Institute of Education.

Index of Doctoral Dissertations International. **Ann Arbor, MI.: Xerox University Microfilms, 1956–date.**

Published as the issue 13 of *Dissertation Abstracts International* each year, this work consolidates into one list all dissertations accepted by American, Canadian, and some European universities during the academic year, as well as those available in microfilm. It indexes by author and key words selected from dissertation titles.

Reader's Guide to Periodic Literature. **New York: H. W. Wilson Co., 1900–date.**

Issued twice each month, *Reader's Guide* indexes by subject and author articles of a popular and general nature. Prior to 1929, *Reader's Guide* covered many of the educational periodicals. By 1929, the number of educational periodicals had become so great that the *Education Index* was established as a more specialized guide. *Reader's Guide* may be helpful to students in education for finding references to articles in areas outside the field of professional education.

Abridged Readers' Guide to Periodic Literature. **New York: H. W. Wilson Co., 1935–date.**

Fifty-six selected periodicals most likely to be found in smaller libraries are indexed here.

New York Times Index. **New York, 1913–date.**

This index is published biweekly with annual cumulation, and it classifies material in the *New York Times* alphabetically and chronologically under subject, title, person, and organization name. It is also useful in locating materials in other newspapers because it gives a clue to the date of events. Complete issues of the *New York Times* are available in microfilm form in many libraries.

Subject Index to the Christian Science Monitor. **Boston: Christian Science Monitor, 1960–date.**

This publication is issued monthly with annual cumulations.

Social Sciences Index. **New York: H. W. Wilson Co., 1974–date.**

This guide indexes 263 periodicals.

Humanities Index. **New York: H. W. Wilson Co., 1974–date.**

Formerly published as *Social Sciences and Humanities Index* (1965–1973), the *Humanities Index* lists 260 periodicals. These two indexes, each issued quarterly and cumulated annually, index alphabetically by subject and title articles from more than 260 periodicals, including many published outside the United States.

Physical Education/Sports Index. **Albany, NY: Marathon Press, 1978–date.**

This quarterly covers more than 100 journals. Since *Education Index* and *Current Index to Journals in Education* cover fewer than 10 physical education journals, these indexes provide an important additional source.

Rehabilitation Literature. **Chicago: The National Society for Crippled Children and Adults, 1940–date.**

Published monthly, this index lists material concerning the physically handicapped.

ABSTRACTS

Another type of reference guide is the abstract, review, or digest. In addition to providing a systemized list of reference sources, it includes a summary of the contents. Usually the summaries are brief, but in some publications they are presented in greater detail.

Dissertation Abstracts International. **Ann Arbor, MI.: Xerox University Microfilms, 1955–date.**

Dissertations accepted by most universities in the United States and Canada and some in foreign countries are indexed by author and key word. Libraries or individuals may purchase complete xerographic or microfiche copies of any dissertation.

Master's Abstracts International. **Ann Arbor, MI.: Xerox University Microfilms, 1962–date.**

Issued semiannually, this guide abstracts those master's degree theses that are available on microfilm.

Resources in Education. **Washington, D.C.: Superintendent of Documents, Government Printing Office, 1966–date.**

This monthly abstract journal prepared by the National Institute of Education reports new and completed research projects gathered by the 16 Educational Research Information Centers (ERIC).

Completed Research in Health, Physical Education and Recreation Including International Sources. **Washington, D.C.: American Alliance for Health, Physical Education and Recreation, 1958–date.**

Issued annually, this work indexes by subject and title abstracts of studies conducted throughout the world.

Child Development Abstracts and Bibliography. **Chicago: University of Chicago Press, 1927–date.**

Issued every four months and cumulated every three years, this publication abstracts more than 20 journals.

Exceptional Child Education Resources. **Arlington, VA.: Council for Exceptional Children, 1969–date.**

Issued quarterly, this publication indexes and abstracts books, periodicals, and government documents.

Psychological Abstracts. **Washington, D.C.: American Psychological Association, 1927–date.**

Issued bimonthly and indexed annually by subject and author, this publication has excellent signed summaries of psychological research reports. The December issue provides annual cumulative author and subject indexes. Beginning in 1963, each issue is also indexed by both subject and author. Libraries may also provide a cumulative subject index (1927–1960) and a cumulative author index (1927–1963).

Annual Review of Psychology. **Palo Alto, CA.: Annual Reviews, 1950–date.**

Each issue of this annual volume contains critical reviews of the literature in some 15 topical areas of contemporary psychology. Each review is written by a recognized authority on the topic. Although different authors writing in different years may vary considerably in their interpretation and handling of the same topic, all aim for comprehensive coverage of new developments.

Psychological Bulletin. **Washington, D.C.: American Psychological Association, 1904–date.**

Issued bimonthly, the *Bulletin* evaluates reviews of research literature and methodology.

Sociological Abstracts. **San Diego, CA.: Sociological Abstracts, Inc., 1952–date.**

Issued five times a year and cumulated annually, the *Abstracts* cover all areas of sociology, including educational sociology. The work abstracts articles and presents book reviews from several hundred periodicals, both domestic and foreign.

Social Work Research and Abstracts. **New York: National Association of Social Workers, 1965–date.**

Published quarterly, this volume indexes by subject, title, and author. It combines published research with the previously published journal, *Abstracts for Social Workers.*

National School Law Reporter. **New London, CT.: Croft Educational Services, 1955–date.**

The biweekly publication abstracts court decisions on school law.

RESEARCH-ORIENTED PERIODICALS

There are many publications in education and in closely related areas that report research activity. Some of these publications are exclusively research-oriented. Others present both research reports and feature-type articles. It is possible that beginning researchers may not be familiar with many of the specialized publications that deal with a problem area selected. Browsing through these periodicals provides an effective introduction to the field. It is also possible that the student many find recent and current reports that have not yet appeared in the appropriate index.

The following list of periodicals may be helpful to those who are planning a research project.

Education

Administrative Science Quarterly
Adolescence
Adult Education
Adult Jewish Education
Alberta Journal of Educational Research
American Association of University Professors Bulletin
American Behavioral Scientist
American Biology Teacher
American Education
American Educational Research Journal
American Vocational Journal
Arbitration in the Schools
Arithmetic Teacher

Audio-Visual Communications Review
Audio-Visual Language Journal
Black Scholar
Bulletin of the National Association of Secondary Schools Principals
Business Education Forum
Business Education Quarterly
California Journal of Educational Research
Catholic Educational Review
Character Education Journal
Child Care Quarterly
Child Development
Child Study Journal
Child Welfare

Children Today
Childhood Education
Civil Rights Digest
Clearing House
College Board Review
Colorado Journal of Educational Research
Community and Junior College Journal
Comparative Education
Comparative Education Review
Computers and Education
Continuing Education
Convergence
Education and Urban Society
Educational Administration Quarterly
Educational Forum
Educational Leadership
Educational Record
Educational Researcher
Educational Research Quarterly
Educational Technology
Elementary School Journal
Evaluation Quarterly
Harvard Educational Review
High School Journal
History of Education Quarterly
Home Economics Research Journal
Human Development
Illinois School Research
Independent School Bulletin
Indian Historian
Integrated Education
International Journal of Aging and Human
    Development
International Journal of Educational Science
Jewish Education
Journal for Research in Mathematics Education
Journal for the Study of Religion
Journal of Afro-American Issues
Journal of Alcohol and Drug Education
Journal of American Indian Education
Journal of Business Education
Journal of Communication
Journal of Computer-Based Instruction
Journal of Creative Behavior
Journal of Drug Education
Journal of Educational Data Processing
Journal of Educational Measurement
Journal of Educational Research
Journal of Educational Statistics

Journal of Experimental Education
Journal of Higher Education
Journal of Home Economics
Journal of Industrial Teacher Education
Journal of Law and Education
Journal of Legal Education
Journal of Leisure Research
Journal of Library Research
Journal of Negro Education
Journal of Religion
Journal of Research and Development in
    Education
Journal of Research in Mathematics Education
Journal of Research in Music Education
Journal of Research in Science Teaching
Journal of Social Studies Research
Journal of Teacher Education
Junior College Education
Junior College Journal
Kappa Delta Pi Record
Library Resources and Technical Services
Library Quarterly
Mathematics Teacher
Measurement in Education
Merrill Palmer Quarterly
Microfilm Review
Modern Language Journal
Multivariate Behavioral Research
National Business Education Quarterly
National Catholic Educational Association
    Bulletin
National Education Association Research
    Bulletin
National Elementary Principal
National Society for Programmed Instruction
    Journal
Negro Educational Review
New England Association Quarterly
North Central Association Quarterly
Outlook
Peabody Journal of Education
Phi Delta Kappan
Phylon
Pollution Abstracts
Practical Application of Research
Programmed Instruction
Psychometrika
Public Opinion Quarterly
Religion Teachers Journal

Religious Education
Research in Higher Education
Research in the Teaching of English
Review of Educational Research
Review of Religious Research
School and Society
School Law Journal
School Law Reporter
School Review
School Science and Mathematics
Science
Science Education
Science and Children
Science Teacher
Social Education
Social Science Research
Speech Monographs
Speech Teacher
Teachers College Record
Theory and Research in Social Education
Theory into Practice
Times Educational Supplement
UCLA Educator
Visual Education
Young Children

Sociology

American Anthropologist
American Behavioral Scientist
American Journal of Sociology
American Sociological Review
Ethnology
Federal Probation
Human Relations
Journal of American Indian Education
Journal of Applied Behavioral Science
Journal of Correctional Education
Journal of Educational Sociology
Journal of Experimental Social Psychology
Journal of Marriage and the Family
Journal of Research in Crime and Delinquency
Rural Sociology
Social Behavior and Personality
Social Case Work
Social Education
Social Forces
Social Problems
Social Psychology

Social Work
Sociological Methods and Research
Sociological Record
Sociology of Education
Sociology and Social Research
Sociometry
Teaching Sociology
Urban Education
Urban Review

Psychology

American Journal of Orthopsychiatry
American Journal of Psychiatry
American Journal of Psychology
American Psychologist
Applied Psychological Measurement
Behavioral Disorders
British Journal of Educational Psychology
British Journal of Psychology
Catholic Psychological Record
Cognitive Psychology
Contemporary Educational Psychology
Educational and Psychological Measurement
Genetic Psychology Monographs
Journal of Abnormal Psychology
Journal of Applied Psychology
Journal of Autism and Childhood Schizophrenia
Journal of Clinical Psychology
Journal of Comparative and Physiological Psychology
Journal of Consulting and Clinical Psychology
Journal of Counseling Psychology
Journal of Creative Behavior
Journal of Educational Psychology
Journal of Experimental Child Psychology
Journal of General Psychology
Journal of Genetic Psychology
Journal of Humanistic Psychology
Journal of Mental and Nervous Disease
Journal of Personality
Journal of Personality and Social Psychology
Journal of Personal Assessment
Journal of Psychiatric Research
Journal of Psychology
Journal of Research in Personality
Journal of School Psychology
Journal of Social Psychology

Journal of Verbal Learning and Behavior
Learning and Motivation
Mental Hygiene
Pastoral Psychology
Perceptual and Motor Skills
Personnel Psychology
Psychiatry
Psychoanalytic Quarterly
Psychological Abstracts
Psychological Bulletin
Psychological Monographs
Psychological Record
Psychological Reports
Psychological Review
Psychology in the Schools
Psychology of Women Quarterly
Small Group Behavior
Transactional Analysis Journal

Health and Physical Education

American Journal of Nursing
American Journal of Occupational Therapy
American Journal of Physical Medicine
American Journal of Public Health
Athletic Journal
Health and Education Journal
Health Education
Journal of the American Dietetic Association
Journal of the American Medical Association
Journal of the American Physical Therapy
  Association
Journal of Clinical Nutrition
Journal of Continuing Education in Nursing
Journal of Drug Education
Journal of Health and Social Behavior
Journal of Health, Physical Education and
  Recreation
Journal of Medical Education
Journal of Mental Health
Journal of Nursing Education
Journal of Nutrition
Journal of Pediatrics
Journal of Rehabilitation
Journal of School Health
Nursing Mirror
Nursing Outlook
Nursing Times

Nutrition Today
Quarterly Review of Pediatrics
Registered Nurse
Research Quarterly of the American Alliance
  for Health, Physical Education and Recreation
School Health Review

Guidance and Counseling

American Vocational Journal
British Journal of Guidance and Counseling
California Personnel and Guidance Association
  Journal
Canadian Counsellor
Counselor Education and Supervision
Elementary School Guidance and Counseling
Focus on Guidance
Guidance Clinic
Measurement and Evaluation in Guidance
Personnel and Guidance Journal
School Counselor
School Guidance Worker
Vocational Guidance Quarterly

Special Education

Academic Therapy
American Annals of the Deaf
American Journal of Mental Deficiency
Braille Book Review
Education and Training of the Mentally
  Retarded
Education of the Visually Handicapped
Exceptional Children
Exceptional Parent
Focus on Exceptional Children
Gifted Child Quarterly
Gifted Pupil
Hearing and Speech Action
International Journal for the Education of the
  Blind
Journal of Learning Disabilities
Journal of Mental Deficiency Research
Journal of Special Education
Journal of Speech and Hearing Disorders
Journal of Speech and Hearing Research
Language, Speech and Hearing Services in
  Schools
Learning Disorders

Mental Retardation
New Outlook for the Blind
Sight Saving Review
Special Education
Teacher of the Blind
Teaching Exceptional Children
Training School Bulletin
Volta Review

Reading

American Journal of Optometry
Elementary English

English Journal
Initial Teaching Alphabet Bulletin
Journal of the Association for the Study of
    Perception
Journal of Reading
Journal of Reading Behavior
Journalism Quarterly
Reading Horizons
Reading Improvement
Reading Quarterly
Reading Research Quarterly
Reading Teacher
Reading World

AUTHOR INDEX

N.B.: Asterisked page numbers denote a reading at end of Chapters.

SUBJECT INDEX